新航道学校指定新托福（TOEFL® iBT）培训教材

LISTENING

新托福听力金牌教程

TOEFL® iBT

（基础版）

Xintuofu Tingli Jinpai Jiaocheng

[韩] 金贤株
[韩] 崔怡玲
[韩] 金琉贤
[美] Henry John Amen Ⅳ
[美] Carey Groleau
[美] John Boswell

高等教育出版社·北京
HIGHER EDUCATION PRESS BEIJING

图字：01-2009-7941号

图书在版编目（CIP）数据

新托福听力金牌教程：基础版/（美）格里奥（Groleau，C.）等著. —北京：高等教育出版社，2010. 10（2015. 11 重印）
（新航道托福自学辅导系列）
ISBN 978-7-04-030364-3

Ⅰ. ①新… Ⅱ. ①格… Ⅲ. ①英语－听说教学－高等教育－教材 Ⅳ. ①H319. 9

中国版本图书馆 CIP 数据核字（2010）第 195340 号

策划编辑 洪志娟　　责任编辑 唐灵依　　翻　　译 万　晓　沈晓玲　　封面设计 周　末
版式设计 孙　伟　　责任校对 唐灵依　　责任印制 尤　静

出版发行	高等教育出版社	地　　址	北京市海淀区中关村大街 28-1 号
社　　址	北京市西城区德外大街 4 号		海淀文化艺术大厦 A 座 3 层
邮政编码	100120	邮　　编	100086
网　　址	http://www.hep.edu.cn	电　　话	010-62117066
印　　刷	北京四季青印刷厂	传　　真	010-62117166
开　　本	787×1092　1/16	网　　址	http://www.newchannel.org
印　　张	33. 5	版　　次	2010 年 10 月第 1 版
字　　数	832 000	印　　次	2015 年 11 月第 8 次印刷
经　　销	新航道国际教育集团	定　　价	68.00 元（含光盘）

物 料 号　30364－00

丛 书 序

托福考试自1981年进入中国，至今在中国已有近30年的历史。托福考试在中国的发展也从侧面反映了中国英语教育发展的进程。回首往昔，1981年中国第一次托福考试仅有数十人参加；着眼现在，2009年数据显示中国托福考生人数已逼近20万。过去的近30年中，中国的众多学子和有志之士在顺利通过这门考试后奔赴异国他乡，到美国或其他国家的大学去读书，从此改变了自己人生的轨迹。

一、托福帝国——从纸质考试到网络考试

托福是一个帝国，然而这个帝国也曾经没落过。由于旧托福考试存在种种局限：缺乏口语考试、考试形式和内容过于单一、写作考试题型和体例十几年无一变，使得托福考试本身陷入了僵化的困局。而此时，作为托福的竞争对手，英国的雅思考试异军突起，托福帝国岌岌可危。

面对竞争，ETS在潜心研究了几年之后，推出了TOEFL-iBT考试，也就是新托福，完成了从纸质考试到网络考试的华丽转身。这一考试在技术上和内容上都走在了全世界英语考试的前面。技术上，新托福考试是全世界首次采用英特网进行的全球性考试，而技术的先进使得考试的多样化和灵活性成为可能；内容上，它把听、说、读、写完美地结合到了一起，做到了听中有说、写中有听、读中有写，纵横交错，互相结合。

二、新托福——新挑战新机遇

自2006年新托福进入中国以来，中国考生的平均成绩在76-78分之间徘徊（满分为120分）。在全球考生中，总体成绩处于中等或中等略为偏下。而从听、说、读、写四项单项成绩来看，中国学生的强项是阅读，高于全球平均水平；写作成绩和全球平均分持平；而听、说两项成绩则是薄弱环节，分数低于全球平均分。

无疑，随着托福的改革，中国学生将面对的是一场更艰难的考试，不仅考试内容难度加大，同时还对中国学生的英语能力提出了更为全面的要求。这对中国学生来说既是一次考验，又是一次提升自己的机会。如果中国学生能够在新托福的考试中取胜，不仅能够大幅提高自己的英语水平，同时到了国外后也能够轻而易举地进入学习状态。

此外，以往的美国大学对中国学生的托福高分已经产生了偏见，因此托福高分已不再成为中国学生进入美国大学的优势之一。现在随着新托福的出现，中国学生可以和全世界考托福的学生一起，用真正的实力，再次证明中国学生依然拥有优秀的英语水平。挑战就是机遇，很多的美国大学已把新托福考试的入门分数定在了相当合理的分数线上，这给了中国学生一次很好的机会：只要我们能够在新托福考试中证明自己，我们的人生就有可能多一次光辉灿烂的选择。

三、新教材——为你的梦想插上翅膀

顺利通过新托福考试，去理想的国度留学是众多中国学生追寻的梦想。然而中国学生在准备新托福考试时存在一些致命误区，譬如认为考托福就是背单词、没有打好基础就直接做真题等等。鉴于此，经过深入的分析和探索，我们从韩国引进了这套丛书，改编成《新托福金牌教程》系列。本系列丛书共包括四本：《新托福阅读金牌教程（基础版）》、《新托福听力金牌教程（基础版）》、《新托福口语金牌教程（基础版）》和《新托福写作金牌教程（基础版）》，涵盖听、说、读、写全部四个方面，特别适合基础较为薄弱的学生，帮助他们打好基础、循序渐进，最终在新托福考试中拿到高分。此外，本系列丛书还融入了分阶段学习的理念和方法，引导学生科学合理地安排学习计划和学习内容，从而使备考更有效果。与此同时，由于听、说、读、写各项技能的自身特点和考查方式的不同，针对不同技能的每本书又各具特色。相同的理念，独特的风格，从而将四本书融为一个有机的整体。你可以根据自己的需要选择合适的那一本，也可以全部拿来系统复习、细细研读，无论怎样，你都会从中受益。

新托福考试不只是一项考试，它也是学习英语的一个契机。本系列教程的意义不仅局限在帮助中国学生通过考试，它更重要的使命在于传授一种学习理念、灌输一种让学生受益终身的学习方法。正如我们将本系列丛书命名为“金牌教程”一样，也同样希望每一位读者都能通过学习积累，获得人生的“金牌”！

最后祝愿大家顺利通过新托福考试，圆自己的留学梦！

新航道国际教育集团总裁兼校长

2010年10月

目　录

basic training 分题型听力训练

step-up training 分主题听力训练

本书使用说明

在结束了基本的分题型听力训练之后，您可以进一步进行分主题听力训练。请根据下面的栏目构成进行学习，它们将帮助您取得最佳的学习效果。

By Theme Types

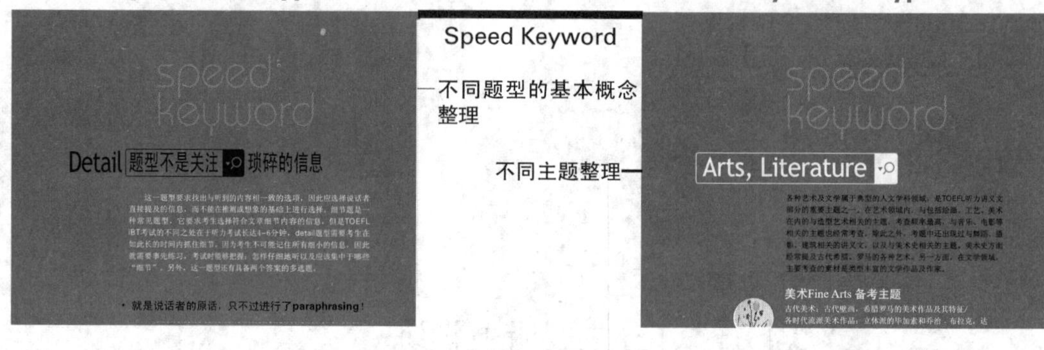

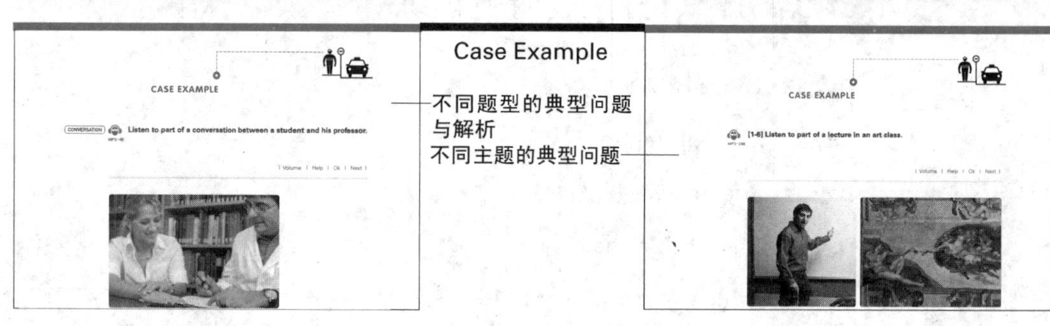

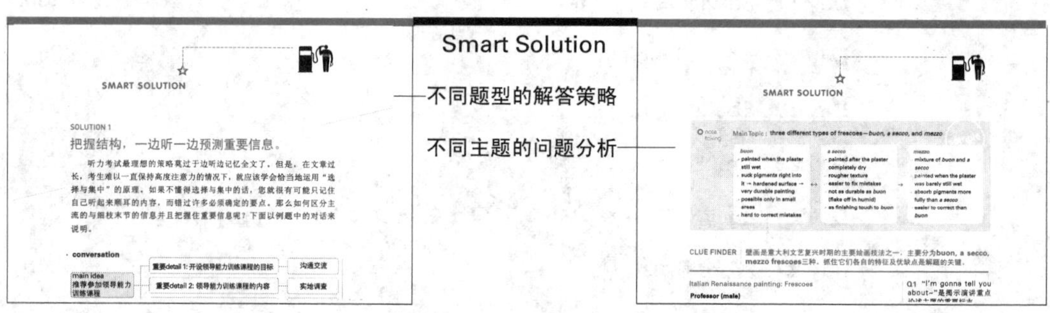

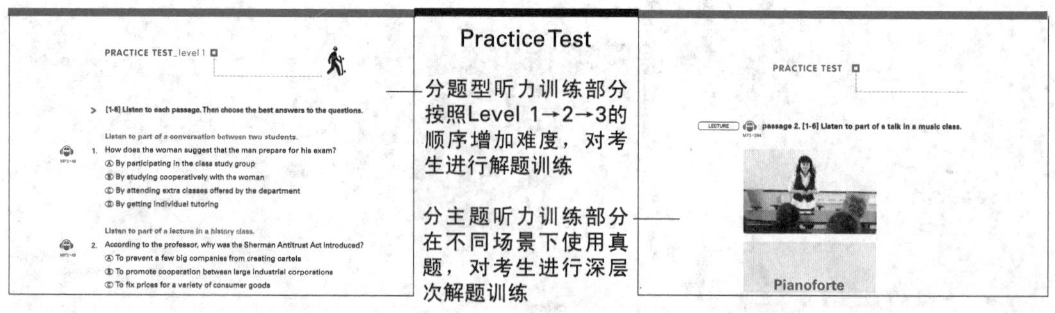

PRACTICE TEST_level 1
Practice Test
分题型听力训练部分按照Level 1→2→3的顺序增加难度，对考生进行解题训练
分主题听力训练部分在不同场景下使用真题，对考生进行深层次解题训练
PRACTICE TEST
Pianoforte

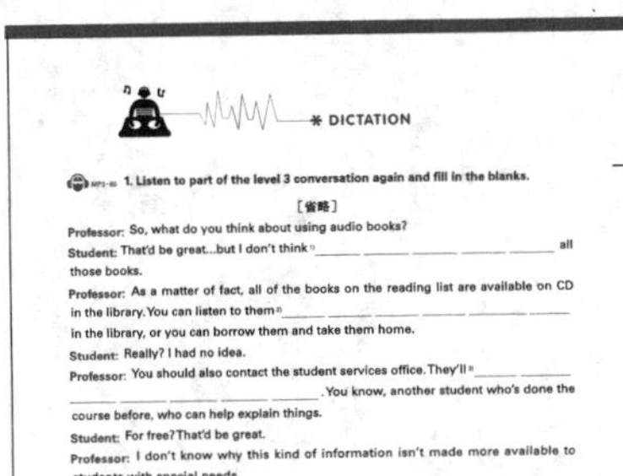

✱ DICTATION

MP1-46 1. Listen to part of the level 3 conversation again and fill in the blanks.

[省略]

Professor: So, what do you think about using audio books?

Student: That'd be great...but I don't think ¹⁾ ______ ______ ______ ______ ______ all those books.

Professor: As a matter of fact, all of the books on the reading list are available on CD in the library. You can listen to them ²⁾ ______ ______ ______ ______ ______ ______ in the library, or you can borrow them and take them home.

Student: Really? I had no idea.

Professor: You should also contact the student services office. They'll ³⁾ ______ ______ ______ ______ ______ ______ ______. You know, another student who's done the course before, who can help explain things.

Student: For free? That'd be great.

Professor: I don't know why this kind of information isn't made more available to students with special needs.

Dictation Oral Expression

通过听写与常用口语表进行额外的听力练习

Smart Source

通过真题背景知识提高对听力文章的理解

smart source

Fine Arts 美术

1 Fresco painting 壁画

壁画是一种绘画技法，它是指在墙壁上涂上灰泥plaster，再将颜料pigment在水里调匀后进行的绘图方法。西洋壁画的技法分为湿壁画（湿性壁画）buon fresco，干壁画（干性壁画）a secco fresco及中性壁画mezzo fresco三种。在灰泥风干前进行绘制的为湿壁画，灰泥风干后进行绘制的为干壁画，而混合使用前两种技法的即为中性壁画。著名的壁画作品有米开朗琪罗在罗马拜占庭的西斯廷教堂Sistine Chapel穹顶绘制的《天地创造》(God creates Adam)。

2 Cubism 立体派/立体主义

立体派是20世纪初叶活动于巴黎的艺术流派，由帕布罗·毕加索(Pablo

DAY 10 DAY 02~09 Review Test II

请完成下列题目，复习前面学过的各类型问题。

passage 1. [1-5] Listen to part of a conversation between a student and a librarian.

Volume | Help | Ok | Next

◀ Review Test

从分题型听力训练部分与分主题听力训练部分挑选出一定量的内容，组成实战练习，帮您及时复习之前所写的内容。

◀ MP3

教材内容全部录入MP3

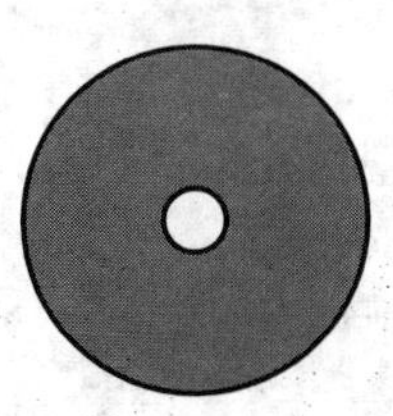

◀ Digital Book

提供涵盖教材内容、视频课堂及MP3的电子书，让您更加熟悉并适应托福iBT考试。

进度安排

本书基本按照25天完成的进度编排。您可以按照此进度进行训练，也可以根据个人水平与实际情况做如下调整：

9天集中训练计划

以解题训练为主，缩短学习时间

在备考时间不甚充裕的情况下，可以采用以下计划来进行集中的解题训练。在不间断的情况下，需要根据此计划进行连续9天集中学习。平均每天至少需要5~6个小时以上的复习时间，因此保证每天的学习时间是至为重要的。

Day		
1st Day 01. Diagnostic Test 解题练习与状态评估	2nd Day 02. Main Idea类型 Day 03. Detail 类型 Day 04. Function 类型	3rd Day 05. Attitude 类型 Day 06. Review Test I （前4种题型复习）
4th Day 07. Organization 类型 Day 08. Connecting Contents 类型	5th Day 09. Inference 类型 Day 10. Review Test II （所有题型复习）	6th Day 12. Office Hours Day 13. Arts, Literature Day 14. Life Science I
7th Day 15. Physical Science Day 16. Review Test III （前4种主题复习）	8th Day 17. Service Encounters Day 18. Life Science II Day 19. Social Science	9th Day 20. America Day 21. Review Test IV （后4种主题复习）

如果复习时间充裕

第一次接触iBT考试，或者想要从头到尾准备所有内容的话，可以选择这种一周学习5天、休息2天的模式。

Week	Day				
1st week	1st Day 01 Diagnostic Test	2nd Day 02 P. 24 ~ 31	3rd Day 02 P. 32 ~ 37	4th Day 03 P. 40 ~ 47	5th Day 03 P. 48 ~ 53
2nd week	6th Day 04 P. 56 ~ 63	7th Day 04 P. 64 ~ 69	8th Day 05 P. 72 ~ 79	9th Day 05 P. 80 ~ 85	10th Day 06 Review Test I
3rd week	11th Day 07 P. 94 ~ 101	12th Day 07 P. 102 ~ 107	13th Day 08 P. 110 ~ 117	14th Day 08 P. 118 ~ 123	15th Day 09 P. 126 ~ 133
4th week	16th Day 09 P. 134 ~ 139	17th Day 10 Review Test II	18th Day 11 Word Brush-up	19th Day 12 Case Example Smart Source	20th Day 12 Practice Test
5th week	21st Day 13 Case Example Smart Source	22nd Day 13 Practice Test	23rd Day 14 Case Example Smart Source	24th Day 14 Practice Test	25th Day 15 Case Example Smart Source
6th week	26th Day 15 Practice Test	27th Day 16 Review Test III	28th Day 17 Case Example Smart Source	29th Day 17 Practice Test	30th Day 18 Case Example Smart Source
7th week	31st Day 18 Practice Test	32nd Day 19 Case Example Smart Source	33rd Day 19 Practice Test	34th Day 20 Case Example Smart Source	35th Day 20 Practice Test
8th week	36th Day 21 Review Test III	37th Day 22 Word Brush-up			

关于 TOEFL iBT

iBT（internet-based test）是通过电脑完成、为了弥补一直以来尽管PBT(paper-based test)取得高分但实际英语实用能力不足的欠缺而进行的考试，最大特点是增加了口语和写作考试内容。

TOEFL iBT的基本信息

1. 考试的构成

① 考试内容：分reading，listening，speaking，writing4项必考内容

② 考试顺序：reading（60~100分钟）-listening（60~90分钟）-休息（10分钟）-speaking（约20分钟）-writing（约50分钟）一共需要约4个小时

③ 分数范围：各项满分分别为30分，共120分

2. 应考信息

① 考试费：以官方网站信息为准

② 报名方法：登录www.ets.org或者 http://toefl.etest.net.cn网站报名

③ 考试场所：全国ETS指定考试中心

④ 考试日期和次数：周六或周日，一个月2~4次，一年30~40次

⑤ 进考场时间：9:30

⑥ 考试证件：以官方网站信息为准

⑦ 查询成绩：从考试日开始15天后（周末、公休日除外）可以在官方网站上确认成绩，选择邮寄的话，需要8~12周

⑧ 成绩有效期：2年

⑨ 考场注意事项：根据考号确定本人的考场，请参考考试时间，提前到达考场。

TOEFL iBT构成

	文章构成	问题类型	考题数
Reading	3篇700词长短的文章 part 1（文章1）-part 2（文章2、3）-如有附加题的情况（文章4、5）	共9个类型	每段文章12~14道题，共36~42道题
Listening	1个题目（1段3分钟长短的对话文） 2个4~6分钟的讲义文 2个题目（如有附加题的情况，一共3个题目）	共7个类型	对话文5道题 讲义文6道题 基本共34道题
Speaking	独立型问题2个 综合型问题4个	共6个类型	共6道题
Writing	综合型问题1个（20分钟） 独立型问题1个（30分钟）	共2个类型	共2道题

关于iBT听力

由于考试采取iBT网考形式，因此熟悉实际考试界面非常重要。主要结构与答题技巧请参照tip部分。

iBT听力的界面构成

1. 说明与试题界面

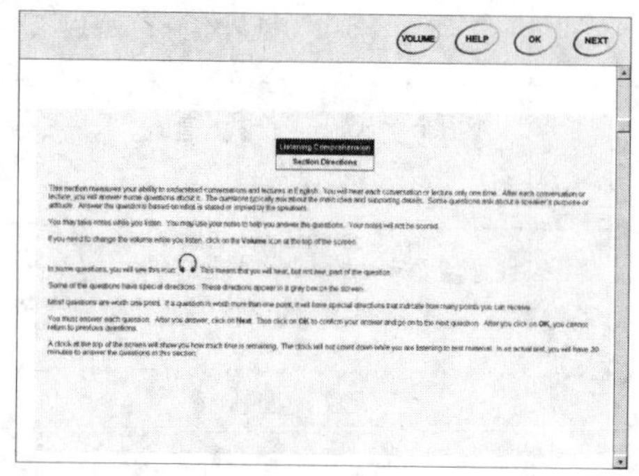

说明部分将介绍试题结构。

2. 听力开始时的画面

听力开始时将出现①画面及②进度指示条。

3. 试题界面

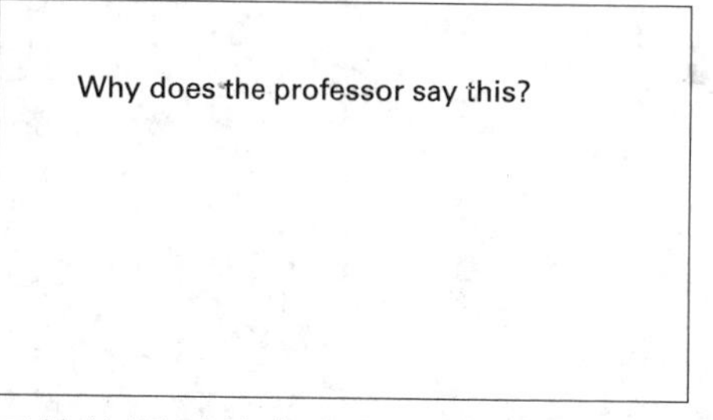

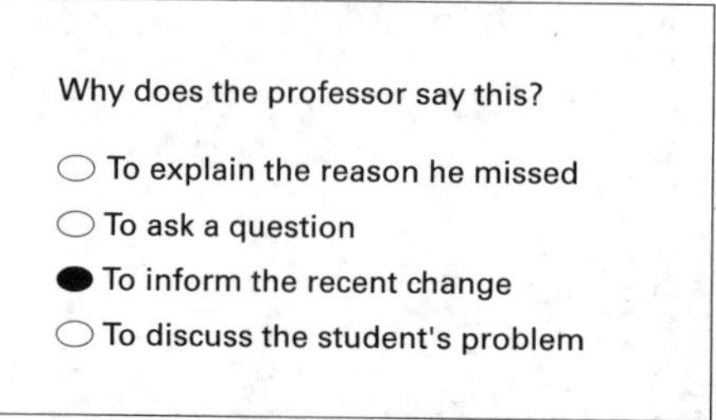

开始答题时首先出现问题，然后试题被读出，但需要注意此时界面上不会出现选项。

4. 图像界面

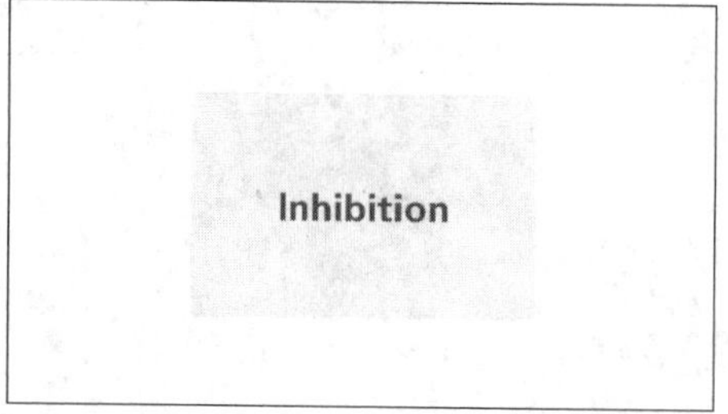

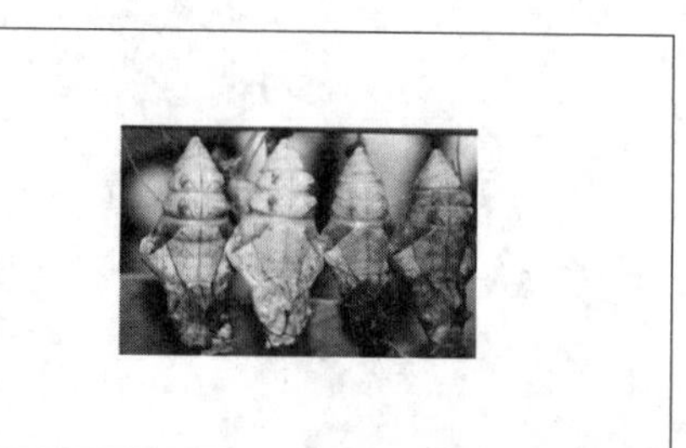

讲义文部分界面上还会出现关键词或相关幻灯片。

iBT听力的题型分布

下面是听力部分一篇讲义文的原文，清楚明晰地说明各题型的分布情况以及何处需要做笔记。

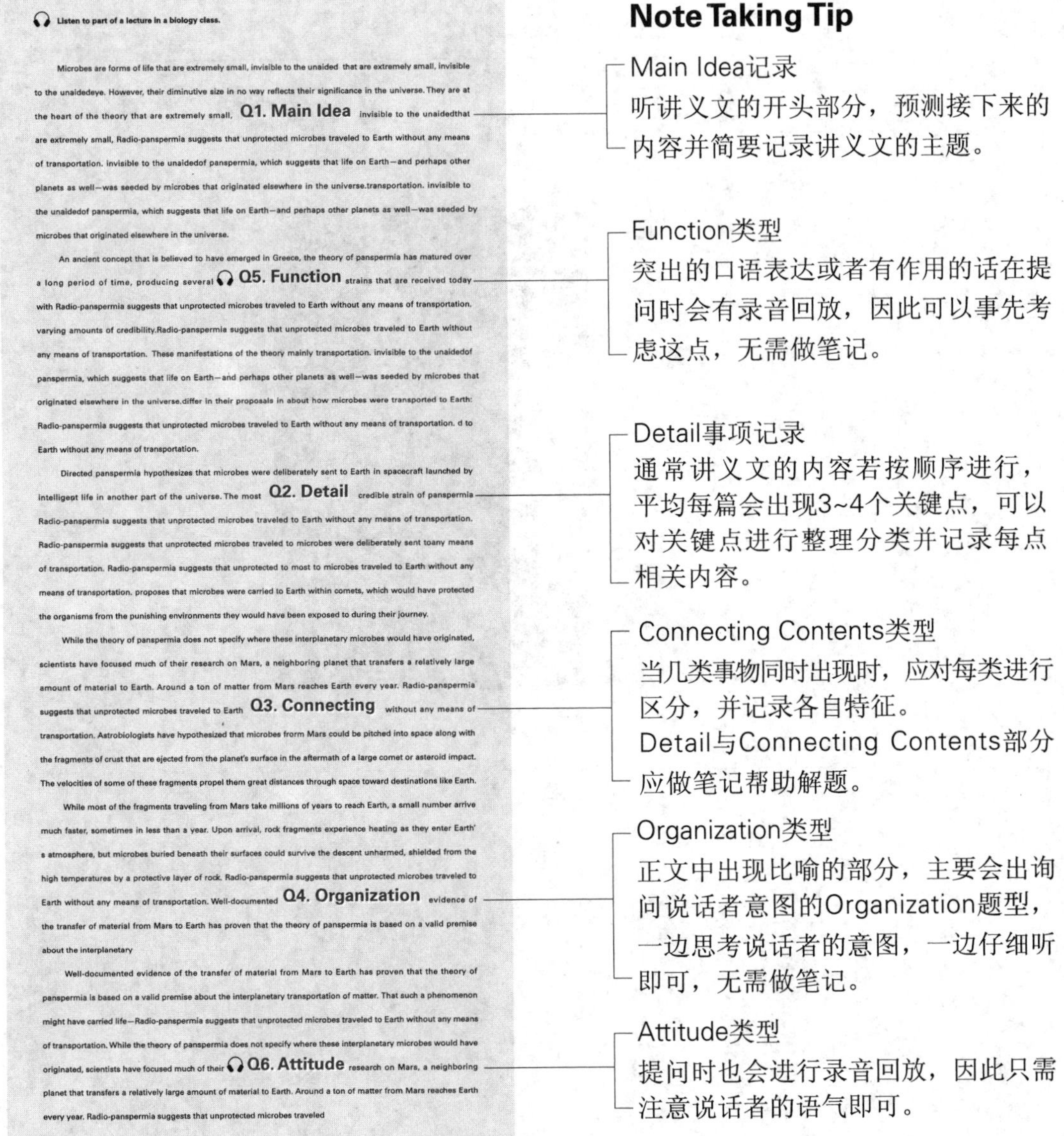

Listen to part of a lecture in a biology class.

Microbes are forms of life that are extremely small, invisible to the unaided that are extremely small, invisible to the unaidedeye. However, their diminutive size in no way reflects their significance in the universe. They are at the heart of the theory that are extremely small, **Q1. Main Idea** invisible to the unaidedthat are extremely small, Radio-panspermia suggests that unprotected microbes traveled to Earth without any means of transportation. invisible to the unaidedof panspermia, which suggests that life on Earth—and perhaps other planets as well—was seeded by microbes that originated elsewhere in the universe.transportation. invisible to the unaidedof panspermia, which suggests that life on Earth—and perhaps other planets as well—was seeded by microbes that originated elsewhere in the universe.

An ancient concept that is believed to have emerged in Greece, the theory of panspermia has matured over a long period of time, producing several **Q5. Function** strains that are received today with Radio-panspermia suggests that unprotected microbes traveled to Earth without any means of transportation. varying amounts of credibility.Radio-panspermia suggests that unprotected microbes traveled to Earth without any means of transportation. These manifestations of the theory mainly transportation. invisible to the unaidedof panspermia, which suggests that life on Earth—and perhaps other planets as well—was seeded by microbes that originated elsewhere in the universe.differ in their proposals in about how microbes were transported to Earth: Radio-panspermia suggests that unprotected microbes traveled to Earth without any means of transportation. d to Earth without any means of transportation.

Directed panspermia hypothesizes that microbes were deliberately sent to Earth in spacecraft launched by intelligent life in another part of the universe. The most **Q2. Detail** credible strain of panspermia Radio-panspermia suggests that unprotected microbes traveled to Earth without any means of transportation. Radio-panspermia suggests that unprotected microbes traveled to microbes were deliberately sent toany means of transportation. Radio-panspermia suggests that unprotected to most to microbes traveled to Earth without any means of transportation. proposes that microbes were carried to Earth within comets, which would have protected the organisms from the punishing environments they would have been exposed to during their journey.

While the theory of panspermia does not specify where these interplanetary microbes would have originated, scientists have focused much of their research on Mars, a neighboring planet that transfers a relatively large amount of material to Earth. Around a ton of matter from Mars reaches Earth every year. Radio-panspermia suggests that unprotected microbes traveled to Earth **Q3. Connecting** without any means of transportation. Astrobiologists have hypothesized that microbes frorm Mars could be pitched into space along with the fragments of crust that are ejected from the planet's surface in the aftermath of a large comet or asteroid impact. The velocities of some of these fragments propel them great distances through space toward destinations like Earth.

While most of the fragments traveling from Mars take millions of years to reach Earth, a small number arrive much faster, sometimes in less than a year. Upon arrival, rock fragments experience heating as they enter Earth's atmosphere, but microbes buried beneath their surfaces could survive the descent unharmed, shielded from the high temperatures by a protective layer of rock. Radio-panspermia suggests that unprotected microbes traveled to Earth without any means of transportation. Well-documented **Q4. Organization** evidence of the transfer of material from Mars to Earth has proven that the theory of panspermia is based on a valid premise about the interplanetary

Well-documented evidence of the transfer of material from Mars to Earth has proven that the theory of panspermia is based on a valid premise about the interplanetary transportation of matter. That such a phenomenon might have carried life—Radio-panspermia suggests that unprotected microbes traveled to Earth without any means of transportation. While the theory of panspermia does not specify where these interplanetary microbes would have originated, scientists have focused much of their **Q6. Attitude** research on Mars, a neighboring planet that transfers a relatively large amount of material to Earth. Around a ton of matter from Mars reaches Earth every year. Radio-panspermia suggests that unprotected microbes traveled

Note Taking Tip

Main Idea记录
听讲义文的开头部分，预测接下来的内容并简要记录讲义文的主题。

Function类型
突出的口语表达或者有作用的话在提问时会有录音回放，因此可以事先考虑这点，无需做笔记。

Detail事项记录
通常讲义文的内容若按顺序进行，平均每篇会出现3~4个关键点，可以对关键点进行整理分类并记录每点相关内容。

Connecting Contents类型
当几类事物同时出现时，应对每类进行区分，并记录各自特征。
Detail与Connecting Contents部分应做笔记帮助解题。

Organization类型
正文中出现比喻的部分，主要会出询问说话者意图的Organization题型，一边思考说话者的意图，一边仔细听即可，无需做笔记。

Attitude类型
提问时也会进行录音回放，因此只需注意说话者的语气即可。

- Basic Comprehension Questions
- Pragmatic Understanding Questions
- Connecting Information Questions

会再次回放录音的function与attitude题型最后出现，其他题型会根据听力内容按顺序出现。

DAY 01  Diagnostic Test

请尝试解答以下问题，测试目前水平。

MP3•01

passage 1. [1~5] Listen to part of a conversation between a nurse and a student.

Volume I Help I OK I Next

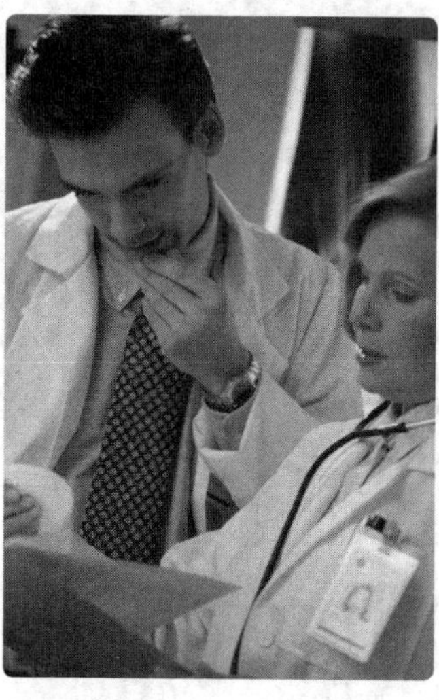

1. Why is the man at the health office?
   Ⓐ To change his flu shot appointment
   Ⓑ To take an immediate vaccination
   Ⓒ To set up a flu shot appointment
   Ⓓ To ask about the health insurance policy

2. Why does the man avoid getting his shot on a specific day?
   Ⓐ He has an athletic competition the next day.
   Ⓑ His health insurance will not cover the flu shot.
   Ⓒ He must go to the Bakersville clinic for the flu shot.
   Ⓓ There are no more free flu shots available at the campus clinic.

3. When can a student go to the Bakersville clinic?
   Ⓐ If the campus clinic is under renovations
   Ⓑ If the student is a competitive varsity athlete
   Ⓒ If the student has premium health insurance coverage
   Ⓓ If the campus clinic cannot handle its students' needs

Listen again to part of the conversation. Then answer the question. 

4. Why does the woman say this:
   Ⓐ To imply it is more convenient than the campus clinic
   Ⓑ To convince the student it is a good alternative
   Ⓒ To notify the student of the exact distance to the clinic
   Ⓓ To discourage the student from visiting the clinic on Friday

Listen again to part of the conversation. Then answer the question. 

5. What can be inferred about the man when he says this:
   Ⓐ He is relieved that the appointment has been booked.
   Ⓑ He is confused about why he has to go off campus.
   Ⓒ He is not sure about the procedure for getting a shot.
   Ⓓ He is uncertain about how to get to the clinic.

MP3•04

passage 2. [1~6] Listen to part of a talk in a zoology class.

Volume I Help I OK I Next

Metacommunication

1. What is the talk mainly about?

Ⓐ Different types of vocal communication among animals

Ⓑ The role communication behaviors play in animal mating

Ⓒ Different interpretations of the meaning of animal communication

Ⓓ The forms and functions of animal communication

2. How does the professor illustrate the concept of animal body language?

Ⓐ By describing a type of feeding behavior exhibited by a common gull

Ⓑ By explaining several gestures that have universal meanings in the animal world

Ⓒ By reminding the class of a species of bird which the students are already familiar with

Ⓓ By comparing the gestures of the herring gull with gestures made by human parents

3. What does the professor imply about the behavior of a cat rubbing against an object?
   Ⓐ It is essentially the same as the vocal calls of frogs and monkeys.
   Ⓑ It is something that is only observed in domesticated pets.
   Ⓒ It is one of the best understood examples of animal communication.
   Ⓓ It is a way of conveying information to other animals through smell.

4. What are two key functions of animal communication mentioned in the talk? Click on 2 answers.
   Ⓐ Conveying an intent to either stand up or yield to another animal
   Ⓑ Attempting to attract potential prey from the surrounding area
   Ⓒ Expressing confusion about the intentions of another animal
   Ⓓ Letting others know the true meaning of the next communication

Listen again to part of the talk. Then answer the question. MP3•05

5. Why does the professor say this:
   Ⓐ To introduce a new theme for discussion
   Ⓑ To show that he will deviate from the main issue
   Ⓒ To indicate that he is unfamiliar with the subject matter
   Ⓓ To terminate his digression from the main topic

Listen again to part of the talk. Then answer the question. MP3•06

6. What does the professor mean when he says this:
   Ⓐ He thinks the students should be able to grasp the idea easily.
   Ⓑ He wants the students to pay particularly close attention to an upcoming point.
   Ⓒ He thinks the students may be having trouble understanding his point.
   Ⓓ He wants to answer students' questions before moving on to another idea.

MP3・07

passage 3. [1~6] Listen to part of a lecture in a history class.

Volume I Help I OK I Next

Gypsum

1. What aspect of the ancient Mayans does the professor focus on in the lecture?

Ⓐ A theory about Mayan migration into South America

Ⓑ A method the Mayans used to deal with drought

Ⓒ A theory about why Mayan cultural influence persists

Ⓓ A possible cause of the Mayan empire's decline

2. What does the professor say happened to the Mayan people between 800 and 900 AD? Click on 2 answers.

Ⓐ They migrated to South America.

Ⓑ They abandoned their cities.

Ⓒ They mysteriously disappeared.

Ⓓ They were wiped out in a flood.

Ⓔ They suffered from severe droughts.

3. What does the professor suggest is the primary evidence supporting the climate change theory?

Ⓐ Gypsum levels in lake sediment

Ⓑ Analysis of fossils in rock formations

Ⓒ Proof that canals and reservoirs were built in the region

Ⓓ Archaeological evidence of famine and disease

4. What does the professor imply about the Mayans' control over local water sources?

Ⓐ It enabled them to withstand harsh weather conditions.

Ⓑ It meant that their water supply never dropped to low levels.

Ⓒ It caused their water supply to become polluted with minerals.

Ⓓ It indicated that they relied too heavily on water.

Listen again to part of the lecture. Then answer the question. MP3·08

5. Why does the professor say this:

Ⓐ To make sure that the students have already read about these theories

Ⓑ To indicate that he will compare the different hypotheses next class

Ⓒ To suggest that he will not elaborate on these points in the lecture

Ⓓ To show that he does not think these theories are very convincing

Listen again to part of the lecture. Then answer the question.  MP3·09

6. What can be inferred about the professor?

Ⓐ He doubts the validity of the evidence used to support the climate change theory.

Ⓑ He believes that the climate change theory is quite reasonable.

Ⓒ He does not believe that there was a significant climate change at the time.

Ⓓ He is sure that other factors besides climate change also played a role.

basic training

分题型听力训练

听力考试会出现哪些题型？

DAY 02 Main Idea

DAY 03 Detail

DAY 04 Function

DAY 05 Attitude

DAY 06 Review Test I (Day 2~5)

DAY 07 Organization

DAY 08 Connecting Contents

DAY 09 Inference

DAY 10 Review Test II (Day 2~9)

Holiday! Word Brush-up

DAY02

Main Idea

- CASE EXAMPLE - 例题
- CASE EXAMPLE解析- 例题解析
- SMART SOLUTION - 题型攻略专题
- PRACTICE TEST - 练习
- DICTATION - 听写

speed keyword

Main Idea 题型相当于为文章添加标题

这一题型要求找出可以概括全文的主题，选择可以做所听文章标题的答案即可。conversation与lecture部分都是以此种题型开始提问的，其中conversation部分通常以询问学生的拜访目的为主，lecture部分通常以询问演讲的主旨为主。鉴于英美国家人士习惯开门见山的逻辑方式，文章的话题通常会在开头部分出现，但是也会出现要求听完全文才了解整体大意的问题，尤其在演讲部分。

- 不可错过文章开头哦！
- 此题型一定会在每篇文章的开头出现哦！

An important early development in American film was the spread of nickelodeons shortly after the…uh, turn of the century. Popular interest in film was booming at the time, but there were few venues for screening. That's why lots of small, storefront, purpose-built movie theaters, known as nickelodeons, began popping up everywhere.

At first, small shops and restaurants were also converted into, ah, makeshift venues for showing movies. But nickelodeons—so-called after a "nickel," a five-cent coin, which was the price of admission, and "odeon," the Greek word for theater—uh…nickelodeons were much more suitable for watching movies. They generally had fewer than 200 seats.

What is the talk mainly about?

CASE EXAMPLE

CONVERSATION  **Listen to part of a conversation between a student and a professor.**

MP3 • 13

| Volume | Help | OK | Next |

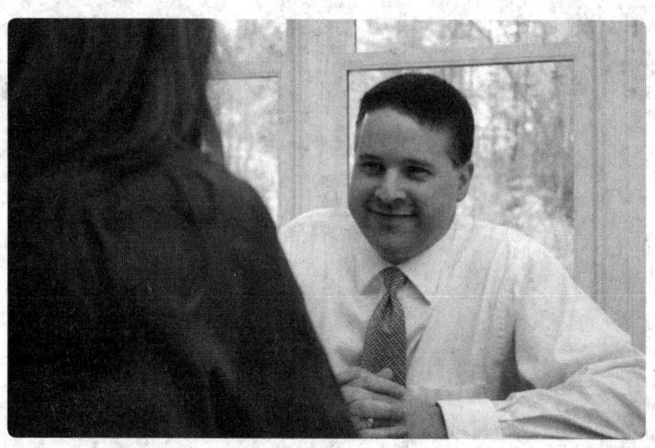

note taking

学生去办公室拜访了教授。请注意听教授让学生来办公室谈话的原因，记录对话要点。

Topic:

> Why did the professor call the woman to his office?

Ⓐ To draw her attention to a student grant

Ⓑ To interview her for a graduate program

Ⓒ To tell her that she got a student fellowship

Ⓓ To talk about an upcoming assignment

LECTURE  **Listen to part of a lecture in a film class.**

MP3 • 14

| Volume | Help | OK | Next |

note taking 这是一堂电影学课。请记录教授希望重点传达的演讲主题。

Topic:

> What is the talk mainly about?

Ⓐ A brief history of movie theaters around the world

Ⓑ A description of an early form of movie theaters

Ⓒ A comparison of different types of movie theaters

Ⓓ A timeline of the evolution of multiplex theaters

CASE EXAMPLE 解析

[SCRIPT] **Narrator** : Listen to part of a conversation **between a student and a professor.**
情景:Office Hours

● 通过对话开头部分判断情景为office hours或service encounters。

Professor (male) : Come in, Erica. I wanted to talk to you about something...

Student (female) : *[pre-empting her]* Professor Klein, **if it's about the assignment on Newton's Laws, please don't worry.** I'm well ahead of schedule on that.
Distraction

● 在对话中故意分散考生注意力的distraction也会首先出现。

Professor : That's good to hear...but no, **I actually wanted to talk about a new departmental fellowship.** It's being given to top students in the sciences next semester. It's worth 3,000 dollars towards tuition. **I wondered if you might be interested in applying for it.**
谈话目的：关键词
真正的谈话目的

● 但是下面面谈的真正原因就会出现了。I wanted to talk about…是引导主题的代表性句型，可是需要注意的是，这类句型经常只出现关键词，而具体内容放在下面的句子中。

Student : *[enthusiastically]* Sure. Absolutely. So, uh, what's this fellowship about?

Professor : It's a new initiative the department has launched to try and get more out of the top students.

> 教授为什么让学生来研究室？

Ⓐ **为了让学生关注奖学金**

Ⓑ 面谈研究生院项目的相关事宜

Ⓒ 告知学生，她获得了奖学金

▶ 谈论的是奖学金的申请机会，而不是授予决定

Ⓓ 为谈论下一个话题做准备▶即首先出现的distraction部分内容

● 尤其要注意不能选择Ⓒ。文章中的关键词fellowship在错误选项中也出现了，但要注意对话不是在谈论已经做出授予决定的奖学金。

Answer Ⓐ

note taking

Topic : The opportunity to apply for the fellowship *or* **奖学金申请建议**

[SCRIPT] **Narrator** : Listen to part of a lecture in a **film class.**
讲义文涉及领域：电影

● 通过讲义文涉及的领域推测下面讲话的主题。

Professor (male)

An important early development in American film was the spread of nickelodeons shortly after the...uh, turn of the century. Popular interest in film was booming at the time, but there were few venues for screening. That's why lots of small, storefront, purpose-built movie theaters, known as nickelodeons, began popping up everywhere.
讲座主题：最初形态的电影院—五分钱电影院

● 开头介绍最早的电影院—五分钱电影院。如果开头部分是讲义文主题，则接下来的内容都会是对这一主题的说明。

At first, small shops and restaurants were also converted into, ah, makeshift venues for showing movies. But nickelodeons—so-called after a "nickel," a five-cent coin, which was the price of admission, and "odeon," the Greek word for theater—uh...nickelodeons were much more suitable for watching movies. They generally had fewer than 200 seats.

● 说明"五分钱电影院"的名称由来及其特征→确定内容是关于五分钱电影院的。

> 讲义文的主要内容是什么？

Ⓐ 简要的世界电影院史 ▶过于笼统

Ⓑ 说明最早形态的电影院

Ⓒ 比较几种不同形态的电影院 ▶除了五分钱电影院未出现其他形态的电影院

Ⓓ 多媒体电影院的演变过程

● 大部分错误选项都与电影院的内容相关，但是没有具体到电影院的哪些层面。尤其像Ⓐ这样内容范围过大的选项通常都是错误的。

Answer Ⓑ

note taking

Topic : nickelodeon—the early form of theater

TIP Main Idea 题型询问文章的主题。主题是文章的核心信息，通常在理解了一半以上的内容后即可充分把握，因此不一定要做笔记，但连续记录文章要点的确可以提高考生的注意力。

SMART SOLUTION

SOLUTION 1

关键词会在开头出现。

错过文章的开头对解题有致命危险，因为通常讲义文在开头部分会出现关键词，而对话在前半部分会揭示拜访的目的。尤其是在如下一些介绍话题的信号词(signal words)之后，往往会出现可以概括全文的关键词。

· 引出对话目的信号语句，例如：

I am here to talk about... 我来是想谈一谈…：揭示拜访目的时最常用的句型。
I'm interested in... 我对…感兴趣：询问特定的课程或项目等。
I've got some questions about... 我有一些关于…问题：针对演讲内容提问时。
I wonder if you can... 不知道您/你是否可以…：请别人参与讨论等。

· 引出演讲关键词的信号语句，例如：

Today, I want to talk about... 今天，我想谈一谈…
In this class we are going to talk about... 今天的课上，我们将谈一谈…
Last time we discussed.... Today, we are going to move on... 上次课上，我们已经讨论过…。今天，我们接着来探讨…。
以上都是提到上次话题时经常使用的句型。

SOLUTION 2

关键词不一定是答案。

但这并不意味着关键词就一定是正确答案。一起来看前面case example对话中的相关部分。

I actually wanted to talk about a new departmental fellowship. It's being given to top students in the sciences next semester. It's worth 3,000 dollars towards tuition. **I wondered if you might be interested in applying for it.**

这部分的关键词是fellowship，但是因为在所有的选项中都很有可能出现这个关键词，因此仅凭这点就去判断正确答案是不恰当的。区分正确与错误答案的关键点在于对关键词的进一步细节描述。上面的对话中，applying for it (fellowship)就是揭示说话者意图的核心细节。尤其是在讲义文中，通常前面部分仅仅会出现关键词，这就需要听完全文后总结出主题，并不能因为获取了关键词就掉以轻心。正确答案的构成模式是“**关键词+具体内容**”，因此需要仔细地通听全文来确定主题。

SOLUTION 3

正确答案会抽象地表述。

主题贯穿于讲义文的全部内容，但是在答案选项中，却只能凝炼为一句话，因此会多少采用抽象的表达方式，选项中就会出现历史、区别、比较、方法或过程之类的表述。

The **history** of the early railroad 早期铁路史
The **difference** between a tornado and a hurricane 龙卷风与飓风的区别
How pearls are formed 珍珠的形成方式

当4个选项都包含相同的关键词时，通常情况下，内容最具体的选项即为答案。需要注意的是讲义文的时间只有4~6分钟，因此内容范围不会非常大。来看前面case example中的答案选项。

Ⓐ A brief history of **movie theaters** around the world
Ⓑ A description of an early form of **movie theaters**
Ⓒ A comparison of different types of **movie theaters**
Ⓓ A timeline of the evolution of multiplex **theaters**

由于4个选项中都出现了关键词theaters，所以此时应将注意力集中于各选项都分别涉及了theaters的哪个层面。正确答案Ⓑ把表述范围限定于电影院的早期形态，内容最为具体。

SOLUTION 4

熟悉典型错误。

下面是main idea题型的典型性错误。

- 关键词或细节与文章内容不符：not correct
- 仅涉及了文章的部分内容：minor

答案选项即使包含了文章内容的一部分，但仍无法囊括全部的，就无法被看作为合适的主题。尤其需要注意的是minor型的错误。

PRACTICE TEST_level 1

> **[1-8] Listen to each passage. Then choose the best answers to the questions.**

Listen to part of a lecture in a paleontology class.

MP3 • 15

1. What is the lecture mainly about?

Ⓐ Climate changes during the Pleistocene epoch

Ⓑ Historic extinctions of large mammal species

Ⓒ Possible causes of the Pleistocene extinctions

Ⓓ A pattern of advancing and retreating glaciers

Listen to part of a lecture in an economics class.

MP3 • 16

2. What is the talk mainly about?

Ⓐ A recently formulated theory of economics

Ⓑ How businesses maximize their earnings

Ⓒ The relationship between cost, output, and price

Ⓓ Why some firms have difficulty making a profit

Listen to part of a lecture in an art class.

MP3 • 17

3. What is the talk mainly about?

Ⓐ The characteristics of ancient Egyptian statuary

Ⓑ Naturalism in the artistic work produced in ancient Egypt

Ⓒ The religious function of ancient Egyptian sculpture

Ⓓ Materials commonly used by sculptors of the ancient world

Listen to part of a lecture in an astronomy class.

MP3 • 18

4. What is the talk mainly about?

Ⓐ The average lifespan of red and blue stars

Ⓑ How the temperature of a star affects its color

Ⓒ What a star's color indicates about its rate of burning

Ⓓ How much fuel is required to sustain stars

Listen to part of a lecture in a biology class.

MP3•19

5. What is the talk mainly about?
   - Ⓐ The differences between mutualism and other types of symbiosis
   - Ⓑ The mutually beneficial relationship between two life forms
   - Ⓒ The breakdown of cellulose as it occurs in ungulates
   - Ⓓ The enzymes found in the digestive tracts of hoofed animals

Listen to part of a lecture in an architecture class.

MP3•20

6. What aspect of Central Park does the professor mainly discuss?
   - Ⓐ Its effects on life in nineteenth-century New York City
   - Ⓑ Its similarities to public grounds in London and Paris
   - Ⓒ The architectural contest by which its design was chosen
   - Ⓓ Its planning and construction by New York officials

Listen to part of a lecture in an art class.

MP3•21

7. What is the discussion mainly about?
   - Ⓐ One way in which an artist influenced people's views about art
   - Ⓑ The principal philosophy behind the artwork of the Dadaists
   - Ⓒ How artistic interpretation evolved during the twentieth century
   - Ⓓ The method an artist used to create revolutionary works of art

Listen to part of a lecture in a psychology class.

MP3•22

8. What is the talk mainly about?
   - Ⓐ The requirements necessary for normal childhood development
   - Ⓑ The emotional bond between an infant and a caregiver
   - Ⓒ The natural instincts displayed by both babies and their caregivers
   - Ⓓ The importance of availability and responsiveness for babies

CONVERSATION  **1. Listen to a conversation between a student and a facilities coordinator.**

MP3 • 23

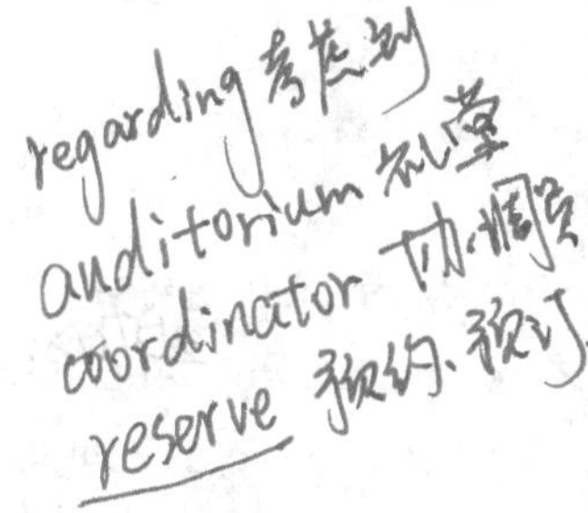

note taking

Why does the woman go to the facilities office?

Ⓐ To request that the department move some of its equipment off the stage

Ⓑ To reserve the auditorium for a performance by the university jazz band

Ⓒ To purchase tickets for the graduation ceremony and pick up a program

Ⓓ To find out how many people will be attending the band performance

LECTURE  **2. Listen to part of a lecture in an engineering class.**

MP3 • 24

note taking

What aspect of photovoltaic cells does the professor mainly discuss?

Ⓐ How they are used to power technological devices

Ⓑ How they have made semiconductors more efficient

Ⓒ The process by which they create an electrical current

Ⓓ The history of their development by the energy industry

CONVERSATION  **1. Listen to part of a conversation in the student services office.**

MP3 • 25

note taking

Main Idea Why is the student at the student services office?

Ⓐ To get information about an upcoming conference

Ⓑ To reserve campus space for an event

Ⓒ To file an objection to an auditorium expansion

Ⓓ To change her previous booking of a conference room

CONVERSATION  **2. Listen to part of a conversation between a student and a professor.**

MP3 • 26

note taking

Main Idea Why does the student go to see the professor?

Ⓐ To inquire about the final exam

Ⓑ To get advice about graduate school options

Ⓒ To discuss a master's degree program

Ⓓ To request a letter of recommendation

LECTURE 3. **Listen to part of a lecture in a literature class.**

MP3 • 27

note taking

Main Idea What is the lecture mainly about?

Ⓐ How *The Good Earth* differs from other works of American literature

Ⓑ Why Buck is considered an important American author

Ⓒ Buck's unique background and her most famous book

Ⓓ The writings and lives of Chinese-American authors

LECTURE 4. **Listen to part of a lecture in a biology class.**

MP3 • 28

note taking

Main Idea What is the talk mainly about?

Ⓐ Differences among the venoms produced by snakes

Ⓑ Three families of venomous snakes

Ⓒ Two ways that snakes deliver venom

Ⓓ The most dangerous snake species in the world

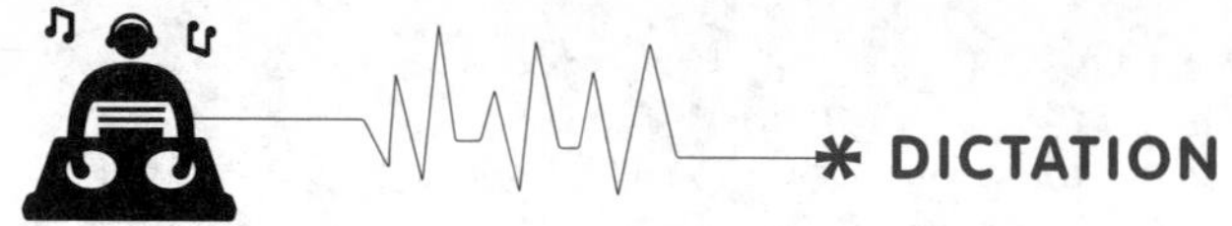

✱ DICTATION

MP3·29 1. Listen to part of the level 2 lecture again and fill in the blanks.

Professor: Class, today we're gonna be talking about technology that helps us use 1) ______. Does anyone in here know what this—this technology is called? It's called photovoltaics. Um, a lot of you are probably familiar with photovoltaics because you've seen 2) ______ or know how photovoltaic cells work. That's actually what I want to talk about today: the functioning of photovoltaic cells.

Basically, it's like this: light strikes the photovoltaic cells and causes 3) ______...and when we capture these freed electrons, we've got an 4) ______.

Let me go over it a little further. Photovoltaic cells—um, I'm going to 5) ______ to PV from now on, OK? So...PV cells are composed of semiconductors. For those of you who don't know, a semiconductor is a material that becomes 6) ______.

When sunlight hits the semiconductor, the energy sometimes 7) ______. So you have 8) ______ moving around the semiconductor, and you have a "hole" in the atom where the electron used to be.

It's actually possible to 9) ______ to increase the number of free electrons or the number of holes. Um, I'm not really going to explain this because we don't have much time. What's important to know is that PV cells 10) ______: one that's been treated to increase the number of free electrons, and one treated to increase the number of holes. So...as a result, 11) ______ between the two layers that causes electrons to move in one direction. If we provide a path from one layer to the other, electrons will flow along it, providing us with a current or electricity. This is how PV cells provide us with electricity.

答案参见ANSWER BOOK P336

MP3·30 2. Listen to part of the level 3 lecture again and fill in the blanks.

［省略］

Professor: OK. All venomous snakes, uh, they use...it's kind of like a saliva. They use this saliva-like venom to kill or, um, 1) ______. And their venom is delivered through...fangs in the mouth.

2) ______ belong to a, um, a family called elapids.

Elapids can really range in size...from just eighteen centimeters to six meters in length. In appearance, elapids are long and thin. They also have smooth scales, and their—their eyes have round pupils.

Elapids 3) ______ ______ ______ ______ ______ ______. These fangs are, um, they're located at the front of the mouth...and the venom they emit comes from venom glands at the back of the upper jaw. When elapids have their mouths closed, their fangs, um, they fit into a kind of—a kind of 4) ______ ______ ______ ______. Elapid venom is usually a neurotoxin, um, which means that 5) ______ ______ ______ ______ ______ ______.

As I said earlier, elapids are some of 6) ______ ______ ______ ______ ______.

An elapid species known as the black mamba is considered to be the most dangerous snake in the world. Um, and it's fast...and really large. It can also be 7) ______ ______ ______ ______ ______ ______. Its venom—its venom isn't the most toxic, but when the black mamba bites, um, it delivers quite a bit of it. Now, the most venomous land snake is also an elapid. 8) ______ ______ ______ ______ ______ ______, and its venom is quite—quite potent. The venom from 9) ______ ______ ______ ______ ______ ______ could kill, um, about one hundred people—or 250,000 mice.

［省略］

答案参见ANSWER BOOK P341

oral expression

MP3•31

Listen to the expressions and sentences in the script below and repeat.

come to a close 结束	As the Pleistocene epoch **came to a close,** some major events were happening.
put A in charge of *doing* 让A负责…	Professor Cox **put me in charge of reserving** the auditorium for our spring concert.
It'll be all yours. 完全听你的。	There's nothing taking place on that day at the auditorium. So **it'll be all yours.**
big deal 大事，重大问题	That's not really a **big deal.**
now that you mention it 既然你提了	Yes, **now that you mention it,** I know of it.
drop off 带…过来	When should I **drop** my résumé **off**?
It's estimated to be 据估计…	**It's estimated to be** actually a hundred times more powerful than any land snake's venom.

DAY03

Detail

- CASE EXAMPLE - 例题
- CASE EXAMPLE解析- 例题解析
- ☆ SMART SOLUTION - 题型攻略专题
- □ PRACTICE TEST - 练习
- * DICTATION - 听写

speed keyword

Detail 题型不是关注琐碎的信息

这一题型要求找出与听到的内容相一致的选项，因此应选择说话者直接提及的信息，而不能在推测或想象的基础上进行选择。细节题是一种常见题型，它要求考生选择符合文章细节内容的信息，但是TOEFL iBT考试的不同之处在于听力考试长达4~6分钟，detail题型需要考生在如此长的时间内抓住细节。因为考生不可能记住所有细小的信息，因此就需要事先练习，考试时能够把握：怎样仔细地听以及应该集中于哪些“细节”。另外，这一题型还有具备两个答案的多选题。

- 就是说话者的原话，只不过进行了**paraphrasing**！

An important early development in American film was the spread of nickelodeons shortly after the…uh, turn of the century. Popular interest in film was booming at the time, but there were few venues for screening. That's why lots of small, storefront, purpose-built movie theaters, known as nickelodeons, began popping up everywhere.

At first, small shops and restaurants were also converted into, ah, makeshift venues for showing movies. But nickelodeons—so-called after a "nickel," a five-cent coin, which was the price of admission, and "odeon," the Greek word for theater—uh…nickelodeons were much more suitable for watching movies. They generally had fewer than 200 seats.

According to the professor, what is...?

只会拿支撑主题的信息提问！

CASE EXAMPLE

CONVERSATION  **Listen to part of a conversation between a student and her professor.**

MP3 • 46

| Volume | Help | OK | Next |

note taking 学生去办公室拜访了教授。教授想给她提个建议，请记录与此建议有关的两条重要信息。

Topic:

Details:

①

②

> Why does the university offer the leadership course?

Ⓐ To teach students how to do field research

Ⓑ To help students develop advanced leadership skills

Ⓒ To reward students who show great achievement in their studies

Ⓓ To facilitate communication between students and the administration

LECTURE  **Listen to part of a lecture in a computer science class.**

MP3•47

| Volume | Help | OK | Next |

note taking 在计算机工程课上，大家就机器鱼进行了探讨，请总结并记录机器鱼的三个特征。

Topic:

Details:

①

②

③

> According to the professor, what are some features of the robotic fish at the London Aquarium? Click on 2 answers.

Ⓐ It moves without the aid of remote controls.

Ⓑ It is over one meter long.

Ⓒ It imitates the appearance of a real fish.

Ⓓ It locates charging stations and recharges its batteries.

CASE EXAMPLE 解析

[SCRIPT] **Narrator** Listen to part of a conversation between **a student and her professor.** 情景：Office Hours

Student (female) Professor Kho. You wanted to see me?

Professor (male) Yes, Rebecca. **It's about the university leadership course**... 关键词：领导能力训练课程 **I'd like to nominate you for it.** 主题：推荐学生参加领导能力训练课程

Student *[curious]* The university leadership course?

Professor Yeah, it's a course **designed to set up a...a kind of dialogue between the administration and the student body.** Detail 1：课程目标 You know, so the university can find out how to meet the needs of the students.

Student *[surprised]* Ah, okay. And, uh, I'd be one of the student representatives?

Professor *[confirming]* Uh-huh. The enrollment is limited to students nominated by their professors.

Student *[honored]* Wow. That's a big responsibility. Uh, what would my role be as a...as a participant in the course?

Professor Essentially you'll be **doing field research—talking to students about campus issues and, uh, gathering their feedback.** Detail 2: 课程内容

- 首先引出了推荐学生参加领导能力训练课程的主题。
- 由于学生是第一次听到关于领导能力训练课程的介绍，因此考生应该明白文章一定会就开设课程的目的以及课程包含的内容进行说明，也就可以推测出detail题型一定会就两个细节中的一个进行提问。当听到designed to这一信号句型时就应明白，接着一定会出现关于课程目标的内容。

> 学校为什么开设领导能力训练课程？

Ⓐ 为了教授学生实地考查的方法

▶ 提及了field research一词，但它并不是课程目标

Ⓑ 为了挖掘学生高超的领导潜力

Ⓒ 为了给学业成绩优异的学生提供补充

Ⓓ 为了加强学生与行政部门的沟通

- 理解问题的意思十分重要，应注意询问的是开设领导能力训练课程的目标，而不是课程内容等其他细节。

Answer Ⓓ

note taking

Details : ① leadership course 的开设目标——加强学生与行政部门的沟通

② leadership course 的课程内容——field research, talk to students ab. campus issues

TIP 恰当地运用缩略语有助于节约时间，尤其像about, from等常用介词，可以统一略写为ab.,fr.等。

[SCRIPT] **Narrator** Listen to part of a lecture in a **computer science class.**
演讲涉及领域：计算机工程

Professor (male)

Scientists at the University of Essex—in the UK—they **developed a robotic fish** (关键词与主题) that runs on batteries. They introduced it to the London Aquarium in 2005, and, uh, since then, many visitors to the aquarium have been fooled into thinking it's a real fish. How? Well, firstly, it **looks just like a real fish** (Detail 1: 机器鱼的特征1). It's been equipped with synthetic scales, fins and everything. But **it also acts like a real fish** (Detail 1: 机器鱼的特征2), too. It can move around in the water in...in a natural way, darting around and changing direction quickly. **It's not controlled by another device** (Detail 1: 机器鱼的特征3)**, though. It uses artificial intelligence, in the form of sensors,** to, uh, to control its own movement. The sensors help it to avoid obstacles and respond to changes in its environment. Uh, in the future, the scientists are hoping to improve on this intelligence. **They want to build a fish that can seek out charging stations and recharge its own battery, just like when a real fish looks for food.** (Detail 2: 今后开发的内容)

● 讲义文开头部分引出主题。

● 机器鱼的三点特征：讲义文中对核心对象进行特征列举之后，涉及的各项特征几乎都会出现于detail题型中，因此对列举的项目一定要做笔记。

> 依据教授的说法，伦敦水族馆里的机器鱼有什么特征？请点击选择两个选项。

Ⓐ 可以不依赖遥控器活动。

Ⓑ 超过1米。

Ⓒ 模仿真鱼外形。

Ⓓ 需要去充电所充电。

▶ 这是今后开发的内容，不是机器鱼现有的特征。

● 正确选项 Ⓐ - moves without the aid of remote controls 是通过把原文中的It's not controlled by another device进行paraphrasing得来的。

Answer Ⓐ, Ⓒ

note taking

Details : ① looks like a real fish *or* 形似真鱼

② acts like a real fish *or* 动似真鱼

③ uses artificial intelligence *or* 应用了人工智能手段

TIP 可以不选择英语做笔记。在用英文写下核心关键词之后，选择又好写又容易理解的中文也利于提高效率。

SMART SOLUTION

SOLUTION 1

把握结构，一边听一边预测重要信息。

听力考试最理想的策略莫过于边听边记忆全文了。但是，在文章过长、考生难以一直保持高度注意力的情况下，就应该学会恰当地运用“选择与集中”的原理。如果不懂得选择与集中的话，您就很有可能只记住自己听起来顺耳的内容，而错过许多必须确定的要点。那么如何区分主流的与细枝末节的信息并且把握住重要信息呢？下面以例题中的对话来说明。

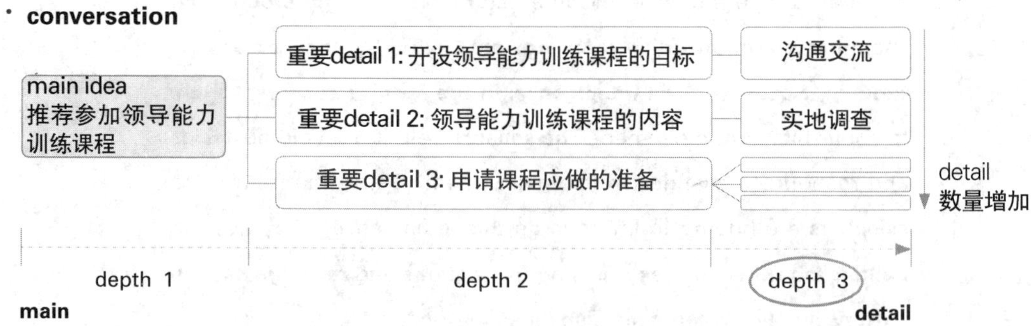

TOEFL detail题型一定不会就文章的非中心部分内容提问。如上图所示，若顺着箭头向右，则信息逐渐变得具体与细节化，TOEFL detail题型主要提问的内容通常为从主题向右延伸两级的depth 3层次的信息。从整篇文章来看，这些信息与主题直接相关，是最实际的信息。这一层次的信息在对话中通常是考生的烦恼或问题以及相应的建议或解决对策；在讲义文中则表现为具体阐释讲义文的三四个核心内容。

SOLUTION 2

记录列举的特征、例子及原理等。

在听力考试的时候，考生常常觉得听懂了全文，但是一开始答题却又觉得力不从心。这是因为考生在掌握了depth 2层次的内容后，便会感觉理解了全文，而实际出现的问题却在考查更深一层的内容。如此，考生在仅仅理解了大致内容的情况下做题，就会发现信息是不够的。下面再以之前case example中的讲义文为例来分析。

- **lecture**

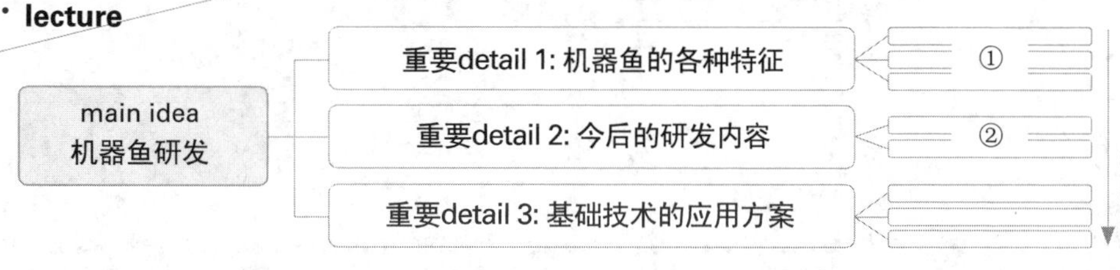

听文章的时候，考生会觉得似乎可以记住所有细节，但是实际上，到录音结束的时候就会发现一些信息已经互相混淆，变得不甚清晰。因此对于像①②部分一样分类列举的信息，一定要做笔记。

SOLUTION 3

正确答案经过paraphrasing。

正确答案通常不会直接引用原文，而会将原文的表达进行paraphrasing。因此，对与原文遣词造句一致的选项应加以甄别。下面来看一看case example的正确答案是怎样由原文改写而来的。

example 原文	正确答案选项
designed to 1) **set up a**...a kind of **dialogue**	To 1) **facilitate communication** between...
2) **looks just like** a real fish	It 2) **imitates the appearance** of a real fish.
It's 3) **not controlled by another device**, though.	It 3) **moves without the aid of remote controls.**

1) set up a dialogue → facilitate communication

2) looks like → imitates the appearance

3) not controlled by another device → moves without the aid of remote controls

SOLUTION 4

熟悉典型错误。

错误选项通常原封不动地引用了对话或讲义文中的词句，但是内容却与原文无关。下面是detail类型问题的典型性错误。

- 叙述的内容与对话或讲义文内容不符：**not corret**
- 叙述的内容在对话或讲义文中未提及：**not mentioned**
- 叙述的内容在对话或讲义文中有提及但是不相关：有的错误选项涉及到原文内容，但是与问题没有直接联系。

PRACTICE TEST_level 1

> **[1-8] Listen to each passage. Then choose the best answers to the questions.**

Listen to part of a conversation between two students.

MP3-48

1. How does the woman suggest that the man prepare for his exam?

Ⓐ By participating in the class study group

Ⓑ By studying cooperatively with the woman

Ⓒ By attending extra classes offered by the department

Ⓓ By getting individual tutoring

Listen to part of a lecture in a history class.

MP3-49

2. According to the professor, why was the Sherman Antitrust Act introduced?

Ⓐ To prevent a few big companies from creating cartels

Ⓑ To promote cooperation between large industrial corporations

Ⓒ To fix prices for a variety of consumer goods

Ⓓ To boost industrial production in 19th century America

Listen to part of a talk in a botany class.

MP3-50

3. According to the professor, what affects the direction that plant stems and roots grow in?

Ⓐ The orientation of the seed

Ⓑ The force of gravity

Ⓒ The direction of the sun

Ⓓ The density of the soil

Listen to part of a conversation between a student and a financial aid advisor.

MP3-51

4. Why does the advisor suggest that the man visit the student help desk?

Ⓐ To inquire about taking out a loan

Ⓑ To check out the scholarships that are available

Ⓒ To find out if he qualifies for an allowance

Ⓓ To get advice on managing a budget

Listen to part of a lecture in a geography class.

MP3 • 52

5. According to the professor, what should people be most concerned about?

Ⓐ The loss of biological diversity in most parts of the world

Ⓑ The environmental impact of losing rainforests

Ⓒ The carbon dioxide emissions from development projects

Ⓓ The changing climatic conditions in rainforests around the world

Listen to part of a talk in a law class.

MP3 • 53

6. According to the professor, why were animals executed in public in medieval Europe?

Ⓐ To help people feel safe from animal attacks

Ⓑ To deter other animals from committing crimes

Ⓒ To send a warning to animal rights' defenders

Ⓓ To show that trials were not necessary for animals

Listen to part of a conversation between a professor and a student.

MP3 • 54

7. Why has the woman decided to drop the class?

Ⓐ She does not find it interesting.

Ⓑ She wants to run for the student council.

Ⓒ She cannot fit it in her schedule.

Ⓓ She plans on changing her major.

Listen to part of a lecture in an environmental science class.

MP3 • 55

8. According to the professor, why are biofuels beneficial for the environment?

Ⓐ Their usage is proven to be completely carbon neutral.

Ⓑ They can reduce greenhouse gas emissions substantially.

Ⓒ Their production is more efficient than the refinement of fossil fuels.

Ⓓ They do not emit any dangerous gases except carbon dioxide.

PRACTICE TEST_level 2

CONVERSATION  **1. Listen to part of a conversation in a library.**

MP3• 56

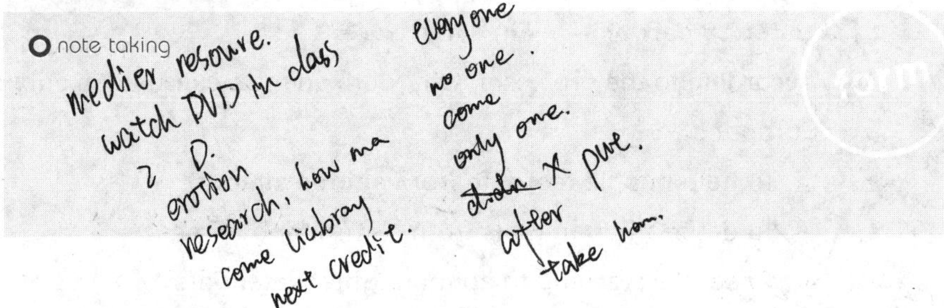

1-1. Which of the following pieces of information does the librarian request from the student? Click on 2 answers.

Ⓐ The student's name

Ⓑ The class the DVD is for

Ⓒ The name of the student's professor

Ⓓ The reference number for the DVD

1-2. According to the librarian, why are library materials placed on reserve?

Ⓐ To make them easier for the library staff to locate

Ⓑ To prevent students from other classes from using them

Ⓒ To make them available for extra-credit projects

Ⓓ To ensure that all students have a chance to use them

LECTURE  **2. Listen to part of a lecture in a botany class.**

MP3•57

note taking

2-1. What does the professor say about the sharp taste of garlic?

Ⓐ It is attractive to birds and insects.

Ⓑ It is created when garlic is damaged.

Ⓒ It is toxic to some animals.

Ⓓ It is present only in certain types of garlic.

2-2. According to the professor, how has garlic been used for medicinal purposes? Click on 2 answers.

Ⓐ To prevent muscular injuries

Ⓑ To treat wounds in place of antibiotics

Ⓒ To reduce cholesterol levels

Ⓓ To help patients recover after heart attacks

CONVERSATION MP3 • 58 **1. Listen to part of a conversation between a student and a professor.**

note taking

Main Idea **1-1.** Why does the woman go to see her professor?

Ⓐ To complain that there is too much material on the reading list

Ⓑ To explain that she is having trouble in class and needs some help

Ⓒ To ask for help with her paper on learning disabilities

Ⓓ To report that there are no audio books in the campus bookstore

Detail **1-2.** Which of the following does the professor mention as resources available to the student? Click on 2 answers.

Ⓐ Audio books on loan at the library

Ⓑ Special classes that have a smaller reading component

Ⓒ Audio books for sale in the bookstore

Ⓓ A tutor available at no cost to the student

Detail **1-3.** What does the professor say about students with special needs?

Ⓐ They sometimes have difficulty handling the extra demands of graduate school.

Ⓑ They often struggle to cope with the workload if they do not seek extra help.

Ⓒ They are usually advised to take classes that include media assistance.

Ⓓ They are disadvantaged because the college does not provide enough resources.

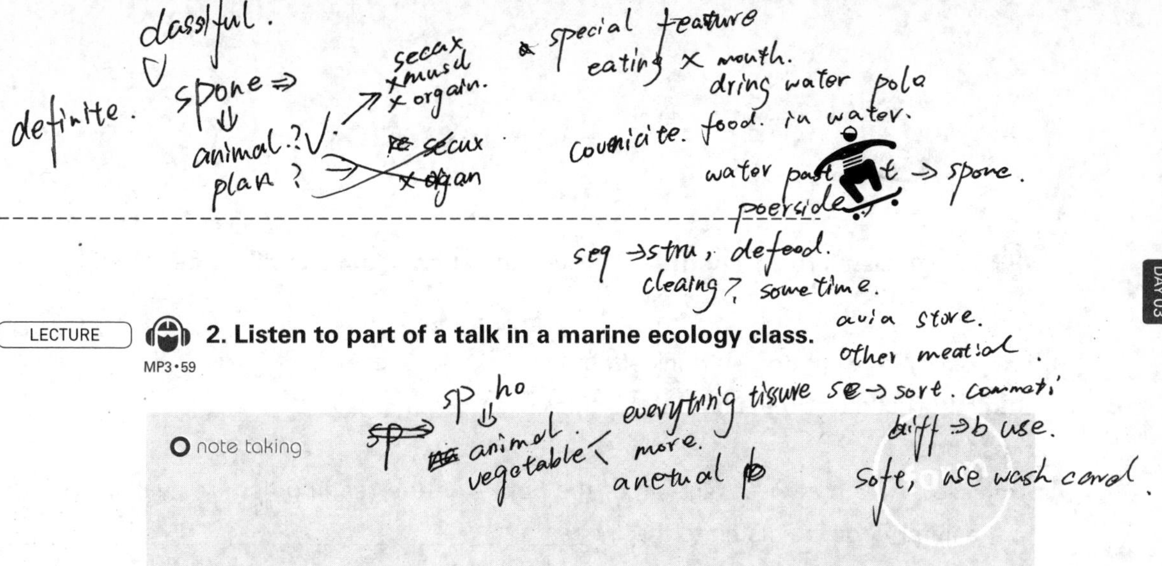

LECTURE

2. Listen to part of a talk in a marine ecology class.

MP3•59

note taking

Main Idea **2-1.** What is the discussion mainly about?

Ⓐ Different uses of sponges
Ⓑ The differences between plants and sponges
Ⓒ The characteristics of animal sponges
Ⓓ Common misconceptions about sponges

Detail **2-2.** According to the professor, why do people sometimes mistakenly classify sponges as plants? Click on 2 answers.

Ⓐ They are immobile.
Ⓑ They cannot obtain food.
Ⓒ They lack basic organs.
Ⓓ They are comprised of tiny cells.

Detail **2-3.** According to the professor, what is the purpose of the pores of sponges?

Ⓐ To purify the water that enters the body of the sponge
Ⓑ To obtain food for the sponge
Ⓒ To defend the sponge against predators
Ⓓ To provide the sponge with skeletal support

Detail **2-4.** According to the professor, what are loofah sponges?

Ⓐ Natural sponges with skeletons too hard to be useful commercially
Ⓑ Synthetic sponges that absorb more water than natural ones
Ⓒ Animal sponges with soft skeletons made of spongin
Ⓓ Natural sponges made out of a type of vegetable

MP3·60 **1. Listen to part of the level 3 conversation again and fill in the blanks.**

[省略]

Professor: So, what do you think about using audio books?

Student: That'd be great...but I don't think 1)_______ _______ _______ _______ _______ all those books.

Professor: As a matter of fact, all of the books on the reading list are available on CD in the library. You can listen to them 2)_______ _______ _______ _______ _______ _______ in the library, or you can borrow them and take them home.

Student: Really? I had no idea.

Professor: You should also contact the student services office. They'll 3)_______ _______ _______ _______ _______ _______ _______. You know, another student who's done the course before, who can help explain things.

Student: For free? That'd be great.

Professor: I don't know why this kind of information isn't made more available to students with special needs.

Student: Actually, I didn't 4)_______ _______ _______ _______ _______ _______.

Professor: Why not?

Student: I guess I didn't want anyone to think I wanted special treatment. And it never gave me too much trouble in high school...of course I had to work a little harder... I thought I could handle a university workload, too. I guess I was wrong. I just didn't realize 5)_______ _______ _______ _______ _______ _______.

Professor: First of all, it's not special treatment. It's the law for schools to provide services to students with disabilities...all types of disabilities. Look, I'm really glad you told me about this. Some students with learning disabilities are ashamed of it, and they shouldn't be. Then they 6)_______ _______ _______ _______ _______. Sometimes it's too late for them to catch up, and they end up having to repeat. Others 7)_______ _______ _______ _______ _______.

[省略]

答案参见ANSWER BOOK P351

MP3·61 **2. Listen to part of the level 3 lecture again and fill in the blanks.**

[省略]

Professor: Well, you've 1)_______ _______ _______ _______ _______ _______ why people believe that sponges are...um, plants. [pause] But, actually, they're animals.

[pause] They are sessile...and, uh, they don't have any, um, [2] ________ ________ ________ ________ ________ ________. Basically, they're a collection of cells working together. They're extremely simple...some of the most [3] ________ ________ ________ ________ ________, but they've evolved some special features. Like, uh, sponges have a pretty unique way of...uh...eating. They don't have mouths, right? So, they've got to get food some other way. And they do that by...by drawing water in through these, um, [4] ________ ________ ________ ________ ________ ________ ________. So, as the water goes through the pores and into the sponge, um, food particles are filtered out of the water. The water gets, um, it gets passed out of the sponge through other openings in the, um, the sponge body. Nifty, eh?

The cells that make up the sponge's pores are called porocytes...and they're just, um, one of many different types of cells that can be found in sponges. [5] ________ ________ ________ ________ ________ ________ ________ ________ ________—those are called, um, choanocytes. Um, and then there are the spicules...those are rods that are used for, um, for structure...or for defense.

Student A: So...spicules are [6] ________ ________ ________ ________ ________ ________?

Professor: Yes, that's right.

［省略］

答案参见ANSWER BOOK P352

oral expression

MP3 • 62

Listen to the expressions and sentences in the script below and repeat.

stressed out 精神压力大	What's wrong? You look **stressed out**.
come up 临近，来临	I know you have heaps of papers to write and exams **coming up**.
keep up with 保持，跟上	I hardly have time to **keep up with** the weekly readings.
put A on reserve 预留A，事先准备好A	Professors usually **put** materials **on reserve** when they assign everyone in their class to watch it.
can afford to *do* 可以负担得起	I don't think I **can afford to order** all those books.
available to A A是可以获取的	You should start using the resources **available to** you.
write down 记录，写下	I want you to **write down** a definition for a word I'm about to give you.

DAY04

Function

- CASE EXAMPLE - 例题
- CASE EXAMPLE解析- 例题解析
- SMART SOLUTION - 题型攻略专题
- PRACTICE TEST - 练习
- DICTATION - 听写

speed keyword

Function题型是有关如何解读字里行间的意义。

听力部分是由conversation与lecture组成的，都原汁原味地保留了日常口语(spoken language)的特点。尽管涉及的是学术性的内容，但使用的都是口语独有的表达，并且语气、语调等对把握意义起着重要的作用。function题型考查的不是对话或讲义文的正文部分，而是关注口语有何功能，是如何推动谈话进行的。因此，对于这一题型，最重要的就是紧跟对话的脉络，准确把握情境。

- 再次录音回放！
- 找出隐含的意思或说话者的意图！

An important early development in American film was the spread of nickelodeons shortly after the…uh, turn of the century. Popular interest in film was booming at the time, but there were few venues for screening. That's why lots of small, storefront, purpose-built movie theaters, known as nickelodeons, began popping up everywhere.

At first, small shops and restaurants were also converted into, ah, makeshift venues for showing movies. But nickelodeons—so-called after a "nickel," a five-cent coin, which was the price of admission, and "odeon," the Greek word for theater—uh…nickelodeons were much more suitable for watching movies. They generally had fewer than 200 seats.

Why does the professor say this:

What does the professor mean when he says this:

每篇会有1~2个此题型

CASE EXAMPLE

  MP3·75 **Listen to part of a conversation between a student and a director of a dormitory.**

| Volume | Help | OK | Next |

note taking 学生去找宿舍的楼长谈话。他们在讨论什么活动，遇到了哪些问题？请记录。

Event:

Issues:

Listen again to part of the conversation. Then answer the question.  MP3·76

> What does the student mean when he says this:

Ⓐ Food will not be served at the open-mic night.

Ⓑ The residents are unlikely to want food or beverages.

Ⓒ The open-mic night will be fairly easy to coordinate.

Ⓓ It will be too complicated to prepare tea and coffee.

LECTURE  **Listen to part of a lecture in an art history class.**

MP3 • 77

| Volume | Help | OK | Next |

note taking 这是一堂美术史课。课堂内容的素材是什么，与其有关的一个关键词语是什么？请记录。

素材：

关键词语：

Listen again to part of the lecture. Then answer the question.  MP3 • 78

> Why does the professor say this:

Ⓐ To define a term he just introduced

Ⓑ To emphasize an important point in the lecture

Ⓒ To indicate that the information will be tested

Ⓓ To remind students of a concept from earlier in the course

CASE EXAMPLE

[SCRIPT] **Narrator** Listen to part of a conversation **between a student and a director of a dormitory.**

情景：Service Encounters

Student (male) Ms. Hines, I was thinking about starting a community event here in the dorm.

Director (female) *[interested]* I'm listening...

Student I thought **an open-mic night** would be a good idea.

对话主题：open-mic之夜

● 出现对话主题。

Director Great idea. Hmm...but where could you stage it?

Student How about in the main lounge? It's usually empty after 5.

Director OK. Good. MP3·76 **And were you thinking about having some beverages or food available at the open-mic night?**

Student 回放 ***[hesitantly]* Well, that would make things a little more complicated...but it might be possible to serve coffee and tea or something. Something simple.**

● 像这样用录音回放的句子，通常受语境的影响很大，所以应考虑到语境与语调，理解其内在意义。

Director Right. That sounds better than trying to coordinate some sort of food service.

> 请重听对话的一部分，回答下列问题。

学生这样说想表达的意思是?

［犹豫不定地］嗯，那样的话事情就有点儿复杂了…但是，像咖啡、茶之类简单的东西还是可以的。

Ⓐ open-mic之夜不提供食品。

Ⓑ 住宿生不想要食品和饮料。

Ⓒ 筹备open-mic之夜会比较轻松。

Ⓓ 准备咖啡或者茶会十分麻烦。

● 学生委婉地说："像咖啡、茶之类简单的东西还是可以的。"从这句话中可以听出，只提供简单的饮料，并不会正式供应食品等。

Answer Ⓐ

note taking

Event: a community event in the dorm → open-mic night

Issues: preparing food → just simple beverages

[SCRIPT] **Narrator** Listen to part of a lecture in an **art history** class.
讲义文涉及领域：美术史

Professor (male)

This week we'll be discussing **Paleolithic art**, and the first thing I want to say about Paleolithic art is that... MP3·78 **well, whenever art historians discuss Paleolithic art, there's always a focus on its portability.** **So, remember, when we're talking about Paleolithic art, um, we'll be getting into the issue of...portability.**
讲义文主题：旧石器时代的艺术

可携带性、轻便

Let me clarify what I mean by portability. The art that comes from the Paleolithic Period is really small—small enough to pick up and carry. Paleolithic art isn't characterized by those large figure sculptures we associate with...say...Greek art. No. We're talking about miniature three-dimensional sculptures.

- 出现讲义文主题。
- 旧石器时代的艺术也涉及到便携性的问题，并且用whenever, when we are talking about等表达进行了强调。解答function题型需要熟悉各种典型的口语表达。

> 请重听演讲的一部分，回答下列问题。

教授为什么这么说？

所以，请大家记住，当我们谈起旧石器时代的艺术时，嗯，我们会涉及到便携性的问题。

Ⓐ 为了定义刚刚引入的用语。
Ⓑ 为了强调演讲的核心内容。
Ⓒ 为了告知学生考试中会出现这部分内容。
Ⓓ 为了让学生回忆起以前课堂上曾提到过的概念。

- 根据remember一词，可以看出说话者强调“便携性”是旧石器时代艺术的核心特征。

Answer Ⓑ

note taking

素材：Paleolithic art *or* 旧石器时代艺术
用语：portability *or* 便携性

TIP function题型不是考查听力正文部分的内容，而是关注考生是否理解了口语的功能，因此不需要另外做笔记。但是考生需要抓住文章脉络，把握情境，并正确地理解说话者的意图或者内在含义，同时整理相应的要点。

SMART SOLUTION

SOLUTION 1

有两种function题型。

function题型又可以大致分为两种，其中的每一种类型都可以轻松地通过问题与选项识别出来。

	问题的形式	选项的形式
理解说话者的意图	Why does A say this:	to使用不定式表现意图 e.g. Ⓐ To define a term he just introduced Ⓑ To emphasize an important point in the lecture Ⓒ To indicate that the information will be tested Ⓓ To remind students of a concept from earlier in the course
理解表达的真正含义	What does A mean when A says this:	主语不同的句子 e.g. Ⓐ Food will not be served at the open-mic night. Ⓑ The residents are unlikely to want food or beverages. Ⓒ The open-mic night will be fairly easy to coordinate. Ⓓ It will be too complicated to prepare tea and coffee.

SOLUTION 2

理解情境十分重要。

在录音回放部分，可以做多种解释的口语表达经常出现。如果考生能够将不同情境的常用口语表达核对归类，在做题的时候，就更有精力集中于不同情境中的各种口语表达。平时多做听力训练，反复听文章，坚持把握文章脉络，把握口语化的表达和语调的变化，这样会令考生受益匪浅。现将考试中经常出现的一些情境整理如下：

· 引导学生回答问题

Come on, we've already dealt with this point last class. 好吧，我们上次课已经讨论过这一点。

come on通常在引导他人行动时使用，**go ahead, I'm listening** 等表达也在类似的情境中使用。

· 讲义文中防止跑题

I don't want to get too far off topic here. 我不想就这点谈得太远。

We've got a lot to get through today and only limited time. 我们今天要说的很多，但是时间有限。

· 重新回到话题

Getting back to what I was saying. 话说回来。

· 更正所说的话

We're going to review the details next Tuesday...I'm sorry...hm...next Thursday. 我们下周二再来复习细节部分…不好意思…嗯…下周四。

· 确认学生是否理解

I don't need to explain the difference between them, do I? 不需要我解释两者的差异了，对吧？

说话者在确认已知的事实时经常使用反义疑问句。文章中出现的反义疑问句经常成为考点，需要多加注意。

· 鼓励学生

The thing is, you are the expert on this issue. 关键是你才是这个问题的专家。

经常用于强调学生非常了解某方面的问题，来鼓励学生。

SOLUTION 3

熟悉表现说话者意图的各种动词。

询问说话者意图的问题，选项经常使用to不定式的句型。这时常用的动词有describe, demonstrate, express, explain, address, show, tell等。现将其作用整理如下：

· 对比：**contrast**
· 强调：**emphasize**
· 定义：**define, clarify**
· 道歉：**apologize**
· 要求：**request**
· 举例：**give an example**
· 提醒、告知：**remind, let A know**
· 更正：**correct**
· 提问：**ask, inquire**
· 避开、拒绝：**avoid, decline, refuse**

PRACTICE TEST_level 1

[1-8] Listen to each passage. Then choose the best answers to the questions.

Listen to a conversation between a student and a professor.

MP3•79

1. Why does the professor say this:

Ⓐ To explain something about the group project

Ⓑ To encourage the man to share his concern

Ⓒ To suggest a way to solve the man's problem

Ⓓ To apologize for being unable to help the man

Listen to part of a lecture in an astronomy class.

MP3•80

2. Why does the professor say this:

Ⓐ To cast doubt on the validity of the research

Ⓑ To summarize recent research about conditions on Mars

Ⓒ To point out that important research is often resisted at first

Ⓓ To indicate that scientists doubt there is life on Mars

Listen to a conversation between a student and an advisor.

MP3•81

3. Why does the student say this:

Ⓐ To show he understood the professor's statement

Ⓑ To remind himself of the requirements he has already met

Ⓒ To indicate that he has not taken the required course

Ⓓ To suggest a course he would like to add to his schedule

Listen to part of a lecture in an architecture class.

MP3•82

4. Why does the professor say this:

Ⓐ To provide a term for the concept he just described

Ⓑ To shift the discussion to a different topic

Ⓒ To share his opinion about the subject matter

Ⓓ To repeat a term he introduced earlier

Listen to a conversation between a student and an administrator.

MP3 • 83

5. Why does the administrator say this:

Ⓐ To inquire whether the woman meets the requirement
Ⓑ To encourage the woman to change her major to art
Ⓒ To indicate that the woman has made a mistake
Ⓓ To express surprise at the woman's request

Listen to part of a lecture in a literature class.

MP3 • 84

6. What does the professor mean?

Ⓐ She wants to focus on a particular tale from the epic.
Ⓑ She does not think the stories will interest the students.
Ⓒ She does not want to spend time discussing the plot.
Ⓓ She thinks the students have already read the text.

Listen to a conversation between a student and a professor.

MP3 • 85

7. What does the professor mean when he says this:

Ⓐ He thinks the woman will require extra time.
Ⓑ He wants the woman to promise to hand in the report on time.
Ⓒ He does not want to grant the woman an extension.
Ⓓ He does not want to discuss the issue right now.

Listen to part of a lecture in a biology class.

MP3 • 86

8. What does the professor mean when she says this:

Ⓐ She does not think the students are surprised by her statement.
Ⓑ She wants to know how much the students already know about lizards.
Ⓒ She thinks the information she just mentioned is new to the students.
Ⓓ She wants the students to answer her question about how lizards walk.

CONVERSATION  **1. Listen to part of a conversation between a student and a professor.**

MP3 • 87

note taking

Listen again to part of the conversation. Then answer the question. MP3 • 88

1-1. Why does the professor say this:

Ⓐ To assure the woman she should not be worried

Ⓑ To show how disappointed he is with the woman

Ⓒ To encourage the woman to keep guessing

Ⓓ To indicate that he understands the woman's concern

Listen again to part of the conversation. Then answer the question. MP3 • 89

1-2. What does the professor mean when he says this:

Ⓐ He thinks the woman has fully considered the offer.

Ⓑ He wants the woman to turn in her proposal now.

Ⓒ He does not think the woman should reject the idea immediately.

Ⓓ He wants the woman to show him her proposal first.

LECTURE  **2. Listen to part of a talk in an art class.**

MP3 • 90

note taking

Listen again to part of the talk. Then answer the question. MP3 • 91

2-1. What does the man mean when he says this:

Ⓐ He wants the professor to display the artistic pictures again.

Ⓑ He thinks that photography certainly qualifies as an art form.

Ⓒ He wants the professor to give examples of some controversial images.

Ⓓ He thinks the images shown in class have been too similar to each other.

Listen again to part of the talk. Then answer the question. MP3 • 92

2-2. Why does the professor say this:

Ⓐ To let the students know that she is moving on to another topic

Ⓑ To get the students to tell her the specific date of the occurrence

Ⓒ To remind the students of a time period they have previously studied

Ⓓ To encourage the students to try to answer her question

PRACTICE TEST_level 3

CONVERSATION

MP3·93

1. Listen to part of a conversation between a student and a professor.

note taking

Main Idea **1-1.** Why does the woman go to see her professor?

Ⓐ To talk about the problems she is having with her thesis advisor

Ⓑ To get advice about applying to grad school

Ⓒ To ask him to write a letter of reference

Ⓓ To find out how to get a good letter of recommendation

Detail **1-2.** Why is the professor reluctant to do what the woman wants?

Ⓐ He thinks that she needs to improve her performance in class.

Ⓑ He does not know her well enough to report worthwhile information.

Ⓒ He knows that she had a bad relationship with her thesis advisor.

Ⓓ He is too busy with his departmental responsibilities to help her.

Listen again to part of the conversation. Then answer the question. MP3·94

Function **1-3.** What does the professor mean when he says this:

Ⓐ The advisor should not suggest unnecessary changes to the student's thesis.

Ⓑ The advisor was very disappointed with the student's work on the thesis.

Ⓒ The advisor is obligated to write the student a good recommendation.

Ⓓ The advisor's comments do not necessarily mean she dislikes the student's work.

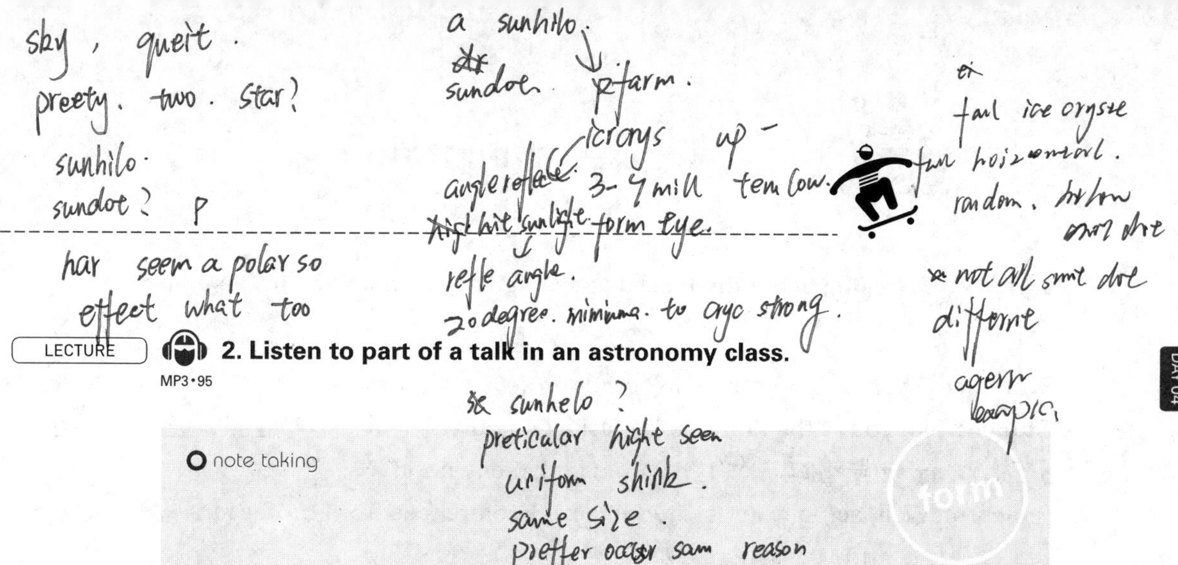

LECTURE 2. Listen to part of a talk in an astronomy class.

MP3 • 95

note taking

Main Idea 2-1. What is the discussion mainly about?

Ⓐ The physical appearance of sun halos

Ⓑ Similarities between sun halos and aurora borealis

Ⓒ The formation of sun halos and sun dogs

Ⓓ Atmospheric dust crystallization

Listen again to part of the talk. Then answer the question. MP3 • 96

Function 2-2. Why does the professor say this:

Ⓐ To review material from a previous lecture

Ⓑ To emphasize important lecture material

Ⓒ To define a term she introduced earlier

Ⓓ To correct the student's misinformation

Detail 2-3. According to the professor, what are two necessary conditions for the creation of a sun halo? Click on 2 answers.

Ⓐ Ice crystals of identical size and shape

Ⓑ Completely still atmospheric conditions

Ⓒ Thin and high cirrus cloud formations

Ⓓ The sun being at a low angle of orientation

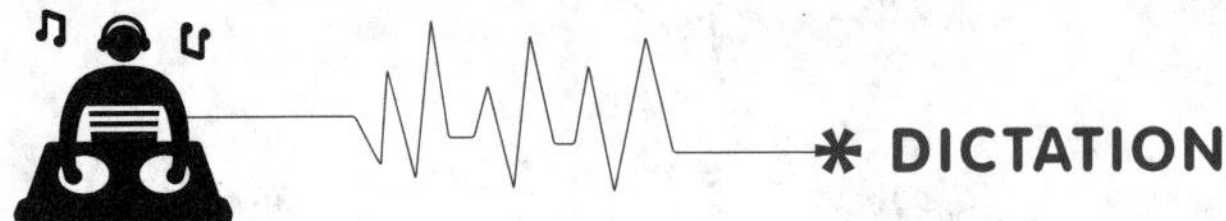

✱ DICTATION

MP3·97 Listen to part of the level 3 conversation again and fill in the blanks.

［省略］

Professor: So, have you asked any other professors?

Student: No, you're the first one I've asked. I figure [1] ________ ________ ________ ________ ________ it would look really good.

Professor: Well, actually, most students seek references from professors [2] ________ ________ ________ ________ ________ ________.

Student: I got a really good mark in your class.

Professor: Well, sure, but I have a lot of good students. I would suggest you [3] ________ ________ ________...someone who knows you personally and who knows your work. Someone who has actually worked with you.

Student: So...you'd rather not?

Professor: Look, I'll be honest with you. I'll do it, but it won't be a good reference. It's not like [4] ________ ________ ________ ________ ________, but I just don't know enough about you to make it sound good. I'll tell you something about reference letters. Nobody writes a bad one, but the people reading the letters read more into what you don't say than what you do say. See what I'm saying?

Student: Yeah...even if you don't say anything bad, it still looks bad if you don't say [5] ________ ________ ________ ________ ________.

Professor: Right...I mean...I can say that you are a hard worker and a good student, but your grades already say that for you. What the grad schools are looking for in a reference letter is [6] ________ ________ ________ ________ that your grades don't say.

Student: OK, I see what you mean.

Professor: And...think about it...if they get a reference from [7] ________ ________ ________ ________, and not from someone who has worked closely with you...what does that say?

Student: I guess [8] ________ ________ ________ ________ ________ ________ ________ ________ with those professors who I have worked closely with.

［省略］

答案参见ANSWER BOOK P360

MP3·98 Listen to part of the level 3 lecture again and fill in the blanks

［省略］

Professor: It really is quite something, huh? A perfect example of today's topic! Sun halos. And we'll briefly look at sun dogs too. Does anyone know [1] ________ ________

______ ______ ______?

Student B: I always thought those effects could be viewed from [2] ______ ______ ______ ______...or from the North Pole—like the northern lights. But if people here saw it yesterday, then I guess not.

Professor: Just to clarify, the northern lights—more accurately known as aurora borealis—they can only be seen [3] ______ ______ ______ ______ ______ ______ ______. You can also see something similar—called aurora australis—you can see that near the South Pole too. Uh...anyway, those effects aren't what I was referring to...Okay, so anyone else? *[pauses]* Alright then, what appeared in the sky yesterday is called a sun halo. That's [4] ______ ______, ______ ______ ______ ______ ______ ...and those two spots...those are sun dogs...but I'll talk about those later. Sun halos are formed...they're formed when light from the sun is [5] ______ ______ ______ ______ ______ ______ ______. These, um, ice crystals are found in thin, upper level cirrus clouds. Maybe, uh...three to six miles straight up. There, the temperature is so low that [6] ______ ______ ______ ______ ______ to form ice...and these ice crystals, they act like prisms. There are millions of these crystals in that atmospheric layer. OK. Now, can anyone tell me...why do these ice crystals [7] ______ ______ ______ ______ ______?

[省略]

答案参见ANSWER BOOK P362

oral expression

MP3•99

Listen to the expressions and sentences in the script below and repeat.

Expression	Sentence
I presume 我猜…	I see...um...in psychology, **I presume**?
be honest with you 说实话(否定意义的内容)	I'll **be honest with you**. It won't be a good reference.
it would seem like 那就好像	I guess **it would seem like** I had a bad relationship with those professors.
work out 做出（计划，事情等）	We'll see if we can **work** something **out**.
quite something 了不起的	It really is **quite something**, huh?
what I was referring to 之前提及的	Uh...anyway, those effects aren't **what I was referring to**.
give an account 说明	Yeah, well...I'm **giving a** fairly general **account** here.

DAY05

Attitude

- CASE EXAMPLE - 例题
- CASE EXAMPLE解析-例题解析
- SMART SOLUTION - 题型攻略专题
- PRACTICE TEST - 练习
- DICTATION - 听写

speed keyword

Attitude 题型是对说话者的心理把握。

这一题型与function类型一样，都着眼于考查口语的功能。但与function类型不同的是，此题型尽管也要求考生深入理解情境，但是更注重考生关注说话者的语气以及理解说话者隐含的心理，即要求考生了解说话者看待对象的视角，结合文章的整体脉络和说话者的语调判断其确定程度、情感及好恶等心理状态。说话者会站在特定的立场上对对象进行描述，这在对话中不会直接说出来，但是这是有效沟通必不可少的要素，应该好好把握。所以平时应多听多练，熟悉这些口语要素。

• 留心突出强调的或者突然出现语调变化的部分！

An important early development in American film was the spread of nickelodeons shortly after the…uh, turn of the century. Popular interest in film was booming at the time, but there were few venues for screening. That's why lots of small, storefront, purpose-built movie theaters, known as nickelodeons, began popping up everywhere.

At first, small shops and restaurants were also converted into, ah, makeshift venues for showing movies. But nickelodeons—so-called after a "nickel," a five-cent coin, which was the price of admission, and "odeon," the Greek word for theater—uh…nickelodeons were much more suitable for watching movies. They generally had fewer than 200 seats.

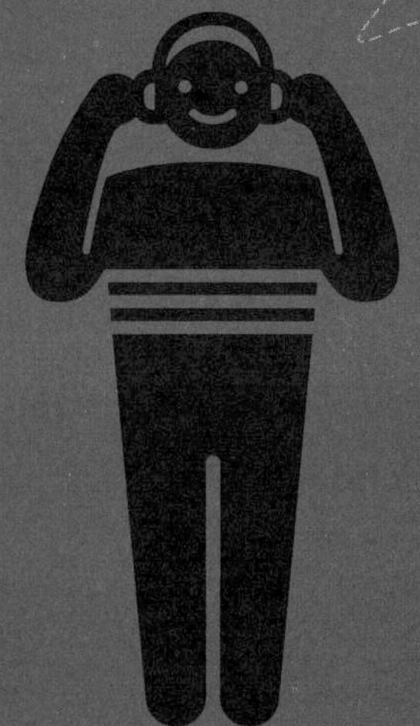

What can be inferred about the professor?

What is the professor's attitude toward…?

每篇有0~1个问题

CASE EXAMPLE

 **Listen to part of a conversation between a student and a clerk.**

MP3 • 120

| Volume | Help | OK | Next |

note taking

学生来到了大学校园服务中心。他为什么来，工作人员反应如何？请记录。

Purpose:

Clerk's response:

Listen again to part of the conversation. Then answer the question.  MP3 • 121

> What does the clerk mean when she says this:

Ⓐ She expects the man to provide proof of his registration.

Ⓑ She doubts that the group is large enough to be officially recognized.

Ⓒ She does not want the man to proceed with the fundraiser.

Ⓓ She is worried that the man's group might not be registered.

LECTURE  **Listen to the following discussion in part of a literature class.**

MP3 • 122

| Volume | Help | OK | Next |

note taking

文学课上，大家正在探讨一位美国作家和他的作品，请记录提及的作家、作品及其作品的两个代表性特征。

作家及作品：

特征：

①

②

Listen again to part of the lecture. Then answer the question.  MP3 • 123

> What does the professor imply when he says this:

Ⓐ He is not sure about the detail that the student referred to.

Ⓑ He feels that the student's answer is not relevant to the topic.

Ⓒ He is impressed at the extent of the student's background knowledge.

Ⓓ He expects students to elaborate on their submissions in class.

CASE EXAMPLE

[SCRIPT] **Narrator** Listen to part of a conversation between **a student and a clerk.**
情景：Service Encounters

Clerk (female) Hello. Welcome to the university services center. What can I do for you?

Student (male) Hi. I'm here on behalf of the Colleges Combating Cancer organization. We're planning a fundraiser for next semester, **and I just wanted to make sure we've got everything in order.**
主题：查看活动的筹备情况

Clerk MP3·121 **Colleges Combating Cancer? Is that a new group?**
1st Replay

Student Yeah. We formed this semester, actually.

Clerk Is your group registered with the university? ***[doubtfully]***
2nd Replay

Only registered organizations can fundraise on campus...

Student *[assuredly]* Don't worry—we're official.
正确答案线索

Clerk Great. Now the first thing you need to obtain is written approval from our office.

● 情景是学生为了筹备募捐活动来到了大学校园服务中心。

● 说话者的语气有些特别，话中有话。这种情境下，解题的线索经常出现在语调突出的部分，因此从一开始就要留心听。

> 请重听对话的一部分，回答下列问题。

工作人员为什么这样说？

［怀疑地］只有注册过的社团才可以在校园里募捐…

Ⓐ 希望学生出示注册凭证。

Ⓑ 怀疑此社团是否具备可以正式认证的规模。

Ⓒ 学生不希望募捐活动能开展。

Ⓓ 怀疑学生所在的社团是否已注册。

● 服务中心的工作人员首先询问了学生社团是否已注册，然后又强调只有注册社团才可以募集捐款，由此可以看出她是在怀疑社团是否注册。

Answer Ⓓ

Purpose: preparing for the fundraiser *or* 筹备募捐活动
Clerk's response: wanna make sure if the org. is reg. *or* 确认此社团是否已注册

TIP 笔记的内容只要自己能看懂就可以了，因此长单词可以只记开头部分。
例如把organization和registered简单记为org.和reg.即可，答题时完全可以识别出来。

[SCRIPT] **Narrator** Listen to the following discussion in part of a **literature class.**
讲义文涉及领域：文学

Professor (male) Today we're looking at **Jack Kerouac's *On the Road*.** Tell me, what did you notice about the book?
主题与关键词

Student A (female) Well, the writing is very free, and...unstructured.

Professor Yeah, it's basically just a stream of consciousness, right? Or as Kerouac himself called it: "spontaneous prose." So, uh, can you guess what influenced him? MP3·123 **What other cultural trends were occurring in the early 50s, when the book was written?**

Student B (male) ***[uncertainly]*** **Maybe rock'n'roll?**

Professor **Uh, well...it's true that rock'n'roll was coming onto the scene then. But, think about the characteristics of spontaneous prose—the improvisation, free association...**
2nd Replay
正确答案线索

Student A *[enthusiastically]* You must mean jazz music!

Professor Right!

● 教授不是对学生大致介绍杰克·克鲁亚的作品，而是把问题交给学生，引导他们自己抓住要点。

● 当学生说出的不是教授想要的答案时，经常会在这里出attitude或function题型。需要留心委婉的表达和语气。

> 请重听对话的一部分，回答下列问题。

教授这样说是想暗示什么？

嗯，是啊……摇滚是从那时开始登上舞台的。

Ⓐ 不是十分清楚学生提到的内容。

Ⓑ 觉得学生的回答与主题不符。

Ⓒ 学生背景知识丰富，给教授留下了深刻的印象。

Ⓓ 希望学生详细说明自己在课堂上提出的问题。

● 教授犹豫地说出了Uh, well...之类的词，并且对学生的回答进行很长地说明。由此可见，学生的回答不是教授所期待的答案。

Answer Ⓑ

note taking

作家及作品：杰克·克鲁亚的《On the road》

特征：① free / unstructured / stream of consciousness / spontaneous prose

② influenced by jazz

TIP 如①，最好将归为同一主题的种种特征整理为一项。

SMART SOLUTION

SOLUTION 1

把握住表现特殊语调和情感的部分。

在日常口语中，说话者为了表现自己的情感状态，会使用不同的语气(tone of voice)或语调(intonation)。出题的时候，这些语调特殊的部分经常被拿来做文章，因此解题时应该首先把握住这些内容。在原文中，它们通常是[ ] 符号中的说明，或者是表现情感的形容词、表达犹豫的词句等内容。

- **情感状态(feelings)**

[doubtfully] Only registered organizations can fundraise on campus...
不能完全相信对方，十分怀疑时

- **确定程度(degree of certainty)**

[doubtfully] Uh...just a minute, let me check the list again.
因为不能准确无误地记忆信息，所以想要再次确认名单时

- **好恶(likes and dislikes)**

The material the class deals with...that part's great.
表示满意课堂内容时

- **意见(personal opinion)**

Is there any way to prove the theory?
委婉地表达自己认为没有依据可以证明。像上面这句话一样，说话者在讲义文中介绍理论后，会说明此理论是有争议的(disputed)，还是被普遍认同的(generally accepted)。这是全文重要的信息，经常被考查。即使是同一个问句，因为语调的不同，可能是提问，也可能只是表示疑问，这些都需小心判断。

- **通过犹豫表达的否定性意见**

Hmm...I guess some scientists actually subscribe to that theory.
Uh, well...it's true that rock'n'roll was coming onto the scene then.
通过犹豫表达对方说的并不是自己所期待的答案时

SOLUTION 2

熟悉选项中出现的情感表达。

attitude题型提问方式多样，因此难以通过提问来判断出问题的类型。

但是，却可以用答案选项轻松地辨别出attitude题型。这些选项通常都以说话者为主语，内容涉及说话者的情感或态度。下面来熟悉一下此时常用的表达。

态度	说话者	与态度相关的表达
积极的情感	She / He	is interested 感兴趣 is impressed 印象深刻 is amused /is excited 乐于 likes 喜欢 /wants 想
消极的情感		is surprised 惊讶 /is confused 迷惑 is embarrassed 尴尬，难为情 is worried /is concerned 担心，忧虑 is upset /is annoyed 生气 is frustrated 失望 is reluctant 勉强
确定的程度		is unsure /is uncertain 不确定 is doubtful 怀疑 / is confident 确信

SOLUTION 3

熟悉典型错误。

这一题型与function题型一样，句子表面的意思常常与内层的含义不同，因此仅仅表达表面意义(literal meaning)的选项常常是错误的。

Student A(male): Deborah, are you done with the biology report?
黛博拉，你生物报告写完了吗？

Student B(female): Oh my gosh! Isn't it supposed to be done by next week?
哦，天呐！不是到下周才交的吗？

在上面的情境中，女生并不是在确认交报告的期限，而是发现自己忘了写报告。她感到非常吃惊。在这种情况下就会出现仅仅表现句子表面意思的错误选项，需加以甄别。

- **表面意义**：She wants to make sure of the due date of the report. （**典型错误**）
- **内层含义**：She is surprised to be reminded of the deadline of the report. （**正确答案**）

PRACTICE TEST_level 1

[1-8] Listen to each passage. Then choose the best answers to the questions.

Listen to a conversation between a student and a professor.

MP3 • 124

1. What is the professor's attitude toward the student's proposal?

   Ⓐ He would be pleased to be involved with the student's group.

   Ⓑ He doubts that he is the appropriate person to advise the club.

   Ⓒ He is excited about the student's idea for a new club.

   Ⓓ He is reluctant to make a commitment to the student's club.

Listen to part of a lecture in an environmental studies class.

MP3 • 125

2. What can be inferred about the professor?

   Ⓐ She expects the students to offer more examples of petroleum products.

   Ⓑ She will not talk about the general characteristics of petroleum.

   Ⓒ She is uncertain of the process by which petroleum forms.

   Ⓓ She is concerned that students have no background knowledge of petroleum.

Listen to a conversation between a student and a professor.

MP3 • 126

3. What is the professor's attitude toward the student?

   Ⓐ She is frustrated that the student will be missing class on Friday.

   Ⓑ She expects the student to do a makeup assignment instead of taking the test.

   Ⓒ She is disappointed with the student for not telling her about the problem earlier.

   Ⓓ She is annoyed that the student cannot take the test with her other class.

Listen to part of a lecture in a social science class.

MP3 • 127

4. What is the professor's opinion of informal social control?

   Ⓐ It is more successful than formal control.

   Ⓑ It is not found in all societies.

   Ⓒ It does not work with all the members of a group.

   Ⓓ It affects a person's behavior to some degree.

Listen to a conversation between a student and a dormitory administrator.

MP3 • 128

5. What can be inferred about the man?

Ⓐ He is upset about what the woman told him.

Ⓑ He is concerned that he misunderstood the woman.

Ⓒ He expects the woman to elaborate on the problem.

Ⓓ He is embarrassed about the condition of his room.

Listen to part of a lecture in an environmental studies class.

MP3 • 129

6. What is the professor's attitude toward the Green Belt Movement?

Ⓐ She would like to be personally involved in the organization.

Ⓑ She feels that the Green Belt Movement receives more credit than it deserves.

Ⓒ She expects that the Green Belt Movement will thrive for many years to come.

Ⓓ She is impressed by the accomplishments of the Green Belt Movement.

Listen to a conversation between a student and an advisor.

MP3 • 130

7. What can be inferred about the woman when she says this:

Ⓐ She does not want to choose a specific major right now.

Ⓑ She is not sure she has heard the advisor correctly.

Ⓒ She is disappointed to see physics is not provided as a major.

Ⓓ She is unprepared to select a specific major.

Listen to part of a lecture in a literature class.

MP3 • 131

8. What does the professor mean when he says this:

Ⓐ He expects that the students are familiar with European-American tricksters.

Ⓑ He is concerned that the students have not studied Native American tricksters.

Ⓒ He is not planning to discuss European-American tricksters at this time.

Ⓓ He is not sure if he needs to explain the trickster character more.

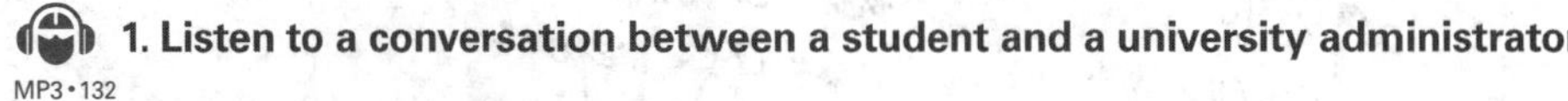

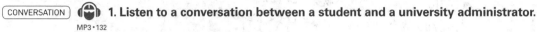

CONVERSATION **1. Listen to a conversation between a student and a university administrator.**

MP3・132

note taking

Listen again to part of the conversation. Then answer the question.  MP3・133

1-1. What can be inferred about the student?

Ⓐ He doubts that the administrator will be able to help him.

Ⓑ He is not sure where the administration office is located.

Ⓒ He is concerned that he is not acquainted with the administrator.

Ⓓ He is certain he has finally arrived at the correct office.

Listen again to part of the conversation. Then answer the question.  MP3・134

1-2. What can be inferred about the student?

Ⓐ He is annoyed that there is a form to fill out.

Ⓑ He is worried that the earnings report will pose a problem.

Ⓒ He thinks he may have already filled out an earnings report.

Ⓓ He is not familiar with the form the administrator mentioned.

LECTURE  **2. Listen to part of a talk in a meteorology class.**

MP3 • 135

note taking

Listen again to part of the talk. Then answer the question.  MP3 • 136

2-1. What can be inferred about the professor?

Ⓐ She does not consider this issue relevant to the discussion.

Ⓑ She is concerned that the student has misunderstood her.

Ⓒ She expects that the student knows the answer to the question.

Ⓓ She is not sure about the exact numerical data for the answer.

Listen again to part of the talk. Then answer the question.  MP3 • 137

2-2. What does the student mean when he says this:

Ⓐ He is not sure he heard the professor correctly.

Ⓑ He is surprised by the professor's claim.

Ⓒ He is unsure what point the professor is trying to make.

Ⓓ He is concerned the professor has omitted some information.

PRACTICE TEST_level 3

CONVERSATION **1. Listen to part of a conversation between a student and an advisor.**

MP3 • 138

note taking

Main Idea **1-1.** What is the student's problem?

Ⓐ She needs to find an internship.

Ⓑ She is dissatisfied with her internship.

Ⓒ She feels the internship is too demanding.

Ⓓ She wants more guidance in her internship.

Detail **1-2.** How does the man suggest that the woman overcome the problem?

Ⓐ By dropping her current internship and picking up another one in the summer

Ⓑ By providing the therapist with informal feedback about the training

Ⓒ By working with another therapist that she gets along with better

Ⓓ By setting up an appointment to talk to the therapist about her concerns

Listen again to part of the conversation. Then answer the question. MP3 • 139

Attitude **1-3.** What can be inferred about the student?

Ⓐ She is frustrated by the therapist's attitude.

Ⓑ She is unimpressed by the therapist's skills.

Ⓒ She is concerned about working with another intern.

Ⓓ She is worried about speaking with the therapist.

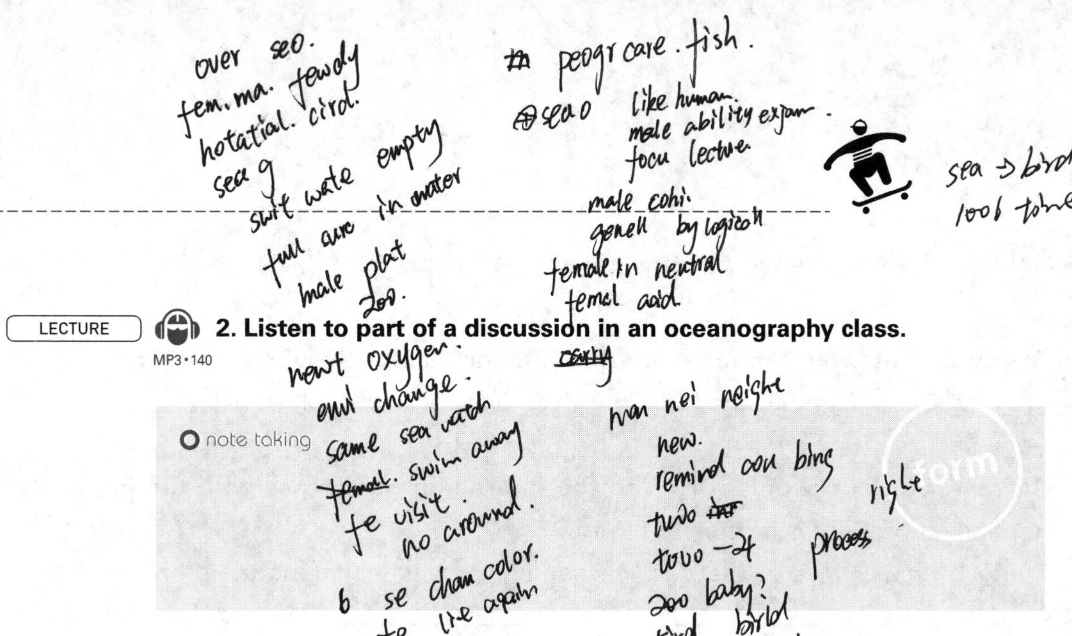

LECTURE **2. Listen to part of a discussion in an oceanography class.**

MP3 • 140

note taking

Main Idea **2-1.** What aspect of seahorses does the professor mainly discuss?

Ⓐ The distinct male and female shapes

Ⓑ The way that they reproduce

Ⓒ The lifecycle they go through

Ⓓ The courtship behavior they exhibit

Detail **2-2.** According to the discussion, what are two behaviors associated with the initial seahorse courtship? Click on 2 answers.

Ⓐ Holding tails

Ⓑ Moving water through the egg pouch

Ⓒ Floating to the surface in pairs

Ⓓ Meeting regularly every morning

Listen again to part of the discussion. Then answer the question. MP3 • 141

Attitude **2-3.** What can be inferred about the student?

Ⓐ She is doubtful the professor is giving valid information to the students.

Ⓑ She is surprised at the information that the professor has just provided.

Ⓒ She is already familiar with the biological facts covered in the lecture.

Ⓓ She is curious about the method scientists used to discover this fact.

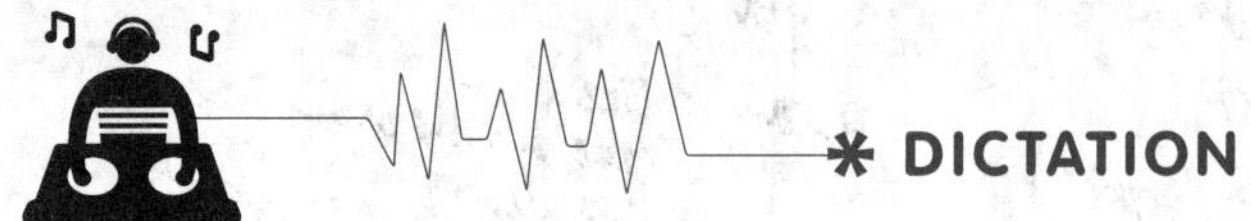

MP3•142 **Listen to part of the level 3 conversation again and fill in the blanks.**

［省略］

Advisor: Tell me about your relationship with the therapist you're working with.

Student: Oh, she's great, and I think we get along well. I can tell she's 1)______ ______ ______ ______.

Advisor: So your problem is with the internship itself—not with the Freemont Rehabilitation Center or the staff there?

Student: *[thinking]* Yeah. That's right. The people definitely aren't the problem. In fact, 2)______ ______ ______ ______ ______ ______ ______. I've met some wonderful people there.

Advisor: Well, that's good news. When you have a 3)______ ______ ______ ______ ______ ______ ______ ______, you'd be surprised how much you can accomplish. Why don't you just talk to them about it?

Student: You're right. I guess I didn't think about that before. I felt like the internship 4)______ ______ ______ ______ ______ ______, and I was powerless to, um, to change it.

Advisor: Well, that's certainly not the case. You know, the therapist you're working with may not even realize that you've got some...reservations about the internship. Other interns she had in the past may have 5)______ ______ ______ ______ ______ ______ ______.

It's up to you to tell her that you 6)______ ______ ______ ______ ______.

Student: *[concerned]* I agree with what you're saying...but the last thing I want to do is seem ungrateful. I really, really appreciate her help...and that 7)______ ______ ______ ______ ______ ______ ______. If I express dissatisfaction with the internship, she may...I don't know...think I don't appreciate her help.

Advisor: I don't think that'll be an issue. She's a professional, and above all, she wants to help you get the experience you need to become a physical therapist. So if you have some ideas about how the internship could help you reach that goal, I'm sure 8)______ ______ ______ ______ ______ ______.

［省略］

答案参见ANSWER BOOK P375

MP3•143 **Listen to part of the level 3 lecture again and fill in the blanks.**

［省略］

Professor: After the, um, 1)______ ______ ______, the male and female pair will float up toward the surface of the water. Then the female seahorse, um, 2)__________ ________ __________ __________ __________ __________ of her...her male partner. The number of eggs she delivers may be around 200, and they, um, they're 3)______________ ________ __________ __________. While inside the pouch, the eggs get nutrients and oxygen...and the temperature is kept just right. Over the course of the pregnancy, the, um, the environment inside the pouch changes a little bit...so that at the end of the pregnancy, it's pretty much the same as the surrounding seawater. That way 4)________ ____________ ________ ____________ ________ ________ ____________ when they're born.

Anyway, after the female deposits the eggs, she, um, she swims away. 5)____________ ________ ________ ____________, the female seahorse will, um, she'll come back to visit her partner every morning. But most of the time she's not around. On her morning visits, the two seahorses do this...this other kind of courtship, I guess. It lasts for about six minutes or so, and the seahorses might swim around together and, uh, change color and 6)________ ________ ________ ________. After that, the female leaves again for the day. Now, when 7)________ ________ ________ ________ ________, it's usually at night. He pushes the offspring out of the pouch, and then he'll be ready for a new pregnancy right away.

[省略]

答案参见ANSWER BOOK P375

oral expression

MP3•144

Listen to the expressions and sentences in the script below and repeat.

have a second to *do* 抽出几分钟做…	Professor Peterson, do you **have a second to talk**?
Would you consider *doing*您可以考虑做…吗?	**Would you consider being** an advisor for a new club I'm starting?
be much of相当多的/地…	It actually wouldn't **be much of** a time commitment.
come to the right place 找对地方了	You've **come to the right place**. I'm a university administrator.
be supposed to *do* 已经定好了可以…	**I'm supposed to get** some information for the drama club's upcoming performance.
You could say that. 你可以这么说。(委婉的肯定)	A: It sounds like it's not what you expected. B: **You could say that.**
the last thing I want to do 最不想做的事情	**The last thing I want to do** is seem ungrateful.

DAY 06 DAY 02~05

Review Test I

请完成下列题目，复习前面学过的各类型问题。

MP3 • 165

passage 1. [1~5] Listen to part of a conversation in a professor's office.

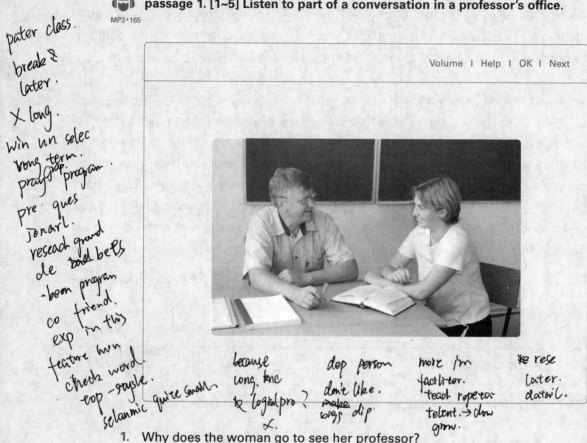

Volume | Help | OK | Next

1. Why does the woman go to see her professor?

Ⓐ To find out where he went to graduate school

Ⓑ To ask about an artist featured in an art magazine

Ⓒ To get information about a graduate program

Ⓓ To ask for a letter of recommendation

◎答案/解析 P. 379

2. What does the professor say about the University of Cellex?

Ⓐ The art department there is bigger than any other department on the campus.

Ⓑ The student will probably feel unhappy at such a small university.

Ⓒ The art department there is unable to afford state-of-the-art technology.

Ⓓ The ratio of professors to students in its ceramics program is very favorable.

3. What does the professor believe is the most important consideration when choosing a graduate school?

Ⓐ The size of the graduate program

Ⓑ The quality of the professors

Ⓒ The style of work promoted by the school

Ⓓ The success of its graduates

Listen again to part of the conversation. Then answer the question.  MP3・166

4. What does the student mean when she says this:

Ⓐ She does not want the professor to miss his faculty meeting.

Ⓑ She thinks it would be best to come back in the afternoon.

Ⓒ She does not want to return to meet with the professor later.

Ⓓ She thinks the professor's faculty meeting will be brief.

Listen again to part of the conversation. Then answer the question.  MP3・167

5. Why does the professor say this:

Ⓐ To give himself time to research the topic

Ⓑ To indicate that he needs to attend to other matters

Ⓒ To urge the student to think about the issue by herself

Ⓓ To let the student know he is available to talk any time

MP3 • 168

passage 2. [1~6] Listen to part of a talk in an architecture class.

Volume | Help | OK | Next

Bungalow

1. What is the discussion mainly about?

Ⓐ A style of British house that is becoming popular again in the U.S.

Ⓑ Bungalow houses in the United States

Ⓒ An internationally popular house style that originated in India

Ⓓ The features of traditional bungalows in India

2. What was the main characteristic of the traditional bungalow?

Ⓐ It had features designed to improve the flow of air through the house.

Ⓑ It included a mixture of Indian and British colonial aspects.

Ⓒ It made use of materials that reflected heat to keep it cool inside.

Ⓓ It was sturdily built to provide people with shelter.

3. How did the British change the traditional bungalow? Click on 2 answers.

Ⓐ By adding columns

Ⓑ By placing it on stilts

Ⓒ By using stone as a building material

Ⓓ By making it a one-story building

4. According to the professor, why did bungalows become popular in the United States in the 20th century?

Ⓐ They were cheaper to build.

Ⓑ They were appropriate for the new American lifestyle.

Ⓒ Their blueprints were sold in housing magazines.

Ⓓ They had a central living room.

Listen again to part of the discussion. Then answer the question.  MP3・169

5. Why does the professor say this:

Ⓐ To show his uncertainty about the information

Ⓑ To introduce the topic for discussion

Ⓒ To encourage the students to conduct more research

Ⓓ To clarify a previous comment

Listen again to part of the discussion. Then answer the question.  MP3・170

6. What does the professor mean when he says this:

Ⓐ He wants the students to focus on more modern developments.

Ⓑ He thinks the students already know the history of housing developments.

Ⓒ He does not want to give too much background information.

Ⓓ He thinks the students will cover this material in another class.

passage 3. [1~6] Listen to part of a lecture in a zoology class.

MP3 • 171

Volume | Help | OK | Next

Mandrill: Mandrillus

1. What is the talk mainly about?

Ⓐ The mystery of olfactory communication

Ⓑ The feeding habits and locations of mandrills

Ⓒ Mandrill communication methods

Ⓓ Differences in the behavioral cues of primates

2. According to the professor, why do mandrills travel up to twenty square miles a day?

Ⓐ They are eluding predators.

Ⓑ They are searching for sustenance.

Ⓒ They are hunting small rodents.

Ⓓ They are marking and increasing their domain.

◎答案/解析 P.382

3. What difference between male and female mandrills is mentioned in the talk?
Ⓐ The shape of their cheeks
Ⓑ The texture of their fur
Ⓒ The size of their noses
Ⓓ The brightness of their features

4. According to the professor, what is commonly misconstrued?
Ⓐ When a mandrill draws back its lips and reveals its teeth
Ⓑ When a mandrill shows a grooming or mating desire
Ⓒ When an adult female mandrill rubs her chest against a tree
Ⓓ When a dominant male mandrill picks through another's fur

Listen again to part of the talk. Then answer the question.  MP3 • 172

5. What does the professor mean when he says this:
Ⓐ He wants the students to challenge this assertion.
Ⓑ He thinks this number is very impressive.
Ⓒ He does not think this information is reliable.
Ⓓ He wants the students to make their own estimate.

Listen again to part of the talk. Then answer the question. MP3 • 173

6. Why does the professor say this:
Ⓐ To show he is disappointed in his students
Ⓑ To indicate the lecture material is important
Ⓒ To remind students he wants a transcript of his lecture
Ⓓ To warn students exam time is drawing near

DAY07

Organization

- CASE EXAMPLE - 例题
- CASE EXAMPLE解析-例题解析
- SMART SOLUTION - 题型攻略专题
- PRACTICE TEST - 练习
- DICTATION - 听写

speed keyword

Organization题型就是把握局部的作用

organization题型不仅考查考生对文章中一般性信息的掌握，还会考查考生是否在听的同时把握了文章整体的脉络。通常，这一题型会询问整篇文章的结构方式或者一个段落的结构方式，但最为常见的是提问某个特定部分在整体环境中所担当的角色。原则上来讲，conversation和lecture部分都会出现这种题型，但实际上还是主要出现在结构逻辑性强的lecture中。

- 留心局部在整体中起到的作用！

An important early development in American film was the spread of nickelodeons shortly after the…uh, turn of the century. Popular interest in film was booming at the time, but there were few venues for screening. That's why lots of small, storefront, purpose-built movie theaters, known as nickelodeons, began popping up everywhere.

At first, small shops and restaurants were also converted into, ah, makeshift venues for showing movies. But nickelodeons—so-called after a "nickel," a five-cent coin, which was the price of admission, and "odeon," the Greek word for theater—uh…nickelodeons were much more suitable for watching movies. They generally had fewer than 200 seats.

Why does the professor mention… ?

主要在讲义文中出现，平均每篇会有1道题。

CASE EXAMPLE

CONVERSATION **Listen to part of a conversation between a student and a professor.**

MP3 • 177

| Volume | Help | OK | Next |

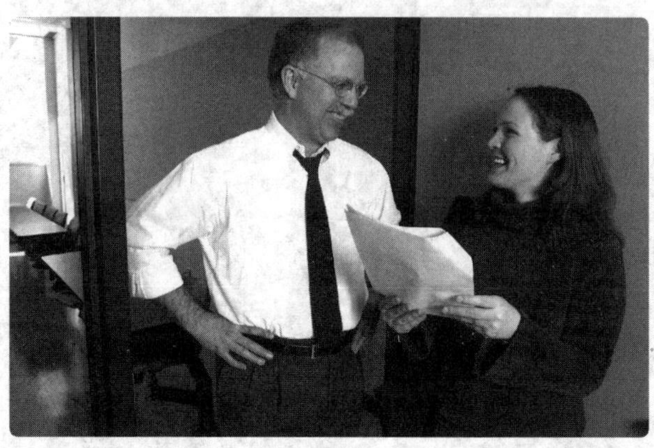

note taking

学生去找教授寻求论文写作的建议。请记录学生遇到的问题和教授给出的建议。

Problem:

Suggestion:

> How does the professor explain that the student's proposal is a bad idea?

Ⓐ By contrasting it with successful papers written by other students

Ⓑ By mentioning the problems with gathering data for case studies

Ⓒ By explaining that his proposed topic is far too broad

Ⓓ By reiterating the name and main purpose of the course

LECTURE **Listen to part of a lecture in a history class.**

MP3 • 178

| Volume | Help | OK | Next |

note taking

在关于金字塔是如何建造的古代历史课上，教授谈到了提供劳动力的人群。她谈到了哪些内容？请记录。

About laborers:

> Why does the professor mention movies about ancient Egypt?

Ⓐ To give an example of the importance of ancient Egyptian architecture

Ⓑ To correct a common misconception about the construction of the pyramids

Ⓒ To illustrate what a pyramid construction site probably looked like

Ⓓ To trace the history of pyramid construction in ancient Egypt

CASE EXAMPLE 解析

[SCRIPT] **Narrator** Listen to part of a conversation between **a student and a professor.** 情景：Office Hours

Student (female) Professor Mboto, can I have a word? It's about the **final paper.** 关键词：期末报告

Professor (male) Sure. What about it?

Student Well, I'm writing about the negative environmental consequences of urban spread.

Professor Sounds interesting.

Student Yeah, **but I'm not quite sure how to attack it**... you know, because there's so much data about different cities all over the world. So, uh, I thought **maybe I might focus on a particular city as a case study. Like, say, LA or Mexico City.** 主题：期末报告的写作方法 学生的立场

● 学生的烦恼是不确定如何写期末报告。因为一篇报告里容纳不了很多城市，她询问教授只挑选一座城市来写是否可行。

Professor Hmmm...**this class is called "Global Environmental Issues." I think your focus should be broader.** 教授的意见和建议

Student So it's better to talk about international trends?

Professor I think so. I'm afraid you'll have to look through lots of data sets and employ your analytical skills.

Student OK.

● 教授提醒了学生这门课希望达到的目标，建议她把范围扩大一些。

> 教授是用何种方式表达他认为学生想法的不足之处？

Ⓐ 与其他学生写的优秀报告做比较。

Ⓑ 提起搜集研究案例资料的困难。

Ⓒ 说明学生提议的主题太过宽泛。

Ⓓ 再次重复课程的名称和主要目标。

● 教授提醒学生课程名称中有"global"一词，试图说服她考虑到课程名称，相应地扩大写作范围。

Answer  Ⓓ

note taking

Problem: Too many cities to deal with → want to focus on a particular city

Suggestion: Global Environmental Issues → focus should be broader

[SCRIPT] **Narrator** Listen to part of a lecture in **a history class.**
讲义文涉及领域：历史

Professor (female)

We're still puzzling over **how the Egyptians managed to construct the pyramids**. Without any modern machinery, they transported, lifted and positioned literally millions of stone blocks, each weighing around two and a half tons. *[impressed]* It's just an amazing feat of engineering.
主题：埃及金字塔的建造方法

● 这篇讲义文主要介绍古埃及金字塔的建造之谜。

We think it probably took about 20,000 people 20 years just to complete the Great Pyramid at Giza. And where did all these laborers come from? **You may have seen some movies about ancient Egypt that show slaves building the pyramids...but, actually, we think now that slaves probably weren't involved.** Peasant farmers probably did most of the construction labor.
举例：电影里的情景与实际情况的比较

● 在电影里，建造金字塔的劳动力是奴隶，讲义文揭示了：事实上，建造金字塔的劳动力是农民。

> 教授为什么提到有关古埃及的电影？

Ⓐ为了举例说明古埃及建筑的重要性。

Ⓑ为了纠正大家对金字塔建造的普遍性误解。

Ⓒ为了说明建造金字塔现场的景象。

Ⓓ为了追寻建造古埃及金字塔的历史遗迹。

● 这道题在询问例子中的电影在文章整体中所起的作用。举这个例子是为了说明电影里看到的内容是不符合事实真相的。

 Ⓑ

O note taking

About laborers: slaves in movies (X) → possibly peasant farmers (O)

TIP 有效地使用简便的缩略语或符号有助于对文章意思的理解。因果关系经常使用→表示，比较或对照经常使用↔表示。

SMART SOLUTION

SOLUTION 1

提前预测哪些要点会成为问题。

organization题型关注的不是文章表述的内容(what is said)，而是进行说明的方式(how it's said)。因此，在解题时，仅靠对文章内容做笔记是不够的，重要的是需要边听边提前预测哪些要点会成为问题。

·讲义文的开头和结尾部分

不是所有的讲义文都先开门见山地用Today I'm going to talk about...直接明示当天的主题，然后预告下次讲义文的主题，接着就结束的。在实际生活中，有时说话者会向学生提问以激发他们的兴趣，有时说话者会举些特定的例子；结束的时候也经常采取提出另一问题的方式。因此应该细心确认文章的开头和结尾处有无什么需要注意的要点。这种问题通常会以如下的方式提问。

e.g. How does the professor introduce the topic?

→ By asking some questions to the students

→ By contrasting A and B

·说明新概念的部分

当讲义文中出现新的概念或用语时，说话者几乎不会简单地以“A means B”的方式进行说明。为了将新概念讲得更加浅显易懂，教授通常会在说明方式上做出多种尝试，因此需要注意说明方式。

e.g. How does the professor explain "A"?

→ By giving a general definition of A

→ By demonstrating the difference between A and B

·看起来与正文关联不大的例子或比喻出现的部分

通常，为了让说明更加易于理解并具有说服力，说话者经常会举例子或者打比方。这些部分的内容经常被用来提问。

e.g. Why does the professor mention A?

→ To give an example of X

→ To show that ...

→ To emphasize the importance of X

TIP 这时，要注意不能单纯地依据to之后使用的动词判断答案的正误，即不能因为哪里出现了例子，就不假思索地选择To give an example of X为正确答案。在这种情况下，判断的核心点应该是X的具体内容，而不是to不定式部分。

SOLUTION 2

熟悉讲义文的几种基本叙述方式。

讲义文展开自身逻辑的叙述方式可以归结为几类。从表面看来，每个讲义文好像都采用了各不相同的逻辑展开方式。而事实上，它们大体都不会超出以下整理的几种类型，不同之处仅仅在于讲义文的整体或局部对它们进行了何种方式的运用。

· 运用于整体的叙述方式

顺序的叙述方式：这是最普通的叙述方式。它把一个对象或概念分要点进行叙述。这种情况下需要注意的是在一个话题向另一个话题过渡的地方，会出现let's move on to..., another thing we need to discuss等提示词语。

按照年代的叙述方式：在说明历史事件的行进或演变过程时经常使用，会以带有数字、时间等状语为标志依次整理要点。

分小项的叙述方式：用来一边对照和比较几个项目，一边对它们进行叙述。关键在于需要分类整理各项都具有哪些特征。使用on the other hand, in contrast to, unlike等作为比较-对照标志的概率很大。

· 运用于局部的叙述方式

除了以上几种运用于整体的叙述方式，局部还使用了下定义、列举、联系因果、举例、比较及对照等叙述方式。

SOLUTION 3

各题型训练。

就算是对同一个要点进行提问，问题和选项的形式也可以出现多种变化。因此，即使问题的形式有所改变，也应该一听就能识别出organization题型。下面以case example中的问题举例如下：

e.g. Why does the professor mention movies about ancient Egypt?

→ To correct a common misconception about the construction of the pyramids

How does the professor explain the construction of the pyramids?

→By contrasting it with Hollywood depictions

What point does the professor make when he mentions movies about ancient Egypt?

→The people who constructed the pyramids were peasants not slaves.

PRACTICE TEST_level 2

LECTURE

1. Listen to part of a talk in a zoology class.

MP3 • 179

note taking

1-1. How does the professor introduce her discussion of color blindness in monkeys?

Ⓐ By asking the students if any of them are color-blind

Ⓑ By listing several different types of color blindness

Ⓒ By pointing out the advantages of being color-blind

Ⓓ By describing the characteristics of capuchin monkeys

Listen again to part of the talk. Then answer the question. MP3 • 180

1-2. Why does the professor say this:

Ⓐ To make sure that the student fully understands red-green color blindness

Ⓑ To ask the student to describe his experience with color blindness to the class

Ⓒ To find out about a condition that she has never actually experienced

Ⓓ To persuade the student to clarify his definition of red-green color blindness

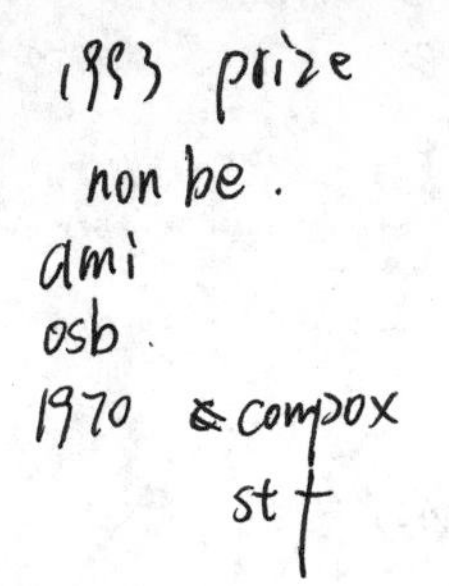

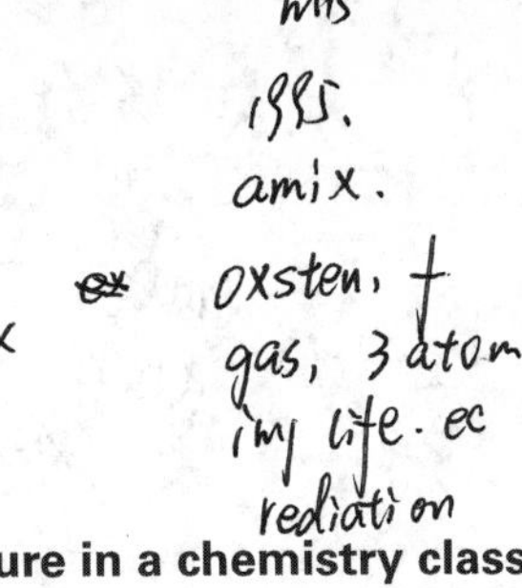

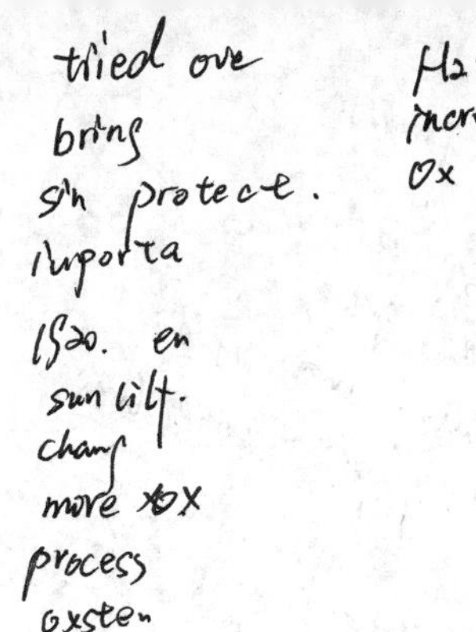

LECTURE **2. Listen to part of a lecture in a chemistry class.**

MP3 • 181

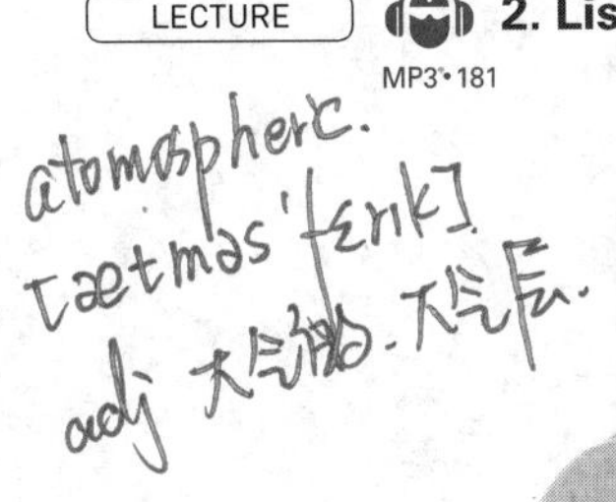

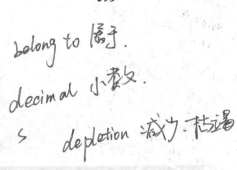

note taking

2-1. What was the subject of Crutzen's groundbreaking research?

Ⓐ The effect of ozone depletion on the Earth's atmosphere

Ⓑ The devastating impact of nitrous oxide on ozone

Ⓒ The part played by OH and HO_2 in ozone decomposition

Ⓓ The factors that influence the formation of ozone

2-2. Why does the professor mention Sidney Chapman and Marcel Nicolet?

Ⓐ To explain why three scientists won the Nobel Prize in Chemistry in 1995

Ⓑ To give examples of researchers who were influenced by Crutzen's work

Ⓒ To provide background information about early ozone research

Ⓓ To name two scientists who researched together with Crutzen

PRACTICE TEST_level 2

LECTURE **3. Listen to part of a lecture in a geology class.**

MP3 • 182

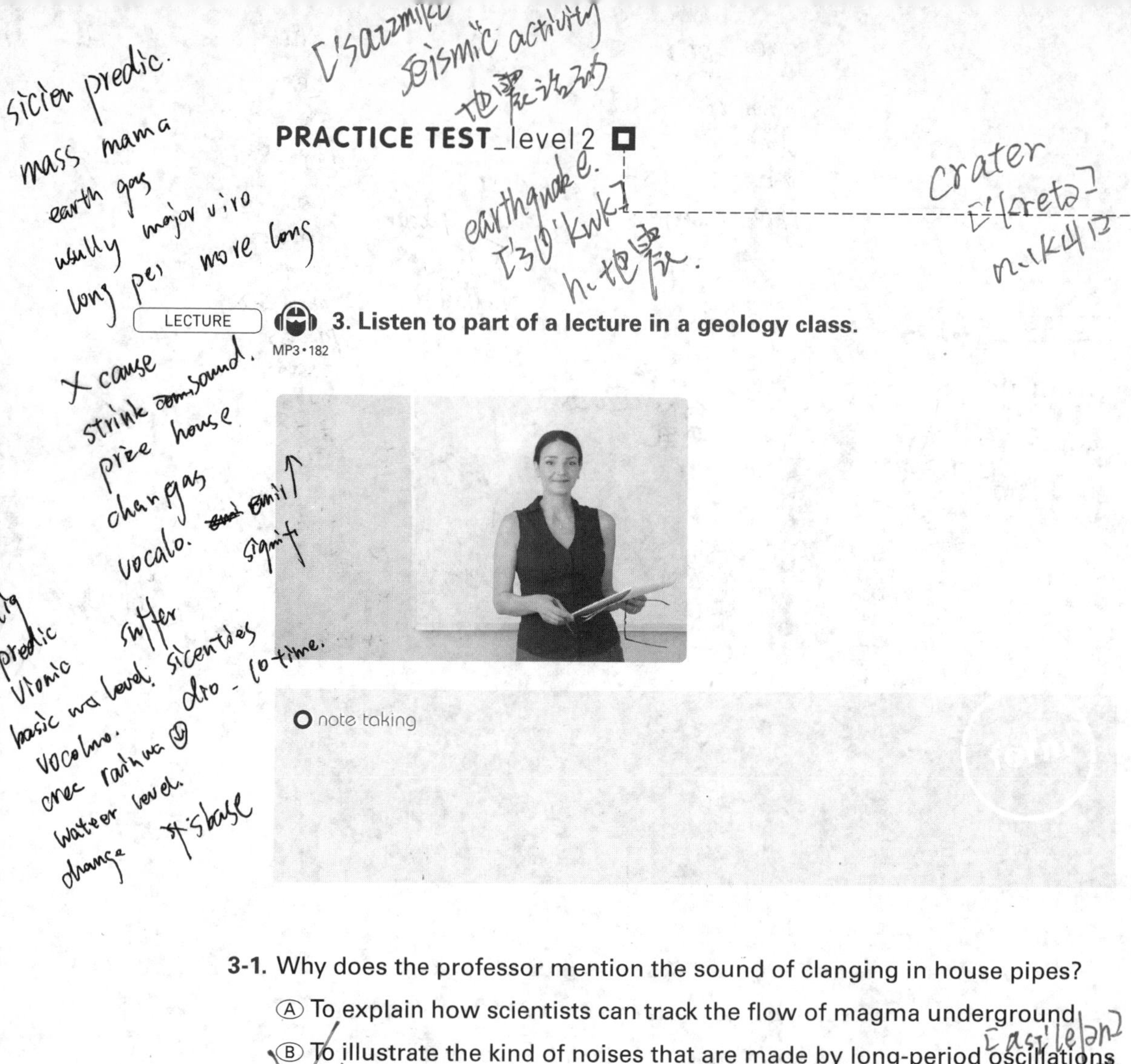

note taking

3-1. Why does the professor mention the sound of clanging in house pipes?

Ⓐ To explain how scientists can track the flow of magma underground

Ⓑ To illustrate the kind of noises that are made by long-period oscillations

Ⓒ To compare the impact of violent earthquakes with those of longer and milder ones

Ⓓ To show how the layers under the surface are affected by volcanic eruptions

3-2. According to the professor, what phenomena occur before a volcanic eruption? Click on 2 answers.

Ⓐ There is a violent earthquake.

Ⓑ The volcanic cone begins to emit toxic gases.

Ⓒ There are elevated sulfur dioxide emission levels.

Ⓓ The water level in the crater lake spikes and dips.

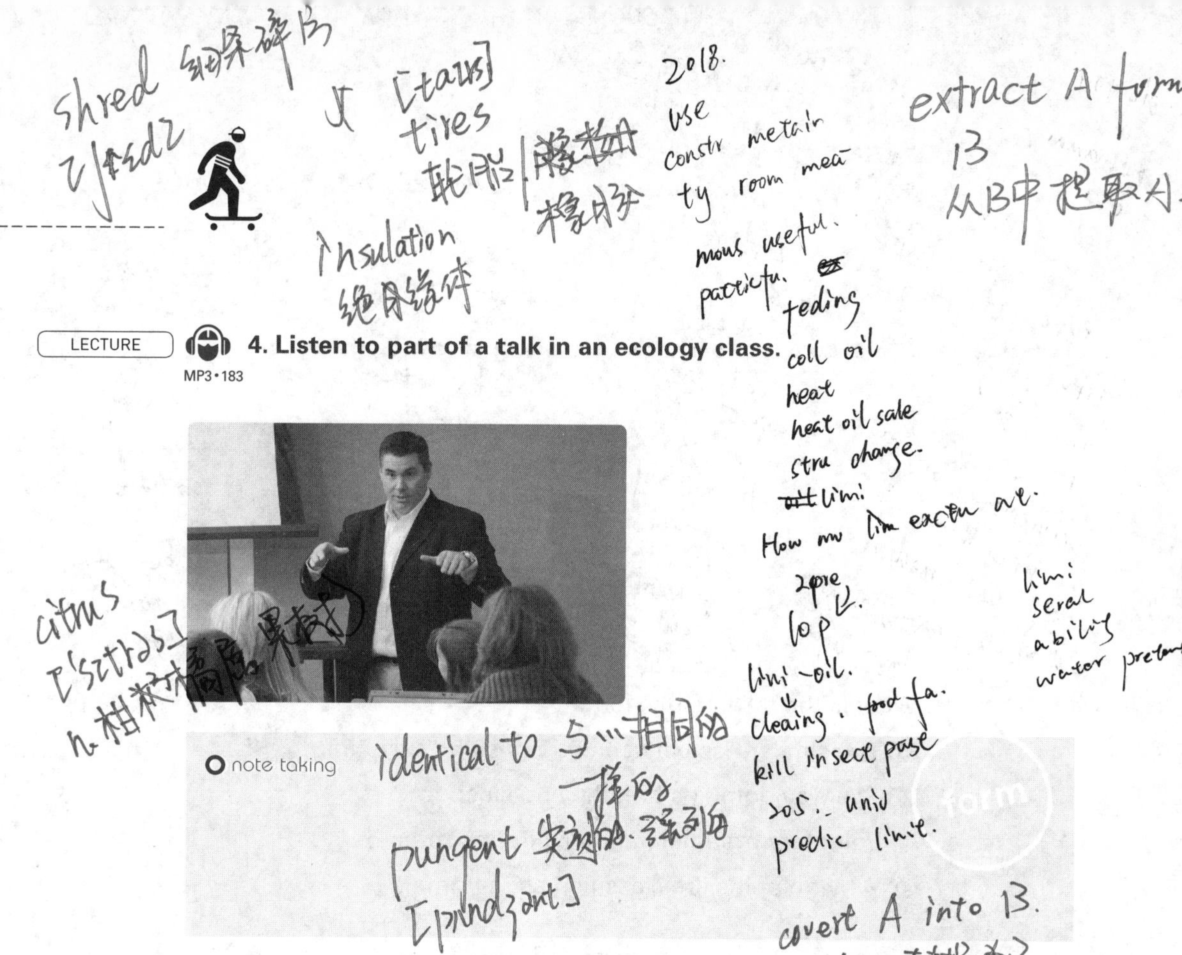

LECTURE **4. Listen to part of a talk in an ecology class.**

MP3 • 183

note taking

DAY 07

4-1. Why does the professor ask about uses for waste tires?

Ⓐ To focus the discussion on a topic he will provide more information about
Ⓑ To encourage the students to think more broadly about the subject
Ⓒ To show the impact of the environmental movement on waste management
Ⓓ To describe the effect of Manfredi's discovery on the scientific community

4-2. According to the professor, how can limonene be used for practical purposes? Click on 2 answers.

Ⓐ In the construction of houses
Ⓑ In the production of plastics
Ⓒ As a potential prevention of cancer
Ⓓ As an additive in motor oil

PRACTICE TEST_level 3

LECTURE 1. Listen to part of a talk in a marine biology class.

MP3 • 184

note taking

Main Idea 1-1. What is the talk mainly about?

Ⓐ The similarities between humans and dolphins

Ⓑ The way dolphins breathe and sleep

Ⓒ Voluntary breathers and involuntary breathers

Ⓓ Why dolphins are classified as mammals

Organization 1-2. What point does the professor make when she mentions that humans are involuntary breathers?

Ⓐ The brains of dolphins and humans are similar.

Ⓑ Human respiratory systems are more sophisticated.

Ⓒ The breathing behavior of humans is very different from that of dolphins.

Ⓓ Dolphins breathe mainly in three different ways.

Detail 1-3. What do scientists believe about the brain-wave activity of sleeping dolphins?

Ⓐ It is similar to the brain-wave activity of conscious dolphins.

Ⓑ It indicates that dolphins likely experience dreams.

Ⓒ It does not reflect the typical patterns associated with REM sleep.

Ⓓ It suggests that sleeping dolphins are not aware of their surroundings.

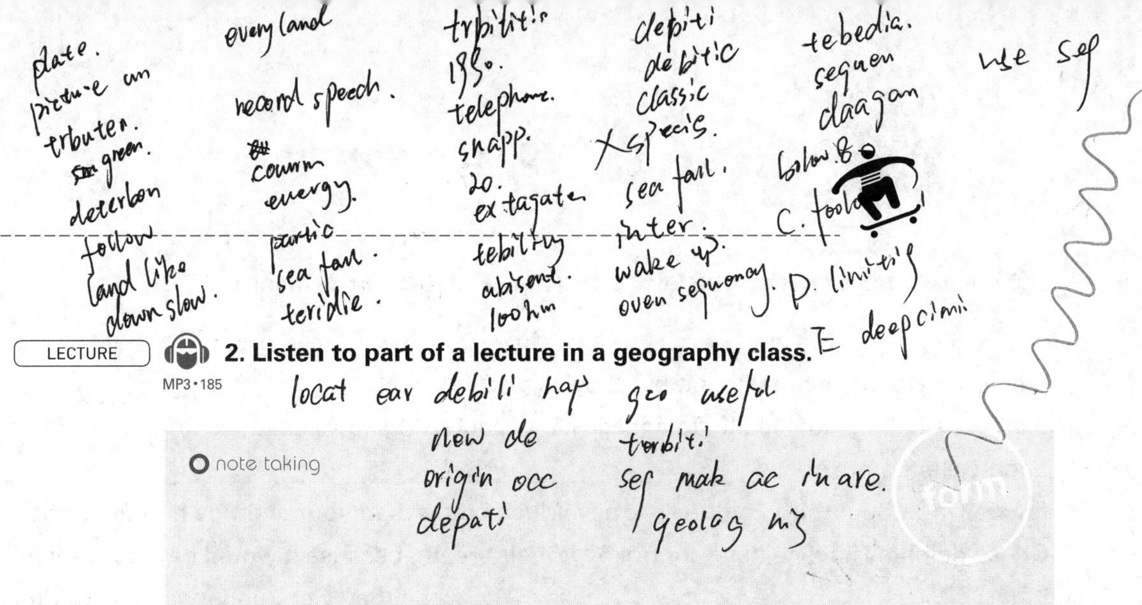

LECTURE 2. Listen to part of a lecture in a geography class.

MP3 • 185

note taking

Organization **2-1.** Why does the professor tell the students to picture a snow avalanche?

Ⓐ To demonstrate the composition of the materials in a turbidity current

Ⓑ To emphasize the dangers posed by turbidity currents on the ocean floor

Ⓒ To explain the geological conditions that trigger turbidity currents

Ⓓ To use a familiar illustration to explain how turbidity currents behave

Detail **2-2.** According to the lecture, what are the characteristics of turbidity currents? Click on 2 answers.

Ⓐ They are affected by the flow of currents in the sea.

Ⓑ They occur in geologically active underwater regions.

Ⓒ They can trigger earthquakes or other seismic events.

Ⓓ They leave behind accumulations of sediments.

Listen again to part of the lecture. Then answer the question.  MP3 • 186

Function **2-3.** Why does the professor say this:

Ⓐ To elaborate on the idea that he has just mentioned

Ⓑ To check whether the students understand the material

Ⓒ To encourage the students to participate in the class

Ⓓ To indicate the content that he is covering is complex

DAY 07

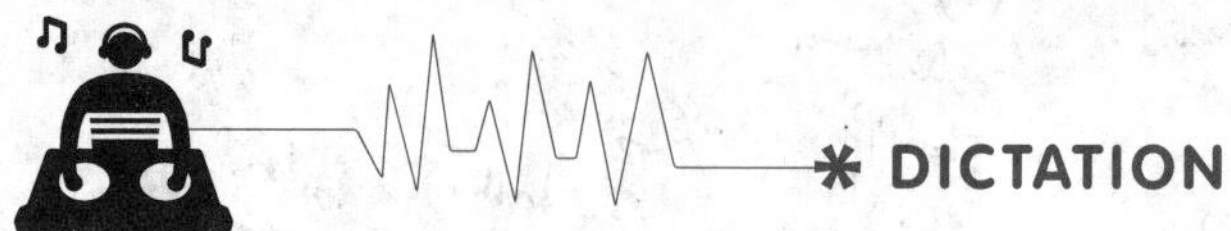

MP3·187 Listen to part of the level 3 talk again and fill in the blanks.

［省略］

Professor: Dolphins breathe air, but they've got 1)________ ________ ________ ________ that's—well, that's adapted to, to aquatic life of course. It allows dolphins to spend a while underwater before 2)________ ________ ________ ________ ________ ________ ________ for air. Oh...about thirty minutes, I'd say. Much better than your average human, right? OK, so dolphins have to have control over their breath, because it would be inconvenient 3)________ ________ ________ ________ ________ while they were underwater, wouldn't it? So, they aren't like humans... they're what we call "voluntary breathers." You know... humans don't have to think about taking a breath every time they need to...it just happens automatically. We're "involuntary breathers." So, actually, even if you decide not to breathe, 4)________ ________ ________ ________ ________ ________ ...uh, you'll fall into unconsciousness and start breathing again. This works out well for us, right? I mean, consider 5)________ ________ ________ ________ ________ ________ if our bodies didn't automatically breathe for us when we were asleep.

But, actually, that brings me to an interesting point about dolphins...how do they sleep? If they're voluntary breathers...that means they have to be conscious in order to breathe. But one of the characteristics of mammals that, uh, that you didn't mention earlier is that they need to 6)________ ________ ________ ________ ________ —to sleep. So... what's the solution? Well, amazingly, a dolphin's brain only sleeps a half at a time. Um, 7)________ ________ ________ ________ ________ ________ ________, scientists have been able to measure the electrical activity in dolphins' brains. And, um, so based on electroencephalography—that's what the technique is called—uh, we've learned that half of a dolphin's brain can be asleep while the other half is awake. And that's 8)________ ________ ________ ________ ________ ________ ________ their, their voluntary breathing process and yet, um, still get enough, uh, enough sleep—and they go to sleep like this for about eight hours a day.

［省略］

答案参见ANSWER BOOK P392

MP3·188 Listen to part of the level 3 lecture again and fill in the blanks.

［省略］

Professor: All right, now I want to talk a bit about 1)________ ________ ________ ________ ________ turbidity current—the turbidites. So these turbidites are clastic—you know, consisting of broken, mixed up fragments 2)________ ________ ________ ________

—and so not really a specific type of rock or anything...nope, they are a jumbled mix of whatever was picked up from the seafloor by the turbidity current.

Uh...but what's really interesting about these turbidites is the way they're 3)______ ______ ______ ______ ______. We can describe these layers using what's known as the Bouma Sequence—so-called because it was discovered by marine geologist Arnold Bouma. So the, uh, turbidite 4)______ ______ ______ ______ ______ ______ which make up the Bouma Sequence. They're labeled A, the very bottom, through E, the top. 5)______ ______ ______ ______ ______ ______ ______ ______. So at the bottom we have "A". These are massive sand grains with a very, um, gravelly base. "B" is 6)______ ______ ______ ______ ______ ______. "C"...are you following me? "C" has cross-laminated sands..."D" has, um, laminated silts. And finally, "E" is mainly comprised of deep-sea muds. You got all that down?

Uh, while it's useful to know about the Bouma Sequence, it's rare to see a turbidite which follows this exact sequence. Can anyone guess why? Well, what do we know about turbidites? They're 7)______ ______ ______ ______ ______ ______, right? And in these areas, turbidity currents are pretty common, right? You see, what happens is, new turbidity currents come along and 8)______ ______ ______ ______.

［省略］

答案参见ANSWER BOOK P395

oral expression

MP3 • 189

Listen to the expressions and sentences in the script below and repeat.

be better at *doing* 更擅长…	The color-blind monkeys **were better at spotting** the hidden insects than those with normal vision.
put in context 放入背景/语境中考查	Let's **put** their work **in context** by talking for a little bit about ozone.
more often than not 经常，通常	**More often than not**, these earthquakes are what are called long-period oscillations.
let A in on the secret 告诉A…	Well, I suppose I could share some information with you...**let** you **in on the secret**.
get the image in mind 想象出样子	Has everyone **got this image in mind**?
get down 写下来，记录…	And finally, E is mainly comprised of deep-sea muds. You **got** all that **down**?
end up *doing* 最终以…收场	So, you **end up having** overlapping turbidites in the same place.

DAY08

Connecting Contents

- CASE EXAMPLE - 例题
- CASE EXAMPLE解析-例题解析
- SMART SOLUTION - 题型攻略专题
- PRACTICE TEST - 练习
- DICTATION - 听写

speed keyword

Connecting Contents题型就是连结信息。

这一题型与detail类型一样，解题线索都是文章中直接出现的信息。但与detail题型不同的是，正如connecting contents的这个标题所显示的，这一题型要求考生把分散开来的各信息按照异同分类，或者按顺序对它们进行排列，以期用一个立体的网络(Web)形态去理解。如果细心考查就会发现，解答这一题型相当于在“掌握信息”过程的基础上，再经历一个处理“信息间的联系”的过程。

- 以图表形式出题
- 留心出现比较、对照或者分类内容的部分！

An important early development in American film was the spread of nickelodeons shortly after the...uh, turn of the century. Popular interest in film was booming at the time, but there were few venues for screening. That's why lots of small, storefront, purpose-built movie theaters, known as nickelodeons, began popping up everywhere.

At first, small shops and restaurants were also converted into, ah, makeshift venues for showing movies. But nickelodeons—so-called after a "nickel," a five-cent coin, which was the price of admission, and "odeon," the Greek word for theater—uh...nickelodeons were much more suitable for watching movies. They generally had fewer than 200 seats.

Click in the correct box for each phrase.

平均每篇出现0~1道题，这里分布的分数可能超过1分。

CASE EXAMPLE

CONVERSATION  **Listen to part of a conversation between a student and a receptionist.**

MP3 • 196

| Volume | Help | OK | Next |

note taking

学生来到了学校行政办公室。她有什么疑问，工作人员又告诉她应该准备哪两样东西，不需要准备什么？请记录。

Problem

Required

Not Required

> In the conversation, they discuss what the man will need to bring to the vehicle impound to retrieve his car. Indicate whether each of the following is Required or Not required by clicking in the correct boxes.

	Required	Not required
Ⓐ A vehicle release form		
Ⓑ A driver's license		
Ⓒ Car registration details		
Ⓓ Payment for the penalty charge		

LECTURE  **Listen to part of a lecture in an anthropology class.**

MP3 • 197

| Volume | Help | OK | Next |

DAY 08

note taking 人类学课上，大家正在讨论某个部落的面具。请将面具的特征按眼睛和嘴巴归为两类。

1. Eyes

2. Mouth

> In the lecture, the professor mentions some specific characteristics of the facial features of Pwo masks. Indicate which characteristic refers to each feature by clicking in the correct boxes.

	Eyes	Mouth	Both
Ⓐ Remains slightly open			
Ⓑ Sticks out from the rest of the face			
Ⓒ Conveys a sad image			
Ⓓ Resembles an oval in shape			

CASE EXAMPLE 解析

[SCRIPT] **Narrator** Listen to part of a conversation between **a student and a receptionist.**
情景:Service Encounters

Student (female) *[sounding annoyed]* Excuse me. I parked in front of Charlotte Hall—and now **my car's been towed.**
问题

Receptionist (male) Ah, you parked in one of the temporary spaces?

Student *[sheepishly]* Yep...**So how do I get it back?**
来的目的：找回被拖走的车

Receptionist Well, the campus administration uses a local towing company, Jake's Impound.

Student I know...they're located just up the road, aren't they?

Receptionist Right.

Student So, uh, what do I need to show them...car registration details?
Distraction

Receptionist No, just your **driver's license.** And you'll **have to pay** to get your car out of the impound.
准备物件1 准备物件2

Student Of course.

Receptionist And for the car release charge...that's $80.

Student $80! Oh man! I should have just paid for parking in the first place.

● 学生在校园里违章停的车被拖走了，为了找回车，她来到了相关办公室。

● 为了找回被拖走的车，学生需要准备一些东西。这些重要的信息不仅与学生的造访目的直接相关，还被列举出来，因此一定会出题，需要做笔记。

> 在对话中，学生和行政人员为了取回车辆的事情进行了一番谈话。学生需要带什么去车辆保管所呢？请在下面的表格中选择出需要和不需要的东西。

	Required	Not required
Ⓐ车辆移交文书		√
Ⓑ驾驶执照	√	
Ⓒ车辆登记信息		√
Ⓓ支付罚款	√	

● Ⓒ是作为distraction出现的选项，Ⓐ是直译car release而出现的容易引起混淆的选项。

note taking

Problem: towed car *or* 车辆牵引、拖挂
Required: driver's license / fee
Not Required: car registration info.

sample

TIP 列举的项目可以自己选择符号标记，一般经常使用/符号标记。

[SCRIPT] **Narrator** Listen to part of a lecture in an **anthropology class.**
演讲涉及领域：人类学

Professor (female)

The **masks that are made to represent Pwo,** they're said to symbolize (关键词) the, um, the ideal mother and woman. **The eyes are usually almond-shaped and appear to be, um, half closed.** (罗列眼部特征) There are—there're pronounced eye sockets. They're sort of sunken into the mask. Often there are **tears falling from the eyes. These tears—they represent the sadness mothers experience** when—when their sons enter adulthood. **As for the mouth, well it's usually open just a little.** (罗列嘴部特征) This means you can see some teeth that are triangular in shape. The, uh, the **lips are quite full and fleshy...they protrude quite a long way out.**

• 教授在介绍Pwo部落的面具。

• 讲义文在介绍面具的耳目口鼻时，讲了眼睛和嘴巴的几个特征，由此应该可以轻松的预测与这些特征有关的题目，然后分眼睛和嘴巴两项做笔记。

> 演讲是关于Pwo部落面具的内容。教授提到了面具各部分的特征。以下部分具有哪些特征？请在相应的栏目中标记。

	眼睛	嘴巴	两者皆是
Ⓐ微微张开。			√
Ⓑ从脸上突出。		√	
Ⓒ传达出悲伤的感情。	√		
Ⓓ椭圆形。	√		

• 请注意Both一栏，考生不仅需要知道眼睛和嘴巴各自的特征，还需要将两者的共同点联系起来进行整理。所有选项都是将原文略微paraphrase得来的。

O note taking

1. Eyes: ① almond-shaped
② half closed
③ sunken into the mask *or* 陷进去的
④ tears → mother's sadness

2. Mouth: ① open a little → can see teeth
② lips → protrude *or* 突出的

TIP 如上，在预测到会出现特征列举，并对各项及各项特征进行整理时，应注意要采用简明的形式，不混淆上层栏目和细节特征。

SMART SOLUTION

SOLUTION 1

了解连结基本信息的方法。

为了构筑信息之间的联系，需要两种以上可以进行比较的信息或者将信息依次连结，如下表所示。

· YES / NO

列举与同一对象相关和无关的内容时，经常使用YES和NO两项对信息进行分类。根据情况，有时也会用REQUIRED / NOT REQUIRED的形式分类。

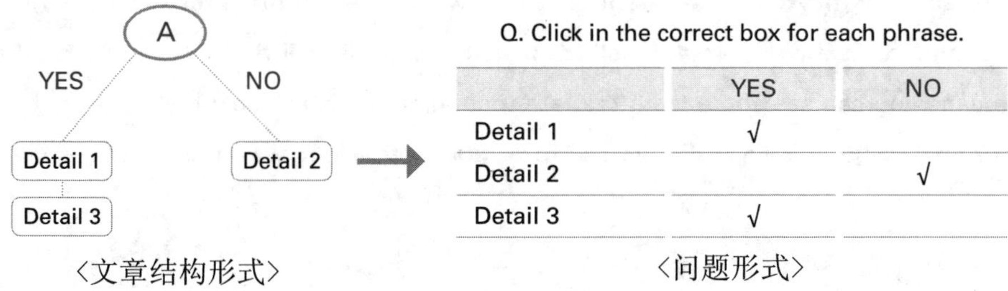

Q. Click in the correct box for each phrase.

	YES	NO
Detail 1	√	
Detail 2		√
Detail 3	√	

〈文章结构形式〉 〈问题形式〉

· 按项目分类

当出现了几个小主题并就其中每一个的几种特征和属性进行列举时，需要能够将对象和相应的属性连接起来。

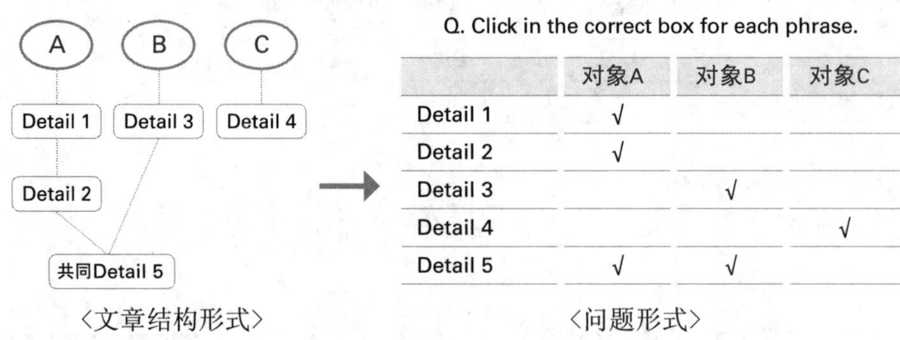

Q. Click in the correct box for each phrase.

	对象A	对象B	对象C
Detail 1	√		
Detail 2	√		
Detail 3		√	
Detail 4			√
Detail 5	√	√	

〈文章结构形式〉 〈问题形式〉

此时，识别将分项对事物特征进行列举的标志如下。

- 列举共同要素时：similarly, likewise, and
- 表现对比或区别时：on the contrary, on the other hand, however, whereas, in comparison to [with], 比较级

• 顺序的过程

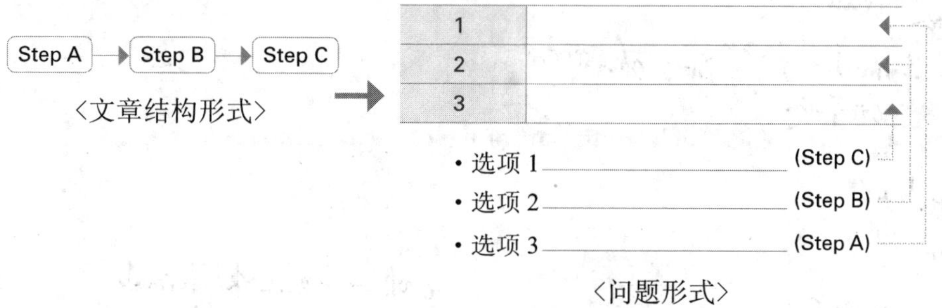

当文章中出现顺序的关系时，需要将图框外的选项按顺序拖入框中的1、2、3栏。此时，识别文章中将出现顺序关系的标志如下：

• 首先：primarily, first, first of all
• 之前：prior to, before
• 接着：then, later, next, subsequently

SOLUTION 2

预测文章的结构，并适当做笔记。

解答问题的线索都分布在文章中，因此在听力开始时提前预测全文的结构，并适当地做笔记十分重要。请牢记SOLUTION 1中介绍的3种连结信息的方法，练习根据开头和脉络预测文章的结构形式。

• **YES / NO形式**

这是最常见的类型。在列举同一对象的对立属性时，分两项做笔记。前面case example对话部分是典型的例子。

• **按项目分类的形式**

通常，按照英语文章的逻辑结构，信息在由概括向具体过渡时，文章开头会出现classify、type、group一类的词语说明将会出现几项信息。请留心项目的数量，准备好适当地做笔记。讲义文中，教授会使用如下的一些句子。

e.g. Let me explain 3 types of A 让我来说明一下A的三种类型。
This can be divided into two groups: A and B 这可以分为两类：A和B。

• **按顺序的说明形式**

通常，在按照时间顺序记叙年代或对某些对象的形成及演变过程进行说明时，经常使用顺序的说明形式。

e.g. 虚假记忆(false memory)的形成过程，沙丘(sand dune)的形成过程

PRACTICE TEST_level 2

LECTURE **1. Listen to part of a lecture in a music class.**

MP3 • 198

note taking

1-1. How does the professor explain the achievements of Miles Davis?

Ⓐ By describing the range of instruments he mastered

Ⓑ By going into detail about some of his best-known releases

Ⓒ By explaining the style he demonstrated on one of his albums

Ⓓ By citing contemporary jazz musicians' impressions of him

1-2. In the lecture, the professor describes three of Miles Davis's albums. Match the phrases below to the album they describe. Click in the correct box for each phrase.

	Birth of the Cool	*Kind of Blue*	*Bitches Brew*
Ⓐ Took inspiration partly from classical music			
Ⓑ Received mixed reactions from the jazz community			
Ⓒ Was characterized by a free and unstructured sound			
Ⓓ Featured the use of electronic equipment			
Ⓔ Was noted for its highly elaborate composition			

LECTURE

2. Listen to part of a lecture in a meteorology class.

MP3 • 199

2-1. What is the talk mainly about?

Ⓐ The requirements necessary for the formation of hurricanes

Ⓑ The various types of disastrous weather phenomena

Ⓒ The formation of hurricanes and tornadoes and their characteristics

Ⓓ The similarities between hurricanes and tornadoes

2-2. Indicate whether each of the following phrases is related to hurricanes or tornadoes. Click in the correct box for each phrase.

	Hurricanes	Tornadoes
Ⓐ Range in size from several feet to a couple of miles		
Ⓑ Reach maximum wind speeds of 300 miles per hour		
Ⓒ Generally persist for several days		
Ⓓ Develop over warm bodies of water		
Ⓔ Occur most frequently in North America		

LECTURE  **3. Listen to part of a lecture in a biology class.**

MP3 • 200

note taking

3-1. Why does the professor mention inaccessible terrain?

Ⓐ To explain one of the difficulties of gauging the populations of endangered animals

Ⓑ To illustrate the actions that must be taken when a population is first deemed endangered

Ⓒ To emphasize that mark-and-recapture is only one of many techniques for gathering population data

Ⓓ To describe why it is so important that populations of animals be estimated from time to time

3-2. In the lecture, the professor describes the mark-and-recapture method of estimating animal populations. Indicate whether each of the following is a step in the process. Click in the correct box for each phrase.

	YES	NO
Ⓐ A team of scientists situate themselves in a specific area.		
Ⓑ Scientists use complicated algorithms to determine how many individuals to mark.		
Ⓒ The team finds as many species as possible and marks them.		
Ⓓ The animals are observed over the course of several months.		
Ⓔ Later, the researchers note the number of marked and unmarked animals in the region.		

LECTURE **4. Listen to part of a talk in a sociology class.**

MP3 • 201

note taking

DAY 08

4-1. In the lecture, the professor describes the philosophies of cultural relativism and cultural absolutism. Match the sentences below to the theory they describe. Click in the correct box for each phrase.

	Cultural Relativism	Cultural Absolutism
Ⓐ There can never be a general consensus about what is right and wrong.		
Ⓑ Some actions should be condemned regardless of the context in which they are performed.		
Ⓒ Every society has its own culturally-based norms and ethics.		
Ⓓ Essential values can be derived from human nature.		

Listen again to part of the talk. Then answer the question.  MP3 • 202

4-2. Why does the professor say this:

Ⓐ To suggest that she agrees with the man

Ⓑ To express surprise at the man's opinion

Ⓒ To imply that the man has made an error

Ⓓ To summarize the man's point of view

PRACTICE TEST_level 3

LECTURE **1. Listen to part of a discussion in a health class.**

MP3 • 203

note taking

Main Idea

1-1. What is the discussion mainly about?

Ⓐ How the growth of plaque can lead to tooth loss

Ⓑ The function of plaque in protecting tooth enamel

Ⓒ How a dentist removes plaque from teeth

Ⓓ The differences between plaque and tartar

Connecting Contents

1-2. In the discussion, the professor describes the problems associated with gum disease. Indicate whether each of the following is mentioned as a symptom of the disease. Click in the correct box for each phrase.

	YES	NO
Ⓐ Bacteria colonize the mouth and form tartar.		
Ⓑ Gums become a deeper red and bleed easily.		
Ⓒ Tissue surrounding the sulcus becomes swollen.		
Ⓓ The ligaments holding teeth are weakened.		
Ⓔ The oral infection spreads to other parts of the body.		

Listen again to part of the discussion. Then answer the question.  MP3 • 204

Function

1-3. Why does the professor say this:

Ⓐ To invite the students to draw a conclusion

Ⓑ To indicate that there is no time to explain the final step

Ⓒ To imply that the next step is not what students would think

Ⓓ To find out if the students need extra explanation

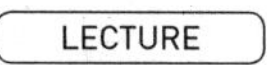

 **2. Listen to part of a lecture in a geology class.**

MP3 • 205

DAY 08

Main Idea

2-1. What is the lecture mainly about?

Ⓐ The importance of underwater volcanoes

Ⓑ The characteristics of different types of underwater lava

Ⓒ The differences between underwater lava and lava on land

Ⓓ The formation of the ocean floor

Connecting Contents

2-2. In the lecture, the professor describes several different types of lava. Indicate whether each of the following phrases relates to pillow, lobate, or sheet lava. Click in the correct box for each phrase.

	Pillow	Sheet	Lobate
Ⓐ Occurs in places where the sea floor is quite flat			
Ⓑ Expands like a water balloon			
Ⓒ Moves quickly over the ocean floor before solidifying			
Ⓓ Looks similar to surface pahoehoe lava			
Ⓔ Has a surface that is usually smooth and even			

Listen again to part of the lecture. Then answer the question.  MP3 • 206

Attitude

2-3. What does the professor mean when she says this:

Ⓐ She is worried that the students are not enjoying the lecture material.

Ⓑ She does not expect the students to take the exercise too seriously.

Ⓒ She is concerned that the students will not like the activity.

Ⓓ She is sure that this content will not appear in the final exam.

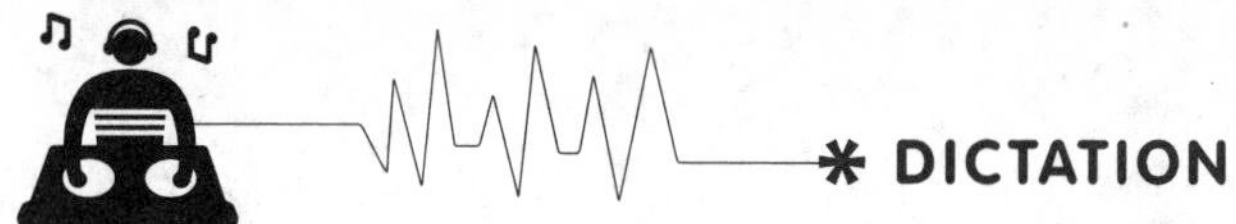

MP3·207 Listen to part of the level 3 discussion and fill in the blanks.

Professor: I'm sure you're all aware of [1]______ ______ ______ ______ ______. We—we need to brush and floss regularly and visit our dentist once a year in order to clean away plaque and to have cavities filled. [2]______ ______ ______, but exactly why is it so important to get rid of plaque?

Student: Well, it causes cavities, for one thing. I think it's a type of bacterium.

Professor: Actually, it's more than one type. It's like a—[3]______ ______ ______ ______ ______ ______ ______. There can be up to 400 different species of bacteria in plaque. Oh, by the way, plaque does serve a function. It protects [4]______ ______ ______ ______ ______ ______ ______ ______. Anyway, even though it serves a function, it needs to be kept in check.

Student: I have a question. What's the difference between plaque and tartar?

Professor: Good question. Basically, tartar is plaque [5]______ ______ ______. That means that it becomes hardened, and it really sticks to teeth. So, whereas plaque can pretty much be removed with a toothbrush, you'll probably have to see your dentist to remove tartar. And once you have tartar the situation gets worse. You see, tartar is rough, unlike the tooth surface. The rough surface provides a much—a much better home for plaque. So the bacteria [6]______ ______ ______ ______ ______ in the tartar, and the, uh, the problem gets worse. Now, who can tell me what might happen if plaque is allowed to—to [7]______ ______ ______ ______ ______?

Student: You could develop gingivitis.

Professor: Very good. And what's that? What is gingivitis?

Student: It's a, um, a gum disease, I think.

Professor: That's true. Gum disease is...well, it's a disease that affects your gums. And it's [8]______ ______ ______ ______. Now, gingivitis is an early form of gum disease. It's an, um, an inflammation of the gums. The earliest sign of gingivitis is, well, inflammation —your gums become reddish in color...redder than normal, I mean...and will probably be very sensitive and bleed easily. And [9]______ ______ ______ ______. The good news is that gingivitis is reversible. It's possible to get rid of gingivitis by taking good care of your teeth.

［省略］

答案参见ANSWER BOOK P401

MP3·208 Listen to part of the level 3 lecture again and fill in the blanks.

［省略］

Professor: So, lava flows underwater look a bit different from how they look on land.

There are [1]______ ______ ______ ______ __________ ______, and they're called pillow lava, lobate lava, and sheet lava. The factors that affect the shape of the lava flow are: A, the speed of the eruption—that is, [2]______ __________ ______; B, the incline of the sea floor where the eruption occurs; and C, the viscosity of the lava, um, [3]______ ______ __________ ______ __________. So a liquid with a high viscosity moves very slowly. Remember that. High viscosity equals slow movement. Got that?

So, pillow lava, as the name suggests, looks like a pillow. It has a high viscosity so it's slow moving, and it solidifies very quickly into formations that are [4]______ ______ ______ ______ ______. What happens is, when the eruption occurs...um, if it's a slow eruption... the outer layer of the lava solidifies almost instantly, so you get something like a bubble of solidified lava with liquid lava on the inside. The liquid lava on the inside [5]______ __________ ______ ______ ______ ______ and causes it to inflate, sort of like when you fill a balloon with water. Sometimes the inner lava will burst through, and a new pillow will be created much like the first. Pillow formations generally occur where there's very little incline, or uh, slope, of the ocean floor. So again, we've got a low effusion rate, a pretty flat sea floor, and high viscosity.

[省略]

答案参见ANSWER BOOK P403

oral expression

MP3 • 209

Listen to the expressions and sentences in the script below and repeat.

start with 从…开始讲	I'll **start with** *Birth of the Cool*, released in 1957.
be considered to 被认为是…	*Kind of Blue* **is** generally **considered to** be his best selling album.
be more likely to 更有可能…	Most animals, especially rare ones **are more likely to** be endangered.
pretty neat 很不错	It's possible to get a fairly accurate estimation of whether a species is endangered or not. **Pretty neat**, huh?
That's what I'm saying. 那正是我想说的。	A: You're saying that there're no absolute rights or wrongs. B: **That's what I'm saying.**
when it comes to A 至于A，A方面	What about **when it comes to** issues like slavery or torture?
for one thing 首先，第一	A: But exactly why is it so important to get rid of plaque? B: Well, it causes cavities, **for one thing**.

DAY09

Inference

- CASE EXAMPLE - 例题
- CASE EXAMPLE解析-例题解析
- SMART SOLUTION - 题型攻略专题
- PRACTICE TEST - 练习
- DICTATION - 听写

speed keyword

Inference题型就是综合信息。

这一题型要求考生搜集散布在文章中的细节信息，并由此推导出文章中没有直接提及的内容。为了推导出关于相应对象的正确结论，最重要的就是充分地积累可使用的准确信息，并且有效地对它们加以综合利用。此题型的部分问题类似于询问说话者态度的attitude题型，但不同之处在于解答inference类型问题的基础是综合利用更加多元的信息。

• 推导，但是要能在原文中找到依据。

An important early development in American film was the spread of nickelodeons shortly after the...uh, turn of the century. Popular interest in film was booming at the time, but there were few venues for screening. That's why lots of small, storefront, purpose-built movie theaters, known as nickelodeons, began popping up everywhere.

At first, small shops and restaurants were also converted into, ah, makeshift venues for showing movies. But nickelodeons—so-called after a "nickel," a five-cent coin, which was the price of admission, and "odeon," the Greek word for theater—uh...nickelodeons were much more suitable for watching movies. They generally had fewer than 200 seats.

What does the professor imply about X?

预测about之后会出现的推导对象。

平均每篇出现0~1个此类问题。

CASE EXAMPLE

  **Listen to part of a conversation between a student and an administrator.**

MP3 • 216

| Volume | Help | OK | Next |

note taking

学生来找学校的工作人员谈什么问题？请记录。

Problem:

> What can be inferred about the man?

Ⓐ He was assigned the wrong room at the beginning of the year.

Ⓑ He would prefer not to live in a university dormitory again.

Ⓒ He has not yet tried to work out his housing problem on his own.

Ⓓ He is already familiar with the official policy on room changes.

 **Listen to part of a lecture in a zoology class.**

MP3•217

| Volume | Help | OK | Next |

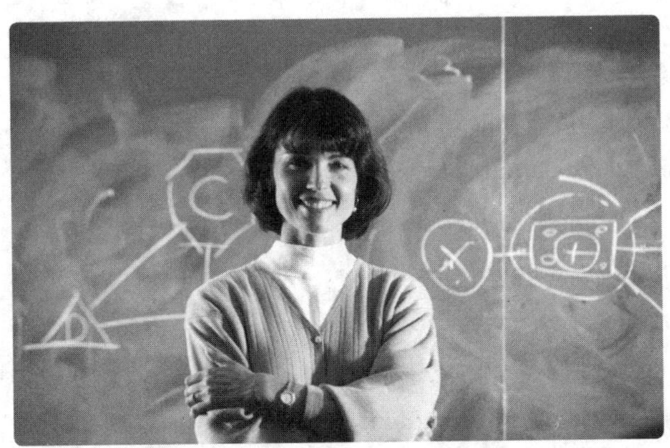

DAY 09

note taking

动物学课上，教授正在讲解恒温动物和变温动物。主题句和例子的主要内容是什么？请试着总结一下。

Topic:

Example:

> What can be inferred from the professor's description of human behaviors?

Ⓐ People imitate behaviors normally exhibited by ectotherms.

Ⓑ Humans rely on internal factors to regulate temperature.

Ⓒ The distinction between endothermic and ectothermic is not rigid.

Ⓓ An animal's classification is largely based on its behavior.

CASE EXAMPLE 解析

[SCRIPT] **Narrator** Listen to part of a conversation between **a student and an administrator.**
情景:Service Encounters

Administrator (female) Hello. How can I help you today?

Student (male) Hi. **I've come to discuss my housing situation.**
关键词：住宿问题

Administrator *[encouraging him to go on]* Sure—

Student *[pause]* The thing is, **I wanna move to a new dorm.**
问题：宿舍变更

Administrator *[disapprovingly]* In the middle of the semester?

Student Yes, I understand that can be arranged.
根据1

Administrator *[with emphasis]* Only in a few specific cases. Room assignments are meant to be for the entire school year. The school prefers you find a way to work out whatever problem you're facing. Moving to a new room is considered a—a final option.

Student Yeah. It says that several times in the student handbook.
根据2

● 在学期中间，学生想换宿舍。工作人员提出了严格的校务规定，表现出了不支持的立场。从学生的反应来看，他已经很了解那些校规了。

> 可以推测出学生？

Ⓐ 他在学期刚开始的时候被分错宿舍了。

▶没有提及此项作为申请变更宿舍的理由，此选项错误。

Ⓑ 他不想再住在大学宿舍里了。

▶仅仅希望变更宿舍，此选项错误。

Ⓒ 他没有尝试着自己解决住宿问题。

▶文章中没有提及，此选项错误。

Ⓓ 他已经对更换房间的正式规定十分熟悉了。

● 因为需要进行推测的对象是学生，因此需要依据学生所说的话来进行选择。从学生说的话中可以推测出的内容仅为Ⓓ项。

Answer Ⓓ

note taking　Problem: wanna move to a new dorm *or* 宿舍变更

[SCRIPT] **Narrator** Listen to part of a lecture in a **zoology class.**
讲义文涉及领域：动物学

Professor (female)

We classify an animal as **endothermic** (关键词1) if it regulates its temperature internally. Whereas an **ectotherm**, (关键词2) it regulates its temperature externally—by lying in the sun to warm up, or going in the water to cool down...those sorts of things. **But actually, it's a little more complicated than that. Endotherms also employ a lot of ectothermic responses to regulate their temperature.** (主题：恒温动物也会表现出变温动物的特征)

Just think about humans. (Supporting example) Broadly speaking, **we're endothermic, but** we rely on lots of outside factors to keep our temperature steady. **We swim to cool off in summer. And, uh, in winter, we wear warm clothes. These are *[with emphasis]* ectothermic responses.** You see what I'm saying?

- 恒温动物与变温动物的基本定义
- 注意连词but，它正式揭示出了主题。
- 教授以人类的行为为例，说明了为什么说恒温动物也具备变温动物的特征。

> 从教授对人类行为的描述中，可以推测出？

Ⓐ 人类主要模仿变温动物表现出的行为。

▶只是表现出变温动物的部分特征，此选项错误。

Ⓑ 人类需要依靠内在因素调节体温。

▶常识性的内容经常为错误选项。

Ⓒ 恒温动物与变温动物之间的区别不是固定不变的。

Ⓓ 动物主要依据行为分类。

▶讲义文前半部分出现了classify一词，但是一般的动物分类并不是讲义文的主要内容，因此该选项错误。

- 说话者以人类行为举例是为了说明什么？这需要根据语境推测。即根据讲义文前半部分同时出现了有关恒温动物和变温动物特征的内容，可以看出正确答案是Ⓒ选项。

Answer Ⓒ

note taking

Topic: endotherm / ectotherm 区别的复杂性

Example: Human behaviors: 显示变温动物的特征（夏季→游泳，冬季→暖和的衣服）

sample

SMART SOLUTION

SOLUTION 1

边听边预测需要作出推论的对象。

边听边预测考点，这一点对依据什么进行推论十分重要。需要作推论的对象大部分都是与文章整体的核心概念相关的，因此需要将出现在文章各部分的线索进行整合，推导出新的结论。
此题型最普遍的提问形式是使用imply或infer的如下形式：

- What does the professor **imply** about X?
- What can be **inferred** about X?

此时，关键是需要推论的对象X是什么，该对象通常是conversation中的核心主题之一，lecture中最具有代表性的是核心概念或用语。

- What does the professor imply about **enrolling in the course**?
  由对话的中心话题可以作何推论
- What can be inferred about the **respiratory systems of plants**?
  由讲义文的核心概念可以作何推论

如上所示，需要作推论的对象通常都与文章的整体内容相关。为此，进行相关的练习是最重要的。需要学会一边听较长的文章，一边综合各种信息。

SOLUTION 2

熟悉正确及错误答案的类型。

基本说来，所谓推论都需要经历一个综合信息的复杂过程。虽然正确及错误答案的区别可能会不明显，但是熟悉以下一些提示的话会对解题有所帮助。

- **正确答案是将听到的文章内容完全综合后再陈述(restatement)。**
- **因为需要作推论，如果只是文章中的表达，或对原文的重复也一般不是正确答案。**
- **有逻辑跳跃的推论并非答案。因为必须以文章中出现的“事实”为依据做推论，所以一定是可以在文章中找到依据的内容。**

SOLUTION 3

理解进行推论的基本方法。

有各种联系并综合信息的方法，以下两种最典型。

· 因果关系(cause and effect)

由原因推出结果是最普遍的推论方法。

Junk foods are full of bad things like fat and salt which of course, cause heaps of health problems, so the junk food consumption is beginning to decrease.
垃圾食品充满脂肪和盐分，会导致各种健康问题，所以垃圾食品的消耗量已开始减少。

→There's more awareness now about the benefits of a nutritious diet.
现在，人们越来越认识到健康饮食的好处。

· 概括(generalization)

通过具体的事实或例子推导出具有普遍性的结论。

Water, land and air are getting increasingly polluted and soil erosion is leading to desertification. 对水、土地和空气的污染正变得越来越严重，并且土壤侵蚀正在导致沙漠化。

→The planet's natural ecosystems are being severely degraded.
地球的自然生态系统正在遭受严重的破坏。

SOLUTION 4

切莫忽略推测未来行动的问题。

推测未来行动或事件的问题有时也会出现，往往要求考生预测说话者的下一个行为或者下一次讲义文的主题。此时，解题的线索经常出现在文章的结尾部分。当与未来行动有关的内容出现时，它很可能成为考点，因此需要特别留心。

	情景	问题
conv.	学生下周要去拜访教授，给教授看他写的报告的初稿 I'll be here to show you my first draft next week.	What will the student probably do next week?
lecture	教授在讲义文末尾提及下次讲义文主题 Let me finish the last part of this topic next class.	What might the professor discuss next class?

DAY 09

PRACTICE TEST_level 1

> [1-8] Listen to each passage. Then choose the best answers to the questions.

Listen to part of a conversation between a student and a parking official.

MP3•218

1. What can be inferred about the college's parking policy?

Ⓐ The administration strictly enforces it.

Ⓑ It was implemented two weeks ago.

Ⓒ Many students are confused by it.

Ⓓ It varies from dorm to dorm.

Listen to part of a lecture in an art class.

MP3•219

2. What does the professor imply about Romanticism?

Ⓐ It is something that the students will learn more about later.

Ⓑ It was mainly concerned with dramatic themes.

Ⓒ It followed immediately after the Naturalism movement.

Ⓓ It was a fairly minor movement that she will not cover in depth.

Listen to part of a conversation between a student and a professor.

MP3•220

3. What does the professor imply about next week's lab assignment?

Ⓐ It is going to address subject matter that is unfamiliar to the students.

Ⓑ A three-person team will have an easier time completing it.

Ⓒ Much of the work will require help from him.

Ⓓ It cannot be done by a group of two people.

Listen to part of a lecture in an astronomy class.

MP3•221

4. What can be inferred about Pluto?

Ⓐ It is no longer regarded as the ninth planet in the solar system.

Ⓑ Its orbit is further from the sun than Eris's is.

Ⓒ It is actually the moon of a much larger planet.

Ⓓ Its status as a dwarf planet is currently under question.

Listen to part of a conversation between a student and a bookstore clerk.

MP3 • 222

5. What does the clerk imply?

Ⓐ There may be a job available for the student during the summer.

Ⓑ The student should look for jobs elsewhere on campus.

Ⓒ She may be quitting her job after the semester ends.

Ⓓ The bookstore is currently hiring student employees.

DAY 09

Listen to part of a lecture in a zoology class.

MP3 • 223

6. What does the professor imply?

Ⓐ The appearance of reindeer is not important to the lecture.

Ⓑ "Reindeer" and "caribou" are two terms for the same animal.

Ⓒ The students should be familiar with the appearance of caribou.

Ⓓ Caribou are more common in the wild than reindeer.

Listen to part of a conversation between a student and a professor.

MP3 • 224

7. What does the professor imply about the teaching assistant position?

Ⓐ It will enable the man to receive extra credits in her class.

Ⓑ It requires the assistant to be available for questions on weekdays.

Ⓒ It is something that most of her graduate students do.

Ⓓ It would not be difficult for the man to fit into his schedule.

Listen to part of a lecture in a geography class.

MP3 • 225

8. What does the professor imply about Alaska's oriented thaw lakes?

Ⓐ They are oriented in opposite directions.

Ⓑ They have not been studied in person.

Ⓒ Their recent growth is due to global warming.

Ⓓ Their formation was understood recently.

PRACTICE TEST_level 2

CONVERSATION  **1. Listen to part of a conversation between a student and a registrar.**
MP3 • 226

note taking

1-1. Why did the registrar call the woman into his office?

Ⓐ To notify her of a change in her schedule

Ⓑ To inform her that her class has been canceled

Ⓒ To explain the requirements for her major

Ⓓ To discuss her options after graduation

Listen again to part of the conversation. Then answer the question.  MP3 • 227

1-2. What does the woman imply when she says this:

Ⓐ Professor Ogawa is her primary reason for enrolling in the course.

Ⓑ She will not consider changing her schedule around.

Ⓒ She has a time conflict with the period the registrar mentioned.

Ⓓ The change in her advanced finance class is unfair.

LECTURE  **2. Listen to part of a talk in a history class.**

MP3 • 228

note taking

2-1. What does the professor imply about the annual flooding of the Nile?

Ⓐ It allowed the ancient Egyptians to accumulate staple crops for trade.

Ⓑ It was supplemented by an unpredictable and powerful rainy season.

Ⓒ It led the ancient Egyptians to create flood barriers around their cities.

Ⓓ It provided farmers with the water they needed to grow crops.

2-2. Why does the professor mention nilometers?

Ⓐ To illustrate how important the Nile's flooding was in ancient Egyptian life

Ⓑ To explain how predictions about the floods affected taxes

Ⓒ To suggest that the flooding of the Nile is still not fully understood today

Ⓓ To discuss how the yearly floods were stopped

1. Listen to part of a conversation between a student and a professor.

MP3•229

note taking

Main Idea

1-1. Why does the student go to see the professor?

Ⓐ To get approval on her chosen thesis topic

Ⓑ To receive advice on selecting a thesis subject

Ⓒ To find out when Professor Donnelly will guest lecture

Ⓓ To discuss a slide shown in the last class

Listen again to part of the conversation. Then answer the question. 

Attitude

1-2. What does the professor mean when he says this:

Ⓐ He is concerned because the proposal is due soon.

Ⓑ He is excited to read her proposal.

Ⓒ He is annoyed the student is so far behind schedule.

Ⓓ He is interested to hear the student's explanation.

Listen again to part of the conversation. Then answer the question. 

Inference

1-3. What can be inferred about the university?

Ⓐ It requires students to submit a thesis for every advanced course.

Ⓑ It forbids students from writing similar papers for more than one class.

Ⓒ It has a clear policy against copying from other students' papers.

Ⓓ It penalizes students who do not complete assignments on time.

LECTURE  **2. Listen to part of a talk in an engineering class.**

MP3•232

note taking

Main Idea **2-1.** What is the talk mainly about?

Ⓐ The discovery of the two different kinds of smart fluids

Ⓑ The ways to affect the viscosity of smart fluids

Ⓒ The potential uses of smart fluids in medical technology

Ⓓ The two types of smart fluids and some of their uses

Inference **2-2.** What does the professor imply about smart fluids in the past?

Ⓐ They were used in a wider variety of industries than they currently are.

Ⓑ They were not thought of as practical commercial products.

Ⓒ They were studied by some of the world's top engineers.

Ⓓ It was not possible to create them with the technology of the time.

Detail **2-3.** Which of the following are mentioned in the lecture as uses of MRFs?

Click on 2 answers.

Ⓐ As artificial biological tissues

Ⓑ In the suspension systems of automobiles

Ⓒ In the inner mechanics of surgical tools

Ⓓ In the joints of prosthetic legs

DAY 09

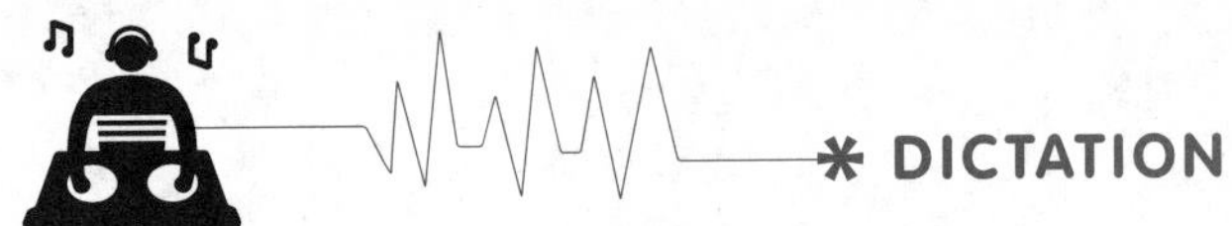

MP3 • 233 **Listen to part of the level 3 conversation again and fill in the blanks.**

［省略］

Professor: I see. Hmmm...you know you have to [1]______ ______ ______ ______ on Monday, right?

Student: Yeah, which is why [2]______ ______ ______ ______ ______ ______. I mean, it's not like I haven't been thinking about it...I just can't seem to narrow it down. Maybe you could help get me started?

Professor: That's what I'm here for. Remember to choose something you are willing to research over the course of five months. [3]______ ______ ______ ______, so make sure you're truly interested in your topic. What are some of the topics you've been considering?

Student: Well, um...I guess I've tried narrowing it down to something on, er, the original influences of Byzantine art, or, um, the meaning of [4]______ ______ ______ ______...and yeah, the last one was about, uh, the achievement of color in ancient Greek pottery.

Professor: Very interesting...I really like your idea about exploring Egyptian symbolism. It's a very rich topic. Although, all three [5]______ ______ ______ ______ ______ ______ ______ ______.

Student: Yeah...that's the problem. I'm equally interested in all three. I wonder if there's something you'd prefer reading...

Professor: Me? Oh, *[chuckling]* I would find pleasure in reading about any of those. What's important is that you focus on something that you enjoy and can [6]______ ______ ______ ______ ______ ______.

［省略］

答案参见ANSWER BOOK P411

MP3 • 234 **Listen to part of the level 3 talk again and fill in the blanks.**

［省略］

Professor: *[chuckling]* Well...at one time, these smart fluids were considered to be, um, nothing more than a—a novelty. Something that was really interesting to study...but that probably wouldn't have any real, uh, applications. But recently, there have been [1]______ ______ ______ ______ ______ ______. So now, some of the uses of MRFs are, um, in automotive design...um, in the suspension system, which is [2]______ ______ ______ ______ ______ that's, uh, that's transmitted from the road to the car.

You see…well, this isn't really what I want to focus on today, but, uh... *[changing his mind]* Well, it's important, so I'll just briefly tell you about some of the advantages. Um, by using MRFs, automotive designers [3]________ ________ ________ ________ ________ ________ ____________ ________ in their suspension systems. That's because MRFs can rapidly adapt. Um, they can [4]______ ______ __________ _______ _______ _______ 500 times in one second. So, in a car's suspension system then, the MRF can change its, its viscosity to best absorb the, uh, specific amounts of shock that [5]______ ______ __________ ______.

Student A: *[interrupting enthusiastically]* I remember reading about some kind of technology that's been used in prosthetics—like artificial legs or something—um, and it uses a smart fluid [6]______ ______ ______ _______ _______ _______… Do you know what I'm talking about?

Professor: Yes, you're right. It is related to MRFs. Some artificial limbs, um, use MRFs [7]____________ _______ ____________ that can automatically detect the—the wearer's walking speed. And it can even detect things like, um, whether the wearer is walking up stairs or—or going up a slope, and it'll [8]______ _______ ___________ ___________.

［省略］

答案参见ANSWER BOOK P414

oral expression

MP3 • 235

Listen to the expressions and sentences in the script below and repeat.

not surprisingly 并不令人惊奇	Naturalism, **not surprisingly** considering the name, is all about representing life accurately and naturally in art.
I was wondering if … 我猜想或许…	My friend Yvonne just transferred into this class, and **I was wondering if** I could switch to be with her.
not too long ago 不久之前	There was a time **not too long ago** when Pluto was considered to be the ninth planet in our solar system.
be impressed that 很欣慰… 对…印象/感受很深	In fact, I've **been** so **impressed that** I'd like to offer you an opportunity.
narrow down 缩小（范围/领域）	I've tried **narrowing** it **down** to something on the original influences of Byzantine art.
stumble on [onto] (偶然地，意外地）发现…	Anyway, I think we've **stumbled onto** the solution to your dilemma.
be worn out 疲惫，耗尽力气	No thesis, thank goodness. I'd **be** so **worn out**.

Review Test II

请完成下列题目，复习前面学过的各类型问题。

MP3·250

passage 1. [1~5] Listen to part of a conversation between a student and a librarian.

Volume | Help | OK | Next

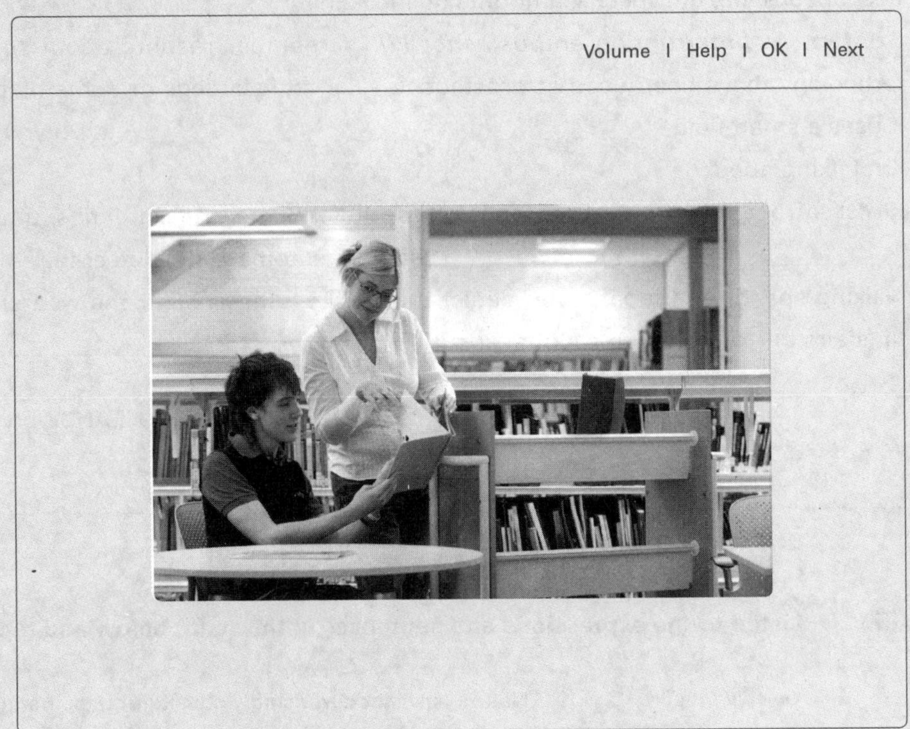

1. Why does the man go to the library?

Ⓐ To check out a book about the MLA citation format

Ⓑ To find out which citation style is required in the class

Ⓒ To ask for assistance in formatting his bibliography

Ⓓ To find out what style guides are available

◎答案/解析 P.416

2. Why does the librarian ask for the name of the man's professor?
Ⓐ To decide what citation style would be best to use
Ⓑ To check whether the style guide has been reserved
Ⓒ To determine how many sources he will need to cite
Ⓓ To find out which course books he is required to read

3. Based on information from the dialogue, indicate whether each of the following would be covered in *the MLA Handbook for Writers of Research Papers*. Click in the correct box for each phrase.

	YES	NO
Ⓐ The placement of periods in a bibliography		
Ⓑ The proper location for the publishing date		
Ⓒ The order in which multiple authors should be listed		
Ⓓ The correct use of italics		
Ⓔ The procedure for checking out style guides		

Listen again to part of the conversation. Then answer the question.  MP3•251

4. What can be inferred about the student when he says this:
Ⓐ He is not sure he heard the librarian correctly.
Ⓑ He needs time to remember which citation style is required.
Ⓒ He is uncertain what the librarian means.
Ⓓ He expects the librarian to know what citation style to use.

Listen again to part of the conversation. Then answer the question.  MP3•252

5. What does the librarian imply when she says this:
Ⓐ Few students come in to use the reference materials.
Ⓑ No one has ever asked to check out the reference materials.
Ⓒ Students cannot take the reference materials out of the library.
Ⓓ It does not take long to use the reference materials.

MP3 • 253

passage 2. [1~6] Listen to part of a lecture in an engineering class.

Volume | Help | OK | Next

Ceramics

1. What is the lecture mainly about?
   Ⓐ Construction materials used in space shuttles
   Ⓑ The process for creating ceramic materials
   Ⓒ Some important applications of ceramics
   Ⓓ New developments in ceramic products and use

2. What characteristic of ceramic-coated tiles explains their use in spacecraft?
   Ⓐ The low cost and ease of their construction
   Ⓑ Their ability to withstand extreme temperatures
   Ⓒ The fact that they can be reused indefinitely
   Ⓓ Their capacity to maintain heat inside the craft

◎答案/解析 P.418

3. How does the professor emphasize the importance of ceramics in construction?

Ⓐ By focusing on a single building and how ceramics are used in it

Ⓑ By listing the positive aspects of specific ceramic materials

Ⓒ By describing the history of ceramic use in the industry

Ⓓ By comparing ceramics to other construction materials

4. Indicate whether each of the following is mentioned in the lecture as a use for ceramics. Click in the correct box for each phrase.

	YES	NO
Ⓐ Ornamental china and pottery		
Ⓑ Temperature gauges in machinery		
Ⓒ Components in high-tech computers		
Ⓓ Surfaces in home design		
Ⓔ Internal parts of racing vehicles		

Listen again to part of the lecture. Then answer the question.  MP3•254

5. What can be inferred about the professor?

Ⓐ She thinks the differences are just trivial.

Ⓑ She doesn't want to be repetitive.

Ⓒ She is concerned the man has misunderstood the lecture.

Ⓓ She does not want to get off topic.

Listen again to part of the lecture. Then answer the question.  MP3•255

6. Why does the professor say this:

Ⓐ To get the students to come up with more examples

Ⓑ To emphasize the importance of the point

Ⓒ To show that there are a lot of additional uses

Ⓓ To ask the students to define a term from the talk

 **passage 3. [1~6] Listen to part of a lecture in a literature class.**

MP3 • 256

Volume I Help I OK I Next

Evelyn Waugh

1. What is the talk mainly about?

Ⓐ Common themes in twentieth-century British literature

Ⓑ Evelyn Waugh's education at Oxford University

Ⓒ The life of a British novelist and his first work

Ⓓ The success enjoyed by the book *Decline and Fall*

2. How does the professor introduce the basic concept of *Decline and Fall*?

Ⓐ By explaining the origin of the book's name

Ⓑ By describing Evelyn Waugh's family

Ⓒ By listing Waugh's post-university jobs

Ⓓ By discussing Waugh's life while writing the book

◎答案/解析 P.420

3. Based on information in the lecture, indicate whether the statements below about the main character are included in *Decline and Fall*. Click in the correct box for each sentence.

	YES	NO
Ⓐ He received low grades and dropped out of Oxford.		
Ⓑ He was mistreated by college officials.		
Ⓒ He took up a career in teaching.		
Ⓓ He married into high society and became wealthy.		
Ⓔ He was engaged to a woman involved in illegal activities.		

4. According to the professor, what two aspects of English society are criticized in *Decline and Fall*? Click on 2 answers.

Ⓐ The legal system
Ⓑ Educational institutions
Ⓒ The social elite
Ⓓ Human trafficking

Listen again to part of the lecture. Then answer the question. 

5. What can be inferred when the professor says this:

Ⓐ Waugh had a lot of problems with his professors.
Ⓑ Waugh was not a very talented student.
Ⓒ Waugh's failure was his own fault.
Ⓓ Waugh clearly had some kind of personality disorder.

Listen again to part of the lecture. Then answer the question. 

6. Why does the professor say this:

Ⓐ To imply this part of the story is remarkable
Ⓑ To show Waugh invented his own literary style
Ⓒ To hint at what will come next
Ⓓ To make the students guess about the plot

type A. [1~30] Listen and fill in the blanks. When the word is repeated add the Chinese meaning.

MP3 • 262 [1~5]

01 have a completely ____________ reason ____________

02 establish international ____________ ____________

03 ____________ the term to NGO ____________

04 ____________ from the bottom of a lake ____________

05 prevent heat from ____________ into space ____________

MP3 • 263 [6~10]

06 the most ____________ theory ____________

07 at the opposite end of the ____________ ____________

08 trigger a ____________ on the ocean floor ____________

09 cause ____________ extinction events ____________

10 ____________ onto the solution to your dilemma ____________

MP3 • 264 [11~15]

11 starve a country into ____________ ____________

12 be forced to ____________ their great empire ____________

13 usually ____________ tombs and temples ____________

14 a popular ____________ for New Yorkers ____________

15 act as a ____________ to others ____________

◎答案/解析 P.424

MP3 • 265 [16~20]

16 produce greenhouse gas ____________ ____________

17 ____________ on just two legs ____________

18 sunlight that is ____________ by ice crystals ____________

19 Maathai's pretty ____________ work ____________

20 have a tendency to avoid ____________ ____________

MP3 • 266 [21~25]

21 let the air ____________ well ____________

22 ____________ rotating columns of air ____________

23 some complex mathematical ____________ ____________

24 be used as a cleaning ____________ ____________

25 feature a special ____________ structure ____________

MP3 • 267 [26~30]

26 reduce the ____________ of food ____________

27 a sudden warm ____________ ____________

28 ____________ the resistance of human skin ____________

29 maintain optimal ____________ levels ____________

30 ____________ of 17th century ____________

type B. [1~30] Listen the definition for each word and choose the correct word.

01 Ⓐ nasal Ⓑ olfactory Ⓒ organic Ⓓ fragrant

02 Ⓐ rephrase Ⓑ emphasize Ⓒ hypothesize Ⓓ energize

03 Ⓐ emotive Ⓑ pastoral Ⓒ serene Ⓓ ideal

04 Ⓐ mundane Ⓑ effective Ⓒ freguent Ⓓ exhaustive

05 Ⓐ conductive Ⓑ transferable Ⓒ automatic Ⓓ receivable

06 Ⓐ atrocious Ⓑ respective Ⓒ aggressive Ⓓ venomous

07 Ⓐ substance Ⓑ component Ⓒ gland Ⓓ intestine

08 Ⓐ relative Ⓑ underprivileged Ⓒ inadequate Ⓓ deficient

09 Ⓐ submit Ⓑ vindicate Ⓒ realize Ⓓ offset

10 Ⓐ incorporate Ⓑ exchange Ⓒ inspect Ⓓ retrieve

11 Ⓐ meteorite Ⓑ phenomenon Ⓒ pathogen Ⓓ comet

12 Ⓐ gender Ⓑ community Ⓒ species Ⓓ primate

13 Ⓐ permit Ⓑ confirmation Ⓒ receipt Ⓓ report

14 Ⓐ affect Ⓑ incite Ⓒ incur Ⓓ induce

15 Ⓐ faze Ⓑ swish Ⓒ veer Ⓓ grate

◎答案/解析 P.424

MP3 • 269 [16~20]

16 Ⓐ fertilize Ⓑ harvest Ⓒ feed Ⓓ diversify

17 Ⓐ destructive Ⓑ stifling Ⓒ perpetual Ⓓ pliable

18 Ⓐ expertise Ⓑ groundwork Ⓒ impulsion Ⓓ improvisation

19 Ⓐ impart Ⓑ fabricate Ⓒ coin Ⓓ direct

20 Ⓐ irritate Ⓑ debate Ⓒ contempt Ⓓ speculate

21 Ⓐ soil Ⓑ estate Ⓒ terrain Ⓓ boundary

22 Ⓐ proponent Ⓑ supervisor Ⓒ commentator Ⓓ participant

23 Ⓐ useful Ⓑ remedial Ⓒ hospitable Ⓓ appointed

24 Ⓐ precede Ⓑ facilitate Ⓒ forewarn Ⓓ imagine

25 Ⓐ polluted Ⓑ intriguing Ⓒ hygienic Ⓓ negligent

26 Ⓐ indecency Ⓑ commitment Ⓒ brutality Ⓓ provocation

27 Ⓐ grateful Ⓑ outrageous Ⓒ passionate Ⓓ needy

28 Ⓐ bereavement Ⓑ reception Ⓒ legacy Ⓓ leftover

29 Ⓐ gala Ⓑ amusement Ⓒ demonstration Ⓓ memorial

30 Ⓐ descend Ⓑ mobilize Ⓒ orbit Ⓓ vault

step-up training

分主题听力训练

听力考试的文章会出现哪些主题？

DAY 12 Office Hours

DAY 13 Arts, Literature

DAY 14 Life Science I

DAY 15 Physical Science

DAY 16 Review Test III (Day 12~15)

DAY 17 Service Encounters

DAY 18 Life Science II

DAY 19 Social Science

DAY 20 America

DAY 21 Review Test IV (Day 17~20)

Holiday! Word Brush-up

DAY12

Office Hours

- **CASE EXAMPLE** - 例题
- **SMART SOLUTION** - 主题补充专题
- **PRACTICE TEST** - 练习
- **DICTATION** - 听写
- **SMART SOURCE** - 主题资料库

speed keyword

Office Hours

按照字面意思解释，office hours指的是在工作时间中，教授用来和学生进行私人面谈的时间。在大部分的美国院校里，每一名教授都会确定office hours，或者学生也可以通过电子邮件向教授预约见面谈话的时间。TOEFL iBT考试中，office hours是指学生就各种与学术有关的问题而与教授进行的交谈。对话的主题大致可分为学术问题和其他学科相关事项。美国的大学不仅设置负责讲课的教授，还会设置指导大学新生学科问题等的指导教师并且与此相关的内容也会经常出现。

学业相关Academics 备考主题

作业建议/提交作业期限延迟/考试相关咨询/成绩咨询/课堂内容提问

学科研修相关Course requirements 备考主题

课程选择相关咨询/职业计划咨询/经济支持咨询

CASE EXAMPLE

MP3 • 270

[1-5] Listen to part of a conversation between a student and a professor.

| Volume | Help | OK | Next |

1. Why does the student go to see his professor?

Ⓐ To talk about yesterday's lecture

Ⓑ To discuss his upcoming graduation

Ⓒ To find out how to apply for a pharmaceutical internship

Ⓓ To get advice about finding a job after college

2. Why is the student worried about his work experience?

Ⓐ None of his jobs have been related to his major.

Ⓑ He has had trouble working in the field of biology in the past.

Ⓒ He has only worked in volunteer positions.

Ⓓ The professor does not think his jobs were valuable.

3. What can be inferred about the student's plans for the spring semester?

Ⓐ He hopes to do an internship with a pharmaceutical company.

Ⓑ He is going to perform some field work for one of his classes.

Ⓒ He intends to submit his application for graduate school.

Ⓓ He will begin looking for employment opportunities.

Listen again to part of the conversation. Then answer the question. 

4. Why does the student say this:

Ⓐ To repeat something he stated earlier

Ⓑ To show that he wants to discuss a complex issue

Ⓒ To emphasize the seriousness of the problem

Ⓓ To clarify something he just said

Listen again to part of the conversation. Then answer the question. 

5. What can be inferred about the student?

Ⓐ He is excited about going to graduate school.

Ⓑ He is uncertain about the prospect of doing an internship.

Ⓒ He doubts that he is qualified to do an internship.

Ⓓ He is concerned that too many other students do internships.

SMART SOLUTION

note taking

Main Topic : advice on job-searching in pharmaceutical fields

Purpose		Problem		Solution
- asking for advice on job searching after grad	→	- want to work in phar. fields after grad, but no work experience	→	- positive about ①internship ②grad school

TIP 在对话部分，大部分情况下，学生都是带着问题去找教授面谈的。因此先准备如上的三个框(purpose, problem, solution)再开始听力也不失为一个好办法。

CLUE FINDER 学生想从事制药业相关领域的工作，但是由于缺乏实际经验而感到苦恼。教授一听到这些，就建议他去实习或者读研来接触相关领域。

...

Purpose: asking for advice on job searching after grad

Professor(female) OK. What can I do for you then?

Student(male) Um...it's about graduation. Q4 **No—I mean... let me start over.** Um, it just occurred to me the other day that...that I'm going to graduate in less than a year.

...

Professor Q1 **So...are you looking for advice about how to use your biology degree to find a job?**

Student **Yeah, that's exactly what I'm wondering about.**

...

Professor Right. That certainly is a popular field to get into these days. A lot of those pharmaceutical corporations are...hugely influential...in the world of medicine. And they're always looking for well-educated people to bring on board.

OK. Q2 **The next thing I'll ask is whether you have any specific work experience...either in pharmaceuticals or in a related field.**

Q1 大部分对话的开头都会出现"What can I do for you?"，这个问题是揭示学生来访原因的标志。对此的回答是第1题的解题线索。

第1题Main Idea类型问题

这里，学生采用了委婉的表达方式，但是通过教授随后的再次确认可以更加确信学生的造访目的。

Q4 在出现了"I mean..."一类口语表达的部分后，经常出题考查说话者的意图。

第4题Function题型

"I mean..."是为了补充说明前面出现过的内容时使用的表达。可以看出说话者试图再次解释"毕业"为什么会成为苦恼。

Q2 所有的conversation篇章都是以学生的"问题"和"解决方案"为中心构成的，这两部分信息一定会被命题考查。

Problem: no work experience

Student **Um, no...and that's one of the things I'm, uh, most concerned about. I mean...every job I've ever had is totally unrelated, uh...waiting tables, working in the university bookstore. Nothing I've done even comes close to the kind of position I hope to get after school.**

Professor I see. But you know...that might not be as big a problem as you think it is. A lot of firms don't expect recent college graduates to have tons of experience. The quality of your education and your academic performance matter a lot...and I'd say you're doing pretty well in those categories.

But there are some things you can do to increase your odds. Um...one of the best is to do an internship.

Student Q5 ***[unsure]*** **An internship? Don't students usually do those during the summer? It's September now, and I graduate next May.**

Professor Well...you're right that summer internships are pretty popular. But there are plenty of organizations that offer them during the rest of the year too.

...

Solution: positive about internship

Student Q3 **Actually, my schedule next semester should be pretty light, and that internship sounds like an excellent opportunity.** Thanks for letting me know about it.

Professor Oh, of course. And don't forget...you can always apply for internships after you graduate as well. Some of them give stipends to participants...in case you're worried about money. I'll be more than happy to help you research your options if you'd like.

...

第2题 **Detail** 题型
学生希望在制药业工作，但是他没有任何相关领域的工作经验，因此对能否顺利就业感到忧虑。

Q5 如［*unsure*］，在语气有变化的部分，经常会有问题考查说话者的态度。

第5题**Attitude**题型
请注意当教授提到相关领域可能会提供实习机会时，学生有何反应。综合考虑到语气的不确定以及时间方面的不妥，可以推断不确定教授的建议能否成为现实。

Q3 学生对教授给出的建议作何选择？这也是核心信息之一，经常出题考查。尤其是如果两人间的对话涉及了未来的行动，经常会考查推论题。

第3题**Inference**类型问题
考虑到下一学期的课程安排会相对轻松，学生也觉得教授建议的实习职位是个非常好的机会，由此应该可以推测出他希望在春季学期中进行实习。

Answer 1 Ⓓ 2 Ⓐ 3 Ⓐ 4 Ⓓ 5 Ⓑ

PRACTICE TEST

CONVERSATION MP3•273 **passage 1. [1-5] Listen to part of a conversation between a student and a professor.**

1. What does the man need from his professor?

Ⓐ A letter of reference for an employment opportunity

Ⓑ Information on different cancer research institutes

Ⓒ A recommendation for a field of study to enter

Ⓓ Advice on applying for funding for his research

2. What does the professor imply about the man's career goals?

Ⓐ He might change his mind about them later.

Ⓑ They may be difficult to realize.

Ⓒ It is likely he will be successful with them.

Ⓓ He needs a more detailed plan to realize them.

3. Where does the man plan to work?

Ⓐ In a federal institution

Ⓑ On a grant review board

Ⓒ At a local university

Ⓓ With a medical company

4. What are two tips the professor gives the man about creating his grant proposal? Click on 2 answers.

Ⓐ Make sure its focus is not too broad.

Ⓑ Write it for audiences with different levels of expertise.

Ⓒ Do not let it distract you from your research.

Ⓓ Make it as comprehensive and thorough as possible.

Listen again to part of the conversation. Then answer the question. 

5. Why does the man say this:

Ⓐ To ask the professor to elaborate on a point she just made

Ⓑ To indicate he is more interested in the application itself than in choosing a grant

Ⓒ To let the professor know that he has not decided on a career path yet

Ⓓ To prove he has done a lot of research about which grants he is eligible for

DAY 12

CONVERSATION MP3 • 275 **passage 2. [1-5] Listen to part of a conversation between a student and a professor.**

1. Why does the woman go to see her professor?

Ⓐ To discuss a piece of literature she read for class

Ⓑ To ask about the deadline for a writing assignment

Ⓒ To hear suggestions on improving a creative writing piece

Ⓓ To get advice on how to write a short story

2. What does the professor think about the narrator of the story?

Ⓐ His voice should be more uniform.

Ⓑ His actions should be explained in greater detail.

Ⓒ The introduction to his character is unnecessary.

Ⓓ He should be changed to a woman.

3. How did the writing about the setting differ from that about the character?

Ⓐ The explanation of the character is more realistic.

Ⓑ The writing about the character is less successful.

Ⓒ The descriptions of the setting are more direct.

Ⓓ The writing about the setting uses more imagery.

DAY 12

Listen again to part of the conversation. Then answer the question.  MP3・276

4. Why does the woman say this:

Ⓐ To explain the reasoning behind her work

Ⓑ To show that the professor has made a mistake

Ⓒ To acknowledge a problem with her writing

Ⓓ To suggest that the professor misunderstood her

Listen again to part of the conversation. Then answer the question.  MP3・277

5. What does the woman imply when she says this:

Ⓐ She will make the change that the professor recommended.

Ⓑ She prefers a different style of writing than the professor.

Ⓒ She did not understand what the professor was saying at first.

Ⓓ She will have to think further about the professor's advice.

PRACTICE TEST

CONVERSATION MP3 • 278 **passage 3. [1-5] Listen to a conversation between a student and a professor.**

1. Why does the student go to see her professor?

Ⓐ To inquire about an extra-credit opportunity

Ⓑ To discuss an upcoming lecture she will miss

Ⓒ To apologize for neglecting an assignment

Ⓓ To review the content of a lecture

2. What does the professor say about today's lecture on cultural transference?

Ⓐ It was designed for students who had already read about the topic.

Ⓑ It is one of the most difficult topics they will cover in class.

Ⓒ It is closely related to the student's experience with her roommates.

Ⓓ It was problematic for many other students in the class.

3. What does the student imply about her roommates?

Ⓐ They demonstrate dialect accommodation.

Ⓑ They have some questions about cultural transference.

Ⓒ They have noticed changes in the way she speaks.

Ⓓ They have trouble understanding her accent.

DAY 12

Listen again to part of the conversation. Then answer the question.  MP3•279

4. What can be inferred about the professor when he says this:

Ⓐ He would prefer to help the student at another time.

Ⓑ He is certain the student can understand the material without help.

Ⓒ He hopes the student will try harder in class.

Ⓓ He is reluctant to fulfill the student's request.

Listen again to part of the conversation. Then answer the question. 

5. Why does the professor say this:

Ⓐ To remind the student of something he mentioned earlier

Ⓑ To criticize the student for failing to prepare for class

Ⓒ To give the student an extra homework assignment

Ⓓ To let the student know he has high expectations for her

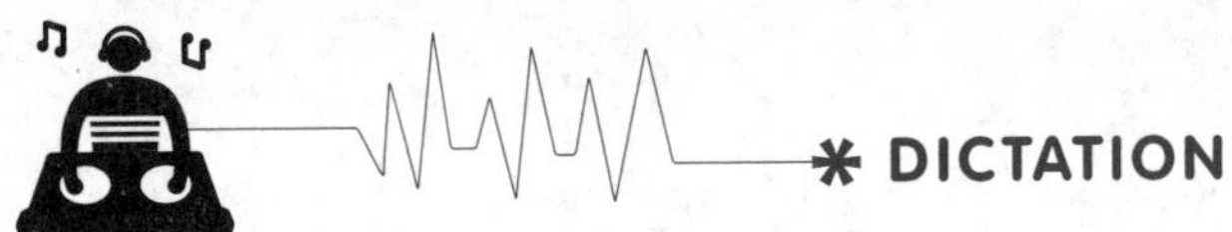

MP3·281 **1. Listen to part of the practice test conversation again and fill in the blanks.**

［省略］

Professor: In that case, you should visit the office of sponsored research at whatever institution you plan to be working with. They'll let you know about [1]______ ________ ______ ________ ________ they have for the application process.

Student: Got it.

Professor: Oh, another thing to consider is what kind of grant is best for you. Even though you know you want to apply for an NIH grant, there're still a lot of options. Um, at this point in your career [2]________ ______ ______ ________ ________ ______...

Student: *[interrupting]* Right, I know. So when it comes time to actually apply, what sorts of things do I need to be thinking about?

Professor: You'll want to clearly define your project [3]______ ______ ______ ______, ________, ______ ______. I'm assuming you're not at this stage yet...?

Student: No...I'm really just [4]______ ______ ______ ________ ______. But I'm hoping to design my research project this semester, and I want to be thinking about this stuff as I develop my proposal.

Professor: That's a good idea. Well, after you've defined your plan, it's time to write the proposal. [5]______ ______ ________ ______ ______. The first people who review your proposal are going to make the decision about [6]________ ______ ______ ________ ________ ________. Chances are, the primary reviewers aren't going to be familiar with your field. So you have to present your proposal in a way that'll [7]______ ______ ______ ______ ________ ______ ______ who don't really know anything about cancer research.

Student: I see. That sounds pretty difficult.

Professor: Yes, it can be. But you've also got to keep in mind that after the primary reviewers see your proposal, experts in your field will go over it. So, your proposal has to [8]______ ______ ________ ______ ______ too.

Student: You've given me a lot to think about. Are there any last pointers you have for me?

Professor: Um, well, above all, make sure [9]______ ________ ______ ______ ______ ______. Don't try to cover too much ground. And leave out anything that's not absolutely essential. I can help you with that when you get to that point. For now, I'd recommend working on [10]________ ______ ______ ________ ______.

Student: Thanks. You've been really helpful.

答案参见ANSWER BOOK P433

 MP3 • 282 **2. Listen to part of the practice test conversation again and fill in the blanks.**

［省略］

Professor: Well, I [1]________ ________ ________ __________ ________ ________ ________.
However, uh, as long as you took good notes during my lecture...um, once you go back and do the reading, you should be able to [2]________ ________ ________ ________ ________ ________.

Student: OK, thanks, I'll do that. If I still have questions afterward, can I come see you again?

Professor: Sure. Now, make sure you also do next week's reading before you show up to class, OK? We'll be [3]__________ ________ __________ ________ __________ __________, and I'll need everyone to be caught up.

Student: OK, I definitely will. Um...what'll we be covering, if you don't mind my asking?

Professor: Next week's topic is dialect accommodation.

Student: Dialect accommodation...could you give me a little preview of what that is? It might help me prepare for class better.

Professor: Sure, OK. Dialect accommodation is what happens when...um, as we saw tonight, when a small group [4]__________ __________ ________ ________ __________ __________, it starts to [5]________ ________ ________ ________ __________ ________ ________ ________. But in this case, we're talking about speech...a way of speaking, and that's called a dialect.

Student: *[surprised]* [6]________ ________... I've been thinking a lot about dialects lately.

Professor: Really? Why's that?

Student: Well, um, I have two roommates in my dorm room. One's from New York City, and the other's from the Deep South...and, well, they both have these totally different and, uh, distinct accents. It's like nothing I've ever heard before...I mean, except on TV.

Professor: Ah, I see. That must be a very interesting experience...[7]________ ________ __________ ________ ________ __________ __________ __________ like that all the time.

Student: Yeah, it really is. But the strange thing is, as the semester's gone on, um, I've noticed that their accents are changing. Like...each of my roommates has started saying [8]________ ________ ________ ________ ________ ________ ________ than like their original accent. You know...'cause I don't really have an accent.

Professor: Very interesting. You know what? [9]________ ________ ________ __________ ________ ________ ________ __________. You see...most students here speak with a fairly... sort of...standard accent, I guess you could call it. So, yeah, your roommates are both in the minority, and they're starting to trade in some of their native speech patterns to, to [10]__________ ________ ________ ________ ________. That's pretty much what dialect accommodation is all about.

［省略］

答案参见ANSWER BOOK P437

smart source

Academics 学术

1 Faculty 教职员

从职务划分，大学的教职员可分为以下几类：院长dean（学院的行政总管），系主任director，普通教授professor，副教授associate professor，助理教授assistant professor以及讲师lecturer等。此外，还有提供面谈与指导的指导教师advisor以及特别为指导论文而设置的教师thesis advisor/director。

2 Assignment 作业

与作业有关的内容是对话中频繁出现的话题。学生会向教授询问如何写作业的主题subject和概要outline，也会在上交最终定稿hand in a final copy之前，携带自己的初稿rough draft向教授询问有关修改revision方面的意见。那么，教授会向学生推荐值得参考的材料reference，或者对学生的研究research方法提供指导。此时，教授通常会建议学生不要简单地堆砌搜集到的资料data/resources，而是要按自己的想法重新组织结构并添加自己的意见。教授通常还会建议学生注明引用部分的出处cite a reference。除了为完成作业寻求帮助以外，学生也会为了延缓上交作业的期限to request an extension on a due date去办公室咨询教授。

3 Class 课程

学生在课堂上遇到难以理解的内容或者想就课堂内容提问的时候，会去办公室向教授求教。此时，教授可能会进行补充说明detailed explanation，或者推荐与课程有关的参考材料reference，或者增加阅读作业reading assignment以帮助学生理解课堂内容。除此以外，学生出于个人原因缺勤课程miss the class时，也会去要讲义handout或材料，有时也会去找教授商议取消选课申请drop a course/withdraw from a course。

- 多样的授课方式：在美国的大学，授课方式不但有教授在很多学生面前单向传授学习内容的讲座lecture，还有以教授和学生间活跃的交流构成的讨论课discussion，以及以研究为中心的workshop，研讨会seminar等。

4 Test & Grade 考试与成绩

学生为了咨询考试相关事项去办公室找教授的场景经常出现。通常，他们会询问课堂上的测试quiz，以及期中考试midterm exam和期末考试final exam的主题或范围。也会咨询开卷考试open-book test［exam］或者带回考试take-home test［exam］等考试方式。如果学生由于个人原因错过了考试，有时候也会以补考make-up test或撰写报告report/paper来弥补。此时，通过考试等方式的评价evaluation结果以GPA(Grade Point Average)形式呈现，学生无法接受自己的成绩时，也会向教授申请变更成绩change the grade。

●不同学期的表达方式：美国大部分院校采取的都是2学期制或4学期制。2学期制的学期称为semester，分为9月~12月(fall term)以及1月~6月(spring term)两学期，每学期有12周。而4学期制的学期称为quarter，分别从10月、1月、4月和7月开始，各有10周。另外，学生还可以利用夏季学期summer session(7月~9月)提前修得学分credit或补充学分。

Course Requirements 课程研修

5 Undergraduate/Graduate Studies 本科与研究生课程

大学的课程大体上可分为本科课程与研究生课程。本科阶段为4年，学生修完4年学业的话，根据专业的不同，可以获颁学位degree—人文科学领域Humanities的B.A.(Bachelor of Arts)和自然科学领域Science的B.S.(Bachelor of Science)。如果学生进入研究生院研修硕士课程的话，根据专业的不同将有机会取得M.A.(Master of Arts)或M.S.(Master of Science)的学位。如果他继续在专业领域从事研究的话，可以最终取得博士学位Ph.D.(Doctor of Philosophy)。

●本科各年级学生的称谓：本科一年级学生freshman，二年级学生sophomore，三年级学生junior，四年级学生senior。学生在进入四年级之后，需要提交称为senior essay的毕业论文。

6 Course Selection 课程选择

学生经常会为了商量选课事宜而拜访教授。选课的范围包括基础必修课程core curriculum或general education，为了以后确定专业，在大一和大二必须提前选择的先修课程prerequisite，为了毕业而必须选择的必修课程requirement，以及按照自己意愿选择的选修课程elective等。教授会参考课程难度、专业紧密度，以及是否能认证为专业学分count toward the major等因素给予学生必要建议。

●选课证明proof of approval：在某些课程中，为了尽可能降低学生中途退课的可能性，在选课之前，学生需要从负责课程的教授或指导教师处领取选课证明。

7 Career Planning 职业规划

学生常常会为了进行职业规划咨询career counseling而去拜访指导教师advisor。通常，教师会就此给予几种建议：如推荐学生读研究生graduate school或专业研究生professional school，去实习internship，研修第二专业double major，参与教授的项目project with the faculty，做交换生exchange student等。教授指导学生独立考虑各种可能性，并做出最适合自己的选择。

有时候，学生也会为了了解有关交换生exchange student，语言研修language course abroad/language study abroad，以及实习internship等信息去咨询教授。当学生想获取一般性的信息general information时，教授会说明申请程序或资格等；当学生想处理文件document方面的事务时，教授会说明需要的文件种类，或者直接为学生写推荐信a letter of reference/a letter of recommendation，或者就写好的附信cover letter，自我介绍a letter of self-introduction，简历resume等与学生进行探讨。

8 Financial Aid/Assistance 经济支持

大部分美国大学都有多样的经济支持项目financial aid program，因此学生常常会为了申请奖学金scholarship或补助金grant之类的经济支持而去办公室拜访教授。此时，学生既会寻求与奖学金或补助金相关的信息，也会为此拜托教授写推荐信a letter of reference/a letter of recommendation。有时，为了勉励学业成绩优秀的学生，教授会亲自让学生来办公室谈话，鼓励并推荐他申请application奖学金。在实际的听力考试中，在与奖学金发放有关的场景中，有时学生只是得到了推荐，有时学生是确定可以得到奖学金，因此需要准确把握具体情况。

●多样的奖学金：各大学奖学金设置情况不同，但是通常都给予博士课程Ph.D.的学生包括学费tuition、医疗费health care、住房补贴housing在内的各种生活费用living cost的奖学金组合fellowship package或全额奖学金full funding。此外，特别要注意的是补助金grant是为研究提供经济支持的，因此为了申请grant就要上交submit学业计划书statement of purpose，说明研究特定领域的理由，具体的研究课题，以及毕业后的计划。此外，还有fellowship, grant, financial support等奖学金形式，学生参与研究项目或实习等还可以得到报酬stipend。

Theme Vocab

MP3 • 283

Faculty 教职员

dean （专科大学/学院）院长
lecturer 讲师
advisor 指导教师

Assignment 作业

rough draft 初稿
hand in a final copy 提交终稿
cite a reference 注明引用部分
request an extension on a due date 申请延期提交
term paper 期末报告
dissertation 学位论文
senior essay 本科毕业论文
miss the class 缺勤
drop a course /**withdraw from a course** 取消选课

Test 考试

take-home test 带回考试
make-up test 补考

Courses & Career 课程与职业

credit 学分
prerequisite 先修课程
requirement 必修课程
elective 选修课程
count toward the major 认证为专业学分
proof of approval 选课证明
double major 第二专业
project with the faculty 教授的研究项目
exchange student 交换生
a letter of reference /**a letter of recommendation** 推荐信
cover letter 附信（简述主要经历的申请文件）
résumé 简历

Financial Aid / Assistance 经济支持

scholarship, fellowship 研究费，报酬
stipend 报酬
grant 研究补助金
tuition 学费
health care 医疗费
housing 住房补贴
full funding 全额奖学金

DAY13

Arts, Literature

- CASE EXAMPLE - 例题
- SMART SOLUTION - 主题补充专题
- PRACTICE TEST - 练习
- DICTATION - 听写
- SMART SOURCE - 主题资料库

speed keyword

Arts, Literature

各种艺术及文学属于典型的人文学科领域，是TOEFL听力讲义文部分的重要主题之一。在艺术领域内，与包括绘画、工艺、美术在内的与造型艺术相关的主题，考查频率最高，与音乐、电影等相关的主题也经常考查。除此之外，考题中还出现过与舞蹈、摄影、建筑相关的讲义文，以及与美术史相关的主题。美术史方面经常提及古代希腊、罗马的各种艺术。另一方面，在文学领域，主要考查的素材是类型丰富的文学作品及作家。

美术Fine Arts 备考主题

古代美术：古代壁画，希腊罗马的美术作品及其特征/
各时代流派美术作品：立体派的毕加索和乔治·布拉克，达达主义/
绘画技法：壁画

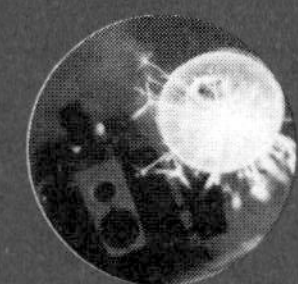

电影Movies及摄影Photo 备考主题

电影的发展历程/多种角度/五分钱电影院/银版摄影法

音乐Music 备考主题

各时代流派的古典音乐/钢琴的历史/爵士乐：繁音拍子(ragtime)

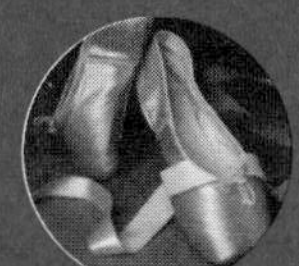

舞蹈Dance 备考主题

舞蹈家伊莎多拉·邓肯/现代舞代表舞蹈家玛莎·葛莱姆

文学作品Literature 备考主题

各时代流派的文学作品/主要英美作家：奥斯卡·王尔德/马克·吐温

CASE EXAMPLE

MP3•288

[1-6] Listen to part of a lecture in an art class.

| Volume | Help | OK | Next |

1. What is the talk mainly about?

Ⓐ The process of creating a *buon* fresco

Ⓑ The influence of the artists of the Italian Renaissance

Ⓒ Some of the advantages of fresco painting

Ⓓ A type of Italian Renaissance painting

2. Why does the professor mention the Sistine Chapel?

Ⓐ To give an example of a fresco that is easily recognizable

Ⓑ To suggest that frescoes were once the most popular kind of Italian art

Ⓒ To introduce some background information about a master Renaissance painter

Ⓓ To name some of the great works from the Italian Renaissance

3. Indicate whether each of the following is mentioned in the lecture as a feature of *buon* frescoes. Click in the correct box for each phrase.

	YES	NO
Ⓐ Are painted on recently laid plaster that has not yet dried		
Ⓑ Require a plaster surface that has been roughened		
Ⓒ Can be repainted without too much trouble if a mistake is made		
Ⓓ Can only be worked on in small sections at a time		
Ⓔ Are better preserved than other types of Renaissance paintings		

4. According to the lecture, what are the main advantages of *mezzo* frescoes?

Ⓐ They represent colors accurately and are very durable.

Ⓑ They absorb pigments quite well and can be corrected easily.

Ⓒ They last for centuries and can be painted all at once.

Ⓓ They did not require the use of sand or a binder.

Listen again to part of the lecture. Then answer the question. MP3・289

5. What does the professor mean when he says this:

Ⓐ He thinks the students need a better explanation of the new term.

Ⓑ He wants to discuss something else before moving on to *buon* frescoes.

Ⓒ He does not want to talk about *buon* frescoes during the lecture.

Ⓓ He realized he skipped important points about *buon* frescoes.

Listen again to part of the lecture. Then answer the question. MP3・290

6. Why does the professor say this:

Ⓐ To warn the students that his Italian is poor

Ⓑ To let the students know where frescoes originated

Ⓒ To introduce the Italian meaning of the term

Ⓓ To get help with the literal meaning of *a secco*

SMART SOLUTION

note taking

Main Topic : three different types of frescoes—*buon, a secco*, and *mezzo*

buon		*a secco*		*mezzo*
- painted when the plaster still wet - suck pigments right into it → hardened surface → very durable painting - possible only in small areas - hard to correct mistakes	↔	- painted after the plaster completely dry - rougher texture - easier to fix mistakes - not as durable as *buon* (flake off in humid) - as finishing touch to *buon*	→	- mixture of *buon* and *a secco* - painted when the plaster was barely still wet - absorb pigments more fully than *a secco* - easier to correct than *buon*

CLUE FINDER | 壁画是意大利文艺复兴时期的主要绘画技法之一，主要分为***buon, a secco, mezzo frescoes***三种。抓住它们各自的特征及优缺点是解题的关键。

Italian Renaissance painting: Frescoes

Professor (male)

OK, class...we've been talking a lot this week about Italian Renaissance painting. Q1 **But there's a type we haven't discussed yet, and it's one of the most important: frescoes.** They're the paintings—often quite large—the ones done on the walls and ceilings of churches and government buildings.

Fresco举例: Michelangelo's painting on the Sistine Chapel ceiling

Q2 **I know everyone's familiar with Michelangelo's giant painting on the Sistine Chapel ceiling...that's a fresco.** Q1 **Obviously, um, frescoes were a big part of Italian Renaissance painting, and I'm gonna tell you about a couple of different kinds.**

So...let's start with the *buon* fresco—or "true fresco." Q5 **Oops, wait a second. Let me back up.** We need to take a look at how frescoes were made first. Before painting on a fresco could start, the surface needed to be prepared. I'm talking about the wall, the ceiling...whatever...and the painter would put a plaster mixture on it. Do you have an idea what this is, plaster? It's a mixture of gypsum or lime, water, sand...maybe some fibers...

...

Q1 "I'm gonna tell you about..."是揭示讲义文重点，论述主题的重要标志。

第1题Main Idea题型

从"a couple of different kinds"可以推导出将要具体介绍壁画的种类。

Q2 如果出现了例子，就需要集中注意力，边听边考虑这个例子在全文中的作用。

第2题Organization题型

教授举西斯廷大教堂的例子，是因为教堂穹顶上有最广为人知的壁画杰作。他想通过学生都很熟悉的例子，对他们生疏的概念—"壁画"进行说明。

Q5 留心讲义文中间涉及了其他话题，或者重复了某些部分的内容。

第5题Function题型

由"Oops, wait a second.（唉呀，请稍等）"可以看出，在正式开始具体介绍湿壁画之前，还有需要说明的事项。

Features of *buon* fresco

Where was I? Ah, the *buon* fresco. Q3 **So, *buon* frescoes were painted onto a smooth layer of plaster before it had a chance to dry.** And because the plaster was still wet, it sucked the color pigments right into it. Then, when it dried, the pigments were trapped within the hardened surface...making a very durable painting. Q3 ***Buon* frescoes are the ones that've been best preserved since the time of the Renaissance.**

Of course, this type of fresco had its, its disadvantages. Q3 **Since it had to be painted before the plaster dried, only small areas could be done at a time.** These were called *giornata*, meaning "day's work." Um, each day, a layer of plaster was spread over the *giornata* and...um, and that was the area the painter worked on all day.

...

Features of *a secco* fresco

Now, there's a second type of fresco known as *a secco*. Q6 **Anyone here speak Italian?** Um, *secco* means "dry," and that tells you a lot about this painting style. These frescoes were painted on that same mixture of plaster...but after it had completely dried. Typically, um, the plaster layer would be left rough—it wouldn't be smoothed down as much. And after it was dry, the painter would rub it with sand to roughen it up even more.

...

Features of *mezzo* fresco

OK, real quick, let me tell you about a third type of fresco—*mezzo* fresco. Basically, think of it as a mixture of *buon* and *a secco* frescoes...with a combination of the, the advantages and disadvantages of both. Q4 **Um, *mezzo* frescoes were painted when the plaster was just barely still wet, meaning the pigments were absorbed more fully than in *a secco* frescoes...but not as much as in *buon* frescoes. But the painter could correct mistakes in a *mezzo* fresco easier than in a *buon* fresco.** Um, the *mezzo* fresco style became really popular at the end of the sixteenth century, after the Renaissance...but we'll be talking more about that era next week.

Q3 此部分在列举湿壁画的特征。在罗列3个以上相关对象的特征时，这部分内容被作为detail或connecting contents类型问题的可能性就很大。此时，最好做笔记记录列举的内容。

第3题Connecting Contents题型

connecting contents类型问题的正确答案大部分都是经过paraphrase的。第3题YES一栏中的"has not yet dried", "better preserved than other types", "be worked on in small sections"是分别由讲义文中提及的湿壁画特征"before it had a chance to dry", "best preserved", "small areas could done"转述而来的。

Q6 如"Anyone here speak Italian?"一样，教授在讲课时直接向学生们提问的部分经常作为回放题考查。教授提问并不是为了获知问题的直接答案，因此不能只从字面意思解析问题，而是要把握说话者隐藏的意图。

第6题Function题型

因为仅凭secco的意大利语意思，就可以知道壁画的特征，教授就是为了表明这一点才提问的。

Q4 列举中性壁画特征的部分。

第4题Detail题型

此处听力的重点是把握湿壁画与干壁画技法结合之后的优点。

Answer 1Ⓓ 2Ⓐ 3YES →Ⓐ, Ⓓ, Ⓔ / NO →Ⓑ, Ⓒ 4Ⓑ 5Ⓑ 6Ⓒ

PRACTICE TEST

CONVERSATION MP3•291 **passage 1. [1-5] Listen to part of a conversation between a student and a professor.**

1. Why does the man go to see his professor?

Ⓐ To complain about his grade on the last exam

Ⓑ To request help with understanding some material

Ⓒ To ask for a textbook that will help him learn more

Ⓓ To apologize for missing so many classes last month

2. What are two functions of low-angle shots mentioned by the professor?
Click on 2 answers.

Ⓐ Showing the vulnerability of a character

Ⓑ Causing the audience to feel fear about what they are seeing

Ⓒ Displaying action to the audience panoramically

Ⓓ Establishing that a character possesses power

3. Why will the professor e-mail the man later?

Ⓐ To let him know when her office hours are

Ⓑ To suggest some materials he can view outside of class

Ⓒ To provide him with notes from the lectures he missed

Ⓓ To tell him about an assignment she gave students in the last class

DAY 13

Listen again to part of the conversation. Then answer the question. 

4. What does the professor imply when she says this:

Ⓐ Many students could not follow her lecture on the different types of camerawork.

Ⓑ The man should have no problem learning the purpose of different camera angles.

Ⓒ The man is fortunate to have already seen examples of the camerawork in class.

Ⓓ It will be difficult for the man to understand camera angles without seeing the clips.

Listen again to part of the conversation. Then answer the question. 

5. Why does the man say this:

Ⓐ To raise questions about what he recently learned from the professor

Ⓑ To explain that he is unfamiliar with the terms the professor is using

Ⓒ To indicate uncertainty about what the professor said

Ⓓ To make sure he has grasped the professor's point

PRACTICE TEST

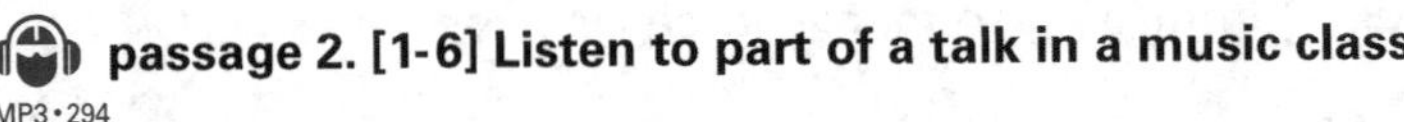

LECTURE **passage 2. [1-6] Listen to part of a talk in a music class.**

MP3•294

Pianoforte

1. What is the talk mainly about?

   Ⓐ Eighteenth-century composers who wrote music for the piano

   Ⓑ The differences between the piano and the harpsichord

   Ⓒ The popularity of stringed keyboard instruments during the eighteenth century

   Ⓓ The invention and development of the early piano

2. What does the professor say about the harpsichord and the clavichord?

Ⓐ They changed Western music more than any other instrument.

Ⓑ They were less versatile than the piano but more popular.

Ⓒ They were early stringed keyboard instruments replaced by the piano.

Ⓓ They often accompanied groups of musicians playing other instruments.

3. According to the professor how did Cristofori's piano differ from modern pianos? Click on 2 answers.

Ⓐ It was not movable.

Ⓑ It used strings that were narrower.

Ⓒ It produced louder sounds.

Ⓓ It had a more fragile body.

4. Why does the professor mention Johann Sebastian Bach?

Ⓐ To demonstrate the influence of the piano

Ⓑ To explain the limitations of the harpsichord

Ⓒ To give an example of an early proponent of the piano

Ⓓ To emphasize that the piano was not popular at first

5. Indicate which of the following are mentioned in the talk as later improvements on Cristofori's piano design. Click in the correct box for each phrase.

	YES	NO
Ⓐ Expansion of the keyboard to include seven or more octaves		
Ⓑ The introduction of special wooden hammers		
Ⓒ The introduction of foot pedals for special effects		
Ⓓ The replacement of wooden hammers with metal mallets		
Ⓔ The production of the Viennese model by German and Austrian companies		

Listen again to part of the talk. Then answer the question. MP3 • 295

6. Why does the professor say this:

Ⓐ To give the students a hint that will help them figure out the answer

Ⓑ To ask the students if they know the full name of the piano

Ⓒ To provide an answer to the student's question

Ⓓ To find out what the students already know about the piano

PRACTICE TEST

LECTURE  **passage 3. [1-6] Listen to part of a lecture in a literature class.**

MP3 • 296

Oscar Wilde

note taking

1. What is the lecture mainly about?

Ⓐ Details about the life and work of Oscar Wilde

Ⓑ Oscar Wilde's influence on other writers of the time

Ⓒ The work of Oscar Wilde to support gay rights

Ⓓ The writing style of Oscar Wilde's essays

2. What are two ways in which Wilde was involved with aestheticism?
Click on 2 answers.
Ⓐ He wrote about it in some of his plays.
Ⓑ He authored essays on the subject.
Ⓒ He spoke about it in different countries.
Ⓓ He created art using peacock feathers.

3. How does the professor explain Wilde's most famous work?
Ⓐ By providing historical background for the story
Ⓑ By going over the key characters
Ⓒ By describing how it was based on his real life
Ⓓ By contrasting it with other things he wrote

4. In the lecture, the professor describes Oscar Wilde's career. Indicate whether each of the following belongs to his career. Click in the correct box for each phrase.

	YES	NO
Ⓐ A playwright who criticized social values		
Ⓑ An honored novelist of his time		
Ⓒ A president of a university in London		
Ⓓ A celebrity famed for his personality and humor		

Listen again to part of the lecture. Then answer the question.  MP3•297

5. What does the professor mean when he says this:
Ⓐ He does not think it is necessary to define the term.
Ⓑ He does not want to discuss aestheticism further.
Ⓒ He thinks the idea of aestheticism requires more explanation.
Ⓓ He wants to give the students a homework assignment.

Listen again to part of the lecture. Then answer the question. MP3•298

6. What can be inferred about the professor?
Ⓐ He disagrees with the law that Wilde was subjected to.
Ⓑ He enjoys Wilde's writing but disapproves of his private life.
Ⓒ He is uncomfortable discussing this subject with the class.
Ⓓ He is uncertain what happened to Wilde at the end of his life.

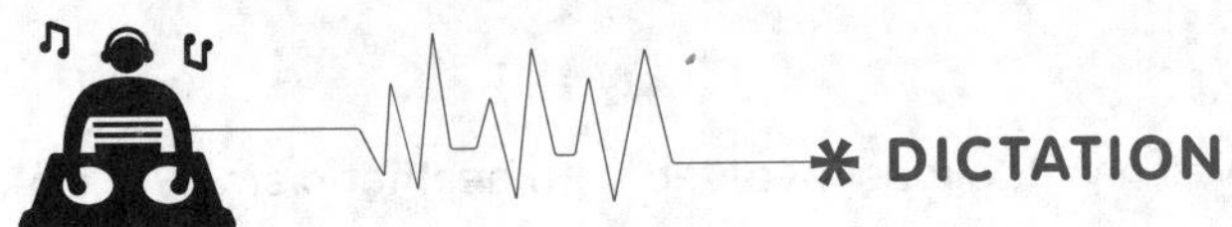

DICTATION

MP3·299 **Listen to part of the music talk again and fill in the blanks.**

［省略］

Professor: So let me talk a little about how all this came about. An instrument designer by the name of Bartolomeo Cristofori, who lived in Italy...um, 1)______ ______ ______ ______ ______ ______ ______...sometime just after 1700, but it's important to understand this was a bit different than what we would recognize as a piano today. Actually, it really resembled the harpsichord more than the modern piano. Um, its body was small and rather delicate, its strings were thinner, and it was somewhat quiet compared to today's pianos...although it still 2)______ ______ ______ ______ over the harpsichord. Another fact to keep in mind is that Cristofori's piano wasn't well received at first.

Student A: Wait...but didn't you say it 3)______ ______ ______ ______ ______ on the harpsichord? Why didn't people like it?

Professor: It was a little rough. Um...like, some notes were always softer than others, 4)______ ______ ______ ______ ______ ______ ______ ______. Johann Sebastian Bach was actually one of the first musicians to try out the piano, and he wasn't impressed with it.

But, you see, as the eighteenth century went on, other instrument makers 5)______ ______ ______ ______ Cristofori's design...getting all the bugs out of it. In particular, there were some German and Austrian companies that began producing pianos more like what we see today—a large, sturdy body, with 6)______ ______ ______ ______ ______ ______ ______ when they were struck. They created the so-called Viennese model, which is what Mozart wrote all his piano pieces on. I mean...this is when the piano really 7)______ ______ ______ ______ ______ ______. Composers realized it allowed them to express so much emotion...by playing at different volumes as well as through special effects made possible by using foot pedals. And its full sound meant it could be played for audiences in large concert halls...and 8)______ ______ ______ ______ playing other instruments too.

Student B: So is this Viennese model the same piano we usually see today?

Professor: Not quite. There were still a lot of 9)______ ______ ______ ______ the 1800s. Um, that's when English and American builders began introducing popular piano designs. Also, you started to see expanded keyboards, ones that 10)______ ______ ______ ______ ______ ______ ______ ______ the, the older models with just five.

［省略］　　答案参见ANSWER BOOK P445

MP3·300 **Listen to part of the literature lecture again and fill in the blanks.**

Professor: Class, last time we went over the life and work of William Butler Yeats, remember? Well, today we're gonna continue our study of nineteenth-century, um, Irish poet-dramatists, with a discussion of Oscar Wilde. Is everyone ready to begin? I suppose I should start off by letting you know that, um, as well-known as Oscar Wilde was for his...his literature, he was 1) ________ ________ ________ ________ ________... and his celebrity. I mean, he was...he was 2) ________ ________ ________...someone lots of people had heard of. It's almost as though Wilde became famous for being famous! OK. Well, Wilde first started to develop his, um, reputation while he was studying at universities in Ireland and England. He, uh, 3) ________ ________ ________ ________ ________ ________, like decorating his room with peacock feathers...and dressing in flamboyant costumes. What you have to understand is this: Oscar Wilde was involved in a movement known as aestheticism. Aestheticism—it basically promoted the idea of "art for art's sake." I know some of you must be wondering, "Well, what's that mean?" It's a slogan for people who believe that art doesn't need to have some kind of 4) ________ ________ ________ ________—the only reason it need exist is to be beautiful; to be art. This movement was 5) ________ ________ ________ ________ ________, and Wilde became a kind of, um, spokesperson for it. In 1879, he began teaching aestheticism in London, and in the 1890s he toured the United States and Canada too, giving lectures related to the movement. And he put out a series of essays that expanded on his beliefs about aestheticism. At the same time, though, he was starting to make it big as a playwright. Um...he 6) ________ ________ ________ ________ ________ that became very popular: *Lady Windermere's Fan, A Woman of No Importance,* um...*An Ideal Husband,* and *The Importance of Being Earnest.*

All of these plays were successful, but *The Importance of Being Earnest* is 7) ________ ________ ________ ________ ________ ________. Let me tell you a little bit about the story of the play before I go on to discuss, um, how it fits into Wilde's life and career. The main character's name is Jack Worthing. He basically represents the society that Wilde lived in, and its Victorian values...things like 8) ________ ________ ________ ________ ________ ________. Wilde represents Victorian morality as hypocritical, um, by making Jack into a very hypocritical character. Jack 9) ________ ________ ________ ________ ________ ________ ________ by creating himself an alter-ego...so he is free to 10) ________ ________ ________ ________ ________ ________ his, um, his reputation.

［省略］

答案参见ANSWER BOOK P447

DAY 13

smart source

Fine Arts 美术

1 Fresco painting 壁画

壁画是一种绘画技法。它是指在墙壁上涂上灰泥plaster，再将颜料pigment在水里调匀后进行的绘图方法。西洋壁画的技法分为湿壁画（湿性壁画）buon fresco，干壁画（干性壁画）a secco fresco及中性壁画mezzo fresco三种。在灰泥风干前进行绘制的为湿壁画，灰泥风干后进行绘制的为干壁画，而混合使用前两种技法的即为中性壁画。著名的壁画作品有米开朗琪罗在罗马拜占庭的西斯廷教堂Sistine Chapel穹顶绘制的《天地创造》(God creates Adam)。

2 Cubism 立体派/立体主义

立体派是20世纪初叶活动于巴黎的艺术流派，由帕布罗・毕加索(Pablo Picasso)和乔治・布拉克(Georges Braque)创立。这一流派的特征是将各种自然形态分解为基础的几何形象，采用二维的平面结构，它对之后的美术、设计以及建筑等产生了深远的影响。

- 帕布罗・毕加索

毕加索活跃在绘画、雕刻、陶艺等各美术领域，为20世纪现代美术的发展做出了巨大的贡献。他的作品大致经历了初期、蓝色时期Blue Period、桃色时期（玫瑰色时期）Rose Period、立体派Cubism时期、古典主义Classicism时期以及超现实主义Surrealism时期。他与布拉克都是立体派的代表性人物，立体派也促使他成为了20世纪最伟大的艺术巨匠之一。他的代表作有开创了立体主义时代的《阿维尼翁的少女》和《格尔尼卡》。

- 乔治・布拉克

乔治・布拉克与毕加索共同开创并推进了立体派，是对20世纪美术发展起决定性影响的艺术家。他初期曾是一名野兽派fauvisme画家，但在1907年见到了毕加索的作品《阿维尼翁的少女》之后，思想受到了极大的启发，决心与毕加索一同创立立体派，并将立体主义由分析立体主义analytic cubism发展为综合立体主义synthetic cubism。其代表作有《弹吉他的男人》、《小提琴及水罐》及《埃斯塔克的房子》等。

3 Nickelodeon 五分钱电影院

镍币电影院即五分钱电影院之意，指的是20世纪初期社区的小型电影院。1905年Harry Davis与John P. Harris在匹兹堡开辟了名为“五分钱”的电影院，人们只要花费五分镍币的费用就可以连续观看放映的电影。这一举动大获成功，五分钱电影院也随之成为了电影院的代名词。五分钱电影院通常放映时间在15到20分钟左右，放映不同风格和不同主题的电影。之后，随着城市的不断扩大，电影界经历整合，更大型与便捷的影院应运而生，五分钱电影院随之慢慢衰退。

4 Angle 角度（相机的角度）

电影中的角度指的是照相机/摄像机在拍摄对象时所维持的角度。通常可分为以下5种。

角度	定义	主要用途	示例
视线角度 eye level	摄像机/照相机镜头与被摄物体眼睛的高度一致	是可以最为精确地描述被摄物体的角度，在说明普通情景或场面时使用	
高角 high angle	摄像机/照相机的位置高于被摄物体，使观众的视线向下	有在一连串的场面中被支配的感觉，常常用来暗示被摄物体处于危险或无能为力的状态中	
低角 low angle	可以放大被摄物体，加速其移动的效果	可以提升被摄物体的重要性，从而表现出恐惧、敬畏或尊敬的感觉。经常用于宣传电影或英雄电影中	
斜角 oblique angle	向一侧歪斜摄像机/照相机进行摄影	经常用于描述心理上的紧张、变化或波动，从而常用于暴力或混乱的场面	
鸟瞰视角 bird's eye view	仿佛鸟从天空中俯瞰的视角，是极端的高角	与万能的神一般，可以跃至画面的上方展现的视角，有大胆粗犷的表现力	

Music 音乐

5 The history of Piano 钢琴的历史

- 拨弦古钢琴Harpsichord或德西马琴Cembalo

拨弦古钢琴或德西马琴是钢琴的前身，是一种使用铁杵拨动琴弦以发音的键盘乐器。它盛行于16~18世纪，曾是欧洲最为重要的乐器之一，但随着可以调节音强高低的钢琴的出现及普及而退出了历史舞台。

- 古钢琴Clavichord

在钢琴出现之前，古钢琴与拨弦古钢琴同样作为钢琴类乐器使用。如果按压它的键盘，末端细小的金属片就会敲击琴弦发声。

- 钢琴Piano

典型的键盘乐器keyboard instrument钢琴piano是pianoforte的简称，这一名称原始意思为强弱的表现。钢琴巨大的共鸣箱中有超过85根金属琴弦string，如果按压与之相连的键盘，木头制作的小锤wooden hammer就会敲击琴弦发声。它是在18世纪初期由克里斯多夫里(Cristofori)发明的。

·键盘弦乐器：钢琴、拨弦古钢琴以及古钢琴都属于键盘乐器keyboard instrument，因为发生时同时使用琴弦所以也被称为键盘弦乐器stringed keyboard instrument。

Literature 文学

6 Epic of Gilgamesh 吉尔伽美什史诗

《吉尔伽美什史诗》是世界上最早的巴比伦史诗，以楔形文字cuneiform在12块粘土板clay tablet上写成。《吉尔伽美什史诗》讲述了与吉尔伽美什有关的故事，吉尔伽美什2/3是神，1/3是人，是一个统治古代国家乌鲁克的传奇君王。史诗中描写了反抗人类文明的斗争、爱情及冒险的故事。其中“大洪水”的故事与《圣经·创世纪》中的故事“诺亚方舟”Noah's ark相似，且广为人知。

7 Oscar Wilde 奥斯卡・王尔德

爱尔兰剧作家、小说家、诗人及短篇小说家，后期因成为维多利亚时代最为成功的剧作家playwright而闻名于世。他同时还是唯美主义aestheticism的代表作家，以不同寻常的才华与华美优雅的行为而备受关注，十分擅长座谈与演讲。可是，他因为涉嫌有同性恋倾向而受到了审判，在经历“昆斯贝里侯爵事件”之后，其作家的身份开始逐渐没落。最终，王尔德在庭审中败诉，两年服刑期满后由英国来到巴黎，在那里度过了悲惨的余生。

8 Evelyn Waugh 伊夫林・沃

英国著名作家，代表作有讽刺小说satirical novels《衰落与瓦解Decline and Fall》《罪恶的躯体Vile Bodies》《一把尘土A Handful of Dust》等。他的小说大部分是以自己的亲身经历为素材创作的，早期作品主要致力于讽刺富有的上流社会，后期作品讽刺了人性的不合理并探讨了天主教在现代社会的意义。

9 Mark Twain 马克・吐温

马克・吐温是著名的美国作家，原名塞缪尔・朗格赫・克莱门斯(Samuel Langhorne Clemens)，马克・吐温为其笔名pen name。他出生于弗罗里达州，4岁时搬家至密西西比河边的一个小城市。密西西比河周边的自然风貌给幼年的马克・吐温留下了深刻的印象，对他日后成为作家产生了不可磨灭的影响。他的代表作有《汤姆・索亚历险记Adventures of Tom Sawyer》,《密西西比河上的生活Life on the Mississippi》,《哈克贝利・芬历险记Adventures of Huckleberry Finn》等，是对美国式自由灵魂的赞歌。作为一名社会讽刺作家Satirist，他还写作了《亚瑟王宫里的康涅狄格佬A Connecticut Yankee in King Arthur's Court》, 以及《王子与乞儿The Prince and the Pauper》等。马克・吐温比其他任何美国作家都更为努力地发掘了文学的力量，更酣畅淋漓的表现了美国式的场面，更大限度地开启了英语的潜力。海明威(Ernest Hemingway)曾称赞他道：“所有的美国文学都源于《哈克贝利・芬历险记》”。

10 Paleolithic Art 旧石器时期的美术

这一时期遗留的美术作品有丰富的洞穴壁画Cave paintings以及著名石像雕塑《威廉多夫的维纳斯》Venus of Willendorf。洞穴壁画主要描绘鹿、野牛等动物，可能是为祈愿在打猎中轻松猎取野兽而绘制。

- 拉斯考克斯洞穴 Cave of Lascaux

法国多尔多涅州拉斯考克斯洞穴里发现的壁画被推测大概绘制于公元前15000~10000年。拉斯考克斯洞穴壁画绘制于洞穴很深的内壁上，描绘了马、牛和鹿等成群的动物。可见它并不是为了视觉欣赏的需要而绘制的图画，而是为了实现祈福、祭礼及宗教功能的画作。画中的动物雄壮有力，栩栩如生。

- 阿尔达米拉洞穴 The Cave of Altamira

阿尔达米拉洞穴位于西班牙北部，深度约270米。此处的壁画利用了洞穴表面起伏不平的特点，将鹿、马、猪等动物刻画的栩栩如生，体现了祈愿富饶和多产的旧石器时代绘画的最高水平。

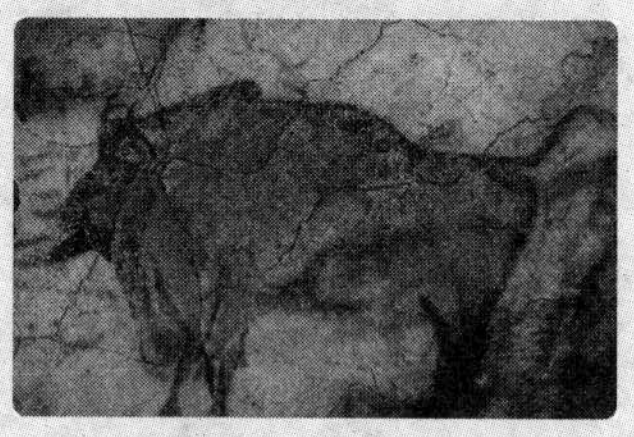

- 威廉多夫的维纳斯 Venus of Willendorf

《威廉多夫的维纳斯》是在奥地利威廉多夫发现的石像雕塑statuette.该雕塑以石灰岩limestone为材料，高11厘米。这座女人像细致地雕刻了头发，但是故意忽略了脸部轮廓。乳房、腹部及臀部塑造得十分丰满，但是臂膀及腿则十分孱弱，彼此不成比例proportion。可以看出，它很有可能是当时人们为了祈愿富饶和多产而雕刻的象征性物品。

11 Architecture of Ancient Greece 古希腊建筑样式

- 多里斯风格建筑 Doric Style

多里斯风格建筑是爱奥尼亚以及哥林多风格建筑等三大样式中最为古老的一种，特点是突出简洁与雄伟。

- 爱奥尼亚风格建筑 Ionic Style

受东方建筑风格的影响，爱奥尼亚风格建筑以女性化的轻快优雅为特点，立起高而细的柱子column，细节部分多装饰，与男性化的多里斯建筑截然不同。

Doric Ionic Corinthian

- 哥林多风格建筑 Corinthian Style

哥林多风格建筑起源晚于以上两种式样的建筑，特点是柱头有美丽的仿佛缠绕生长的莨苕叶Acanthus leaves样花纹。整体式样与爱奥尼亚风格建筑接近，但是更为华丽。

12 Renaissance Art 文艺复兴时期艺术

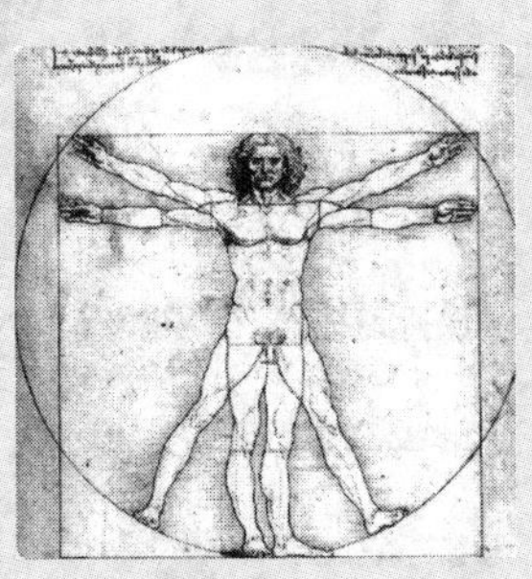

文艺复兴Renaissance一词原意为“再生”或“复活”，这里文艺复兴时期美术指的是从15至16世纪整个欧洲兴起的绘画或雕塑sculpture领域的革新性变化。这场文艺界的大复兴始于15世纪初，以意大利的雕塑sculpture为中心，倡导人性的复活、对自然的再发现以及个性解放等。代表性人物包括波提切利(Botticelli)、雷奥纳多·达芬奇(Leonardo da Vinci)、拉斐尔(Raffaello)以及米开朗基罗(Michelangelo)等。以这一时期为基点，绘画中开始使用透视法perspective。此外，以科学的方法对人体进行研究的活动也开始变得活跃。

DAY 13

Theme Vocab

MP3・301

Fine Arts 绘画

painting 绘画
sculpture 雕刻
pigment 颜料
Cubism 立体派
cave paintings 洞穴壁画
style 风格

Film 电影

perspective 远近法，透视法
proportion 比例
oblique angle 斜角

Music 音乐

string 弦
stringed keyboard instrument 键盘弦乐器

Literature 文学

epic 叙事诗
clay tablet 粘土板
cuneiform 楔形文字
aestheticism 唯美主义
playwright 剧作家
satirical novels 讽刺小说
pen name 笔名

DAY14

Life Science I

- CASE EXAMPLE - 例题
- SMART SOLUTION - 主题补充专题
- PRACTICE TEST - 练习
- DICTATION - 听写
- SMART SOURCE - 主题资料库

speed keyword

Life Science I

生命科学研究存在于自然界中的各种各样的生命体中。根据研究对象的不同，这门学科可以细分为植物学、动物学、昆虫学、藻类学、海洋生物学以及微生物学等。研究古生物化石的古生物学的一部分以及关注生物的系统与分类的分类学(taxonomy)也是生命科学范畴内研究的内容。

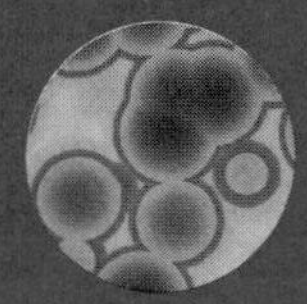

普通生物学General Biology 备考主题

生态界的物质循环/动植物的细胞结构

植物学Botany 备考主题

依赖授粉的植物繁殖/依赖光合作用的新陈代谢/植物的向性/食虫植物：捕蝇草

动物学Zoology 备考主题

冬眠/共生/变温动物与恒温动物/沙漠动物的特征及生态/候鸟的迁徙方式

昆虫学Entomology 备考主题

蜜蜂的8字舞/昆虫的保护色：蛾/蚂蚁社会的等级/昆虫的变态

古生物学Paleontology 备考主题

各地质时代特征：洪积世/恐龙的灭绝原因/古代化石：花化石

CASE EXAMPLE

MP3 • 306

[1-6] Listen to part of a discussion in a botany class.

| Volume | Help | OK | Next |

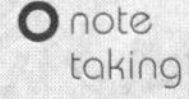

1. What is the discussion mainly about?
   Ⓐ Two opposing views on the value of exotic species
   Ⓑ A comparison of native and invasive species
   Ⓒ How to choose the best species for a given environment
   Ⓓ Attempts made to control the spread of introduced species

2. What are two examples of the way that introduced species can disrupt an environment? Click on 2 answers.

Ⓐ By altering the natural flow of water in wetlands

Ⓑ By providing food for species of agricultural parasites

Ⓒ By growing quickly and killing off native species

Ⓓ By spreading non-native diseases among native species

3. In the lecture, the professor mentions some introduced species that are beneficial to humans. Indicate whether each of the following is a beneficial introduced species. Click in the correct box for each phrase.

	YES	NO
Ⓐ Purple loosestrife		
Ⓑ Tomatoes		
Ⓒ Sawgrass		
Ⓓ Southeast Asian wheat		
Ⓔ Swamp rose mallow		

4. Why does the professor discuss the economic role of crops in Florida?

Ⓐ To argue against the eradication of introduced species

Ⓑ To explain how species can be introduced naturally

Ⓒ To show that some regions are more vulnerable to introduced species

Ⓓ To describe the risks of allowing introduced species to spread

Listen again to part of the discussion. Then answer the question. 

5. Why does the professor say this:

Ⓐ To express dissatisfaction with the student's comment

Ⓑ To give students an idea of what he will discuss next

Ⓒ To ask students to debate an issue with him

Ⓓ To request that the student elaborate on her comment

Listen again to part of the discussion. Then answer the question. 

6. What can be inferred about the professor?

Ⓐ He is sure the students are already aware of this fact.

Ⓑ He is very confident about the figure.

Ⓒ He wants to make sure the students write down the information.

Ⓓ He finds the figure he is relating to be amazing.

SMART SOLUTION

note taking MainTopic : pros and cons of introduced species(exotic plants)

cons		pros
- reduce biodiversity by killing off native plants - destroying an ecosystem e.g. purple loosestrife(change water flow)	↔	- food supply e.g. corn, wheat, rice - natural process - economic role e.g. tomato, citrus in Florida

CLUE FINDER 讲义文在介绍外来植物时，阐释了对待外来植物的两种相反立场。一种观点认为外来植物是破坏生态系统的威胁，因此必须根除；另一种观点认为它们可以提供粮食供给，创造经济附加值，因此不应该被消灭。

Native species vs. Introduced species

Professor (male)

Q1 **Class, I thought we'd, uh, spend some time today going over the issue of native versus introduced—or exotic—plants.** It's been a debate in the world of biology, and a lot of questions have been raised—how should we feel about introduced species? Is it better to plant only native species?

...

Disadvantages of introduced species

Professor

Getting back to your comment...it's true that introduced species have a bad reputation. Q5 **Since you brought it up, we may as well start off by discussing this side of the debate**—the side that says native plants are best and introduced species are bad and should be, um, eliminated. It's a logical position when you consider that introduced species can upset entire ecosystems, interfere with agriculture, and—as you said—reduce biodiversity by killing off native plants.

...

Student B (male)

Oh...now I understand. Q2 **So introduced species essentially take over and end up replacing native populations that just can't compete with them.**

Q1 句子"We'd spend some time today going over..."是揭示讲义文主题的标志，对此应接着确认下面的话题。

第1题Main Idea题型

要留意这里不是在单纯地比较native species和exotic species，因此Ⓑ选项不正确。此处不是单纯地比较外来品种和本地品种，而是介绍必须根除外来品种的正反方观点。

Q5 "Since you brought it up（既然提到了）"一类的口语表达预示着下面讨论的方向将发生转变，请注意这类表达的功能。

第5题Function题型

因为有学生正好提起了外来品种的消极影响，教授也顺势想从正反两方面开始探讨。

Q2 对外来品种的支持和反对两种立场是引导讲义文进行的核心轴。考生应该预测出会考查两种立场的根据，并相应地做笔记。

...

Professor

It's an introduced species from Europe that grows and multiplies at a tremendous rate in wetlands and brings about drastic changes. Plants native to the United States—like swamp rose mallow and endangered orchids— Q2 **they can't compete and lose a lot of their habitat to purple loosestrife, which actually ends up changing the water flow and affecting other species in the ecosystem—birds, amphibians...algae.**

...

Professor

Exactly. Q1 **On the other side of the debate are people who question the labeling of introduced species as "bad" and, um...they actually take issue with the whole "native versus introduced" opposition. They feel it's just not that simple.**

Advantages of introduced species

You see, the thing is, not all introduced species are the same. There are a few that are aggressive and invasive, but most of them aren't. Actually, we rely on introduced species every day for things like food, shelter, and medicine. Q6 **Consider this: 98 percent of the U.S. food supply comes from introduced species. 98 percent!** Among other things, there's corn that originated in Mesoamerica, Q3 **wheat native to Southeast Asia,** and rice from Asia and Africa—all of it introduced to the United States from other places!

...

Professor

Yes. So if we actively prevent the introduction of new species, we're, um, we're stopping a natural process. Q3 Q4 **Besides, is there really any harm in planting tomatoes and citrus trees in Florida, a place where they aren't native? Those two introduced crops have an economic role...and, more importantly, they don't pose a threat to important native plants like sawgrass.** If an introduced species gets along well with native plants and doesn't disturb the ecosystem, is there really any reason why it should be eradicated?

第2题Detail题型

正确答案Ⓐ中的altering the natural flow of water是由原文中的changing the water flow转述而来，正确答案Ⓒ中的killing off native species是由原文中的take over and end up replacing native population转述而来的。

Q6 正如"98 percent!"中的感叹号所展示的，此部分出现了说话者特别的语调，因此很有可能会被命题考查说话者的情感状态。

第6题Attitude题型

说话者先介绍粮食的很大一部分来源于外来品种，然后又引出了98%这一数值。由此可见他认为这一数值高得惊人。

Q3 此处列举了支持和反对灭除introduced species两种立场的根据。由此，考生应该边听边预测可能会出题要求对两种立场的相关细节事项进行联系。

第3题Connecting Contents题型

因为有学生正好提起了外来品种的消极影响，教授也顺势想从正反两方面开始探讨。

Q4 以佛罗里达州的番茄和柑橘属植物为例解说。如果发现哪部分出现了例子，就需要提高警惕，把握例子在全文中的作用。

第4题Organization题型

佛罗里达州的番茄和柑橘属植物都是外来品种，但是带来了经济收益。以此来尝试反驳灭除外来品种的论点。

DAY 14

Answer 1 Ⓐ 2 Ⓐ, Ⓒ 3 YES → Ⓑ, Ⓓ / NO → Ⓐ, Ⓒ, Ⓔ 4 Ⓐ 5 Ⓑ 6 Ⓓ

PRACTICE TEST

LECTURE  **passage 1. [1-6] Listen to part of a talk in a zoology class.**

MP3 • 309

Dormancy

note taking

1. What is the talk mainly about?

   Ⓐ Forms of dormancy that help animals deal with difficult environments

   Ⓑ Adaptations that enable mammals to cope with winter conditions

   Ⓒ Types of hibernation in different species of mammals

   Ⓓ The differences between predictive and consequential dormancy

2. Why does the professor mention chipmunks?

Ⓐ To suggest that they are more closely related to bears than most people realize

Ⓑ To illustrate why only small mammals can enter a state of dormancy

Ⓒ To give background information about the metabolism of land mammals

Ⓓ To give an example of how hibernation affects a specific animal

3. What does the professor say about bears?

Ⓐ They experience a form of consequential dormancy.

Ⓑ They are unlike other large mammals because they become dormant.

Ⓒ They are vulnerable to heat and may estivate during periods of extreme heat.

Ⓓ They become dormant in the winter but do not actually hibernate.

4. Indicate whether each of the following is mentioned in the lecture as a cause that triggers dormancy. Click in the correct box for each phrase.

	YES	NO
Ⓐ Periods of above-average temperatures		
Ⓑ The arrival of a new predator in the region		
Ⓒ Lack of rainfall and scarcity of food		
Ⓓ A seasonal decrease in sunlight		
Ⓔ An unseasonable change in temperature		

DAY 14

Listen again to part of the talk. Then answer the question. 

5. Why does the professor say this:

Ⓐ To encourage the student to elaborate on his example

Ⓑ To indicate that there is some debate surrounding this issue

Ⓒ To suggest that the student's statement is not entirely accurate

Ⓓ To give the student a chance to correct his mistake

Listen again to part of the talk. Then answer the question. 

6. What does the professor mean when she says this:

Ⓐ She does not think "consequential dormancy" is a familiar term to the students.

Ⓑ She does not want to spend a lot of time going over consequential dormancy.

Ⓒ She wants to remind the students of what they learned last time.

Ⓓ She thinks the students can infer the meaning of consequential dormancy.

PRACTICE TEST

LECTURE  **passage 2. [1-6] Listen to part of a lecture in a zoology class.**

MP3 • 312

1. What is the lecture mainly about?

Ⓐ Different types of badgers and their characteristics

Ⓑ Adaptations that make badgers skillful diggers

Ⓒ Similarities between badgers and large carnivores

Ⓓ The pattern of coloration in badgers' fur

2. How does the professor introduce her discussion of the badger?

Ⓐ By mentioning some well-known North American carnivores

Ⓑ By listing the animal's most notable physical characteristics

Ⓒ By disproving a common misconception people have about the badger

Ⓓ By asking the students what they already know about the mammal

3. What does the professor say about badgers' face masks?

Ⓐ They evolved to mimic the coloration of skunks.

Ⓑ They are unique to individual badgers.

Ⓒ They warn predators to keep their distance.

Ⓓ They indicate that badgers are poisonous to some predators.

4. What are two characteristics of badgers mentioned in the lecture? Click on 2 answers.

Ⓐ Sharp fangs and strong jaws for fending off predators

Ⓑ Sturdy legs and large paws suitable for sprinting

Ⓒ Reddish-brown fur covering the main portion of the body

Ⓓ Dangerous claws that are designed for digging and obtaining prey

Listen again to part of the lecture. Then answer the question.  MP3•313

5. What does the professor imply?

Ⓐ Badgers are not the only animals to display this kind of patch.

Ⓑ There is some uncertainty about the origin of the name "badger."

Ⓒ The term "badge" was likely derived from the common name of the species.

Ⓓ Badgers generally feature tri-colored patterns on their fur.

Listen again to part of the lecture. Then answer the question.  MP3•314

6. Why does the professor say this:

Ⓐ To let the students know that they might want to write down the point

Ⓑ To introduce a term that is more familiar to the students

Ⓒ To remind the students that they studied aposematism in another class

Ⓓ To encourage the students to look up a biological concept

PRACTICE TEST

LECTURE  **passage 3. [1-6] Listen to part of a lecture in a biology class.**

MP3 • 315

Bioluminescence

1. What aspect of bioluminescence does the professor mainly discuss?

Ⓐ The characteristics of animals that produce it

Ⓑ Its use as camouflage in the animal kingdom

Ⓒ The purposes it serves in different species

Ⓓ A theory explaining its evolutionary origins

2. How does the professor explain the meaning of the term "luminescence?"
   Ⓐ By discussing why it is more common in water than on land
   Ⓑ By illustrating the chemical reaction responsible for it
   Ⓒ By providing a simpler and more familiar word for it
   Ⓓ By contrasting it with a different type of light production

3. Which organisms are given as examples of bioluminescence that scientists have yet to understand? Click on 2 answers.
   Ⓐ a certain type of earthworm
   Ⓑ tiny plankton in the ocean
   Ⓒ specific species of fireflies
   Ⓓ insects and arachnids

4. In the lecture, the professor mentions several specific uses of bioluminescence in animals. Indicate whether each of the following is one of these uses. Click in the correct box for each phrase.

	YES	NO
Ⓐ Chasing away attackers		
Ⓑ Sending messages about the location of a food source		
Ⓒ Making it difficult for predators to see a fish swimming above it		
Ⓓ Enticing potential prey to approach		
Ⓔ Helping an animal to stand out in dark waters		

DAY 14

5. According to the professor, why does each species of firefly exhibit a specific pattern of flashes?
   Ⓐ To communicate with their young shortly after birth
   Ⓑ To establish species-specific territories during the mating season
   Ⓒ To discourage predators from feeding on their larvae
   Ⓓ To ensure that only individuals from the same species mate with each other

Listen again to part of the lecture. Then answer the question. MP3·316

6. Why does the professor say this:
   Ⓐ To cast doubt on some scientific data about bioluminescence
   Ⓑ To suggest that students have already studied the topic
   Ⓒ To let students know he has finished discussing the issue
   Ⓓ To apologize for his lack of knowledge about bioluminescence

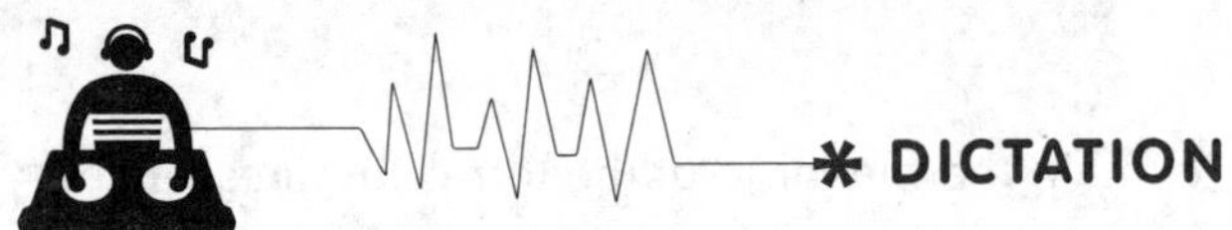

✱ DICTATION

MP3·317 **Listen to part of the zoology lecture again and fill in the blanks.**

［省略］

Professor: OK, so that's a [1] ______ ______ ______ ______ ______ ______ for you. But what I'm going to focus on today is more about their physical appearance... specifically, their coloration. Because badgers..., um, this isn't just true for American badgers, other species in Europe and Asia share [2] ______ ______ ______ ______ ______ ______—badgers have a very interesting color pattern in their fur. Let's see. So, most of the badger's body is a single, solid color: grayish-silver usually. But, um, when it comes to their heads...things get more interesting. See, badgers have a very interesting pattern of black and white stripes on their faces. Their cheeks are [3] ______ ______ ______ ______ ______ ______ ______...um, this patch is also called a badge and may have something to do with how the animal got its name. Each cheek has a darkish patch. Then, the center of the face [4] ______ ______ ______ ______ ______ ______ ______ ______ ______ that starts at the snout and runs straight up between the eyes and onto the top of the head. Um...in some species, this stripe [5] ______ ______ ______ ______ ______ ______ ______ ______ ______. This pattern of colored fur makes for a very distinctive face...also called a mask. And the big question is: why do badgers have these strange masks? What [6] ______ ______ ______ ______ ______ here? Well, to answer that question, I have to explain the idea of aposematism. Um...you might have heard of this [7] ______ ______ ______ ______ ______—warning coloration. Basically, some species develop distinctive color patterns that serve as visual warnings to other animals—particularly predators—to stay away. You know...for example, certain moths display color patterns that [8] ______ ______ ______ ______ ______ ______...that they aren't worth catching and eating. Or, um, poisonous snakes and frogs may be brightly colored to warn animals that any encounter with them will mean trouble. That's aposematism. Oh, and another good example of this is the skunk, which is actually similar in many ways to the badger. Um, the skunk has its own color patterns of black and white stripes ...and this warns other animals that it's capable of defending itself. [9] ______ ______ ______ ______ ______ ______ ______. Now, the badger does have glands that produce a similar scent, but it can't actually spray it like the skunk. Instead, the badger's mask is warning predators that it's a fierce fighter and will defend itself and [10] ______ ______ ______ ______ ______.

［省略］

答案参见ANSWER BOOK P456

MP3·318 **Listen to part of the biology lecture again and fill in the blanks.**

［省略］

Professor: If you're wondering 1)________ ________ ________—why they glow, you're not the only one. Scientists have long been studying the purpose of, um, of bioluminescence. There's been a lot of progress, but we're still uncertain about some things. For example, there're a couple of species of earthworms that, that 2)________ ________ ________ ________—and we just don't know why. I mean, there isn't any apparent reason to it. Oh, and in the ocean there's the mystery of dinoflagellates—single-celled plankton—that glow when disturbed, often lighting up huge areas in the ocean. Think the size of the state of Connecticut. Anyway, we're not, um, 3)________ ________ ________ ________ ________ ________ ________. But—that's enough about what we don't know. Why don't we move on to our, um, theories about the function of bioluminescence?

All right. One main purpose of bioluminescence is camouflage...um, particularly among marine organisms. The ability to glow helps these organisms 4)________ ________ ________ ________ ________. It sounds counterintuitive, doesn't it? That glowing could actually help an animal blend in...but that's how it works. Just imagine you're swimming underwater in the ocean. What do you see when you look below you? Everything is dark and murky, right? What if you look upward, toward the surface? It's very bright... isn't it? When viewed from below, organisms in the ocean really 5)________ ________ ________ ________ ________ ________ ________ ________ ________. However...if they emit light on the underside of their bodies, they're better able to 6)________ ________ ________ ________ ________ ________ ________ ________.

OK. Another very important use of bioluminescence is for communication. If you've ever seen fireflies flashing outside at night, you've witnessed this. Male and female fireflies exchange flashes 7)________ ________ ________ ________ ________ ________. They use their flashes to locate one another. The interesting thing about firefly flashes is that they're species specific. I mean, different species have different flash patterns—that way no one, um, 8)________ ________ ________ ________ ________ ________ ________ ________.

Actually, I guess the behavior of fireflies that I just mentioned is very similar to another function of bioluminescence: attraction. Fireflies use their bioluminescent capabilities to attract mates, while other types of organisms—especially marine ones—they luminesce in order to attract prey. The anglerfish...maybe you've seen pictures of anglerfish before—they've got a very odd, very distinctive appearance, so I'm sure you'd remember it. See...they have this, this 9)________ ________ ________ ________ ________ ________. It's a filament that has a little bioluminescent growth at the end of it. The anglerfish can 10)________ ________ ________ ________ ________ in order to attract prey.

［省略］

答案参见ANSWER BOOK P458

smart source

General Biology 普通生物学

1 Ecosystem, Ecological system 生态系统

生态系统是指特定地域内所有的生物以及它们周围的阳光、空气、土壤等无机环境。生物生活的整个空间被称为生物圈biosphere，生物的群落主要有根据气候条件形成的生物群体——生物社会biome。生物分为生产者producer，消费者consumer和分解者decomposer。吸收太阳热能直接制造能量的绿色植物，消耗生产者制造有机物的动物，以及分解生产者或消费者尸体和排泄物的细菌或菌类生物分别属于以上三类。

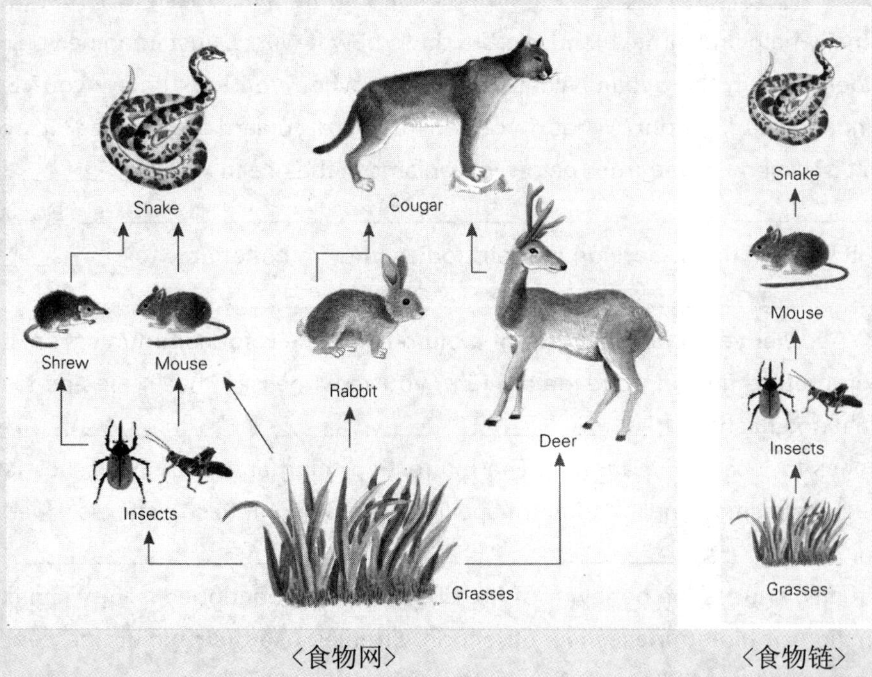

〈食物网〉 〈食物链〉

- 物质循环cycle of material：将生态系统内的生物之间或者生物与非生物之间物质的储存、转化、迁移的往返流动。生物需要的一切物质都是通过生产者从非生物环境中获取，经由食物链food chain转移至消费者，最后再依靠分解者回归环境的。这个循环过程即物质循环。
- 食物网food web：因为大部分生物的食物来源都比较广泛，因此单一的食物链food chain几乎不可能存在，而是相互形成食物网。

2 Cell 细胞

细胞是生命体结构及功能的基本单位。它是由原生质protoplasm构成的，原生质包括细胞核nucleus和细胞质cytoplasm。细胞核内有染色丝chromatin thread和磷元素phosphorus，染色丝含有丰富的脱氧核糖核酸deoxyribonucleic acid，磷元素含有丰富的核糖核酸ribonucleic (RNA) acid。

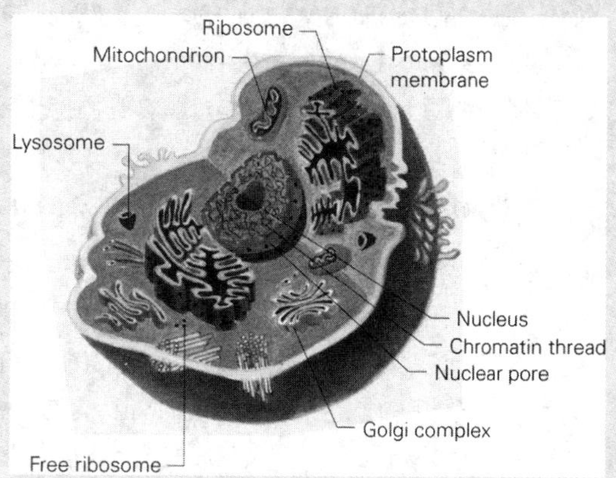

- 原生质protoplasm：指细胞里包括细胞核以及细胞质在内的“活着的物质系统”，由水分、蛋白质、脂质、其他有机物以及无机离子等构成。
- 后成质metaplasm：指细胞质内的液泡、碳水化合物、蛋白质、脂肪、脂质及结晶等非活性物质。因与生命现象没有直接关联而区别于原生质。
- 液泡vacule：像口袋一样的细胞器官，里面装有细胞液。
- 脱氧核糖核酸deoxyribonucleic acid：DNA，组成基因的材料。
- 染色体chromosome：细胞分裂时细胞核中出现的粗线状或棒状结构，承载着遗传物质。

DAY 14

Botany 植物学

3 Anabolism Catabolism 同化作用与异化作用

同化作用指生命体内部进行新陈代谢metabolism时的物质合成过程。典型的同化作用有绿色植物利用光能将二氧化碳和水分合成有机物organism的光合作用photosynthesis，以及将土壤中的硝酸根离子NO_3^-和铵根离子NO_4^+合成蛋白质protein的氮元素同化过程。与同化作用anabolism相反，将有机高分子organic matter分解resolve成无机低分子的过程称为异化作用catabolism。典型的异化作用有呼吸作用respiration。

- 光合作用Photosynthesis：绿色植物利用光能将二氧化碳与水分合成有机物的过程，受光的强度、二氧化碳浓度及温度等因素影响。

4 Tropism 植物的向性

植物在生长过程显示出的一种生长运动，指植物受到各种刺激stimulation而向特定方向弯曲的现象，向性根据刺激类型的不同分为以下几类。

- 向地性gravitropism：植物对于重力的反应，根向下，茎向上的生长现象。
- 向水性hydrotropism：植物应激于水的向性。
- 趋光性phototropism：植物应激于光的向性。

5 Insectivorous [insect-eating] Plants 食虫植物

食虫植物是对具备特别的器官organ捕捉昆虫insect并消化以摄取养分的植物的统称。这种特殊的器官可分为三类，第一类是具有叶子变形而成口袋状的捕虫囊mucus，第二类是高黏度的如饭勺般开闭的捕虫叶，第三类是可以分泌粘液的腺毛glandular hair。在托福考试真题中，出现过捕蝇草flytrap。捕蝇草“flytrap”这一名称来自于这种植物具有捕捉苍蝇这类昆虫的特性，它自己生长于土壤贫瘠的地方，因此无法只依赖光合作用或是根的吸收得到充足的养分供给，于是要通过捕食昆虫摄取必要养分。

6 Pollination 授粉

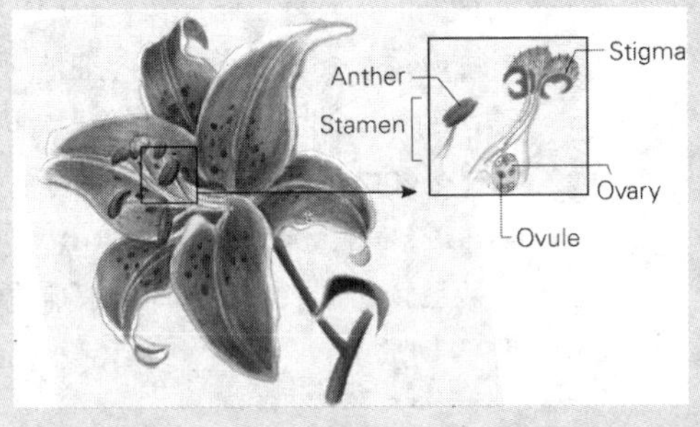

授粉指的是种子植物seed plant的雄蕊stamen产生花粉pollen，花粉经雌蕊的花柱style而达到其底部胚珠ovule的过程。雄蕊产生的花粉如果掉落在雌蕊柱头stigma上，就会生成花粉管，花粉管pollen tube一直向下生长到达子房ovary内部的胚珠。那么花粉管内的两个精子就会分别与胚珠内的卵细胞核与极核结合而形成受精卵。受精卵分为胚embryo和胚乳endosperm，它长大即成为果实。这一过程因为有两个精子参与受精而被称为双受精double fertilization。

Zoology 动物学

7 Dormancy 动物的休眠

当光照时间变短，气温降低并且觅食prey变得困难时，动物就会进入冬眠hibernation状态，以保存体力，度过寒冷而漫长的冬天。普通动物进入完全的冬眠true hibernation状态时，体温会降至5℃以下，代谢量减少，呼吸breathing减慢。采取深度冬眠deep hibernation的动物有蛤蟆、蛇、乌龟以及花栗鼠

chipmunk等。与之不同，休眠dormancy指的是深度不及冬眠的非活动状态。通常被看做冬眠动物的熊、狸或臭鼬raccoon等，即使是在冬天，如果温度上升，也会醒来活动，因此准确来说应看做休眠动物。反之，动物在像夏天一样的高温或降水量低的情况下进入的休眠状态称为夏眠estivation。

- 预测休眠predictive dormancy：根据日照变短的现象提前预知冬季的来临而主动开始的冬眠。
- 相应休眠consequential dormancy：无法预测季节，冬季来临之后才进行的冬眠，气温较高或者其他气候条件允许的话冬天仍然可以活动。

8 Endotherm恒温动物 Ectotherm 变温动物

哺乳类mammal及鸟类bird等动物的体温body temperature不受外界气温影响，保持恒定，它们被称为恒温动物endotherm。外界温度低时，它们会在体内产生热量；外界温度高时，它们会加快排汗perspiration或呼吸respiration散热emit来维持体温。与之相反，爬行类reptile与两栖类amphibian变温动物ectitherm，体温会随外界环境external environment变化，自我调节体温的能力有限。因此，它们在体温的上升或下降超过一定限度时，新陈代谢metabolism会受阻，像青蛙、蜥蜴lizard以及蛇等动物就会进入休眠dormancy或夏眠estivation。

9 Meerkat 海岛猫鼬

海岛猫鼬生活在土壤soil坚硬、多岩石的干燥arid地带，一个洞穴cave最多可容纳30只猫鼬。它们为了警戒guard天敌猛禽的袭击，会用两爪站立观察周围，因此有“沙漠哨兵”之称。繁殖期breeding season为每年9~10月，产仔期为11~12月，一胎产仔2~5只。杂食性omnivorous，通常以蚂蚁、硬壳虫及蝗虫等昆虫为食，分布disperse在从安哥拉西南部直到非洲南部的地域。易饲养，在南非共和国，人们有时候会为了消灭elimination家鼠而饲养它们。海岛猫鼬为了对抗天敌natural enemy、保护种群而站岗放哨，以利他行为altruistic闻名。但是也有与此相反的观点。

Entomology 昆虫学

10 Termite白蚁 Leaf-cutter Ant 切叶蚁

白蚁属白蚁目昆虫，与普通蚂蚁不同，体内共生着可以助其消化纤维质fiber的微生物microorganism，因此可以啮噬木头，给木质住宅及其他房屋造成危害，被认定为害虫vermin。像普通蚂蚁一样，白蚁社会由蚁后、工蚁及兵蚁构成，但与蚂蚁和蜜蜂不同的是，白蚁群里除蚁后外还存在蚁王。白蚁的天敌natural enemy有黑猩猩、野猪和蚂蚁等，其中蚂蚁甚至连行使繁殖功能reproduction的蚁后都不放过，是白蚁可怕的天敌。另一种蚂蚁—切叶蚁leaf-cutter ant体长约25毫米，主要分布于中美洲的热带雨林tropical rain forest，下颚如剪刀般长且尖。它会利用下巴将树叶细细切碎，在上面栽培蘑菇作为食粮。

11 Honey bee communication 蜜蜂的信息传递

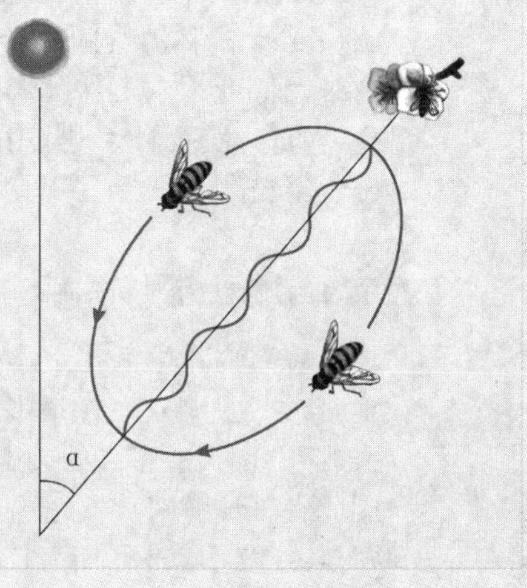

德国昆虫学家卡尔·冯·弗里奇(Karl Ritter von Frisch)发现了蜜蜂honey bee传递信息的方式。若蜂群中采集食物的工蜂发现花蜜，就会回到蜂巢beehive中，吐出一点花蜜让其他蜜蜂品尝，并跳舞告知花蜜的位置及方向。据其研究，若花蜜所在位置与巢穴的距离在80~100米以内，蜜蜂跳圆圈舞round dance；当花蜜位置与巢穴的距离超过100米时，蜜蜂跳8字舞waggle dance。其他蜜蜂根据花蜜的味道和舞蹈的类型飞往有食物的地方，此时以太阳为判断方向的重要基准。蜜蜂有根据太阳的移动认知recognition时间的能力，因此可以以太阳为基准设定方向而判定食物的位置。

Paleontology 古生物学

12 Pleistocene Epoch 洪积世

洪积世亦称为更新世。地质时代大致分为前寒武纪Precambrian era、古生代Paleozoic era、中生代Mesozoic era，以及新生代Cenozoic era。这其中第四时期的新生代又可以再分为两世epoch，即洪积世与冲积世Alluvial epoch。关于洪积世的具体时间存在两种学说，一说认为是1~250万年前，另一说认为是1~160

万年前。这一时期以显著的火山活动与人类祖先的出现闻名。此外，这一时期冰河期glacial epoch与间冰期interglacial epoch反复交替，气候呈周期性periodical变化，地球上动植物界产生剧变，曾在美洲全境盛极一时的哺乳类动物和灌木中生活的乳齿象，冻原地区生活的猛犸象灭绝，出现了牛、骆驼、大象、犀牛等新的哺乳类动物。

13 Flower Fossil 花化石

与动物化石相比，花化石的发现时期相对较晚。2002年，在中国北京的东北部发现了花化石。专家预测estimate这一化石至少形成于距今1亿2500万年前。基于这样的发现discovery使古代ancient花的研究也成为可能。尤其是相关研究显示，与世界上最早的花化石之一对应的真花可能栖息在水中underwater。由此，花是由水生植物进化revolve而来的观点也被提出。时至今日，还有一种普遍的假说认为，开花植物flowering plant不是由陆生植物，而很可能是由水生植物进化而来的。化石的发现为这种假说提供了科学依据scientific evidence。实验中，研究人员发现花化石的大小并不一定与真花大小相符，通常花化石的大小比相应的真花要小。对此，有两种假说，一种认为花经历了很大的进化，另一种认为花可能因为森林火灾而在干燥缩小后才成为化石。

Theme Vocab

MP3• 319

General Biology 普通生物学

ecosystem, ecological system 生态系统
biome 生物社会
producer 生产者
consumer 消费者
decomposer 分解者
nucleus 细胞核
chromosome 染色体

Botany 植物学

anabolism 同化作用
catabolism 异化作用
metabolism 物质代谢，新陈代谢
photosynthesis 光合作用
protein 蛋白质
tropism （植物的）向性
insectivorous plants 食虫植物
mucus 黏液
pollination 授粉
double fertilization 双受精
stamen 雄蕊
pollen 花粉

Zoology 动物学

dormancy （动物的）休眠状态，不活动状态
estivation 夏眠
hibernation 冬眠
perspiration 汗
respiration 呼吸
reptile 爬行类
amphibian 两栖类
omnivorous 杂食性

Entomology 昆虫学

vermin 害虫
beehive 蜂窝
waggle dance 摇摆舞，8字舞

Paleontology 古生物学

Paleozoic Era 古生代
Mesozoic Era 中生代
Cenozoic Era 新生代
Pleistocene Epoch 洪积世
Alluvial Epoch 冲积世

DAY15

Physical Science

- CASE EXAMPLE - 例题
- SMART SOLUTION - 主题补充专题
- PRACTICE TEST - 练习
- DICTATION - 听写
- SMART SOURCE - 主题资料库

speed keyword

Physical Science

生命科学Life Science以生命体为研究对象。相反，自然科学Physical Science以自然界中存在的非生命体和物质之间的作用为研究对象。其中有代表性的学科有物理学、化学、天文学、地质学等。这一领域经常考查考生在日常生活中不熟悉的内容，因此将各备考主题细化分类，再进行背景知识的整理会对解答问题有所帮助。

天文学Astronomy/宇宙科学Cosmology 备考主题

星体的形成/星体年龄测定/火星勘察/特洛伊小行星群

地质学Geology/地震学Seismology/地理学Geography/海洋学Oceanography 备考主题

大陆漂移说/冻土地带的永久冻土层/沙漠地带特征/火山活动与熔岩/岩石的形成及各种类特征/运用碳-14年代测定法测定岩石的地质学年龄

化学Chemistry 备考主题

物质的基本特性及物质间的转化/无机化学

物理学Physics 备考主题

光的性质/热的性质/声波的性质/电磁波/真空的发现

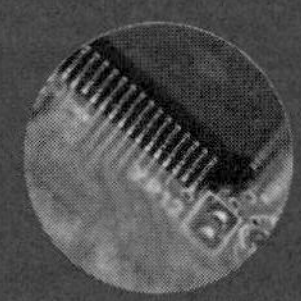

工程学Engineering 备考主题

化工陶瓷/替代能源/计算机发展过程

CASE EXAMPLE

MP3 • 324

[1-6] Listen to part of a talk in a geography class.

| Volume | Help | OK | Next |

1. What is the lecture mainly about?

Ⓐ The formation of alpine glaciers

Ⓑ The impact of water erosion caused by rivers

Ⓒ The geographical differences between America and Europe

Ⓓ The ways valleys are created

2. Based on the information in the lecture, indicate whether the statements below apply to the formation of river valleys. Click in the correct box for each statement.

	YES	NO
Ⓐ They are characterized by a distinctive V-shape.		
Ⓑ Their size is mainly determined by the depth of the river.		
Ⓒ The river's gradient affects the speed with which they develop.		

3. According to the professor, what is the Grand Canyon an example of?

Ⓐ A valley created by a river with an extreme gradient

Ⓑ A valley formed by the combined effects of uplift and downcutting

Ⓒ A valley which is lower than sea level at its deepest point

Ⓓ A valley left behind after a glacier has receded

4. According to the professor, what does the type of rock in the riverbed usually affect?

Ⓐ The shape of the valley

Ⓑ The size of the floodplain

Ⓒ The gradient of the river

Ⓓ The length of the channel

5. How does the professor explain the impact of glacial ice?

Ⓐ By likening it to a piece of modern machinery

Ⓑ By reporting the dimensions of U-shaped valleys

Ⓒ By contrasting it with other natural phenomena

Ⓓ By comparing the sizes of different glaciers

Listen again to part of the talk. Then answer the question.  MP3 • 325

6. What does the professor mean when she says this:

Ⓐ She does not think this week's reading was difficult.

Ⓑ She wants the students to do the reading next week.

Ⓒ She thinks the students should already know this information.

Ⓓ She is not going to look back over old material.

DAY 15

SMART SOLUTION

note taking Main Topic : two ways that valley are formed

Fluvial formation		Glacial formation
- V-shaped - by downcutting(vertical erosion) - steeper gradient → faster process → steeper valley - geological uplift + downcutting → e.g. Grand Canyon - its shape depends on the type of rocks on the riverbed → e.g. Finger Lakes	↔	- U-shaped - by glacial ice - enormous pressure & force by glacier → slowly move down slope * like giant bulldozer - huge divot behind → e.g. Yosemite Valley

CLUE FINDER 讲义文介绍了河流侵蚀型河谷与冰川侵蚀型河谷的形成原理。考生需能够区分各类型河谷的形成原理及形态差异。

Two ways that valleys are formed: fluvial vs. glacial

Professor (female)

All right, class. Q1 **Today we're going to be talking about the formation of valleys.** This topic was used as the essay question on the final exam last year, so it's definitely a good idea to pay close attention. It's a, uh, really important and interesting topic. Q1 **So, uh, anyway, there are basically two ways that valleys are formed. There's fluvial formation—that's formation by a river—and there's glacial formation.**

Fluvial formation: 河流侵蚀性河谷的形成

We'll start by looking at fluvial formation, because it's a little more complex. The first thing I want you to note is the shape of river valleys. Q2 **If you took a cross section of one, you'd notice it would come to a narrow point at the bottom, right? So, uh, this is why river valleys are known as V-shaped valleys.** They get their shape because of downcutting. You all know what I mean by downcutting, don't you? *[surprised]* No? Q6 ***[annoyed]*** **It was one of the main topics in this week's reading...** ***[pause]*** Downcutting is the vertical erosion that is caused by rivers.

...

Q1 "Today we're going to be talking about..."是介绍讲义文主题的标志句。

第1题Main Idea题型

正确答案ⒹThe ways valleys are created中的created是原文中formation，formed转述而来的。

Q2 此处对两种河谷形成方式进行了说明，并列举了各方式的几个特征。因此，考查能否区分各类型特征的细节detail或相关内容connecting contents的问题出现几率很高。

第2题Connecting Contents题型

Q6 如[*annoyed*]所显示的，说话者的语调变强了，并且出现了与讲义文脉络无关的内容。这样的部分经常被用来考查说话者的态度或者话语功能。

第6题Attitude题型

downcutting是本周阅读材料的主题。如果学生好好读过了材料应该知道，可是学生的反应却是不知道，教授因此而感到不满意。

Fluvial valley 1 2: Black Canyon & Grand Canyon

Q2 **Of course, the steeper the gradient of the river, the faster this process occurs, and the steeper the valley is, too.** ... But, uh, speaking of the Colorado...it helped create the Grand Canyon, which is a good example of another type of valley. You see, other dramatic river valleys can occur when there is also geological uplift in the region. We say this, uh, "rejuvenates" the river. So, the Colorado River had reached its base level thousands of years ago, but then there was uplift created by the Rocky Plateau. This increased the Colorado's gradient, and then it started downcutting again. At the same time, the land kept being pushed up by the collision of two tectonic plates, Q3 **and, uh, with a combination of these forces, we ended up with the Grand Canyon.**

Fluvial valley 3: Finger Lakes

Oh, and just before we move on to talk about glacial valley formation, Q4 **there's one further point I'd like to cover: how the type of material on the riverbed can have an impact on the shape of a river valley.** It's pretty obvious, really. Some types of rock are more resistant to erosion than others. So, uh, a riverbed comprised mainly of soft rocks like limestone for instance, tends to erode very quickly. On the other hand, harder stone erodes pretty slowly. So, uh, some of the tributaries that run into the Finger Lakes of New York, for instance, have created fairly wide and flat-bottomed valleys, even though their gradients are fairly steep.

Glacial formation

OK, so that's all clear? Good. Let's take a look at glacial formation now then. Rather than a V-shape, glaciers tend to form U-shaped valleys. ... Q5 **In fact, I want you to think about glaciers as being like giant bulldozers. I use this image because a glacier has so much weight and power behind it. You see, using this massive force, it acts like a bulldozer on the earth around it. Like a bulldozer, it flattens everything in its path, gouging out a huge divot where it has been. Then, when the glacier recedes, the wide, flat bottomed U-shaped divot remains—and we have a valley.**

...

Q3 对于各类型河谷的细节特征和典型事例应做笔记。此处，教授举了大峡谷的例子，对它独特的形成方式进行了详细说明。由此，考生应该可以预测到可能会考查相关内容。

第3题Detail题型

科罗拉多大峡谷是河流侵蚀型河谷，它是由向上隆起和向下侵蚀两种方式混合作用而成的，因此正确答案是Ⓑ。

Q4 从“there's one further point I'd like to cover”可以看出说话者将要引入新的要点。当新的要点出现时，请记录新一段落的重点。

第4题Detail题型

这一部分说明了河底的质地会对河谷地貌产生的影响。河底如果是由坚硬的岩石构成的，就会形成“wide and flat-bottomed valleys”。由此可见，河底岩石的种类会对河谷的形态产生很大影响。

Q5 出现比喻或例子的部分几乎都会以organization题型进行考查。尤其是一些难度高的概念，要运用上下文知识来理解，托福讲义文的篇章常把这些概念用熟悉的素材进行举例说明。

第5题Organization题型

此处将冰川挤压地表的力量比喻为推土机来说明，由此可见正确答案为Ⓐ。

DAY 15

Answer **1** Ⓓ **2** YES →Ⓐ, Ⓒ / NO →Ⓑ **3** Ⓑ **4** Ⓐ **5** Ⓐ **6** Ⓒ

PRACTICE TEST

CONVERSATION MP3 • 326 **passage 1. [1-5] Listen to a conversation between a student and a professor.**

Chemistry Report

note taking

1. Why does the student go to see the professor?

Ⓐ To clarify the requirements for a course paper

Ⓑ To receive feedback on her mid-semester report

Ⓒ To get help choosing a topic for an assignment

Ⓓ To request an extension on a project deadline

2. Why does the professor recommend avoiding spectroscopy?

Ⓐ It is not covered in the course textbook.

Ⓑ He is not an expert in the subject.

Ⓒ It is too unoriginal as an assignment topic.

Ⓓ The class has not studied it yet.

3. What does the professor imply about general reports?

Ⓐ They are very challenging to write.

Ⓑ They are usually boring to read.

Ⓒ They are not detailed enough.

Ⓓ They are too broad to cover issues properly.

DAY 15

4. What does the student decide to focus on?

Ⓐ The differences between leuco dyes and liquid crystals

Ⓑ Color indicators on batteries

Ⓒ General information about thermochromism

Ⓓ Bottle labels that change color according to the temperature

Listen again to part of the conversation. Then answer the question. 

5. Why does the professor say this:

Ⓐ To let the student know that advanced level courses are very prescriptive

Ⓑ To justify his decision not to give students specific guidelines

Ⓒ To imply he is not the right person to give the student some advice

Ⓓ To emphasize how wide-ranging the subject area is

PRACTICE TEST

LECTURE  **passage 2. [1-6] Listen to part of a lecture in a geology class.**

MP3 • 328

note taking

1. What is the lecture mainly about?

Ⓐ The role of tectonic plates in the formation of volcanoes

Ⓑ The existence of hotspots on Earth and Mars

Ⓒ Differences between Olympus Mons and Earth's shield volcanoes

Ⓓ Shield volcanoes of the Hawaiian Islands

2. According to the professor, why are shield volcanoes more like hills than peaks?

Ⓐ They have been eroded for millions of years.

Ⓑ They do not often produce explosive eruptions.

Ⓒ They expel lava that is very fluid.

Ⓓ They form in oceans rather than on continents.

3. Why does the professor discuss plate tectonics?

Ⓐ To emphasize that Earth has more volcanoes than Mars

Ⓑ To describe the event that occurs before a shield volcano erupts

Ⓒ To illustrate the force responsible for the creation of Olympus Mons

Ⓓ To explain why volcanoes on Earth are much smaller than Olympus Mons

4. What does the professor imply about the islands at the end of the Hawaiian Island chain?

Ⓐ They were over the hotspot a long time ago.

Ⓑ They will become active volcanoes again in the future.

Ⓒ They have not yet passed over the hotspot.

Ⓓ They were once larger than the big island is now.

Listen again to part of the lecture. Then answer the question. 

5. What does the professor mean when he says this:

Ⓐ He wants to hear the students' opinion on this issue.

Ⓑ He wants to surprise the students with some new information.

Ⓒ He thinks today's topic will arouse the students' interest.

Ⓓ He thinks the subject matter might be familiar.

Listen again to part of the lecture. Then answer the question. 

6. What does the professor mean when he says this:

Ⓐ He wants the students to know that the Hawaiian Islands have been dormant for some time.

Ⓑ He thinks the Hawaiian Islands are a good example of the effect of tectonic plates on volcanoes.

Ⓒ He wants to discuss a point that is not directly related to plate tectonics.

Ⓓ He thinks the Hawaiian Islands are worth visiting for their educational value.

LECTURE **passage 3. [1-6] Listen to part of a discussion in an astronomy class.**

MP3 • 331

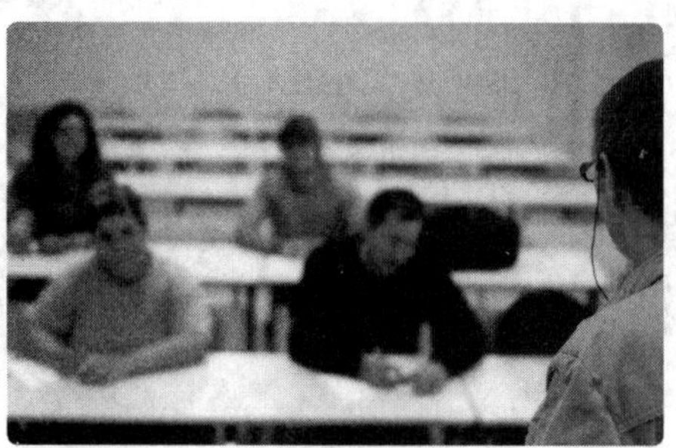

Zone of Avoidance

note taking

1. What is the discussion mainly about?
   Ⓐ The distribution of galaxies throughout space
   Ⓑ The portion of the sky that appears to be devoid of galaxies
   Ⓒ Infrared and x-ray observations of the Milky Way
   Ⓓ The formation of the zone of avoidance

2. According to the professor, what is responsible for the zone of avoidance?

Ⓐ Gas in the Earth's atmosphere

Ⓑ Matter in the Milky Way

Ⓒ A massive black hole

Ⓓ Large clouds where stars form in space

3. According to the discussion, what can high energy X-rays do?

Ⓐ They can detect black holes in distant galaxies.

Ⓑ They can retrieve infrared signals and store the data.

Ⓒ They can penetrate through the dust and gas in our galaxy.

Ⓓ They can emit electromagnetic waves.

4. Why does the professor mention 2MASS and the Chandra x-ray observatory?

Ⓐ To provide background information about the discovery of the zone of avoidance

Ⓑ To explain why scientists are unable to see through the Milky Way

Ⓒ To give an example of how the zone of avoidance prevents astronomical discoveries

Ⓓ To demonstrate that scientists have some knowledge of what is beyond the zone of avoidance

Listen again to part of the discussion. Then answer the question. MP3·332

5. Why does the professor say this:

Ⓐ To indicate that he does not understand what the woman means

Ⓑ To suggest that the woman's answer is not correct

Ⓒ To show that there is scientific uncertainty about the issue

Ⓓ To encourage the woman to elaborate further

Listen again to part of the discussion. Then answer the question. MP3·333

6. What does the student mean when he says this:

Ⓐ He wants to move on to the next point.

Ⓑ He is certain his guess is correct.

Ⓒ He wants the professor to repeat the question.

Ⓓ He is offering a suggestion.

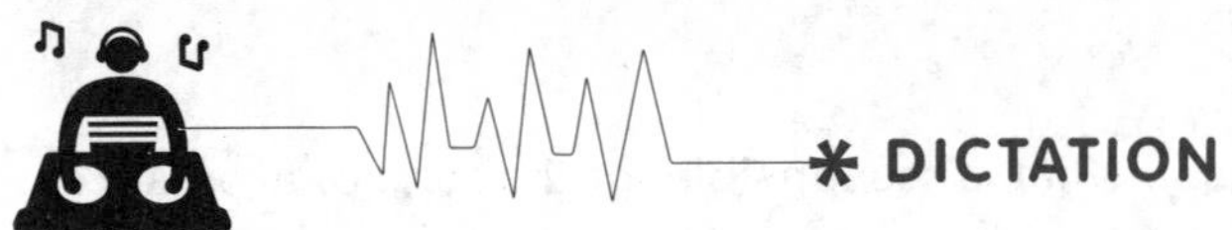

MP3·334 **Listen to part of the geology lecture again and fill in the blanks.**

[省略]

Professor: Another thing about these shield volcanoes is that they don't really... uh...explode, when erupting. So the lava coming out of shield volcanoes isn't, isn't 1)______ ______ ______ ______ ______ ______. Do you understand? The, the Hawaiian Islands are examples of shield volcanoes on Earth.

But, you might ask, why is Olympus Mons so much larger than volcanoes on Earth? Well, we think it's probably related to plate tectonics. As you know, Earth's surface is composed of these huge tectonic plates that are constantly moving. And, as far as anyone can tell right now, Earth is 2)______ ______ ______ ______ ______ ______ ______ that experiences this. We aren't really sure, but it's possible that some planets might have once had, um, this kind of plate-tectonic activity in the past...but probably, probably with some differences from what we see on Earth. OK, uh...but that's not really the topic for today, so let me get back to comparing Olympus Mons with Earth volcanoes.

You see, many shield volcanoes are formed over "hotspots," which are 3)______ ______ ______ ______ ______ where, where conditions deep within the planet cause volcanic activity at the surface. For example, the Hawaiian Islands are over one of Earth's hotspots. Now, the reason I mentioned plate tectonics is that, on Earth, tectonic plates keep the 4)______ ______ ______ ______ ______ over a hotspot.

So no single area of crust is ever...uh...permanently over a hotspot. And this means that, over time, um, volcanoes that were 5)______ ______ ______ ______ ______ ______. Right? Because the tectonic plate they're on moves away from the heat source—the hotspot.

Actually, the Hawaiian Islands illustrate this fact beautifully. See, this island chain has been formed as its tectonic plate—the Pacific plate—has slowly moved over a hotspot. Now, the speed of the plate is, of course, uh, pretty slow...about 52 kilometers per every million years. But as a result of this, um, movement, we can 6)______ ______ ______ ______ ______ that are actually the remains of volcanoes that formed as the tectonic plate traveled over the hotspot. Hawaii, the big island, is the youngest...so it's still right over the hotspot, and it, it hasn't 7)______ ______ ______ ______ ______ ______. Older islands at the end of the chain are smaller because they've become dormant and had a longer time to erode.

So that's why there's a limit to the size of these volcanoes on Earth. They remain over hotspots for...for a period of time, and then they 8)______ ______ ______ ______ ______ ______.

[省略]

答案参见ANSWER BOOK P465

MP3·335 **Listen to part of the astronomy lecture again and fill in the blanks.**

［省略］

Professor: Any other guesses, then?

Student B: 1)________ ____________ ____________...how about a region where there just weren't any galaxies?

Professor: That's it. The astronomers discovered this...this band in the sky where there were hardly any galaxies. Pretty strange, they thought. They 2)________ ________ ________ ________ ________ ________, uh, the "zone of avoidance" because it's...it's almost as though, um, as though galaxies just avoid the region. What do you think the cause of this...this zone of avoidance might be?

Student B: Well, could it be like...like a huge black hole or something?

Professor: Uh...no. Let me give you a hint. The zone of avoidance isn't 3)________ ________ ________ ____________ ________ ____________...

Student B: Maybe there's something covering up the galaxies...so that we can't see them, even though they're there.

Professor: Yes. That's correct. So...what is it that's covering up 4)________ ________ ______ ________ ________ ____________ ____________?

Student B: Is there something in the Earth's atmosphere that's...that's 5)____________ ________ ________ ________ ________?

Professor: No...it's not in the Earth's atmosphere. Any last guesses?

Student A: Oh, I think I know. Is it our galaxy that's causing the problem? I mean, is it part of the Milky Way that's preventing us from seeing clearly outside our own galaxy?

Professor: That's exactly what the problem is. See, the Milky Way is very large. I mean, it's between 80,000 and 100,000 light years wide. And about, um, about 1,000 light years thick. 6)________ ________ ________ ____________ ________ ________ a lot of gas and dust floating around in the plane of the disk, so there's an awful lot of stuff in the way if you're trying to look out across the, uh, the plane of the Milky Way 7)________ ________ ________ ________. That's what the zone of avoidance is...it's the dust and gas clouds in the band of the Milky Way. It blocks about 20 percent of the sky beyond our galaxy.

Student B: Wow. So we don't have any information about 20 percent of the sky outside the Milky Way?

Professor: Well, not exactly. See, even though we can't see through it, uh— 8)____________ ____________ ________ ________ a lot more of what's behind all the dust and gas. Between, um, 1997 and 2001, the Two Micron All-Sky Survey, also known as "2MASS," 9)________ ________ ________ ________ ________ and discovered new galaxies that had been, well, hidden behind the zone of avoidance.

［省略］

答案参见ANSWER BOOK P467

DAY 15

smart source

Astronomy 天文学

1 Star formation 星体的形成

宇宙空间的灰尘或气体等星际物质在受到银河旋转、星体引力、光压力等影响下，稠密地聚积起来，形成星云。这样的星云随着密度的增加，会产生向内的中心引力而整体旋转，一边旋转一边收缩。星云密度逐渐增加，旋转速度也逐渐变快，星云内部就会产生密度大小不一的部分，密度大的部分持续受到向心的重力作用，最终形成星体。

2 Calculating a star's age 星体的年龄测定

星体随着年龄的增长，颜色会按照蓝色→白色→黄色→橘黄色→红色的顺序变化。通常，带有蓝色的星体有50,000℃，红色的星体有3,500℃左右。即，星体的年龄越高，温度越低。此外，星体内存在的铍元素随着时间的流逝会不断增加，最近也利用这点测定星体年龄。2004年，一个国际研究团体利用尖端望远镜测定了铍的量，并正式发表了研究结论，宣称银河系的年龄大约为128~144亿年。

3 Mars exploration 火星勘察

美国火星探测器“水手”号第一次实现了火星勘察。1965年，“水手4”号探测器observation通过近距离观测，监测到火星表面surface存在多个火山口fireball。而“水手9”号则通过拍摄火星表面，监测到除了火山口外，也存在火山volcano。20世纪70年代，苏联的无人探测器“火星3”号以及美国的探测器“海盗1”、“海盗2”号接连在火星表面着陆，直接对火星表面进行了勘测。1997年，美国航空航天局NASA发射了宇宙飞船spacecraft“火星探路者”Pathfinder，其上搭载了装备有光谱测量仪器spectral apparatus的火星车“索纳杰”Sojourner。它在火星表面运行了83天，向地球传送了大量有关火星地质构成、化学构成及大气情况的信息。

4 Trojan Asteroid 特洛伊小行星群

特洛伊小行星群与太阳和木星Jupiter共同形成一个正三角形equilateral triangle，其位置正好在正三角形的顶点vertex，即拉格朗日点处Sagrangian

Point。拉格朗日点是太阳和木星的引力平衡点balance，有数十个小行星sateroid在木星的前后形成行星群cluster。

Geology 地质学/Seismology 地震学/Geography 地理学

5 Continental drift 大陆漂移说

阿尔弗雷格·魏格纳提出了大陆漂移说理论，认为现在的陆地是由一个被称为“原大陆”的巨大原始板块断裂漂移而形成的。

• 构造板块tectonic plate：构成大陆并且漂移的地壳crust表层，具体指地球内部的构造层次中包括地壳及地幔lithosphere在内的岩石圈，依据地球表面是由几个板块构成的板块构造论plate tectonics而产生的概念。

6 Tundra 冻土地带

指一年中的大部分时期地表冰冻，植物vegetation的生长繁衍期不超过60天，最热的月份温度不超过10度，年降水量precipitation低于380毫米的地带。北极地区的冻原arctic tundra占整个地球冻土地带的1/10左右，并且存在因严寒而形成的永久冻土层permafrost，深达90~456米。在长约两个月的夏季，冻原的地表会稍许解冻thaw，土地变湿变软soggy，植物主要藉此生长。但是，尽管如此，由于生长期短，主要生长的植物只有苔藓lichen以及矮小的草本植物和灌木等。

• 永久冻土层permafrost：指超过半年的月平均气温average temperature都在零度以下below freezing，并且土地一年都保持冰冻状态的地带。

DAY 15

7 Desert 沙漠地带

沙漠依据地表的成因分为岩石沙漠rocky desert和沙粒沙漠sand desert。岩石的表面被风侵蚀erosion process，并由于气温的变化风化weathering崩坏destroyed，最终变成细小的物质而被风搬运。这样形成的沙漠称为岩石沙漠。岩石沙漠中分布有岩屑detritus（岩石由于侵蚀、风化作用而产生的细小的岩石碎屑），因此又被称为卵石沙漠pebble desert，特点是没有沙粒。沙粒沙漠是岩层或者石头在风化之后碎裂而成的。变成微小颗粒的沙子堆积形成沙丘sand dune，这些沙丘再在风力作用下移动而渐渐形成广阔的沙漠。

8 Lava 熔岩

火山volcano喷发erupt时，把地下深处形成的岩浆magma（岩石在高温下熔化生成的物质）喷出地表形成熔岩。熔岩中的物质有的流动性liquidity强，有的黏稠度高。熔岩整体的黏性viscosity由其化学组成chemical compostiton、气体含量、温度及结晶度crystallization决定，不同黏稠度的熔岩形成不同种类的火山。黏稠度很高的熔岩单层厚度可达600米，但是被覆面积（覆盖大地的面积）却并不大，形成钟状tholoide火山或塔状belonite火山；中等黏稠度的熔岩形成圆柱形的火山体circular cone（例如：菲律宾马荣火山、日本富士山）；黏稠度低的熔岩单层厚度不过几米，可是被覆面积大、斜坡平缓，形成盾状（盾牌形状）火山shield volcano（例如：夏威夷冒纳罗亚山）；黏稠度非常低的熔岩一次会大量喷发，覆盖大面积的地表（例如：美国哥伦比亚河玄武岩、印度德干高原玄武岩）。

9 Rock 岩石

- **沉积岩**sedimentary rock：由风化和沉积作用形成的沉积物sediment受重力影响向低处移动硬化而形成的岩石。
- **变质岩**metamorphic rock：在地球内部的高温高压作用下，由一种石头自然变质成的另一种石头。代表性的变质岩有片麻岩、石灰岩及大理岩等。
- **岩浆岩**igneous rock：也是在高温高压作用下形成的岩石，但不是从固体状态，而是由液状的炽热岩浆冷却凝固形成的岩石。

sedimentary rock

metamorphic rock

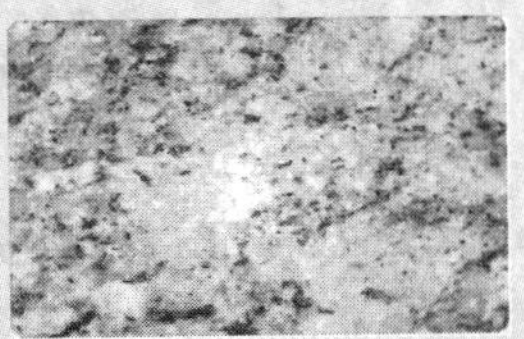
igneous rock

- **深成岩**plutonic rock：是岩浆岩的一种，因为岩浆在地下深处凝固而生成，因此结晶crystal颗粒大。
- **玄武岩**basalt：化学成分与辉长岩相似，硅氧化物的含量达50%左右，是一种较轻的岩浆岩。
- **钟乳石**stalactite：溶洞cave洞顶上垂下的冰柱状矿物质，以石灰岩质limestone洞窟里悬挂的石灰岩质钟乳石最为常见。
- **石笋**stalagmite：饱含着碳酸钙的水从溶洞洞顶滴下，沉积在洞底形成的圆柱形cylindrical突出protruding物。
- **石化作用**lithification：生物的遗体或沉积物像石头一样硬化的过程。

10 Radiocarbon dating method 碳-14年代测定法

自然界中的植物为了获取能量生长而吸收二氧化碳carbon dioxide，进行光合作用photosynthesis。动物通食物链food chain取食植物，而又被另一动物捕食。如此，基本上所有生物体内都存在碳元素。在这些碳元素中，带有放射性radioactive的被称为放射性碳radiocarbon，即碳-14，它从生命体死亡disappear的瞬间开始衰减decay。科学家们于1940年研究出来源于动植物的碳-14消失或衰减所需的时间，其后威拉德・利比(Willard Libby)藉此第一次测定出了碳-14的半衰期the half-life of radiocarbon。半衰期指骨骼、硬壳shell或碳元素样品中的碳-14含量减半所消耗的时间。此后，碳-14年代测定法不仅被应用于地质学，还被广泛应用于海洋学、大气学以及考古学等诸多领域。

Oceanography 海洋学

11 Upwelling 涌升现象

海洋表层的海水seawater在风力作用下移动，深层的海水即上升至表层补偿流出的部分，此过程称为涌升现象。从深海deep water涌升的海水温度water temperature低、密度density高，稳定住许多海洋表层的有机物质organic matters，这些物质经光合作用photosynthesis而被分解decomposition，成为浮游植物phytoplankton的养分nutrients。因此，存在涌升现象的区域，海洋表层的浮游植物数量会急剧增加。浮游植物是海洋生态系统中的生产者，它们增多的话，沙丁鱼或鳀鱼等鱼类也会相应地增多，涌升区域upwelling zone即形成黄金渔场productive fisheries。存在涌升现象的代表性海域有秘鲁沿海、智利沿海、美国加利福利亚州沿海、非洲西南海岸以及阿拉伯海沿岸等地区。

12 El Nino 厄尔尼诺现象/La Nina 拉尼娜现象

厄尔尼诺源于太平洋，指南美洲秘鲁及厄瓜多尔西岸的热带海洋地区tropical region水温超过常年的一种异常气候现象abnormal climate change。而与之相反，拉尼娜指东太平洋海域的水温低于常年水温0.5℃，并且时间持续5个月以上的现象。厄尔尼诺来袭时，温暖的海水推开蕴含养分的冷海水，相应海域的植物及鱼类数量急剧下降decline。与之相比，拉尼娜现象发生得更加频繁，由于水温低，会促使寒冷地域愈加寒冷，从而造成长时期雨季monsoon或干旱drought等气候异常现象。

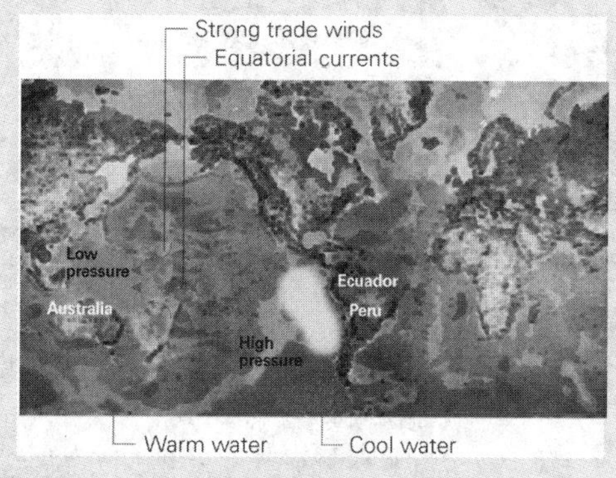

Chemistry 生物学

13 Solution 溶液/Solvent 溶剂/Solute 溶质

溶液solution的意思是均匀混合了两种以上物质的混合物mixture。通常指气体gas、液体liquid或固体solid状态的溶质solute溶解在液体状态的溶剂solvent里所形成的混合物。溶剂是溶解溶质形成溶液的物质，通常是液体。溶质指的则是溶剂中含有的其他成分ingredient。此外，在一定条件下，某一物质无法再溶解liquefaction的状态称为饱和saturation。

Physics 物理学

14 Vacuum 真空

意大利科学家首次发现了真空。如果向长约1米、一端封闭的玻璃管内注入水银mercury，未封闭的另一端用手指堵住，再倒置在盛有水银的容器container中。那么，玻璃管内的水银面就会下降至一定的高度（约760毫米）。这是因为玻璃管内的水银柱在作用于容器水银面的大气压atmospheric pressure作用下，会维持一定的高度。这时，在玻璃管上方，就形成了除少量水银蒸汽steam以外，不存在其他任何物质的真空vacuum。

15 Infrared rays 红外线/Ultraviolet rays 紫外线/Visible rays 可见光线

- 红外线infrared rays：红外线指的是用光谱仪spectrum分散dispersion太阳光时，存在于红色频谱末端以外的电磁波electromagnetic wave。它比可见光线或紫外线热作用强，因此又称为热光线thermic rays。
- 紫外线ultraviolet rays：紫外线指的是用光谱仪分散太阳光时，比可见光线波长wavelength短，肉眼无法看见的电磁波。因为化学作用chemical reaction强，它又被称为化学光线。
- 可见光线visible rays：波长在人肉眼可见范围内的电磁波。

Engineering 工程学

16 Ceramics 化工陶瓷

化工陶瓷是对热加工制造的无机质inorganic非金属材料non-metallic的统称。与金属材料material相比，它克服了化学性缺陷，具有坚固、耐高温的特点。通常，化工陶瓷技术被广泛应用于陶瓷pottery、水泥cement、砖brick和瓷砖tile等建筑材料construction material、绝缘体insulation材料，甚至火箭、人工卫星satellite的组件component等范围。最近，化工陶瓷通过调节结构内的微小minute

结晶粒子particle，克服了如普通陶瓷般易碎的缺点drawback，正在成为代替complement普通金属必须使用的新材料new material，备受各方关注。

17 Alternative energy 替代能源

替代能源指代替逐渐枯竭的石油petroleum、煤炭coal以及天然气natural gas等化石燃料fossil fuel的能源，又被称为可再生能源renewable energy。近来，地球环境的污染问题日益凸显。与化石燃料相比，替代能源是可以显著减少环境污染environmental pollution的清洁能源clean energy，因此受到关注。

- 生物燃料：指利用吸收阳光Sun rays进行光合作用的有机物organic matter（主要为植物），以及食用该有机物进行生产的所有生物有机体biomass而取得的能源。这种能源不仅使用谷物、淀粉类植物、草本植物、林木、禾杆、稻糠、甘蔗sugar cane以及甜菜sugar beet等农作物，甚至还可以使用动物的排泄物excretion、尸体dead body以及食物残渣等。典型的有使用大豆油、棕榈油以及废弃食用油等植物性油脂vegetable oil制造的生物柴油机bio-diesel。
- 燃料电池：指把氧化氢气、甲烷及甲醇等燃料生成的化学能转化为电能的电池。

Theme Vocab

MP3・336

Astronomy 天文学

interstellar matter 星际物质
nebula 星云
star cluster 星团
galaxy 银河系
asteroid 小行星

Geology 地质学/Seismology 地震学/Geography 地理学

crust 地壳
plate tectonics 板块构造论
precipitation 降水量
permafrost 永久冻土层
erosion 侵蚀
sand dune 沙丘
lava 熔岩
sedimentary rock 沉积岩
metamorphic rock 变质岩
igneous rock 岩浆岩

Chemistry 化学

solution /**solvent** /**solute** 溶液/溶剂/溶质
gas /**liquid** /**solid** 气体/液体/固体
saturation 饱和

Physics 物理学

atmospheric pressure 大气压
infrared rays /**ultraviolet rays** 红外线/紫外线

Engineering 工程学

inorganic 无机的
insulation 绝缘体
alternative energy 替代能源
fossil fuel 化石燃料

Review Test III

passage 1. [1~5] Listen to part of a conversation between a student and a professor.

MP3 • 341

Volume I Help I OK I Next

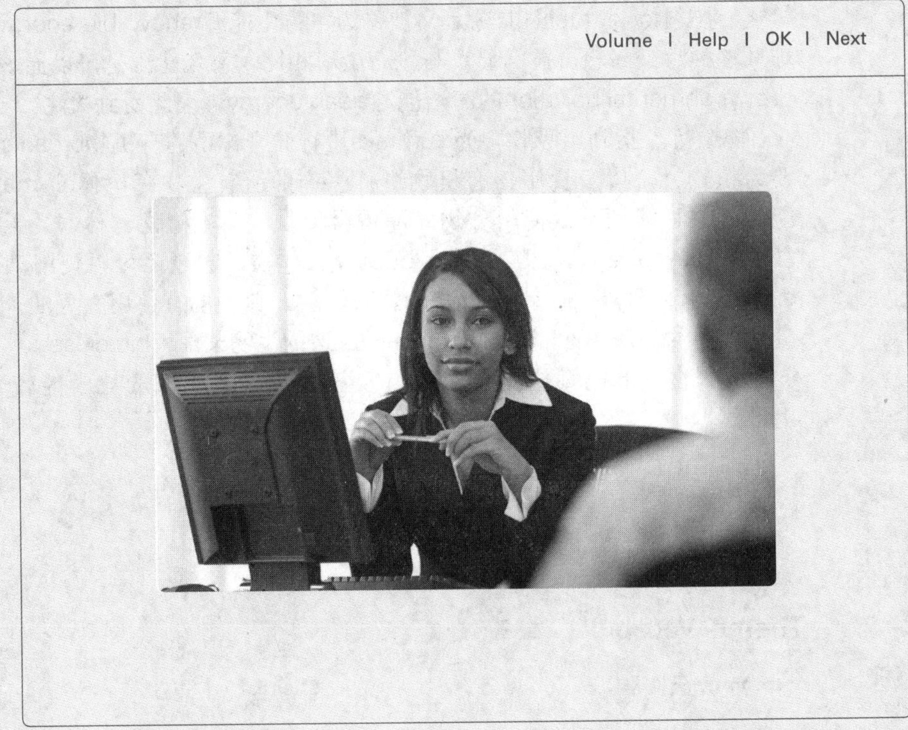

◎答案/解析 P469

1. Why does the man go to see his professor?

Ⓐ To find out the topic of the take-home exam

Ⓑ To get ideas for the upcoming essay

Ⓒ To pick up a copy of the take-home exam

Ⓓ To explain that he will miss next week's exam

2. What does the professor say about the length of the paper?

Ⓐ There are no official requirements for the length of the paper.

Ⓑ The paper should not be more than ten pages in length.

Ⓒ There is a minimum page length but no maximum page length.

Ⓓ The minimum page length is five pages.

3. What does the professor say about sources?

Ⓐ It is OK to consult with other people in the class.

Ⓑ It is not acceptable to use Internet sources.

Ⓒ It is inappropriate to use outside sources.

Ⓓ It is necessary to cite whatever sources are used.

Listen again to part of the conversation. Then answer the question.  MP3•342

4. What does the student mean when he says this:

Ⓐ He wants the professor to know what his plan for the exam is.

Ⓑ He thinks the professor needs to know where he will take the test.

Ⓒ He wants the professor to provide more instructions.

Ⓓ He thinks the professor should give more days to finish the paper.

Listen again to part of the conversation. Then answer the question.  MP3•343

5. Why does the professor say this:

Ⓐ To inform the student that he should choose the number of sources

Ⓑ To find out how many sources the student plans to use

Ⓒ To ask for the student's opinion before setting a requirement for sources

Ⓓ To imply that the student should already know about the minimum number of sources

MP3 • 344

passage 2. [1~6] Listen to part of a discussion in an astronomy class.

Volume | Help | OK | Next

Trojan Asteroids

1. What is the discussion mostly about?
   Ⓐ Recent discoveries of new Trojan asteroids
   Ⓑ Parallels between the Trojan War and astronomy
   Ⓒ The location and distribution of Trojan asteroids
   Ⓓ The development of astronomy since ancient times

2. What is so interesting about Max Wolf's technique for finding asteroids?

Ⓐ It required special camera equipment.

Ⓑ It was especially rudimentary.

Ⓒ It is still used today by astronomy experts.

Ⓓ It was kept a secret for many years.

3. How does the professor explain the orbit of the Trojan asteroids?

Ⓐ By comparing it to that of other asteroids

Ⓑ By using the example of a household object

Ⓒ By providing the students with statistical data

Ⓓ By contrasting it with Jupiter's orbit

4. Why do the Trojan asteroids not bump into Jupiter?

Ⓐ They are pulled closer to the sun than Jupiter.

Ⓑ They follow an elliptical rather than circular orbit.

Ⓒ They circle the sun at the same speed as Jupiter.

Ⓓ Their movement is affected by perturbations from other planets.

Listen again to part of the discussion. Then answer the question.  MP3・345

5. Why does the professor say this:

Ⓐ To warn the students that the subject matter is rather complicated

Ⓑ To lead into further discussion on the Trojan Horse

Ⓒ To show he is disappointed with the student's answer

Ⓓ To indicate that the origin of the term is surprisingly simple

Listen again to part of the discussion. Then answer the question.  MP3・346

6. What can be inferred from the professor when he says this:

Ⓐ He will need to check his facts before commenting further.

Ⓑ He does not want to confuse the students with minor details.

Ⓒ He thinks the students probably already know this information.

Ⓓ He wants to talk about this point in a later lecture.

MP3 • 347

passage 3. [1~6] Listen to part of a lecture in a biology class.

Volume | Help | OK | Next

Mangroves

1. What is the lecture mainly about?

Ⓐ Various functions of mangrove roots

Ⓑ The threat of mangrove endangerment

Ⓒ Mangrove adaptations for survival

Ⓓ The benefits of viviparous reproduction

2. Why does the professor begin the lecture with a talk about saltwater forests and waterlogged swamps?

Ⓐ To review a previous lesson on mangrove habitats

Ⓑ To clarify which aspect of mangroves he will discuss

Ⓒ To answer a question someone posed in the previous class

Ⓓ To compare mangroves to other common saltwater plants

◎答案/解析 P477

3. According to the professor, why are lenticels important?
   Ⓐ They allow the plant to take in and store air.
   Ⓑ They collect and convert nutrients found in saltwater.
   Ⓒ They stabilize the soil surrounding the plants.
   Ⓓ They increase the amount of oxygen in aboveground air.

4. According to the professor, what is special about propagules?
   Ⓐ They photosynthesize through their parent plant.
   Ⓑ They are able to root in almost any type of soil.
   Ⓒ They can expel excess salt via special pores in their leaves.
   Ⓓ They can change their density to float and root.

Listen again to part of the lecture. Then answer the question. MP3 • 348

5. Why does the professor say this:
   Ⓐ To indicate she expects the students to know this basic information
   Ⓑ To imply that the course material is too easy for the students
   Ⓒ To discredit a theory the students were taught before
   Ⓓ To solicit responses to her lecture from the students

Listen again to part of the lecture. Then answer the question. MP3 • 349

6. What does the professor mean when she says this:
   Ⓐ The root system is too complicated to discuss in detail.
   Ⓑ Mangrove reproduction is a far more interesting topic.
   Ⓒ Mangrove trees possess many unique characteristics.
   Ⓓ The reproduction system is closely related to the root structure.

DAY17

Service Encounters

- CASE EXAMPLE - 例题
- SMART SOLUTION - 主题补充专题
- PRACTICE TEST - 练习
- DICTATION - 听写
- SMART SOURCE - 主题资料库

speed keyword

Service Encounters

在校园生活中，学生经常需要和大学员工以及各项业务负责人打交道。他们经常会与学校的员工对话，有时还会在学生公寓中与宿舍分配人员或同一个系的同学对话。但是不论是在什么样的场景中，这些对话都不是一般性的聊天闲谈，而都是为了解决一定的问题而带有明确目的的。

学业相关Division of Academic Affairs 备考主题

选课申请、变更或取消/季节学期/学分确认/毕业要点确认

学生服务中心Student Services Center 备考主题

各种证明开具/语言研修、实习、打工兼职等咨询/现场实践学习咨询

图书馆Library，多媒体中心Media Center 备考主题

书籍、多媒体等参考资料的借出及延期

宿舍Dormitory/学生公寓Residence Hall 备考主题

房间变更/设施修理问题/停车场使用

保健诊疗中心Health Care Center 备考主题

疫苗接种/诊疗

课外活动Extracurricular Activities 备考主题

社团活动/慈善募捐及慈善晚会等活动筹备

CASE EXAMPLE

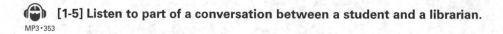

[1-5] Listen to part of a conversation between a student and a librarian.

MP3 • 353

| Volume | Help | OK | Next |

1. What does the man need from the library?

Ⓐ Access to the online catalogue for the film collection

Ⓑ Spanish-language films to watch for his class

Ⓒ A replacement college library card

Ⓓ Information about the library's circulation policies

2. What does the woman imply about the online catalog?

Ⓐ The man should have checked it before coming to the library.

Ⓑ It does not contain listings for Media Collections.

Ⓒ It is more convenient than checking on a resource in person.

Ⓓ Students can use it to check out books and films.

3. Why will the man check out only one film now?

Ⓐ He found the others are already reserved for a class.

Ⓑ He plans to watch another one in the library's viewing room.

Ⓒ He cannot watch two films in the time allotted him.

Ⓓ He is not allowed to check out more than one at a time.

Listen again to part of the conversation. Then answer the question. 

4. Why does the man say this:

Ⓐ To make sure he is in the correct area

Ⓑ To ask the woman's advice about something

Ⓒ To explain why he has come to the library

Ⓓ To let the woman know he is lost

Listen again to part of the conversation. Then answer the question. 

5. What can be inferred about the man when he says this:

Ⓐ He expects the woman to make an exception for him.

Ⓑ He is worried that he may not be able to use the library.

Ⓒ He is pleased by the information the woman gives him.

Ⓓ He is not planning to borrow anything from the library.

SMART SOLUTION

note taking

Main Topic : checking out media resources from a library

initial check		purpose		problems & solutions
circulation policy at Media Collections	→	looking for three Spanish films for a class	→	- not a student at the Univ. → can check out as an affiliate borrower - can borrow only two films at a time → two films first, the third one later *using the online catalogue first - should return within 1 day → just take one at this time

CLUE FINDER 在某大学的多媒体资料室里，其他学校的学生想借3盘DVD。本对话的主要内容是关于该学生想使用的材料的规定和外校人员借阅资料的规则。

Checking circulation policy

Librarian (female) Can I help you find something in the library's film and music collections?

Student (male) Um, I'm not sure. I've actually never been to this part of the library before. Q4 **This is Media Collections, right?**

Librarian Yep. We occupy the entire ground floor of the Norton-Oliver Library. We have videos, DVDs, CDs, LPs...Are you, um, just browsing around or are you looking for something specific? I can answer whatever questions you have about the film and music resources here.

Student Thanks. Um, what's the circulation policy for, um, for items in Media Collections?

Librarian Well, that depends. Are you a student here?

Student Q5 **Uh, no. I just live in the community. *[concerned]* Am I ineligible to borrow from the library?**

Librarian Well...I'm afraid you won't be able to take any films or music outside the library if you don't have valid university identification.

对图书馆里的资料阅览咨询是十分常见的情境，经常出现特定资料的阅览、图书馆的使用方法等相关咨询。

对话内容是关于多媒体资料的使用。对话开始时，并未直接出现学生来访的目的，有关借阅的基本事项首先出现。

Q4 "This is the Media Collections, right?" 这样的口语根据情境可以进行不同的解读，因此很可能用来出题考查，应边听边留心。关键是要把握对话的前后脉络以及说话者在话中蕴含的意图。

第4题Function类型问题

如果只看相应的句子，可能会认为这句话是在回想所在的地点，但是从学生是第一次来图书馆的事实可以看出，他是为了确认自己是否找对了地方而提问的。

Q5 两个人对话时，语调有变化的部分很可能被出

Student	*[disappointed]* Oh. I see. ...

Purpose of the visit

Student	OK. Q1 **Well, I'm looking for three Spanish films my teacher said I could find here.** Do you have, like a, a foreign-language section?

Problems and solutions

Librarian	Yes, we do, but, um...I'm afraid affiliate borrowers are only permitted to check out two items at once.
Student	That's OK. I'll just pick up the third one when I return the first two. ...
Librarian	Let me just type that in here. *[while typing]* Q2 **Are you familiar with the online catalogue? You can view all of our books and DVDs and videos online by going to the library website and clicking on the link to the catalog. That way you can check the status of a book or film or whatever before you come over to the library. You know...to make sure it's not already checked out.**
Student	OK, great. I'll do that next time. ...
Student	Thanks. Oh, wait a minute. Q3 **How long can I check them out for?**
Librarian	**Um, you get them for one night. They have to be back by noon tomorrow.**
Student	**Oh, really? I don't think I'm going to have enough time to watch two films tonight. I'd better just check out one of them.** ...

题考查。[*concerned*]一词标明了说话者的心理状态，应该予以把握。

第5题Function题型

因为不是本校的学生，学生担心自己没有借阅的资格。

Q1 "I'm looking for..."是揭示来访具体目的的标志性语句。

第1题Main Idea题型

学生是第一次来这个图书馆，因此在开头首先询问了circulation policy（借阅规定）。但是要注意学生来图书馆的真正目的是因为课程需要，来借西班牙语电影光盘。

Q2 这里出现了online catalog这一新的要点。因为是与使用资料室相关的重要内容，一定要仔细听这一部分。

第2题Inference题型

图书管理员说可以通过网上目录提前确认图书等资料借出与否，提示这比直接找资料更加简便。

Q3 有关问题解决的部分。尤其是当行动有所变化时，有何变化，为何变化等问题经常出现。

第3题Detail题型

学生原来想借两部电影，但是在得知借出期限只有一天之后，觉得没有足够的时间看两部电影，决定只借一部。

DAY 17

Answer 1Ⓑ 2Ⓒ 3Ⓒ 4Ⓐ 5Ⓑ

PRACTICE TEST

CONVERSATION

MP3 • 356

passage 1. [1-5] Listen to part of a conversation between a student and a Residence Life clerk.

note taking

form

1. Why does the woman go to see the Residence Life clerk?

Ⓐ To get in contact with the painters of the dorm

Ⓑ To request a transfer to a different residence hall

Ⓒ To ask the clerk to unlock her room for some painters

Ⓓ To inquire about a delay in a maintenance project

2. Why were the two painters unable to work on the wall?

Ⓐ The forms were not filed with the correct office.

Ⓑ They were given an incorrect address.

Ⓒ No one was available to let them in.

Ⓓ They were late for the scheduled service.

3. Why does the woman fill out another maintenance request form?

Ⓐ To complain about the maintenance staff

Ⓑ To have a second wall in her suite repainted

Ⓒ To rectify an omission on the previous one

Ⓓ To add her name to her roommate's

Listen again to part of the conversation. Then answer the question. 

4. What can be inferred about the woman?

Ⓐ She is upset at having had to submit requests repeatedly.

Ⓑ She is hopeful that the man will help her submit a request.

Ⓒ She thinks the man should know when the requests were submitted.

Ⓓ She does not remember exactly when the requests were submitted.

Listen again to part of the conversation. Then answer the question. MP3•358

5. Why does the woman say this:

Ⓐ To apologize for misinterpreting the man's statement

Ⓑ To express surprise at the information the man shared

Ⓒ To indicate that she did not hear what the man said

Ⓓ To ask the man to check the information again

CONVERSATION **passage 2. [1-5] Listen to part of a conversation between a student and a bookstore employee.**

MP3•359

1. Why does the student approach the bookstore employee?

Ⓐ To determine which books she needs for her English classes

Ⓑ To see about ordering a book from a publisher

Ⓒ To find out where to purchase a used book

Ⓓ To get help finding a book for her class

2. Why is the student late in purchasing her book?

Ⓐ She joined the class after the semester started.

Ⓑ Her professor was supposed to order her a copy.

Ⓒ She did not realize there was a textbook for the course.

Ⓓ Professor Lawson did not assign the book until recently.

3. What are two possible solutions to the woman's problem suggested by the bookstore employee? Click on 2 answers.

Ⓐ Borrowing the textbook from the library

Ⓑ Checking the student message boards

Ⓒ Asking her professor to order her a copy

Ⓓ Placing an order with the campus bookstore

Listen again to part of the conversation. Then answer the question.  MP3 • 360

4. What does the student imply when she says this:

Ⓐ The books do not appear to be shelved in order.

Ⓑ The employee should know where to find the book.

Ⓒ The book she is looking for is not in its proper place.

Ⓓ She already knows where the book is located.

Listen again to part of the conversation. Then answer the question.  MP3 • 361

5. Why does the employee say this:

Ⓐ To let the student know she has other options

Ⓑ To indicate that there may be a problem ordering the book

Ⓒ To express sympathy for the student's situation

Ⓓ To apologize for not ordering the book beforehand

PRACTICE TEST

CONVERSATION MP3·362 **passage 3. [1-5] Listen to part of a conversation between a student and a basketball coach.**

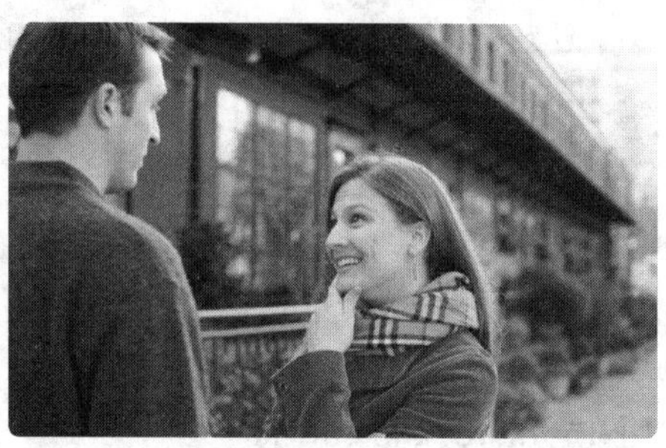

1. Why does the coach want to speak with the woman?

Ⓐ To update her about decisions made while she was gone

Ⓑ To find out if she had a good trip home

Ⓒ To get her opinion about changing the team's uniforms

Ⓓ To talk about why she missed the last practice

2. Why did the team want to change their uniforms?

Ⓐ To simplify the design

Ⓑ To get more comfortable uniforms

Ⓒ To feature the university's mascot

Ⓓ To make the school colors more obvious

3. What are two duties of the team captain mentioned by the coach? Click on 2 answers.

Ⓐ Organizing training activities during team practices

Ⓑ Facilitating communication between the coach and the team

Ⓒ Helping the team stay positive in the face of adversity

Ⓓ Choosing new players to add to the team

Listen again to part of the conversation. Then answer the question. 

4. Why does the student say this:

Ⓐ To verify that the coach is talking to her

Ⓑ To express her disagreement with the decision

Ⓒ To encourage the coach to explain what he means

Ⓓ To show the coach she understood what he said

Listen again to part of the conversation. Then answer the question. MP3·364

5. What can be inferred about the coach?

Ⓐ He fears that the student will not be available to lead the team.

Ⓑ He hopes the student thinks over what he says.

Ⓒ He understands the student's doubts about being team captain.

Ⓓ He has confidence in the student's ability to lead the team.

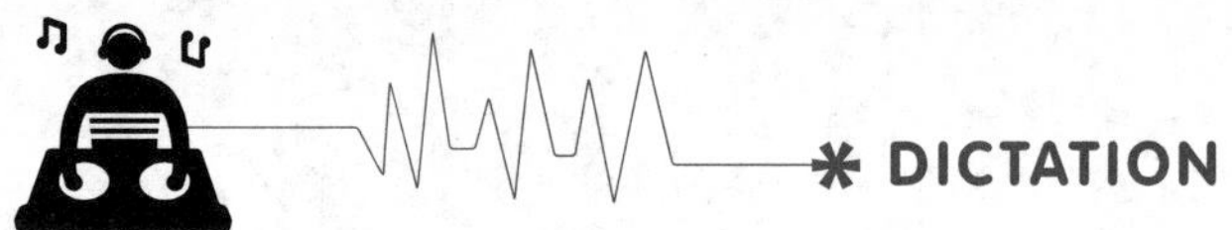

MP3 • 365 **Listen to part of the practice test conversation again and fill in the blanks.**

[省略]

Student: Um, the paint in the common room of my suite is peeling off all over the place. 1)________ ________ ________ ____________ ____________. My roommates and I have been trying to get maintenance up to our suite to repaint the wall, but it's been more than two weeks and nothing's happened.

Clerk: I see. When 2)________ ________ ________ ________ ____________?

Student: Actually, we submitted two requests. One right after it happened...um, on the 21st. And then we submitted a second request on the 28th. It's already November 4th and we still haven't seen anyone from the maintenance department.

Clerk: OK. Let me just look for 3)________ ____________ ________ ____________ ________ ____________, and I'll see if I can figure out what the problem is here. What's your name?

Student: It's Sam Russo, but I didn't submit the documents. It was my roommate, Denise Lombardi.

Clerk: *[looking through some papers]* OK. Denise Lombardi... *[pause]* Are you in suite 301?

Student: Yeah, that's our suite.

Clerk: OK. Yeah, I have the documents here. One submitted on the 21st and the other submitted on the 28th. *[scanning the documents]* Um...it looks like 4)____________ ________ ________ ________ ________ ________. And according to what it says here, two painters were sent to suite 301 after all.

Student: *[surprised]* What? Then why hasn't 5)________ ________ ________ ____________ ________?

Clerk: Well, I'm not sure. Let me give the maintenance department a call and find out what happened. This will just take a minute... I'll be right back. *[pause]* I spoke with the maintenance department on the phone, and they said the first painter went to the suite on Thursday the 23rd at 10:30 in the morning, and the second painter went up there on Wednesday the 29th at two in the afternoon.

Student: Oh. Well no one was home then. 6)________ ________ ________ ________ ________ ________ ________ ________ ________ ________. Couldn't someone from Residence Life here let the painters into our suite?

Clerk: Well, yes, we can do that. If we have the permission of someone in the suite. But when your roommate...um, when Denise filled out the form she didn't check the permission box to let us 7)________ ________ ________ ________ ____________ ____________.

Student: Oh...so that's the problem.

Clerk: Yeah. Just an oversight. Would you like to fill out another request form? Hopefully 8)______ ______ ______ ______ ______ ______.

［省略］

答案参见ANSWER BOOK P481

MP3·366 **Listen to part of the practice test conversation again and fill in the blanks.**

［省略］

Student: Thanks. I hope I didn't miss too much at practice while I was away.

Coach: Actually, that's why I need to talk with you. You see, there was a team meeting after practice on Saturday afternoon, and...well, the rest of the girls 1)______ ______ ______ ______ ______ our team uniforms.

Student: Ah, you talked about that already? Yeah, we were all thinking that it'd be better to have uniforms that feature the school colors more...instead of the plain purple ones we have now. But I didn't realize the team was going to 2)______ ______ ______ ______ ______.

Coach: Yeah, they felt it'd be best to get started on it as soon as possible.

Student: So...what did you think of the idea?

Coach: I think it's fantastic. In fact, I've already spoken with the university athletic director, Mr. Sato. 3)______ ______ ______ ______...um, the new design and everything. The new uniforms should be here in time for our first game.

Student: *[excited]* Oh, that's great! Well, then, I'm glad the girls brought it up with you ...even if I had to miss the discussion.

Coach: Good. Now...there was one other thing that was decided during the team meeting. And...um, it has 4)______ ______ ______ ______ ______ ______ ______.

Student: *[surprised and nervous]* M—me?

Coach: You were 5)______ ______ ______ ______ ______ this year!

Student: *[shocked]* Ah! Really? I can't believe it! That's so wonderful!

Coach: I thought you'd be excited.

Student: You bet I am. Oh, that's such a wonderful honor. I mean...I know I've been on the team for three years and a lot of the girls look up to me, but...I just can't believe it.

Coach: Well, you should. You 6)______ ______ ______ ______ ______, and I can't think of anyone else I'd rather have in the position.

Student: Thanks so much, Coach. That means a lot.

Coach: Now, it's not simply a title, you know. There're a lot of 7)______ ______ ______ ______ ______ ______ being team captain.

［省略］

答案参见ANSWER BOOK P485

DAY 17

smart source

1 Division of Academic Affairs 学生事务处

学生为了各项学业事务academic affairs去学生事务处找负责登记的职员registrar。通常，申请选课apply/sign up/register、变更选课change a shedule、取消withdraw选课申请或者放弃drop选课等与登记registration有关的事务最为常见。有时，学生也会为了处理与季节学期summer session/winter session、转系transfer或与毕业graduation相关的事务，前往确认学分credit。

2 Student Services Center 学生服务中心

学生服务中心是为了帮助学生更有效地进行大学生活而设立的机构，它负责开具成绩证明transcript、毕业证明certificate of graduation、学位证diploma等各种证书或证明文件academic certificates，也负责发放学生证student ID card等。此外，这一机构还负责校务或者咨询服务counseling services，不仅提供保管信件mailing service等琐碎的服务，还提供语言研修language study [course] abroad、交换生exchange student、实习机会internship等更有实质性帮助的服务。

3 Library / Media Center 图书馆/多媒体中心

大一新生freshman或者新的转学生transfer来到图书馆或多媒体中心，向图书管理员librarian询问图书借出check out及返还return的情景十分常见。尤其是借出的情况，教授经常会为听课的学生提前预约书籍put material on reserve或多媒体参考资料。若出借时间超过overdue借期，借书人就需要缴纳罚款fine/late fee。

4 Dormitory / Residence Hall 宿舍/学生公寓

学生为了处理与宿舍有关的事务会找宿舍管理员housing officer或者维护管理人maintenance staff谈话。通常，谈话的内容都是学生在宿舍生活时遇到的种种不便inconvenience，如与室友roommate的矛盾、噪音noise问题、房间变更申请、假期房间空置问题或者内部设施facilities问题等。很多美国大学的宿舍都设置在校内on campus或学校附近，学生在宿舍里可以使用网络、有线电视等设备，并且可以使用有固定菜单meal plans的校内食堂cafeteria。通常，这些宿舍或公寓的名字都是如Williams Hall或McGill Hall一样的固有名词，做听力的时候要留心不要与人名混淆。

5 Part–time Job 打工/兼职

学生经常在餐厅或者商店打工兼职part-time job，或者兼职校内工作campus job。在校内工作时，他们经常在图书馆、书店、校内食堂等地方打工，并且经常为了考试或其他急事而调整工作日程。

6 Campus Bookstore 校内书店

为了购买或预订课程需要的教材，学生会去校内的书店，经常会与书店店员对话。这时，经常出现学生需要的书没有库存out- of-stock的情境。对此，书店的店员会提出追加订货reorder、复印copy或购买旧书used book等建议。

7 Health Care Center 保健诊疗中心

为了治病或接种vaccination/immunization病毒性感冒flu、乙肝hepatitis B等疫苗，学生会去校内保健诊疗中心campus clinic。这时，经常出现与护士谈话预约时间的情境。

8 Extracurricular Activities 课外活动

在实际的美国大学生活中，学生在学业之外还会进行丰富多彩的课外活动。社团club或学生会student government [council]会举办host各种文化节festival、校友alumni访问母校homecoming day、慈善募捐晚会fund-raising party以及学术会议academic conference等活动。因此，听力考试中经常会出现与此相关的对话。通常，内容都是与活动筹备相关的，例如为预订场地与学校职员就场地venue大小、日程以及茶点refreshments准备进行商议等。

Theme Vocab

MP3 • 367

Division of Academic Affairs 学业事务处

registrar 学籍注册员，登记员
sign up 听课申请(=**register**)
transfer 转课，转系

Student Services Center 学生服务中心

transcript 成绩证明单
certificate 证明
issue a student ID card 发放学生证
check out 借出
return 返还
put material on reserve （教授）预借资料
fine /**late fee** 滞纳金

Dormitory /Bookstore 宿舍/书店等

on campus 校内
meal plans 餐单
out-of-stock 没有库存
reorder 追加订货
health care center 保健诊疗中心
vaccination 疫苗接种(=**immunization**)

Extracurricular activities 课外活动

student government[council] 学生会
alumni 校友

DAY18

Life Science II

- CASE EXAMPLE - 例题
- SMART SOLUTION - 主题补充专题
- PRACTICE TEST - 练习
- DICTATION - 听写
- SMART SOURCE - 主题资料库

speed keyword

Life Science II

正如之前所讨论过的，生命科学是考查从微生物到人类的所有生命体的大范围学科。在Life Science I中，我们已经对微生物以及动植物方面的一些主题进行了考查。在本章中，将会对以海洋生物及人体为对象的一些内容和最近尤为重要的环境、生态等经常出现的话题进行整理。

海洋生物学Marine Biology 备考主题

丰富的海洋生物生态/发光生物

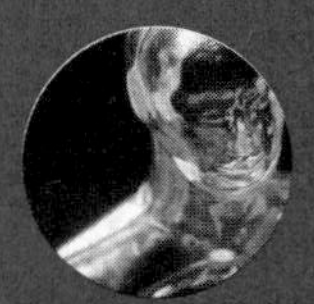

生理学Physiology 备考主题

人体/构成人体的器官的特征：脑、荷尔蒙、感觉器官

保健学Public health 备考主题

睡眠/生物体节律/运动反射神经/各种营养成分对人体的影响

环境学Environmental Studies、生态学Ecology 备考主题

各种污染：大气污染与水质污染/生态破坏与处于灭绝危机中的生物/富营养化

CASE EXAMPLE

[1-6] Listen to part of a talk in a paleontology class.

MP3·372

| Volume | Help | OK | Next |

Endotherm
Ectotherm

1. What aspect of dinosaurs does the professor mainly discuss?
   Ⓐ Why some species were different than others
   Ⓑ How they evolved special features over millions of years
   Ⓒ Which of two physiological types they were
   Ⓓ How they were able to generate their own body heat

2. How does the professor correct the misconception that dinosaurs were certainly cold-blooded?

Ⓐ By discussing the work of paleontologists in past decades

Ⓑ By explaining the process of animal metabolism

Ⓒ By mentioning hard evidence that contradicts this notion

Ⓓ By citing the example of a similar modern animal

3. In the lecture, the professor lists evidence in support of the theory that dinosaurs were endothermic. Indicate whether each of the following is evidence for the theory. Click in the correct box for each statement.

	YES	NO
Ⓐ The surrounding environment controlled their body temperature.		
Ⓑ Their limbs gave them an erect posture.		
Ⓒ Most species were large and had relatively short lifespans.		
Ⓓ Their metabolic rates may have varied substantially.		
Ⓔ Today's fast-moving species are mostly endothermic.		

4. What are two reasons the professor gives for why dinosaurs could have been ectothermic? Click on 2 answers.

Ⓐ They grew at a rapid rate.

Ⓑ A hot climate existed at the time.

Ⓒ Their skin is similar to that of the modern ectotherms.

Ⓓ Modern reptiles exhibit similar behavioral characteristics.

Listen again to part of the talk. Then answer the question.  MP3•373

5. What can be inferred about the woman when she says this:

Ⓐ She is sure that her initial answer was correct.

Ⓑ She is reconsidering her opinion on the issue.

Ⓒ She misunderstood the professor's question.

Ⓓ She disagrees with the professor's assessment.

Listen again to part of the talk. Then answer the question. MP3•374

6. Why does the man say this:

Ⓐ To make sure he understands what the professor is saying

Ⓑ To express agreement with the professor's point

Ⓒ To indicate he has something to add to the discussion

Ⓓ To raise a question about the professor's argument

SMART SOLUTION

note taking

Main Topic : a long debate about whether dinosaurs were warm-blooded or cold-blooded

Dinosaurs were warm-blooded (endothermic)?	↔	Dinosaurs were cold-blooded (ectothermic)?
*reconsider that dinosaurs were cold-blooded(since Bakker's article in 1968) - move at fast speeds → high metabolic rates - erect limbs(like modern endotherms) - fast growth rate(large body) & short lifespan		- warm climate of the Mesozoic era - scales like modern ectotherms

CLUE FINDER 文章介绍了有关恐龙到底是温血动物（恒温动物）还是冷血动物（变温动物）的争论。教授从客观角度列举了两种观点各自的根据，但更着力于阐释恐龙是恒温动物的假说。

Long debate about dinosaurs: warm-blooded or cold-blooded?

Professor (male) I have a question for you, class. Q1 **Dinosaurs—were they warm-blooded or cold-blooded?**

Student A (female) Um—they were cold-blooded, of course.

Professor Are you sure?

Student A Q5 ***[uncertainly]* Well, that's what I'd always assumed. But, uh, I guess you wouldn't have asked us if it were that simple.**

Professor ...But in the past couple of decades, most of the evidence we've been finding suggests that the opposite might actually have been true. Dinosaurs might've been fast and active, with high metabolisms.

...

First assertions that dinosaurs were warm-blooded

Student A Q2 **OK. So what caused scientists to reconsider their belief about dinosaurs being cold-blooded?**

Professor **Well, a young paleontologist named Robert Bakker had a lot to do with it. He published an article in 1968 called "The Superiority of Dinosaurs," which suggested that dinosaurs were much more active than generally believed...and warm-blooded. Bakker's assertions generated a lot of interest, and soon others**

Q1 文章的主题并不一定都是在"要介绍…"之类的标志性语句后揭示出来的。尤其是在对话式的课堂上，教授也经常会向学生提问，来揭示课上将要探讨的核心内容。
第1题Main Idea题型

Q5 与文章的内容无关，对话式的口语特点凸显的部分大都会成为考点，需要留心。通过综合考虑***[uncertainly]***的语调与情境，考生应该可以推测出说话者的感情。
第5题Attitude题型
教授一旦反问学生是否肯定恐龙是冷血动物，学生立刻就显得不十分自信了。

Q2 此时，教授将要进入正题了。请边听边留心这里和前面内容的关系。由于已经提出了恐龙可能是温血动物，因此可以推测下文会出现这种假设的根据。

began looking into the possibility that dinosaurs may have been, um, warm-blooded creatures.

...

Evidence for "warm-blooded" hypothesis

Professor Absolutely. Q3 First, when we look at the range of modern animals around the globe, there's a certain trend: metabolic rate is proportional to speed. From what we know about dinosaurs, it seems that they were designed to move at fast speeds. So there's a natural assumption, then, that dinosaurs might've also had high metabolic rates, as that would fit the trend we see among modern animals.

Student B Q6 Well, that doesn't really seem like, um, hard evidence.

Professor ... Q3 If you look at modern animals, it's pretty much only, um, endotherms like birds and mammals that have erect limbs. Oh, and another factor that supports the endothermic theory is their growth rate. As you know, some of them grew to be extremely large, so they probably had to grow quite quickly. And what we know about modern animals tells us that endothermic animals grow faster than ectothermic animals. From what we can tell, dinosaurs seem to have had faster growth rates than similarly sized modern reptiles, and similar growth rates to modern endothermic animals. Does everyone follow?

...

Evidence for "cold-blooded" hypothesis

Professor Oh, well sure. Nothing's been decided yet. Q4 Some people look at the climate of the Mesozoic era—which was probably a lot warmer than today's climate—and they take that as a sign that dinosaurs probably didn't need to be endothermic because the climate was so mild. They would've been warm enough. Furthermore, from what we can tell about dinosaurs' skin, they had scales...which is just like today's modern ectotherms.

...

第2题Organization题型
为了支持恐龙可能是温血动物的假说，教授列举了具体的理论以及学者的事例。

Q3 教授列举了恐龙可能是温血动物的根据。像这样分几点进行罗列的部分很有可能成为**detail**或**connecting contents**类型的问题，听的时候要做笔记。
第3题Connecting Contents题型
来看原文内容在表格的YES栏目中是怎样被换成另一种说法表述的。

Q6 请留心用委婉的方式表达否定意思的部分。
第6题Function题型
hard evidence意为"确凿的证据"，学生觉得教授举出的温血动物论的依据并不充分，用此词表达了这种否定的意见。

Q4 这篇文章尽管着重介绍了恐龙的温血动物论，但是也同样列举了冷血动物论的依据。在这样使用对照方式进行的文章当中，反论的部分也是重要的论点，经常被用来考查细节性的信息。
第4题Detail题型

DAY 18

Answer 1 Ⓒ 2 Ⓐ 3 YES → Ⓑ, Ⓒ, Ⓔ / NO → Ⓐ, Ⓓ 4 Ⓑ, Ⓒ 5 Ⓑ 6 Ⓓ

PRACTICE TEST

LECTURE  **passage 1. [1-6] Listen to part of a lecture in a marine biology class.**

MP3 • 375

Incirrina

note taking

1. What is the lecture mainly about?

Ⓐ The intelligence and memory of the octopus

Ⓑ Forms of camouflage common among the suborder of Incirrina

Ⓒ Methods the octopus uses to capture prey

Ⓓ Ways the octopus manages to elude predators

2. Indicate whether each of the following is mentioned in the lecture as one of the octopus's survival techniques. Click in the correct box for each phrase.

	YES	NO
Ⓐ Slipping away through small openings in rocks or coral		
Ⓑ Releasing a cloud of ink to confuse prey's senses		
Ⓒ Secreting a harmful toxin from one of its tentacles		
Ⓓ Taking on the appearance of an inanimate bit of debris		

3. Why does the professor mention the eyesight of the octopus?
Ⓐ To emphasize the unusual quality of the octopus's senses
Ⓑ To compare the octopus's chemoreceptors with similar senses
Ⓒ To illustrate the special adaptations aquatic animals have to their environment
Ⓓ To explain why the octopus needs so many defensive tricks

4. According to the professor, how does the octopus differ from other invertebrates? Click on 2 answers.
Ⓐ It can detect the presence of chemicals in the water.
Ⓑ It has well developed problem-solving skills.
Ⓒ It has a sense of smell and a sense of taste.
Ⓓ It has a number of special survival techniques.
Ⓔ It is capable of memorizing information.

Listen again to part of the lecture. Then answer the question.  MP3・376

5. What does the professor mean when he says this:
Ⓐ He wants the students to learn the word for an upcoming test.
Ⓑ He thinks the term is probably unfamiliar to the students.
Ⓒ He does not want to spend time writing down terms for the students.
Ⓓ He thinks the students have already studied the term.

DAY 18

Listen again to part of the lecture. Then answer the question.  MP3・377

6. Why does the professor say this:
Ⓐ To imply there are different opinions on what he has just discussed
Ⓑ To introduce another way the octopus can escape a predator
Ⓒ To compare the intelligence of the octopus with that of its predators
Ⓓ To ask the students to make a guess about the behavior of the octopus

LECTURE  MP3 • 378 **passage 2. [1-6] Listen to part of a lecture in an environmental studies class.**

Salmon

1. What is the lecture mainly about?

   Ⓐ How wild salmon have made a comeback in recent years

   Ⓑ The decline of wild salmon populations due to human activities

   Ⓒ The relationship between salmon farms and the environment

   Ⓓ The differences between wild and farmed salmon populations

2. What does the professor say about Atlantic wild salmon?

Ⓐ They are less hardy than their relatives in the Pacific Ocean.

Ⓑ Their situation is more dire than that of Pacific wild salmon.

Ⓒ They are currently only found in protected rivers and lakes.

Ⓓ Their populations were drastically reduced in the early 20th century.

3. Indicate whether each of the following is mentioned in the lecture as a factor contributing to the loss of wild salmon populations. Click in the correct box for each phrase.

	YES	NO
Ⓐ The damming of rivers, which inhibits salmon reproduction		
Ⓑ The capture of wild salmon for introduction into salmon farms		
Ⓒ A lack of nutrients in the water due to the disappearance of bears and birds		
Ⓓ Habitat loss and habitat degradation caused by human development		
Ⓔ Water loss caused by prolonged periods of droughts in recent decades		

4. According to the professor, how do farmed salmon affect wild salmon?

Ⓐ By competing with them for food and other resources

Ⓑ By bolstering their dwindling wild populations

Ⓒ By introducing diseases to which they have no immunity

Ⓓ By adding more resilient genes to the gene pool

Listen again to part of the lecture. Then answer the question. 

5. What does the professor imply when she says this:

Ⓐ The situation for salmon is not as bad as it might at first appear to be.

Ⓑ Her discussion will be solely focused on wild salmon.

Ⓒ Other wild species of fish are also on the decline.

Ⓓ Wild salmon and farmed salmon deal with different circumstances.

Listen again to part of the lecture. Then answer the question. 

6. Why does the professor say this:

Ⓐ To quantify the environmental damages caused by farmed salmon

Ⓑ To emphasize the economic value of the salmon industry

Ⓒ To encourage the students to take the problem more seriously

Ⓓ To correct her previous comment about wild salmon

PRACTICE TEST

LECTURE  **passage 3. [1-6] Listen to part of a lecture in a biology class.**

MP3 • 381

Neuron

note taking

1. What is the lecture mainly about?
   Ⓐ Why the neuron is structured the way that it is
   Ⓑ Major breakthroughs in the history of neurology
   Ⓒ Newly discovered treatments for serious neurological diseases
   Ⓓ How neurons relay information in the human nervous system

2. In the lecture, the professor describes the process of synaptic transmission. Indicate whether each of the following occurs in the process. Click in the correct box for each statement.

	YES	NO
Ⓐ A neuron's dendrites receive a signal.		
Ⓑ Signals pass over gaps between neurons called synapses.		
Ⓒ The axon of a neuron transmits a message to another neuron.		
Ⓓ A neuron's cell body communicates directly with a synapse.		
Ⓔ The brain receives a signal sent by individual neurons.		

3. Why does the professor mention Santiago Ramón y Cajal?
   Ⓐ To identify the founder of the study of neurology
   Ⓑ To provide a timeframe for a discovery about neurons and synapses
   Ⓒ To describe the process by which scientists study neurons
   Ⓓ To suggest that research into neurons is still controversial

4. What are the features of Alzheimer's mentioned in the discussion? Click on 2 answers.
   Ⓐ It can lead to the onset of Parkinson's disease.
   Ⓑ It causes people to struggle while performing familiar tasks.
   Ⓒ It inhibits synaptic transmission in the brain.
   Ⓓ Its main symptom is a gradual loss of motor control.

Listen again to part of the lecture. Then answer the question. MP3・382

5. Why does the professor say this:
   Ⓐ To indicate that she will go over information some students may have already learned
   Ⓑ To check whether or not the students have completed introductory biology courses
   Ⓒ To ask for students' opinions on some of the information she just presented
   Ⓓ To suggest that the students may have difficulty understanding the lecture topic

Listen again to part of the lecture. Then answer the question. MP3・383

6. What can be inferred about the professor?
   Ⓐ She wants to criticize how knowledge about neurons is applied.
   Ⓑ She thinks the students are familiar with ongoing medical research.
   Ⓒ She thinks the students should read about neurological diseases for homework.
   Ⓓ She wants to begin discussing a different aspect of neurology.

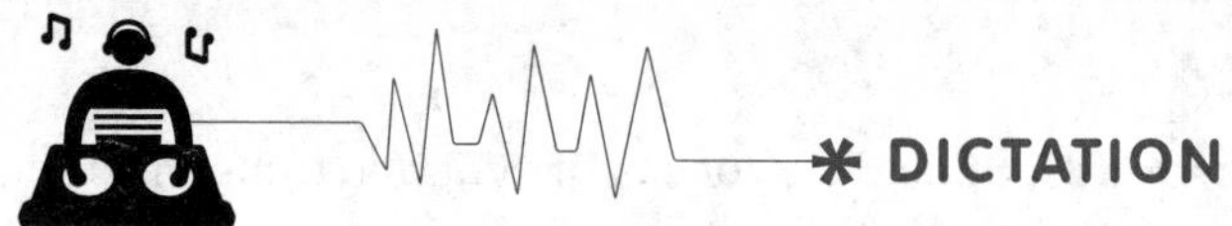

MP3·384 **Listen to part of the biology lecture again and fill in the blanks.**

［省略］

Professor: Let's continue with the idea of escaping predators for a minute. Um, what does an octopus do if there aren't any rocks or coral around to hide in? How can it get away? Well, it turns out the animal is 1)________ ________ ________ ____________...it can make itself appear to be something else. For example, say an octopus is crawling along the seafloor...which, by the way, is how they usually travel. Um, so it's crawling along, and suddenly a predator shows up. The octopus can arrange its body in such a way that 2)________ ________ ________ ________ ________ ________ ____________...or some other uninteresting piece of debris. Moving slowly, in sync with the waves, it'll gradually just drift away, and the predator will be none the wiser.

Pretty neat. But what if the predator isn't fooled? In that case, 3)________ ____________ ________ ________ ________ ________ ________. It has another method of locomotion, which, um...it's called jet propulsion. It'll draw in water through its gills, and then 4)________ ________ ________ ________ ________ ____________ ____________ its mouth. This'll send the creature shooting forward at up to 25 miles per hour. That's pretty fast, but the drawback is the octopus can only use its jet propulsion for a short time before tiring out.

Luckily, it has 5)________ ________ ________ ____________ ________. One of these...the octopus can release a cloud of dark ink into the water. Um, not only does this obscure the vision of the predator, it also obscures smell...important since a lot of 6)________ ____________ ________ ________ ________ during hunting. So the ink cloud basically throws the predator off the octopus's trail. OK, then...one more. In, um, 7)________ ____________ ____________, the octopus will actually detach one or more of its arms. That's right...just let them go. They'll wiggle around in the water, 8)____________ ____________ ________ ____________ ________ ________ for the octopus to escape. Oh...and conveniently, the arms grow back.

Now...how about avoiding predators all together? This is where the octopus's 9)________ ________ ________ ________ ________ ________. First of all, it has fairly good eyesight... which is a bit unusual for undersea creatures. Um...its eyes aren't positioned like ours. They're 10)____________ ________ ____________ ________ ________ ________ ________, greatly increasing its field of vision.

［省略］

答案参见ANSWER BOOK P491

 MP3• 385 **Listen to part of the biology lecture again and fill in the blanks.**

［省略］

Professor: So...a general explanation of neurons is that they're cells that make up the nervous system. The nervous system—this [1]______ ______ ______ ______ ______, basically the spine and the brain...and then there's the peripheral nervous system, which includes nerves that run throughout the body. Anyway, um, neurons... they [2]______ ______ ______ ______ ______ ______ within the nervous system.

But let's get a little more specific, OK? Starting with the structure of neurons. You can break them down into three parts: the cell body, the axon, and the dendrites. Is any of this sounding familiar to you? The cell body has the [3]______ ______ ______, like DNA, ribosomes, and mitochondria. The axon is sort of like a long strand...and it's the axon that's [4]______ ______ ______ ______ to other neurons. Then there are the dendrites—little branch-like threads that, um, stick out of the neuron. Most neurons have thousands of dendrite branches, and, um, their job is to receive messages from other neurons. Axons send, dendrites receive. Got it?

OK, that [5]______ ______ ______ ______ ______...which is the process by which neurons transmit information. So...what's a synapse? Well, you see...neurons aren't actually in physical contact with each other. They're separated by a small gap, and it's this gap that's called a synapse. Um, synapses essentially [6]______ ______ ______ ______ ______ that, um, that makes the components of our nervous system function, for example, our brain. What happens is [7]______ ______ ______ ______ ______ ______ ______ in order to travel from one neuron to the next. There're 100 billion neurons in the brain, all making connections with other neurons... and that's, um, basically how our brains work—how we think. Fascinating, isn't it? I mean, your entire nervous system is actually [8]______ ______ ______ ______ ______—separate neurons that aren't, um, physically connected. And yet they can [9]______ ______ ______ ______ ______ synaptic transmission.

Actually, you know...at one point, we used to think the brain was more of a connected, um, meshwork. It wasn't until the late nineteenth century that the breakthrough discovery of neurons was made. It was a Spanish physician named Santiago Ramón y Cajal who first realized that—that neurons were separated by gaps—synapses. His theory about neurons became [10]______ ______ ______ ______ ______...and now it's pretty much universally accepted, though it did [11]______ ______ ______ ______ ______ ______ ______.

［省略］

答案参见ANSWER BOOK P495

DAY 18

smart source

Marine Biology 海洋生物学

1 Dolphin Communication 海豚的通信

在与其他海豚dolphin交流communication时，海豚会使用一定频率frequency的声波交换信息。种群不同，声波sound wave的频率也不一样。海豚收发声波的能力十分强。它通过脑袋前方的椭圆形oval器官organ向外部发送声波，通过下巴下半部分的声窗acoustic window接收返回的声波，之后再对声波信号进行分析来实现相互间的通信。除此之外，海豚还可以根据超声波碰撞物体后返回的速度、声音与音量等确定recognize周围有哪些种类的物体以及它们所处的位置。在考试真题中，出现过相关的试题，即说话者在介绍了海豚为了相互通信使用的三种声音类型之后，要求考生将它们与相应的例子联系起来。

2 Bioluminescence 生物发光

指像萤火虫firefly一样的生物体自己发光的现象。发光的生物体从细菌bacteria、甲虫bug到鱼fish都有，种类繁多。海洋oceanic生物中的发光生物尤其多，比如说腔肠动物coelenterate中的海蜇、海仙人掌、管水母等，软体动物mollusk中代表性的有海鸥贝、火星望潮、火鱿鱼等。发光的目的主要被解释为自我保护和防止defense捕食者predator侵害，而对于具体的发光机制mechanism，目前还没有明确的解释，如果生物种类species不同，其发光机制也体现出差异性。现在，人们认为一种被称为荧光素luciferin的物质如果在生物体内氧化oxidation，就会发光。在考试真题当中，曾有文章介绍过两种类型的发光生物，它们都为了自我保护而发光。其中的一种会在捕食者出现的瞬间发光，引起捕食者慌乱而趁机逃走；另一种则在黝黑的水下发出明亮的光作为伪装camouflage，让水面上的捕食者无法觉察到自己的存在。通过对这两个例子进行说明，文章之后有题目考查各自的细节事项。

●警戒色warning color：也叫做警告色，指与周围环境颜色相比，十分显眼、强烈并且华丽的身体颜色。警戒色是为了警示捕食者自己是危险的生物，从而摆脱危险。

3 Fin 鱼鳍

鱼的鳍由平行parallel或者呈放射状伸出的鳍棘支撑，而鳍肉又由鳍条支撑。鱼鳍大致可以分为奇鳍unpaired fin和偶鳍faired fins两种。

●奇鳍unpaired fin：位于鱼身体的正中央，始于背部，然后环绕鱼尾，直达肛门anus的鳍。中间间断，形成背鳍dorasl fins、尾鳍tail fins和臀鳍anal fins。尾鳍是推进propulsion鱼身体前进的舵，背鳍和臀鳍则起保持方向的作用。

●偶鳍paired fin：鱼身体两侧成对的鳍，有胸鳍和pecroral fins腹鳍pelvic fins两种。胸鳍通常紧贴鳃线gill之后，而腹鳍则通常位于肛门左右。对于这样的偶鳍，有的观点认为它们原来各是连续的一只鳍，中间消失之后剩下的两边各自形成了现在的胸鳍和腹鳍。偶鳍的作用相当于四肢动物的腿。

Physiology 生理学

4 Organ Systems 器官系统

构成动物身体的主要器官相互影响联系。它们虽然不能独立工作，但是可以根据主要功能加以分类。

●消化系统digestive system：将摄取的食物磨碎break down，吸收养分nutrients，排泄excrete出剩下的物质。

●神经系统nerious system：由神经细胞nerve cell构成，快速传达transmission身体因体内外变化而受到的刺激，并且生成相应的反应。神经元neuron是传达信号最基础的细胞，此外还有称为胶质细胞glian cell的神经辅助细胞。

●呼吸系统respiratory system：呼出二氧化碳CO_2，吸入emission氧气O_2的一系列器官。典型的有嘴、支气管bronchus及肺lung等。

●循环系统circulatory system：由血液blood系统和淋巴lymph系统组成，并起着促使血液及淋巴循环circulate的作用。

DAY 18

5 Synapse 突触

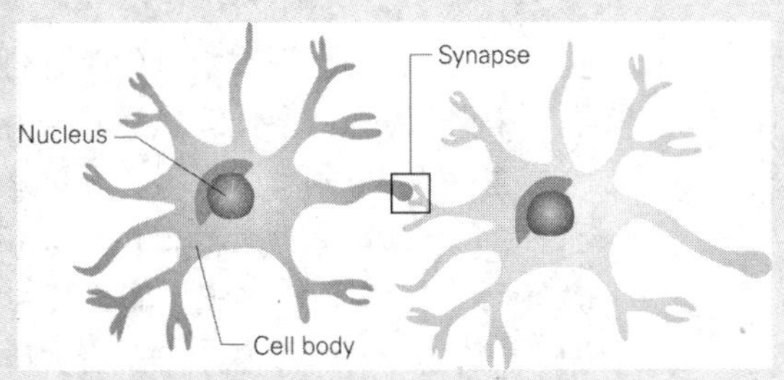

神经元neuron是传递刺激或兴奋的基本神经单位，由细胞核nucleus所在的神经细胞体cell body、从其他细胞接收信号的树状突dendrite及向其他细胞发送信号的轴索axon三部分构成。神经元与神经元之间并不是直接连结的，一个神经元轴索的末端与另一神经元的树状突之间会有20毫米左右的间隙，这一部分被称为突触synapes。轴索的末端会分泌称为乙酰胆素acetylcholine的化学物质，经过突触，传达至树状突，并通过这一过程向神经细胞传递刺激与兴奋。

6 Sleep Disturbance 睡眠障碍

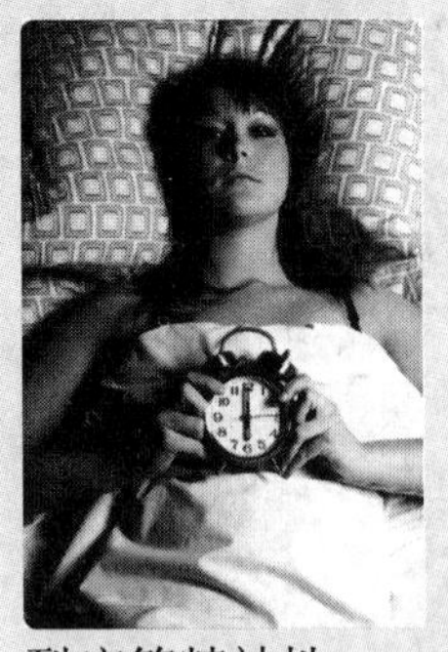

指睡眠在量quantitative和质qualitative两方面存在障碍。根据伴随睡眠量的症状或异常行为，睡眠障碍可分为以下几类。

●失眠症insomnia：入睡时间超过30分钟，或者一夜之中睡着再醒来的情况反复5次以上，抑或一周凌晨醒来2～3次以上。引起失眠的原因有噪音noise或气温等环境性environmental因素，疼痛ache、发痒itchness或睡眠无呼吸等生理性physical因素，以及脑动脉硬化、躁郁症或精神分裂症等精神性mental因素。

●过眠症hypersomnia：指睡眠量过大、睡眠时间过久的状况。睡觉的时候会有疾病发作、出现幻觉、梦以及睡眠麻痹等症状。

●快速眼动睡眠REM/睡眠行为障碍sleep behavior disorder：睡觉时，把抡胳膊或踢腿等梦中的行为实际做出来的病症，可能是由于承担肌肉运动的大脑部分受到损伤或压力过大导致的。

●嗜眠症narcolepsy/somnolence：睡意突然来袭，无法抵挡，瞬间就进入睡眠状态的现象。多见于青少年期，大部分属于遗传疾病genetic disease。

●时差病jet lag：主要出现在需要长途飞行或黑白颠倒轮班的工作人群当中。有无法入眠、慢性疲劳、压力大及忧郁等症状。

7 Dementia 痴呆

指大脑cerebrum的神经细胞大范围损伤，智力intelligence显著下降decline的状态，伴随有记忆力、理解力及计算能力calculation等思维能力的整体衰退、强迫症等特定的行为障碍behavioral disorder，以及心理psychological状态不安等情感障碍。

●阿尔兹海默氏病Alzheimer's disease：是退行性的大脑疾病，主要出现在老年人群中。它会导致大脑的整体性萎缩、脑室扩张等，引起智力减退、行动障碍、情感障碍等典型性痴呆症状，并最终导致死亡。

●帕金森氏病Parkinson's disease：与老年痴呆同为中枢神经系统central nervous system的退行性老年疾病，可能是由遗传因素引起的。主要症状是运动障碍，可能因渐进性的肌肉麻痹paralysis导致手臂、腿脚无法移动，以致日常行为动作的丧失，严重时甚至会导致患者无法眨眼，面无表情。

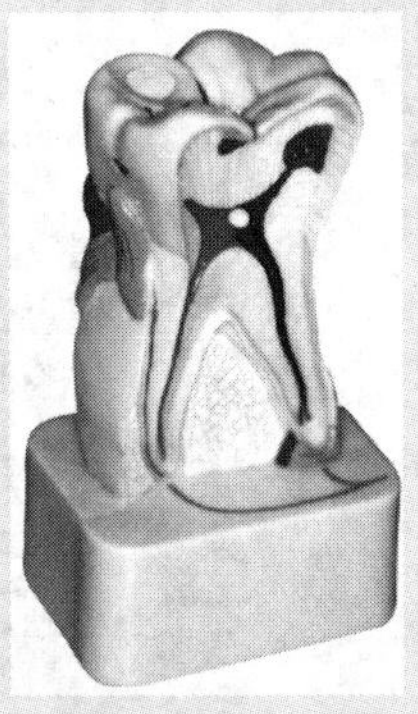

8 Oral Plaque 齿菌斑

出现在牙齿表面的黄色粘着状细菌bacteria层。牙菌斑

plaque的危害与其说是它本身存在毒性toxicity，对身体有威胁，还不如说是由于无法通过刷牙彻底地清洁牙齿，容易造成龋齿cavities、牙周炎periodontis、牙龈炎gingivitis等牙齿疾病。如果不规律性地清洁齿菌斑，而任其发展的话，就会形成牙垢tartar，严重的甚至会导致有牙龈gum出血现象的牙龈炎。唾液saliva原本起着中和口腔内酸性环境的作用。但是随着时间流逝，如果齿菌斑越积accumulation越多，唾液的中和作用neutralization就会变得难以实现，最终导致齿菌斑内部的微生物microorganism分泌酸acids，损伤覆盖牙齿表面的牙釉质enamel。

Theme Vocab

MP3• 386

Marine Biology 海洋生物学

frequency 频率
bioluminescence 生物发光
firefly 萤火虫
predator 捕食者
oxidation 氧化
warning color 警戒色
fin 鳍
unpaired fin 奇鳍
paired fins 偶鳍
gill 鳃
anus 肛门

Physiology 生理学

organ system 器官系统
digestive system 消化系统
nervous system 神经系统
respiratory system 呼吸系统
circulatory system 循环系统
dendrite 树状突
axon 轴索

Public Health 保健学

sleep disturbance 睡眠障碍
insomnia 失眠
itchiness 发痒
hypersomnia 过眠症
narcolepsy, somnolence 嗜眠症
genetic disease 遗传病
dementia 痴呆
cerebrum 大脑
behavioral disorder 行动障碍
oral plaque 齿菌斑
cavities 龋齿
gum 牙龈
saliva 唾液
neutralization 中和作用
microorganism 微生物

DAY 18

Environmental Studies 环境学

9 Water Pollution 水质污染

●生物需氧量(BOD)：Biology Oxygen Demand. 好氧性生物（需要氧气的微生物）在一定时间内，分解水中有机物所使用的氧气量，被用作衡量水污染程度的指标。

●化学耗氧量(COD)：Chemical Oxygen Demand. 衡量被污染的水体水质的指标。

●硝化生化需氧量(NBOD)：Nitrification Biochemical Oxygen Demand衡量河川、污水或工业废水污染浓度的指标，指硝酸菌的耗氧量。

10 Salmon Farming 鲑鱼养殖

近来，养殖鲑鱼salmon farm的渔场对生态系统ecosystem的破坏正成为严重的环境问题。养殖鲑鱼时，如果鲑鱼长到了一定程度，就要放生release。此时，养殖的鲑鱼farmed salmon就会与野生鲑鱼wild salmon混杂在一起，前者就可能向后者传播它们无法免疫immunity的病毒或疾病。此外，由于养殖的鲑鱼和野生鲑鱼体质特征trait不同，两者之间可能发生争斗，结果导致后者的数量急剧减少，最终危害生物多样性biodiversity。在托福真题中，曾经介绍过关于鲑鱼是否处于濒危endangered状况的争论controversy——把养殖的鲑鱼也算在内的话，鲑鱼的整体数量并不算少，但是如果只计算纯种的野生鲑鱼，则已经达到了濒危状况。

11 Eutrophication 富营养化

在江、河、湖等水体环境oceanic ecosystem中，藻类algae植物伴随着营养物质的增加而迅速增殖proliferation的现象。如果生活污水waste water、工业废水或家畜livestock的排泄物feces等流入江河或海洋，水中氮nitrogen、磷phosphorous等营养元素就会增加。如果此类营养物质增多，它们的循环速度circulation也会相应变快，海藻类植物的光合作用photosynthesis量也就会迅速增加，结果导致它们的生长growth与繁殖reproduction速度加快，引起水体富营养化。富营养化的水体根据海藻类植物种类的不同，会呈现出红、绿、褐等不同颜色。海水由于海藻类植物的迅速增殖proliferation而变红的现象被称为赤潮red tide。在托福真题中，曾有内容对富营养化的定义、特征及原因等进行过整体性的说明，并提出为了防止富营养化现象的出现，需要全社会共同努力。

12 Bioremediation 生物净化

生物净化指利用微生物净化purification被污染contaminated的土壤及水体的方法。随着工业废水industrial waste等污染物pollutant的急剧增多，生态环境本身具有的自净作用self-purification也达到了极限。为了解决这个问题，人们引进了生物净化这一方法。其基本原理是将从生物学角度来看的有害harmful物质进行分解decompose或构造简化simplify，让它们变成安全的物质。微生物microorganism为了获取生长所必需的碳元素carbon或电子electron，会灵活利用周围的硝酸盐、硫酸盐或铁等污染物pollutant。利用这一点，人们想出了在污染严重的区域培养微生物，降解有害物质toxic substance的方法。最近，这一方法也被用来复原restore被放射性物质radioactive material或重金属heavy pollution污染的区域。生物净化会二次污染secondary pollution的可能性相对较小，具有方便现场on-site处置、能源投入量少的优点。

Theme Vocab

MP3 • 386

Environmental Studies 环境学

water pollution 水质污染
Biology Oxygen Demand（BOD） 生化需氧量
release 放生
farmed 养殖的(↔**wild**)
immunity 免疫力
trait 特征
biodiversity 生物多样性
endangered 处于灭绝危机的
eutrophication 富营养化
algae（海）藻类
waste water 工业废水
nitrogen 氮
phosphorous 磷
growth and reproduction 生长和繁殖
proliferation 增殖
red tide 赤潮
contaminate 污染
purification 净化
self-purification 自净作用
decompose 分解
pollutant 污染物
toxic substance 有害物质
radioactive material 放射性物质
heavy metal 重金属
restore 复原
secondary pollution 二次污染
on-site 现场

DAY 18

DAY19

Social Science

- CASE EXAMPLE - 例题
- SMART SOLUTION - 主题补充专题
- PRACTICE TEST - 练习
- DICTATION - 听写
- SMART SOURCE - 主题资料库

speed keyword

Social Science

社会科学是以经验的方式理解各种社会现象的学科，包含经济学、历史学、政治学等。在TOEFL听力考试中，文章试图从经济、心理、历史层面去考查从古代社会到现代社会的各种社会问题。

经济学Economics/经营学Business Management 备考主题

美国大萧条/罗斯福新政/胡佛大坝/单体垄断与寡头垄断/各种经济理论

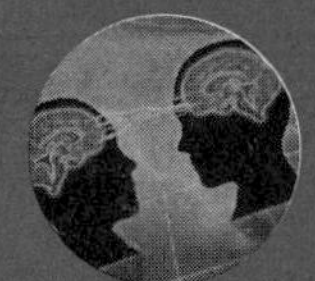

心理学Psychology 备考主题

让·皮亚杰的认知发展阶段理论/行为主义/约翰·杜威的教育理论/性格

历史学History 备考主题

古代文明：苏美尔、埃及的历法/中世纪的封建制度/古登堡的活字印刷术

经历了工业革命后的工业面貌变化/城市化及工业化对社会产生的影响

人类学Anthropology 备考主题

不同地质时代的人类进化/史前时期的生活方式/原始社会的生活面貌

CASE EXAMPLE

MP3 • 391

[1-6] Listen to part of a lecture in a business studies class.

| Volume | Help | OK | Next |

1. What is the lecture mainly about?
   Ⓐ Why companies originally developed
   Ⓑ The history of companies and common types
   Ⓒ Differences between corporations and companies
   Ⓓ The three most popular types of companies

2. Why does the professor mention the British East India Company?

Ⓐ To emphasize the global impact of companies

Ⓑ To note that companies contributed to Britain's colonial success

Ⓒ To give an example of a famous colonial company

Ⓓ To suggest that companies are ancient entities

3. What does the professor say about companies in today's world?

Ⓐ Tax issues are promoting changes in the organization of most companies.

Ⓑ The explosion of consumer products has led to the creation of more small companies.

Ⓒ Trends that began during the Industrial Revolution have largely ended.

Ⓓ The largest companies often acquire smaller companies.

4. The professor describes the differences between corporations and partnerships. Indicate whether each of the following is mentioned in the lecture as a characteristic of a corporation or a partnership. Click in the correct box for each phrase.

	Corporation	Partnership	Neither
Ⓐ Exists as a legal entity separate from its owners			
Ⓑ Prevents shareholders from losing their investments in the event of bankruptcy			
Ⓒ Does not make anyone financially responsible for its failure			
Ⓓ Allows its owners to save money on tax payments			

Listen again to part of the lecture. Then answer the question. MP3 • 392

5. What does the professor imply?

Ⓐ The reasons she mentioned compelled ancient businesspeople to form companies.

Ⓑ Modern scholars are not entirely sure why the first companies evolved the way they did.

Ⓒ Ancient India and Rome were relatively late in developing their first companies.

Ⓓ The concept of the company was simultaneously developed in India and Rome.

Listen again to part of the lecture. Then answer the question. MP3 • 393

6. What does the professor mean when she says this:

Ⓐ She thinks the concept is easy to understand.

Ⓑ She wants to expand on this definition later.

Ⓒ She wants the students to research more on the issues by themselves.

Ⓓ She does not think the issue is important.

SMART SOLUTION

note taking

Main Topic : The history of companies and the three types of modern companies

Early Co.
conduct business effectively (e.g. India & ancient Rome)

→

Colonial Co.
- similar to modern Co.
- permission from home government
- extracting resources and monopolizing trade (e.g. British East India company)

→

Modern Co. (after the Industrial Revolution)

corporation	partnership	limited liability Co.
- legally separate entities	- owners are fully responsible - tax benefits	- combination of corporation and partnership

CLUE FINDER 说话者在以年代顺序概括了公司的起源和演变而来的面貌之后，介绍了当今社会最具代表性的“股份公司”、“合资公司”以及“有限责任公司”。

The origin of companies

Professor (female)

I'd like to...to take a step back from our ongoing discussion of the global economy to give you a little background on something that's so, um, fundamental to us that it's...it's hard not to take it for granted. Q1 **I'm talking about the company. Where did companies come from...and why?**

...

The history of companies

First of all, it gave their business a life of its own. Even if the founders of the business died, the, uh, the company would live on. Also, it set out a fair and structured method for entrepreneurs to pool their resources in order to conduct their business more effectively.

Q5 **So, um...it's no wonder then that we see companies appearing well over 2,000 years ago—in India, ancient Rome of course... perhaps even before that.**

...

Companies in the colonial period

Moving forward...it wasn't really until the colonial period that we started seeing companies with a lot of the features we might recognize today. ...

Q1 从“**I'm talking about the company.**”这一句话可以听出文章的主题是有关“公司”的。但是因为这里只是概括性地提及了讲义文的主题，因此想要知道具体论述了公司的哪些层面就需要听完全部内容再进行总结。

第1题Main Idea题型

Ⓐ和Ⓓ是只涉及了讲义文一部分内容的典型错误选项。

Q5 如“**It's no wonder**（这并不奇怪）”加入了个人评价的部分很有可能被用来出题考查说话者话中隐含的意思。

第5题Inference题型

为了向人们介绍设立公司的理由，以2000年前的印度或古罗马为补充事例进行介绍，解释了公司出现的必然性。

Q2 **Think of the British East India Company...probably the most famous example of this type of business organization—and the most powerful.**

...

The trend of modern companies

OK, then...um, the rise of the modern company really took off after the Industrial Revolution, which, um...it made so many new technologies possible, and companies stepped in to deliver these countless new products to the public. Q3 **In recent history, we've seen a trend toward consolidation. That is, a powerful company will buy up other smaller companies and form a super-company...**

...

The most common types of modern companies

Q1 **What I do want to talk about quickly are the...the three most common types of companies in today's world...at least, in the U.S.** Um...often when we call an organization a "company," we're really talking about a "corporation." Q4 **The key feature of corporations is they exist independently of their founders, their employees, and their shareholders. They're legally defined as separate entities.** What does that mean? Well, everyone involved with the corporation enjoys something called limited liability. ... Q4 **But beyond that, no one is financially responsible for the corporation's failure.** Understand?

Now, contrast that with a partnership. In a partnership, the owner or owners are fully responsible for the company. ... Q4 **But, um, then partnerships also have some benefits that corporations lack...mainly dealing with the taxes they have to pay. In short, corporate profits are often taxed twice—once as income for the corporate entity, and again as income for the shareholders. General partnerships...their income's only taxed once.**

OK, very quickly...there're also limited liability companies, and these basically combine the good points of both corporations and partnerships. Um, owners have limited liability, but they also get the tax benefits enjoyed by partnerships. Q6 **That's a very simplified explanation, but I'm afraid it's all we have time for today.**

Q2 讲义文的重点部分转入殖民地时期的公司。这时，又举出了其他的例子。

第2题Organization题型

介绍殖民地时期公司的典型事例——著名的英国东印度公司。

Q3 在谈完殖民地时期的公司之后，接着开始论述现代公司。通过这些内容，可以看出说话者是在以时间的顺序说明公司面貌的变化，因此很可能会出现考查各时期特征的题目。

第3题Detail题型

Q4 说话者首先概括了公司的起源及其在各时代的特征，然后又介绍了当今所有公司最具代表性的三种类型。像这样出现了两个以上项目并对它们进行对比的时候，很可能会出现要求联系各项特征的问题。所以请记笔记，对相关的细节事项做整理。

第4题Connecting Contents题型

解此类题很重要的技巧是边听边关注出现对比的部分（例如：股份公司与合资公司股东或职员是否担责、缴纳税金是否有优惠等）。

Q6 请留意讲义文结尾部分的口语性表达。“I'm afraid ...”这一口语表达的是说话者没有办法，感到很可惜的感情。由此可以看出她希望下节课再就“**limited liability companies**”进行进一步说明的意图。

第6题Function题型

Answer 1 Ⓑ 2 Ⓒ 3 Ⓓ 4 Corporation → Ⓐ, Ⓒ / Partnership → Ⓓ / Neither → Ⓑ 5 Ⓐ 6 Ⓑ

PRACTICE TEST

LECTURE  **passage 1. [1-6] Listen to part of a talk in a psychology class.**

MP3 • 394

Inhibition

note taking

1. What is the talk mainly about?

Ⓐ A psychological phenomenon that regulates human behavior

Ⓑ Different impulse-control disorders studied by psychologists

Ⓒ A landmark experiment that proved a controversial theory

Ⓓ The ways in which culture affects self-control in humans

2. How does the professor introduce his description of self-control?
Ⓐ By giving details about the history of its study
Ⓑ By suggesting that it has been observed in many animals
Ⓒ By elaborating on a commonplace experience as an example
Ⓓ By reminding students of a situation that took place in the classroom

3. What are two key findings of Walter Mischel's marshmallow experiment mentioned in the lecture? Click on 2 answers.
Ⓐ Self-control is related to performance on intelligence tests.
Ⓑ Pigeons demonstrate less self-control than humans do.
Ⓒ There are variations in people's ability to control their actions.
Ⓓ Society values self-control over impulsiveness.

4. In the lecture, the professor describes some functions of social inhibition in humans. Indicate whether each of the following is a function of social inhibition. Click in the correct box for each phrase.

	YES	NO
Ⓐ Enhances our natural survival instincts		
Ⓑ Increases our chances of experiencing success in life		
Ⓒ Allows us to interact with others in a positive way		
Ⓓ Assists us in telling the difference between right and wrong		
Ⓔ Helps us create plans and organize our thoughts		

5. What does the professor imply about obsessive gambling and attention-deficit/hyperactivity disorders?
Ⓐ They are potential results of a lack of inhibition.
Ⓑ They can be cured through psychological treatment.
Ⓒ They are triggered by traumatic childhood events.
Ⓓ They are caused by other impulse-control disorders.

Listen again to part of the talk. Then answer the question. MP3 • 395

6. Why does the professor say this:
Ⓐ To support a point he just made
Ⓑ To imply that the topic is already a familiar one
Ⓒ To question the conclusion drawn by the man
Ⓓ To correct a mistake the man made

PRACTICE TEST

LECTURE  **passage 2. [1-6] Listen to part of a talk in a history class.**

MP3•396

1. What is the talk mainly about?

   Ⓐ The inventions of two ancient civilizations

   Ⓑ The historical development of glass production

   Ⓒ Uses of crafts in the ancient world

   Ⓓ Two breakthroughs in glass manufacturing

2. Why does the professor mention glazes on ceramics?

Ⓐ To give an example of a craft that preceded glassmaking

Ⓑ To name the first evidence of manmade glass

Ⓒ To explain why there are few early examples of glass to study

Ⓓ To introduce the components that make up glass

3. What does the professor say about decorative glass beads dating to 2500 BC?

Ⓐ They were carved out of volcanically produced glass.

Ⓑ They are the first true examples of synthetic glass.

Ⓒ They predate ceramic pottery in Europe.

Ⓓ They have not been found in Egypt or Mesopotamia.

4. Indicate whether each of the following is mentioned in the lecture as a factor that makes it difficult to determine where glassmaking originated. Click in the correct box for each phrase.

	YES	NO
Ⓐ Mesopotamia and Egypt were closely linked by trade.		
Ⓑ Historians have found early glass in two different places.		
Ⓒ Glassmaking facilities have been found in Egypt but not Mesopotamia.		
Ⓓ Ancient glass ornaments have not been adequately preserved.		
Ⓔ Volcanic glass was available long before people learned to produce it themselves.		

5. What does the professor imply about the revolution that made glass a commonplace product?

Ⓐ It was an important step toward the larger Industrial Revolution.

Ⓑ It was facilitated by cultural exchange between Europe and the Middle East.

Ⓒ It was prompted by an increase in the influence of religion in European society.

Ⓓ It was the result of new techniques that made glassmaking more efficient.

DAY 19

Listen again to part of the talk. Then answer the question. MP3•397

6. Why does the professor say this:

Ⓐ To find out if other students are wondering the same thing

Ⓑ To suggest that the history of glass has not been thoroughly studied

Ⓒ To indicate that no one has determined this fact for certain

Ⓓ To encourage the students to research the issue on their own

PRACTICE TEST

LECTURE  **passage 3. [1-6] Listen to part of a lecture in a politics class.**

MP3 • 398

Bureaucracy

note taking

1. What is the lecture mainly about?

   Ⓐ Problems and dangers associated with bureaucracies

   Ⓑ The history and features of bureaucracies

   Ⓒ Popular misconceptions about bureaucracies today

   Ⓓ The development of the world's earliest bureaucracies

2. Why does the professor mention the military?

Ⓐ To identify the origin of the term "bureaucracy"

Ⓑ To contrast its purpose with that of other bureaucracies

Ⓒ To illustrate the concept of bureaucratic organization

Ⓓ To explain why bureaucracies are widely criticized

3. What are two characteristics of bureaucracies according to the scholar Max Weber? Click on 2 answers.

Ⓐ Their members are chosen based on written referrals.

Ⓑ They are run by employees who receive payment for their work.

Ⓒ Power is held by specific individual members.

Ⓓ Their operations proceed according to documented regulations.

4. In the lecture, the professor describes the functions of historical bureaucracies in ancient Sumer and China's Qin Dynasty. Match each function to the correct civilization. One choice will not be used. Click in the correct box for each phrase.

	Ancient Sumer	Qin Dynasty
Ⓐ Establishing an entrance examination system for officials		
Ⓑ Promoting the development of written language		
Ⓒ Setting up a system of criminal punishments		
Ⓓ Controlling corruption in government agencies		
Ⓔ Facilitating tax collection		

Listen again to part of the lecture. Then answer the question.  MP3·399

5. Why does the professor say this:

Ⓐ To identify a common bias associated with a term

Ⓑ To contrast the United States with other countries

Ⓒ To offer his own opinion about bureaucracies

Ⓓ To cast doubt on a popular idea

Listen again to part of the lecture. Then answer the question. MP3·400

6. What does the professor mean when he says this:

Ⓐ He thinks the concept is unimportant to the lecture topic.

Ⓑ He wants the students to pay close attention to the next point.

Ⓒ He does not think he has to explain the term.

Ⓓ He thinks it is not the right time to explain the word.

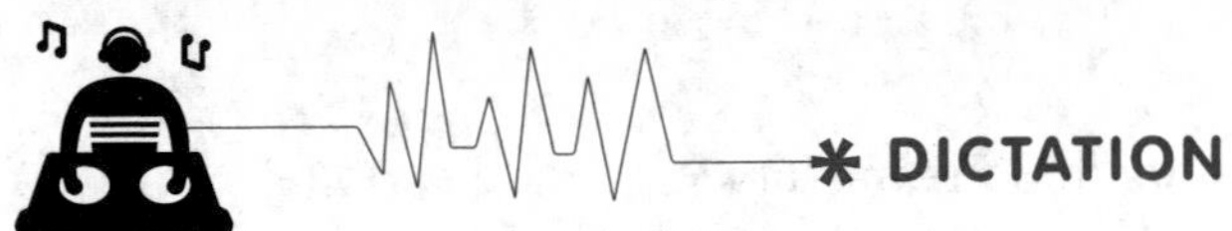

✱ DICTATION

MP3•401 **Listen to part of the history lecture again and fill in the blanks.**

［省略］

Professor: 1) ______ ______ ______ ______ ______ ______ we have comes in the form of pottery glaze...the stuff added to the outside of ceramic pottery that 2) ______ ______ ______ ______ ______. We're talking as early as 5000 BC here.

Student B: Are glazes considered to be glass? The two things sound pretty different to me.

Professor: Yes, well, that's very true. But what the glazes represent is the ability to create glass, because the ingredients are pretty much the same. There's the silica first of all—sand, in other words. Then to that you add 3) ______ ______ ______ ______ ______ ______ ______ and add strength and color.

So, as I was about to say, the first true human-made glass appeared around 2500 BC 4) ______ ______ ______ ______ ______ ______. The problem for historians, though, is they're found in both Egypt and Mesopotamia...and no one knows for sure where they appeared first.

For the next 1,500 years, development in glassmaking in both of these places seems to 5) ______ ______ ______ ______ ______. In 1500 BC, glass crafters figured out how to make hollow containers out of glass. They did this 6) ______ ______ ______ ______ ______ ______ ______ ______, then either dipping this core into melted glass...uh, or spreading the liquid glass over the core with a special tool. Once the glass cooled, the clay core would be removed. Now...this often worked better in theory than reality. A lot of times, it was impossible to remove the core completely, 7) ______ ______ ______ ______ ______ ______ ______ ______ ______ ______. So, as I was saying earlier, the first glass looked a lot different from the stuff we're used to.

But back to the big debate. We're just not sure 8) ______ ______ ______ ______ ______ happened in Egypt or Mesopotamia.

Student B: Why is it so hard to tell?

Professor: Well, these civilizations were very close to one another, and they traded with each other all the time. So, for example, if Mesopotamian glassmakers figured out 9) ______ ______ ______ ______ ______ ______, this knowledge would've been very quickly transported to Egypt, 10) ______ ______ ______.

［省略］

答案参见ANSWER BOOK P504

 MP3·402 **Listen to part of the politics lecture again and fill in the blanks.**

[省略]

Professor: Bureaucracy is simply the formal control structure found in large organizations ...like the military, as I mentioned, and also in organizations like governments, corporations, schools...that kind of thing. In a bureaucracy, there's 1)______ ______ ______ ______ ______ that control how just about all the procedures within the organization are carried out. Bureaucracy also 2)______ ______ ______ ______ ______ ______ ______ ______ ______ ______ to different, um, offices or groups within the organization. The, um, the point of bureaucracy is to, to have everything organized in the most efficient way possible.

One of the most famous scholars of bureaucracy, Max Weber...he identified certain characteristics that, um, that define a bureaucracy. Here they are: First, it has written rules that help 3)______ ______ ______ ______ ______ ______ ______. Second, there's a clear hierarchy—you know what I mean by "hierarchy," right? Good. Third, power in the organization is associated with certain positions and offices, not the individuals themselves. Fourth, new employees are hired 4)______ ______ ______ ______ ______ ______ ______ on an entrance examination. Fifth, record keeping and communication within the organization must be 5)______ ______ ______. And finally...um, staff within the organization must be paid for their work.

OK, so now you have a basic idea of what bureaucracy is, and some of its features. Let's move on and talk a little bit about 6)______ ______ ______ ______. Well... the term itself came from the word "bureau," which, um, during the 18th century, was used in Western Europe to mean an office. The second half of the term, the "cracy" part, comes from the Greek "kratos," um, which means something like "power" or "rule." Now, although the concept of bureaucracy has changed over time, the basic idea has been around for quite a while. In fact, its development seems to be 7)______ ______ ______ ______ ______ ______ ______. One of the earliest examples of, um, of bureaucracy can be found back in ancient Sumer, where a bureaucracy made up of priests developed to deal with, well, property-related issues and to collect taxes. That sort of thing. Of course, none of this would've been possible without written records...and the Sumerians are 8)______ ______ ______ ______ ______ ______ ______ ______ ______. They used picture-like characters known as cuneiforms, which they inscribed on, uh, on clay tablets to produce the official written records for their early bureaucracy.

[省略]

答案参见ANSWER BOOK P506

smart source

Economics 经济学 & Business Management 管理学

1 The Great Depression 大萧条

第一次世界大战之后，美国经济从表面上看呈现出一派繁荣景象，但是实际上却正由于生产过剩overproduction与大量失业unemployment而处于危险的脆弱状态。在这样的环境中，1929年10月24日，纽约市华尔街上的“纽约证券交易所New York Stock Exchange”发生股价暴跌stock market crash，物价随之立即暴涨inflation，企业纷纷破产bankruptcy，失业增加，最终导致国家经济活动几乎停滞。这严重地打击了工业部门，不仅导致了技术发展的暂时性退步，还对欧洲乃至世界造成了非常恶劣的影响。

●罗斯福新政The New Deal：指罗斯福总统(Franklin Delano Roosevelt)为带领美国走出经济大萧条the Great Depression所提出的政策，又称为3R(Relief, Recovery, Reform)政策。政府积极地介入intervention市场，试图通过管制垄断monopoly企业，调整农产品的过度生产等方式引导经济恢复，并实施了如田纳西河流域开发、胡佛大坝Hoover Dam建设等大规模公共设施建设public work，创造就业机会create jobs并开拓其他地域。

●灰盆地区Dust Bowl：20世纪30年代，在美国中南部的俄克拉荷马州、德克萨斯州、堪萨斯州以及新墨西哥州地区，人们只要开垦出大型农场，就会无一例外地遭遇土壤侵蚀erosion、干旱drought以及沙尘暴dust storm侵害，从而导致大规模损失的事件，它是经济大萧条的余波，这一词汇也用以指那一时期。很多人因此而移居加利福尼亚地区，加利福尼亚州也以此为契机在政治及经济方面得到了很大发展。

2 Monopoly and Oligopoly 单体垄断与寡头垄断

指企业或企业经营者作为市场支配者，在特定市场中的占有率过高或基本没有竞争者competitor的状况。判断是否存在垄断或寡头经济，可以综合考虑市场占有率market share的多少、是否存在进入市场的壁垒及其程度、竞争企业的相对规模等因素。

●单体垄断monopoly：指在市场中，个人或企业对一定的产品或服务拥有排他性的权限。垄断性企业不为消费者考虑，而是为了实现自身利润的最大化maximize profit给产品或服务定价。这种行为有损公平竞争的原则fair competition，成为市场问题。

●寡头垄断oligopoly：与单体垄断形态相似，指由少数的供应方供应产品的状况。通常，为数不多的几家巨型企业supercompany控制着绝大部分的商品供给，他们通过价格联盟collusion、企业联合cartel以及其他各种协议谋求共存。典型的例子有手机市场、石油市场、家电及汽车市场等。

3 Moratorium and Default 延期偿付与违约

延期偿付moratorium指一个国家因为战争、自然灾害natural disaster或经济萧条等原因无法顺利地偿还从外国借来的贷款loan，所以由政府出面延长还款期限的情况。而违约default指的是尽管已经到了偿还期限，但是无法还款的无偿付能力状态insolvency。通常，政府如果预计到可能产生违约，就会对外宣称延期偿付，重新调整偿还贷款的期限。但即使支付时间得以推迟，这种做法还是会对国家的国际信誉有所损害，使国家在对外贸易方面蒙受损失。

●重新约定rescheduling：指为了提高后期偿还债务redemption of a debt的可能性，债务国与外国的债权金融机构进行商议，以豁免债务或延长还款期等债务调整过程。

4 Green Marketing 绿色经营

过去，企业销售商品的战略重点仅仅是满足顾客的要求或需要。但是现在与此不同，出现了绿色经营，它指的是提倡社会生态学均衡Social-ecological Balance与环境安全性environmentally safety的企业市场活动。典型例子有生产磁带等化学产品的3M公司，它通过3P(Pollution, Prevention, Pays)项目发起了防止公害运动。3M公司认识到防治环境污染最终是与收益相关的，因此为了生产出环境友好型的eco-friendly产品，该公司从设计环节开始付出了很多努力，最终成功生产出降低了一半以上的环境污染度的产品。此外，实施绿色经营的典范还有世界性快餐企业麦当劳。它引入了运用3R(Reduce, Recycle, Reuse)原理的程序，运作各项活动，实施对大量不同包装与容器的再利用。

Psychology 心理学

5 The theory of cognitive development 认知发展阶段论

认知cognition指把从外部获取的信息通过符号化等各种方法变形处理之后储存在记忆中，之后再引出使用的过程。瑞士心理学家让・皮亚杰Jean Piaget认为人要经过四个认知发展阶段达到理智上的成熟。根据他的理论，这四个阶段分别为感觉运动阶段sensory-motor period、前运算阶段preoperational period、具体运算阶段concrete operations period以及形式运算阶段formal operations period。

●感觉运动阶段sensory-motor period：从出生到2岁。这一阶段的儿童主要依靠自己的肌肉动作和感觉学习事物，开始模仿或记忆等思考活动，行为从单纯的反射行为渐渐过渡到有目的性的行为。

●前运算阶段preoperational period：2～7岁。这一时期的幼儿语言能力逐渐发达，能以表象进行思维。思考及语言表达的自我思想是这一阶段的突出特点。

●具体运算阶段concrete operations period：7～11岁，在这一阶段，儿童可以有逻辑地解决具体问题，排列并分类处理各种信息。

●形式运算阶段formal operations period：自11岁开始，到这一阶段，个体能进行形式命题思维，能够有逻辑地解决抽象性问题、复杂的语言命题以及假说性质的问题，思考方式也变得有科学性。

6 Attachment 依附

依附是由英国儿童精神分析师J.M.波尔比定义的术语，它指的是为了维持与爱恋对象的关系而做出的行为。母亲和孩子之间相互给予并接受无限的爱意affection，他们是依附关系的典型。哺乳类或鸟类动物从出生之时开始就会本能地对母亲产生依恋，并同时对陌生对象抱有恐惧。而人类的婴儿在出生6个月左右就会对特定人物产生依附情绪，并对未知事物产生茫然的恐惧。这时，婴儿如果经历了巨大的恐惧或者不安，长大以后就有可能诱发情绪障碍emotional disorder。在托福听力真题中，提到过让照顾孩子的人外出或离开，把孩子独自留下后观察孩子出现的反应的实验。说话者通过这个实验介绍了positive attachment与negative attachment两种类型的依附情绪，以及依附对儿童精神成长产生的影响。

7 Grice's Cooperative Principle(=Gricean Maxims) 格赖斯会话合作原则（=格赖斯准则）

语言哲学家保罗·格赖斯定义的准则，指双方要让对话自然地进行，必须遵循的四项前提。但是在实际会话情境中，通常认为通过舍弃某一原则，或着重使用某一原则的方法可以更好地传达意思，使会话更有效。

●质量原则Maxim of Quality：保证会话内容是真实可靠的信息。

●数量原则Maxim of Quantity：保证会话中提供的信息量对于目前对话的目标充分但不多余。

●关联原则Maxim of Relation：对话中提供的信息围绕目的，紧扣主题。

●方式原则Maxim of Manner：使用清晰并不会引起歧义的表达，明白易懂、逻辑性地表达。

History 历史

8 Medieval Feudalism 中世纪的封建制度

指从9世纪到13～14世纪西欧的统治体制。从政治角度看，领主lord分封土地——即采邑fief给封臣vassal，作为回报，封臣保护领主，并向他宣誓效忠fealty，这是一种提供军事力量military service的契约contract关系。从经济角度看，领主和农民peasant之间以土地land为媒介收取或缴纳封建税收feudal dues，他们处于一种“支配-从属”形态的生产体制之中。通常，封建制度因为极端束缚restriction与剥削exploitation农民，被认为是必须打破的旧制度（法国的旧体制Ancien Régime）。但是，也有积极的观点认为，因为这种制度是以领主与封臣之间相辅相成的complimentary关系为基础建立的，所以也对社会的发展做出了一定贡献。

9 Egyptian Calendar 埃及历法

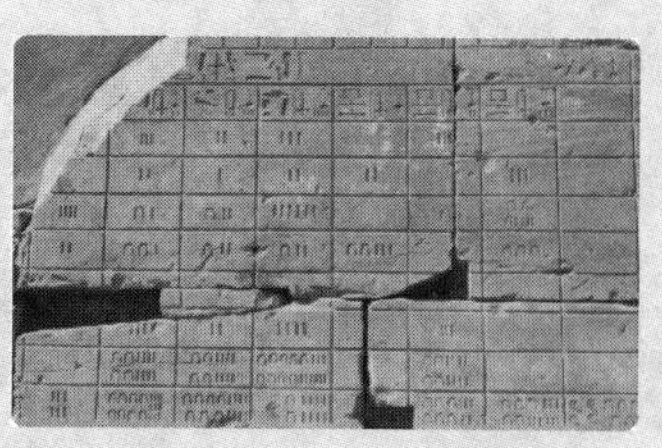

古代埃及人观察到尼罗河会十分有规律性地泛滥，他们就利用这一点很早就创造出了自己的历法。天空中最亮的恒星fixed star——天狼星Sirius在天亮之前会从东边升起，尼罗河通常会从这时开始泛滥。埃及人以此为基础，计算calculation出一年的时间为365.25天，即以天狼星偕日升为一年的开始，再加上12个30天的月份及年底额外的5天。但是，这种历法由于是以恒星为基准计算的，与太阳历solar calendar相比缺少闰日leap day。至今在埃及和埃塞俄比亚的部分埃及土著教会中仍在使用这种历法。

10 Sumer 苏美尔

古代地区名，相当于今天底格里斯河与幼发拉底河交汇的伊拉克地区，是公元前3000年世界最早文明civilization的诞生地。苏美尔人发明了一种象形文字pictograph，后来这种文字发展为楔形文字cuneiform。他们使用12进制duodecimal system与阴历lunar calendar，并制定出了称为“苏美尔法”的法典。此外，还有很多的遗物relic可以显示出苏美尔人高超的技术水平和优秀的艺术水准。例如世界上最早的叙事史诗epic《吉尔伽美什史诗Epic of Gilgamesh》就是他们优秀文学艺术造诣的代表。苏美尔地区不生产除黏土以外的其他资源resource，因此完全依靠贸易获取矿石与贵金属precious metal。他们的贸易trade领域东至印度河流域，西至安纳托利亚、叙利亚与埃及，也正是这样的远途贸易推动了苏美尔文明Sumerian culture传播spread over至东方各国。苏美尔文明在公元前2000年左右达到鼎盛时期renaissance，但是之后因为气候干燥arid，土壤盐分含量salinity上升，农业agriculture的根基被破坏而开始走向衰退。

11 Gutenberg's movable type printing 古登堡活字印刷术

公元7～8世纪左右，在中国诞生了于木板上镌刻文字的木板印刷术woodblock printing。木板印刷术传入欧洲，并一直被使用到14世纪。但是，木板印刷的模板存在使用寿命短、文字模糊、体积大等缺点drawback，并不适合inappropriate欧洲柔软的纸质。当时，欧洲普通群众的公民citizenship意识正处于成长阶段，他们对文化知识的渴求thirst for knowledge越来越强烈，因此对出版物publication的需求量demand也很大。在这样的情况下，德国的宝石加工师古登堡(Johannes Gutenberg)在美因兹开设了一家印刷厂，正式开始使用金属活字印刷movable metal type printing技术。这种更为可靠且标准化standardized的印刷技术革新revolutionize了书籍的制作book-making过程，并且使得书籍的大量生产mass production成为了可能，同时它也被看做是推动宗教改革the Protestant Reformation与文艺复兴the Renaissance的原动力。

12 Industrial Revolution 工业革命

工业革命指从1760年开始，于1840年左右结束的一场生产技术革新innovation，以及由此引起的社会、经济变化。很早以前，英国就开始进行活跃的海外贸易overseas trade与商业活动，并由此积累accumulation了充足的资本capital，用以发展技术。除此之外，英国还从海外殖民地colony获取丰富的abundant资源和燃料，并且通过公有土地私有化的“圈地运动”迫使农民离开了农村，进入城市，得到了充足的劳动力labor force。当时，市场对棉纺织品cotton fabrics的需要剧增，借助机器的发明及技术的革新，纺织业自然而然地得到了发展。以此为开端，机器产业machine industry、制铁业iron industry以及煤炭产业也得到了快速的发展。詹姆斯·瓦特(James Watt)发明的蒸汽机steam engine给交通及运输方式transportation带来了革新，这也激发了工业的进一步发展。之后，源于英国的工业革命不仅对欧洲，甚至对整个世界都产生了深远的影响，并最终引发了19世纪末美国与德国的第二次产业革命，使钢铁、化学、汽车及电气产业都得到了极大的发展。

Anthropology 人类学

13 Human evolution 人类的进化

对于人类的进化，学界存在着许多错综复杂的观点与主张。通常认为在新生代Pleistocene Epoch的第四期—洪积世，会使用工具并直立行走walk erect的人类第一次出现。洪积世经历了四次交替的冰河期glacial age与间冰期interglacial epoch，气候和动植物的种类已经演变为与今天相似的形态。这一时期出现的人类mankind根据出现时期的不同分为南猿Australopithecus、爪哇猿人Java man与北京人Peking man、尼安德特人Neanderthal man以及智人Homo sapiens。据推测，被认为是最原始的primitive人类的南猿生活在距今约200或100万年前，而爪哇猿人与北京人生活在距今约40~50万年前的第二间冰期，尼安德特人则生活在第三到第四间冰期初期。而与今天的人类最为相似的智人出现于洪积世的最后一个冰河期。

14 Prehistory 史前时期

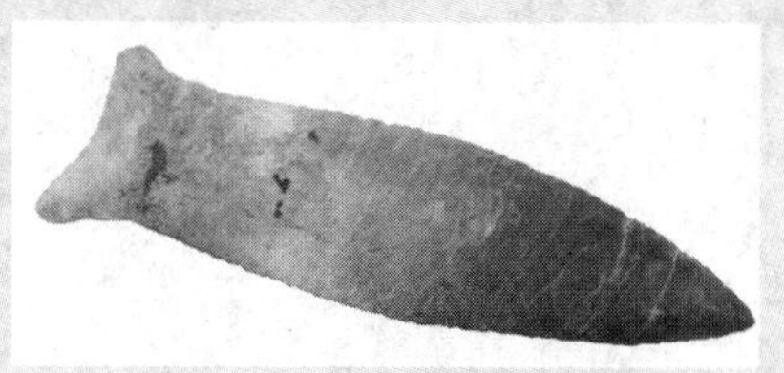

史前时期prehistory指不存在文献史料记载的人类原始时代primitive times。通常，从考古学角度来看，人类历史是按照“旧石器时代Paleolithic era→新石器时代Neolithic era→青铜器时代Bronze Age→铁器时代Iron Age”的顺序发展演变的。由于在不同的地区，文献出现的时期不同，文化或技术的发展形式也不一样，我们很难明确地划分出史前时期。但是，学界通常都一致同意至少把首次出现打制石器工具knapped stone tool的旧石器时代与农耕agriculture文化开始的新时期时代看做史前时期。如果观察旧石器时代的社会面貌，你就会发现，当时人们主要以群居移动生活为主，社会平等egalitarian society，不存在阶级hierarchy。这一时期，人类尚未开始农业耕作，主要依靠狩猎hunting、捕鱼fishing以及采集gathering/foraging生存，并在搭建于洞穴或江边的窝棚mud hut中生活。从新石器时代起，人类开始使用以磨制石器sharpened stone与骨头制成的工具。尤其是随着农耕文化与定居生活的开始，人类生活的面貌也发生了巨大改变。后来就把这一时期称为“新石器革命Neolithic Revolution”。随着农业生产的开始，同一血统的人们聚居在一起，形成了氏族tribe与部落，它是之后社会与国家的起源origin。

Theme Vocab

MP3・403

Economics经济学&Business Management管理学

stock market crash 股价暴跌
public work 公共事业
create jobs 创造就业岗位
monopoly单体垄断/**oligopoly**寡头垄断
collusion 共谋/**cartel** 企业联合
insolvency 无力偿还

Psychology 心理学

cognition 认知
sensory 感觉的
attachment 依附

History 历史

feudalism封建制度
cuneiform 楔形文字
duodecimal system 十二进制
movable type printing 活字印刷术
woodblock printing 木板印刷术
mass production 大量生产
The Protestant Reformation 宗教改革
accumulate capital 资本积累
glacial age 冰河期
interglacial epoch 间冰期
Paleolithic era 旧石器时代
Neolithic era 新石器时代

DAY20

America

- CASE EXAMPLE - 例题
- SMART SOLUTION - 主题补充专题
- PRACTICE TEST - 练习
- DICTATION - 听写
- SMART SOURCE - 主题资料库

speed keyword

America

作为考查学生在美国大学完成学业能力的考试，TOEFL考试经常把与美洲大陆相关的内容当作考试素材。America是一个范围广泛的概念，它不仅指现代美国，通常还包括称为印第安人的美洲原住民，直至拉丁美洲大陆的古代文明。在TOEFL考试中，留意这一点，并将美国分为独立战争前与独立战争后来看，把握美洲大陆的历史潮流尤为重要。不仅如此，备考时，从文化、艺术及工业的角度对核心的变化进行一些整理也十分有益。

美国史US History 备考主题

英国殖民地时期/独立初期的美国：独立宣言、托马斯·杰弗逊总统和路易斯·克拉克探险/西部开拓：（靠近未开发地带的）边远地区、淘金热/南北战争与林肯总统/南北战争后跨大陆铁路建设/经济萧条：罗斯福总统与新政，胡佛坝的建设

美洲原住民Native American 备考主题

北美洲最初的文化——古代克洛维斯文化/普魏布勒族/纳瓦伙族印第安人

拉丁美洲Latin America 备考主题

古代玛雅文明/秘鲁的纳斯卡文化

CASE EXAMPLE

MP3・408

[1-6] Listen to part of a talk in an American history class.

| Volume | Help | OK | Next |

1. What is the talk mainly about?

   Ⓐ The influence Jefferson had on American academia

   Ⓑ The role Jefferson played in founding the United States

   Ⓒ Jefferson's experiences as an ambassador in France

   Ⓓ Jefferson's achievements as an architect

2. Indicate whether each of the following is mentioned in the lecture as a characteristic of neo-classicism. Click in the correct box for each phrase.

	YES	NO
Ⓐ Could be seen in the architecture of France		
Ⓑ Was inspired by themes from ancient Rome		
Ⓒ Combined features from European and Asian traditions		
Ⓓ Was born of the ideals of the emerging United States		
Ⓔ Was intended to be relevant for modern times		

3. What does the professor say about the architecture of the University of Virginia campus?

Ⓐ They were designed to evoke the grandeur of Greek and Roman history.
Ⓑ They were intended to stimulate discussion and learning.
Ⓒ They were predominantly French in design.
Ⓓ They were modeled after important buildings in Washington D.C.

4. Why does the professor mention the architecture of U.S. federal buildings?

Ⓐ To illustrate the significance of the neo-classical ideals she mentioned earlier
Ⓑ To suggest that Jefferson's politics affected his approach to architecture
Ⓒ To list some lesser known examples of Jefferson's work
Ⓓ To explain the importance of the University of Virginia in American architecture

Listen again to part of the talk. Then answer the question.  MP3 • 409

5. Why does the professor say this:

Ⓐ To initiate a discussion of a specific one of Jefferson's designs
Ⓑ To indicate that she is not ready to discuss an important point yet
Ⓒ To suggest that her previous comment is not relevant to the lecture
Ⓓ To let the students know what to expect for next class

Listen again to part of the talk. Then answer the question. MP3 • 410

6. What does the professor mean when she says this:

Ⓐ She wants the students to deduce how Jefferson studied architecture.
Ⓑ She thinks the students should know more about the topic than they seem to.
Ⓒ She wants the students to provide a definition of "classical architecture."
Ⓓ She thinks some of the students in the class have studied classical architecture.

SMART SOLUTION

note taking

Main Topic : Thomas Jefferson's architectural achievements

1) background	2) his architectural works	3) influences
- mostly self-taught (by books) - study classical arch. in France *neo-classicism(reinterpret ideals of ancient Greek & Rome)	- e.g. campus of the Univ. of Virginia → synthesize various influences into neo-classical arrangement *"academical village"	- huge impact → determine the direction of American design e.g. govt. bldg. & univ. campus → feature neo-classical elements

CLUE FINDER 这篇讲义文介绍了美国著名政治家、第3任总统托马斯・杰弗逊在建筑方面的成就。重点就三个方面进行了介绍，分别是影响他的新古典主义、由他设计的建筑物以及对美国建筑史的意义。

Professor (female) Well, class. I think we did a pretty good job last time summing up the political achievements of Thomas Jefferson. Who wants to list some of those, just to refresh our memories?

...

Thomas Jefferson as an architect

Professor Very good. And don't forget his influential views on the philosophy known as republicanism. Q1 **But today I want to shift our focus slightly. Because...it's obvious Jefferson had a profound impact on America as a politician. But, you see, he was also a philosopher—a thinker...and one of the subjects he contributed greatly to was architecture.** In fact, one of his designs has been recognized by the American Institute of Architects as being the country's most significant architectural achievement. Q5 **But I'll get to that in a second.**

...

Background

... He was also able to study classical architecture firsthand, and you all should be able to tell me when that was. Q6 **Anybody?**

Student B (male) Um...he...went to France, right? As the U.S. ambassador? That was in the 1780s, I think. Maybe he got to

Q1 "today I want to shift our focus slightly（今天，让我们稍微转移一下我们的关注点）"是介绍讲义文主题的标志性语句。尤其是通过这种表达，可以推测出说话者将要从一个和当今不同的角度论述问题。

第1题Main Idea类型问题

美国第3任总统托马斯・杰弗逊通常是以政治家的身份闻名于世的，但是这篇文章却从全新的角度，介绍了作为建筑家的托马斯・杰弗逊以及他对美国建筑产生的影响。

Q5 请注意讨论展开的脉络以及标志性的语句。"**I'll get to that in a second**（我们稍后就来谈谈那些）"这一表达显示说话者将要暂停现在讨论的内容，将话题转向另一内容。因此，可以推测出下面要介绍的内容可能是建筑学的成就有关的。

第5题Function类型问题

在介绍托马斯・杰弗逊在建筑学方面的成就之前，先介绍他的建筑风格等背景知识。

study some of the architecture over in Europe.

His architectural works

Professor Right...that's exactly what I meant. As we discussed, Jefferson was American ambassador to France from 1785 to '89. Q2 **So some of the architectural styles he read about—um, much of which belonged to the school of neo-classicism—a lot of that type of architecture was on display in Paris and other parts of France. Do you all know what neo-classicism refers to?**

Student A (male) **It's based on, um, Roman ideals, isn't it? Styles and, and ideals that were popular in ancient Rome?**

Professor **Yeah, pretty much. "Ideals" is a good word. Neo-classicism emphasizes the ideals of the classical world... ancient Greece and Rome, but it doesn't just seek to copy those ideals. Proponents of neo-classicism wanted to take them and reinterpret them for modern times.** That's something Jefferson was very interested in.

...

Professor Yes, they sure are. I mentioned just a minute ago that one of his works has been called the most significant architectural achievement in America, remember? And that would be the central campus of the University of Virginia, a school which Jefferson actually founded.

...

Professor ... Jefferson referred to this campus as his "academical village," where residents could devote themselves to the pursuit of knowledge. Q3 **All the diverse styles he included in the buildings...they were meant to inspire debate and encourage academic investigation.**

...

The influence of his works

Professor Q4 **Because it really determined the direction of American design. That's why most government buildings in the U.S., from town halls to courthouses to the federal buildings in Washington...as well as college campuses everywhere—they all feature this strikingly neo-classical style.**

...

Q6 教授是以提问的方式推动教学进行的，请留心。
第6题Function题型
教授向学生确认他们是否有人知道托马斯·杰弗逊直接接触建筑学的时间，并藉此希望有学生可以谈一谈托马斯·杰弗逊接触建筑学的来龙去脉。

Q2 杰弗逊的建筑设计极大地受到neo-classicism（新古典主义）的影响，很可能会出题考查与此主题相关的事项。
第2题Connecting Contents题型
〈文章中出现的neo-classiciam的特征〉
1) was on display in Paris and other parts of France
2) emphasizes the ideals of the classical world such as ancient Greece and Rome
3) reinterpreted ancient ideals for modern times

Q3 杰弗逊设计过弗吉尼亚大学校园里的长椅，说话者正以此为例对他的设计加以说明。听力考试中不会出现考查太过于细节化的事项，因此同试图记住所有建筑的配置相比，更应该边听边关注杰弗逊设计的最终目的。
第3题Detail题型

Q4 说话者在此处举出了一个例子，详细介绍了杰弗逊设计的建筑风格。
第4题Organization题型
说话者提到美国大多数行政建筑都是新古典主义风格，以此为例说明了杰弗逊的建筑设计决定了美国建筑史上的一种潮流。

Answer 1 Ⓓ 2 YES → Ⓐ, Ⓑ, Ⓔ / NO → Ⓒ, Ⓓ 3 Ⓑ 4 Ⓓ 5 Ⓑ 6 Ⓐ

CONVERSATION MP3·411 **passage 1. [1-5] Listen to part of a conversation between a student and a librarian.**

note taking

1. What does the man need from the library?

Ⓐ A list of academic journals kept by the library

Ⓑ Permission to access the library's journal database

Ⓒ Advice on how to check out journals

Ⓓ Research resources for a major assignment

2. According to the woman, what are two benefits of having digital journals instead of physical ones? Click on 2 answers.

Ⓐ Digital journals contain the most up-to-date articles.

Ⓑ It is easier to access complete articles in digital journals.

Ⓒ Digital journals do not take up as much space in the library.

Ⓓ It does not cost the library anything to obtain digital journals.

3. What topic will the man's thesis address?

Ⓐ Recent advancements in the American education system

Ⓑ Characteristics of research journals in the digital age

Ⓒ The decisions of U.S. courts in the 1960s and '70s

Ⓓ Freedom of expression for American minority groups

Listen again to part of the conversation. Then answer the question. 

4. Why does the woman say this:

Ⓐ To suggest that the man does not need to visit the JSTOR site

Ⓑ To indicate that the man does not need to pay for access

Ⓒ To deny the man's request to use the online site

Ⓓ To explain that the man is not eligible for the site

Listen again to part of the conversation. Then answer the question. 

5. What can be inferred about the man?

Ⓐ He is confused about the process described by the woman.

Ⓑ He does not feel confident about his computer skills.

Ⓒ He suspects that the woman's instructions are incorrect.

Ⓓ He is not sure how to access the library website.

LECTURE  **passage 2. [1-6] Listen to part of a lecture in an American art class.**
MP3 • 414

Nazca

note taking

1. Which aspect of the Nazca does the professor mainly discuss?
   Ⓐ The characteristics of the ceramic art they created
   Ⓑ Their relationship to the Inca and other peoples of the Andes
   Ⓒ The influence of their iconography on their pottery designs
   Ⓓ Some of the central themes found in their art

2. Why does the professor mention the Nazca lines?

Ⓐ To introduce certain concepts present in all Nazca art

Ⓑ To give background information about the Nazca's environment

Ⓒ To explain what caused the Nazca civilization to disappear

Ⓓ To suggest why students may have heard of the Nazca culture

3. What does the professor say about the pictures adorning Nazca pottery?

Ⓐ They were created with solid colors.

Ⓑ They were used in place of a written language.

Ⓒ They remained largely unchanged over the centuries.

Ⓓ They were different than those seen in the Nazca lines.

4. In the lecture, the professor describes the features of Nazca pottery. Indicate whether each of the following is true about the features of this culture's pottery. Click in the correct box for each sentence.

	YES	NO
Ⓐ Most resembled plants, animals, and other natural forms.		
Ⓑ Early bottles were made in the shape of the human body.		
Ⓒ Some were created in order to produce sound.		
Ⓓ Those used in burial rituals were double-spouted jugs.		
Ⓔ They most often did not serve utilitarian purposes.		

5. What are two ways in which the style of Nazca pottery changed over time? Click on 2 answers.

Ⓐ From emphasizing the Mythical Killer Whale to focusing on the Harvester

Ⓑ From displaying only coastal themes to including different highland images

Ⓒ From a concentration on realistic designs to more supernatural motifs

Ⓓ From the use of three standard colors to a greater variety

Listen again to part of the lecture. Then answer the question. MP3•415

6. Why does the professor say this:

Ⓐ To indicate what she will discuss next

Ⓑ To apologize for omitting some information

Ⓒ To identify a common misconception

Ⓓ To make sure the students have understood everything so far

LECTURE  **passage 3. [1-6] Listen to part of a talk in an American history class.**

MP3·416

Democracy

note taking

1. What is the talk mainly about?

   Ⓐ Democratic Native American societies

   Ⓑ The formation of the U.S. government in 1776

   Ⓒ The system of government in colonial America

   Ⓓ The structure of the English Parliament

2. Why does the professor mention the English Parliament?

Ⓐ To point out the differences between the U.S. and English democracies

Ⓑ To suggest that England inherited democracy from Greece

Ⓒ To emphasize the connection between republics and monarchies

Ⓓ To call attention to a democratic element of the English monarchy

3. Indicate whether each of the following is mentioned in the lecture as a characteristic of U.S. colonial governments. Click in the correct box for each phrase.

	YES	NO
Ⓐ Allowed every citizen to vote on political issues		
Ⓑ Functioned as representative democracies		
Ⓒ Were established to gain profits from domestic agriculture		
Ⓓ Made the decisions on small local matters		
Ⓔ Engaged in conflict with the English monarchy in the 1600s		

4. According to the professor, why did England permit self-governance among the U.S. colonies from the outset?

Ⓐ The colonies agreed to model their governments after England's.

Ⓑ England was unable to enforce its own laws from overseas.

Ⓒ England was temporarily preoccupied with domestic disorder.

Ⓓ Self-governance was more efficient than ruling from a distance.

Listen again to part of the talk. Then answer the question. 

5. What does the professor imply when he says this:

Ⓐ The student should have been paying closer attention.

Ⓑ The student did not prepare properly for class.

Ⓒ The student has revealed the misconception he wants to expose.

Ⓓ The student's answer was almost correct.

Listen again to part of the talk. Then answer the question. 

6. Why does the professor say this:

Ⓐ To suggest that democracy is one of the most widely practiced forms of government

Ⓑ To define a word that the students are likely unfamiliar with

Ⓒ To warn the students their understanding of democracy may not be complete

Ⓓ To ask the students for their interpretations of the concept of democratic government

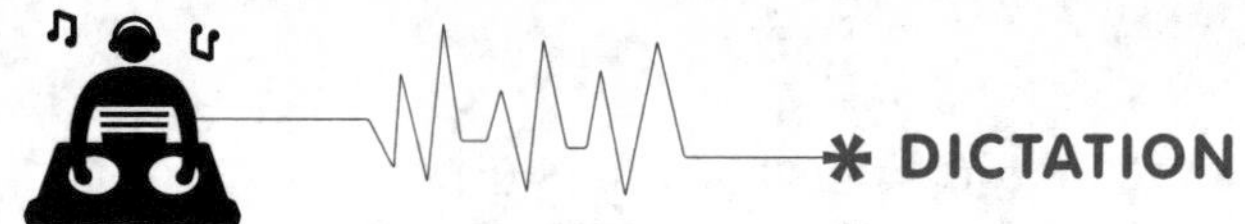

MP3•419 **Listen to part of the American art lecture again and fill in the blanks.**

［省略］

Professor: Um, Nazca pottery is known for its use of color. It's also important to note that the Nazca had no system of writing. Instead, they used iconography—or symbolic signs and images—to communicate. In studying Nazca pottery...um, it gives us a chance to study 1)_____ _____ _____ _____ _____ _____ _____.

Some of the iconography seen on Nazca ceramics is based in nature, with motifs like, uh, like plants, animals, birds—that sort of thing. Then 2)_____ _____ _____, which sort of anthropomorphize or give human-like features to the different spirits the Nazca believed in.

From what we can tell, Nazca ceramics were used for 3)_____ _____ _____ _____ _____ _____. Oh, some of it was ceremonial...some of it was used in burial contexts...and some of it shows scratches and wear from use—so 4)_____ _____ _____ _____ _____ _____ _____ _____, um, burial practices and such.

OK, moving on... Oh, we haven't talked much about the shapes of Nazca pottery, so let's do that. Well, there're the kind of 5)_____ _____ _____ _____ _____ _____ _____ _____, like bowls and jars and plates and things like that, but there're also interesting effigy vessels, which resemble human or animal figures. The most esteemed shape of all was the, uh, the double spout bottle—sort of like a round jug with two spouts on top. These jugs generally had the 6)_____ _____ _____ _____ _____ _____ of all the Nazca pottery forms. And there was also an assortment of other types of ceramic shapes, like panpipes, drums, and whistles.

As you might imagine, Nazca pottery changed over time. The culture began around 100 BC, and early Nazca pottery was 7)_____ _____ _____ _____, usually, um—thin-walled vessels...most commonly bottles in the shape of a human effigy. Sometimes it would be adorned with, uh, thick and uneven slip—uh, that's a 8)_____ _____ _____ _____ _____ _____ _____. Um, and remember how I said Nazca pottery is polychrome? Well, at first only three colors were used—red, white, and black. But later on, as many as 12 colors were used. For quite some time, um, naturalism and realism prevailed in Nazca ceramic designs. Eventually, though, 9)_____ _____ _____ _____ _____. Later pottery designs suggest that the culture experienced some changes in social organization as well...and they perhaps 10)_____ _____ _____ _____ _____ _____ _____ _____ _____ _____ _____ _____.

［省略］

答案参见ANSWER BOOK P515

MP3·420 **Listen to part of the American history lecture again and fill in the blanks.**

［省略］

Professor: Exactly. And what's a representative democracy?

Student B: Um, 1) ______ ______ ______ ______ ______ ______ to represent them...and their interests. Like the U.S. Congress.

Professor: Uh-huh. And these representatives, while they're 2) ______ ______ ______ ______ ______ ______ ______ ______, they don't just carry out 3) ______ ______ ______ ______ ______ ______. No. They have the power to take actions that they feel will benefit the people they represent. And that's what we mean by representative democracy.

Student A: So I guess the governments of the American colonies were representative democracies...not direct ones.

Professor: Yes, that's right. Any idea why that would be? Where that influence came from? No? Well, England of course. I mean, the people founding these colonies were English after all. So when it came time to 4) ______ ______ ______ ______ ______...they simply went with what they knew. And England—it was a monarchy, yes, but partially democratic as well. There was the English Parliament, 5) ______ ______ ______ ______ ______ ______ ______, um, for passing laws and such. We saw something similar in the colonies.

Student B: So all of the colonies shared the same type of government?

Professor: Well...they were all similar in that they were representative democracies. But beyond that there were actually a lot of differences. Because...um, each colony was founded by a different group...and for a different purpose. Take, uh, the Jamestown colony in Virginia. That was set up in 1607 by a commercial organization...6) ______ ______ ______ ______ ______ ______ ______ ______. Shortly after that, in New England, several colonies were established with a focus on religion. But then...in both of these cases, the colonists chose to form representative democracies based on the English model.

Student B: Why did England let the colonies have their own governments in the first place? It seems like they'd want to have more control over them...you know, 7) ______ ______ ______ ______.

Professor: Yeah, that's a good point. In fact, the colonies were given a lot more liberties than you'd expect, partly because England was 8) ______ ______ ______ ______ ______.

［省略］

答案参见ANSWER BOOK P518

DAY 20

smart source

US History 美国史

1 Colonial period 殖民时期

与西班牙和法国相比，英国在美洲大陆的殖民活动开始的相对较晚，直到1607年英国才在弗吉尼亚virginia建立了最早的英属殖民地colony。从1607年至1733年，英国在北美一共建立了13个殖民地thirteen colonies。之后，英国又在法国印第安人战争French and Indian War（1754~1763）中取得了胜利，从而将法国势力逐出了北美洲大陆。战争看似是以英国的领土扩大告终的，但实际上却使英国本土与美国殖民地之间的矛盾激化。美国随之于1775年向英国宣战，开始了独立战争the Revolutionary War，于1776年发表了《独立宣言》the Declaration of Independence并通过1783年的巴黎和约Treaties of Paris正式取得对其独立国家身份的承认。

2 Frontier（靠近未开发地带的）边远地区

在美国历史上，西部有待开拓的地区被称为边远地区frontier。边远地区最初是指平均每平方英里人口数量在2~6名及以下地区之间的分界线boundary line/border line。通常用以指代文明化程度不高uncivilized的地区。这一边远地区始于东部的13个州，到达阿巴拉契亚山脉Appalachian Mountains，然后越过密西西比河Mississippi River以及中部大草原Great Plains继续向西延伸。开拓这一地区的最重要的目的即为提高经济生活质量。美国于19世纪中叶取得了太平洋沿岸Pacific coast领土，之后又在加利福尼亚州发现了金矿gold mine，掀起了一阵淘金热Gold Rush。随着这些事件的发生，以原来的边远地区为基点，向西延伸出了许多待开发地区。

3 Gold Rush 淘金热

淘金热指19世纪在美国的部分地区发现金矿以后，人们为了寻找黄金蜂拥而至的现象。这一事件始于1828年佐治亚州的淘金热Georgia Gold Rush，之后随着弗吉尼亚州发现了黄金的消息传开，西部随即掀起了淘金热。来自美国其他地区、欧洲、中南美洲以及夏威夷等地约10万人移居加利福尼亚州。这一事件被称为加利福尼亚淘金热California Gold Rush。

4 National Emblem of the United States 美国国徽

美国政府从1782年起正式开始在公职文件中采用刻画的国徽。国徽分正obverse反reverse两面，正面画有巨大的白头秃鹰bald eagle。这只秃鹰胸部画有美国国旗，左爪擎着有13片树叶的橄榄枝olive branch，右爪紧握13根箭arrow，头上还顶着13颗星星。这些数字13都象征着加入《独立宣言》的13个殖民州thirteen colonies。作为美国的标志，国徽被印刷在1美元纸币one-dollar bill的背面以及护照passport等处。

5 Thomas Jefferson 托马斯·杰弗逊

托马斯·杰弗逊是美国第三任总统the third President of the United States。他起草了美国1776年发表的《独立宣言》，任期内致力于确保宗教、言论及出版的自由，完成了路易斯安那购地Louisiana Purchase及刘易斯、克拉克远征Lewis and Clark Expedition。从政界隐退之后，于1819年创立了弗吉尼亚大学University of Virginia并倾注了大量的心血，亲自设计了校园建筑并制定了教学课程curriculum。他生前亲自书写了日后闻名于世的墓志铭epitaph，“美国独立宣言的起草者、弗吉尼亚新教自由法的起草者、弗吉尼亚大学之父托马斯·杰弗逊安息于此”。

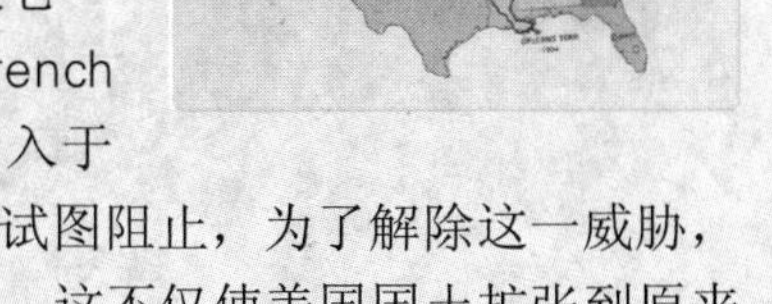

●路易斯安那购地Louisiana Purchase

指1803年，美国总统托马斯·杰弗逊从拿破仑一世手中购买了北美大陆中南部广阔的法国领地French territory路易斯安那的事件。美国的贸易船只出入于新奥尔良港port of New Orleans，法国和西班牙试图阻止，为了解除这一威胁，托马斯·杰弗逊向法国购买了路易斯安那的土地。这不仅使美国国土扩张到原来的两倍，还成为了之后西部开拓的催化剂。

●刘易斯与克拉克远征Lewis and Clark Expedition

在购入了路易斯安那地区之后，托马斯·杰弗逊决定于1804至1806年组织探险队沿密苏里河Missouri River直到太平洋Pacific Ocean的地区考查。梅里韦瑟·刘易斯(Meriwether Lewis)上尉与威廉·克拉克(William Clark)少尉领导了这次探险，这一远征也因此以他们的名字命名。这次远征是对西部海岸west coast最早的探察。探险队考查了该地区的水路waterway，收集了动植物zoological and botanical specimens及矿物标本mineral specimens，调查了印第安部落Indian tribes的实际情况，对积累科学知识做出了贡献，并且促进了西部地区的移民与贸易。

6 Sherman Antitrust Act 谢尔曼反托拉斯/反垄断法

1890年，美国国会U.S. Congress为了防止企业垄断monopoly与联合cartel制定了此法，它是美国最早的反垄断法。19世纪，石油和铁路等是当时的主要产业部门，其市场却被少数大资本家所垄断，丧失了竞争。为了克服这些弊病，俄亥俄州的参议员senator约翰·谢尔曼John Sherman提交了反垄断禁止法案。虽然这一法案的内容十分简单，只有8条规定，但它却是反托拉斯法的重要法律来源sources of law。它与之后制定的法克莱顿反托拉斯法Clayton Act（1914），以及联邦交易委员会法Federal Trade Commission Act一起，成为世界反垄断母法。

Native American 美洲原住民

7 Clovis Culture 克洛维斯文化

众所周知，亚洲人沿着白令海Bering Sea来到美洲，他们是美洲大陆最早的移民，并且由于在新墨西哥地区的克洛维斯附近最早发现了他们的使用的石器，所以他们的文化又被称为克洛维斯或古印第安文化Paleoindian culture。但是，在东北亚地区并未发现克洛维斯人制作的精巧石制矛头spearhead。这种石器主要用于宰杀猛犸象mammoth，是美洲特有的一种石器。通常认为，大约1万3千年前，一块巨型陨石meteorite在整个北美洲上空爆炸。克洛维斯人和猛犸象等大型哺乳类动物mammal都在那场灾难中灭亡extinction。可是最近，通过碳-14测定法radiocarbon dating得到一种新的主张，即克洛维斯人可能不是美洲大陆最早的移民。

8 Pueblo 普魏布勒族

普魏布勒族是美洲印第安种族Native American的一支，为史前Prehistory阿纳萨齐族Anasazi的后裔。他们主要分布在美国以及新墨西哥州地区，居住在以黏土clay烧制的公寓式村落中，大部分从事种植玉米等农业生产活动。普魏布勒族原是母系氏族，但是因为生活在干燥地区arid region，需要比之前更强有力的统帅。所以村落形式的社会形态得以强化，亲族组织变为双系形态。1600年前，为了抵御西班牙人的入侵，他们进行了顽强抵抗revolt，但是很快就被镇压下去。虽然他们于17世纪成为了天主教徒catholic，但是仍旧举行传统宗教活动，至今依然忌讳与白人通婚，他们的文明并没有被美国的文明同化assimilation，依然在独立发展。

9 Navajo textiles[weaving] 纳瓦伙族纺织品

纳瓦伙族是北美印第安种族Navajo people中的一支，以纺织品出名，尤以毛毯blanket与小毯rug最为突出。纳瓦伙族的纺织品原来是以实用性utilitarian为目的，但是进入19世纪末期，织造工weaver开始以观光tourism及出口export为目的进行制作。纳瓦伙族的纺织品以美丽的几何图案geometric pattern和华丽的色彩闻名。

Latin America 拉丁美洲

10 Nazca Culture 纳斯卡文化

纳斯卡文化是繁荣于秘鲁南部纳斯卡地区的史前文化（BC300～AD800），

绚丽的陶器pottery、纺织品textile以及高超的手工艺技术是这一文化的标志。其中，纳斯卡陶器尤以鸟、鱼、人和神的图案闻名。此外，人们还发现了分布在沙漠中间的纳斯卡线Nazca line。抽象的线条及动物图案幅原辽阔，只有从飞机上才能看到它们的全貌。

11 Mayan Civilization 玛雅文明

玛雅文明的发源地是从危地马拉高原highland到尤卡坦半岛peninsula的美洲中部地区。它是古代玛雅族人创造的文明，始于公元前2000年左右，并于公元300至900年达到繁盛期。玛雅人观测天体的方法以及使用的历法calender十分先进。他们建造了作为神殿使用的金字塔pyramid以及许多其他的石制建筑，并使用数字0～20的二十进制base-20/vigesimal。但是，奇怪的是玛雅文明在公元9世纪以后突然消逝。对此，存在非自然理论non-ecological theory与自然理论ecological theoty两种假说。非自然理论认为玛雅文明突然消逝的原因是人口爆炸overpopulation、外敌入侵foreign invasion、农民起义peasant revolt以及主要贸易通道trade route崩毁等。而自然理论则认为可能是自然灾害environmental disaster、传染病epidemic disese及气候变化climate change等。尽管如此，目前还没有任何明确的证据可以证明这些假说。

Theme Vocab

MP3•421

US History 美国史

Colonial period 殖民地时期
the Revolutionary War 独立战争
the Declaration of Independence 独立宣言
frontier（靠近未开发地带的）边远地区
gold mine 金矿
Gold Rush 淘金热
National Emblem of the United States 美国国徽
bald eagle 秃鹰

Native American /Latin America 美洲原住民/拉丁美洲

Navajo people 纳瓦伙族印第安人
textile 纺织品
rug 小毯
weaver 织造工
geometric pattern 几何图案
prehistory 史前时代
Mayan Civilization 玛雅文明
base-20 20进制

Review Test IV

passage 1. [1~5] Listen to part of a conversation between a student and an administrator.

MP3 • 426

Volume | Help | OK | Next

◎答案/解析 P.520

1. Why does the man go to the Information Technology Services Center?
   Ⓐ To ask if he can use a computer in the lab
   Ⓑ To learn how to use his share of university server space
   Ⓒ To find out his campus e-mail address and password
   Ⓓ To request a tutorial about building his own webpage

2. Why does the man want to create a webpage?
   Ⓐ He wants to learn more about website design.
   Ⓑ He needs to complete it as part of a class project.
   Ⓒ He will set up an online community for his dormitory.
   Ⓓ He will use it to sell items over the Internet.

3. What does the woman say about designing webpages?
   Ⓐ Many resources on it can be found on the university website.
   Ⓑ It may be difficult to do without any experience.
   Ⓒ It cannot be done without formal instruction.
   Ⓓ She can give the student written instructions on it.

Listen again to part of the conversation. Then answer the question.  MP3•427

4. What can be inferred about the woman?
   Ⓐ She assumes the student has a technical question.
   Ⓑ She wants the student to talk with someone in the computer lab.
   Ⓒ She thinks the student has come to use the computer lab.
   Ⓓ She does not want to help the student with his question.

Listen again to part of the conversation. Then answer the question.  MP3•428

5. What does the woman imply when she says this:
   Ⓐ He should join a class to get this information.
   Ⓑ She cannot figure out which classes he attends.
   Ⓒ The professors explain the instructions in class.
   Ⓓ It is easy for students to find this information themselves.

MP3・429

passage 2. [1~6] Listen to part of a talk in an American history class.

Volume | Help | OK | Next

The Great Seal

1. What is the talk mainly about?

Ⓐ The origin of the Great Seal of the United States

Ⓑ The history of the bald eagle in North America

Ⓒ The symbols contained in the design of the Great Seal

Ⓓ The use of the bald eagle as a national symbol in America

2. Indicate whether each of the following is mentioned in the lecture as being an image included in the Great Seal. Click in the correct box for each phrase.

	YES	NO
Ⓐ An eagle with its wings and legs spread out		
Ⓑ An olive tree with an eagle perched on it		
Ⓒ Arrows that represent the colonies		
Ⓓ A shield that bears a design like the U.S. flag		
Ⓔ A striped banner that symbolizes peace		

◎答案/解析 P.523

3. What does the professor mention about the national emblem?
Ⓐ It was first devised for the design of the national flag.
Ⓑ It is used either as part of the Great Seal or individually.
Ⓒ It was chosen to symbolize peace and morality.
Ⓓ It took a long time for the Government to select it.

4. Why does the professor discuss a letter written by Benjamin Franklin?
Ⓐ To demonstrate that some did not approve of using the bald eagle as the national emblem
Ⓑ To give details about the process of selecting a national emblem and creating the Great Seal
Ⓒ To argue that the bald eagle has been the national emblem since the country's founding
Ⓓ To answer the student's question about why a bird was selected as the national emblem

Listen again to part of the talk. Then answer the question. 

5. Why does the professor say this:
Ⓐ To discourage the students from consulting their books
Ⓑ To see whether the students have done the reading
Ⓒ To explain a section from the students' textbook
Ⓓ To request confirmation of a particular statistic

Listen again to part of the talk. Then answer the question. 

6. What can be inferred about the professor when he says this:
Ⓐ He thinks the letter is a joke.
Ⓑ He wants the students to be serious.
Ⓒ He thinks the letter is surprisingly harsh.
Ⓓ He thinks there is a mistake in the letter.

MP3·432

passage 3. [1~6] Listen to part of a lecture in an environmental studies class.

Volume | Help | OK | Next

Charcoal

1. What is the lecture mainly about?

   Ⓐ The negative effects of using wood as a fuel source

   Ⓑ The fuel sources used in sub-Saharan Africa

   Ⓒ The production of charcoal and its advantages

   Ⓓ The history of charcoal use in Europe and Africa

2. What are two beneficial events that occur when wood is baked to make charcoal? Click on 2 answers.

   Ⓐ Water content is diminished.

   Ⓑ Methane, hydrogen, and tars are removed.

   Ⓒ Carbon volume is reduced.

   Ⓓ The burning point gets lowered.

◎答案/解析 P.526

3. Indicate whether each of the following is mentioned in the lecture as a cost of using charcoal as a fuel source. Click in the correct box for each phrase.

	YES	NO
Ⓐ Deforestation caused by sourcing wood to make charcoal		
Ⓑ The emission of toxic gases as it burns		
Ⓒ Various air pollutants emitted during the formation of charcoal		
Ⓓ High costs incurred in building its processing facilities		

4. Why does the professor mention premature deaths in sub-Saharan Africa?

Ⓐ To emphasize the importance of using charcoal instead of wood
Ⓑ To compare the region's death rate to those of other areas
Ⓒ To support the use of various fuel sources in sub-Saharan Africa
Ⓓ To highlight a serious drawback of relying on charcoal for fuel

Listen again to part of the lecture. Then answer the question. 

5. What can be inferred about the professor when she says this:

Ⓐ She is sure the situation is not as bad as it seems.
Ⓑ She is hopeful about a solution to the problem.
Ⓒ She is not confident about the accuracy of the result.
Ⓓ She is concerned about the situation.

Listen again to part of the lecture. Then answer the question. 

6. What can be inferred from the professor's comment?

Ⓐ Both charcoal and wood are unsustainable as sources of fuel.
Ⓑ Charcoal has a few irreversible drawbacks as a fuel source.
Ⓒ Most people now use alternate fuels instead of charcoal.
Ⓓ It is worthwhile making the effort to convert wood into charcoal.

type A. [1~30] Listen and fill in the blanks. When the word is repeated, add the Chinese meaning.

MP3 • 438 [1~5]

01 flaming ____________ from the blast ____________________

02 ____________ the nucleus inside an oyster's shell ____________________

03 be deeply ____________ with the cycles of life ____________________

04 some ____________ qualities of exotic species ____________________

05 ____________ estivation in many reptiles ____________________

MP3 • 439 [6~10]

06 spray a ____________ and unpleasant scent ____________________

07 a lure that ____________ from anglerfish's head ____________________

08 vertical ____________ that is caused by rivers ____________________

09 ____________ an enormous amount of pressure ____________________

10 the steepness of the glacier's ____________ ____________________

MP3 • 440 [11~15]

11 rely on Internet sources ____________ ____________________

12 a slightly ____________ distribution of asteroids ____________________

13 a species that is ____________ to the habitat ____________________

14 the _______ policy for items in Media Collections ____________________

15 ____________ books and DVDs stored out back ____________________

◎答案 P.530

MP3 • 441 [16~20]

16 boost ___________ among the younger players ___________

17 ___________ to the amount of the property ___________

18 ___________ between the species and the posture ___________

19 another method of ___________ called jet propulsion ___________

20 ___________ resources from the subcontinent ___________

MP3 • 442 [21~25]

21 ___________ trade in the region ___________

22 control the basic ___________ impulse ___________

23 see a trend toward ___________ ___________

24 a desirable personality ___________ ___________

25 a word that ___________ a negative image ___________

MP3 • 443 [26~30]

26 ___________ around the library's online database ___________

27 face ___________ in American culture ___________

28 an ___________ of other types of ceramic shapes ___________

29 ___________ with civil conflict at that time ___________

30 reduce the impact of ___________ ___________

type B. [1~30] Listen the definition for each word and choose the correct word.

MP3•444 [1~15]

01 Ⓐ stipend Ⓑ feat Ⓒ fund Ⓓ practice

02 Ⓐ patterned Ⓑ virtual Ⓒ sophisticated Ⓓ supposed

03 Ⓐ reverence Ⓑ deity Ⓒ temptation Ⓓ increment

04 Ⓐ established Ⓑ numerous Ⓒ versatile Ⓓ encouraging

05 Ⓐ fracture Ⓑ dependence Ⓒ reconfiguration Ⓓ realization

06 Ⓐ diverse Ⓑ flamboyant Ⓒ sufficient Ⓓ cheerful

07 Ⓐ hypocritical Ⓑ irresponsible Ⓒ redeemable Ⓓ elective

08 Ⓐ admission Ⓑ prerequisite Ⓒ manual Ⓓ provision

09 Ⓐ descend Ⓑ surge Ⓒ waver Ⓓ submerge

10 Ⓐ core Ⓑ secretion Ⓒ production Ⓓ creature

11 Ⓐ remains Ⓑ details Ⓒ reparations Ⓓ premises

12 Ⓐ physiology Ⓑ metabolism Ⓒ capability Ⓓ immunity

13 Ⓐ omnivorous Ⓑ ambivalent Ⓒ bilingual Ⓓ egalitarian

14 Ⓐ replenishment Ⓑ congestion Ⓒ saturation Ⓓ opposition

15 Ⓐ insulate Ⓑ offend Ⓒ protect Ⓓ circulate

◎答案 P.530

MP3 • 445 [16~20]

16 Ⓐ buttress Ⓑ repeal Ⓒ eradicate Ⓓ invade

17 Ⓐ inhospitable Ⓑ reliant Ⓒ covert Ⓓ local

18. Ⓐ impressive Ⓑ nocturnal Ⓒ inferior Ⓓ deluxe

19 Ⓐ bloom Ⓑ luminescence Ⓒ enlightenment Ⓓ infection

20 Ⓐ reproduction Ⓑ inference Ⓒ disease Ⓓ camouflage

21 Ⓐ noteworthy Ⓑ responsive Ⓒ calculating Ⓓ relentless

22 Ⓐ geographical Ⓑ sterile Ⓒ dormant Ⓓ logical

23 Ⓐ exceptional Ⓑ opposing Ⓒ fragile Ⓓ concise

24 Ⓐ consider Ⓑ peruse Ⓒ occur Ⓓ germinate

25 Ⓐ silence Ⓑ residue Ⓒ dispersion Ⓓ property

26 Ⓐ urgent Ⓑ distinct Ⓒ divergent Ⓓ impeccable

27 Ⓐ contour Ⓑ measurement Ⓒ impact Ⓓ physique

28 Ⓐ repellant Ⓑ concentric Ⓒ reflective Ⓓ defective

29 Ⓐ vibrant Ⓑ convex Ⓒ located Ⓓ intentional

30 Ⓐ fable Ⓑ bibliography Ⓒ anecdote Ⓓ conjecture

answer book

答案及解析

DAY01 Diagnostic Test

P.14

Answer passage 1 > 1 (C) 2 (A) 3 (D) 4 (B) 5 (C)

passage 2 > 1 (D) 2 (A) 3 (D) 4 (A), (D) 5 (D) 6 (C)

passage 3 > 1 (D) 2 (B), (E) 3 (A) 4 (D) 5 (C) 6 (B)

MP3·01 **passage 1. [1-5] Listen to part of a conversation between a nurse and a student.**

Student (male) Q1 **Excuse me, is this where I sign up for a flu shot?**

Nurse (female) **Oh, hello. Yes, it is. Just give me one second while I put this away...*[pause]* OK. Sorry, so you wanted to get a flu shot today?**

Student **Uh, well not today. I want a flu shot, but I'm not ready to take it now. I was hoping for sometime early next week.**

Nurse We aren't giving out free flu shots past this weekend though, so you'll have to do it beforehand. And as I look at the schedule...we only have time for it today. All the other time slots are booked. I'm sorry.

Student *[hesitant]* Oh, but hmm...I don't know. There's really no time we can do it later?

Nurse I'm afraid not. We only have a limited number of free shots and it seems everyone else has signed up for the later times. It's not such a big deal having it done now, is it?

Student Q2 **It's just that I'm on the swim team and we have a meet tomorrow morning. I tend to get a bit weak and sick after the flu shot, so I'd prefer to do it when I don't have anything particular to do the following day.**

Nurse I understand. However, I really can't do anything at the moment. It's today or, um, you can get it done after next week, but I'm afraid you'll have to pay for it.

Student No way! I don't want to pay extra if I have health insurance. University is costing me an arm and a leg already as it is...

Nurse I understand. *[typing]* I'm sorry, I didn't catch your name...what was it?

Student Jeff. Jeff Gormley. Do you want my student ID?

Nurse Yes, please. *[typing on keyboard]* Are you still living at 524 Albert St., apartment 401?

Student Yeah.

Nurse Alright, here's the thing. I really can't fit you in anywhere at this campus clinic...but I might be able to sign you up at the Bakersville clinic, off-campus. Q4 MP3·02 **Would you be willing to go to the other clinic on Friday for your free shot?** <u>**It's only a short ten-minute bus ride away.**</u>

Student I guess so. Are you sure I can do that? Does my college health insurance policy cover it?

Nurse Q3 Q5 MP3·03 **Yes. It's something we try to avoid if we can accommodate student needs on campus. However, if there are extenuating circumstances, we'll send them there. And you have a completely legitimate reason for wanting**

to take the shot later.

Student  **So can I just show up at the clinic and they'll give me the shot?**

Nurse Well, don't forget your student ID. I signed you up for Friday at 11:00 a.m. Is that alright?

Student Yes, that works for me. Thanks so much for your help.

MP3 • 10

sign up for 申请…，在…注册
flu shot 流感疫苗注射
give out 分发
beforehand 提前，事前
time slot （从几点到几点的）一段时间
big deal 大事

meet （运动）会
cost an arm and a leg 花了很多钱
fit A in 将A加进去，（根据日程）预先记下A
insurance policy 保险单[证明]

accommodate needs 满足需要
extenuating 情有可原的，有正当理由的
legitimate 妥当的，合理的
show up 出现，到场

◎ 解析

1. 学生为什么来医疗所？
   (A) 为了变更注射流感疫苗的预约。**(not correct)**
   (B) 为了立刻注射流感疫苗。**(not correct)**
   (C) 为了预约接种流感疫苗。
   (D) 为了询问有关医疗保险的问题。**(not correct)**

Main Idea

请看标记Q1的语句。护士问学生是否愿意今天接种疫苗，而学生回答说今天不想，希望在下个星期的前半段接种。由此，就可以看出学生来医疗保健所的目的是为了“预约”接种流感疫苗，所以正确答案是(C)。虽然学生的最终目的是接种疫苗，但是他并不想今天接种，因此(B)选项错误。

2. 学生为什么不希望在特定的一天接种疫苗？
   (A) 因为第二天有运动比赛。
   (B) 因为自己的医疗保险不包括流感疫苗接种。**(not correct)**
   (C) 因为如果想要注射流感疫苗，就需要去贝克斯维尔医疗所。**(not correct)**
   (D) 因为在校内的医疗所里已经不能再接种免费的流感疫苗了。**(not correct)**

Detail

请看标记Q2的语句。因为第二天早上有游泳比赛，所以如果今天注射了疫苗，第二天的体力和精神就可能会受到影响。因此学生希望在第二天没什么特别安排的时候再接种疫苗，正确答案是(A)。(B)选项错误，因为只要在规定期限内注射疫苗，医疗保险都有效。此外，(C)和(D)虽然符合对话内容，但是并不是学生不预约今天的理由，所以错误。

3. 学校的学生在哪些情况下可以去贝克斯维尔医疗所。
   (A) 当校内医疗所在整修时。**(not correct)**
   (B) 当学生是优秀的学校代表队选手时。**(not correct)**
   (C) 当学生享受医疗保险优惠时。**(not correct)**
   (D) 当校内医疗所无法满足学生需求时。

Detail

请看标记Q3的语句。护士说当校内医疗所无法满足学生需要时，就会把他们转到贝克斯维尔医疗所。所以正确选项是(D)。

4. 护士为什么这样说？

It's only a short ten-minute bus ride away.

(A) 为了暗示那个地方比校内的医疗所便利。
(B) 为了说服学生去那里接种疫苗是好的替代方案。
(C) 为了告诉学生到那里具体的路程。
(D) 为了阻止学生周五去那家医疗所。

Function

护士一边询问学生想不想周五去贝克斯维尔医疗所接受免费的疫苗注射，一边说“It's only a short ten-minute bus ride away（坐公交车只需要十分钟就到了）”。可见，她在强调贝克斯维尔医疗所距离学校非常近，去那里是一个很好的替代方案。因此，正确答案是(B)。

5. 从学生下面说的话可以推测出？

So can I just show up at the clinic and they'll give me the shot?

(A) 他在预约成功后感到放心了。
(B) 他不明白为什么一定要去校外的医疗所。
(C) 他不清楚接种疫苗的程序。
(D) 他真的不知道怎么去那家医疗所。

Attitude

请看标记Q5的语句。护士根据实际情况，建议学生去贝克斯维尔医疗所，但是没有提供其他方面的信息。因此，学生并不知道去了那家医疗所之后应该怎么做，所以他问道“So can I just show up at the clinic and they'll give me the shot?（那么我只要去了，他们就会给我打针的是吗？）”学生这样问了之后，护士提醒他不要忘带学生证，这是对接种疫苗程序的补充说明。因此，正确答案应该选(C)。

 MP3·04 **passage 2. [1-6] Listen to part of a talk in a zoology class.**

Professor (male) Is everyone ready to begin? Let's get started... Q1 **today's topic is a very interesting one: animal communication. Basically, what we're talking about here is any behavior carried out by an animal that has an effect on the behavior of another animal.** The animal world is quite diverse, isn't it? Well, accordingly, the forms of communication we've found within it are also very diverse. Q2 **Probably the most obvious and best-known form of animal communication is body language, where animals move parts of their bodies in order to, um, to communicate with each other. One example of this form of communication is demonstrated by the herring gull—a gull commonly seen along the coast in Asia, Europe, and North America. Parent gulls, um, have distinctive body movements that enable them to, to communicate with their young about food.** See, when a parent returns to its nest with food, it makes this motion with its beak—it taps its beak on the ground in front of its chick. When the chick sees this movement, it immediately starts a, a begging response, and then the parent regurgitates food for the young bird. So...body movement is one form of animal communication. Can anyone think of another form?

Student A (female) What about birds' songs? Whenever I hear a bird singing, it always seems to me that it's communicating with other nearby birds. I don't know if that's actually the case...but is that an example of vocal animal communication?

Professor Great. Yeah, bird songs are probably the most recognizable form of vocal communication in animals. Q5 MP3·05 **A lot of interesting research has been conducted on the possibility of bird songs actually being a language...with rules and structure.** Um, but I'm sort of getting off track here—that's not what I want to focus on today. Anyway, you're right about birds—their songs are certainly a form of vocal communication. But birds aren't the only animals that use vocal communication. I mean, other animals such as frogs and monkeys also use vocal calls.

OK. Does anyone else have any ideas about other forms of animal communication?

Student B (male) I'm not exactly sure what kind of communication this would be, but when dogs urinate to mark their territory—is that a means of communication?

Professor Excellent. That's a very good example. Q3 **You're talking about olfactory communication—probably the form of animal communication that's least obvious to us. See, animals can deposit scents through their urine or feces...or through special scent glands on their bodies. Think of cats. Have you ever seen a cat rubbing against a chair or your leg?** All right, Q1 **let's move on and talk a little about the function of animal communication.**

Q4 **There're actually lots of different functions of animal communication.** Q4(A) **One function is to express aggression or submission, often in situations where two animals are competing over food, territory, or prospective mates. This sort of, um, behavior is known as agonistic behavior.** Another function of animal communication is to, to initiate courtship rituals. See, many species attract or communicate with a potential mate by making certain displays...or—or producing certain calls, for example. Pretty neat, huh? There're still other functions of animal communication—um, but we really can't cover them all today.

Q4(D) **OK. There's one more, um, purpose of animal communication that I want to mention, though...and that's metacommunication.** Q6 MP3·06 **Metacommunication is a form of communication that changes the meaning of a separate communication the animal's about to perform.** Is that confusing? I think it's sort of a difficult concept to understand without an example. Take dogs. Dogs can make a special signal—like a play face—that lets another dog know that the aggressive behaviors they're about to undertake are done in play...that they aren't actually meant to be interpreted as aggressive. Understand?

Student A So...this metacommunication...it's always used in conjunction with another form of communication? To add information to the second communication?

Professor Exactly...good. OK. Let's just finish up by talking briefly about interpreting animal communication. Can they communicate emotions, for example? Well... it's hard to know exactly. Some researchers may interpret it one way, and some the other. But I'd say the majority of scientists believe that animals use forms of communication to convey attitudes like excitement, playfulness, contentment... uncertainty...that sort of thing. It's surprisingly similar to human communication, isn't it?

MP3 • 11

carry out 实施，履行	**urinate** 小便，排尿	**prospective**
diverse 多样的，各种各样的	（←**urine** 尿，小便）	未来的，将来的
herring gull [鸟类]银鸥	**territory** 领域，留鸟区	**agonistic** 争斗的
distinctive 独特的，特有的	**means** 方式，手段	**initiate** 开始
tap 轻拍，轻敲	**olfactory** 嗅觉的	**courtship** 求爱
chick 雏鸟	**feces** 大便，排泄物	**ritual** 仪式
begging 乞求	**gland** 分泌器官，分泌腺	**undertake** 着手做
regurgitate 反胃，呕吐	**aggression** 攻击，侵略	**interpret** 理解，解释
recognizable 可识别的，可辨认的	**sbumission** 屈服，投降	**in conjunction with** 与…一起，与…有关
	compete over 竞争…	**contentment** 满足

◎解析

1. 讨论的主题是什么？
   (A) 动物之间利用声音进行交流的各种类型。**(minor)**
   (B) 交流行为在动物的交配中所起的作用。**(minor)**
   (C) 解析动物采取的交流方式所具有的意义。**(minor)**
   (D) 动物交流的方式及其功能。

Main Idea

教授首先说明了今天讲义文的主题是动物交流，然后举例说明了肢体语言、听觉、嗅觉及元信息传递等类型的动物交流方式，并说明了各自的作用。因此，正确答案是(D)。其他选项中的内容在讲义文中也有涉及，但要注意只是局部的内容。为了有效地解决Main Idea类型的问题，考生需要把握贯通全文的整体脉络。为此，一定要专心听讲义文开头部分出现的today's topic is一类的标志性语句。

2. 教授是以何种方式说明动物肢体语言的概念的？
   (A) 描述在海鸥中常见的喂食行为。
   (B) 介绍动物界中具有普遍意义的几种行为。
   (C) 让学生联想他们熟知的某种鸟类。
   (D) 比较银鸥的动作与人类父母的动作。

Organization

请看标记Q2的语句。这里，说话者介绍到肢体语言是动物为了传达信息而移动身体部位的行为。之后，他以银鸥为例，介绍了银鸥运用肢体语言向雏鸟传达有关食物信息的行为。所以，教授是在通过银鸥中常见的喂食行为说明动物肢体语言的概念，正确答案为(A)。

3. 教授提到了猫将身体贴着物体摩擦的行为，他希望通过这样的例子暗示什么？
   (A) 这与青蛙和猴子发出声音基本属于一类行为。**(not mentioned)**
   (B) 这是仅在宠物身上观察到的行为。**(not mentioned)**

Inference

请看标记Q3的语句。教授一边介绍动物利用嗅觉进行交流的方式，一边告诉学生动物会通过大、小便或身体里的特殊气味分泌器官遗留气味。接着，他问学生是否见过猫在椅子或人的腿上摩擦身体，并通过这个引

(C) 这是动物的交流方式中最容易被理解的。**(not correct)**

(D) 动物可以通过气味向其他动物传递信息。

出猫在使用嗅觉方式进行信息传达。所以，正确答案是(D)。在选项里，原文中的scent被换成了smell，communication被换成了conveying information to other animals的表达。教授并没有说利用声音和气味的交流方式是一样的，但是说利用嗅觉的信息传达方式是最难理解的，所以(A)与(C)选项不合适。

---

4. 讲义文中提到的动物交流的两项重要功能是什么？请选择两个正确答案。

(A) 向其他动物传达自己想要对抗或让步的意图。

(B) 引诱周围可以成为食物的东西。**(not mentioned)**

(C) 向其他动物表达不明白它们的意图。**(not mentioned)**

(D) 向其他动物揭示接下来交流的真正意义。

Detail

教授在讲义文中主要介绍了metacommunication等动物交流的三种功能。交流是两只动物在相互竞争的情境中进攻或认输意图的标志，是动物求偶的仪式，也是狗与狗之间发送特定信号的标志，表示下面攻击性的行为其实是玩笑等。与第一条及第三条对应的(A)与(D)是正确答案。请看标记Q4的语句，其中的aggression与submission在选项(A)中分别被改成了stand up与yield；其中的the meaning of a separate communication the animals about to perform在选项(D)被改成了the true meaning of the next communication。

---

5. 教授为什么说下面这句话？

Um, but I'm sort of getting off track here–that's not what I want to focus on today.

(A) 为了介绍讨论中新的主题。

(B) 为了表明讲义文的内容将要离开主要话题。

(C) 为了表明自己并不了解这一主题。

(D) 为了停止讨论偏题的话题。

Function

教授在讨论的前半部分介绍了动物的几种交流方式，并说到鸟的歌声也是其中的一种。但鸟类的歌声到底是不是语言呢？对此，有很多有趣的研究。教授提到了这些内容，但是觉得这些都是跑题的内容，所以不再多说了。因此，正确答案选(D)。

---

6. 教授为什么说下面这句话？

Is that confusing?

(A) 他认为学生应该可以轻松地掌握这一概念。

(B) 他希望学生可以集中注意力听下面要说的内容。

(C) 他发现学生理解自己的论点可能有困难。

(D) 在将内容转移至另一话题之前，希望学生可以回答提问。

Attitude

教授一边解释metacommunication这一概念，一边询问学生Is that confusing?(不太明白吗？)。之后，教授发觉不举例子说明这一概念多少有些让人难以理解，所以就举了狗的例子。因此，教授问这句话是担心学生不理解metacommunication的概念，正确答案选(C)。

 MP3·07 **passage 3. [1-6] Listen to part of a lecture in a history class.**

Professor (male)

OK, what I'd like to talk about today is...I'd like to talk some more about the Mayans, about the ancient Mayan empire. The Mayans were, uh, were an advanced culture that inhabited a large area of Central America, basically from the Yucatan peninsula in what is now Mexico...all the way, all the way down to what is now Honduras, and they did so roughly during the period between 250 and 900 AD. They were a sophisticated culture, admired for their art, the architecture of their vast cities, and their fascination with astronomy.

Q1 **But I don't want to talk about the Mayan civilization itself today. What I want to talk about is the collapse of the Mayan civilization and about a particular theory as to why it happened.**

Q2(B) **The mighty Mayan empire, with all its art and culture, more or less suddenly disappeared at, um, at some point between 800 and 900 AD...a thriving civilization, suddenly gone. Fifteen million people mysteriously left behind great cities to fall into ruin.** But, um, an important distinction to make here before we go any further...is that contrary to some popular myths, the Mayans themselves, the Mayans themselves didn't actually disappear. In fact, they're still around today, living in Mexico and various countries in Central America. There are millions of descendants of the people who built those great cities that they later abandoned. Well, what disappeared was their civilization. While elements of the Mayan society continued on for hundreds of years, the civilization was never again the dominant force or the cultural center that it once was. And for quite some time, scientists and archeologists have been debating what actually happened.

There have been...um, there have been many theories discussed. Q5 MP3·08 **Some scientists have argued that it was due to, um, overpopulation, or to disease or war.** **And, uh, you can learn about these hypotheses in more detail in this week's reading.** **But I want to look at an interesting theory that recently received some hard scientific support—the climate change theory.** There is now evidence that there was a 200-year period of drought, a series of extended droughts, actually. Q2(E) **There were three consecutive severe droughts between 810 and 910 AD**... and it is hypothesized that these droughts, which undoubtedly led to famine and disease, ultimately spelled the end of the great Mayan civilization.

Q3 **Scientists have backed up this theory with data they acquired by examining sediment—that is, tiny particles of solid matter that accumulate in liquid—from the bottom of a lake in the Yucatan. Their studies showed that the sediment from the period of the Mayan collapse was particularly high in gypsum.** Now the reason why—why this is significant—is that gypsum, a fairly common mineral, is known to generally dissolve in water before it can reach the bottom of a lake. Unless, of course, the water level of the lake is abnormally low...such as in a time of drought.

Q6 MP3·09 **Now, uh, it's possible that a high level of gypsum could also indicate something else, like, uh, gypsum is often associated with volcanic activity, for instance. But let's just say that the most likely explanation for the unusual concentration of gypsum was an extended period of drought...a climate change.**

So the, er, the next question...the next question that we should be asking ourselves is this: why would these droughts, as severe as they seem to have been, wipe out such a thriving civilization? Well, one possibility is the Mayans' great dependence on water. Most of the Mayan settlements, their cities and towns, relied on lakes, ponds, and rivers for their drinking water and for the water to irrigate their crops...grow their food. In order to deal with the dry summers of the region, they built a system of canals and reservoirs to gather and store rainwater. Q4 **In fact, it was this control over reservoirs, it would seem, that gave the Mayans one of their many edges over competing civilizations.**

But...as history seems to have proven, there is a fine line between control and dependence. If indeed this theory is true, uh, the Mayans had grown too dependent on water, and when the drought stretched on and on, they were forced, eventually, to abandon their cities, to dismantle their great empire and move on.

MP3•12

inhabit 居住，栖息
peninsula 半岛
sophisticated 复杂的，高级的
fascination 迷恋，着迷
collapse 崩溃，衰落
thriving 繁盛，茂盛
distinction 区别；特征
descendant 子孙，后代
abandon 抛弃
archeologist 考古学家
hypothesis 假说，假设 (*pl.* hypotheses)

hard （证据，信息等）确凿的
consecutive 连续的，连贯的
hypothesize 做假设
famine 饥荒
spell 招致（不好的结果）
back up 支持（主张等）
sediment 沉淀物，沉积物
accumulate 积聚，堆积
gypsum 石膏
dissolve 溶解
be associated with 与…有关联

concentration 浓度
wipe out 清除
dependence on 对…的依存（度）
settlement 定居点
irrigate 灌溉（农田等）
canal 运河，人造水路
reservoir 蓄水池；水库
edge 优势，有利
dismantle 解体

◎解析

1. 在讲义文中，教授着重介绍了玛雅人的什么方面？
   (A) 一套玛雅人向南美移民的理论 **(not correct)**
   (B) 玛雅人应对干旱曾采用的一种方法 **(minor)**
   (C) 一套解释玛雅文化影响力仍旧存在的理论 **(not mentioned)**
   (D) 玛雅帝国衰落的可能原因

Main Idea
请看标记Q1的语句。教授在今天讲义文中想介绍的不是玛雅文明本身，而是玛雅文明的衰落及解释这一现象的特定理论。因此，正确答案选(D)。在这里，应留意并把握开头出现的but一类表转折的标志性词语。(B)选项内容文章中虽有涉及，但是并不能看做讲义文的主题，因此错误。

2. 教授介绍了公元800~900年间发生在玛雅人身上的哪些事情？请选择两项正确答案。
   (A) 他们移居南美。**(not correct)**
   (B) 他们丢弃了自己的城市。
   (C) 他们神秘地消失了。**(not correct)**
   (D) 他们被洪水彻底摧毁了。**(not correct)**
   (E) 他们曾经历严重的干旱。

Detail
请看标记Q2(B)的语句。公元800~900年间，1500万人离开了大城市。再看标记Q2(E)的语句。从公元810~910年间，曾有三次严重干旱。因此，正确答案为(B)和(E)。请注意，原文中的left behind在(B)选项中被表述成abandoned。与一般概念不同，在讲义文中，教授认为玛雅人并未消失，而是至今仍生活在中美洲不同的国家之中。而对于玛雅文明的消亡，教授介绍了干旱导致的饥荒或疾病等原因。因此，(A), (C)和(D)选项不正确。

3. 对于气候变化理论，教授介绍了什么主要的论据？

(A) 湖水沉积物中的石膏含量

(B) 对岩层中化石的分析 **(not mentioned)**

(C) 那一地区曾建过运河和蓄水池的证据 **(not correct)**

(D) 饥荒和疾病的考古学依据 **(not correct)**

Detail

请看标记Q3的语句。教授介绍到，科学家对从尤卡坦半岛一处湖底取得的沉积物进行了调查，并将此作为解释玛雅文明衰落的主要依据。即科学家对玛雅文明衰落之时的沉积物进行了分析，发现其中石膏的含量非常高，但是考虑到石膏易溶于水的性质，就可以推断出当时水资源一定很匮乏。因此，正确答案选(A)。而玛雅人曾建造过运河及蓄水池的事情只是历史事实，并不能证明气候变化理论。此外，干旱之后又接连发生饥荒和疾病的事情也只不过是另一种推测，所以(C)和(D)不是正确答案。

4. 针对玛雅人对当地水资源的管理，教授暗示了什么？

(A) 这帮助玛雅人渡过了恶劣的气候条件。**(not correct)**

(B) 这意味着玛雅人的水供应从未降至过低水平。**(not mentioned)**

(C) 这导致那一地区的水资源被矿物质污染。**(not mentioned)**

(D) 这显示出玛雅人过于依赖水。

Inference

请看标记Q4的语句。这里介绍到与竞争文明相比，玛雅人对蓄水池的管理虽然是他们先进的表现之一，但结果却造成了他们对水的过分依赖。因此，正确答案选(D)。原文中的too dependent在选项中被表述为relied too heavily。玛雅人为了度过干燥的夏天，构筑了运河及蓄水系统并试图对水进行管理，但是随着干旱的持续，过于依赖水的玛雅人最终选择了遗弃自己的城市。因为提到了这一假说，(A)选项不正确。

5. 教授为什么这样说？

And, uh, you can learn about these hypotheses in more detail in this week's reading.

(A) 为了确认学生都已经读过这些理论。

(B) 为了表明下节课他会接着比较不同的理论。

(C) 为了表明在讲义文中，他将不会再仔细展开这一论点

(D) 为了显示他并不认为这些理论具有说服力

Function

对于玛雅文明的衰落，有人口爆炸、疾病、战争等很多假说与理论。教授提到可以通过阅读材料了解这些理论，而从But开始，本次讲义文会重点整理介绍气候变化理论，暗示着将不再说明其他理论。因此，正确答案选(C)。

6. 对于教授可以推测出什么？

(A) 怀疑支持气候变化理论的证据的可靠性。

(B) 认为气候变化理论相当具有说服力。

(C) 不相信当时曾有显著的气候变化。

(D) 认为除气候变化以外，其他因素也起到过影响。

Inference

对于石膏含量高这一现象，教授提出可能的原因还有火山活动。但是，从let's just say一词可以看出他的态度是更相信干旱这一原因。因此，正确答案选(B)。

Answer level 1 > 1 (C) 2 (B) 3 (A) 4 (C) 5 (B) 6 (D) 7 (A) 8 (B)
level 2 > 1 (B) 2 (C)
level 3 > 1 (B) 2 (D) 3 (C) 4 (B)

level 1

MP3·15 **1. Listen to part of a lecture in a paleontology class.**

Professor (female)

Q1 **Class, you know the Pleistocene epoch...the period of geologic time that ended about 10,000 years ago.** And, um, as it came to a close, some major events were happening. Namely, animal extinctions—a lot of them. Primarily large mammals...mammoths, sloths, big cats. Q1 **The problem for modern-day paleontologists is...we're not exactly sure what caused these species to disappear.** Q1 **Some feel they were the result of climate change.** Because... if you know something about the Pleistocene, it was an epoch of active glaciation...glaciers growing, shrinking. And this indicates some pretty dramatic shifts in climate that presumably would've been difficult for animals to adapt to. Q1 **OK, and there are others who think the spread of disease could've been responsible. But, um, to me the most intriguing theory is that these big mammals...they actually may've been hunted to extinction by humans.** Interesting, isn't it?

Q1讲义文的主要内容是？
(A) 洪积世时期的气候变化
(B) 历史上大型哺乳类动物的灭绝
(C) 可能导致洪积世动物灭绝的原因
(D) 冰川的扩张及后退形态

MP3·32
Pleistocene epoch 洪积世（也称为更新世。新生代第四期的前半期，是人类祖先出现的时期。）
come to a close 结束
extinction 灭种，灭绝
sloth 树獭
paleontologist 古生物学家
glaciation 冰河作用，冻结成冰
glacier 冰河，冰川
shrink 萎缩，缩小
intriguing 激发兴趣的，引人入胜的

MP3·16 **2. Listen to part of a lecture in an economics class.**

Professor (male)

Q2 **What's the primary goal of any commercial organization? To bring in as much revenue as possible. So how do firms decide the best way to meet this goal?** Well, there're a few basic concepts to be considered. The first is cost...the amount of money the firm must expend in order to manufacture its products. The second is output level, referring to the quantity of products that are produced. And finally, price. How much does the firm need to charge for its products? Q2 **The key is to balance these factors in such a way that the firm's costs are as small as possible...and its revenue is as**

Q2讲义文的主要内容是？
(A) 最近建立的经济学理论
(B) 企业使自身利益最大化的方法
(C) 费用、产量与价格之间的关系
(D) 部分企业难以创造利润的原因

MP3·33
primary 最先的，最重要的
commercial 商业的，交易的
revenue 收益，收入

large as possible. And that's a simplified explanation of what we mean by profit maximization.

meet a goal 实现目标
output （一定时间内的）产量，出品量
refer to 指的是…，指称
quantity 量，数量
charge 定价，附加费用
profit maximization 利润最大化

 MP3·17 **3. Listen to part of a lecture in an art class.**

Professor (female)

Q3 **I'd like to continue on the topic of ancient sculpture today with a discussion of Egyptian statues.** Um, although a lot of different types of material were used, such as clay, wood, and ivory, stone was the most common sculptural material. The artists of ancient Egypt tended to create statues that strongly resemble the cube shape of the original stone they were carved from; they were rigid, not particularly reminiscent of the round shapes you actually see when you look at the human form. So they don't appear very, um, naturalistic. But that wasn't really the point. See, we think Egyptian sculpture was mainly decorative in purpose because it usually adorned tombs and temples.

Q3讲义文的主要内容是？
(A) 古埃及雕塑的特点
(B) 古埃及艺术作品中体现出的自然主义
(C) 古埃及雕像的宗教性机能
(D) 古代社会雕塑家乐于使用的材料

MP3·34
sculpture 雕塑
statue （通常较大型的）雕像
carve 雕刻，刻
rigid 刚硬的，僵硬的
reminiscent 使人想起…的
naturalistic 自然的
adorn 装饰，装扮

 MP3·18 **4. Listen to part of a lecture in an astronomy class.**

Professor (male)

Q4 **It's possible to make a generalization about the connection between a star's color and how fast it burns. Blue stars are usually pretty young stars, since blue indicates that the star is burning very hot and therefore very fast.** Fast burning stars use up all of their fuel within a couple hundred million years, so they die relatively young as far as stars go. Q4 **Red stars, on the other hand, are quite cool and slow burning.** They burn so slowly that they might survive for hundreds of billions of years. You can't tell the age of a red star by color alone—it could be very young or very old.

Q4讲义文的主要内容是？
(A) 红星与蓝星的平均寿命
(B) 星体的温度对其颜色所产生的影响
(C) 由颜色体现出的星体燃烧速度
(D) 为了维持生命，星体需要的燃料量

MP3·35
generalization 一般化，普遍化
connection 联系，关系
relatively 相对的，比较的
tell A by B 通过B区分A

MP3·19 **5. Listen to part of a lecture in a biology class.**

Professor (female)

Q5 **Class, are you familiar with mutualism? It's the symbiotic relationship you sometimes find between organisms—uh, that's beneficial to both.** One example of mutualism in animals is the kind you see between ungulates, or hoofed animals, and the bacteria in their digestive tract. See, these ungulates often eat food that contains cellulose, a plant carbohydrate that they're unable to break down on their own. But the bacteria in their intestinal tract possess the right enzymes to break down cellulose into a form that the hoofed animal can use. So both animals benefit. The ungulate gets food that it can use, and the bacteria receive nourishment and a place to live.

Q5讲义文的主要内容是？

(A) 互利共生与其他共生关系的区别

(B) 两种生物之间的相互利益关系

(C) 有蹄类动物在体内分解纤维素的作用

(D) 有蹄类动物消化器官内发现的酶

 MP3·36

mutualism 互利共生（不同种类的生物互惠互利共同生活的关系）

symbiotic relationship 共生关系

organism 生物（体）

ungulate 有蹄类动物（**=hoofed animal,** 有兽蹄的动物）

digestive tract 消化道

carbohydrete 碳水化合物

intestinal 肠的

enzyme [生化]酶

nourishment 养分，营养

 MP3·20 **6. Listen to part of a lecture in an architecture class.**

Professor (male)

In the mid-1800s, the city of New York was looking to establish its... its international credentials. One way city officials chose to do this was by imitating the famous European public grounds...like those in London and Paris. Q6 **This is how New York's Central Park was born. In the middle of Manhattan, 843 acres of rocky, swampy terrain were set aside by the city for the new park.** There was a contest...different architects submitted their designs for the park, and a winner was selected. The winning design was in the English pastoral tradition. Rolling meadows punctuated with carriage paths, pedestrian and horse trails, manmade lakes...it was a pretty huge undertaking. After two years of construction, the park opened in 1859...and it's been a popular retreat for New Yorkers ever since.

Q6教授主要介绍了中央公园的什么方面？

(A) 对19世纪纽约生活产生的影响

(B) 与伦敦和巴黎的公园的相似之处

(C) 公园设计的征集比赛

(D) 依靠纽约市政府实现的工程策划与建设

MP3·37

establish credentials 获得名誉，获取信任

swampy terrain 沼泽地

set aside （根据政府的命令把土地等）划定为保护区

pastoral 田园的，乡村的

rolling 倾斜平缓的

meadow （广阔的）草地，牧场

be punctuated with 由于…而被打断，中断

pedestrian 行人，步行者

trail 小径，小路

manmade 人工的，人造的
undertaking 事业，承担的事情
retreat 休息处，避暑地

MP3·21 **7. Listen to part of a lecture in an art class.**

Professor (female)

Q7 **Class, the artist Marcel Duchamp is most often classified along with the Dadaists...those early-twentieth-century artists who shook up the art world.** They liked to create pieces out of everyday objects, calling attention to the existence of art within the mundane. I mean...one of Duchamp's most famous works is simply a urinal, which he signed and titled "Fountain." But he remained a major artistic figure long after the end of Dadaism. Q7 **And...uh, one of his lasting legacies is his notion about interpreting art.** You see, Duchamp never liked to explain the meaning behind his art. Instead, he preferred for viewers to create their own interpretations. These interpretations, he felt, were works of art in themselves...and more important than anything he could say about the art he made.

Q7讲义文的主要内容是？
(A) **一名艺术家是如何影响人们看待艺术的视角的**
(B) 达达主义艺术家的作品中铺垫的主要哲学理念
(C) 20世纪诠释艺术方式的进化
(D) 一名艺术家为了创作新颖的作品而使用的方法

MP3·38
shake up 给…带来巨大影响，震动
call attention to 引发对…的关注
mundane 平凡的，日常的
urinal 小便池
fountain 喷泉，泉
Dadaism 达达主义（20世纪初期以欧洲和美国为中心兴起的虚无主义艺术思潮）
legacy 遗产，遗留之物
notion 观念，概念

MP3·22 **8. Listen to part of a lecture in a psychology class.**

Professor (male)

Q8 **If you've ever spent any time around infants, you've probably noticed that there's a really special, um, relationship between the baby and his or her primary caregiver.** The baby seeks out contact with the caregiver and gets upset if the caregiver leaves. Psychologists believe that this attachment is really important in the development of the child—caregivers who're present and responsive, um, provide the infant with a sense of security, so they're more comfortable exploring the world. They know that if they encounter something frightening or threatening, the caregiver'll be there to offer protection. Q8 **This attachment the baby feels for its caregiver is essential for its survival.**

Q8讲义文的主要内容是？
(A) 正常的婴儿成长中必需的因素
(B) **婴儿与其照看者之间的感情纽带**
(C) 婴儿及其照看者都体现出的天生本能
(D) 陪伴婴儿并给予其行为反馈的重要性

MP3·39
infant 婴儿，幼儿
primary 主要的，基础的
caregiver 照看者，监护人
attachment 依恋，爱恋
responsive 有反应的，关心的

MP3·23 **1. Listen to a conversation between a student and a facilities coordinator.**

Student (female) Hi. This is the...facilities office, isn't it?

Coordinator (male) That's right. What can I help you with?

Student Um... Q1 **I'm here to talk about an event at, at Danvers Auditorium.**

Coordinator Oh, you must mean the graduation ceremony. Are you here to buy tickets, or did you need a program schedule?

Student What? Um, no... Q1 **I'm not here about graduation. It's regarding a music concert, actually...the university jazz band.**

Coordinator Hmm...I'm not aware that any jazz band concert has been scheduled in Danvers Auditorium...

Student Right, I know. Q1 **Professor Cox, the bandleader, put me in charge of reserving the auditorium for our spring concert. It's supposed to be on May 2nd.**

Coordinator Ah-ha. Now I understand. Q1 **So you need to book the auditorium for a university jazz band concert...on May 2nd**...let me see...OK. According to my schedule, there's nothing taking place on that day at the auditorium. So it'll be all yours.

Student Great.

Coordinator So...can you give me a little information about the concert? I mean...how much space do you need...and how many people do you expect to attend?

Student Let's see. Well, there're 57 of us in the band. We've played at Danvers before, and I think we usually take up the whole stage. It's a big group.

Coordinator OK...we have some equipment stored on stage right at the moment, but I'll make sure that's put into storage before the performance, so you should have no problem fitting everyone on the stage. Also, how many people do you expect to attend?

Student Yeah...I'm not really sure about that. Professor Cox didn't mention anything to me.

Coordinator Don't worry about it. That's not really a big deal. Just...if there'll be a lot of people, we need to

Q1学生为什么来学校设备中心？
(A) 为了请他们移走舞台上的部分设备。
(B) 为了预订可以举办大学爵士乐队演出的礼堂。
(C) 为了购买毕业典礼入场券并领取日程表。
(D) 为了了解会有多少人来看乐队演出。

MP3·40

facillties 〈复数形式〉设施，设备
coordinator 协调员，管理员
auditorium 礼堂
graduation ceremony 毕业典礼
regarding 考虑到…，关于…
put A in charge of *doing* 让A负责…
reserve 预约，预订(=**book**)
take place （活动或演出）开始，举行
take up （时间或空间）填满，占有
store 保管，储存
（←**storage**保管处，仓库）
right at the moment 在这个时候，现在
on hand 在手边，在近处

	prepare...have more staff on hand, that kind of thing. But I can contact Professor Cox about that and get the information myself.
Student	OK, thanks. Do you need anything else?
Coordinator	Nope. I think that's it.
Student	Thank you very much.

 MP3·24 **2. Listen to part of a lecture in an engineering class.**

Professor (female)

Dictation 开始 Class, today we're gonna be talking about technology that helps us use [1]*sunlight to meet our energy needs.* Does anyone in here know what this—this technology is called? It's called photovoltaics. Q2 **Um, a lot of you are probably familiar with photovoltaics because you've seen [2]*solar panels in use* or know how photovoltaic cells work. That's actually what I want to talk about today: the functioning of photovoltaic cells.**

Q2 **Basically, it's like this: light strikes the photovoltaic cells and causes [3]*atoms to eject their electrons*...and when we capture these freed electrons, we've got an [4]*electric current that can be used as electricity.***

Let me go over it a little further. Photovoltaic cells—um, I'm going to [5]*abbreviate the term* to PV from now on, OK? So...PV cells are composed of semiconductors. For those of you who don't know, a semiconductor is a material that becomes [6]*electrically conductive under certain conditions.*

When sunlight hits the semiconductor, the energy sometimes [7]*knocks an electron free from its atom.* So you have [8]*a negatively charged electron* moving around the semiconductor, and you have a "hole" in the atom where the electron used to be.

It's actually possible to [9]*treat a semiconductor with chemicals* to increase the number of free electrons or the number of holes. Um, I'm not really going to explain this because we don't have much time. What's important to know is that PV cells [10]*contain two layers of semiconductors*: one that's been treated to increase the number of free electrons, and one treated to increase the number of holes.

So...as a result, [11]*there's an electrical field at the boundary* between the two layers that causes electrons to move in one direction. If we provide a path from one layer to the other, electrons will flow along it, providing us with a current or electricity. Q2 **This is how PV cells provide us with electricity.** Dictation 结束

Q2教授介绍了光电池的哪些方面？

(A) 光电池是如何应用于电力技术设备的。

(B) 光电池是如何使半导体效能更高的。

(C) 光电池产生电流的过程

(D) 光电池在能源工业领域的开发历史

MP3·41

meet a need 满足一项要求

photovoltaics [工程学]光电转换工程学（模仿利用阳光制造的太阳能电池的原理，将光能转化为电能的工程学技术）

solar panel 太阳能电池板

photovoltaic cell 光电池(**=photocell,** 如果以光照射半导体，就会产生电流。利用这一原理将光能转换为电能的电池。)

functioning 功能，作用

atom 原子

eject 排出，喷出

electron 电子

electric current 电流

electricity 电，电力，电气

abbreviate A to B 简称A为B，将A简略说成B

semiconductor 半导体

conductive 传导性的，有传热性的

under certain conditions 在特定的环境下

knock A free from B 击打A使其脱离B

negatively charged 带有负电荷的（↔**positively charged** 带有正电荷的）

free electron 自由电子

electrical field 电场

MP3·25 **1. Listen to part of a conversation in the student services office.**

Student (female) Hi...I need to speak to someone about renting rooms. Are you the facilities coordinator?

Coordinator (male) Yes, that's me. Renting rooms you say? What's this for?

Student Oh, let me explain. My name's Margaret Trent. Q1 **I'm the operations director this year for the annual "Women In Business Conference" held on campus.**

Coordinator Yes, now that you mention it, I know of it. I saw posters up for it all last year. Q1 **So you're looking to book facilities, right?**

Student Q1 **That's right. It's not taking place until the end of the year, but I know I have to put in the request early.**

Coordinator Definitely. Do you know how many attendees you're expecting, including speakers?

Student This year, we're expecting...hmmm...maybe 500? Last year we were in Shuster Hall, but it felt really crowded. This time, I was hoping to book Hartman Auditorium and Clement Hall. Could you put in the request for December 14th through the 17th, please?

Coordinator OK...let me check. *[pauses while looking at the computer database]* Hmmm...that's odd. It says here that Hartman Auditorium's already been booked on December 14 for a benefit performance.

Student Oh no, that's the night we wanted to hold our opening gala. *[frustrated]* I don't even know what group would be holding a charity event at that time. I checked with the Student Clubs Association, and they assured me nobody else was holding anything that would conflict with our conference.

Coordinator Yeah, I think it's a bit strange. I've been the only one here since March and nobody's come to see me about such an advanced booking. There must be some mistake. *[starts clicking on computer]*

Q1学生为什么来服务中心？
(A) 为了了解即将召开的会议的相关信息。
(B) 为了预订校内场地举办活动。
(C) 为了提出有关礼堂扩建的异议。
(D) 为了变更上一次预订会议室的相关事项。

MP3·42

operation 运营，调整
put in 提交…，申请…
attendee 参加者，出席者
benefit performance （为了募集捐款的）慈善活动（=charity）
gala 特别演出，庆祝
assure 向…保证，使确信
advanced booking 提前预约

Student What about Clement Hall? Is that available?

Coordinator Yes, that location is free. I can schedule your conference there tentatively, and then it will need to be approved by the registrar. But that shouldn't be a problem. Now about Hartman... *[typing]* Ah! Now I see... *[somberly]* It's not good news, I'm afraid.

Student Who booked it?

Coordinator Apparently, an external group has booked it. The City can access our system because it's a public college. It says here the Mackenzie Autism Foundation has booked it for a charity concert.

Student I'm not sure what to do. What do you think? Are there any other facilities that can hold more than 500 people on campus?

Coordinator Actually...do you know Ellis Auditorium?

Student Yes, but it's definitely not big enough. I had two classes there last semester.

Coordinator Yeah, right now its capacity isn't as great as Hartman's. However, next month we're beginning an expansion project on Ellis Auditorium. So by mid-October, it'll be just as big, if not bigger, than Hartman.

Student Really? That's perfect. Can you put in my request to book Ellis for the conference then?

Coordinator *[typing]* OK, it's done. So, unless the registrar decides to cancel your booking for some reason, it should be fine. It's all yours.

Student Great. Thanks for your help!

MP3·42

available （物体或空间等）可以使用的
tentatively 试验性地，临时地
registrar （大学）负责教务的职员
somberly 昏暗的，阴沉的
external 外部的
access （电脑系统等）进入，接近
autism 自闭症
capacity （建筑等的）容量，承受能力
expansion 扩张，扩大

MP3·26 **2. Listen to part of a conversation between a student and a professor.**

Professor (male) Please come in, Sarah. How are you?

Student (female) Hi, Professor Dalton. I have a favor to ask of you, if you don't mind.

Professor *[reluctantly]* If this is about the final exam, I'm afraid I can't give out any hints. The departmental policy is very strict on fairness.

Student Oh, it has nothing to do with that. Q2 **I was actually hoping you could write me a reference letter for my law school application.**

Professor *[flattered]* Oh, I'd be happy to do it, but I thought

Q2学生为什么去找教授？
(A) 为了询问期末考试的相关情况。
(B) 为了听取读研方面的建议。
(C) 为了商议硕士学位课程方面的情况。
(D) 为了请教授帮忙写推荐信。

MP3·43

fairness 公正性，公平性
have nothing to do with 与…无关，与…没有关联

you were going to go for a master's in English literature. Your thesis was impressive, and I think you'd make an excellent candidate.

Student Really? Thanks, but I've done a lot of thinking, and I think a law degree would serve me better in the future. *[sheepishly]* Sorry...it's just that... that I want to help out with my family business later on. Having a law background would be useful.

Professor Oh, you don't need to apologize. I would just have been delighted to work with you next year. Now, back to the reference letter...do I need to fill out anything?

Student Well, I have this here...*[shuffling papers]* You'll need to fill out this form. Then write a short letter of recommendation.

Professor Alright, that's pretty standard. I enjoy writing these... Did you bring along a résumé?

Student A résumé? No...why would you need my résumé?

Professor Well, it's useful for me to refer to while I'm writing your recommendation. Then I could see what else you've done and what your interests are.

Student Oh, I'm sorry. I didn't know it was important... When should I drop one off?

Professor I'll be at an out-of-town conference until Friday night... Actually I should get going soon to make my train...so anyway, I won't be coming back to my office until after the weekend. You can just leave it in my mailbox and I'll pick it up when I get in on Monday.

Student Monday? That might be a bit late. Hmmm...my application is due next Friday and I wanted to have everything prepared early.

Professor Well, I guess I could write the recommendation without your résumé. It would just be more helpful to me to make it more personal.

Student I completely understand. Hmm...*[coming up with an idea]* What about e-mail? I could e-mail it to you later today, if that will help.

Professor That's a good suggestion, I didn't think about that. Sure. E-mail it to me as soon as you can. Then I'll be able to work on the letter over the

reference letter 推荐信(=letter of recommendation)
application 申请书，申请志愿
flattered 高兴的，愉快的
master's 硕士学位
impressive 印象深刻的，优秀的
candidate 候选人，申请攻读学位者
sheepishly 羞怯地，怯懦地
later on 之后，以后
be delighted to *do* 很高兴…
fill out a form 填表格
résumé 简历，履历表
drop off 带去，带给（物品等）
out-of-town 市外的，在其他城市的
due （一定期限）预期的，（一定时间）期限的

weekend and get it back to you on Monday.

Student OK. I will send it to you when I get home tonight. Thank you so much again for helping me out.

Professor It's my pleasure.

MP3·27 **3. Listen to part of a lecture in a literature class.**

Professor (male)

Well, let's get started. Q3 **Today we'll be talking about Pearl S. Buck, an American author. Maybe you've heard of her. She was an American author who lived...oh...from around—say, the 1890s to the 1970s.**

There's something about this author that makes her stand out from other American authors. See, she grew up in China...and spent much of her life there. That qualifies as unusual, wouldn't you say? Now, what circumstances brought her to China? Well, when she was just a baby—about three months old. Her parents were missionaries, Presbyterian missionaries...and they moved the family to China from their home in West Virginia. Buck—well, at this point in her life, uh, before she was married, her name was Pearl Comfort Sydenstricker—anyway, she was a baby when she moved to China, so you can probably imagine that Chinese culture was, was basically her first culture. And the Chinese language was essentially her first language. But she spoke English, too. And it's a good thing she did... otherwise her novels would be inaccessible to a lot of Americans, right?

Q3 **So...let's look at her writing, shall we?** Buck once said, "I can only write what I know, and I know nothing but China, having always lived there," and, true to her words, she wrote a lot about China. See, after she got married in 1917, she moved with her husband to a rural town in the Anhui province. It was in this impoverished community that Buck gathered the principal material she would later use in her writings. Q3 **The book that she's most famous for is a...a novel called *The Good Earth*.** It was published in, uh, in 1931. *The Good Earth* is a story that centers on the life of Wang Lung who is a Chinese peasant...a farmer around the year 1900. Wang Lung uses the earth to make a living, and the book follows his life...as he lives in poverty, then earns money...uh, and gradually loses his connection to the land... The book was very well received after its publication and it was translated into many languages. It even won the Pulitzer Prize in 1932.

I think I'll tell you a little about the writing style in this novel. It's something that a lot of people talk about when they bring up *The*

Q3讲义文的主要内容是？

(A)《大地》与其他美国文学作品的区别

(B) 赛珍珠被看做重要的美国作家的理由

(C) 赛珍珠的独特背景及其著名作品

(D) 中国派美国作家的作品与人生

MP3·44

stand out 突出

qualify 赋予权利，给予权利

circumstances 〈复数形式〉情况，（生活）环境

missionary 传道士，传教士

Presbyterian ［宗教］长老教的，长老教会的

be inaccessible to 难进入…，从…切断联系的

province 州，省，地方

impoverished 贫穷的，赤贫的

principal 非常重要的，主要的

center on 以…为中心，以…为重点

peasant 佃农，小耕农

connection to 与…联系，与…关联

publication 出版，发行

Good Earth. You see, Buck's writing style in this novel is very... well...it's rather plain; simple and direct. Not like...oh...stream-of-consciousness writing, which was pretty popular in the early twentieth century. There aren't really any subplots or anything either. The writing just—it just takes you from start to finish. And there's nothing wrong with that...but this kind of writing style has led people to wonder, "Why is it like that?" Some people think that the style is really, ah, really similar to the kind of style that you might find in Chinese novels. Other people suggest similarities with the writing in the Bible. And if you look at Buck's personal history, as I described it...you might see that it's certainly possible that, uh, that both of these sources could have influenced her writing style.
Another aspect of her style is—well, since she's writing about a peasant farmer and his family, it's about people who might not be able to read or write...so her dialogue reflects the characters in her book. And her writing style seems appropriate for telling this story. The simplicity and directness—that might be based on how the main character Wang Lung, how he would have told his story himself...in his own words. Actually, *The Good Earth* is celebrated for its character portrayal. You see, Buck really tried to convey a full sense of the individuals in the story. Her characters are consistent... but they're also complex. They're not just stereotypes of peasants or anything like that. I think that her character portrayal is probably a big factor in making Buck such a classic and celebrated American author.

stream-of-consciousness [文学]意识流，使用意识流技巧的（根据主人公的感觉、想法、记忆、联想等意识进行的实验性小说展开方式，也称为“意识的流动技巧”）
subplot （戏曲，小说等的）次要情节
source 根源，出处
reflect 反映
appropriate for 适合…
celebrated 被庆祝的
character portrayal 人物描写
convey 传达，搬运
consistent 一贯的，持续的
stereotype 典型，固定观念

MP3·28 **4. Listen to part of a lecture in a biology class.**

Professor (female)

Did you know there are about 3,000 types of venomous snakes in the world? And of those, um, those 3,000 types, about 500 are venomous. Dictation 开始 OK. All venomous snakes, uh, they use...it's kind of like a saliva. They use this saliva-like venom to kill or, um, [1] *immobilize their prey.* And their venom is delivered through...fangs in the mouth.

Q4 [2] ***The most deadly venomous snakes* belong to a, um, a family called elapids.** Elapids can really range in size...from just eighteen centimeters to six meters in length. In appearance, elapids are long and thin. They also have smooth scales, and their—their eyes have round pupils.

Elapids [3] *deliver venom through their hollow fangs.* These fangs are, um, they're located at the front of the mouth...and the venom

Q4 讲义文的主要内容是?
(A) 不同毒蛇的区别
(B) 三种类型的毒蛇
(C) 蛇喷射毒液的两种方式
(D) 世界上最致命的蛇的种类

MP3·45
venomous 有毒的，分泌毒液的（←**venom** 毒液，有毒物质）
saliva 口水，唾液
immobilize 使不能移动，使麻痹
fang （肉食性动物的）犬齿，尖牙
elapid 眼镜蛇科的毒蛇
range （变化等的）范围，幅度

they emit comes from venom glands at the back of the upper jaw. When elapids have their mouths closed, their fangs, um, they fit into a kind of—a kind of [4]*slot in the mouth.* Elapid venom is usually a neurotoxin, um, which means that [5]*it affects an animal's nerve cells.* As I said earlier, elapids are some of [6]*the most deadly venomous snakes.* An elapid species known as the black mamba is considered to be the most dangerous snake in the world. Um, and it's fast...and really large. It can also be [7]*quite aggressive if it feels threatened.* Its venom—its venom isn't the most toxic, but when the black mamba bites, um, it delivers quite a bit of it. Now, the most venomous land snake is also an elapid. [8]*It's appropriately named the fierce snake,* and its venom is quite—quite potent. The venom from [9]*one bite of the fierce snake* could kill, um, about one hundred people—or 250,000 mice.[Dictation 结束] But the most venomous snake of all lives in the water. It's, of course, an elapid known as the Belcher's sea snake. The venom from this snake is, um, it's estimated to be actually a hundred times more powerful than any land snake's venom.

Q4 **OK...let's talk about another family of venomous snakes—the viperids.** Viperids are somewhat stocky and have short tails. Their heads are, um, are sort of distinctively shaped...uh, triangular, actually. And their pupils are thin slits...not round like elapids.

Viperids eject their venom through hollow fangs, similar to elapids. They've also got venom glands that are, um, that are at the back of the upper jaw, but there's a big difference—uh, between the fangs of elapids and viperids. See, viperids' fangs are located on a bone that, um, that can actually rotate. This means that the fangs can fold back against the roof of the mouth. So, um, when a viperid isn't using its fangs, they get tucked away. And the venom of viperids isn't usually a neurotoxin like in elapids. No...instead of attacking nerve cells, what it does is, is break down an animal's tissue. Uh, actually, this is quite beneficial for viperids, um, because they're sort of bad at digesting things...so the venom actually helps out the digestive process by, um, by essentially digesting the prey from the inside out.

Q4 **Now, there's just one more group of venomous snakes I want to—to mention. The family known as colubrids.** A lot of colubrids aren't venomous...but I thought it was important to mention them, uh, because there are some types of—of venomous snakes that are colubrids. Colubrids are, uh, somewhat smaller than other snakes and have...oval-shaped heads.

Unlike elapids and viperids, colubrids usually have, um, have fangs that are in the back of their mouths. Uh, since many colubrids aren't venomous, I'll, um, I'll just tell you about a specific species of colubrid that is venomous: the boomslang. Like a typical colubrid,

scale 鳞片，外皮
pupil 瞳仁，瞳孔
hollow 中空的，空洞的
emit 喷出，放射
slot 狭长孔 (=**slit**)
neurotoxin [医学]神经性毒素（麻痹神经等的对神经有害的毒物）
nerve cell 神经细胞
toxic 有毒的，有毒性的
appropriately 合适的，适合的
fierce 凶猛的
potent 强有力的，有效力的
stocky 矮胖的，健壮结实的
distinctively 独特的
trangular 三角形的
eject 喷射，吐出
tuck away 把…藏入
tissue （肌肉或神经等的）组织
oval-shaped 椭圆形的
grooved 表面有沟槽的，带纹道的
hemoglobin 血红素
molecule 分子
red blood cell 红血球

the boomslang has fangs in the back of the mouth, and, uh, the fangs are grooved, not hollow. The venom from boomslangs is a hemotoxin. Now, that means that, um, the venom destroys an animal's hemoglobin, which is the molecule in your red blood cells that carries oxygen. So the boomslang's venom basically destroys its victim's blood.

Answer

level 1 > 1 (D) 2 (A) 3 (B) 4 (C) 5 (B) 6 (B) 7 (C) 8 (B)

level 2 > 1-1 (B), (C) 1-2 (D) 2-1 (B) 2-2 (B), (C)

level 3 > 1-1 (B) 1-2 (A), (D) 1-3 (B) 2-1 (C) 2-2 (A), (C) 2-3 (B) 2-4 (D)

level 1

MP3·48 **1. Listen to part of a conversation between two students.**

Student A (female) Greg, what's wrong? You look stressed out.

Student B (male) Yeah, I've been trying to study for our biology final. I just know I'm gonna fail.

Student A *[reluctantly]* Oh, do...do you need some help studying? I could help you go over the material.

Student B Uh...no. I wouldn't want to impose like that. I know you have heaps of papers to write and exams coming up, too.

Student A Uh, OK. If you insist. Q1 **Then, uh, why don't you find yourself a tutor? Like, one of the better students in our biology class. Or perhaps someone who took the course last year.**

Student B That's a thought.

Student A Just post a note on the bulletin board in the biology department. I'm sure someone will reply soon.

Student B Great idea!

Q1 女生向男生提供了什么备考建议？
(A) 参加学习小组聚会。
(B) 和自己一起学习。
(C) 去听系里提供的补充课程。
(D) 接受个人辅导。

MP3·63

stressed out （压力堆积导致的）精神紧张
final 期末考试
impose 强加，附加
heaps of 很多的
post 贴出，公示
bulletin board 布告牌
reply 回答，答复

MP3·49 **2. Listen to part of a lecture in a history class.**

Professor (female)

So, what was the Sherman Antitrust Act of 1890 all about? Well, in order to understand it, we need to look back at why it was introduced, and the business practices that were common around the late 19th century. You see, a few large American corporations had set up cartels, which, uh, dominated a number of industries, most famously in the case of the railroads. These major companies were forming what were called "trusts"—which were, as I say, basically cartels—and, uh, the basic purpose was to fix prices. Obviously, uh, this wasn't very good for consumers, right? Because prices were kept artificially high by these arrangements. Q2 **So, uh, legislators**

Q2 根据教授的介绍，美国为何引入《谢尔曼反垄断法》？
(A) 为了禁止几家大公司联手垄断。
(B) 为了促进大公司之间的合作。
(C) 为了稳定不同消费品的价格。
(D) 为了活跃19世纪美国的商业生产。

decided to make it illegal for companies to...uh, to cooperate in this way, against the interests of consumers, by bringing in the Sherman Antitrust Act.

MP3-64

look back 再重新看…
business practice 商业惯例
corporation 公司，法人企业
cartel 卡特尔，企业联合
fix 稳定（价格或利率等）
legislator 立法者
interests 〈复数形式〉利益，优惠
bring in 引入…

MP3·50 **3. Listen to part of a talk in a botany class.**

Professor (male)	Q3 **So you know stems grow up, and roots grow down, right? But why? Why do they grow this way?**
Student A (female)	Well, I guess it's just the way the seed is oriented in the soil. You know, soil's normally pretty flat.
Professor	Really? What about plants that grow on steep mountains? The stems shoot up and the roots grow down there, too. In fact, if you turned a potted plant on its side, you would still find the stems growing up, and the roots down!
Student B (male)	Then is it because of the sun? Plants need sunlight, so it could affect their growth.
Professor	Good try. But that's not the answer I was looking for. Q3 **The real reason is gravity. It's the Earth's gravitational force that determines the orientation of plant growth.** So, uh, we call this phenomenon gravitropism.

Q3根据教授的介绍，什么因素会影响植物根茎的生长方向？
(A) 种子的向性
(B) 重力
(C) 太阳的方向
(D) 土壤密度

MP3-65

orient 以…为方向的
flat 平坦的，平地的
steep 陡峭的
potted 盆栽的
gravity 重力
gravitational force 万有引力
determine 决定
phenomenon 现象
gravitropism 向地性

MP3·51 **4. Listen to part of a conversation between a student and a financial aid advisor.**

Advisor (female)	Hi there. Welcome to the financial services desk.
Student (male)	Hi. I need to organize a student loan. Uh...how do I go about it?
Advisor	Well, firstly, let's establish whether you really need a loan. It's best to avoid getting in debt if possible, right?
Student	Yeah, but, I'm pretty sure. I have no other choice, what with living costs and tuition and fees and everything.

Q4负责财务方面工作的职员为什么让学生去问询处？
(A) 为了咨询贷款问题。
(B) 为了确认是否能拿奖学金。
(C) 为了了解是否有资格补充津贴。
(D) 为了听取管理预算方面的建议。

Advisor	OK. So you've checked out all the scholarships available in your department?
Student	Yep.
Advisor	Q4 **And you can't get a student allowance?**
Student	Huh?
Advisor	Uh...students from underprivileged backgrounds are entitled to an allowance of up to $150 a week.
Student	*[sounding intrigued]* Really?
Advisor	Could that apply to you?
Student	Well...maybe. How do I find out?
Advisor	Q4 **Go visit the student help desk. They'll explain the system and let you know if you're eligible.**
Student	OK. Thanks.

MP3-66

financial 财政的，金融的
loan 贷款
establish 确认（是否具有真实性）
in debt 负债的
living costs 生活费
allowance 津贴，补助
underprivileged 低收入阶层的，无法享受适当权益的
be entitled to 有享受…的权利
apply to 适用…
eligible 有资格的

MP3-52 **5. Listen to part of a lecture in a geography class.**

Professor (male)

OK, so we're losing more and more rainforest to logging and development. So what? What's the big deal? Well, for one thing, it robs the world of biological diversity. Lots of animal and plant species that used to thrive in the rainforest are either endangered or have died out completely. So, uh, the preservation of this diversity is one reason the rainforests are so important. Q5 **But, uh, from a selfish, human perspective, there's a more important reason than that. You see, plants absorb carbon dioxide—the main cause of the greenhouse effect, climate change...call it what you want. And rainforests are the biggest CO_2 consumers of all. So, uh, if we keep destroying our rainforests, carbon dioxide levels will skyrocket. And this could have disastrous consequences for conditions here on Earth.**

Q5根据教授的介绍，人们最担心什么？
(A) 世界大部分地区生物多样性遭受的破坏。
(B) 破坏热带雨林给环境造成的影响。
(C) 开发导致的二氧化碳排放。
(D) 全世界热带雨林的气候环境变化。

MP3-67

rainforest 热带雨林
logging 伐木，木材
rob A of B 抢夺A的B
biological diversity 生物多样性
thrive 繁荣，兴旺
endangered 处于灭绝危机中的
die out 灭绝
preservation 保存，保护
perspective 观点，立场
absorb 吸收，吸取
greenhouse effect 温室效应
skyrocket 猛涨的
disastrous consequences 灾难性的后果
conditions 〈复数形式〉环境

MP3·53 6. Listen to part of a talk in a law class.

Professor (female)	Uh, I thought I'd start off today's class with something fun. So, uh, who can tell me about the famous "animal trials?"
Student (male)	Do they have something to do with animal rights?
Professor	*[with emphasis]* No, not that. These were cases where the animals themselves were on trial.
Student (male)	No way!
Professor	*[laughing]* You see, back in the middle ages, in medieval Europe, people really put animals on trial for crimes. Like, uh, if a pig attacked someone, they'd be tried in court—like a proper case. As if they were human.
Student	*[jokingly]* And were they found guilty?
Professor	*[laughing]* Almost always. Q6 **And, uh, afterwards, they'd face a public execution. You know, to warn other animals...to, uh, to act as a deterrent to others!** It just seems silly, doesn't it? These days, we have rules to defend animal rights. But we'd never try animals like people.

Q6根据教授的介绍，中世纪欧洲为什么将动物公开处以刑罚？
(A) 为了让人们不再担心受到动物攻击。
(B) 为了防止其他动物犯罪。
(C) 为了警告动物保护主义者。
(D) 为了显示动物不需要审判。

MP3·68
trial 审理，审判（←**try**审判）
medieval 中世纪的
court 法庭
proper 真的，与实际相符的
be found guilty 被判决有罪
afterwards 以后，之后
public execution 公开处以刑罚
deterrent （不让某种行为进行的）遏制的
defend 保护

MP3·54 7. Listen to part of a conversation between a professor and a student.

Professor (male)	Jenny, you wanted to see me?
Student (female)	Yes. I, uh, need to get you to sign something for me.
Professor	OK.
Student	It's, uh...it's a form. You know, to say I'm dropping this class.
Professor	*[shocked]* You're dropping this class? Why? Are you not enjoying it or something?
Student	No, it's not that. Q7 **I just have too much going on now that I'm on the student council. I hardly have time to keep up with the weekly readings, let alone the assignments.** You understand, right?
Professor	You know this is a required class for English lit majors? You won't be able to graduate unless you complete it.
Student	Yeah, I'm planning to take it next semester,

Q7学生为什么想要撤销选课？
(A) 因为对课程内容不感兴趣。
(B) 因为想参加学生会选举。
(C) 因为日程排得太满。
(D) 因为计划变更专业。

MP3·69
drop 撤销，取消（选课等）
council 委员会，议会
keep up with （不落后）跟上…
let alone 更不用说…
required class 必修科目
complete 修完

	when I won't have such a busy schedule.
Professor	OK, I see you've thought it through. Now, uh, where's this form you want me to sign?
Student	Thanks, professor.

MP3·55 **8. Listen to part of a lecture in an environmental science class.**

Professor (female)

Today's topic is biofuels—fuels like ethanol and biodiesel, which are extracted from plants. Now, you've probably all heard about some controversy surrounding biofuels. But, uh, I want to discuss their benefits first. And, uh, their primary advantage is that they're more environmentally friendly than traditional fossil fuels like coal and oil. Q8 **Specifically, biofuels produce much smaller greenhouse gas emissions—they reduce emissions by up to 60 percent.** Pretty impressive, eh? It was initially hoped that biofuels could be completely carbon neutral—um, that the amount of carbon dioxide they emit could, uh, could actually be offset by the amount of carbon dioxide that the crops absorb. But, um, of course they need to use energy to process the fuel, too, so it doesn't quite work out. Uh, but anyway, the most important thing to note is that biofuels are much better for the environment overall.

Q8根据教授的介绍，生物燃料为什么对环境有益？
(A) 因为生物燃料被证实使用时不产生二氧化碳。
(B) 因为可以相当大地降低温室气体排放量。
(C) 因为生产生物燃料比精炼化石燃料更加有效。
(D) 因为除了二氧化碳他们不排放其他有害气体。

MP3·70
biofuel 生物燃料
extract from 从…精炼
controversy 争议，争论
surrounding 围绕…
environmentally friendly 亲环境的，有利环境的
fossil fuel 化石燃料
greenhouse gas 温室气体
emission 排出，排放（←**emit** 排放）
neutral 中性的，不带特定成分的
offset 抵消，补偿
work out 正常起动，正常动作
note 注意

level 2

 MP3·56 **1. Listen to part of a conversation in a library.**

Student (female)	*[hesitantly]* Excuse me.
Librarian (male)	Oh, hello. Welcome to the media resources department.
Student	I'm not sure, but I think this is where I need to be—um, I need to watch a DVD for one of my classes...
Librarian	Yes, you're in the right place.
Student	Oh, good.
Librarian	Q1-1 **OK, so what class do you need it for, and,**

Q1-1图书管理员向学生要求了以下哪些信息？请选出两个正确选项。
(A) 学生姓名
(B) 需要DVD的课程
(C) 教授姓名
(D) DVD资料的号码

	uh, who teaches that class?
Student	The class is Introduction to Volcanology; Geology 201 with Professor Kaiser.
Librarian	*[confirming]* Spelt K-A-I-S-E-R? OK. And the name of the DVD?
Student	It's, ah...hang on. Let me check. *[pause]* It's called *Eruptions and their Impact on the Environment.*
Librarian	OK, thanks. Let me go retrieve this for you. I'll be right back. *[pause] [returning]* You said this was on reserve for Professor Kaiser? I'm sorry... but we don't seem to have any materials for her class on reserve.
Student	But she told me to come to the library to get this DVD.
Librarian	Is it something that everyone in the class has to watch for an assignment?
Student	No. I'm doing it for an extra credit, since I missed a class last week.
Librarian	Ah-ha, that's why it's not on reserve. Q1-2 **See, professors usually put materials on reserve when they assign everyone in their class to watch it. That way, since no one person can check it out, everyone can come here and view it.** But since you're the only one watching this particular DVD...your professor didn't put it on reserve. It's probably just in the general section. Wait a minute.
Student	OK.
Librarian	*[returning]* Yes, we do have it after all. And, uh, you can take it home with you if you like, since it's not on reserve.
Student	I can check it out? Great.
Librarian	OK. I just need your student ID.

Q1-2 根据图书管理员的说法，图书馆的资料排列放置在指定资料一类的原因是？
(A) 为了图书馆工作人员找起来方便。
(B) 为了不让选其他课的学生使用。
(C) 为了能让学生选择给额外学分的课题时使用。
(D) 为了给所有学生使用的机会。

MP3·71
media resources （日报、音乐或影音等）多媒体资料
retrieve 找回；恢复
on reserve 给某（些）人保留［预约］
assignment 课题，任务（←**assign**布置任务）
extra credit 额外学分
check out 从（图书馆）借…

MP3·57 **2. Listen to part of a lecture in a botany class.**

Professor (male)

Let's, uh—let's begin. I'm going to talk about garlic. That's right, garlic...the plant. I'm sure you all know a bit about it already. It's, uh, it's a plant that's related to onions and lilies and has a similar appearance...with a bulb and green shoots. And, of course, garlic

Q2-1 关于大蒜强烈的气味，教授说了什么？
(A) 大蒜的气味是为了引诱鸟或昆虫的。
(B) 大蒜的气味是大蒜有损伤时才散发的。
(C) 对某些动物来说，大蒜的

has a distinctive flavor, so it's often used as a seasoning in cooking. Q2-1 **Interestingly, it actually makes that sharp garlic flavor when it gets damaged—for instance, when someone bites into it, or chops it up, or crushes it.** See, when that happens, a process occurs in the cells of the garlic that, uh, that causes compounds in the, um, the garlic to break down. And that's what makes that—that hot flavor you taste when you bite into a, a raw piece of garlic. And you know what? That garlic flavor is actually a defense mechanism. It evolved for the purpose of—of defense against animals that would eat the plant...like birds or insects. You see, garlic is pretty unappetizing to most animals. *[jokingly]* But...well, that defense mechanism didn't work on humans, I guess.

Also, garlic is believed by many people to have some medicinal qualities...and it appears as a healing agent throughout history. Like, one particularly good example was in World War II. Q2-2(B) **Medics used garlic when they were out of antibiotics...because it had been proven that garlic could kill germs. They used garlic to, ah, to fight against infections in the wounds, and it helped some of the injured soldiers to recover.**

Q2-2(C) **More recently, scientific research has shown that, um, that garlic can lower cholesterol and, um, reduce high blood pressure.** Of course, high cholesterol and high blood pressure often lead to heart attacks as well as, uh, a whole host of other diseases. So, uh, you can see why this is causing excitement in the medical community, can't you?

气味是有毒的。
(D) 只有特定种类的大蒜带有气味。

Q2-2根据教授的介绍，大蒜是如何用于医疗途径的？请选择两项正确答案。
(A) 为了防止肌肉损伤。
(B) 为了代替抗生素治疗伤口。
(C) 为了降低胆固醇数值。
(D) 为了帮助心脏病患者恢复。

MP3·72
bulb 球根
shoot 芽
distinctive 特别的
seasoning 佐料，调味料
chop 切，剁碎
compound 化合物，混合物
defense mechanism 防御机制
unappetizing 引不起食欲的
medicinal 有药效的
healing agent 愈合剂
medic 医生
antibiotic 抗生物质
germ 细菌，病菌
infection 感染，传染
a whole host of 数量多的

level 3

MP3·58 **1. Listen to part of a conversation between a student and a professor.**

Student (female) Can I talk to you for a minute?

Professor (male) Sure, have a seat.

Student Q1-1 **The thing is...I have a learning disability, and I'm having a little trouble keeping up in class.**

Professor What kind of learning disability is it?

Student Dyslexia...I have trouble reading.

Professor I'm glad you came to talk to me so early in the term. We've actually got some great resources for students with dyslexia here at the university. Tell me, specifically which aspect of the course are you having problems with?

Q1-1学生为什么去找教授？
(A) 因为阅读目录上的材料太多，学生觉得不满。
(B) 因为学习课程有困难，学生需要帮助。
(C) 因为学生在写关于学习障碍的论文，需要向教授请求帮助。
(D) 因为学生想告诉教授校内书店不出售有声书籍。

Student Mainly the reading list. I go home and start reading as soon as I'm finished with classes, and sometimes I don't finish till midnight.

Professor I understand. And how are you doing in the actual lectures? Any trouble taking notes or understanding my handwriting?

Student No, if the class was based wholly on the lectures I would be fine.

Professor Dictation 开始 So, what do you think about using audio books?

Student That'd be great...but I don't think [1] *I can afford to order* all those books.

Professor Q1-2(A) **As a matter of fact, all of the books on the reading list are available on CD in the library. You can listen to them** [2] ***in one of the special booths*** **in the library, or you can borrow them and take them home.**

Student Really? I had no idea.

Professor Q1-2(D) **You should also contact the student services office. They'll** [3] ***set you up with a free tutor.*** **You know, another student who's done the course before, who can help explain things.**

Student For free? That'd be great.

Professor I don't know why this kind of information isn't made more available to students with special needs.

Student Actually, I didn't [4] *report my disability on my application.*

Professor Why not?

Student I guess I didn't want anyone to think I wanted special treatment. And it never gave me too much trouble in high school...of course I had to work a little harder...I thought I could handle a university workload, too. I guess I was wrong. I just didn't realize [5] *how much reading would be involved.*

Professor First of all, it's not special treatment. It's the law for schools to provide services to students with disabilities...all types of disabilities. Look, I'm really glad you told me about this. Q1-3 **Some students with learning disabilities are ashamed of it, and they shouldn't be. Then they** [6] ***get overwhelmed with the workload.*** **Sometimes**

Q1-2根据教授的说法，在如下的资料和资源中，学生可以使用哪些？请选择两项正确答案。

(A) 图书馆可借的有声书籍

(B) 阅读量小的特殊课程

(C) 书店里出售的有声书籍

(D) 可以向学生提供免费辅导的教师

Q1-3关于需要特别帮助的学生，教授说了什么？

(A) 他们有时在解决研究生阶段更难的课业方面会遇到困难。

(B) 没有个人学业辅导帮助的话，他们在消化理解大量的课业方面会遇到困难。

(C) 建议他们经常选择有多媒体辅助的课程。

(D) 因为大学不能向他们提供足够的资源，他们的利益会受损。

MP3·73

learning disability 学习障碍
dyslexia 诵读困难
wholly 完全地，全部地
afford to *do* 可以承担得起…
booth （进行语言学习时使用的）小房间
set up with 准备好…
treatment 对待，待遇
workload 工作量
get overwhelmed with 被…所压倒

it's too late for them to catch up, and they end up having to repeat. Others [7]*get discouraged and drop out.* Dictation 结束

Student Oh, that won't happen to me. I'm really determined to get a bachelor's degree. I don't know if I'll ever be able to go to grad school or anything but...

Professor *[interrupting]* Why not?

Student I don't know...that just seems impossible for someone like me.

Professor Not at all. From what I've seen, you seem like a very capable student.

Student *[honored]* Really?

Professor Absolutely. And if you keep working hard—and actually start using the resources available to you, you could make an excellent candidate for graduate school.

Student Wow! Thanks, professor.

MP3·73

catch up 挽回（落后的局面），追上

end up *doing* 结果…，最终…

drop out 退学，落榜

be determined to *do* 坚定地决定…

bachelor's degree 学士学位

grad school 研究生院（**=graduate school**）

capable 有能力的

MP3·59 **2. Listen to part of a talk in a marine ecology class.**

Professor (female) Q2-1 **OK, class. I want you to write down a definition for a word I'm about to give you. Get ready...OK. "Sponge."** *[pause]* Has everyone finished their definitions? OK, let's see. Fred, will you read me what you've written down?

Student A (male) I wrote: "A primitive sea animal belonging to the group porifera."

Professor So, sponges are animals.

Student A Right.

Professor *[addressing the rest of the class]* Is that correct? Let's see a show of hands. Are sponges animals? *[counting hands]*...four...five. OK. Who thinks sponges are plants? *[counting again]*...six... seven. Interesting. Um, Otis, can you tell me a little bit about why you've classified sponges as, um, as plants?

Student B (male) Right. I think sponges are plants because they... they resemble plants. Q2-2(A) **They're sessile—y'know they don't move around and, uh, they don't have organs...**

Professor Dictation 开始 Q2-2 **Well, you've [1]*summed up some of the reasons* why people believe that sponges are...um, plants.** Q2-1 *[pause]* **But, actually,**

Q2-1讲义文的主要内容是？
(A) 海绵的各种用途
(B) 植物与海绵的区别
(C) 动物海绵的特性
(D) 对海绵的大众性误解

Q2-1根据教授的介绍，人们有时候错把海绵当做植物的原因是？请选择两项正确答案。
(A) 因为它不动。
(B) 因为它们无法捕食。
(C) 因为它们缺乏基本的器官。
(D) 因为它们是以很小的细胞构成的。

they're animals. ***[pause]*** They are sessile...and, uh, Q2-2(C) **they don't have any, um,** [2]***muscles or nerves or other organs.*** **Basically, they're a collection of cells working together. They're extremely simple...some of the most** [3]***primitive animals on the planet,*** **but they've evolved some special features.** Like, uh, sponges have a pretty unique way of...uh...eating. They don't have mouths, right? Q2-3 **So, they've got to get food some other way. And they do that by...by drawing water in through these, um,** [4]***these little pores on the sponge walls.*** **So, as the water goes through the pores and into the sponge, um, food particles are filtered out of the water.** The water gets, um, it gets passed out of the sponge through other openings in the, um, the sponge body. Nifty, eh?

The cells that make up the sponge's pores are called porocytes...and they're just, um, one of many different types of cells that can be found in sponges. [5]*The cells that filter out food in the water*—those are called, um, choanocytes. Um, and then there are the spicules...those are rods that are used for, um, for structure...or for defense.

Student A So...spicules are [6]*like the skeleton of the sponge?*

Professor Yes, that's right.[Dictation 结束]

Student B I'm curious... Are the sponges we use for cleaning the same as these...animal sponges?

Professor Yes, sometimes. Of course, uh, most of the sponges available at stores are made from synthetic materials. But, uh, certain types of natural sponges have spongin skeletons—you know, like their skeletons are kinda soft and springy—and, uh, these skeletons are also used commercially. In fact, there are lots of different species of, um, of sponges that are used. Some of them are really, um, really soft...and others are coarser and used for, um, washing cars...or something like that. Um, see, all of the, uh, the animal matter gets taken off...and what's left is a sponge that can be used for household chores.

Student B Is it the same thing with loofah sponges? You

Q2-3根据教授的介绍，海绵孔的用途是？
(A) 净化流入海绵体内的水。
(B) **帮助海绵获取食物**。
(C) 帮助海绵防御天敌。
(D) 为海绵的身体提供骨骼支撑。

MP3-74

sponge 海绵
primitive 原始的
porifera 海绵动物
classify A as B 把A分类为B
sessile 黏着的，着生的
sum up 总结…，整理…
pore (小)孔，气孔
filter 过滤
nifty 俊俏的，漂亮的
porocyte 孔细胞
choanocyte 环细胞
spicule 针状体，针骨
rod （长）棍，棒
skeleton 骨骼，骨骼
synthetic 合成的
natural sponges 天然海绵
spongin 海绵质
springy 有弹力的
coarse 粗糙的，粗劣的
household chores （琐碎的）家务活
loofah sponge 丝瓜络
ridge gourd [植物]丝瓜
xylem （植物的）木质部

know, the ones people use in bathrooms.

Professor Oh, um...they're a bit different. Q2-4 **They're natural sponges, but they aren't made from animal sponges. Loofah sponges are actually from a vegetable.** The vegetable has a couple of names...Chinese okra...the ridge gourd. Um, what happens is, everything but the xylem—that's the tissue that carries water throughout the plant—everything but that gets removed... and what you're left with is a natural spongy material.

Q2-4根据教授的介绍，丝瓜络是？
(A) 骨骼过于坚硬而无法投入商业用途的天然海绵
(B) 比天然海绵吸水性更强的合成海绵
(C) 由海绵质构成的具有柔软骨骼的动物海绵
(D) 使用一种蔬菜制成的天然海绵

Answer level 1 > 1 (B) 2 (A) 3 (C) 4 (A) 5 (A) 6 (C) 7 (C) 8 (C)
level 2 > 1-1 (A) 1-2 (C) 2-1 (B) 2-2 (D)
level 3 > 1-1 (C) 1-2 (B) 1-3 (D) 2-1 (C) 2-2 (D) 2-3 (A), (C)

level 1

MP3·79 **1. Listen to a conversation between a student and a professor.**

Professor (female)	Q1 MP3·100 **Kyle, you have a question about the upcoming group project?**
Student (male)	**Um...yeah. I'm not sure it's something you can help me with, though...**
Professor	**Well, there's only one way to find out.**
Student	OK. It's just...I've never written a research paper as part of a group before. How are we supposed to divide up the work?
Professor	Usually...um, usually what happens is everyone does research on their own, then you put together what you find and decide the direction of the paper.
Student	Oh...OK. That makes sense, I guess.
Professor	Of course, every group is different. But as long as you're open to listening to the ideas of your team members, I'm sure the assignment will go fine.

Q1教授为什么说下面这句话?
Well, there's only one way to find out.
(A) 为了说明一些关于小组课题的事情。
(B) 为了鼓励学生和大家一起分享自己的忧虑。
(C) 为了向学生提供一个解决问题的办法。
(D) 因为无法帮助学生而向他道歉。

MP3·108
upcoming 即将到来的，这次的
research paper 研究报告，研究论文
be supposed to *do* 认为应该…，被期望…
divide up 把…分开
put together 把…放在一起，把…组成整体

 MP3·80 **2. Listen to part of a lecture in an astronomy class.**

Professor (male)

The prospect of life on Mars is pretty exciting. It's almost impossible not to wonder if maybe, at some point in the distant past, our rocky neighbor once supported life. Q2 MP3·101 **Some research on Mars meteorites that've landed on Earth once generated speculation that maybe the meteorites contained evidence of life on the red planet. However, um, those findings have been nothing but controversial.** Yet certain types of life forms on Earth provide scientists with hope that the extreme conditions on Mars aren't too inhospitable for life: hardy microbes known as "extremophiles"

Q2教授为什么说下面这句话?
However, um, those findings have been nothing but controversial.
(A) 为了质疑研究的真实性。
(B) 为了总结最近有关火星环境的研究。
(C) 为了指出重要的研究开始都会遇到一些挫折。
(D) 为了暗示科学家怀疑火星上存在生命。

survive in the most difficult environments on Earth. If there is life on Mars, maybe it would be similar in form to these types of organisms.

MP3·109

meteorite [地质]陨石
speculation 推论，推测
red planet 红色星球（红星的俗称）
controversial 有争议的
inhospitable 不适于生存的，荒凉的
microbe 微生物
extremophiles 嗜极微生物，极端微生物（生活在各种极端恶劣环境下的微生物）

MP3·81 **3. Listen to a conversation between a student and an advisor.**

Advisor (female)	So you've thought about the classes you want to take for your last semester?
Student (male)	Yeah. I've got my ideal schedule all mapped out. Here's what I have so far.
Advisor	*[looking over the schedule]* OK...let's see here. *[pause]* Looks pretty good so far. According to my records, you've already obtained the credits for your major and your general requirements for the College of Arts and Sciences.
Student	That's right. Are there any other requirements I need to meet?
Advisor	Q3 MP3·102 **Um, there're the two cultural diversity classes that everyone in the university needs to take. East Asian art history will take care of one of them...but—have you taken a race relations class yet?**
Student	***[confused]* Uh...race relations?**
Advisor	Yeah, it looks like you need just one more class. How about Professor Sheldon's course on black poets of the twentieth century?

Q3学生为什么说下面这句话？
***[confused]* Uh...race relations?**
(A) 为了显示他已经理解教授的话了。
(B) 为了提醒自己已经达到的课业要求。
(C) 为了显示自己没有听过那门必修课。
(D) 为了提出一门自己想追加到日程表上的课程。

MP3·110

map out 周密的制定（计划）
credit 学分
meet a requirement 获得必修学分，满足要求
cultural diversity 文化多样性
take care of 处理（事情、责任等）

MP3·82 **4. Listen to part of a lecture in an architecture class.**

Professor (male)

The idea of the garden as a place of beauty and calm goes back a long way...thousands of years. But not until ancient Rome did

Q4教授为什么说下面这句话？
A virtual garden.
(A) 为了给他刚刚说明的概念提供一个专门术语。
(B) 为了改变讨论的主题。

gardens start appearing in the private homes of wealthy citizens. Statues, columns, pools, fountains...all kinds of architectural touches made these gardens exquisite places for their owners to relax. Q4 MP3·103 **But, uh, what about people with less money, those who couldn't afford to build such a garden? Well...what they did was hire a fresco painter to paint the image of a garden, complete with all the things I just mentioned—they'd have this painted on a wall somewhere in their house.** **A virtual garden.** And...the funny thing is, the virtual gardens lasted much longer than the real ones, and most of the things we know about Roman gardens come from the frescoes. The ruins of Pompeii, especially, contain many well-preserved garden paintings.

(C) 为了和大家分享对于这一主题的意见。
(D) 为了重复之前说过的一个专门术语。

MP3·111
statue 雕塑
column 柱，圆柱
exquisite 精美的，精致的
complete with 具备，使完备（特性或特征等）
virtual 虚拟的
ruins <复数形式>遗迹，废墟

MP3·83 **5. Listen to a conversation between a student and an administrator.**

Student (female)	Hi...Mr. Singh?
Administrator (male)	Yes? How can I help you?
Student	Q5 MP3·104 **I'm interested in going on the art department's field trip to the National Museum of Art. Professor Wilcox said I needed to see you about that.**
Administrator	**Oh, OK.** **Now...I assume you know the trip is only open to art majors...**
Student	Yeah...and I just switched over my major to art this semester.
Administrator	Great. Then I need you to fill out this form with your personal information, and, um, I need to collect the trip fee from you now.
Student	How much is that again?
Administrator	Fifteen dollars...and I can only accept cash.
Student	No problem. I have that right here.
Administrator	Great. We'll see you bright and early this Saturday.

Q5管理员为什么说下面这句话？
Now...I assume you know the trip is only open to art majors...
(A) 为了询问学生是否符合要求。
(B) 为了劝说学生把专业换成艺术。
(C) 为了告诉学生她犯错误了。
(D) 为了对学生的要求表示惊讶。

MP3·112
field trip 现场学习，实地考查
switch over 换
fill out a form 填表
bright and early 一大早

MP3·84 **6. Listen to part of a lecture in a literature class.**

Professor (female)

The Epic of Gilgamesh...is quite possibly the oldest surviving work of literary fiction. This, um, this epic poem comes to us from the Sumerian civilization—around 3,000 BC. It's the story of a king...part

Q6教授的意思是？
(A) 她想集中于叙事诗中一个特定的故事。
(B) 她不认为故事会吸引学生。
(C) 她不想花费时间讨论情节。

god, part man...the story of this mighty king and his adventures. Q6 MP3·105 **There're actually some pretty interesting tales contained in the epic, but I'll let you explore those on your own as you read the text at home.** What I want to emphasize today is how influential *The Epic of Gilgamesh* has been. I mean, there are scholars who've shown that it had a tremendous impact on other ancient writings...Homer's *Odysseus*, for one. Possibly even the Bible!

(D) 她认为学生已经读过文章了。

MP3·113

The Epic of Gilgamesh 吉尔伽美什史诗

epic poem 叙事诗，史诗

mighty 有力的

explore 探索，调查

tremendous 巨大的，了不起的

MP3·85 **7. Listen to a conversation between a student and a professor.**

Student (female) Professor Ahman, can I speak with you?

Professor (male) Sure, Alison.

Student I was wondering, uh...would it be possible to get an extension on the due date for my interview report?

Professor Oh, Alison, I don't know...are you having trouble with it?

Student Yeah, kind of. The woman I'm interviewing...she keeps changing her schedule. As of now, I won't be able to meet with her until next Tuesday, which is just three days before the report's due.

Professor I see. And you don't think you could finish it in three days?

Student I'm not sure. I have a lot of work in my other classes.

Professor Q7 MP3·106 **Well, let's just see what happens. Try your best to get the report in on time, but if you really can't, I'll see about giving you a couple extra days.** **<u>But...that's not the ideal scenario, OK?</u>**

Q7教授这样说的意思是什么？

But...that's not the ideal scenario, OK?

(A) 他认为学生还需要一些时间。

(B) 他想让学生保证按时交报告。

(C) 他不想允许学生延期。

(D) 他不想现在就讨论那个问题。

MP3·114

extension （日期的）延期，延长

due date 到期日

keep *doing* 继续…

as of now 到目前为止，此时

on time 按时

ideal 理想的，最好的

MP3·86 **8. Listen to part of a lecture in a biology class.**

Professor (female)

Most animals walk on either two legs or four. Q8 MP3·107 **Birds and primates like us have gone bipedal. But did you know that some**

Q8教授这样说的意思是什么？

Surprising, I know.

(A) 她不认为学生对她所说的感到惊讶。

lizards actually have two? **Surprising, I know.** When you think of a lizard, you picture a creature that walks on four legs, right? Well, that's not always the case for dragon lizards at least. Sure, most of the time you'll find them prowling around on four legs, but when they're in a hurry, they'll sprint on just two legs, taking a bipedal posture that somewhat resembles an upright dinosaur. Scientists think it's an evolutionary consequence of running faster; standing up moves their center of gravity and offers them more maneuverability.

(B) 她想知道学生对蜥蜴了解多少。
(C) 她觉得自己刚才提到的信息对学生来说是新的。
(D) 她希望学生回答蜥蜴如何行走的问题。

MP3·115
primate 灵长类
bipedal 两足的，有两只脚的
dragon lizard 猛龙壁虎
prowl 悄然潜行
sprint 全力疾跑
upright 直立的，竖直的
evolutionary 进化的
consequence 结果
maneuverability 机动性，可操作性

level 2

MP3·87 **1. Listen to part of a conversation between a student and a professor.**

Professor (male)	Sam, thanks for agreeing to meet with me today.
Student (female)	Oh, sure. *[somewhat nervously]* Um...I just hope you didn't call me here to talk about my term paper.
Professor	Actually, that is why I wanted to talk to you today.
Student	Q1-1 MP3·88 ***[very nervous now]*** **Oh no. Did I overlook one of your requirements or did I cite my sources incorrectly?**
Professor	***[chuckling]*** **Sam, calm down. Quite the opposite, actually. Your paper really impressed me.**
Student	*[relieved]* Wow! I'm so glad to hear that. I worked on it for so long...I don't even know what to think of it anymore.
Professor	Well, I think there're lots of other scholars in our field who'd be interested in reading it. Have you heard about the big technology conference

Q1-1教授为什么这样说？
[chuckling] **Sam, calm down. Quite the opposite, actually.**
(A) 为了告诉学生不用担心。
(B) 为了告诉学生自己对她有多失望。
(C) 为了鼓励学生继续猜。
(D) 为了显示自己理解学生担心的事情。

MP3·116
term paper 期末报告[论文]
overlook 忽视，未注意到
cite 引用

that's going to be held here in October?

Student Yes...

Professor I was hoping you'd consider submitting a proposal to make a presentation at the conference, based on the research in your term paper.

Student Wow. *[pause]* I'm really honored that you think my term paper is, uh, good enough to be presented at the technology conference. *[reluctantly]* But, um, I just don't think I could do that. Give a presentation in front of thousands of people, I mean.

Professor I thought you might feel that way, but I strongly urge you to take some time and think it over. It'd be an excellent opportunity for you.

Student *[not persuaded]* It's just...I'm so afraid of speaking in public. I always have been.

Professor The audience is going to be very forgiving and understanding. There'll be other student presentations too, so you won't be the only student there.

Student Um...

Professor Q1-2 MP3·89 **You don't have to make up your mind now. I'll tell you what. Why don't you at least submit a proposal? <u>You can always decide later on not to do it.</u>**

Student **OK. I guess I could do that.**

Q1-2教授的意思是什么？

You can always decide later on not to do it.

(A) 他认为学生已经充分考虑了建议。

(B) 他希望学生现在提交建议书。

(C) 他认为学生不应该现在就拒绝这一想法。

(D) 他希望学生先给自己看建议书。

MP3·116

submit a proposal 提交建议书

I'm honored 我感到很荣幸

urge to *do* 催促去做…，劝…

take some time 拿出一些时间（做…）

think over 仔细考虑

forgiving 宽容的，宽大的

make up one's mind 决定，下决心

MP3·90 **2. Listen to part of a talk in an art class.**

Professor (female) Q2-1 MP3·91 **Class, we've been discussing photography as art, but...did you know there's always been a big debate about whether photography is indeed an art form?**

Student A (male) **<u>That seems strange. I mean, all the pictures we've studied in class are very carefully crafted...very artistic.</u>**

Student B (male) Well...I can see the other side of the argument too. Think about all those amateur photographers out there, snapping quick, random shots. You probably wouldn't consider those images art.

Professor Yes...you've pretty much summed up the

Q2-1学生的意思是什么？

That seems strange. I mean, all the pictures we've studied in class are very carefully crafted...very artistic.

(A) 他希望教授可以再展示一遍艺术照。

(B) 他认为摄影完全有资格被视为一种艺术形式。

(C) 他希望教授可以举一些争议性影像的例子。

(D) 他认为课上看的影像都过于相似了。

debate right there. It all started back in the mid- to late 1800s, when photography was still very young. And people, um, most people saw it simply as a way to document real life. Its images were too sharp, too...well, real, to be art. But one group of photographers—the pictorialists—felt differently. So they decided to show the world just how artistic photography could be. Any idea how they did that?

Student A Well, I guess they could've tried to model their photographs after established art...like paintings.

Professor Q2-2 MP3·92 **Absolutely right. And what style of painting was popular around this time?** **Come on...late 1800s...**

Student B Um...impressionism?

Professor Uh-huh. So the school of pictorialism...these photographers created images that looked strikingly similar to impressionist paintings. You know...shifting focus away from the main subject, concentrating on emotion instead of realism, representing light and shadow...

Student B How did they do that?

Professor Oh, there were various techniques. First of all, they'd compose their shots to mimic the composition of a painting. And then...um, they used special filters and coatings on their camera lenses, a softer focus to blur the image...making the details less sharp. And in the printing process, various chemicals were added to produce different effects. Even...um, they even made scratches on their prints to imitate etching marks or brushstrokes.

And so...they were successful, ultimately. The art world accepted photography, and you started seeing photographs alongside paintings in museums. Of course, the debate continues today, but pictorialism was the first successful argument in favor of photography as art.

Q2-2教授为什么这样说？
Come on...late 1800s...
(A) 为了告诉学生们她要转换主题了。
(B) 为了让学生告诉她时间发生的具体日期。
(C) 为了提醒学生过去学习过的某一特定时期。
(D) 为了鼓励学生尝试回答她的问题。

MP3·117
photography 摄影，摄影术
craft 精心制作
snap 拍照，拍…的快照
pictorialist 绘画主义摄影艺术家
model A after B 照着B的样子做A，模仿B制作A
established 既存的，建立的
impressionism 印象主义
school 学派
strikingly 震惊地，十分
concentrate on 集中…
mimic 模仿
blur （使）变模糊
etching 蚀刻（利用腐蚀技法的版画）
brushstroke 一笔，一划
alongside 在…旁边，和…一起
in favor of 赞成…，支持…

MP3·93 **1. Listen to part of a conversation between a student and a professor.**

Student (female)	Excuse me, can I talk to you for a minute?
Professor (male)	Sure, come on in. What seems to be the problem?
Student	There isn't a problem. Q1-1 **I was just wondering if you could write a reference letter for me.**
Professor	*[hesitant]* A reference letter? Uh...you're asking me? Um...what's it for?
Student	I'm applying to grad school.
Professor	I see...um...in psychology, I presume?
Student	Yes.
Professor	Dictation 开始 So, have you asked any other professors?
Student	No, you're the first one I've asked. I figure [1] *since you're the head of the department* it would look really good.
Professor	Well, actually, most students seek references from professors [2] *who are familiar with their work.*
Student	I got a really good mark in your class.
Professor	Well, sure, but I have a lot of good students. Q1-2 **I would suggest you [3] *ask your thesis advisor*...someone who knows you personally and who knows your work. Someone who has actually worked with you.**
Student	So...you'd rather not?
Professor	Look, I'll be honest with you. I'll do it, but it won't be a good reference. It's not like [4] *I'll maliciously make you sound bad*, but I just don't know enough about you to make it sound good. I'll tell you something about reference letters. Nobody writes a bad one, but the people reading the letters read more into what you don't say than what you do say. See what I'm saying?
Student	Yeah...even if you don't say anything bad, it still looks bad if you don't say [5] *a whole lot that's good.*
Professor	Right...I mean...I can say that you are a hard

Q1-1学生为什么来见教授？
(A) 为了谈她和论文指导老师之间存在的问题。
(B) 为了听听申请研究生院的建议。
(C) 为了请教授帮忙写推荐信。
(D) 为了了解得到好的推荐信的办法。

Q1-2教授为什么不太愿意帮助学生？
(A) 因为他认为学生需要提高学业表现。
(B) 因为他并不足够了解学生，提供不了有参考意义的信息。
(C) 因为他知道学生和论文指导老师关系不好。
(D) 因为系里的事情太忙了，他无法帮助学生。

MP3·118
reference letter 推荐信
apply to 申请…
presume 推定，假定
head of the department 系主任
be familiar with 熟悉…
mark 分数，成绩
thesis advisor 论文指导教授
maliciously 故意地，恶意地
a whole lot 十分，非常

worker and a good student, but your grades already say that for you. What the grad schools are looking for in a reference letter is [6]*all the extra stuff* that your grades don't say.

Student OK, I see what you mean.

Professor And...think about it...if they get a reference from [7]*one of your random professors*, and not from someone who has worked closely with you...what does that say?

Student I guess [8]*it would seem like I had a bad relationship* with those professors who I have worked closely with.[Dictation 结束]

Professor Exactly, it looks as if you are hiding something. Now, is there any particular reason you didn't ask your thesis advisor in the first place?

Student Well...yeah...I don't think she was very happy with my work.

Professor What didn't she like about it?

Student Well, she said my research was sloppy and my review of the literature was incomplete.

Professor Did you take her advice?

Student Yeah, of course.

Professor Q1-3 MP3·94 **Listen to me...she's your advisor. <u>It's her job to point out your mistakes.</u> We don't expect you to do a perfect job on your first thesis, that's why we have advisors.**

Student I guess that makes sense.

Professor If I were you, I would go talk to her. You'll be able to tell if she's going to write you a good reference or not. If you still feel like it's a bad idea, come back and see me. We'll see if we can work something out.

Student OK, I'll do that. Thanks for the advice.

Q1-3教授的意思是什么？
It's her job to point out your mistakes.
(A) 指导教授不应该建议学生对论文做不必要的修改。
(B) 指导教授对学生写作论文的表现十分失望。
(C) 指导教授有义务给学生写一封好的推荐信。
(D) 指导教授的评价不一定意味着她讨厌学生做出的努力。

MP3·118
extra stuff 额外的东西
random 随机的，随便的
in the first place 第一，第一次，一开始
sloppy 草率的，做事马虎的
incomplete 不完整的，不充分的
point out 指出

MP3·95 **2. Listen to part of a talk in an astronomy class.**

Professor (female) If any of you happened to look up into the sky yesterday afternoon, you would've seen something quite extraordinary. Anyone know what I'm talking about?

Student A (male) My mom pointed out this enormous bright ring around the sun. It was actually really pretty...and not only that, but also, there were like, two bright spots on either side of this ring. Not sure if those were stars or comets or something...but I've never seen anything like it.

Professor Dictation 开始 It really is quite something, huh? Q2-1 **A perfect example of today's topic! Sun halos. And we'll briefly look at sun dogs too.** Does anyone know [1] *anything about these atmospheric phenomena?*

Student B (male) Q2-2 MP3·96 **I always thought those effects could be viewed from [2] *somewhere near the equator*...or from the North Pole—like the northern lights. But if people here saw it yesterday, then I guess not.**

Professor **Just to clarify, the northern lights—more accurately known as aurora borealis—they can only be seen [3] *within the polar zone in northern latitudes.*** You can also see something similar—called aurora australis—you can see that near the South Pole too. Uh...anyway, those effects aren't what I was referring to...OK, so anyone else? *[pauses]* Alright then, what appeared in the sky yesterday is called a sun halo. That's [4] *the giant, glowing ring around the sun*...and those two spots...those are sun dogs...but I'll talk about those later.

Sun halos are formed...they're formed when light from the sun is [5] *refracted by ice crystals in the atmosphere.* These, um, ice crystals are found in thin, upper level cirrus clouds. Maybe, uh...three to six miles straight up. There, the temperature is so low that [6] *water crystallizes on dust particles* to form ice...and these ice crystals, they act like prisms. There are millions of these crystals in that atmospheric layer. OK. Now, can anyone tell me...why do these ice crystals [7] *create this peculiar halo effect?* Dictation 结束

Student A Um...It must have something to do with the angle of refraction, right? I mean, when they get hit by sunlight.

Q2-1讨论的主要内容是什么？
(A) 日晕的外观
(B) 日晕与北极光的相似之处
(C) 日晕与幻日的形成
(D) 大气中的灰尘结晶

Q2-2教授为什么这样说？
Just to clarify, the northern lights—more accurately known as aurora borealis—they can only be seen within the polar zone in northern latitudes.
(A) 为了回顾以前讲义文中的素材。
(B) 为了强调重要的讲义文素材。
(C) 为了定义之前说的术语。
(D) 为了纠正学生信息的错误。

MP3·119
happen to *do* 偶然地…
sun halo 日晕（日光通过大气中的冰晶或水蒸气时，经折射而形成的光现象，围绕太阳四周，呈彩色）
sun dog 幻日（太阳两边出现的浅色光）
atmospheric 大气的
phenomenon 现象（**pl. phenomena**）
equator 赤道
aurora borealis 北极光
latitude 纬度
aurora australis 南极光
refract 使折射（←**refraction**折射）
cirrus cloud 卷云（高空中呈纤维状的白色云层）
crystallize 结晶化
dust particle 灰尘微粒
peculiar 奇怪的，异常的

Professor That's right. The reason there's a hole in the center of the ring—you know, around where the sun is—the reason for that is that the sunlight is refracted at an angle. Usually when we see it, it's refracted at an angle of 22 degrees, or somewhere close to that figure. That's what we call the "minimum deviation angle"—the smallest angle at which light is refracted through the crystals. At this angle, the sunlight produces the strongest, most intense halo.

Student B Uh...professor. I'm a little bit confused. If sunlight gets refracted like this by, um, by crystals, why can't we see sun halos all the time?

Professor *[with concern]* Oh, did I not make this clear before? Q2-3(C) ***[assertively]*** **Remember, I said you need a particular cloud formation to get the right kind of ice crystals—high, thin cirrus clouds.** Q2-3(A) **The crystals all need to be uniform in shape—they're flat-faced and hexagonal. Plus, the crystals should be the same size. It's only when they're uniform in size and shape that they refract light in the same way.**

Student B Ah, I see. So it's pretty rare that all these atmospheric conditions occur at the same time.

Professor Well, reasonably rare...not common, at any rate.

Student A Also, you said something before about sun dogs?

Professor Right, thanks...I was just getting to them. Sun dogs. They're the bright spots on the halo, and they're always aligned with the horizon, on either side of the sun. And why do they occur? Well, they form when most of the ice crystals are orientated in a uniform way—when their flat faces are horizontal. So sun dogs occur when the crystals are lying horizontally, but when their orientation is random, you just see a halo...no dogs.

Student A *[confused]* What? But yesterday I saw sun

Q2-3根据教授的介绍，产生光晕的两个必要条件是什么？请选出两项正确答案。
(A) 大小和形状相同的冰晶
(B) 完全静止的大气条件
(C) 稀薄且高的卷云现象
(D) 太阳位于较低的角度

MP3-119

deviation 偏向，偏离
uniform 一律的，统一的
hexagonal 六角形的
be aligned with 与…（直线）平行
orientate 确定方向（←**orientation**方向）
horizontal 水平线上的（←**horizon**水平线）

dogs and a sun halo.

Professor Yeah, well...I'm giving a fairly general account here. I mean, not all the crystals lie completely horizontal and still. At any one moment, there are always some crystals that are orientated in different directions. That's why you still see a bit of a halo when you get sun dogs.

Student A Ah, OK. Got it.

Professor Great. So I hope you found that introduction helpful. There's a, uh, a journal article in this week's reading list that I want you all to look at. It explains this topic in much more detail.

Answer
level 1 > 1 (D) 2 (B) 3 (D) 4 (D) 5 (A) 6 (D) 7 (D) 8 (C)
level 2 > 1-1 (B) 1-2 (D) 2-1 (D) 2-2 (B)
level 3 > 1-1 (B) 1-2 (B) 1-3 (D) 2-1 (B) 2-2 (A), (B) 2-3 (B)

level 1

MP3·124 **1. Listen to a conversation between a student and a professor.**

Student (female) Professor Peterson, do you have a second to talk?

Professor (male) As long as it's quick. I have a class in twenty minutes at Spaulding Hall.

Student No problem. Would you consider being an advisor for a new club I'm starting? It's for raising awareness about autism.

Professor Q1 MP3·145 ***[hesitating]*** **I'm really honored that you're asking me...*[discouragingly]* but I don't have a lot of time this semester.**

Student *[disappointed]* Oh, I see. *[pause]* It's just, I've been so inspired by your class on autism. I thought this club might be something that would interest you. It actually wouldn't be much of a time commitment—we're only looking for an advisor because it's mandatory that new student clubs have an official advisor.

Professor OK, well, let me think it over. I'll give you my answer tomorrow.

Q1 教授对学生的建议态度如何？
(A) 他很乐意加入学生的社团。
(B) 他不确定自己是自己是为社团提供建议的合适人选。
(C) 他对学生创办新社团的主意非常有兴趣。
(D) 他不太情愿对学生的社团做什么承诺。

MP3·153
raise awareness 提高认识，提高认知度
autism 自闭症
inspire 激发灵感，鼓舞
time commitment 时间承诺，投入时间
mandatory 义务的，必需的

MP3·125 **2. Listen to part of a lecture in an environmental studies class.**

Professor (female)

Q2 MP3·146 **Class, you know what petroleum is, I'm sure. The raw material we take out of the ground to create products such as gasoline, plastics, fertilizers, and medicine. But, um...how does petroleum form?** It all starts in a watery environment, where little pieces of dead organic matter mix with sediments like clays and

Q2可以推测出教授什么？
(A) 她希望学生能举出更多石油产品的例子。
(B) 她不会再介绍石油的一般性特征。
(C) 她不确定石油形成的过程。
(D) 她担心学生没有关于石油的背景知识。

sands. Now, over time...as all this material gets buried deeper and deeper under the ground, the sediments get compressed into solid rock, trapping the organic particles...which basically get cooked by the heat present deep in the Earth. Almost like a rock oven. The eventual product is petroleum. In some cases, large amounts of petroleum build up in pockets in the rock called traps, and these traps are what oil companies drill into.

MP3·154

petroleum 石油
raw material 原料，原材料
fertilizer 肥料，化肥
organic matter 有机物，有机体
sediment 沉淀物，沉积物
compress A into B 把A压缩入B
particle 微粒，粒子
drill into 钻孔进入…

MP3·126 **3. Listen to a conversation between a student and a professor.**

Student (male) Professor, would it be possible for me to reschedule a time to take the upcoming exam? I won't be here on Friday because I'm on the lacrosse team and we have an early game.

Professor (female) I see. Well, come in on Monday at 3:30—that's when my other class will be taking the exam.

Student I have a chemistry lab then. Could I do it on Monday evening?

Professor Q3 MP3·147 ***[annoyed]*** **I'd have to make a whole new version of the test just for you, since I never administer the same test more than once.**

Student Oh, I didn't realize it would be such a big deal. I'll tell my chemistry teacher about the situation and see if I can work something out with him, so I can take your test at 3:30 on Monday.

Q3教授对学生的态度如何？
(A) 她很失望学生要缺席周五的课。
(B) 她期望学生完成一项补充课题来代替考试。
(C) 她很失望学生没有早些告诉她问题。
(D) 对学生说不能与其他班学生一起考试，她有些恼怒。

reschedule 重新安排，调整（日程或约定）
upcoming 即将到来的，即将发生的
lacrosse 长曲棍球（与曲棍球相似的一种球类运动）
a whole new version of 全新的…
administer 实施，进行
big deal 大事，严重的问题

 **4. Listen to part of a lecture in a social science class.**

Professor (male)

Every society has certain, certain regulations or rules, and members of the society incur punishment for breaking them. Makes sense, right? It's about social order; rules keep societies functioning. So social control is universal, found in all societies. There're two forms

Q4教授对非正式社会控制有何看法？
(A) 它比正式社会控制更成功。
(B) 它不是在所有社会中都可以看到的。
(C) 它并不适用于集体中的所有成员。

of social control I'd like to mention: formal and informal. Formal social control is carried out by officials, like the police and the court system. Q4 MP3·148 **Informal social control happens at the interpersonal level—when people judge others' behavior by shunning them or criticizing. Sounds simple enough but it works to some extent, since people tend to want to avoid disapproval.**

(D) 它在某种程度上影响一个人的行为。

MP3·156
regulation 规则，规范
incur 招致（处罚或非难等）
court system 司法制度
interpersonal 人与人之间的，人际的
shun 避开，远离
to some extent 在一定程度上，到某种程度
disapproval 不赞同，反对

MP3·128 **5. Listen to a conversation between a student and a dormitory administrator.**

Administrator (female) Benjamin, I'm afraid there was a problem with your dorm room when we inspected it.

Student (male) Oh, no. You're kidding.

Administrator No...there's a large hole in the wall next to the door. I'm afraid we're going to have to charge you for the repairs.

Student Q5 MP3·149 ***[upset]* Wait a minute, that hole was there when I moved in at the beginning of the year.** I filed a report about it and was told I wouldn't be held responsible.

Administrator Oh, is that the case? I didn't notice anything about that when I looked at your move-in report, but I guess I could've missed it. Let me check again and get back to you. If I've made a mistake, I apologize.

Student That's OK...I just don't want to pay for those repairs.

Q5可以推测出学生的态度是什么？
(A) 不同意管理员说的
(B) 由于不理解管理员说的话感到担心。
(C) 希望管理员可以更细致地解释问题。
(D) 对自己房间的状况感到不好意思。

MP3·157
dorm 宿舍(=**dormitory**)
inspect 调查，监督，检查
charge A for B 向A索要B（通常为资费或手续费等）
file a report 申报，提交报告
hold A responsible 向A问责，向A追究责任
move-in report 入住申报

MP3·129 **6. Listen to part of a lecture in an environmental studies class.**

Professor (female)

Are you familiar with Wangari Maathai? She won a 2004 Nobel Peace Prize for her work with the Green Belt Movement, which is actually what I'd like to focus on. It's a Kenya-based non-

Q6对于绿化带运动，教授态度如何？
(A) 她希望直接参与这一组织的活动。
(B) 她认为绿化带运动被过高评价了。

governmental organization that started in 1977 when Dr. Maathai began a grassroots tree-planting program to help overcome deforestation. Q6 MP3·150 **Since then, more than 40 million trees have been planted in Africa, helping to prevent soil erosion, sustain water resources, and generate fair economic development. Another important result of the Green Belt Movement is the way it empowers the women who become involved, and that helps their communities too. So, as you can see, Maathai's work has been, um, pretty inspirational.**

(C) 她希望绿化带运动在今后几年会得以发扬光大。
(D) 她对这一运动所取得的成就印象很深。

MP3·158
non-governmental organization 非政府组织（=**NGO**）
grassroots 平民的，草根的
deforestation 森林破坏
soil erosion 土壤侵蚀，水土流失
sustain 持续，存续
empower 增加（某人的）权利，赋予权利
inspirational 鼓舞人心的，激发灵感的

MP3·130 **7. Listen to a conversation between a student and an advisor.**

Advisor (male)	Well, Samantha...are you ready to choose your major?
Student (female)	I think so. I've given it a lot of thought, and I want to major in physics.
Advisor	Excellent. Q7 MP3·151 **Now, that's a pretty broad field, and here at the university we have several different majors within the physics department. Applied physics, theoretical physics, astronomy...which one did you have in mind?**
Student	***[caught off guard]*** **Uh...actually...that's news to me. I thought physics was a major in itself...that it covered all those subjects.**
Advisor	Well, you'll be able to take classes in all of them, but you do need to decide on one particular area to major in.
Student	*[unsure where to begin]* OK...well...
Advisor	How about this? I have a packet of information from the physics department about the different major options. Why don't you browse through this and come back in a few days when you make your decision?
Student	Good idea. I think I need more time to decide.

Q7从下面这番话，可以推测出什么？
[caught off guard] **Uh...actually...that's news to me. I thought physics was a major in itself...that it covered all those subjects.**
(A) 她并不想现在就选一个具体的专业。
(B) 她并不确信听清楚了指导教授的话。
(C) 她对不能选物理作为专业感到十分失望。
(D) 她还没做好选具体专业的准备。

MP3·159
give A a lot of thought 慎重地考虑A
broad 广泛地，广范围地
applied physics 应用物理学
theoretical physics 理论物理学
have A in mind 考虑A
catch A off guard （意料之外的）趁A不备，使A措手不及
That's news to me. 我第一次听说。
cover 涵盖，包括（主题或领域等）

a packet of information （一捆，一包的）资料集，信息册

browse through 浏览…，翻阅…

MP3·131 **8. Listen to part of a lecture in a literature class.**

Professor (male)

In a lot of Native American lore you find this character repeatedly; the trickster. Q8 MP3·152 **Um, *[pausing]* you also find trickster-like characters in European-American traditions... *[pause]* um, but back to what I was saying—the trickster is a character who breaks the laws of nature or the gods, usually for some beneficial goal.** Now, among Native American cultures, coyote is a pretty common trickster. He appears in a lot of stories, and he's always different. Sometimes he's an animal, sometimes a fool, sometimes a cultural hero, and sometimes even the Creator. This variability is an important aspect of the Native American trickster—he or she embodies the multiplicity of life in a way that you don't find in European-American trickster stories.

Q8在说下面这番话时，教授的意思是什么？

***[pause]* um, but back to what I was saying—**

(A) 他以为学生很熟悉欧洲裔美国文化中的恶作剧妖精。

(B) 他很担心学生没有学习过美国本土文化中的恶作剧妖精。

(C) 他并不准备现在讨论欧洲裔美国文化中的恶作剧妖精。

(D) 他不清楚是否应就恶作剧妖精这一形象进行进一步的解释。

MP3·160

lore 学问和传统，（专门的）知识

trickster 骗子，无赖，恶作剧的妖精（古典小说或神话中出现的淘气鬼或年轻艺人或动物）

the Creator [宗教]创世主

variability 多样性

embody 体现，使具体化

multiplicity 多样性，多重性

level 2

MP3·132 **1. Listen to a conversation between a student and a university administrator.**

Student (male)	*[uncertain whether he is in the right place]* Q1-1 MP3·133 **Um...hi. I'm looking for the, um, the administration office...**
Administrator (female)	**Well, you've come to the right place. I'm a university administrator.**

Q1-2可以推测出什么？

(A) 学生怀疑行政工作人员是否会帮助自己。

(B) 学生不确定行政办公室在哪儿。

(C) 学生因为与行政人员不熟而担心。

(D) 学生确定自己最终找对了办公室。

Student	*[relieved]* Oh, great. I'm pretty unfamiliar with this side of campus, so I was afraid I was lost. Um...anyway, Professor Kahn sent me over here from the theater department. I'm supposed to get some information for the drama club's upcoming performance.
Administrator	Oh, OK. Is the performance taking place on the stage in Billing's Hall?
Student	Yes, that's right. It's next Friday, Saturday, and Sunday. We're doing a modern remake of *Macbeth*.
Administrator	Sounds great. That's one of my favorites. So...what kind of information do you need from me?
Student	Well...we were curious about the university's policy on ticket sales. You see, we're trying to raise money for the annual club trip to London...to visit Shakespeare's Globe Theatre. And we thought if we could charge admission to our play, that'd really help us get closer to our fundraising goal. So...I guess our question is, are we allowed to sell tickets on our own, or does someone in the administration office have to approve it first?
Administrator	I understand. OK. The drama club is part of the university's theater department, right?
Student	That's right.
Administrator	In that case, you can handle the ticket sales completely on your own. But, um, once you've collected all the proceeds, Professor Kahn will have to submit an earnings report here to the administration office. The club will get to keep all the money, but the university just needs a record of it.
Student	Q1-2 MP3·134 **Oh, that sounds good. So we just need a...*[unfamiliar with the term]* what was that again? An earnings report?**
Administrator	Yes. Here. I have a copy I can give you to take to Professor Kahn.
Student	OK, then. I'll do that. Thank you very much for your help.
Administrator	Not at all.

Q1-2可以推测出什么？
(A) 学生对于要填表感到厌烦。
(B) 学生担心收入报告会成为问题。
(C) 学生认为自己可能已经填过收入报告了。
(D) 学生不太清楚行政工作人员是否提到了表格。

MP3·161
administrator 行政工作人员，办公人员
be unfamiliar with 对…不熟悉，对…不了解
send A over （交予任务等）派遣A去…，发送A去…
performance 演出，（业务）表现
raise money 募集资金
annual 每年的，年度的
admission 准许进入，入场费
fundraising 筹款，募款
approve 认可，赞成
proceeds （买卖物品等的）收益，收入
earnings 收入所得，收益

 MP3·135 **2. Listen to part of a talk in a meteorology class.**

Professor (female)	Everyone...I'm sure all of you are aware that the temperature of the planet is...changing.
Student A (male)	Yeah. I'm curious—how much do you think the climate will warm by the end of the 21st century?
Professor	Q2-1 MP3·136 ***[hesitating]* Uh...*[with uncertainty]* Maybe around three to seven degrees Fahrenheit...though it'd probably be safer to estimate between two and eleven degrees Fahrenheit. It's just—there're a lot of factors that could potentially affect how much the climate changes in the near future.** Um, but I'd prefer to refrain from making any more guesses about the future temperature. Could someone, uh, give me an example of a factor that causes climate change?
Student B (male)	Well, one factor is greenhouse gas emissions, since greenhouse gases in the atmosphere prevent heat from dissipating into space.
Professor	You're right. Right now at least, greenhouse gases seem to be the main, um, the main cause of climate change. Particularly carbon dioxide, even though it's actually not the main greenhouse gas—water vapor is. Nonetheless, rising levels of carbon dioxide due to industrialization appear to be the, um, the primary culprit in terms of recent global warming. What else? Who has some other ideas about global climate change?
Student B	Um, what about variations in solar output?
Professor	Well, that's a good point. If you look at the big picture, the sun has been getting brighter and putting out more energy over the course of our planet's history, so naturally that has an effect on Earth's temperature. Similarly, slight changes in Earth's orbit affect how much sunlight reaches the surface and where it hits. Q2-2 MP3·137 **Oh, and another cause of climate change that you haven't mentioned yet is volcanism.**

Q2-1可以推测出教授的态度是什么？
(A) 她不认为这件事与讨论有关。
(B) 她担心学生误解了自己。
(C) 她期待学生知道问题的答案。
(D) 她不确定答案的精确数值。

Q2-2学生这样说的意思是什么？
***[surprised]* You can't mean that volcanoes affect the global climate.**
(A) 他不确定自己是否听对了教授的话。
(B) 他对教授的主张感到惊讶。
(C) 他不清楚教授要表明什么观点。
(D) 他担心教授省略了一些信息。

MP3·162

be aware that 知道…，认识到…
estimate 预测，估计
potentially 潜在的
refrain from *doing* 抑制做…，避免做…
dissipate into 消散于…，消失于…
water vapor 水蒸气
primary culprit 主犯，主要原因
variation 变化，变动
output 排出物，产量
over the course of …期间，…的过程中
volcanism 火山活动，火山作用
eruption （火山）爆发，喷发
massive 大规模的，大量的
devastating 破坏性的，压倒性的
extinction 消灭，灭绝
initiate 开始，开始实施

Student A	**[*surprised*] You can't mean that volcanoes affect the global climate.**
Professor	Indeed they can. In fact, the biggest eruptions can influence the climate for millions of years. Scientists think massive eruptions may have caused devastating extinction events in Earth's history and initiated periods of global cooling.

level 3

MP3·138 **1. Listen to part of a conversation between a student and an advisor.**

Advisor (male)	So, Sandrine, how's your internship this semester working out? Has it been a worthwhile experience so far?
Student (female)	[*hesitantly and with uncertainty*] Um... well...I guess so.
Advisor	[*concerned*] Hmmm...it sounds like it's not what you expected.
Student	Yeah, you could say that.
Advisor	Well, how does the internship differ from your expectations?
Student	Um, I guess I thought that I'd have a lot more responsibility...you know, actually getting to work with patients...like a real physical therapist, with a little guidance, of course.
Advisor	That sounds like a reasonable expectation. That hasn't happened?
Student	Not really. Q1-1 **I mean, I've been working with a therapist and helping her with her patients, but I don't feel like I'm really getting the hands-on experience I thought this internship would—would provide.** I just sort of do what the therapist tells me...you know, instead of making decisions about treatments for patients. So I don't get to test my knowledge as a therapist.
Advisor	I see. Well, the point of the internship is to give you practical experience you can't get from your regular classes. It's an

Q1-1学生的问题是什么？
(A) 她需要找一个实习职位。
(B) 她对现在的实习不满意。
(C) 她认为实习的工作负担过重。
(D) 她希望在实习中得到更多指导。

MP3·163
worthwhile 有意义的，有价值的
physical therapist 理疗师
guidance 指导，引导
reasonable 合理的，正当的
hands-on 实战的
regular class 正规课程

essential part of your education as a physical therapist. So I think it's a big problem that you feel like you're not...um... benefiting from your time at the Freemont Rehabilitation Center.

Student Do you think I should...I don't know...drop the internship and try another one during the summer?

Advisor *[discouragingly]* Well...that's a pretty drastic step. I wouldn't recommend that until all other options have been, um, exhausted. Dictation 开始 Tell me about your relationship with the therapist you're working with.

Student Oh, she's great, and I think we get along well. I can tell she's [1]*really knowledgeable and experienced.*

Advisor So your problem is with the internship itself—not with the Freemont Rehabilitation Center or the staff there?

Student *[thinking]* Yeah. That's right. The people definitely aren't the problem. In fact, [2]*that's the best part of the internship.* I've met some wonderful people there.

Advisor Well, that's good news. When you have a [3]*good working relationship with your employer and coworkers,* you'd be surprised how much you can accomplish. Q1-2 **Why don't you just talk to them about it?**

Student You're right. I guess I didn't think about that before. I felt like the internship [4]*was set up a certain way,* and I was powerless to, um, to change it.

Advisor Well, that's certainly not the case. You know, the therapist you're working with may not even realize that you've got some... reservations about the internship. Other interns she had in the past may have [5]*felt uncomfortable handling patients on their own.* Q1-2 **It's up to you to tell her that you** [6]***prefer a more hands-on method.***

Student Q1-3 MP3·139 ***[concerned]* I agree with what you're saying...but the last thing I want to do is seem ungrateful. I really,**

Q1-2为了解决问题，指导教授提供了什么建议？
(A) 放弃现在的实习，夏天再开始其他的实习。
(B) 向理疗师就训练给予坦率的反馈。
(C) 和与自己可以更好相处的其他理疗师一起工作。
(D) 和理疗师约个时间谈谈自己的问题。

Q1-3可以推测出学生的态度是什么？
(A) 她对理疗师的态度感到失望。
(B) 她觉得理疗师的水平不高。
(C) 她很担心和别的实习生一起工作。
(D) 她很担心和理疗师谈话。

MP3·163

rehabilitation 修复，复兴，回归社会
drop 取消，放弃（课程等）
drastic 激烈的，猛烈的
exhausted 耗尽的，精疲力竭的
get along well 和睦相处
experienced 熟练的，老练的
be set up 被设定好的，计划好的
reservation 制约，条件
handle 处理
ungrateful 不知感激的
volunteer to *do* 自愿做…，主动做…

really appreciate her help...and that [7]*she volunteered to take on an intern.* **If I express dissatisfaction with the internship, she may...I don't know...think I don't appreciate her help.**

Advisor I don't think that'll be an issue. She's a professional, and above all, she wants to help you get the experience you need to become a physical therapist. So if you have some ideas about how the internship could help you reach that goal, I'm sure [8]*she'd be thrilled to hear them.* Dictation 结束

Student OK. I'll give it a try. How do you think I should bring it up?

Advisor Maybe after an appointment with a patient. While you're helping her with the patient, think about tasks that you'd like to try handling on your own. Maybe you want to try showing the patient how to do a certain leg stretch or how to use the gymnastic ball. Well...after the appointment, just suggest that next time you'd like to try doing that on your own to test your skills and to...to build up your confidence. I'm sure she won't mind making adjustments to the internship if you express your suggestions.

Student OK. I'll definitely talk to her when I go in on Thursday. I'm excited to find out what she'll think about my suggestions.

take on 聘用（人员），承担（事情）
be thrilled to *do* 很激动…
bring up 提出（话柄或话题）
gymnastic 体操的，体育的
build up confidence 树立自信，培养自信
make adjustment to 调整…，调节…

MP3·140 **2. Listen to part of a discussion in an oceanography class.**

Professor (male) Remember last time we were talking about, um, about male parental care...how some types of bony fish exhibit patterns of...of paternal care for offspring instead of maternal care? Q2-1 **We're going to continue that discussion of paternal care in fish. Let me give you a hint about our topic: seahorses.** Does anyone know what I might be referring to?

Student A (female) Uh, I think seahorses are—they're like humans because, um, because they carry

Q2-1 教授主要介绍了海马的什么方面？
(A) 公海马与母海马的形态区别
(B) **繁殖方式**
(C) 生长周期
(D) 海马展现出的求爱行为

MP3·164
parental 父母亲的，父母有责任的
paternal 父亲的，父系的（←**paternity**父权，父亲的义务）
offspring 子孙，后代

developing offspring inside them. Um. But, uh, in seahorses, I think it's the male that gets pregnant. Maybe that's going to be the focus of the lecture.

Professor Exactly. Seahorses are sort of like an instance of male paternity to the extreme. It's not the female who carries the offspring, it's the male.

Student B (male) *[expressing doubt]* I have to admit...I've heard about male seahorses being the ones who get pregnant...but it just seems like a myth to me...

Professor I'm not surprised to hear you say that. Seahorses are generally pointed out as a strange exception to a biological rule that female pregnancy is what normally happens in nature. So we hear about that so much that...I don't know...I think it makes male pregnancy in seahorses seem a little bit like a myth or a legend; too strange to be real. But it is indeed real.

Student B So...is it the male or the female seahorse that produces eggs?

Professor The female seahorse produces the eggs, just like in other animals. And she then deposits the eggs into the...the pouch in the male's body where he carries the offspring. Q2-1 **Uh, let me tell you a little bit about the overall reproduction process for seahorses.** First, males and females court for a few days. Q2-2(A) **The kind of, um, of courtship behavior you might see could be...they'll hold tails...** or swim up close beside each other...or maybe circle the same, uh, the same piece of sea grass together. Q2-2(B) **And the male might swish some water through his pouch to show that it's empty.**

Dictation开始 After the, um, [1] *the courtship behavior,* the male and female pair will float up toward the surface of the water. Then the female seahorse, um, [2] *deposits her eggs in the pouch* of her...her male partner. The number of eggs she delivers may be around

Q2-2根据教授的介绍，与海马最初的求爱相关的两种行为是？请选择两项正确答案。
(A) 抓尾巴。
(B) 让水通过孵卵袋。
(C) 结成一对浮上水面。
(D) 规律性地每天早上见面。

MP3-164

maternal 母亲的，母系的
seahorse 海马
refer to 提到…，谈论…
carry 孕育
developing 成长，生长
get pregnant 怀孕
myth 虚构的故事，神话
legend 传说
indeed 真正地，确实
deposit 保存，存放
pouch 口袋，囊
reproduction 繁殖，再生
court 求爱，交往
courtship behavior [ritual] （动物等繁殖期的）求爱行为[仪式]
sea grass 海草
swish 嗖地移动，行进
float 浮在（水面上或空中）
deliver 产（卵），生（孩子）
fertilize 孵化
nutrient 养分，营养

200, and they, um, they're [3]*fertilized in the pouch.* While inside the pouch, the eggs get nutrients and oxygen...and the temperature is kept just right. Over the course of the pregnancy, the, um, the environment inside the pouch changes a little bit...so that at the end of the pregnancy, it's pretty much the same as the surrounding seawater. That way [4]*the offspring aren't shocked by the seawater* when they're born.

Anyway, after the female deposits the eggs, she, um, she swims away. [5]*Throughout the male's pregnancy,* the female seahorse will, um, she'll come back to visit her partner every morning. But most of the time she's not around. On her morning visits, the two seahorses do this...this other kind of bonding, I guess. It lasts for about six minutes or so, and the seahorses might swim around together and, uh, change color and [6]*hold each other's tails.* After that, the female leaves again for the day.

Now, when [7]*the male goes into labor,* it's usually at night. He pushes the offspring out of the pouch, and then he'll be ready for a new pregnancy right away.[Dictation 结束] He can re-mate even just a couple of hours after giving birth. You see, when the female mate comes back for her morning visit, the two will probably start that initial courtship ritual again.

Student B How long does a typical pregnancy last?

Professor Usually about two to four weeks.

Student A **Q2-3** MP3·141 ***[impressed]* So the male gives birth to 200 little babies and then right away gets pregnant again? It sounds tiring.**

Professor I agree. He gives birth...and then he's ready to start the whole process again right away. But what's even more impressive is that some species of seahorses actually give birth to more than that. Scientists found that one seahorse gave birth to, um, to 1,500 offspring at one time.

Q2-3可以推测出学生的态度是什么？

(A) 她怀疑教授向大家提供的信息不准确。

(B) 她对教授刚刚提供的信息感到惊奇。

(C) 她之前就很熟悉讲义文中讨论的生物学事实。

(D) 她很好奇科学家是运用什么方法发现这一事实的。

MP3·164

surrounding 周围的，包围着的

bonding （紧密的）纽带

go into labor 开始生产，开始分娩

mate 配对，配偶，伴儿

give birth 生产，分娩

initial 开始的，初期的

tiring 累人的，令人疲劳的

DAY06 Review Test I

Answer passage 1 > 1 (C) 2 (D) 3 (B) 4 (C) 5 (B)

passage 2 > 1 (C) 2 (A) 3 (A), (C) 4 (B) 5 (B) 6 (C)

passage 3 > 1 (C) 2 (B) 3 (D) 4 (A) 5 (B) 6 (B)

MP3·165 **passage 1. [1-5] Listen to part of a conversation in a professor's office.**

Student (female) Excuse me, Professor Ba?

Professor (male) *[startled]* Oh. Can I help you?

Student Uh, I'm in your pottery class, and I was wondering if you had a minute—

Professor Q4 MP3·166 **Well, I've got a meeting with the art department faculty at 10:00, so you'll have to make it brief...or you could always come back later. I'll be around for a while this afternoon.**

Student **Actually...that's OK. I mean, I think this won't take very long.**

Professor OK then...well, come on in.

Student Thanks.

Professor So, what can I do for you?

Student Well...I remember you said you went to the University of Cellex...

Professor For grad school? Actually, it was Patton University. Wrong town...but the same state.

Student *[disappointed]* Oh...really? I thought it was the University of Cellex. Q1 **See, I was thinking about applying to one of their grad programs.**

Professor Well, I didn't go there, but I do know a little bit about it. Q1 **Did you have a specific question? Or were you just looking for general information?**

Student **I guess just general info. Like, do they have a good ceramics program?** I've been researching art grad schools, but it's hard to, uh, determine which schools have the best programs. I wanted to talk to someone who'd been in the program.

Professor Probably a good idea. I did have a couple of friends in the ceramics program at Cellex, and they had positive experiences with it. Actually, one of my friends who went there is featured in this month's *Potters' Guild*. You should check out her work—that's another good way to get an idea of the school. Look at the work of the students coming out of the program. You know, because you want to go to a good school, but on top of that, you want to go to a school that fits your style.

Student Yeah...that's a good point.

Professor Anyway, the ceramics program at the University of Cellex is quite small, but it's very good. Q2 **The professor-to-student ratio is really high**, and the facilities are beautiful. Their art department recently added a lot of state-of-the-art technology.

Student But do you think it's better to go to a larger program, where you've got more students to interact with and learn from? I'm worried that a small program might feel a little bit...I don't know...stifling after a while.

Professor	I'd say that depends on your personality. Like I said, my friends who attended the grad program there were really happy with it. Me, on the other hand, I probably wouldn't have liked it as much. The ceramics program at Patton University was much bigger. The art department was actually the biggest department on campus.
Student	Well, Q3 **what do you think's the most important thing to consider when choosing a grad program?**
Professor	**Hmm...It's really important to think about the faculty at the school you end up going to. You need to make sure the teachers have a good reputation, that's for sure.** You're at a stage where you're just trying to develop your talent, and you need a good set of teachers to help you do that. Q5 MP3•167 **Then you'll really be able to grow as an artist.**
Student	**Yeah, I know what you're saying. I guess I'll have to do some more research about...**
Professor	***[interrupting and sounding rushed]* Look, uh, why don't you come back later on today? We can discuss your options in more detail then.**
Student	Ah, OK. Sure. Thanks.

MP3•174

pottery 陶艺(=ceramics)，陶瓷器
faculty （大学的）教职员
grad school 研究生院(=graduate school)
feature （在杂志、报纸等上）特别刊载

check out 检查，确认
on top of 不仅…，还有
ratio 比，比率
state-of-the-art 最新的，尖端的
stifling 令人郁闷的

on the other hand 另一方面
end up *doing* 结果…
have a good reputation 名声好，评价好

◎ 解析

1. 学生为什么去找教授？
   (A) 为了了解教授是从哪个研究生院毕业的。**(Minor)**
   (B) 为了询问某本艺术杂志中介绍的艺术家。**(not correct)**
   (C) 为了获取研究生阶段的相关信息。
   (D) 为了拜托教授写推荐信。**(not mentioned)**

Main Idea
请看标注Q1处。学生说自己正在考虑去Cellex大学研究生院继续深造，他想知道关于那所大学的一般性信息。可见，学生是为了询问与研究生学业相关的信息才来拜访教授的。因此，正确答案是(C)。请注意，学生尽管问了教授毕业于哪所学校的研究生院，但是并不是为此来访的，所以(A)选项不正确。提起陶艺杂志中人物报道的不是学生，而是教授，因此(B)也是错误选项。

2. 对于Cellex大学，教授说了什么？
   (A) 那所学校艺术专业的规模比其他任何专业都大。 **(not correct)**
   (B) 学生在那么小的学校里不会感到满足的。 **(not correct)**

Detail
请看标注Q2处。教授说Cellex大学陶艺专业中教授与学生之间的比例真的非常高。因此，正确答案是(D)。正确答案中的very favorable是原文中really high经过paraphrasing而来的。

(C) 那所学校没有将尖端技术引入艺术专业的财政余力。 **(not correct)**

(D) 陶艺专业教授与学生之间的比例十分合适。

Patton大学的美术专业规模最大，而Cellex大学美术专业最近引进了不少尖端设备。因此(A)和(C)都是错误选项。学生担心在教学规模小的专业或项目中学习可能会感到不满意，不是教授，因此(B)也不正确。

---

3. 教授认为选择大学院时最重要的什么？

(A) 大学课程专业的规模 **(not correct)**

(B) 教授队伍的水平

(C) 学校鼓励的研究风格 **(not Mentioned)**

(D) 研究生是否成功 **(not Mentioned)**

Detail

请看标注Q3处。教授说在决定去哪所学校时，有必要先确定对其师资水平的评价。因此正确答案是(B)。她和学生都提到了研究生专业的规模，但是并不认为这是需要考虑的最重要事项，因此(A)选项错误。

---

4. 学生这么说的意思是什么？

Actually...that's OK.

(A) 教授不想缺席教授会议。

(B) 他觉得下午再来更好。

(C) 他不想为了见教授再来一次。

(D) 他认为教授会议很快就会结束。

Attitude

请看标注Q4处。学生在说了Actually...that's OK之后，马上又补充到不会占用多长时间 (this won't take very long)。由此可见，比起以后再来一趟，他希望即使谈得短一些，也要在现在说。因此正确答案是(C)。

---

5. 教授为什么这么说？

[interrupting and souding rushed] Look, uh, why don't you come back later on today?

(A) 为了有时间就那个主题进行一些调查。

(B) 为了告诉学自己还有其他事情。

(C) 为了催促学生自己思考那个问题。

(D) 为了告诉学生自己随时都有谈话的时间。

Function

在对话开头，教授就提到了因为有教授会议不能谈很久。谈话中学生又停下了一次，之后加快了谈话速度，可见谈话是因为其他事情而不能再进行下去。因此，正确答案选(C)。

 MP3·168 **passage 2. [1-6] Listen to part of a talk in an architecture class.**

Professor (male) **Q1 Has anyone ever heard of the term "bungalow?"**

Student A (female) **Yes. It's a, a style of house.** I'm not exactly sure what features it has...but I know it's a kind of house.

Professor **Q5** MP3·169 **Well, you're right. It is a style of house. I'll talk more about the—uh—the typical, um, features of the bungalow in a minute, but first there's something else we've got to go over.** **How much do you know about—about the British Empire?**

Student B (male) You mean the historic British Empire that had colonies all over the world?

Professor Yes, that's the one.

Student B Well...they had a lot of territory in a lot of regions. For a really long time. Um, they were particularly successful—*[revising his statement]* well...I wouldn't call the occupation of someone else's land a success—anyway, the British were able to really establish themselves on the Indian subcontinent.

Professor Good. That's exactly what I want to discuss—the British presence in India. Um, in the 1750s, the British...uh...who had been in India for a while at that time...um, they began to wage war in southern and eastern India. See, they really wanted control over the wealthy province of Bengal. When the British conquered Bengal they became, um, quite powerful. I mean, previously, they had—they had really just been, um, traders...you know, foreign traders in India. Q6 MP3·170 **But once the British conquered the Bengal province, they took on a different role. As, um, well, as a ruling power. And, well, I don't want this to turn into a history class or anything. So before that happens, can anyone guess why I might be giving you this historical background about India?**

Student A I guess it's somehow related to bungalows. Perhaps the, um, the style originated in India...The word "bungalow" sounds like it could be, um, from India, I guess.

Professor Yeah, right. Q1 **The word is from India, and the bungalow style originated there...um, in Bengal. And because of the British, the bungalow style spread across the world.** Let me explain. See, as the British started to settle in India, they—they just used whatever materials were around. They hired local builders to make traditional-style houses using traditional materials. So, um, so what they were living in were, um, bungalows—which had been built in India for a long time. Q2 **These bungalows were designed to, um, to be comfortable in the incredible Indian heat. They were one-story houses...with, um, with spacious rooms that let the air circulate well.** They had a big veranda, too. Um, and often they would be, uh, set on stilts. The stilts had two purposes—to help increase, um, air ventilation and to—to keep bugs and snakes out of the house.

Well, Q3 **over time, the British started to, um, to change these bungalows so that they looked more like the, um, the houses they were used to in England.** Q3(C) **So they started having the bungalows made out of, of stone...** Q3(A) **um, and they added columns to the veranda.** Um, I guess for the most part, though, the bungalow style remained, uh, quite similar to the original form. Because it was well suited for, for the heat in India. Um, eventually, the British brought the bungalow style back to England...and the style kept on spreading.

Student A So...are these bungalows still built now?

Professor Oh, sure. They're a pretty popular style in the U.S. There's a lot of variety...but bungalows in the U.S. have a couple of common features. They've got, um, a low roof with a really gentle slope. Um, they've got a porch with columns...they're usually one story or one-and-a-half stories tall...um, and usually there's a central living room, with bedrooms, a kitchen, a dining room, and bathrooms arranged around that central, um, that living room.

The first bungalow in the U.S. was built in, um, in 1879. Q4 **They became really popular during the 20th century because they, um, they fit the changing American lifestyle of that time.** Families were starting to simplify their lives. I mean, families were working and taking care of the kids...uh, so old concerns—say, like entertaining visitors—these weren't really a part of their lifestyle anymore. So families no longer wanted houses with lots of special rooms for—for entertaining...like a parlor or a music room or a reception room...anything like that. The bungalow design was what people were looking for in a house. And house-design magazines sold a lot of blueprints for various bungalow designs. Between, um, 1880 and 1930, bungalows were extremely popular in the U.S. Although the bungalow craze is over, you can still see a lot of bungalow-style architecture in—in houses made during that time period. And, of course, new bungalows are still being made. The design is still quite appealing to, to some people.

MP3 • 175

go over 探讨，议论
colony 殖民地
occupation 占有，占据
subcontinent 次大陆（主要指包括印度、巴基斯坦及孟加拉在内的整个大陆）
wage war 进行战争

province 地方，省
originate 开始，起源
spacious 宽敞的，广阔的
circulate 循环
stilts 〈复数形式〉（房屋的）支柱
ventilation 通风，换气
column 柱，圆柱

porch 玄关，门廊
concerns 〈复数形式〉关心，关心的事情
parlor 客厅，起居室
blueprint 设计图，蓝图
craze 狂热
appealing 吸引人的，有魅力的

◎ 解析

1. 讲义文的主要内容是什么？
   (A) 在美国再次流行的英式住宅风格 **(minor)**
   (B) 美国的孟加拉式住宅 **(minor)**
   (C) 来源于印度的国际性住宅风格
   (D) 印度传统孟加拉式平房特征 **(minor)**

Main Idea

讲义文首先介绍了孟加拉一词的来源，然后说明这一住宅风格起源于印度，然后传播至世界各地。其中又以英国与美国为例子。因此正确答案为(C)。选项(A)，(B)与(D)在讲义文中也有提及，但只是局部性的内容，因此不正确。

2. 传统孟加拉式平房的主要特征是什么？
   (A) 具备为了改善整个屋子空气流通而设计的特征。
   (B) 混合了印度与英国殖民地风格的特征。 **(not correct)**
   (C) 为了使内部凉爽而使用了反射光和热的材料。 **(not mentioned)**
   (D) 为了给人们提供一个休息场所，建造得十分坚固。 **(not mentioned)**

Detail

请看标记Q2部分的内容。此处介绍了孟加拉式建筑为了适应印度炎热的气候而建为单层的，又为了更好的通风换气建得十分宽敞。通过这些，即可知道传统的孟加拉平房是为了改善通风而设计的。因此正确答案为(A)。随着时间的流逝，英国人将孟加拉式平房建得与英国的房子渐渐相似，但是大部分的孟加拉式平房还是维持了原来的形态。因此(B)选项不正确。

3. 英国人是如何改造传统的孟加拉式平房的？请选择两项正确答案。
   (A) 增加柱子

Detail

标记Q3的部分出现了传统印度孟加拉式平房的特征是如何变化的内容，因此需要仔细听。这部

(B) 建在支柱上。**(not correct)**
(C) 把石头作为建筑材料使用。
(D) 建成单层建筑。**(not correct)**

分介绍到英国人用石头建筑孟加拉式平房，并且在阳台立起柱子。这些都是他们对孟加拉式平房的改造。因此正确答案为(A)和(C)。在支柱上面建房是传统的风格，而孟加拉式平房一直以来都是单层建筑，所以(B)和(D)选项不正确。

4. 根据教授的介绍，为什么孟加拉式平房在20世纪的美国很受欢迎？
(A) 因为建造费用低。**(not mentioned)**
(B) 因为符合美国新的生活形式。
(C) 因为住房杂志上出售设计图。**(not correct)**
(D) 因为中间有卧室。**(not correct)**

Detail
当时，美国生活渐渐转变为以家庭为中心，而孟加拉式平房正好符合了这种生活方式的需要，因此正确答案选(B)。尽管在住宅杂志上出售孟加拉式平房的设计图以及中间有客厅都是事实，但是这并不是它在20世纪的美国受欢迎的原因。所以选项(C)与(D)不正确。

5. 教授为什么这样说？
How much do you know about-about the British Empire?
(A) 为了显示对信息感到不确定。
(B) 为了介绍讲义文的主题。
(C) 为了让学生进一步调查。
(D) 为了明确以前说过的话。

Function
印度曾经是大英帝国的殖民地。录音回放部分之后，讲义文介绍了英帝国对孟加拉式平房建筑的影响以及这一建筑风格在世界范围内的普及。正是为了介绍这两点，教授才提到了大英帝国。因此，教授说这句话是为了介绍接下来讲义文的主题。正确答案选(B)。

6. 教授这样说的意思是什么？
well, I don't want this to turn into a history class or anything.
(A) 他希望学生更加关注现代发展史。
(B) 他认为学生已经知道一些关于住宅发展史的内容。
(C) 他不想介绍过多的背景信息。
(D) 他认为学生在其他课上会学习这部分内容。

Attitude
请注意这是一篇“建筑学”讲义文。即，教授提起大英帝国是因为这一历史事实与主题有关，而历史性的内容应该在历史课上介绍，所以教授在讲义文表现出只介绍“建筑”部分内容的态度。由此可见，教授不想提供太多的历史背景信息，所以正确答案选(C)。

MP3 • 171 **passage 3. [1-6] Listen to part of a lecture in a zoology class.**

Professor (male)

Yesterday we took an in-depth look at the physical characteristics of primates, their shared DNA with humans...the opposable thumb...so if you're just joining us today, please make sure you read chapter 24 of your textbook. Q1 Q5 MP3 • 172 **Today, we're going to focus on the mandrill...the most colorful monkey—or rather, it's not truly a monkey anymore...it's been classified as its own genus, mandrillus—but yes, the most colorful of primates...the mandrill. They are social creatures and have been observed by scientists to live and travel in packs of, uh, up to eight hundred individuals!** **<u>Can you imagine it?</u> Normally though, it's anywhere between twenty and two hundred.** Um, so the mandrills live mostly on the primary forest ground, roaming about the floor looking for food. Q2 **On average they might cover around twenty square miles a day foraging.** And although most of their diet consists of plant matter...you know, like fruits, leaves, roots, bark, grasses...they are omnivorous, so they sometimes eat spiders, snails, worms, ants, and occasionally small ground rodents. What's interesting to note, yes, is that males feed on the ground, while, um, females and young mandrills climb into the trees to eat.

Q1 **The way mandrills communicate has been an interesting focus of research for scientists... they have several types of communication.** Uh, the most obvious ones are verbal, tactile, and visual. Verbal contact is, as maybe you can guess, when they make noises...oh, there are a variety... grunting, crowing, screaming, grinding, growling, and roaring, to name a few...they use these to warn one another, for mating, for guiding or directing, for threatening, or in general, to express the mood of a situation. Tactile communication is...touch. This is mostly used to signify grooming or announce reproductive availability and readiness. For example, uh, with social grooming...an individual will pick through another's fur using its tongue, fingers, and lips.

Visual communication is...hmm...it has a broad range of conveyances. It ranges from behavioral cues to their bright physical colors. As common with many other animals, Q3 **male mandrills are conspicuously more vividly colored than females. Adult males have a bright red nose, blue cheeks, and a rump in hues of blue, red, and purple. Females are similarly, um, colored but much duller and without red noses.** Their fur, both males and females, is kind of a dull olive-grey-black shade. It's been postulated that the brilliant coloration allows mandrills to identify one another while foraging...also to follow and keep together while traveling through the forest.

Q6 MP3·173 **Moving along...is everyone following me here?** **<u>I hope you're taking notes.</u> Anyway, behavioral visuals include when the mandrill yawns, bares its teeth, threat jerks or rushes, or sits and looks a particular way to indicate a grooming or mating desire**...these visual communications can have subtle differences, as researchers have noted. For example, um, a yawn. Sometimes, the animal yawns as a reflex because it's sleepy, very much like humans. But the adult male mandrill also has another type of yawn...an exaggerated, what scientists coin a tension yawn. In this case...uh, it occurs when a rival group or predator is approaching...the mandrill opens its mouth fully to reveal its canines and displays them for a prolonged period of around five seconds. Then it closes its mouth. This cue serves as a warning or threat... Q4 **which is the exact opposite of when the mandrill silently bares its teeth, its canines and premolars. There is a common misconception that this signifies a threat of aggression. In fact, it's actually a sign of friendliness, submission, or peace...kind of a like a grin. Infants perform this display during and before play activities.**

OK, so...we've covered the obvious ones. Now, a lesser-understood form of communication between mandrills is olfactory communication...like smell. A mandrill will rub its chest area against a tree, the ground, a rock...a substrate area. They have a scent gland in their chest and can deposit unique scents. They will raise their chin when doing so...and yeah, all members of a group will do this. Well, all of them except for infants under seven months old. Usually the dominant males and females will repeatedly rub up and down on and return to the same spot. Nobody is sure yet or has come to a conclusion why this is so...but it's been observed. Researchers speculate that it has to do with the wide area of their domain...they almost always mark their sleeping sites. So perhaps marking areas with these scent glands helps facilitate orientation within their home range...

MP3 • 176

in-depth 全面的，深入的
opposable thumb 可相对拇指，与另外的四根手指相对的拇指（灵长类动物使用工具的相关特征之一，通常在介绍此方面内容时出现）
genus [生物]属（科与种之间的分类单位）
roam 漫步
foraging 狩猎，采集
bark 树皮
omnivorous 杂食性的
rodent 啮齿目动物
tactile 触觉的
grunt （猪等）作咕噜声
crow 欢呼
grind 咬（牙）的嘎嘎声响
growl （狗等）嗥叫，（人）咆哮
roar 呼啸，吼叫
signify 示意，表示
grooming 打扮，修饰
conveyance 传达，传递
cue 信号，提示，线索
conspicuously 显眼地
rump 臀部
hue 颜色，色彩
dull 不鲜明的，晦暗的
shade 色度
postulate 假定，假设
coloration 天然色
jerk 猛然一动
reflex 反射
coin 创造，杜撰（新词等）
canine 犬齿
prolonged 延长的，持续的
premolar 前臼齿
submission 屈从，服从
grin 露齿而笑
olfactory 嗅觉的
substrate 地面，基质（=substratum）
gland 分泌腺
speculate 推测，推断
domain 领土，领域
facilitate 使容易
orientation 方向

◎ 解析

1. 讲义文的主要内容是什么？
(A) 利用嗅觉进行交流的秘密 **(minor)**
(B) 山魈选择食物的习性与栖息地 **(minor)**
(C) 山魈的交流方式
(D) 灵长类动物丰富的行动信号 **(not mentioned)**

Main Idea
在讲义文的开头部分，教授首先揭示了讲义文主题是有关山魈的内容。然后，他依次对山魈使用语言、触觉、视觉以及嗅觉的表达意思、相互交流的方式进行了说明。因此正确答案选(C)。讲义文也提到了尚未研究清楚的嗅觉交流方式，选择食物的习性以及生存地，但是这些都是细节性内容，不能作为正确答案。因此，(A)和(B)选项都不正确。

2. 根据教授的介绍，山魈为什么一天之内可能会迁移20平房英里？
(A) 为了躲避天敌。**(not mentioned)**
(B) 为了寻找食物。
(C) 为了捕捉小型啮齿类动物。**(not correct)**
(D) 为了标识并扩张自己的领地。**(not correct)**

Detail
请看标记Q2的部分。这里介绍了山魈为了搜寻食物，平均每天要迁移20平房英里。因此正确答案选(B)。请留意，原文中的foraging在选项中被表述为sustenance。讲义文中尽管也提到了它们是杂食性动物，会以小型啮齿类动物为食，并且以强烈的气味标记自己的领地，但是这些都不是它们移动20平方英里的原因。因此(C)与(D)选项不正确。

3. 讲义文中提到了雌雄山魈的什么区别？
(A) 脸颊的样子 **(not mentioned)**
(B) 皮毛的手感 **(not mentioned)**
(C) 鼻子大小 **(not mentioned)**
(D) 身体部位的亮度

Detail
教授说明了为什么雄山魈的颜色比雌性的艳丽显眼，因此正确答案选(D)。请注意原文中描述色彩部分，vivid这一形容被表述为色彩的亮度。此外，教授仅仅提到了脸颊与鼻子的区别，皮毛有由两种颜色构成，并没有提到有手感有关的内容。因此(A) (B) (C)选项都不正确。

4. 根据教授的介绍，山魈什么时候经常遭到误解？
(A) 山魈将嘴唇咧向后方露出牙齿的时候
(B) 山魈表露抚平毛发或求偶要求的时候 **(not correct)**
(C) 雌山魈在树上蹭胸部的时候 **(not correct)**
(D) 最强的雄山魈给别的山魈抚平毛发的时候 **(not mentioned)**

Detail
教授提到了山魈露出牙齿的两种情况。一种是宽宽地咧开嘴做出紧张地打哈欠的动作，另一种是安静地露出牙齿的动作。其中，静静地露出牙齿的表情常常被视为威胁的意思。但实际上，它只是山魈的一种微笑。因此正确答案选(A)。

5. 教授这样说的意思是什么？
Can you imagine it?
(A) 他希望学生反驳这一观点。
(B) 他认为这一数字惊人。
(C) 他认为这一信息可信。
(D) 他希望学生自己可以推算。

Attitude
请看标记Q5处的内容。教授在介绍了山魈被观测到最多可以800只组成群体移动之后，问道："能想象的出来吗？"可见，他认为这一规模非常之大。因此正确答案选(B)。

6. 教授为什么这样说？
I hope you're taking notes...
(A) 为了表示对学生感到失望。
(B) 为了告诉他们讲义文的内容十分重要。
(C) 为了提醒学生需要讲义。
(D) 为了警告学生考试临近。

Function
教授在确认学生是否理解了讲义文内容之后，又说I hope you're taking notes...（我希望你们能记笔记…）这意味着目前学习的内容十分重要，达到了有必要记录的程度。因此正确答案选(B)。

Answer level 2 > 1-1 (A) 1-2 (B) 2-1 (B) 2-2 (C)
3-1 (B) 3-2 (C), (D) 4-1 (A) 4-2 (B), (C)
level 3 > 1-1 (B) 1-2 (C) 1-3 (C)
2-1 (D) 2-2 (B), (D) 2-3 (D)

level 2

MP3·179 **1. Listen to part of a talk in a zoology class.**

Professor (female) Ready to get started, everyone? Q1-1 **First...is anyone here color-blind?**

Student A (male) Uh, I am.

Professor Great. Would you mind telling us a little bit about the condition?

Student A Sure, um...what would you like to know?

Professor Well...what type of color blindness do you have?

Student A Q1-2 MP3·180 **I'm red-green color-blind.**

Professor **Excellent. That's actually the most common type. Now, what does it mean to be red-green color-blind?**

Student A Um, I'm unable to really distinguish reddish or greenish hues. They kind of look...gray to me, I guess.

Professor Uh-huh. That's because your retinas are missing some photoreceptors...specifically, the ones responsible for detecting red and green. Now, here's another question. Did you know there are advantages to being color-blind?

Student A Really? No, I had no idea.

Student B (male) Wait a minute...advantages? How can there be advantages to not being able to see color?

Professor Well, to answer that, let me describe a study that some researchers from the University of Calgary performed using...using capuchin monkeys. They took two groups of monkeys—one that was color-blind, and one that wasn't. They observed both groups as the individuals hunted for food...um, their food being various camouflaged insects. What they found was that

Q1-1教授是如何引出猴子色盲的话题的？
(A) 通过在班上询问是否有色盲的学生。
(B) 通过列举不同种类的色盲。
(C) 通过指出色盲的好处。
(D) 通过描述中南美卷尾猴的特点。

Q1-2教授为什么这么说？
Now, what does it mean to be red-green color-blind?
(A) 为了确认学生是否完全理解了红绿色盲。
(B) 为了请学生向大家描述色盲的经历。
(C) 为了了解自己从未经历过的状态。
(D) 为了说服学生说明对红绿色盲的定义。

MP3·190
color-blind 色盲的
（←**color blindness** 色盲）
color blindness 普通类型
hue 色调，色彩
retina 视网膜

	the color-blind monkeys were better at spotting the hidden insects than those with normal vision.
Student B	That's really strange. How did they explain the results?
Professor	Well, it's hard to know for sure, but the researchers think color blindness...it kind of renders the insects' camouflage useless. I mean, it's supposed to mimic the colors of the environment so the insects can blend in, right? But, um, if you can't see the colors, you might start to notice other things. Like...differences in texture and brightness between the insects and the background. Now, humans don't go around hunting insects. But the fact that there are so many color-blind people suggests that it may have actually been, uh, advantageous for some early humans to be color-blind.

photoreceptor ［生物］感光细胞（像眼睛中的杆状细胞一样，把光刺激传导至神经细胞的器官）
detect 察觉，感知
capuchin monkey 卷尾猴
camouflage 拟态，伪装
spot 认出，探明（位置等）
vision 视觉，视力
render A useless 使A变得无用
mimic 模仿
blend in 掺入…，混合…
texture 组织，纹理

 MP3・181 **2. Listen to part of a lecture in a chemistry class.**

Professor (male)

In 1995, Paul Crutzen won the Nobel Prize in Chemistry. Does anyone know, um, why he won the Nobel Prize? Well, he won for his work in, um, in atmospheric chemistry. Particularly for his work with, um, ozone. **Q2-1** **See, in 1970, Crutzen showed that—that the, um, the chemical compounds of nitrous oxide—N_2O—um, these compounds speed up the destruction of ozone in the stratosphere.** There wasn't really too much acceptance of his work at first, but it eventually helped other researchers who were also doing atmospheric research. Uh, like Mario Molina and Sherwood Rowland...who in 1995 also got the same award—the Nobel Prize in Chemistry for their work in atmospheric research in relation to ozone depletion.

Let's put their work in context by talking for a little bit about, um, about ozone...and about, um, their field. OK. Ozone is a gas consisting of molecules that are made up of three atoms of oxygen. Everybody knows that ozone is important for life on Earth because it—it protects us from the sun's radiation. You're probably tired of hearing these facts over and over...but they're important...I've got to bring them up. We've all got to remember that the ozone, um, that we simply must protect it. That's why this kind of research is so important.

Q2-1 保罗・克鲁岑具有划时代意义的研究主题是？
(A) 臭氧减少对地球大气的影响
(B) 氧化亚氮对臭氧层的破坏性影响
(C) OH和HO_2在破坏臭氧层方面的作用
(D) 影响臭氧形成的因素

MP3・191
atmospheric 大气的，空气的
compound 化合物，混合物
nitrous oxide N_2O 氧化亚氮
destruction 破坏
stratosphere 平流层（对流圈之上的大气层）
in relation to 与…有关
depletion 减少，枯竭
molecule 分子
radiation 反射线，辐射能

Q2-2 **Now for a little bit of the history of their field...Back in 1930, Sidney Chapman, an English physicist, um, developed a theory about how sunlight causes different forms of oxygen to change into other forms.** But the problem was that the theory predicted there would be much more ozone in the atmosphere than there actually is. So, there had to be some kind of process that reduced the amount of ozone. Q2-2 **Later, a Belgian scientist named Marcel Nicolet explained that OH and HO_2 caused an increase in ozone decomposition.**

Q2-2教授为什么要提悉尼·查普曼与马塞尔·尼科莱特?
(A) 为了解释三位科学家1995年获得诺贝尔化学奖的原因
(B) 为了举例说明哪些科学家受到过克鲁岑研究的影响
(C) 为了提供早期关于臭氧的研究信息
(D) 为了提出两位曾与克鲁岑一起从事研究的科学家

MP3·191
physicist 物理学家
decomposition 分解，解题

 MP3·182 **3. Listen to part of a lecture in a geology class.**

Professor (female)

So, how exactly do scientists predict when volcanic eruptions will happen? Well, earthquakes are the main seismic activity that they look for. Just prior to an eruption, there's a massive buildup of magma under the Earth, and, uh, this puts heaps of pressure on brittle rock in the Earth's crust. It forces it to crack, but, uh, usually not in a major or sudden or violent way. Q3-1 **More often than not, these earthquakes are what are called long-period oscillations—much less severe, but much longer in duration. They don't cause the ground to shake violently or anything. Instead you can just hear these strange clanging sounds coming from below the surface. The sound is a bit like when you hear something clanging in the pipes in your house.**

OK. Another eruption warning sign is changes in gas emissions. Volcanoes constantly emit all types of gases, Q3-2(C) **but when the emissions are found to include higher traces of sulfur dioxide, this is usually significant. See, sulfur dioxide is one of the key volcanic gases. There was a recent case in the Philippines, at, ah, Mount Pinatubo, where scientists...they noted that the amount of sulfur dioxide increased more than 10 times prior to an eruption.**

What's next? Ah, right. Scientists can also use hydraulic measurements to predict likely volcanic activity. Hydraulic measurements—I guess you might not be familiar with the term? *[pausing to check]* Didn't think so. They're basically measurements of water levels. You might think it's a bit strange, right? What have water levels got to do with volcanoes? Well, most volcanoes have craters where rain

Q3-1教授为什么提起家里水管发出的丁零当啷的声响?
(A) 为了说明科学家如何追踪地下岩浆的流动
(B) 为了描述持久震动导致的噪音
(C) 为了比较剧烈的和持续时间长而强度弱的地震带来的冲击
(D) 为了显示地表下的地层会受到火山爆发怎样的影响

MP3·192
seismic activity 地震活动
prior to 先于…
heaps of 很多的…
brittle 易碎的，易破裂的
crust (地球的)表层，地壳
crack 断裂，裂开
oscillation 震动，振幅
clang （丁零当啷地）响
a trace of 微量的

water collects. Q3-2(D) **And, ah, a clear sign of an upcoming eruption is when there's a sudden rise in the water level in the crater lake, and then a sudden drop soon after.** Why? Because changes in gas pressure underground cause the water level to spike.

Q3-2根据教授的介绍，火山爆发前会出现何种现象？请选择两项答案。

(A) 发生强烈的地震。

(B) 火山口首先开始喷发有毒气体。

(C) 二氧化硫气体的排出量增加。

(D) 火山口湖的水位时而上升，时而下降。

MP3·192

sulfur dioxide 二氧化硫
hydraulic 水力的，水压的
crater （火山的）火山口
spike 上冲

 MP3·183 **4. Listen to part of a talk in an ecology class.**

Professor (male) Q4-1 **So, around 250 million tires are discarded every year in America. Does anyone know what they're used for?**

Student A (female) As a...a construction material. They build houses out of waste tires, right?

Professor Q4-1 **Sure. Tires can actually be used for roofing materials...insulation...sealants and so on. But today I want to tell you about another... more unusual way someone has found to reuse tires...or at least one specific material in the tires. One chemist has found a way to extract lemon oil from used tires.**

Student B (male) *[with disbelief]* How is it done?

Professor First, Manfredi—that's the chemist's name, Kirk Manfredi—first he heats up shredded tires and collects the oil that's produced during the heating process. Next, he heats up the oil itself...and it eventually undergoes a structural change and...and becomes chemically identical to limonene—an oil found in citrus fruits like lemons and oranges. *[assuringly]* You know—that pungent oil in the peel.

Student A How much, uh...what did you say it was? Limonene? How much of that can be extracted from a tire?

Q4-1教授为什么询问废旧轮胎的用途？

(A) 为了将讨论集中于一个他将提供更多信息的话题

(B) 为了鼓励学生对主题进行更宽范围的思考

(C) 为了显示环境运动对废弃物管理的影响

(D) 为了说明曼弗雷迪的发现在科学界产生的影响

MP3·193

discard 抛弃，丢弃
construction material 建筑材料
insulation 绝缘体
sealant 密封物，密封剂
extract A from B 从B中提取A
shredded 破碎的，碎成一块一块的
undergo 经历，经过
identical to 与…相同的，一样的
limonene 柠檬油精（一种碳氢化合物，作为与橙子气味相似的香料或原料使用）
citrus 柑橘类
pungent 尖刻的，强烈的，痛苦的
peel 皮，壳

Professor	Right now, Manfredi can convert about 2 percent of the weight of the tire into limonene, but in the future, he hopes to get to 10 percent.	Q4-2根据教授的介绍，柠檬油精有哪些实际用途？请选择两项正确答案。 (A) 住宅建筑施工。 **(B) 生产塑料产品。** **(C) 预防癌症发病可能。** (D) 作为汽车发动机汽油的添加剂。
Student B	Professor, I'm wondering...what can this lemon oil be used for?	
Professor	Well, limonene is used as a cleaning solvent... as a fragrance...as a food flavoring...even as an insecticide to kill unwanted insect pests. What else? Q4-2(B) **Um, actually, in 2005, some researchers at, at Cornell University discovered that it's possible to make plastics out of limonene.** Q4-2(C) **Oh, and recently, at the University of Wisconsin, they found out that limonene is one of several compounds present in plants that actually has the ability to inhibit cancer.** So you can see there're a lot of potential applications for this substance.	MP3·193 **convert A into B** 把A转换为B。 **solvent** 溶媒，溶剂 **insecticide** 杀虫剂 **insect pests** 害虫 **inhibit** 阻止，预防 **application** 应用，适用 **substance** 物质，材质

level 3

MP3·184 **1. Listen to part of a talk in a marine biology class.**

Professor (female)	Class, tell me a little bit about dolphins.	Q1-1讲义文的主要内容是？ (A) 人与海豚的相似之处 **(B) 海豚呼吸与睡觉的方式** (C) 自发呼吸的生物与非自发呼吸的生物 (D) 海豚归类为哺乳动物的依据
Student A (male)	Well, they live in water, obviously, but they're mammals, aren't they?	
Professor	Yes, and how do mammals get oxygen?	
Student B (male)	By breathing air, right?	
Professor	Yes. Q1-1 **Exactly—that's just what I want to discuss.** ***[expressing wonderment for the sake of enthusiasm]*** **How do they do that—breathe air while living in water?**	MP3·194 **mammal** 哺乳动物 **let A in on the secret** 告诉A某种信息，秘密 **handy** 便利的 **respiratory** 呼吸的 **aquatic** 水的，水中的
Student A	Well, I guess I'm not really sure.	
Professor	How about anybody else? Does anybody else have the answer? *[pause]* Oh, no? Well, I suppose I could share some information with you...let you in on the secret. Dictation 开始 Dolphins breathe air, but they've got 1) *a handy respiratory system* that's—well, that's adapted to, to aquatic life of course. It allows dolphins to spend a while underwater before 2) *needing to come up to the surface* for air. Oh...about thirty minutes, I'd say. Much better than your average human, right? OK, so dolphins have to have control over their	

breath, because it would be inconvenient [3]*if their bodies automatically inhaled* while they were underwater, wouldn't it? Q1-2 **So, they aren't like humans...they're what we call "voluntary breathers." You know...humans don't have to think about taking a breath every time they need to...it just happens automatically. We're "involuntary breathers."** So, actually, even if you decide not to breathe, [4]*your body can override your decision*...uh, you'll fall into unconsciousness and start breathing again. This works out well for us, right? I mean, consider [5]*what a hassle it would be* if our bodies didn't automatically breathe for us when we were asleep.

Q1-1 **But, actually, that brings me to an interesting point about dolphins...how do they sleep?** If they're voluntary breathers... that means they have to be conscious in order to breathe. But one of the characteristics of mammals that, uh, that you didn't mention earlier is that they need to [6]*enter regular periods of unconsciousness*—to sleep. So...what's the solution? Well, amazingly, a dolphin's brain only sleeps a half at a time. Um, [7]*by hooking up electrodes to dolphins' heads,* scientists have been able to measure the electrical activity in dolphins' brains. And, um, so based on electroencephalography—that's what the technique is called—uh, we've learned that half of a dolphin's brain can be asleep while the other half is awake. And that's [8]*how they manage to maintain control over* their, their voluntary breathing process and yet, um, still get enough, uh, enough sleep—and they go to sleep like this for about eight hours a day.[Dictation 结束]

Student A When they're sleeping, where are the dolphins? I mean, they have to have access to the surface in order to breathe, so do they, uh, float on top of the water so that they can breathe whenever they have to?

Professor Sometimes, yes. There are actually three ways dolphins commonly sleep. Sometimes they float

Q1-2教授提到人是非自发呼吸型生物时，还表达了何种观点？

(A) 海豚和人类的大脑是相似的。

(B) 人的呼吸方式更加复杂。

(C) 人与海豚的呼吸方式十分不同。

(D) 海豚主要以三种方式呼吸。

MP3·194

inhale 吸入，呼吸

voluntary 自发性的（↔**involuntary** 非自发性的）

override 撤销，推翻

unconsciousness 无意识，失去知觉

hassle 麻烦，困难，问题

hook up 连接（电子器械等）

electrode 电极

float （在水面或空气中）漂浮，飘浮

at the surface, like you—like you suggested, and they have their, um, their blowhole exposed to the air. Other times they swim slowly—you know, guided by the half of their brain that's still awake—and, um, and they just come up to breathe every once in a while. And sometimes they sleep on the bottom—on the ground...um, if the water's shallow. And then they can just float up to the, uh, the surface when they need to.

Student B Professor, do the scientists who study dolphins have any idea what this, this, uh, half-of-my-brain-is-asleep stage might feel like? It must be such a strange sensation!

Professor Well, there've been some guesses made...I think it might be similar to, um, you know that feeling you have as you're falling asleep—you're still aware of some things, and you could wake up if you needed to, but you're just semi-conscious... Maybe it would feel like that.

Student A So, does that mean that dolphins can have... um...waking dreams or something? Do they experience REM sleep just like humans do?

Professor Well, as far as anyone can tell, um, dolphins don't seem to go through REM sleep, which... for those of you who aren't familiar with that, REM is the stage in human sleep when we have dreams. Q1-3 **At least, scientists haven't been able to detect the, uh, the kind of brain-wave activity in dolphins that they think, um, correlates with REM sleep.**

Q1-3对于睡着的海豚的脑电波运动，科学家认为？

(A) 它与清醒的海豚的脑电波运动相似。

(B) 它暗示着梦的存在。

(C) 它不能表现与快速眼动睡眠相关的形式。

(D) 它显示出睡眠中的海豚对周围环境没有意识。

MP3·194

blowhole （鲸的）喷水孔，通风孔

shallow 浅的

sensation 感觉，感受

semi-conscious 半知觉的

REM(Rapid Eye Movement) sleep 快速眼动睡眠（浅睡眠状态，由于大脑处于兴奋状态而产生眼球转动或做梦的现象）

brain-wave activity 脑电波运动

correlate with 与…相关联

MP3·185 **2. Listen to part of a lecture in a geography class.**

Professor (male)

Q2-1 **Everybody, picture a snow avalanche...a huge tide of snow and ice crumbling slowly down a mountainside, destroying everything in its path and picking up more snow along the way. Has everyone got this image in mind? Good. If you can picture this, then you will begin to understand what a "turbidity current" is.**

Turbidity currents are very similar to that snow avalanche, but instead of snow, they are composed of sediment grains found in the sea. Q2-2(B) **These turbidity currents characteristically occur in areas**

Q2-1教授为什么让学生想象雪崩的情景？

(A) 为了说明构成浊流的物质。

(B) 为了强调浊流对海床的威胁。

(C) 为了说明引发浊流的地质条件。

(D) 为了举熟悉的例子说明浊流的流动。

of seismic instability. So, when something like, um, an earthquake or tsunami, triggers a disturbance on the ocean floor, a turbidity current may sometimes follow. This is a landslide of seafloor sediment that cascades downslope, toward the continental shelf. Just like an avalanche, the currents can build up a large amount of speed and momentum. In fact, some turbidity currents have been recorded reaching speeds up to half the speed of sound. Once the slope of the tectonic plate begins to even out, this current begins to slow down. It loses so much energy it can't support the load of sediment it's carrying...and um, the particles begin to settle down onto the seafloor. This is the formation of what's called a "turbidite." More on that later.

But first, just to give you an idea of the speeds turbidity currents can reach...there was an earthquake off the coast of Newfoundland in 1929. Several minutes after the actual earthquake hit, uh, transatlantic telephone cables began to break sequentially...they just kept on snapping...snapping downslope and away from the epicenter of the quake. Twelve cables snapped in twenty-eight places and this allowed investigators to record the locations and times of these occurrences. It was...it was found that a turbidity current had swept 400 miles down the continental slope from the epicenter at a rate of, uh, about 100 kilometers per hour, snapping the poles as it went.

Q2-2(D) Dictation 开始 **All right, now I want to talk a bit about [1]*the sedimentary deposits left by* turbidity current—the turbidites. So these turbidites are clastic—you know, consisting of broken, mixed up fragments [2]*derived from pre-existing rocks*—and so not really a specific type of rock or anything...nope, they are a jumbled mix of whatever was picked up from the seafloor by the turbidity current.**

Uh...but what's really interesting about these turbidites is the way they're [3]*made up of distinct layers.* We can describe these layers using what's known as the Bouma Sequence—so-called because it was discovered by marine geologist Arnold Bouma. Q2-3 MP3·186 **So the, uh, turbidite [4]*is comprised of five separate beds* which make up the Bouma Sequence. They're labeled A, the very bottom, through E, the top.** [5]***<u>You may want to jot down a mini-diagram.</u>*** **So at the bottom we have "A".** These are massive sand grains with a very, um, gravelly base. "B" is [6]*a mixture of parallel bedded sands.* "C"...are you following me? "C" has cross-laminated sands..."D" has, um, laminated silts. And finally, "E" is mainly comprised of deep-sea muds. You got all that down?

Uh, while it's useful to know about the Bouma Sequence, it's rare to see a turbidite which follows this exact sequence. Can anyone guess

Q2-2根据讲义文中的介绍，浊流有哪两个特征？请选择两项正确答案。
(A) 在海里受到海流的影响。
(B) 产生于地质活动活跃的水下区域。
(C) 可能诱发地震或其他与地震有关的灾害。
(D) 会留下沉积物。

MP3·195

avalanche （雪）崩，山崩
crumble 破碎，碎裂
turbidity current 浊流（混合了泥沙的高密度液体因地震等刺激而快速流动的现象）
sediment 沉积物，沉淀 (**=deposit**)
grain 谷粒，细粒
seismic 地震的，因地震而引起的
instability 不稳定性
earthquake 地震 (**=quake**)
tsunami 海啸
trigger a disturbance 引发不安，引发混乱
landslide 滑坡，山崩
cascade 大量流下，瀑布似地落下
downslope 斜坡，斜坡的
continental shelf [地理]大陆架
momentum 冲力，动力
tectonic plate 地壳板块（构成大陆的移动着的地壳表层）
even out 变平
turbidite 浊积相（随着浊流移动并沉淀于海底的物质）
transatlantic 跨大西洋的
sequentially 连续地
snap 突然折断，拽
epicenter 震中，震源地
sweep 扫，席卷
continental slope [地理]大陆斜面
at a rate of 以…的速度[比率]
clastic [地质]碎屑状的，分裂性的
be derived from 起源于…，来自…
jumble 使混乱，使杂乱
be made up of 由…构成(**=be comprised of**)

why? *[pause]* Well, what do we know about turbidites? They're [7]*located near areas of seismic instability,* right? And in these areas, turbidity currents are pretty common, right? You see, what happens is, new turbidity currents come along and [8]*erode the original deposit.* Dictation 结束

So, uh, you know, you end up having overlapping turbidites in the same place. And this is what geologists find particularly useful about the study of turbidites. By looking at the layers and their composition, they're able to work out the sequence of seismic activity in an area. It gives them a much better idea of the region's geological history.

Q2-3教授为什么这样说?
You may want to jot down a mini-diagram.
(A) 为了细致说明刚才提到的内容。
(B) 为了确认学生是否已经理解了内容。
(C) 为了鼓励学生参与课堂。
(D) 为了暗示正在介绍的内容是复杂的概念。

MP3-195

layer 层，层次
sequence 一连串，连续
bed 地层，层（←**bedded** 层上的）
jot down 草草记下，匆匆记下（信息等）
gravelly 多碎石的
parallel 平行的
laminated 由薄片组成的，层压的
silt 沉积土，泥沙，淤泥（被河水搬运，在河边等地堆积的泥沙）
erode 侵蚀
overlap 重叠，重复覆盖

Answer level 2 > 1-1 (B) 1-2 Birth of the Cool → (A), (E) / Kind of Blue → (C) / Bitches Brew → (B), (D)
2-1 (C) 2-2 Hurricanes → (C), (D) / Tornadoes → (A), (B), (E)
3-1 (A) 3-2 YES → (A), (C), (E) / NO → (B), (D)
4-1 Cultural Relativism → (A), (C) / Cultural Absolutism → (B), (D) 4-2 (D)
level 3 > 1-1 (A) 1-2 YES → (B), (C), (D) / NO → (A), (E) 1-3 (A)
2-1 (B) 2-2 Pillow → (A), (B) / Sheet → (C), (E) / Lobate → (D) 2-3 (B)

level 2

 MP3・198 **1. Listen to part of a lecture in a music class.**

Professor (male)

Today we're gonna—I wanna talk about my favorite jazz trumpeter of all time, Miles Davis. Even if you don't know his music, you've probably heard his name before, since he's pretty much one of the twentieth century's most influential jazz artists. Q1-1 **I mean, he was basically part of every developing movement in jazz during the whole second half of the twentieth century. Let me tell you about some of his major albums...**I'll start with *Birth of the Cool*, released in 1957.

Davis's *Birth of the Cool*, uh, was a fresh work that introduced the world to a new form of jazz, cool jazz. Cool jazz—it's like an intellectual form of jazz, understated yet challenging. Q1-2(E) **I mean, there was an emphasis on complex arrangements and intricate harmonies,** and Q1-2(A) **some of it was influenced by classical music.** *Birth of the Cool* featured some nontraditional instruments, too, like the tuba and the French horn.

In 1959, Davis released an album that received a great deal of acclaim. *Kind of Blue* is generally considered to be his best selling album, and many people think it's one of the finest jazz albums ever produced. Q1-2(C) **It's filled with a kind of freedom, which results from its improvisational nature, because musicians weren't working with a complete score, or even chord progressions. Instead, each musician received a set of scales to guide their improvisation.**

Davis's 1970 *Bitches Brew* is in some ways the opposite of *Kind of Blue*. Q1-2(B) **I mean, unlike the beloved *Kind of Blue, Bitches Brew* was terribly controversial.** The controversy centered on the use of electric instruments in jazz. See, Q1-2(D) ***Bitches Brew* included electric piano and guitar;** it represented a, um, a really unconventional

Q1-1 教授是如何介绍迈尔士・戴维斯的成就的？
(A) 通过描述他可以熟练演奏的各种乐器。
(B) 通过详细说明他的一些有名的专辑。
(C) 通过说明他的某张专辑所展示出的风格。
(D) 通过引用同时代爵士乐艺术家对他的评价。

Q1-2在讲义文中，教授描述了迈尔士・戴维斯的三张专辑，请选出对应下列各项的专辑并点击相应的空格。
(A) 由古典乐得到一些灵感。***(Birth of the Cool)***
(B) 在爵士乐界得到了不同评价。***(Bitches Brew)***
(C) 特点是声音自由而不拘于结构。***(Kind of Blue)***
(D) 特点是使用电子乐器。***(Bitches Brew)***
(E) 以及其精巧复杂的构成闻名。***(Birth of the Cool)***

blending of jazz with electric rock... Q1-2(B) **which upset some jazz fans, who considered it an insult to traditional jazz techniques. Nonetheless, it was groundbreaking stuff, and fortunately some audiences recognized it as that.**

MP3·210

trumpeter 喇叭手
the second half 后半，下半期
release 发行，发售
understated 含蓄克制的
intricate 难以理解的，错综复杂的
acclaim 欢呼，喝彩
score [音乐]乐谱
chord [音乐]和弦
scale [音乐]音阶
improvisation 即兴演奏
controversial 争议的
unconventional 非常规的，不依惯例的
groundbreaking 开创性的，划时代的

MP3·199 **2. Listen to part of a lecture in a meteorology class.**

Professor (female)

Q2-1 **Hurricanes and tornadoes...two of the most destructive weather phenomena.** They're extraordinary...both in their power and their ability to destroy lives and property.

Let's start with hurricanes. Um, as you know, hurricanes are massive storm systems that, that form over oceans. How they form...that's a topic for another time...but, um, just understand that a major factor is the presence of warm surface waters. Basically, waters need to be at least 80 degrees Fahrenheit to support a hurricane. Q2-2(D) **So, obviously, we see hurricanes forming most often over warm, tropical waters...usually in the late summer season.** And they're just massive. The distance between the central eye and the outermost bands of clouds...um, it can be anywhere from 135 to 550 miles. Wind speeds also vary, but the strongest hurricane winds ever measured were blowing at 195 miles per hour.

OK, and hurricanes...they won't disappear until their fuel source—warm ocean water—until that's no longer available. So either it moves into an area of cooler water, or it hits land. Q2-2(C) **Most hurricanes last for several days, but they've been known to wander around the ocean for up to a month!**

Great. Now...how are tornadoes different? Of course, they form over land, not water, but the major difference is tornadoes are part of a larger storm system, usually a huge thunderstorm called a supercell. Supercells often spawn these rotating columns of air that stretch vertically from the clouds down to the ground—a tornado. Q2-2(E) **They occur all over the world, but we see the vast majority forming in the U.S. and Canada.**

Q2-1讲义文的主要内容是？
(A) 形成飓风的必要条件
(B) 不同类型的灾难性气候现象
(C) **飓风与龙卷风的形成与特点**
(D) 飓风与龙卷风的相似之处

Q2-2请选择下列各项词组与飓风或龙卷风中哪一个有关并点击相应的空格。
(A) 大小变化范围从几英尺至几英里。
(B) 最高风速为每小时300英里。
(C) 通常持续数天。
(D) 在温暖的水体上方开始形成。
(E) 最频繁出现于北美。

MP3·211

phenomenon 现象 (**pl. phenomena**)
Fahrenheit 华氏的
outermost 最外边的
wander 漫游，闲逛

Tornadoes are relatively small... Q2-2(A) **they can be anywhere from a couple feet to a couple miles wide.** Q2-2(B) **Their winds, though, are typically quite fast...the maximum ever measured being over 300 miles per hour.** Really amazing. But they're pretty short-lived. On average, they only last around ten minutes before dissipating. Within that time, though, they destroy anything in their path.

supercell 超级细胞（伴有持续上升气流的严重脑炎）
spawn 造成，酿成
column 柱，圆柱
vertically 竖直地
dissipate 消散，消失

 MP3·200 **3. Listen to part of a lecture in a biology class.**

Professor (male)

Good afternoon. You're all familiar with the idea of endangered species, aren't you? Of course. And for a species to be considered endangered, what has to happen? Well, scientists have to determine the population is so small...or falling so fast...that they're in danger of dying out forever. But...did you ever wonder how exactly scientists make those judgments?

Um...think about it. Q3-1 **Most animals, especially rare ones that are more likely to be endangered...um, they're not exactly the easiest subjects to observe. They live in varied, often inaccessible terrain. They move around a lot, and they mate and produce offspring. So how do you suppose scientists are able to get accurate data on population trends?** Well...one tool that's proven particularly useful is the mark-and-recapture method. It's a bit complicated to explain... let me give you a specific example.

Take...whales. They live in the vast oceans, far from the watchful eyes of humans. And they travel...they're capable of traveling tremendous distances. Sounds pretty difficult to get an accurate population count, doesn't it? So here's how researchers would use the mark-and-recapture method to do so. Q3-2(A) **First, um, a team would go into a specific region...aboard a ship, in this case.** Q3-2(C) **Over a period of days or weeks, they'd locate as many individual whales from the given species as possible and mark them—by shooting a small needle into a whales' skin...something like that.** Then, several months later, the team goes back to the same region and does it again. Only this time, some of the whales they capture will already be marked. Q3-2(E) **The researchers...they count how many whales are marked and how many are unmarked.** Next, some complex mathematical formulas are applied...too complex to get into today. But, um, from these calculations, it's possible to get a fairly accurate estimation of population size, rate of growth or decline, migration trends...and of course, whether a species is endangered or not. Pretty neat, huh?

Q3-1 教授为什么提起不可接近地带？
(A) 为了说明一项测定濒临绝种的动物数量的困难
(B) 为了说明当一个族群被认为濒临灭绝状态时，必须采取的措施
(C) 为了强调标志回捕法是搜集族群数量的诸多方法之一
(D) 为了说明不断测定动物数量的重要性

Q3-2 在讲义文中，教授介绍了测定动物族群大小的标志回捕法。请判断下列叙述是否为这一方法的步骤并点击正确的空格。
(A) 科学家组队驻扎在一片特定区域。**(YES)**
(B) 科学家通过复杂的演算法决定标记多少动物。**(NO)**
(C) 科研队尽可能多地找到种群并做标记。**(YES)**
(D) 对动物进行长达几个月的观察。**(NO)**
(E) 之后，研究人员统计这一地区标记及未标记的动物数量。**(YES)**

 MP3·212

endangered species 濒临灭绝的物种
die out 灭绝
inaccessible 难以接近的，不可接近的
terrain 地带，地域

mark-and-recapture method 标志回捕法（在特定区域捕捉生物后做标记，再把它们放生。之后重新捕捉，通过其中带有标志的个体比率推测生物种群密度的方法）
watchful 监视的，警惕的
migration 移居，移动

MP3·201 **4. Listen to part of a talk in a sociology class.**

Professor (female) Class, what is value?

Student A (male) Well...that depends on the context.

Professor Very true. Then, what are cultural values?

Student B (male) Cultural values—they're the things or behaviors or conditions that people within a society consider to be important. For example, wealth... or individualism.

Professor OK...but do all societies consider wealth and, um, individualism to be valuable?

Student B Q4-2 MP3·202 **No. Cultural values are relative. They're basically only applicable within their own society. There aren't any absolute values.**

Professor **You're saying that there're no absolute rights or wrongs.**

Student B That's what I'm saying.

Professor OK. What you've just described is the philosophy of cultural relativism. Q4-1(C) **It's a philosophy that, um, says that theories about morality or ethics aren't universal moral truths. Rather, they're relative to different cultures and societies.** Q4-1(A) **So it doesn't make sense to make judgments about the morals of other cultures because morality is a relative concept, and there aren't any absolute rights and wrongs.**

Student A That sounds like a good philosophy in most cases, but what about when it comes to issues like, um, slavery or torture? What about

Q4-1在讲义文中，教授介绍了文化相对主义与文化绝对主义哲学。请判断下列句子分别对应哪种理论并点击相应的空格。
(A) 不会有关于对错的共识。**（文化相对主义）**
(B) 某些行为不论在何种背景下都是应该被否定的。**（文化绝对主义）**
(C) 每一个社会都具有以自身文化为背景的规范与伦理。**（文化相对主义）**
(D) 本质性的价值可以来源于人类的本性。**（文化绝对主义）**

Q4-2教授为什么这样说？
You're saying that there're no absolute rights or wrongs.
(A) 为了表明同意学生说的话。
(B) 为了表示对学生意见的惊异。
(C) 为了暗示学生犯了一个错误。
(D) 为了总结学生的观点。

MP3·213
context 上下文，语境
individualism 个人主义
applicable 可以适用的

apartheid and the holocaust? If we accept the premise of relativism, we have to accept that these violations of human rights aren't wrong—they're something we've simply got to tolerate.

Professor Our principle of tolerance forces us to accept these types of behaviors and practices, right? Q4-1(B) **The issue you just pointed out is exactly what proponents of cultural absolutism criticize about cultural relativism. They argue that there most certainly are moral absolutes—rights and wrongs that we should judge human actions against.** Q4-1(D) **According to their philosophy, certain morals are rooted in human nature or the laws of the universe...** and it doesn't matter what circumstances cause a culture to practice slavery or wage war—these are immoral actions that should be judged. It's actually from moral absolutism that we have the theory of human rights.

cultural relativism 文化相对主义
morality 道德（←**moral** 道德上的）
slavery 奴隶制度
torture 拷问，折磨
apartheid （对黑人的）种族歧视
holocaust [隔离]政策，种族隔离政策
premise 前提
tolerate 默认
（←**tolerance** 默认，宽容）
proponent 支持者
cultural absolutism 文化绝对主义
be rooted in 植根于…
human nature 人类本性，人类本能
wage war 进行战争
immoral 不道德的
human rights 人权

level 3

 MP3·203 **1. Listen to part of a discussion in a health class.**

Professor (female) Dictation 开始 I'm sure you're all aware of [1] *the importance of dental hygiene.* We—we need to brush and floss regularly and visit our dentist once a year in order to clean away plaque and to have cavities filled. [2] *That's common knowledge*, but exactly why is it so important to get rid of plaque?

Student (male) Well, it causes cavities, for one thing. I think it's a type of bacterium.

Professor Actually, it's more than one type. It's like a—[3] *a colony of various kinds of bacteria.* There can be up to 400 different species of bacteria in plaque. Oh, by the way, plaque does serve a function. It protects [4] *the tooth enamel from colonization by certain microorganisms.* Anyway, even though it serves a function, it needs to be kept in check.

Student I have a question. What's the difference between plaque and tartar?

Q1-1讲义文的主要内容是？
(A) 齿菌斑的形成如何一步步损坏牙齿
(B) 齿菌斑保护牙釉质的功能
(C) 牙医如何清除牙齿上的齿菌斑
(D) 齿菌斑与石灰质牙垢的区别

MP3·214
dental hygiene 牙齿卫生
floss 用牙线洁牙
plaque 齿菌斑
cavity 蛀牙的空洞，蛀洞
get rid of 摆脱…，去除…
bacteria 细菌
（*pl.* **bacterium**）
a colony of …的集体，…的集团
serve a function 发挥功能
enamel （牙齿等的）釉质，珐琅质

Professor Good question. Basically, tartar is plaque [5] *that's become calcified.* That means that it becomes hardened, and it really sticks to teeth. So, whereas plaque can pretty much be removed with a toothbrush, you'll probably have to see your dentist to remove tartar. And once you have tartar the situation gets worse. You see, tartar is rough, unlike the tooth surface. The rough surface provides a much—a much better home for plaque. So the bacteria [6] *find a more hospitable home* in the tartar, and the, uh, the problem gets worse. Q1-1 **Now, who can tell me what might happen if plaque is allowed to—to [7] *grow unchecked in the mouth?***

Student You could develop gingivitis.

Professor Very good. And what's that? What is gingivitis?

Student It's a, um, a gum disease, I think.

Professor That's true. Gum disease is...well, it's a disease that affects your gums. And it's [8] *caused by plaque buildup.* Now, gingivitis is an early form of gum disease. It's an, um, an inflammation of the gums. The earliest sign of gingivitis is, well, inflammation— Q1-2(B) **your gums become reddish in color...redder than normal, I mean... and will probably be very sensitive and bleed easily.** And [9] *you'll have bad breath.* The good news is that gingivitis is reversible. It's possible to get rid of gingivitis by taking good care of your teeth. Dictation 结束

But, as I mentioned, Q1-1 **gingivitis is merely an early stage of gum disease. If it's not taken care of, it can progress into a much more serious gum disease: periodontitis.** If you don't treat it, you could eventually lose your teeth. In the early stages of periodontitis, things start happening to the sulcus, which is the space between your gums and your teeth. Q1-2(C) **The tissue around the sulcus swells up and provides still an even better place for bacteria to thrive.** And soon after, the bacteria actually— Q1-2(D) **they actually attack the ligaments that are holding the teeth in place.** Q1-3 MP3·204 **Next, the gum line will erode and ligaments holding the teeth in**

Q1-2在讲义文中，教授描述了牙龈疾病相关的一些问题。请判断下列叙述是否为牙龈疾病的症状并点击相应的空格。

(A) 细菌占据口腔并形成石灰质牙垢。**(NO)**

(B) 牙龈很容易变成深红色并出血。**(YES)**

(C) 牙沟周围的组织浮肿。**(YES)**

(D) 牵引牙齿的韧带变弱。**(YES)**

(E) 空腔感染蔓延至其他身体部位。**(NO)**

Q1-3教授为什么这样说？

You can imagine what the final step is.

(A) 为了引导学生做出一个结论

(B) 为了表明没有时间说明最后阶段

(C) 为了暗示下一个步骤与学生想象的不同

(D) 为了确认学生是否需要额外说明

MP3·214

colonization （动植物）族群
microorganism 微生物
tartar 石灰化的牙斑
calcify 石灰化
hospitable 宜人的，适宜的
gingivitis 牙龈炎
gum disease 口腔疾病
buildup 蓄积，积累
inflammation 炎症
reversible 可逆的，可反转的
periodontitis 齿周炎
sulcus 沟
swell up 肿胀，浮肿
ligament 韧带
erode 侵蚀，磨损
inflamed 发炎的，有炎症的

place become inflamed. **You can imagine what the final step is.**

Student The teeth become loose and fall out?

Professor Yeah, or they will have to be removed by a dentist. Q1-1 **So, as you can see—as if you didn't already know—poor dental hygiene is not only unattractive and unpleasant, it can lead to tooth loss.**

 MP3·205 **2. Listen to part of a lecture in a geology class.**

Professor (female)

OK, what do we remember from our last class about lava? It's hot—very hot...over 1,100 degrees Celsius, and of course, it comes from volcanoes when they erupt...it flows downhill, from the volcano, and keeps flowing until it cools and, um, solidifies, right? These lava flows solidify into rock, thereby adding to the—the size of the volcano. Now, usually when we think about volcano eruptions we think of the ones that happen on the Earth's surface, right? Last class we talked about two types of lava flows—uh, formations of lava—that occur on land. As you probably recall, a lot of the information we have about lava comes from studies of...of Hawaii. Do you remember those Polynesian words I told you about? There was *a'a [pronounced ah-ah]*, lava that cools with a very rough and jagged surface...and there was *pahoehoe [pronounced pa-hoy-hoy]*, lava that cools with a, um, gentle rolling surface.

Anyway, even though we most commonly picture lava flows on land, they actually occur underwater, too. A lot. In fact, most of the ocean's floor is made up of solidified lava.

Dictation 开始 Q2-1 **So, lava flows underwater look a bit different from how they look on land. There are [1]*three main shapes of underwater flows*, and they're called pillow lava, lobate lava, and sheet lava.** The factors that affect the shape of the lava flow are: A, the speed of the eruption—that is, [2]*the effusion rate*; B, the incline of the sea floor where the eruption occurs; and C, the viscosity of the lava, um, [3]*which is basically its stickiness.* So a liquid with a high viscosity moves very slowly. Remember that. High viscosity equals slow movement. Got that?

So, pillow lava, as the name suggests, looks like a pillow. It has a high viscosity so it's slow moving, and it solidifies very quickly into formations that are [4]*like round lumps of lava.* What happens is, when the eruption occurs...um, if it's a slow eruption...the outer

---

Q2-1讲义文的主要内容是？
(A) 海底火山的重要性
(B) 不同海底熔岩的特征
(C) 海底与地上熔岩的区别
(D) 海床的形成

Q2-2在讲义文中，教授描述了不同类型的熔岩。请判断下列描述分别与枕状熔岩、叶状熔岩及片状熔岩中的哪一种对应并点击相应的空格。
(A) 产生于十分平坦的海底。**（枕状熔岩）**
(B) 像水中的气球一样扩张。**（枕状熔岩）**
(C) 凝固前很快地在海底移动。**（片状熔岩）**
(D) 与地面上的绳状熔岩相似。**（叶状熔岩）**
(E) 表面通常光滑而平坦。**（片状熔岩）**

MP3·215
lava 熔岩
Celsius 摄氏
solidify 凝固
Polynesian 波利尼西亚的，波利尼西亚人的
jagged 锯齿状的
effusion 泻出，流出
incline 倾斜，斜坡 (**=slope**)
viscosity 黏度，黏性 (**=stickiness**)
lump 肿块

layer of the lava solidifies almost instantly, so you get something like a bubble of solidified lava with liquid lava on the inside. Q2-2(B) **The liquid lava on the inside** [5]***puts pressure on the outer layer*** **and causes it to inflate, sort of like when you fill a balloon with water.** Sometimes the inner lava will burst through, and a new pillow will be created much like the first. Q2-2(A) **Pillow formations generally occur where there's very little incline, or uh, slope, of the ocean floor.** So again, we've got a low effusion rate, a pretty flat sea floor, and high viscosity. Dictation 结束

Now, at the opposite end of the spectrum, we've got sheet lava. A high effusion rate, a low viscosity, and a steep incline for the lava to flow down means that the lava moves faster. Q2-2(C) **Since it moves faster, it has a chance to flow further before solidifying. So the lava quickly spreads over the ocean floor, filling in cracks and creating sort of a sheet over the ocean floor.** Q2-2(E) **Sheet lava is usually pretty smooth and flat,** but it can be covered in a kind of swirling pattern as well.

Then of course, somewhere in the middle, we've got lobate lava. The effusion rate is moderate, the incline is moderate, and the viscosity is high. Q2-2(D) **You remember what I said about pahoehoe lava? Well, it looks similar to that...kind of bulbous...rolling...but the bulbs are more inflated.**

Q2-3 MP3·206 **Now, I hope you were taking notes because we're going to have a little quiz...** don't panic, it's just for fun. I'm going to show you some pictures of different types of lava flows, and you can tell me what they are and how they were formed.

Q2-3教授为什么这样说？
don't panic, it's just for fun.
(A) 因为她担心学生觉得课堂内容无聊
(B) 因为她不希望学生过于认真对待那项练习
(C) 她担心学生不喜欢答题
(D) 她确定这部分内容不会在期末考试中考查

MP3·215
inflate 使充气，使膨胀
at the opposite end of the spectrum 正相反的情况
crack 裂缝
swirl 打旋，漩涡
bulbous 球根的，球根状的
bulb （球状的）圆形部分
panic 恐慌，惊慌

Answer level 1 > 1 (A) 2 (B) 3 (B) 4 (A) 5 (A) 6 (B) 7 (D) 8 (D)

level 2 > 1-1 (A) 1-2 (C) 2-1 (D) 2-2 (A)

level 3 > 1-1 (B) 1-2 (A) 1-3 (B) 2-1 (D) 2-2 (B) 2-3 (B), (D)

level 1

MP3·218 **1. Listen to part of a conversation between a student and a parking official.**

Student (male) I have a complaint to submit to the parking office.

Official (female) This is the parking office. What's the problem?

Student My car was towed yesterday from my dorm's parking lot...at Culver Hall.

Official OK...and your name is?

Student Mark Liszt. L-I-S-Z-T.

Official Let me just look that up... *[pause]* OK. It says here your car was towed because it had an expired parking permit.

Student Is that all? I know my permit was a couple of weeks expired, but I had no idea the car could be towed just for that.

Official Q1 **Well...the parking agreement you signed clearly states that you have two weeks to renew your permit after it expires. After that, your car can be towed. We can't afford to have students with expired permits parking at our dorms. There's just not enough space.**

Student OK, I see. Then I'd better renew my permit, I guess. Otherwise I'll just run into more trouble.

Q1关于该大学的停车规定，可以推测出什么？
(A) **行政部门严格执行。**
(B) 于两周之前开始执行。
(C) 很多学生不明白这一规定。
(D) 每个宿舍不一样。

MP3·238
complaint 不满，抱怨
submit 提交，呈递
tow 牵引（车辆等）
expire 满期，（期限）终止
permit 许可证
renew 更新

MP3·219 **2. Listen to part of a lecture in an art class.**

Professor (female)

Class, let's get started with today's lecture. OK? Naturalism was a style of painting that began during the middle of the nineteenth century in France. Naturalism, not surprisingly considering the name, is all about representing life accurately and naturally in art. It's about painting what the eye sees, not about idealizing

Q2关于浪漫主义，教授暗示了什么？
(A) 学生之后还会进一步学习浪漫主义。
(B) **浪漫主义主要关注戏剧化的主题。**
(C) 浪漫主义紧接着自然主义思潮出现。

life and dealing with elevated themes. Naturalists wanted to use, um, everyday characters and objects, and they avoided infusing their paintings with too much drama. Q2 **As you know, since we talked about Romanticism last week, an excess of drama was characteristic of the artistic movement that preceded Naturalism.**

(D) 浪漫主义是相对不重要的运动，因此讲义文中不会深入讲解。

MP3·239

Naturalism 自然主义
represent 描写，描绘
idealize 理想化
deal with 处理…
elevated 高尚的，崇高的
infuse A with B 将B注入A，赋予A以B
Romanticism 浪漫主义
excess 超过，过量
precede 先于…，在…之前

MP3·220 **3. Listen to part of a conversation between a student and a professor.**

Professor (male) Cassandra, I noticed you put in a request to change your lab partner...

Student (female) Yeah, my friend Yvonne just transferred into this class. I was wondering if I could switch to be with her.

Professor Ah, I see. But if you do that, what's going to happen to your current partner, Tim?

Student Oh, I guess there isn't anyone else in the class without a partner.

Professor No...um...but I think there's an easy solution. Why don't you keep Tim as a partner, and your friend Yvonne can join you two?

Student Q3 **So we can have a three-person team? Is that OK?**

Professor **It's no problem for me. Actually...you'll probably be thankful for the extra hands once you hear about next week's lab assignment. It's going to be...different. You'll see.**

Student OK, that sounds great to me. I'll let Tim and Yvonne know.

Q3关于下周的实验课题，教授暗示了什么？
(A) 内容将是学生不太了解的主题。
(B) 三个人的小组可以更轻松地完成这一课题。
(C) 大部分的研究工作都需要教授的帮助。
(D) 只有两个人的小组完成不了这一课题。

MP3·240

put in 提交…
lab 实验室(=**laboratory**)
transfer 搬，转换
extra hands 帮手，帮忙的人
assignment 课题，作业

MP3·221 **4. Listen to part of a lecture in an astronomy class.**

Professor (female)

Q4 **There was a time not too long ago when Pluto was considered to be the ninth planet in our solar system. But that was before**

Q4可以推测出冥王星？
(A) 不再被视为太阳系的第九大行星。
(B) 绕太阳公转轨道远于厄里斯星。

astronomers made several interesting discoveries after studying the far edge of our solar system. Uh, let's start with the discovery of Eris, a trans-Neptunian object. Eris's just an object that orbits the sun out toward the edge of the solar system. This object is bigger than Pluto, which started people thinking that maybe the ninth planet should be reclassified. Another issue was the size of its moon Charon, which is so big in comparison to Pluto that astronomers thought it should be considered a dwarf planet rather than a moon.

(C) 实际上是更大的行星的卫星。
(D) 矮星的地位最近受到质疑。

MP3·241
Pluto 冥王星
solar system 太阳系
trans-Neptunian object 海王星外天体
orbit 环绕轨道运行
Charon 卡伦星[天文]（冥王星的卫星）
dwarf planet [天文]矮星（介于小行星与行星中间状态的天体）

MP3·222 **5. Listen to part of a conversation between a student and a bookstore clerk.**

Clerk (female)	Hi there. How can I help you?
Student (male)	I was wondering if you're hiring right now?
Clerk	Well, at the moment we don't need anybody because the semester is coming to an end. But...are you going to be around this summer?
Student	Yeah.
Clerk	And have you worked in customer service before?
Student	I've—well, I've had a couple of jobs before. but none of them were exactly in customer service.
Clerk	That's OK. Let me take down your name and phone number. Q5 MP3·236 **I'll speak with my manager and get back to you if there's a chance we'll be hiring someone to work here over the summer.**

Q5店员在暗示什么？
(A) 暑假可能会有学生可以做的工作。
(B) 学生应该去校内的其他地方寻找工作机会。
(C) 她有可能在学期结束时离职。
(D) 书店目前雇用学生店员。

MP3·242
come to an end 结束
be around 在附近
customer service 顾客服务中心
take down 记下…，写下…

 MP3·223 **6. Listen to part of a lecture in a zoology class.**

Professor (male)

Q6 MP3·237 **Do you know what a caribou looks like? If so, then you know what a reindeer looks like.** They're basically Arctic deer that you'll find ranging through territories above 62 degrees North latitude. Since their habitat is so cold, they're well adapted for winter conditions. Um, they've got a special nasal structure that increases surface area inside the nostrils, so when the animal breathes in, cold air is rapidly warmed before entering the lungs. And what do

Q6教授在暗示什么？
(A) 驯鹿的样子在讲义文中不重要
(B) "reindeer" 与 "caribou" 指代的是同一种动物
(C) 学生对北美驯鹿的样子应该很熟悉
(D) caribou比reindeer在野生环境中更常见。

you think they eat all winter long? Well, one of their main staples is something called reindeer moss, which is a hardy tundra lichen. When conditions are really bad, reindeer decrease their metabolism and reduce their intake of food.

MP3·243
caribou 驯鹿(**=reindeer**)
North latitude 北纬
nasal 鼻的（←**nostril** 鼻孔）
hardy 耐寒的

MP3·224 **7. Listen to part of a conversation between a student and a professor.**

Student (male)	Professor Lee, you wanted to see me?
Professor (female)	Yes, Jamal. First of all, I wanted to tell you your work so far in this graduate seminar has been outstanding.
Student	Oh...thank you.
Professor	In fact, I've been so impressed that I'd like to offer you an opportunity. How would you like to be a teaching assistant for one of my undergrad classes next semester?
Student	A teaching assistant? Wow...I've never considered doing that before. Q7 **Um...my schedule for next semester's pretty busy...**
Professor	**Actually, it sounds like it'd be a lot of work, but it really doesn't involve that much. All you have to do is lead a review session once a week and answer students' questions.** But...why don't you think about it and get back to me?
Student	OK, I'll do that. Thanks.

Q7关于助教的职位，教授暗示了什么？
(A) 他会让学生在自己的课上拿到额外的学分。
(B) 助教需要在工作日随时答疑。
(C) 自己的大部分研究生都做这一项工作。
(D) 学生把助教工作日程合理安排并不难。

MP3·244
first of all 首先
outstanding 优秀的，突出的
teaching assistant 教学助理，助教(**=T.A.**)
undergrad 大学生（**=undergraduate**）
session （授课等的）时间

MP3·225 **8. Listen to part of a lecture in a geography class.**

Professor (male)

Q8 **There're many types of lakes in the world, but here's one you may not have heard of: oriented thaw lakes.** One of the best examples of an oriented thaw lake system is in northern Alaska... picture it—thousands of oval-shaped lakes stretching over hundreds of square miles. OK. Q8 **For a long time, there were two big mysteries about these lakes. One...they're all oriented in the same direction, and two...they grow larger over time. It wasn't until recently that we solved these mysteries.** So...it all has to do with the top layer of frozen soil that covers the ground up there. Sometimes, there's a sudden warm spell, and the frozen layer thaws rapidly. This causes it to weaken, and the soil surrounding the banks of the

Q8关于阿拉斯加向一个方向延伸的融陷湖泊，教授暗示了什么？
(A) 它们都朝着相反方向。
(B) 它们实际上还未被研究。
(C) 它们最近的扩张源于全球变暖。
(D) 最近揭晓它们形成的原理。

MP3·245
oriented 朝着一个方向的
thaw lake 融陷湖泊（永久冻土层局部融化，地面下陷积水而形成的湖泊）

lakes collapses...and they grow. The fact that the lakes are on gently sloping terrain means that their downhill banks collapse more easily...which is why they're all egg-shaped and all pointing the same direction.

oval shaped 椭圆形的 (**=egg-shaped**)
spell （特定天气）持续的时间
thaw 融化
bank 斜坡，斜面
collapse 崩毁，瓦解
gently 温和地
sloping 倾斜的，有坡度的
terrain 地形

level 2

MP3·226 **1. Listen to part of a conversation between a student and a registrar.**

Registrar (male)	Sandra Gomez? Thanks for coming to see me.
Student (female)	Sure. The semester just started and I don't have too much work in my classes yet, so I have plenty of free time.
Registrar	Good. Q1-1 **Well, it's actually your schedule I'd like to talk to you about. Specifically, the schedule of your class with Professor Ogawa... advanced finance.**
Student	Oh, really? OK. Um...I think that meets on Tuesdays and Thursdays at 9:30, right?
Registrar	Yes...I mean, that's when it was initially scheduled for. But, you see, something important has come up for Professor Ogawa. He...he's no longer able to teach the class at that time.
Student	Oh, no. Are you serious?
Registrar	I'm afraid so.
Student	Well...I have to take that class. It's a requirement for my major, and if I don't take it, I won't graduate. What am I going to do?
Registrar	Don't worry, Q1-1 **we're arranging a new time for your session of the class. That's why I called you in today...to see if it'll work for you.**
Student	Q1-2 MP3·227 **I see. When is the new time?**
Registrar	**It's Wednesdays and Fridays from 1:30 to 3:15.**
Student	***[thinking]*** **Wednesdays and Fridays from 1:30...** ***[suddenly concerned]*** **That's not my only option, I hope...**
Registrar	Oh...does that not work for you?
Student	I have another class during that time. It's a required course too, so I can't drop it. Please

Q1-1 注册主任为什么让学生来办公室？
(A) **为了告知学生日程表的变化。**
(B) 为了告知学生她选的课被取消了。
(C) 为了解释专业必修课。
(D) 为了讨论毕业后的去向选择问题。

Q1-2 说下面这句话时，学生在暗示？
[suddenly concerned] **That's not my only option, I hope...**
(A) 她选择那门课最重要的原因是Ogawa教授。
(B) 她不会考虑变更日程表。
(C) **按主任提出的时间注册，会与上课时间有冲突。**
(D) 高级财务课的变更对她不公平。

MP3·246
advanced 高级课程的
initially 最初的，初期的
come up 发生
requirement 必修课 (**=required course**)
drop 取消

	tell me there's some other way to take advanced finance.
Registrar	Well, yes, there is. Professor O'Connor...do you know her? She's teaching the same class. It's an evening class and it meets once a week...on Mondays, from 5:30 to 8 o'clock. How does that sound?
Student	Um...I'm not usually very fond of evening classes, but...is that my only other choice?
Registrar	I'm afraid it is.
Student	I guess it'll have to do, then.
Registrar	OK. Then I'll switch you over to Professor O'Connor's class. Monday evenings, 5:30 to 8. You'll receive confirmation by e-mail later today.
Student	I understand. Well, thanks for taking care of that for me.
Registrar	Certainly.

be fond of 喜欢…，乐于…
switch A over to B 把A变更为B
receive confirmation 得到确定答复，得到确证

2. Listen to part of a talk in a history class.

Professor (female)	In some parts of the world, there's enough natural rainfall to, um, to support agriculture, but in arid regions like, um, like the kind you would've found in ancient Egypt, there just isn't enough natural precipitation to grow staple crops. Yet, somehow, agriculture of the civilization of ancient Egypt thrived there in the rainless Nile River Valley. Class, what do you know about the ancient Nile River?
Student A (male)	Um, I've heard that it flooded annually.
Professor	Right. It flooded its banks predictably every year, when heavy rains in Ethiopia drained downstream to Egypt. The Nile would overflow its banks starting in June, with its peak in September and October. The timing was the same year after year, so farmers knew what was coming. During the flood period, the, uh, the plains surrounding the Nile would be completely inundated. Then, at the end of the flood season—
Student B (male)	*[interrupting]* You had conditions perfect for a crop season.
Professor	That's right. The flood plains—they were perfect for farming. Obviously, Q2-1 **the Nile's seasonal**

Q2-1 关于尼罗河每年的泛滥，教授暗示了什么？
(A) 它使得古埃及人有幸积聚主要农作物。
(B) 它因为不可预测的雨季变得更为严重。
(C) 它引发了古埃及人在城市周围筑造防御洪水的砖墙。
(D) 它为农民提供了必要的农作物种植用水。

MP3·247
arid 干燥的
precipitation [气象]降水（量）
staple 主要的
thrive 繁盛
predictably 可预测的
drain 流出
downstream 向下流
inundate （使）泛滥
（←**inundation** 泛滥）

flooding was essential to ancient Egyptian farmers; I mean, in years where the floodwaters were lower—or even higher than usual, famines would result. Actually, the, um, the conditions of the annual flood were so important that estimates about how much water would come down the Nile during a year's flood season actually affected taxes. **Q2-2 To help get an idea of what to expect in any given year, people ended up building these, um, "nilometers" upriver. Can you guess what a nilometer did? They, um, helped people measure the volume of the river and predict what the annual flood would be like.** At their simplest, nilometers were just columns marked with intervals and set in the water. They originated in ancient Egypt but continued to be used in various forms by later civilizations. Um, these days, though, the Nile has been bound by human engineering so the annual inundation doesn't happen anymore...so nilometers are pointless now.

Q2-2教授为什么要提尼罗河的水位计？

(A) 为了说明尼罗河的泛滥对古埃及人的生活有多重要

(B) 为了说明对尼罗河洪水的预测会对税负产生何种影响

(C) 为了显示直至今日尼罗河的泛滥仍未被完全理解

(D) 为了讨论每年一次的洪水是如何消失的

MP3·247

famine 饥荒
estimate 推定
nilometer 尼罗河水位计
upriver 上流的
interval 间隔
be bound by 被…围绕，被…环绕
pointless 无意义的

level 3

MP3·229 **1. Listen to part of a conversation between a student and a professor.**

Student (female) Are you free now, Professor Lerner?

Professor (male) Sure, Christine. What's up?

Student **Q1-1 It's about my thesis selection...The problem is I haven't chosen anything yet. Q1-2** MP3·230 **There are just too many topics and issues that I'm interested in.**

Professor Dictation 开始 **I see. Hmmm...you know you have to [1]*submit a thesis proposal* on Monday, right?**

Student Yeah, which is why [2]*I'm getting a bit stressed out.* I mean, it's not like I haven't been thinking about it...I just can't seem to narrow it down. Maybe you could help get me started?

Professor That's what I'm here for. Remember to choose something you are willing to research over the course of five months. [3]*It's quite a commitment,* so make sure you're truly interested in your

Q1-1学生为什么去找教授？

(A) 为了征得教授对自己选择的论文主题的同意

(B) 为了听取有关选题的建议

(C) 为了了解唐奈利教授做客座讲座的时间

(D) 为了讨论上节课的幻灯片

MP3·248

thesis proposal 论文开题报告
stressed out 有压力的
narrow down 缩小…
commitment 献身，贡献

topic. What are some of the topics you've been considering?

Student Well, um...I guess I've tried narrowing it down to something on, er, the original influences of Byzantine art, or, um, the meaning of [4] *ancient Egyptian decorative symbolism*...and yeah, the last one was about, uh, the achievement of color in ancient Greek pottery.

Professor Very interesting...I really like your idea about exploring Egyptian symbolism. It's a very rich topic. Although, all three [5] *are perfect for the nature of this assignment.*

Student Yeah...that's the problem. I'm equally interested in all three. I wonder if there's something you'd prefer reading...

Professor Me? Oh, *[chuckling]* I would find pleasure in reading about any of those. What's important is that you focus on something that you enjoy and can [6] *probably benefit from in the future.* Dictation 结束

Tell me something, what other classes are you taking?

Student This semester?

Professor Yes.

Student Well, there's your class...and I'm also taking Romantic literature, Cognitive psych, British colonialism, Latin, and Greek mythology.

Professor You're in Classics 341 with Professor Donnelly?

Student Yes, that's Greek mythology. It's a great course, too. Do you know Professor Donnelly well?

Professor Sure...in fact, I'm planning on inviting him to be a guest lecturer in class next month. There are very particular elements and narratives in Greek artwork that stem from their mythology. Do you remember the slide we looked at last Friday? The ornate vase?

Student *[thinking]* Yeah, I think so. It had tree detailing, right? The artist had etched leaves at the neck and base.

Professor Uh-huh. See, that vase is based on the golden apple myth with Paris and the three goddesses, Aphrodite, Hera, and Athena. Anyway, I think we've stumbled onto the solution to your dilemma, wouldn't you say?

Q1-2教授为什么这样说？
I see. Hmmm...you know you have to submit a thesis proposal on Monday, right?
(A) 因为提交开题报告的截止时间就要到了，他很担心。
(B) 因为他读了学生的开题报告后很激动。
(C) 因为他对学生落后于日程感到恼火。
(D) 因为他有兴趣听学生解释。

MP3·248

decorative 装饰的
rich（有很多可看的东西）饶有兴味的
cognitive psych 认知心理学（**=cognitive psychology**）
colonialism 殖民主义
narrative 叙述，记叙文，故事
stem from 起因于…
ornate 华丽的
etch 蚀刻，深印
stumble onto （未预料到地）与…碰上，发现…

Student	You're thinking I should work on the Greek pottery topic, right?
Professor	Well, it seems the most logical choice now that we can draw a relation between my course and Professor Donnelly's. The information you learn in both classes will overlap.
Student	You're right...wow, I'm surprised I didn't think of this before. I guess I was just too focused on this class and what exactly we've learned to consider the broader picture. This is good...so now my research can help me in both classes. Perfect, two birds with one stone.
Professor	Hmm... Q1-3 MP3·231 **Remember, if you're required to write a thesis for Professor Donnelly, you'd better be very careful what you write about. In fact, you'd do better to write the paper on something completely different. The university policy is very strict on this.**
Student	Oh, of course. Don't worry about it! We just have a final and three tests for that course, anyway. No thesis, thank goodness. I'd be so worn out.
Professor	All right, fine.
Student	I'd better get running now. Thanks so much, sir.
Professor	Thanks, Christine. Have a good day now.

Q1-3关于学校可以推测出什么？
(A) 要求学生对每一门高级课程提交论文。
(B) 不允许学生在一门以上课程中写作相似的论文。
(C) 有禁止抄袭他人论文的明确规定。
(D) 对规定时间内不能完成课题的学生加以处罚。

MP3·248
worn out 疲惫的，精疲力竭的

MP3·232 **2. Listen to part of a talk in an engineering class.**

Professor (female)	So...let's get started. Q2-1 **The thing I want to focus on today is a substance called a smart fluid.** I bet that some of you have—have heard of it, right?
Student A (male)	Yeah, we looked at smart fluids in one of my physics classes last year.
Professor	Great, but I'll go over the topic at a basic level because I think there may be some students who—who've never studied this before. OK. Anyway, smart fluids are fluids that have a property that can be changed when—when an electrical field is applied...or when a magnetic field is applied. Oh...so...by "properties" I mean attributes of the fluid. So, uh, what sort of attributes am I talking about?
Student A	Well, uh, I know...I remember the main one is

Q2-1讲义文的主要内容是？
(A) 两种智能流体的发现
(B) 影响智能流体黏度的方法
(C) 智能流体应用于医学技术的潜在用途
(D) 两种智能流体及它们的几种用途

MP3·249
substance 物质
smart fluid 智能流体（若加以电场或磁场，黏性等特性会产生有变化的流体）
property 属性，性质（**=attribute**）
electric field 电场
magnetic field 磁场

the viscosity of the fluid.

Professor Right, smart fluids can change their viscosity... their, um...basically, they can change their thickness. Uh, OK, but getting back to what I was saying...um, Q2-1 **I mentioned that there are two ways to—to affect a smart fluid. Uh... magnetic fields and electrical fields. The smart fluids that respond to magnetic fields are called magneto-rheological fluids. Um...commonly referred to as MRFs.** And, uh, these MRFs—they're made up of suspensions of tiny little particles in a liquid...and what they do is...they—when a magnetic field is applied, the liquid thickens into a paste. On the other hand, when the magnetic field is taken away, uh, the paste turns back into a liquid. Pretty interesting, huh? Q2-1 **Uh, and, oh yeah—um, the other kind of smart fluid—the electrical-field kind... well, it's the same deal. So, in the presence of an electrical field, electro-rheological fluids—or ERFs—they harden the same way...**

Student B (male) The way you describe MRFs and ERFs, they seem to follow a pretty similar process. Are there any major differences between them?

Professor Well, yeah, there are some differences. See, um, MRFs, they can tolerate really strong forces. And ERFs well, they're not so good with strong forces, but the good thing about ERFs is that the components that generate electrical fields can be really small. You know, compared to magnets, which have to be bigger. So they can be used for more delicate things. You see what I'm saying? Q2-1 ***[confirming]* MRFs and ERFs have slightly different properties, so they're useful for different applications.**

Student B *[interrupting]* Yeah, I was just going to ask about that. I mean, I think I understand how they work now, but how exactly are they used?

Professor Dictation 开始 Q2-2 ***[chuckling]* Well...at one time, these smart fluids were considered to be, um, nothing more than a—a novelty. Something that was really interesting to study...but that probably wouldn't have any real, uh,**

Q2-2关于过去的智能流体，教授暗示了什么？
(A) 它们在更广泛的产业上得以应用
(B) 大家不认为它们是可行的商品。
(C) 世界上最顶尖的工程师在研究它们。
(D) 用那个时代的技术来创造它们是不可能的。

MP3·249
viscosity 黏度，黏性
MRFs(=magneto-rheological fluids) 磁流变液（如果从外部加以磁场，则流体黏度会发生改变的机能性液体）
suspension （液体中的）悬浮物
paste 粉末或面团等固体块状物
ERFs(=electro-rheological fluids) 电流变液（如果从外部加以电场，则流体黏度会发生改变的机能性液体）
tolerate 容忍，包容
delicate 精美的，易碎的
application 适用，应用
novelty 新颖的事物，新奇
automotive 汽车的
suspension system [汽车]挂档装置，驱动装置

applications. But recently, there have been [1]*improvements in the field of technology.* So now, Q2-3(B) **some of the uses of MRFs are, um, in automotive design...um, in the suspension system,** which is [2]*responsible for absorbing the shock* that's, uh, that's transmitted from the road to the car. You see...well, this isn't really what I want to focus on today, but, uh... *[changing his mind]* Well, it's important, so I'll just briefly tell you about some of the advantages. Um, by using MRFs, automotive designers [3]*don't need to use as many mechanical parts* in their suspension systems. That's because MRFs can rapidly adapt. Um, they can [4]*adjust to fluctuating motion and shock* 500 times in one second. So, in a car's suspension system then, the MRF can change its, its viscosity to best absorb the, uh, specific amounts of shock that [5]*the car's exposed to.*

Student A Q2-3(D) ***[interrupting enthusiastically]*** **I remember reading about some kind of technology that's been used in prosthetics—like artificial legs or something—um, and it uses a smart fluid** [6]***in the joint of the limb...*** **Do you know what I'm talking about?**

Professor **Yes, you're right. It is related to MRFs.** Some artificial limbs, um, use MRFs [7]*controlled by sensors* that can automatically detect the—the wearer's walking speed. And it can even detect things like, um, whether the wearer is walking up stairs or—or going up a slope, and it'll [8]*adjust its properties accordingly.*[Dictation 结束]

Uh, now switching over to ERFs...there's some really great technology being developed with these smart fluids, too. One of the most interesting things is the potential for training surgeons. You see, using ERFs that mimic the resistance of human skin and—and other tissues, it's possible to give new surgeons a really good idea of what it will feel like to actually, um, to operate on a person. So...you can tell just from these few examples that, uh, smart fluids have a lot of, uh, potential...in lots of fields. It's pretty impressive, I think.

Q2-3下面哪些是讲义文中提到的磁流变液的用途？请选择两项正确答案。
(A) 充当人造生物组织
(B) 应用于汽车的悬挂系统
(C) 应用于手术器械的内部装置中
(D) 应用于假肢的关节处

MP3·249
fluctuate 波动，来回摆动
prosthetics 弥补术
artificial 人工的，假的
joint 关节
limb 肢体
detect 探查，查明
potential 潜力，可能性
mimic 模拟的
resistance 抗体
operate 做手术

DAY10 Review Test II

P.140

Answer passage 1 > 1 (C) 2 (A) 3 YES → (A), (B), (D) / NO → (C), (E) 4 (C) 5 (C)
passage 2 > 1 (C) 2 (B) 3 (B) 4 YES → (A), (D), (E) / NO → (B), (C) 5 (D) 6 (C)
passage 3 > 1 (C) 2 (A) 3 YES → (B), (C), (E) / NO → (A), (D) 4 (B), (C) 5 (C) 6 (A)

MP3·250 **passage 1. [1-5] Listen to part of a conversation between a student and a librarian.**

Student (male)	Excuse me.
Librarian (female)	Hi. How can I help you?
Student	Q1 **Is this where I come if I need help with citations?**
Librarian	Sure, I can help you out with that.
Student	Q1 **I'm trying to cite these two books here. But I'm just not entirely sure how to do it. Last time I handed in a paper I was penalized for citing my sources improperly. I'm really worried about getting it right this time.**
Librarian	Q4 MP3·251 **OK, sure. I can help you figure out what you need to do. What citation style are you using in your class?**
Student	***[confused, unfamiliar with the term]*** **Citation style? Uh...**
Librarian	**Yeah, you know, like MLA...APA...Chicago...**
Student	None of those sound familiar to me.
Librarian	Q2 **OK, um...well, who is your teacher?**
Student	**Professor Martin.**
Librarian	***[recognizing the name]*** **Oh, Professor Martin in the English Department? Yeah, he'll want you to be using the MLA format. MLA is what English professors usually require. Actually, it's the most commonly used style for humanities and liberal arts studies.**
Student	OK. So can you help me put these books into the MLA citation format? I've always had trouble with bibliographies. And I know the university takes this really seriously, so I don't want to mess it up and accidentally not acknowledge my sources.
Librarian	Right. It's a big deal. Let me show you our collection of citation reference materials. We've got all styles covered, so, say you need help with a bibliography for a psychology class. You can come here to consult our APA style guides.
Student	OK, thanks.
Librarian	So here are all our guides. This whole shelf is full of information that'll help you figure out how to cite your sources.
Student	OK. So what's a good book to help me with my MLA citations?
Librarian	*[looking over the titles]* Uh...oh here's a good one. *The MLA Handbook for Writers of Research Papers.*
Student	Great, thanks.
Librarian	No problem. You'll see that the book is organized by types of sources. Um,

what's the title of one of your books?

Student Oh, um, this one's called *Race Relations in Chicago*.

Librarian And the author?

Student Eileen M. McMahon.

Librarian OK, so that's a single-author book. If you want to cite a book that was written by a single author, you'll look in the "One Author" section of the handbook. Q3 **It'll tell you how to format the entry in your bibliography...like what order to put things in,** Q3(B) **where to put the publishing date,** Q3(D) **what to italicize,** Q3(A) **where to put periods...that sort of thing.** Or, for example, to cite an encyclopedia article, look in the "Encyclopedia" section. That handbook's pretty easy to follow.

Student Q5 MP3·252 **Thanks a lot. This is really helpful. So where do I go to check out the handbook?**

Librarian **Oh...actually, these reference materials are meant to be kept available for all students. But you can go ahead and use them here in the library if you want. Feel free to use those tables over there.**

Student OK, I'll do that. Thanks for your help.

Librarian Oh, it's no problem at all.

MP3·259

citation 引用（文）（←**cite**引用）
hand in 提交
penalize 对…予以惩罚，处以罚金
improperly 不正确的，不适当地
figure out 理解…

humanities 人文学科
liberal arts（大学的）文科
bibliography 参考书目，书志学
mess up 把…弄糟
acknowledge 承认，供认
reference materials 参考材料

encyclopedia 百科全书
check out 借出…
be meant to *do* 照道理/规矩应该…
go ahead 前进，走在前面
feel free to *do* 随自己之意…也好

◎ 解析

1. 学生为什么去图书馆？
   (A) 为了借一本有关MLA引用格式的书 **(not correct)**
   (B) 为了了解课上要求采用何种引用文标记样式 **(not correct)**
   (C) 为了寻求编排参考书目方面的帮助
   (D) 为了了解可以使用哪种形式的指导手册 **(not correct)**

Main Idea
在标记Q1处，学生对图书管理员说自己来是为了获取有关引用的帮助。他想引用自己书里的内容，但是不知道该怎么办。由此可见，学生是为了寻求编排参考书目方面的帮助才来的。因此正确答案选(C)。学生确实是想借有关MLA标记法的书籍，但这是图书管理员推荐的。此外，询问课上要求采用何种引用标记样式的也是管理员推荐的。因此，(A)和(B)选项错误。

2. 图书管理员为什么问学生其教授的名字？

(A) **为了决定使用哪种引用样式最好**

(B) 为了确认是否已经指定了某一样式指导手册 **(not correct)**

(C) 为了判断学生需要引用多少参考文献 **(not correct)**

(D) 为了找出学生按要求应该读的教科书 **(not correct)**

Detail

图书管理员为了帮助学生，问他课上要求何种引用形式。但是学生并不知道。听到这个，管理员就问他负责教授的名字以寻找学生需要的格式。因此正确答案选(A)。

3. 根据对话中的信息，以下各项哪些是<针对写作研究报告的MLA指导手册>？请判断并点击正确的空格。

(A) 参考目录中句号的位置	√	
(B) 刊载出版日期的合适位置	√	
(C) 当作者有多个名字时，记录的顺序 **(not correct)**		√
(D) 斜体的正确使用方法	√	
(E) 指导手册的借用步骤 **(not correct)**		√

Connecting Contents

请看标记Q3部分的内容。<针对写作研究报告的MLA指导手册>一书介绍了标记参考文献的详细方法。例如：出版年份应该写在哪里，什么内容需要用斜体标识，句号应该在哪里等。因此，(A) (B) (D) 为YES。书中没有提到作者不只一名时，记录的顺序，因此(C)为NO。图书管理员告诉学生这本书借不了，而不是在说明借书步骤，因此(E)也为NO。

4. 学生这样说的时候，可以推测出他？

[confused,unfamiliar with the term]

Citation style/ Uh...

(A) 他不确定是否正确理解了图书管理员的话。

(B) 他需要时间回想要求采用的引用格式。

(C) **他不太理解图书管理员的话**。

(D) 他希望图书管理员知道应该使用何种引用格式。

Attitude

请看标记Q4部分的内容。图书管理员刚问学生需要使用何种引用格式，学生就反问道“Citation style?（引用格式?）”接着，图书管理员举例进行了补充说明，可以发现学生对citation style一词感到陌生。因此正确答案选(C)。

5. 图书管理员这样说是为了暗示什么？

Oh...actually, these reference mater-ials are meant to be kept available for all students.

(A) 来使用参考资料的学生很少。

(B) 至今没有一名学生要求借参考资料。

(C) **学生们不可以将参考资料带出图书馆**。

(D) 使用参考资料不需要花费多长时间。

Inference

请看标记Q5部分的内容。学生一问图书管理员借指导手册的方法，管理员就说为了让所有学生都可以使用不外借。也就是说为了所有学生都可以使用它，这本书不能带出图书馆，只能在馆内阅览。因此正确答案选(C)。

 MP3・253 **passage 2. [1-6] Listen to part of a lecture in an engineering class.**

Professor (female) OK. Q1 **Today—today we're going to get into ceramic materials. First, let's talk about what they are...a definition...and then later we'll talk about—about**

what their uses are. OK. A general definition of "ceramic" is, uh, inorganic, non-metallic material...that's formed as a result of heat. Uh—I should mention that glass is often considered to be a ceramic, even though it's a little bit different. Anyway, the word "ceramic" actually goes back to a Sanskrit root meaning "to burn." So the name "ceramic" refers to the fact that ceramics are a product of burning—of heat.

Now traditionally—traditionally we've used the word to talk about clay, and the—the products that we make with clay...like bricks, pottery, and tiles. As you know, clay can be shaped into different forms and then it's heated—heated in a kiln. The high temperatures in the kiln cause permanent changes to the clay objects—um, making them hard and strong. OK. But I don't want to go on defining ceramic materials for too long because—because we've got a lot of ground to cover in class today. Can someone tell me about the uses of ceramics?

Student A (male) Well, I think of clay and pottery, like you said...and I picture ceramics being used mainly for tableware, um, dishware...and maybe sometimes sculptures or jewelry.

Professor Right. Well, Q4(A) **I'm sure many of you are probably picturing porcelain teacups, earthenware plates, decorative statuettes...that sort of thing.** Q1 **But...although pottery may be one of the first things a lot of people think about when—when they hear the word "ceramic"...um, there're plenty—plenty of other uses for ceramics. Many of them are quite...technical. Did you know ceramics are used for things like—like space shuttle components, construction, automobiles...get the idea?**

Student B (male) Wow...ceramics are used on the space shuttles? Can you explain that a little more?

Professor Sure. OK. Q2 **So the first thing you need to understand is that ceramics can—can withstand really high temperatures. I mean, they remain very strong even when they're exposed to—to, say, temperatures above 1,100 degrees Celsius. And this attribute of ceramics is what makes them useful in—in the space shuttles. Ceramics are used in the thermal protection system of the spacecraft.** As you know, when space vehicles re-enter the Earth's atmosphere, they're in some, um, some pretty intense heat, right? Plunging through our thick atmosphere creates a whole lot of heat. Well, scientists designing the—the vehicles that we send into space...they wanted to figure out a way to protect the spacecraft during re-entry so they could be reused on future missions. And they turned to ceramics. So the bellies of the space shuttles—uh, that's the part that's exposed to the intense heat—they're covered in tiles that have special ceramic coatings that—that resist the heat of re-entry...um, when the surface temperature of the craft might reach above 1,200 degrees Celsius. It protects the space shuttle so it's not destroyed or heavily damaged during re-entry.

Student A Q5 MP3•254 **I had no idea about that. I mean...is the ceramic you're talking about the same as your ordinary, everyday ceramic that's used in, um, in pottery? Or is it more high-tech?**

Professor **Uh, yeah...of course there are some differences, but...look, we can talk more**

about this later, but now I—I really need to move on.

Anyway, let me get back on track here. What was I talking about? Oh, the—the other uses of ceramics. OK. Q4(D) **So ceramics often serve a—a structural purpose.** Q3 **Ceramics include materials like bricks, cement...tile...the sorts of things we often use to—um, for construction. These are all really essential materials, right?** Q6 MP3·255 **Take cement: it's used to make roads, bridges, dams, buildings...** <u>**you name it.**</u> Q3 **Brick's great for building with 'cause it's not affected by termites...it doesn't rot...doesn't warp...doesn't rust...doesn't burn...doesn't peel...and so on. Um, and tile...it's hygienic and durable, so it's good for indoor domestic uses like floors and countertops. As you can see, there are a lot of uses.**

OK. And as I mentioned earlier, ceramics are also used in automobiles. And this goes back all the way to the—the 1920s, when they were used in spark plugs. And now, they've actually helped, um, reduce emissions in modern cars. See, there's a ceramic oxygen sensor in the engine that—that helps maintain optimal combustion levels...it makes things more efficient. And you know what else? Q4(E) **The kind of ceramic brake equipment that's usually found in racecars**—because it's so light and heat resistant—um, well, this kind of brake system is starting to appear in high-performance passenger vehicles too. Apparently, these ceramic components are so durable that they're expected to—to last for the entire life of the car.

MP3·260

inorganic 无机的，非生物的
kiln 窑，火炉
permanent 永久的，长久的
ground （研究）领域，问题
cover 处理（特定部分或领域），包括
picture 出现在（脑海里）
tableware 餐具
dishware 碟，盆，餐具
porcelain 瓷器，陶瓷制品
earthenware ［集合性的］陶器
statuette 小雕像，小塑像

space shuttle 宇宙飞船
component 成分，部件，元件
withstand 经受，承受
be exposed to 遭受，暴露于…
attribute 属性，特质
thermal 热的，保暖的
intense 强烈的，强度高的
plunge 突然跌落，猛跌
re-entry 再次进入，再次入场
high-tech 尖端技术的
termite 白蚁
warp 弯曲，弄弯

rust 生锈
peel （油漆、壁纸等）剥落
hygienic 卫生的
durable 持久的，耐用的
countertop （厨房的）工作台面
spark plug （汽车等内燃机的）火花塞，点火栓
emission 排气，排出气体
optimal 最佳的，最优的
combustion 燃烧，氧化
heat resistant 耐热的

◎ 解析

1. 讲义文的主要内容是什么？
   (A) 建造宇宙飞船使用的材料 **(minor)**
   (B) 制作陶瓷的过程 **(minor)**
   (C) 陶瓷的几项重要应用

<u>Main Idea</u>

只知道主题是关于ceramics的内容的话，很难找出正确答案。在标志Q1处，教授说："（首先，我们来了解陶瓷是什么，就是说了解陶瓷的定

(D) 陶瓷制品新的开发与使用 **(not mentioned)**

义。接着，我们再来谈谈陶瓷的用途。）”通过这句话，可以发现教授关注陶瓷的哪些层面。教授在简短定义了陶瓷之后，又介绍了陶瓷不是普通的工艺品，而是具有特殊的用途。也就是详细叙述了陶瓷在宇宙飞船、建筑、汽车方面的应用。因此正确答案选(C)。

2. 包裹陶瓷的瓦具有什么特征，使得它们可以用于宇宙飞船？

(A) 低廉的价格与简单的制造。**(not mentioned)**

(B) 可以抵御极端温度的耐热性能。

(C) 可以反复无限使用的性能。**(not mentioned)**

(D) 可以维持宇宙飞船内部温度的性能。**(not mentioned)**

Detail

在标记Q2处，教授介绍说：“（正是因为陶瓷的这种属性，它才在宇宙飞船中变得十分有用。）”这句话中的this attribute指的就是前面提到的陶瓷可以抵御1100度以上热度的耐热性能。

3. 教授是如何强调建筑中陶瓷的重要性的？

(A) 通过集中介绍某一建筑及陶瓷在其中的应用

(B) 通过列举某种特定陶瓷材料的优点

(C) 通过描述陶瓷应用于工业的历史

(D) 通过比较陶瓷与其他建筑材料

Organization

教授列举了cement,brick,tile等在建筑领域得到灵活运用的陶瓷材料，并一一介绍了它们的优点。这其中，他尤其详细介绍了brick“（不怕白蚁…不烂…不变形…不生锈…不着火…不剥落…等等特点）”。因此正确答案选(B)。

4. 下列哪些项目是讲义文中提到的陶瓷的用途？请判断并点击相应空格。

(A) 装饰用的瓷器与陶器	√	
(B) 机器的温度测量仪 **(not mentioned)**		√
(C) 最尖端的计算机的元件 **(not mentioned)**		√
(D) 住宅的外墙面	√	
(E) 跑车的内部附件	√	

Connecting Contents

在标记Q4(A)处，教授介绍说提起陶瓷，人们通常会想到瓷杯、瓷碗以及装饰用的塑像等。但是如果看Q4(D)部分的内容就会发现，陶瓷还包括砖、水泥以及瓦等，是广泛使用的建筑材料。最后，在Q4(E)中又提到在跑车中发现了用陶瓷制成的刹车。因此，(A)，(D)与(E)是YES。

5. 可以推测出教授？

(A) 她认为区别都很小。

(B) 她不想再重复内容。

(C) 她担心学生没有正确理解课堂内容。

(D) 她不想偏题。

Attitude

教授说：“now I–I really need to move on.”从这句话可以看出，尽管学生提问有技术性应用的陶瓷与普通陶瓷的区别，但是教授认为比起详细解答这一问题，最好还是继续集中于讲义文原本的主题“陶瓷的用途”。也就是教授只想继续说明原来计划好的讲义文主题，因此正确答案选(D)。参考：move on作为转入另一话题或进入下一顺序的标志，经常在讲义文中使用。

6. 教授为什么这么说？

you name it.

(A) 为了让学生举出更多的例子

(B) 为了强调这一要点的重要性

(C) 为了显示陶瓷还有许多其他用途

(D) 为了让学生定义一个讲义文中的用语

Function

"You name it（除此之外随便什么）"这一表现是在列举了好几个同类的东西之后，说明还有很多其他种类的常见表现形式。在这里，教授首先列举了使用cement的有roads, bridges, dams以及buildings等。然后使用这一表现表达还有很多例子。因此正确答案选(C)。即使不知道该词组表达表现的意思，但是看到它出现在列举了很多使用cement的事例之后，应该可以推测出它意味着还有很多例子。

 MP3·256 **passage 3. [1-6] Listen to part of a lecture in a literature class.**

Professor (female)

Q1 **Class, the subject of today's lecture is the British writer Evelyn Waugh.** He's considered by many to be one of the great satirical novelists of the twentieth century.

Uh, Waugh was born in 1903 to quite a literary family; his father was an author and editor, and his brother ended up being a writer, too. Waugh went to Oxford to study history, and scholars believe this phase of Waugh's life really influenced his later writings. Q5 MP3·257 **As it turned out, Waugh didn't get a degree from Oxford, um, because his test scores were low...and he would've had to stay an extra semester. Probably due to the amount of time he spent drinking rather than studying. I mean, he was certainly intelligent enough. He just lacked the discipline.** Anyway, so instead of doing that, he left Oxford in 1924. Sometime later—um, this was after working a couple of jobs—uh, after that Q1 **he published the book that, um, earned him his reputation as an author. It was called *Decline and Fall*.**

Some of you may already be aware of this if you've studied history... Q2 **but, um, the title *Decline and Fall* comes from another book—*The History of the Decline and Fall of the Roman Empire*, which is by Edward Gibbon. As the name suggests, Gibbon's book, uh, describes the decline...um, the decay of ancient Rome. In a way, Waugh parodies that idea...of the, um, decline of a civilization. He's using it to criticize the, the corruption he saw in the social institutions of his country. England. Um, so that's the general concept of the book.** And then, uh, the ideas for some of the events in the novel come from his own experiences. Um, so Waugh's *Decline and Fall* is loosely autobiographical. It's based partly, um, on, well, his time at Oxford...and one of the jobs he had after leaving Oxford—a schoolmaster job.

Um, I'd like to talk more about *Decline and Fall* itself now, so let me introduce the main character a little bit. His name is Paul Pennyfeather. Pennyfeather is a quiet student at Oxford...someone who

stays out of trouble. Now, as I mentioned earlier, Evelyn Waugh was a satirist...and the first bit of satire in *Decline and Fall* comes at the beginning of the story...with an outrageous scenario involving Pennyfeather getting expelled from Oxford for indecency. *[finding the idea humorous and strange]* Indecency! See, Pennyfeather is minding his own business when some drunken upperclassmen basically assault him and steal his pants for a laugh. Q3(B) **Pennyfeather, um, obviously the victim in the situation, gets in trouble for not wearing pants...um, and the college officials turn a blind eye toward the...the drunken exploits of the upperclassmen.** Waugh uses Pennyfeather's expulsion to criticize Oxford, um, suggesting that the university has ridiculous priorities and displays favoritism. Um, remember, he was once a student at Oxford, and he left that institution somewhat unsatisfied.
The next target of, um, Waugh's satirical style is English society at large. Q3(C) **After getting kicked out of Oxford, Pennyfeather goes out into the, um, the real world and becomes a teacher.** He meets a collection of strange characters...with odd, or negative character traits. To Waugh, these people represent the, um, the strangeness that society accepts so easily. Eventually, Pennyfeather gets involved with some members of the, uh, social elite... Q6 MP3•258 **and here the novel starts to get really...fantastical. Pennyfeather is about to marry into the world of the social elite, but before that happens he gets...arrested.** **And you'll never guess what he's arrested for: involvement in the white slave trade.** Q3(E) **Apparently, the rich woman he's engaged to earned her money through, well, human trafficking.** Pretty strange, huh? Eventually, Pennyfeather returns to Oxford—uh, which is ironic considering that he got kicked out...and, um, how tarnished his name became after leaving Oxford. So, um, again, ironically, he's right back where he started at the beginning of the novel. He...he hasn't gotten anywhere.
Q4 **Waugh...he wrote from a, um, moral perspective...and through his satire criticized social institutions that he thought had...had lost their morality, such as educational organizations...um, and the aristocracy.** Waugh highlighted their lack of integrity, um, and he did it in a humorous way: through satire. After *Decline and Fall* was successfully received by the public, um, he published other novels satirizing England's high society...people who he saw as somewhat immoral. That was one of his major themes as a writer.

MP3•261

satirical 讽刺的（←**satirize** 讽刺）
turn out 结果是…，原来是…
discipline 限制，规定
decline 下降，灭亡
be aware of 意识到…，知道…
decay 衰退，腐败
corruption 腐败
loosely 松弛地
autobiographical 自传的，自传性的
schoolmaster 男校长
outrageous 令人惊讶的，反常的

expel A from B （正式地）把A赶出B，从B流放A
indecency 猥亵，猥琐的行为
mind one's own business 管好自己的事情
assault 攻击，强暴
turn a blind eye toward [to] A 故意对A睁一只眼闭一只眼
exploit 英勇（或激动人心、引人注目）的行为
expulsion 开出，驱逐
priority 优先考虑的事，优先权
favoritism 偏袒主义，偏爱
get kicked out of 被赶出…

odd 奇数的，怪异的
trait （人物的）性格，特征
get involved with 给…缠住，连累
human trafficking 人身买卖
tarnish 玷污，败坏（名声、形象等）
moral prospective 道德性观点
aristocracy 上流阶层，贵族阶层
highlight 突出，强调
integrity 正直，诚实

◎ 解析

1. 讲义文的主要内容是什么？
   (A) 20世纪英国文学的常见主题 **(not correct)**
   (B) 伊夫林 • 沃在牛津大学的学生时节 **(minor)**
   (C) 一名英国小说家的人生及其第一部作品
   (D) 小说《衰退与堕落》的成功 **(minor)**

Main Idea

请看标记Q1的部分。教授首先明确说道：“（今天讲义文的主题是英国作家伊夫林 • 沃。）”然后一边介绍作家的处女作，也是一部自传性质的作品——《衰退与堕落》，一边集中介绍作家的作品与人生。

2. 教授是怎样介绍《衰退与堕落》的基本理念的？
   (A) 通过解释书名的来源
   (B) 通过介绍伊夫林 • 沃的家庭
   (C) 通过列举沃大学退学后的职业
   (D) 通过讨论沃写作小说那一时期的生活

Organization

请看标记Q2的部分。教授说：“（这就是书中的基本理念。）”留心此处即可以解题。教授介绍说沃为了批判当时腐败的英国社会，借用了Edward Gibbons著书《The History of the Decline and Fall of the Roman Empire》的题目，讽刺了文明的堕落。因此正确答案选(A)。

3. 根据讲义文的介绍，下列哪些叙述是关于《衰退与堕落》中的主人公的？请判断并点击相应的空格。

(A) 他成绩很差，中途从牛津大学退学了。 **(not correcr)**		√
(B) 他曾经受到大学官员不正确的对待。	√	
(C) 他开始从事教学活动。	√	
(D) 他通过婚姻进入了上层社会并变得富有。 **(not correcr)**		√
(E) 他曾经订婚的女人结婚之前被牵连入狱。	√	

Connecting Contents

请注意这道题考查的不是作家伊夫林 . 沃，而是小说中的主人公Pennyfeather。请看标记Q3的部分。这里说：“（大学官员们对喝醉酒惹是生非的上流阶层纨绔子弟们睁一只眼，闭一只眼，放任他们胡来。）”由此可见，培尼佩德受到了不公平的对待。此外，通过Q3(C)中的“becomes a teacher”与 Q3(E)中的“the rich woman he engaged to... human trafficking”，可以确定(C)与(E)为正确的叙述。因此(B)(C)(E)选项选YES。因为成绩差而中途从大学退学是作家伊夫林 . 沃本人，而培尼佩德在与订婚的女人结婚之前被逮捕了，因此(A)与(D)为NO。

4. 根据教授的介绍，《衰退与堕落》批判了英国社会的哪两个方面？
   (A) 法律体系 **(not mentioned)**
   (B) 教育机构
   (C) 社会精英
   (D) 人身买卖 **(not correcr)**

Detail

请看标记Q4处。教授举教育的例子说明社会制度的腐败“（教育机构…嗯，还有上流社会）”。表示“上流阶层、上流阶级”的aristocracy在答案选项中被表述为the social elite。因此正确答案选(B)与(C)。而human trafficking是小说中主人公培尼佩德受牵连的案件，并不是作家的批判对象。因此(D)选项不正确。

5. 教授这样说时，可以推测出他？

Probably due to the amount of time he spent drinking rather than studying.

(A) 沃与教授之间存在许多问题。

(B) 沃不是一个非常有才华的学生。

(C) 沃的失败是自己的错误造成的。

(D) 沃明显有某种性格障碍。

Inference

接着，教授介绍说："(我的意思是，他肯定够聪明但就是缺少规矩。)"由此可见，沃没能从大学毕业并不是因为智力上的原因，而是因为他的生活缺乏制约。所以他没能取得学业上的成功是自己的原因，因此正确答案选(C)。

---

6. 教授为什么这样说？

And you'll never huess what he's arrested for:

(A) 为了暗示小说的这一部分十分特别。

(B) 为了显示沃创造了自己的小说风格。

(C) 为了暗示接下来的内容。

(D) 为了让学生猜测接下来的内容。

Function

在回放部分，说话者介绍到培尼佩德被逮捕的原因是the white slave trade。在即将与上流社会的女性结婚之时，很难想到他从事白人奴隶买卖。所以，教授说："(你们永远也猜不到他被捕的理由。)"由此可见，这一理由一定非常地特别。所以正确答案选(A)。

type A

Answer

01 **legitimate** 合理的，妥当的
02 **credentials** 名声，证书
03 **abbreviate** 缩写，使省略
04 **sediment** 沉积物，沉淀物
05 **dissipating** 消失的，驱散的
06 **intriguing** 饶有兴味的，迷人的
07 **spectrum** 范围，领域
08 **disturbance** 混乱，不安
09 **devastating** 破坏性的
10 **stumble** （偶然地）绊倒，绊脚
11 **submission** 投降，屈服
12 **dismantle** 解体
13 **adorn** 装饰，使生色
14 **retreat** 休息处，避难所
15 **deterrent** 威慑力量，制止物
16 **emissions** 排放，放出
17 **sprint** 全力疾跑
18 **refracted** 折射的
19 **inspirational** 鼓舞人心的，激发灵感的
20 **disapproval** 非难，反对
21 **circulate** 循环
22 **spawn** 造成
23 **formula** 公式
24 **solvent** 溶媒，溶剂
25 **nasal** 鼻的
26 **intake** 摄取量
27 **spell** （某种天气的）一段持续时间
28 **mimic** 模仿
29 **combustion** 燃烧，氧化
30 **reminiscent** 回忆往事的，发人联想的

type B

Answer

01 (B) **02** (C) **03** (B) **04** (A) **05** (A) **06** (D) **07** (C) **08** (B) **09** (D) **10** (D) **11** (A) **12** (D)
13 (A) **14** (C) **15** (B) **16** (A) **17** (B) **18** (D) **19** (C) **20** (D) **21** (C) **22** (A) **23** (C) **24** (A)
25 (C) **26** (A) **27** (B) **28** (C) **29** (A) **30** (C)

type B [SCRIPT]

01 associated with an animal's sense of smell

(A) nasal(鼻的) **(B) olfactory(嗅觉的)** (C) organic(有机的) (D) fragrant(香的)

02 to put forward an unproven theory to explain something

(A) rephrase(改换措辞表达) (B) emphasize(强调) **(C) hypothesize(假设)** (D) energize(激励)

03 connected with the countryside and agriculture

(A) emotive(感情的) **(B) pastoral(田园生活式的)** (C) serene(静谧的) (D) ideal(理想的)

04 normal and regular, not exciting

(A) mundane(平凡的) (B) effective(有效的) (C) frequent(频繁的) (D) exhaustive(消耗的)

05 capable of conducting heat or electricity

(A) **conductive(传导性的)** (B) transferable(可转移的) (C) automatic(自动的) (D) receivable(可接受的)

06 producing poison to kill prey

(A) atrocious(非常恶劣的) (B) respective(各自的) (C) aggressive(攻击性的，侵略的) (D) **venomous(有毒的)**

07 an internal organ that produces hormones, sweat or saliva to help the body function

(A) substance(物质) (B) component(成分) (C) **gland(分泌腺)** (D) intestine(肠)

08 having worse living conditions and fewer opportunities than most other people

(A) relative(相对的) (B) **underprivileged(低收入层的)** (C) inadequate(不合适的) (D) defi cient(不足的)

09 to ensure that the situation stays the same by opposing another force or action

(A) submit(提交) (B) vindicate(证明) (C) realize(实现) (D) **offset(抵消)**

10 to recover information stored in a computer's memory

(A) incorporate(把…法人化/组成公司) (B) exchange(交换) (C) inspect(检查) (D) **retrieve(检索信息)**

11 a small object made of rock or metal which has landed on Earth

(A) **meteorite(陨石)** (B) phenomenon(现象) (C) pathogen(病原体) (D) comet(彗星)

12 a member of a particular group of mammals including humans, apes and monkeys

(A) gender(性，性别) (B) community(团体) (C) species(种) (D) **primate(灵长类)**

13 an official document that allows you to do something

(A) **permit(许可证)** (B) confirmation(确认) (C) receipt(发票) (D) report(报告)

14 to suffer a penalty or an unpleasant consequence for doing something wrong

(A) affect(影响) (B) incite(激起) (C) **incur(招致)** (D) induce(诱导)

15 to move something quickly through the air so that it makes a quiet sound

(A) faze(烦扰) (B) **swish(嗖地挥动)** (C) veer(改变方向) (D) grate(摩擦，磨碎)

16 to help plants grow and develop

(A) **fertilize(施肥)** (B) harvest(收获) (C) feed(喂养) (D) diversify(使多样化)

17 being extremely hot and uncomfortable, making it difficult to breathe

(A) destructive(破坏性的) (B) **stifling(令人窒息的)** (C) perpetual(永久的) (D) pliable(柔软的)

18 something done after no preparation

(A) expertise(专门知识) (B) groundwork(基本原理) (C) impulsion(推动，冲动) **(D) improvisation(即兴创作，即兴作品)**

19 to invent a new expression that becomes popular

(A) impart (分给) (B) fabricate(制造，组装) **(C) coin(杜撰新词)** (D) direct(指导)

20 to make a guess about a future event despite not having access to all the facts or details

(A) irritate(使恼怒) (B) debate(辩论) (C) contempt(蔑视) **(D) speculate(推测)**

21 an area of land and its natural features

(A) soil(土壤) (B) estate(地产) **(C) terrain(地域，地带)** (D) boundary(分界线)

22 a person who supports a particular side, or who persuades others to do something

(A) proponent(支持者) (B) supervisor(监督者) (C) commentator(评论者) (D) participant(参与者)

23 being friendly and helpful to visitors

(A) useful(有用的) (B) remedial(治疗的，矫正的) **(C) hospitable(招待周到的，好客的)** (D) appointed(指定的)

24 to occur or be present before something or someone, or to go before something in a series

(A) precede(处在前面，领先) (B) facilitate(使容易) (C) forewarn(事先警告) (D) imagine(想象)

25 being very clean and preventing bacteria or germs from spreading

(A) polluted(被污染的) (B) intriguing(饶有兴味的) **(C) hygienic(卫生的)** (D) negligent(随便的，不在意的)

26 behavior that is considered to be sexually offensive

(A) indecency(无理，猥亵) (B) commitment(献身，承诺) (C) brutality(残忍) (D) provocation(挑拨，挑衅)

27 very unusual and funny or shocking

(A) grateful(感激的) **(B) outrageous(令人吃惊的)** (C) passionate(热情的) (D) needy(贫穷的)

28 something you are given by someone after they die

(A) bereavement(丧亲，丧友) (B) reception(欢迎，接待) **(C) legacy(遗产)** (D) leftover(残余物)

29 a performance or festival to celebrate an occasion

(A) gala(节日，庆祝) (B) amusement(娱乐) (C) demonstration(演示，示威) (D) memorial(纪念品)

30 to move along a curved path around a far larger object

(A) descend(下来，下降) (B) mobilize(动员) **(C) orbit(绕轨道运行)** (D) vault(跳跃)

Answer

case example	> 1 (D) 2 (A) 3 (A) 4 (D) 5 (B)
passage 1	> 1 (D) 2 (C) 3 (C) 4 (A), (B) 5 (B)
passage 2	> 1 (C) 2 (A) 3 (C) 4 (A) 5 (A)
passage 3	> 1 (D) 2 (A) 3 (A) 4 (D) 5 (A)

case example

MP3•270 **[1-5] Listen to part of a conversation between a student and a professor.**

Student (male) Professor Stuart, do you have a minute?

Professor (female) Is that you, Miguel? Of course I do...come on in. This is the first time you've stopped by to see me during office hours, isn't it?

Student Yeah...I guess so.

Professor Do you have a question about something we covered in class yesterday? I know my lecture dealt with a lot of different issues...

Student Oh, no. It's nothing like that.

Professor OK. What can I do for you then?

Student Q4 MP3•271 **Um...it's about graduation. No—I mean...let me start over. Um, it just occurred to me the other day that...that I'm going to graduate in less than a year.**

Professor Time goes by so fast, doesn't it?

Student It sure does. But...I'm kind of worried about it. You know... Q1 **I have no idea what I'm going to do with my biology degree after I finish school.** It's like, um, I've been so busy worrying about getting good grades and learning the material...I haven't had any time to consider where it's leading me.

Professor Q1 **So...are you looking for advice about how to use your biology degree to find a job?**

Student **Yes, that's exactly what I'm wondering about.**

Professor OK. I understand how overwhelming this process can be...especially when you're first starting to think about it. Um, hmm...I suppose the first step would be to find out what area of biology

Q1学生为什么去找教授？
(A) 为了讨论昨天的讲义文
(B) 为了讨论即将面临的毕业
(C) 为了了解如何申请制药公司的实习生职位
(D) 为了寻求关于毕业后就业问题的建议

Q2学生为什么对自己的工作经历感到担心？
(A) 因为没有一项与他的专业相关
(B) 过去他在生物学领域工作时遇到过困难
(C) 因为所有的工作经历都是志愿性质的活动
(D) 因为教授不认为它们有价值

MP3·284
deal with 处理（主题或提议等）
start over 从开头重新开始
the other day 有一天，一天
overwhelming 繁重的，累人的

you'd be interested in working in. Have you narrowed it down at all?

Student Actually, yes. That's one thing I've considered.

Professor Excellent. In fact, that's probably the most important part right there. So what field looks good to you?

Student Well, I can see myself working in the pharmaceutical industry. The idea of developing new medicines...that's really appealing. Ideally, I'd like to find a position where I could utilize my minor, too...which is in business administration.

Professor Right. That certainly is a popular field to get into these days. A lot of those pharmaceutical corporations are...hugely influential...in the world of medicine. And they're always looking for well-educated people to bring on board.

OK. Q2 **The next thing I'll ask is whether you have any specific work experience...either in pharmaceuticals or in a related field.**

Student **Um, no...and that's one of the things I'm, uh, most concerned about. I mean...every job I've ever had is totally unrelated, uh...waiting tables, working in the university bookstore. Nothing I've done even comes close to the kind of position I hope to get after school.**

Professor I see. But you know...that might not be as big a problem as you think it is. A lot of firms don't expect recent college graduates to have tons of experience. The quality of your education and your academic performance matter a lot...and I'd say you're doing pretty well in those categories.

Q5 MP3·272 **But there are some things you can do to increase your odds. Um...one of the best is to do an internship.**

Student ***[unsure]* An internship? Don't students usually do those during the summer? It's September now, and I graduate next May.**

Professor Well...you're right that summer internships are pretty popular. But there are plenty of organizations that offer them during the rest of the year, too. In fact, Anderson Pharmaceuticals

Q3可以推测出学生春季学期的计划？
(A) 他希望去制药公司实习。
(B) 在一门课中做一些现场实习勘察。
(C) 他希望提交研究生入学申请。
(D) 他将开始了解实习机会。

Q4学生为什么这样说？
No—I mean...let me start over.
(A) 为了重复之前说过的话。
(B) 为了表明自己想讨论一件复杂的事情。
(C) 为了强调问题的严重性。
(D) 为了阐明自己刚才说的内容。

MP3·284
narrow down 缩小（范围或领域等）
pharmaceutical 制药的，制剂的
appealing 有魅力的，有召唤力的
utilize 灵活利用，运用
minor 第二专业，辅修专业
business administration 经营（学）
bring on board 使进入（公司等特定组织），使进入公司
related field 相关领域
tons of 非常多的
matter 重要的，成为问题的
odds 概率，可能性

here in the city accepts people for fall and spring internships. Q3 **I think the application period for the one in the spring is still open, if you're interested in that. Of course, that might be difficult if you're going to be busy during your final semester.**

Student **Actually, my schedule next semester should be pretty light, and that internship sounds like an excellent opportunity.** Thanks for letting me know about it.

Professor Oh, of course. And don't forget...you can always apply for internships after you graduate as well. Some of them give stipends to participants...in case you're worried about money. I'll be more than happy to help you research your options if you'd like.

Student Thanks so much. I'll do some, um, preliminary searching and let you know what I find out.

Professor Sounds good. But I don't want to let you go without discussing another option too.

Student Oh...what's that?

Professor Have you considered grad school? I know lots of schools offer specialized programs combining biology and business...which is just what you want to do. And they typically involve a lot of field research...which would give you plenty of experience for when you're ready to apply for a job.

Student That's a good point too. Wow. Obviously I have a lot to think about. Why don't I look into this more and come back and see you in a few weeks?

Professor That sounds great. I hope I was able to help.

Student Oh, definitely. Thank you so much again, and I'll see you in class tomorrow.

Professor Great, see you then.

Q5可以推测出学生？
(A) 他很高兴可以读研。
(B) 他不确定有多少可能进行实习。
(C) 他怀疑自己是否有实习资格。
(D) 他担心实习的学生过多。

MP3-284

application period 报志愿[申请]时间
stipend 月薪，工资，报酬
participant 参与者
preliminary 初期的，预备的
specialized 专门的
involve （使）包括，（使）关联
plenty of 很多的…，丰富的…，充分的…
obviously 明显的，明确的（**=definitely**）

passage 1

MP3·273 **[1-5] Listen to part of a conversation between a student and a professor.**

Student (male) Professor Tananger, do you have a moment to talk?

Professor (female) Oh—hello, An. Yes, I have a few minutes free. Why don't you come on in and have a seat. Tell me...what can I help you with today?

Student Q2 **Well, as you know, a lot of my graduate training has focused on programs at the laboratory for cancer research... Well, I've—I've come to the conclusion that I'd like to make a career out of it.**

Professor **You do seem to have the personality for that kind of work. All the work that you've produced here has been of an exceptional standard, so I've got high hopes for you.**

Student Thank you. Q1 **The reason I'm here is—well I know how important grants are for researchers... and since you come from a research background, maybe you could give me some tips about how to apply for grants?**

Professor Sure, I'm more than happy to give you some pointers. Let's see...where to start? Um, well, the first thing you'll want to do is determine where your research belongs. Seek out institutions that are going to value and support your work.

Student I've come up with a list of institutions that are already supporting and funding the kind of research I want to get involved in. I'm hoping to continue working in cancer research.

Professor Very good. I'm happy to hear you've already started the process. Uh, have you identified any grants to apply for?

Student A couple so far. I'm pretty sure I'll apply for a grant from the National Institutes of Health.

Professor An NIH grant? Well, that'll limit where you can conduct your research. Universities and businesses are eligible for NIH grants...but some federal institutions aren't.

Student OK. That's good to know. Q3 **I'm hoping to continue my work here, or at another university**

Q1学生需要教授的什么帮助？
(A) 就业推荐信
(B) 关于不同癌症研究所的信息
(C) 推荐可以进入的研究领域
(D) 关于申请研究经费的建议

Q2对于学生的职业目标，教授暗示了什么？
(A) 学生日后可能改变心意。
(B) 它们可能难以实现。
(C) 学生很有可能会成功地实现自己的目标。
(D) 为了实现目标，学生需要一份更详细的计划。

Q3学生想在哪工作？
(A) 联邦机构
(B) 津贴审查委员会
(C) 当地大学
(D) 医药行业

MP3·285
come to the conclusion that 得出…的结论
make a career 积累事业经验
exceptional 出色的，突出的
grant 津贴，经费
apply for 申请
pointer 建议
seek out 寻找…
come up with 找出了…
get involved in 与…有关
be eligible for 有资格享受…

in the region.

Professor Dictation开始 In that case, you should visit the office of sponsored research at whatever institution you plan to be working with. They'll let you know about [1] *any restrictions and internal procedures* they have for the application process.

Student Got it.

Professor Q5 MP3·274 **Oh, another thing to consider is what kind of grant is best for you. Even though you know you want to apply for an NIH grant, there're still a lot of options. Um, at this point in your career [2] *there're some you wouldn't qualify for...***

Student **[interrupting] Right, I know. So when it comes time to actually apply, what sorts of things do I need to be thinking about?**

Professor You'll want to clearly define your project [3] *in terms of time, resources, and budget.* I'm assuming you're not at this stage yet...?

Student No...I'm really just [4] *at the very preliminary stages.* But I'm hoping to design my research project this semester, and I want to be thinking about this stuff as I develop my proposal.

Professor That's a good idea. Well, after you've defined your plan, it's time to write the proposal. Q4(B) [5] ***Keep your audience in mind.*** The first people who review your proposal are going to make the decision about [6] *whether your project deserves further consideration.* Chances are, the primary reviewers aren't going to be familiar with your field. Q4(B) **So you have to present your proposal in a way that'll [7] *make sense and seem valuable to people* who don't really know anything about cancer research.**

Student I see. That sounds pretty difficult.

Professor Yes, it can be. Q4(B) **But you've also got to keep in mind that after the primary reviewers see your proposal, experts in your field will go over it. So, your proposal has to [8] *appeal to experts and peers* too.**

Student You've given me a lot to think about. Are there any last pointers you have for me?

Professor Q4(A) **Um, well, above all, make sure [9] *your***

Q4对于津贴申请，教授提醒了学生哪两点？请选择两项正确答案。
(A) **主题不要太宽泛。**
(B) **针对具有不同专业水平的审查委员写作。**
(C) 不要偏离自己的研究领域。
(D) 尽可能写得透彻明了。

Q5学生为什么这么说？
Right, I know. So when it comes time to actually apply, what sorts of things do I need to be thinking about?
(A) 为了请教授详细说明刚才的观点。
(B) **为了表明同选择津贴的类型相比，自己更关心申请本身。**
(C) 为了告诉教授他还没有决定职业去向。
(D) 为了证明自己已经做了很多调查，看看自己有资格获得何种津贴。

MP3-285
restriction 制约，限制
internal procedures 内部程序，内部步骤
qualify for 满足…的资格要求
define 下定义
in terms of 从…方面，就…方面
preliminary 准备的，预备的
keep A in mind 牢记A
deserve 有…的价值
primary 第一的，首先的
be familiar with 熟悉…
go over 探讨…
appeal to 对…满意
peer 同事
above all 最重要的

***proposal has a sharp focus.* Don't try to cover too much ground. And leave out anything that's not absolutely essential.** I can help you with that when you get to that point. For now, I'd recommend working on [10] *sketching out your research plan.*

Student Thanks. You've been really helpful.[Dictation 结束]

cover ground 包括领域或主题
leave out 去掉…
sketch out 大致描述…

passage 2

MP3·275 **[1-5] Listen to part of a conversation between a student and a professor.**

Professor (male) Hello, Tara. You're right on time for our appointment. Please, have a seat.

Student (female) Q1 **Thank you, Professor Sandler. Did you have a chance to go over the rough draft of my short story?**

Professor **Yeah, I went over the draft you sent me on Tuesday, and I have a couple of pointers for you to think about while you're revising it.**

Student Great. I think the story still needs a lot of work.

Professor Well, it's coming along well so far, I think. It's not quite polished yet, but it'll get there.

Student So, what kind of feedback do you have?

Professor Overall, the plot is interesting and the story is well written.

Student OK, thanks.

Professor However, I'm interested in why you chose to write the story in the first person, and from a male character's perspective.

Student Yeah...I wanted to try something new. Usually I write in the third person, so I wanted to break out of my usual routine. You don't think it was very successful?

Professor Q2 **Well, I thought that the narrator's voice was, um, inconsistent at times. I mean, sometimes the narrator was very informal and used colloquial speech. But at other times the very literary narrative style I'm used to seeing in your writing showed through.** You might want to read through the story a couple of times looking for these sorts of inconsistencies.

Q1学生为什么去找教授？
(A) 为了讨论一篇为上课阅读的文学作品
(B) 为了询问提交写作作业的截止时间
(C) 为了给自己创作的一篇文章寻求改进意见
(D) 为了询问写作短篇小说的建议

Q2教授对小说的叙述者有何意见？
(A) 他的语气应更具有一贯性。
(B) 他的行为应更详细地解析。
(C) 没有必要对人物进行介绍。
(D) 他应该换成女性。

MP3·286
on time 准时的
rough draft 草案，草稿
revise 修改
（←**revision**修改，纠正）
come along 顺利进行
polished 精炼的，完成的
plot 情节
first person [文学]第一人称
perspective 观点，角度
third person [文学]第三人称
routine 惯例，日常工作
inconsistent 不连贯的，不连续的
（←**inconsistency**不一致）
colloquial 口语的
narrative 叙述的
be used to doing 习惯…

Consider what kind of mood you want to convey and which narrative technique is best suited for the, um, the mood of your piece.

Student OK. I'll do that. But you definitely prefer the, um, the idea of a third-person narrator?

Professor Well, that's not exactly what I'm saying. The first-person narrator in this draft wasn't, um, wasn't real to me because of the inconsistencies I mentioned. If you were able to improve on those, I'm not sure how I'd feel. I'm leaving that up to you.

Student All right. Thanks, I'll think about it.

Professor Q3 **Another issue I had was with the way you established the setting. I think there was too much direct explanation.** I don't want to read sentences like "It was extremely hot out that day." I want to get the impression of heat. Convey it in a more indirect way. For example, you could talk about the character's shirt being sticky with sweat, or you could describe the way grass looks after a couple days of a heat wave. Do you see what I'm saying?

Student Yeah. That makes sense to me. I tried to use that technique to explain the character's personality and appearance...but I guess I lost my focus while I was writing about the setting.

Professor Yes. Q3 **You did a great job with your explanation of the character. I never felt like you were directly explaining his personality.**

Student OK. Great. So I should just take that further... apply it to the whole piece.

Professor Right.

Student Um, is there anything else I should think about while I revise this draft?

Professor Um...I think that's about all. Oh—wait. Q4 MP3·276 **Um, what about getting rid of the first paragraph entirely?**

Student **Really? I thought there needed to be a little bit of, um, introduction before the main sequence of events begins.**

Professor I don't agree. Q5 MP3·277 **I think the second paragraph is much more interesting. Sometimes, it's a good idea to just throw your reader into**

Q3背景描写与出场人物描写有何区别？
(A) 对出场人物的解说更加现实。
(B) 对出场人物的描写较为不成功。
(C) 对背景的描写更加直接。
(D) 背景描写中使用了更多的比喻。

Q4学生为什么这么说？
Really? I thought there needed to be a little bit of, um, introduction before the main sequence of events begins.
(A) 为了解释自己那样写的理由
(B) 为了表明教授犯了一个错误
(C) 为了表示承认自己写的东西有错误
(D) 为了表明教授误解了自己

MP3·286
convey 传达
leave it up to you 托付给你，由你负责
establish 设定，建立
setting （小说，话剧等的）背景
sticky 粘的
heat wave 热浪，热气
sequence of events 一连串的事件
look forward to doing 期待…
final version 最终版本
due 期限，到期

	the action without explaining too much about what's going on.	Q5学生这样说是为了暗示什么？ **OK. I do like that idea now that you mention it. I wouldn't have thought to do that on my own, though. Thanks.** **(A) 她会按照教授建议的修改。** (B) 比起教授给出的建议，她更喜欢其他的写作风格。 (C) 她一开始并不理解教授所说的东西。 (D) 她需要更加深入地考虑教授的建议。
Student	**OK. I do like that idea now that you mention it. I wouldn't have thought to do that on my own, though. Thanks.**	
Professor	Oh, sure. I'm looking forward to seeing your next draft. The work you produce in class is always top quality.	
Student	Thanks a lot. I'm really enjoying creative writing this semester. Oh—when is the final version due again?	
Professor	It has to be finished by next Friday. You still have plenty of time to revise your draft.	
Student	Great. Thanks so much for your suggestions. I think I'll go get started on my revisions.	

passage 3

MP3·278 **[1-5] Listen to part of a conversation between a student and a professor.**

Professor (male)	Laura, good evening.	Q1学生为什么去找教授？ (A) 为了咨询是否有获得额外学分的机会 (B) 为了讨论下节课缺勤的事情 (C) 为了就疏忽了一项作业道歉 **(D) 为了再听一遍对讲义文内容的说明**
Student (female)	Professor Ellis, hi. Thanks for taking time to meet with me after class.	
Professor	It's no problem.	
Student	Q1 **Um...so...I wanted to ask you about some things you talked about in class tonight.**	
Professor	OK, sure. What do you have a question about?	MP3·287 **transference** 转移，传递
Student	Um...well...pretty much all of it. The transference of culture...how a small group over time, um, tends to absorb the culture of the larger group surrounding it. Q4 MP3·279 **I understand the basic idea, but...a lot of the details you were talking about...they were kind of difficult for me to pick up. I was wondering if you could just quickly explain them to me again.**	
Professor	*[unsure how to proceed]* Um...OK...well, I can't go over everything with you again right now. Let's see...did you do the reading assignment for the class?	
Student	No, actually...I haven't had time to do that yet.	
Professor	Ah, well that explains it. Q2 **In my lecture, I was assuming everyone had done the reading...**	

um, so I skipped over all the fundamental stuff so I'd have time to go into more depth on certain issues. But if you didn't do the background reading first, I can see why you felt lost.

Student Yeah, I'm sorry. I guess I should make sure to always prepare for class.

Professor Dictation 开始 Well, I [1] *do assign the readings for a reason.* However, uh, as long as you took good notes during my lecture...um, once you go back and do the reading, you should be able to [2] *fill in any gaps from there.*

Student OK, thanks, I'll do that. If I still have questions afterward, can I come see you again?

Professor Sure. Q5 **Now, make sure you also do next week's reading before you show up to class, OK?**

We'll be [3] *continuing our discussion of cultural transference*, and I'll need everyone to be caught up.

Student OK, I definitely will. Um...what'll we be covering, if you don't mind my asking?

Professor Next week's topic is dialect accommodation.

Student Dialect accommodation...could you give me a little preview of what that is? It might help me prepare for class better.

Professor Sure, OK. Dialect accommodation is what happens when...um, as we saw tonight, when a small group [4] *becomes isolated from its original culture*, it starts to [5] *adopt things from the dominant culture around it.* But in this case, we're talking about speech...a way of speaking, and that's called a dialect.

Student *[surprised]* [6] *How weird...* I've been thinking a lot about dialects lately.

Professor Really? Why's that?

Student Well, um, I have two roommates in my dorm room. Q3 **One's from New York City, and the other's from the Deep South...and, well, they both have these totally different and, uh, distinct accents.** It's like nothing I've ever heard before...I mean, except on TV.

Professor Ah, I see. That must be a very interesting

Q2 今天的讲义文内容与文化转移有关，对于这次讲义文，教授说了些什么？
(A) 它是为已经阅读了解过这一主题的学生设计的。
(B) 它是课上讨论的最难话题之一。
(C) 它与学生及其室友之间的经历紧密相关。
(D) 它对于班上的许多其他学生来说都很难。

Q3 对于自己的室友，学生暗示了什么？
(A) 她们表现出了对其他方言的适应。
(B) 她们对文化转移有些疑问。
(C) 她们注意到了自己说话方式的变化。
(D) 她们很难听懂她的口音。

MP3-287

skip over 跳过
fundamental 基本的，基础的
assign 布置，分配（作业等）
as long as 只要…
fill in 填满…，充满…
dialect 方言
accommodation 适应，调节，膳宿
isolate from 从…孤立，孤立于…
dominant 占优势的
Deep South 美国最南部地区（Georgia, Alabama, Mississipp, Louisiana等州）
distinct 与其它不同的，独特的

experience...[7]*to be exposed to two completely different accents* like that all the time.

Student Yeah, it really is. Q3 **But the strange thing is, as the semester's gone on, um, I've noticed that their accents are changing. Like...each of my roommates has started saying [8]*some things that sound more like me* than like their original accent. You know...'cause I don't really have an accent.**

Professor Very interesting. You know what? Q3 [9]***This ties in perfectly with next week's lecture.*** **You see...most students here speak with a fairly... sort of...standard accent, I guess you could call it. So, yeah, your roommates are both in the minority, and they're starting to trade in some of their native speech patterns to, to [10]*conform to the larger group*. That's pretty much what dialect accommodation is all about.**[Dictation 结束] **Of course, dialects are more than just accents...but it's the same idea.**

Student How funny. I guess I'll be more prepared for next class than I thought.

Professor *[laughing]* I guess so. In fact...are you at all interested in an extra-credit opportunity?

Student Really? Yeah, I can always use some extra credits.

Professor Great. If you can put together a short presentation about your roommates' accents...you know, really analyze the changes you've observed... what's changed and what hasn't and how long it took...um, just a quick five-minute presentation. If you'll present it next class, I'll give you ten extra points on our next test.

Student *[excited]* It's a deal!

Professor Excellent. Q5 MP3·280 **Oh, and Laura... I still expect you to do the reading for next week as well.**

Student **Don't worry, Professor. I won't miss another one. Thanks so much for helping me out.**

Professor My pleasure. See you next week.

Q4当教授这样说时，可以推测出他？
[unsure how to proceed]
Um...OK...well, I can't go over everything with you again right now.
(A) 倾向于利用其它的时间帮助学生。
(B) 确信学生不需要帮助也可以理解材料。
(C) 希望学生上课时更认真。
(D) 他很不情愿满足学生的要求。

Q5教授为什么这样说？
Oh, and Laura...I still expect you to do the reading for next week as well.
(A) 为了提醒学生自己之前讲过的内容
(B) 为了埋怨学生不为上课做准备
(C) 为了给学生布置额外的作业
(D) 为了告诉学生自己对她期望很高

MP3·287
tie in with 与…一致
be in the minority 属于少数
conform to 符合…，顺应…
extra-credit 额外学分
put together 组装…
analyze 分析
It's a deal. 好，赞成/同意。

Answer

case example > 1 (D) 2 (A) 3 YES → (A), (D), (E) / NO → (B), (C) 4 (B) 5 (B) 6 (C)

passage 1 > 1 (B) 2 (B), (D) 3 (B) 4 (D) 5 (D)

passage 2 > 1 (D) 2 (C) 3 (B), (D) 4 (D) 5 YES → (A), (C), (E) / NO → (B), (D) 6 (A)

passage 3 > 1 (A) 2 (B), (C) 3 (B) 4 YES → (A), (D) / NO → (B), (C) 5 (C) 6 (A)

case example

 MP3·288 **[1-6] Listen to part of a lecture in an art class.**

Professor (male)

OK, class...we've been talking a lot this week about Italian Renaissance painting. Q1 **But there's a type we haven't discussed yet, and it's one of the most important: frescoes.** They're the paintings—often quite large—the ones done on the walls and ceilings of churches and government buildings. Q2 **I know everyone's familiar with Michelangelo's giant painting on the Sistine Chapel ceiling...that's a fresco.** Q1 **Obviously, um, frescoes were a big part of Italian Renaissance painting, and I'm gonna tell you about a couple of different kinds.**

Q5 MP3·289 **So...let's start with the *buon* fresco—or "true fresco." <u>Oops, wait a second. Let me back up.</u> We need to take a look at how frescoes were made first. Before painting on a fresco could start, the surface needed to be prepared.** I'm talking about the wall, the ceiling...whatever...and the painter would put a plaster mixture on it. Do you have an idea what this is, plaster? It's a mixture of gypsum or lime, water, sand...maybe some fibers...I can't really get into it now. Just remember that plaster was always applied to the surface, and it helped absorb the colors of the paint and make them stick. OK?

Q1讲义文的主要内容是？
(A) 一幅湿壁画的创作过程
(B) 意大利文艺复兴时期艺术家们的影响
(C) 壁画技法的几个优点
(D) 意大利文艺复兴时期的一种绘画技法

Q2教授为什么提起西斯廷大教堂？
(A) 为了举出一个容易理解的西洋壁画的例子
(B) 为了显示西洋壁画曾是意大利最受欢迎的艺术形态
(C) 为了介绍某位文艺复兴巨匠的背景
(D) 为了提出并讨论文艺复兴的几件杰作

MP3·302
fresco 壁画画法（在刚抹过灰泥的墙上用水彩绘画的技法）西洋壁画
back up 补充说明，证明
plaster 灰泥，灰浆
gypsum 石膏
lime 石灰
fiber 纤维
absorb 吸收，吸入

Where was I? Ah, the *buon* fresco. Q3(A) **So, *buon* frescoes were painted onto a smooth layer of plaster before it had a chance to dry.** And because the plaster was still wet, it sucked the color pigments right into it. Then, when it dried, the pigments were trapped within the hardened surface...making a very durable painting. Q3(E) ***Buon* frescoes are the ones that've been best preserved since the time of the Renaissance.**

Of course, this type of fresco had its, its disadvantages. Q3(D) **Since it had to be painted before the plaster dried, only small areas could be done at a time.** These were called *giornata*, meaning "day's work." Um, each day, a layer of plaster was spread over the *giornata* and...um, and that was the area the painter worked on all day. They usually had about seven to nine hours of working time on each *giornata*. After that, the plaster would harden, and if they weren't finished...well, unfortunately they'd have to scrape off the plaster—along with all their hard work—and start over the next day. Likewise, if they made a big mistake, um...there was no real way to correct mistakes without scraping off the plaster.

Q3下列哪些项目是讲义文中提到的湿壁画的特征？请判断并点击相应空格。
(A) 绘制于刚晾不久还未干的灰泥之上。**(YES)**
(B) 需要打磨粗糙的灰泥面。**(NO)**
(C) 即使画错了也可以轻松地重新画。**(NO)**
(D) 一次只能绘制一小部分。**(YES)**
(E) 比文艺复兴时期的其它绘画作品保存状态更好。**(YES)**

Q4根据讲义文内容，中性壁画的主要优点是？
(A) 颜色鲜明，耐久性强。
(B) 它们可以很好地吸收颜料并且易于修改。
(C) 它们可保存几个世纪并且一次就可以绘制完成。
(D) 它们不需要使用沙子或展色剂。

Q6 MP3·290 **Now, there's a second type of fresco known as *a secco*.** Anyone here speak Italian? Um, ***secco* means "dry," and that tells you a lot about this painting style.** These frescoes were painted on that same mixture of plaster...but after it had completely dried. Typically, um, the plaster layer would be left rough—it wouldn't be smoothed down as much. And after it was dry, the painter would rub it with sand to roughen it up even more. Why? Well, the rougher texture made it easier for the paint pigments to seep into the plaster. But no matter how rough the surface, *a secco* painters always had to use an additional substance, a binder...mixed with the paint to make it stick. Typically, this was made out of egg yolk and some other type of gum or glue.

MP3·302
suck 吸收
pigment 颜料
durable 持久的，耐用的
scrape off （使用刀等工具将外壳或表面）刮去
texture 织物，纺织品
seep into 渗入…，浸润…
substance 物质，内容成分
binder [美术]展色剂（为了使颜料快速分散并干燥而掺入的物质）
egg yolk 蛋黄

The benefit of working *a secco* was that you weren't limited by the drying time of the plaster...and it was a lot easier to fix mistakes. You'd just paint over them. The problem, though, was that *a secco* frescoes weren't nearly as durable as *buon* frescoes. The paint never really integrated into the plaster, so over time it'd flake off, especially in humid conditions. A lot of times, the *a secco* method was just used to add finishing touches to *buon* frescoes...to hide tiny mistakes and make colors more accurate. Because, well, sometimes color would look different in wet plaster than it would after the plaster dried. Blue, for example, was really hard to represent with a *buon* fresco by itself. Um, there're also frescoes done completely *a secco*, but these weren't as common.

OK, real quick, let me tell you about a third type of fresco—*mezzo* fresco. Basically, think of it as a mixture of *buon* and *a secco* frescoes...with a combination of the, the advantages and disadvantages of both. Q4 **Um, *mezzo* frescoes were painted when the plaster was just barely still wet, meaning the pigments were absorbed more fully than in *a secco* frescoes...but not as much as in *buon* frescoes. But the painter could correct mistakes in a mezzo fresco easier than in a buon fresco.** Um, the *mezzo* fresco style became really popular at the end of the sixteenth century, after the Renaissance...but we'll be talking more about that era next week.

Q5教授这样说的意思是？
Oops, wait a second. Let me back up.
(A) 他认为有必要更仔细地向学生解释新的用语。
(B) 在开始讲解湿壁画之前，他想先讲讲其它内容。
(C) 他不想在讲义文中再介绍湿壁画了。
(D) 他意识到自己漏掉了关于湿壁画的重要内容。

Q6教授为什么这样说？
Anyone here speak Italian?
(A) 为了告诉学生自己意大利语说得不好。
(B) 为了告诉学生壁画起源于哪里
(C) 为了解释特定术语的意大利语意思
(D) 为了寻求帮助解释干壁画的字面意思

MP3-302

be limited by 被…限制，制约
integrate into并入…，统合进…
flake off （油漆等）剥落，（碎裂）掉落
humid 潮湿的，有水气的
finishing touch
barely 几乎不…
not as much as 没有达到…的程度

passage 1

MP3·291 **[1-5] Listen to part of a conversation between a student and a professor.**

Professor (female)	Oh, hello. Come on into my office, Franco.
Student (male)	Thanks, Professor Taylor. Are you sure it's all right to talk now? I could always come back later.
Professor	Oh, that's not necessary. It's important to me to be available for my students...after all, that's why I have office hours—so anyone can drop by to get a little extra help.
Student	Great. Thanks a lot.
Professor	I'm guessing you're here to talk about the last exam.
Student	Well...honestly...I wasn't expecting to do very well on it.
Professor	Yes...you missed several classes during the past month.
Student	Yeah...I got the flu this semester and fell way behind in all my classes.
Professor	I see.
Student	Q1 **Anyway, I did the readings and tried to keep up with your class, but I'm not really very good at learning by reading. Honestly, I remember information a lot better when someone is explaining it to me in class.**
Professor	You're not alone. In fact, I'm the same kind of learner. Q1 **I'd be more than happy to go over some of the concepts you missed while you were out sick.**
Student	Thanks so much. I really think that'd help me out.
Professor	Q1 **Is there something specific you'd like to start with?**
Student	Um, yeah. Q4 MP3·292 **The last chapter I read in the textbook was about camera angles, and how they can be used for different effects. I just couldn't really picture it all.**
Professor	**Oh yes. In class, we looked at several clips from movies that demonstrated examples of some different camera angles.** **I'm sure seeing examples of the camerawork would make it a**

Q1学生为什么去找教授？

(A) 为了表达对上次考试成绩的不满

(B) 为了请教授帮助理解教材的某些内容

(C) 为了请教授推荐更利于学习的教材

(D) 为了就上个月的几次旷课道歉

Q2教授提到了低角画面的哪两种功能？请选择两项正确答案。

(A) 展示人物的柔弱。

(B) 引起观众对视觉对象的恐惧。

(C) 全景地向观众展示动作。

(D) 赋予人物力量。

MP3·303

drop by 顺便拜访，顺便去

fall way behind 落后

keep up with （为了不落后）跟上…

go over 重温

be out sick 因病缺勤

clip 片断

demonstrate 展示

camerawork （电影或录影等的）剪辑

lot easier to understand.

Student Yeah.

Professor That's OK, though. We can talk about some of the principles right now, and then I can recommend a couple of films you should check out at the library. That way you'll be able to see some examples too.

Student That sounds good.

Professor OK. Well, the first thing you should know about camera angles is that most movies and television shows use angles that represent eye level. These are called straight-angle shots. People are accustomed to seeing the action this way. It's like you're actually watching it through your own eyes.

Student OK. So when I'm watching a film, the characters would appear directly in front of me pretty much. I wouldn't really be looking up at them or, or down at them.

Professor That's right.

Student But isn't that pretty limiting for filmmakers?

Professor Q5 MP3·293 **Well, I can understand why you might think that, but the audience's expectations about camera angles also create a lot of opportunities. See, if the camera angle is anything other than a straight angle, the people watching feel a little bit uncomfortable.**

Student So you're saying that, just by using a different kind of camera angle, a filmmaker can cause the audience to feel a certain way?

Professor Exactly. The filmmaker can convey moods or emotions this way. For example, if a low camera angle is used—

Student Like you're looking up at the characters?

Professor Right. Q2(B) **If the camera angle is low, the audience will feel awe or reverence, or even fear about what they're seeing.**

Student OK. So when would you want to use this kind of low-angle shot?

Professor Q2(D) **Imagine you were filming a movie about Queen Elizabeth. If you were showing her addressing the nation, you might use a low-angle shot to establish her as a powerful and...**

Q3教授为什么要课后给学生发邮件？
(A) 为了告知学生自己的办公室答疑时间
(B) 为了向学生推荐几种课外阅读材料
(C) 为了向学生提供缺勤的几次讲义文的笔记
(D) 为了说明上节课向学生布置的作业

Q4教授这样说是为了暗示什么？
I'm sure seeing examples of the camerawork would make it a lot easier to understand.
(A) 很多学生都不理解他关于不同摄影技巧的讲义文。
(B) 学生学习不同摄影角度的用途时不会遇到困难。
(C) 学生很幸运地在课上已经看过了相机摄影技法的示例。
(D) 学生不看剪辑将很难理解相机摄影的角度。

MP3·303
principle 原理
check out 借出…
be accustomed to *doing* 熟悉…
convey 传达
awe 敬畏
reverence 尊敬
address 演说，讲义文

	and respected figure.
Student	Or like in *Star Wars*, when Darth Vader is seen towering above the camera? OK, I get it.
Professor	Great. Q2(D) **That's another great example, because Darth Vader is an extremely powerful figure.** Plus, the low-angle shot can sometimes hint that the character has a sinister side.
Student	So then does a high-angle shot do the opposite?
Professor	Yep. Exactly. Where the low-angle shot shows, um, power, the high-angle shot expresses vulnerability. Um, do you think you could come up with an example of a scene where a high-angle shot might be appropriate?
Student	Um...let's see. *[pause]* Vulnerability? *[coming up with an idea]* Yeah. If you had a scene where some traveler finds himself stranded in the desert...I can imagine the camera looking down on this small figure in the sand and producing a mood of despair and hopelessness.
Professor	That's a perfect example. Q3 **Um, let me put together a list of films you might want to watch in order to see some of these camera angles in action. Give me a couple hours to work on that tonight and I'll send you an e-mail later.** How does that sound? I'll include other kinds of camera shots that we haven't gone over yet in class, just so you can get a head start on the material.
Student	Oh, wonderful. Thanks so much for your help.

Q5学生为什么这样说？
So you're saying that, just by using a different kind of camera angle, a filmmaker can cause the audience to feel a certain way?
(A) 为了就最近向教授学习的内容提问
(B) 为了说明自己不熟悉教授使用的术语
(C) 为了表示对教授所说的话有所质疑
(D) 为了确认自己掌握了教授说的要点

MP3·303
towering 高大的
sinister 危险的
vulnerability 弱点
come up with 提出…
appropriate 恰当的
stranded 处于困境的
put together 把…放在一起
in action 操作上地
head start 首先开始

passage 2

 MP3·294 **[1-6] Listen to part of a talk in a music class.**

Professor (female)	Class, I want you to think back to the beginning of the eighteenth century. Some of you may know...there was something that happened around this time that changed the course of Western music forever. Anybody?
Student A (male)	Well, wasn't it around then that the piano was invented?... as a replacement for the harpsichord, I think.
Professor	Yes, you got it pretty much exactly right. Q1

Q1讲义文的主要内容是？
(A) 18世纪的钢琴作曲家
(B) 钢琴与拨弦古钢琴的不同
(C) 18世纪键盘弦乐器的流行
(D) 早期钢琴的发明与演变

The introduction of the piano—that's exactly the eighteenth-century event I was referring to. Q2 And it did replace earlier versions of stringed keyboard instruments, like the harpsichord. There was another one called the clavichord, but we don't need to get into that today. All you need to understand is that these earlier instruments...they worked on the same principle as the piano, but they weren't as, as versatile.

Student B (male) Professor...what is that principle? I've never been entirely sure how the piano is able to make the sound that it does.

Professor That's a good question...I was just about to go over that. Remember that in stringed keyboard instruments, you produce sound by pressing down on the keys, right? When you do this—um, in the case of the piano, pressing a key triggers a small wooden hammer to strike one or more of the strings housed within the instrument. And this produces a sound...a note...got it?

Student A You said that the harpsichord...and...*[struggling for the term]* the other one...the...

Professor The clavichord...

Student A Q6 MP3·295 **Right. Well, you said those two weren't as versatile as the piano. What do you mean?**

Professor **Hmm...let me answer that by telling you something else about the piano. Its full name is the pianoforte. *[pause]* Any ideas?**

Student B Oh...well, piano means "soft" in Italian, and forte means "loud." Right? That's why the piano was so revolutionary, I think. Because the players could control the volume of the music they were playing.

Professor Precisely. Due to some innovations in the design of the hammer mechanism, the piano allowed musicians to play both soft and loud notes...depending on how hard they pressed the key, and this opened up a whole new world of possibility for stringed keyboard instruments. Dictation 开始 So let me talk a little about how all this came about. An instrument designer by

Q2教授介绍了拨弦古钢琴与钢琴的什么内容？
(A) 比起其他乐器，它们给西方音乐带来了最大的改变。
(B) 比起钢琴，它们的功能要少但是受欢迎程度更高。
(C) 它们是被钢琴取代的早期弦乐器。
(D) 它们经常被用于伴奏艺术家团体使用的其他乐器。

Q3根据教授的介绍，克里斯多夫里发明的钢琴与现代钢琴有何不同之处？请选择两项正确答案。
(A) 它不可移动。
(B) 它使用更细的弦。
(C) 它发出的声音更响亮。
(D) 它的形体更脆弱。

MP3·304
replacement 代替
harpsichord 拨弦古钢琴（16~18世纪的键盘乐器，是钢琴的前身）
refer to 涉及
stringed keyboard instrument 带键盘的弦乐器
clavichord 古钢琴（钢琴的前身）
versatile 多功能的，多才多艺的
trigger 诱发，引发（事件）
house （在特定场所或空间内）保管
note （钢琴等的）键，音
revolutionary 革命性的

the name of Bartolomeo Cristofori, who lived in Italy...um, [1] *he's credited with building the first piano*...sometime just after 1700, but it's important to understand this was a bit different than what we would recognize as a piano today. Actually, it really resembled the harpsichord more than the modern piano. Q3(D) **Um, its body was small and rather delicate,** Q3(B) **its strings were thinner**, and it was somewhat quiet compared to today's pianos...although it still [2] *offered a considerable volume increase* over the harpsichord. Another fact to keep in mind is that Cristofori's piano wasn't well received at first.

Student A Wait...but didn't you say it [3] *made a bunch of improvements* on the harpsichord? Q4 **Why didn't people like it?**

Professor **It was a little rough. Um...like, some notes were always softer than others, [4] *no matter how hard you struck the keys.* Johann Sebastian Bach was actually one of the first musicians to try out the piano, and he wasn't impressed with it.**

But, you see, as the eighteenth century went on, other instrument makers [5] *started playing around with* Cristofori's design...getting all the bugs out of it. Q5(E) **In particular, there were some German and Austrian companies that began producing pianos more like what we see today—a large, sturdy body, with [6] *thicker strings that made a fuller sound* when they were struck. They created the so-called Viennese model**, which is what Mozart wrote all his piano pieces on. I mean...this is when the piano really [7] *started living up to its potential.* Q5(C) **Composers realized it allowed them to express so much emotion...by playing at different volumes as well as through special effects made possible by using foot pedals.** And its full sound meant it could be played for audiences in large concert halls...and [8] *accompany groups of musicians* playing other instruments too.

Student B So is this Viennese model the same piano we usually see today?

Q4教授为什么要提起约翰•塞巴斯蒂安•巴赫？
(A) 为了显示钢琴的影响力
(B) 为了说明拨弦古钢琴的局限
(C) 为了举出一个早期钢琴支持者的例子
(D) 为了强调钢琴一开始并不受欢迎

Q5下列项目中哪些是克里斯多夫里钢琴设计后改进的地方？请判断并点击相应空格。
(A) 将键盘扩大至7个八度音 **(YES)**
(B) 引入特殊的木制音锤 **(NO)**
(C) 为了特殊效果引入脚踏板 **(YES)**
(D) 将木制音锤换成金属质地 **(NO)**
(E) 德国与奥地利公司生产的维也纳风格钢琴 **(YES)**

MP3-304

be credited with 得到…的评价
delicate 精美的，脆弱的
a bunch of 很多
be impressed with 受…感动
play around with （当乐子）玩弄…，戏弄…
bug 缺陷
sturdy 坚固的
Viennese 维也纳风格的
piece 乐曲
live up to A's potential 发挥A的全部潜力
accompany 伴随，和…一起

Professor	Not quite. There were still a lot of [9]*improvements being made throughout* the 1800s. Um, that's when English and American builders began introducing popular piano designs. Q5(A) **Also, you started to see expanded keyboards, ones that [10]*comprised seven or more octaves as opposed to* the, the older models with just five.** Dictation 结束 Other changes were things like new materials for the hammers...different pedal effects...things like that. And then there was the rise of the two main piano configurations—the grand piano, which had its strings laid out horizontally, making it a very large instrument...and the upright, whose strings run vertically. Those are usually much smaller. OK, that's it for now, but next time I'll be discussing how the Industrial Revolution affected the development of pianos...mainly by making them much more affordable. But that's next class, OK?	Q6教授为什么这样说？ **Hmm...let me answer that by telling you something else about the piano. Its full name is the pianoforte. *[pause]* Any ideas?** **(A) 为了提示学生找到正确答案** (B) 为了考查学生是否知道钢琴的完整名称 (C) 为了回答学生的疑问 (D) 为了询问学生对钢琴的了解程度 MP3·304 **comprise** 由…构成 **as opposed to** 和…相反，与…相对比 **configuration** 形态 **lay out** 展开…，陈设… **horizontally** 水平地 **upright** 直立地 **vertically** 竖直地 **affordable** 价格合理地

passage 3

 MP3·296 **[1-6] Listen to part of a lecture in a literature class.**

Professor (male)

Dictation开始 Class, last time we went over the life and work of William Butler Yeats, remember? Q1 **Well, today we're gonna continue our study of nineteenth-century, um, Irish poet-dramatists, with a discussion of Oscar Wilde.** Is everyone ready to begin? Q4(D) **I suppose I should start off by letting you know that, um, as well-known as Oscar Wilde was for his...his literature, he was [1]*equally well-known for his wit*...and his celebrity. I mean, he was...he was [2]*a real personality*...someone lots of people had heard of. It's almost as though Wilde became famous for being famous!**

OK. Well, Wilde first started to develop his, um, reputation while he was studying at universities in Ireland and England. He, uh, [3]*adopted some behaviors that attracted attention,* like decorating his room with peacock feathers...and dressing in flamboyant costumes. What you have to understand is this: Oscar Wilde was involved in a movement known as aestheticism. Q5 MP3·297 **Aestheticism—**

Q1讲义文的主要内容是？

(A) 对奥斯卡·王尔德生平及作品的详细介绍

(B) 奥斯卡·王尔德对同时代其他作家产生的影响

(C) 奥斯卡·王尔德支持同性恋的作品

(D) 奥斯卡·王尔德随笔的写作风格

MP3·305

dramatist 剧作家

celebrity 名声，名人

peacock 孔雀

flamboyant 华丽的

aestheticism 欧美[唯美]主义

for A's sake 为了A，看在A的份上

it basically promoted the idea of "art for art's sake." I know some of you must be wondering, well, what's that mean? It's a slogan for people who believe that art doesn't need to have some kind of [4]*utilitarian or moral purpose*—the only reason it needs to exist is to be beautiful; to be art.

This movement was [5]*really influential at the time,* and Wilde became a kind of, um, spokesperson for it. Q2(C) **In 1879, he began teaching aestheticism in London, and in the 1890s he toured the United States and Canada too, giving lectures related to the movement.** Q2(B) **And he put out a series of essays that expanded on his beliefs about aestheticism.** Q4(A) **At the same time, though, he was starting to make it big as a playwright.** Um...he [6]*published some satirical witty plays* that became very popular: *Lady Windermere's Fan, A Woman of No Importance,* um...*An Ideal Husband,* and *The Importance of Being Earnest.*

Q1 Q3 **All of these plays were successful, but *The Importance of Being Earnest* is** [7]*often regarded as his best work.* **Let me tell you a little bit about the story of the play before I go on to discuss, um, how it fits into Wilde's life and career. The main character's name is Jack Worthing.** He basically represents the society that Wilde lived in, and its Victorian values...things like [8]*duty and being a respectable citizen.* Wilde represents Victorian morality as hypocritical, um, by making Jack into a very hypocritical character. Jack [9]*spurns the values he pretends to uphold* by creating himself an alter-ego...so he is free to [10]*behave immorally without fear of ruining* his, um, his reputation.Dictation 结束

Q3 **Now, the secondary character in the story—who may be more the "hero" than Jack—is a man named Algernon Moncrieff.** While Jack represents hypocritical Victorian society, Algernon exemplifies aestheticism. He doesn't worry about morality, he's occupied with his appearance...and all he wants to do is live a beautiful life—characteristics of aestheticism. Um, I really don't want to delve into the plot too much, so suffice it to say that Wilde creates these parallels between Jack and Algernon in order to, uh, compare the two men, and what they represent. Jack deceives people in his life and evades moral constraints while preserving his moral reputation. Algernon, on the other hand—Wilde is almost suggesting that Algernon's deceptions are a form of art. Q4(A) **Do you see how, on some level, the play was a criticism of the morals and values of Oscar Wilde's society...values which he despised?**

Q1 **OK. But let's get back to what I was saying about how this play fits into Wilde's life overall. *The Importance of Being Earnest*** essentially marked the top of his career. However, being such a,

Q2 奥斯卡・王尔德是以哪两种方式参与唯美主义运动的？请选择两项正确答案。
(A) 在自己的几部戏剧作品中写关于唯美主义的内容。
(B) 执笔与唯美主义有关的随笔。
(C) 在不同国家做唯美主义方面的讲义文。
(D) 用孔雀羽毛创作文艺作品。

Q3 教授是以何种方式介绍王尔德最有名的作品的？
(A) 通过提供故事的历史背景
(B) 通过一一介绍出场人物
(C) 通过说明故事有多少成分是以作家自己真实的生活为背景的
(D) 通过与王尔德的其他作品对比

Q4 在讲义文中，教授介绍了奥斯卡・王尔德的生平经历。请判断下列项目是否属于其生平经历并点击相应的空格。
(A) 批评创造社会价值的剧作家 **(YES)**
(B) 当时备受尊敬的小说家 **(NO)**
(C) 伦敦一所大学的校长 **(NO)**
(D) 以个性及幽默闻名的著名人士 **(YES)**

MP3-305
utilitarian 实用性的
spokesperson 发言人
put out 出版
make it big 成功
playwright 剧作家
satirical 讽刺的
Victorian 维多利亚时代的
hypocritical 伪善的
spurn 弃绝，一脚踢开
uphold 支持
alter-ego 另一个自我

um, a prominent personality made him a target for criticism...and trouble. Wilde had a male partner...and the father of this partner was very homophobic, so he continually harassed Wilde. Wilde finally tried to press charges against the father, but this just created a huge scandal. Q6 MP3·298 ***[disapprovingly]* Um, unfortunately, homosexual acts were punishable by prison at that time, so Wilde was tried and sent to jail for two years...simply for his partnership with a man. It pretty much brought an end to his career, and...um, sadly, Wilde died just two years after getting out of jail.** He was only 46 at the time. Well, I'm afraid we've run out of time today, but I'd like you to read Wilde's essay *The Decay of Lying* for next class.

Q5教授这样说的意思是？
well, what's that mean?
(A) 他认为没有必要定义这一术语。
(B) 他不想再讨论唯美主义了。
(C) 他认为有必要对唯美主义做进一步的说明。
(D) 他想给学生布置作业。

Q6可以推测出教授？
(A) 他反对针对奥斯卡・王尔德的法律惩罚。
(B) 尽管喜欢读王尔德的作品，但是对王尔德的生活持批判态度。
(C) 他感到与学生讨论这一主题别扭。
(D) 他不清楚王尔德晚年经历了什么事情。

MP3·305
exemplify 是…的典型，是…的例子
be occupied with 被…所占据
delve into 深入研究…
suffice it to say that （现在）只想说…
parallel between …之间的比较[相关]关系
deceive 欺骗
（←**deception** 欺骗，蒙骗）
evade 逃避，回避
constraint 制约
despise 鄙视，蔑视
prominent 有名的
homophobic 厌恶同性恋的
harass 侵扰，骚扰
press charge 诉讼，控告
homosexual 同性恋的
punishable 可处罚的
try 审判
bring an end to …结束

Answer

case example	> 1 (A) 2 (A), (C) 3 YES → (B), (D) / NO → (A), (C), (E) 4 (A) 5 (B) 6 (D)
passage 1	> 1 (A) 2 (D) 3 (D) 4 YES → (A), (C), (D) / NO → (B), (E) 5 (C) 6 (D)
passage 2	> 1 (D) 2 (A) 3 (C) 4 (A), (D) 5 (B) 6 (B)
passage 3	> 1 (C) 2 (D) 3 (A), (B) 4 YES → (A), (C), (D) / NO → (B), (E) 5 (D) 6 (C)

case example

MP3·306 **Listen to part of a discussion in a botany class.**

Professor (male) Q1 **Class, I thought we'd, uh, spend some time today going over the issue of native versus introduced—or exotic—plants. It's been a debate in the world of biology, and a lot of questions have been raised—how should we feel about introduced species? Is it better to plant only native species?**

Student A (female) I didn't realize there was a debate. Everything I've heard about introduced species is negative. You know...like they're a threat to biodiversity. And native species aren't. It seems clear to me.

Professor OK. Before I respond, could you explain "biodiversity," in case some of your classmates are unfamiliar with the word?

Student A Sure. Biodiversity is...the variety of life on Earth.

Professor Right, and um, most people agree that more biodiversity equals a healthier environment. Q1 Q5 MP3·307 **Getting back to your comment...it's true that introduced species have a bad reputation.** **Since you brought it up, we may as well start off by discussing this side of the debate—the side that says native plants are best and introduced species are bad and should be, um, eliminated.** It's a logical position when you consider that introduced species can upset entire ecosystems, interfere with agriculture, and—as you said—reduce biodiversity by killing off native plants.

Student B (male) Why are introduced species so destructive compared to native species?

Q1讲义文的主要内容是？
(A) 对于外来物种价值的两种不同意见
(B) 本地物种与外来物种的比较
(C) 为特定环境选择最合适的物种的方法
(D) 控制外来物种侵袭的尝试

Q2为了说明外来物种如何破坏生态环境，教授举的两个例子是？请选择两项正确答案。
(A) 通过改变湿地中水流的自然流向
(B) 通过为寄生农作物的生物提供食物
(C) 通过快速生长驱除本地物种
(D) 通过在本地物种之间传播外来疾病

MP3·320
exotic 外来的，异国的
introduced species 外来品种，外来物种
native species 本地品种，当地物种
biodiversity 生物多样性
bring up 提出（问题等）
may as well 做…比较好
eliminate 驱除，消灭
upset 弄翻，倾覆
ecosystem 生态系统
interfere with 干涉…，妨碍…

Professor
Well, introduced species often have no, um, no natural predators in the place where they're introduced. No natural competitors...no natural diseases...no natural parasites...which means they have no natural form of population control. Native species, on the other hand, are subject to population control by these factors, because they've been a part of the environment for a long time and are deeply intertwined with the cycles of life there. Q2(C) **But introduced species have no limiting factors and can grow out of control, unchallenged.**

Student B
Oh...now I understand. Q2(C) **So introduced species essentially take over and end up replacing native populations that just can't compete with them.**

Professor
That's right. So some people say you should only plant native species, since they fit the ecosystem and have built-in population control—unlike introduced species, which in some cases completely transform native ecosystems.

Student A
Like purple loosestrife?

Professor
Yeah. That's a good example.

Student B
What's purple loosestrife?

Professor
It's an introduced species from Europe that grows and multiplies at a tremendous rate in wetlands and brings about drastic changes. Plants native to the United States—like swamp rose mallow and endangered orchids—Q2(A) **they can't compete and lose a lot of their habitat to purple loosestrife, which actually ends up changing the water flow and affecting other species in the ecosystem—birds, amphibians...algae.**

Student B
Wow...all those problems are caused by one introduced species?

Professor
That's right. That's where this side of the argument comes from. I mean, if introduced species are capable of, um, of really destroying an ecosystem in this way...well, then we should avoid them at all cost, and make sure only native species are allowed to grow.

Student B
But, obviously if this is a debate, there must be another side, right? Some redeeming qualities

Q3在讲义文中，教授提到了几种对人类有益的外来物种。请判断下列动植物是否为有益的外来物种并点击相应空格。
(A) 紫色马鞭草 **(NO)**
(B) 番茄 **(YES)**
(C) 芒草 **(NO)**
(D) 东南亚小麦 **(YES)**
(E) 美国芙蓉 **(NO)**

Q4教授为什么提起福罗里达州作物的经济作用？
(A) 为了反驳必须消灭外来物种的观点
(B) 为了说明如何自然地引入外来物种
(C) 为了说明某些地区抵御外来物种的体系十分脆弱
(D) 为了说明容忍外来物种侵袭的危险

MP3-320
predator 天敌
parasite 寄生动物，寄生虫
population control 个体数统计
be subject to 受…管制，在…之下
be intertwined with 与…相互交织，与…相互纠缠
take over （代替）接管，接手
purple loosestrife [植物]紫色马鞭草
multiply 增殖，增加
tremendous 巨大的，极大的
wetlands 〈常用复数形式〉湿地地带
swamp rose mallow [植物]沼泽木槿花，美国芙蓉
endangered （动植物）濒临灭绝的
orchid 兰花
amphibian 两栖类
algae 〈主要为复数形式〉（与海草相似的）藻类
at all cost 无论如何，不惜代价
redeeming （缺点，缺陷）补偿，补充

of exotic species?

Professor Exactly. Q1 **On the other side of the debate are people who question the labeling of introduced species as "bad" and, um...they actually take issue with the whole "native versus introduced" opposition. They feel it's just not that simple.**

You see, the thing is, not all introduced species are the same. There are a few that are aggressive and invasive, but most of them aren't. Actually, we rely on introduced species every day for things like food, shelter, and medicine. Q6 MP3·308 **Consider this: 98 percent of the U.S. food supply comes from introduced species. 98 percent!** Among other things, there's corn that originated in Mesoamerica, Q3(D) **wheat native to Southeast Asia,** and rice from Asia and Africa—all of it introduced to the United States from other places.

Then there's the question of what a native species really is. Some people suggest that any plant growing in the United States before the arrival of European immigrants is a native plant...regardless of its prior history—even if it was introduced to the region by people who arrived before Europeans. What's more, if you look at fossil evidence, you'll find that plenty of species were once "native" to regions far away from the regions where they are considered to be "native" now. Do you see what I'm getting at?

Student A You mean species can be introduced to a new region naturally?

Professor Yes. So if we actively prevent the introduction of new species, we're, um, we're stopping a natural process. Q3(B) Q4 **Besides, is there really any harm in planting tomatoes and citrus trees in Florida, a place where they aren't native? Those two introduced crops have an economic role... and, more importantly, they don't pose a threat to important native plants like sawgrass.** If an introduced species gets along well with native plants and doesn't disturb the ecosystem, is there really any reason why it should be eradicated?

Q5教授为什么这样说？
Since you brought it up, we may as well start off by discussing this side of the debate—
(A) 为了表现对学生的评价不满意
(B) 为了告诉学生自己下节课要讲的内容
(C) 为了邀请学生和自己一起讨论那个事件
(D) 为了要求学生进一步说明自己的评价

Q6可以推测出教授？
(A) 确信学生们已经知道这一事实。
(B) 对数据十分自信。
(C) 希望学生准确记下信息。
(D) 认为自己所说的数据十分惊人。

MP3·320
label A as B 命名A为B，把A归类为B
invasive 侵略的，侵害性的
Mesoamerica 中美洲
immigrant 移民
prior 以前的，之前的
pose a threat to 对…施加威胁
sawgrass [植物]芒草
eradicate 根除，根绝

passage 1

MP3·309 **[1-6] Listen to part of a talk in a zoology class.**

Professor (female) So, class...what've we been talking about for the last week or so?

Student A (male) Q1 **Well, the main subject's been, um...the adaptations animals have evolved that protect them from the harsh conditions of their environment.**

Professor Excellent...well put. Q1 **We're gonna continue with that theme today as we discuss dormancy in animals.**

Student A Q5 MP3·310 **Dormancy...you mean like when bears hibernate for the winter?**

Professor *[thinking about how to phrase her response]* Well, um...uh, kind of. Um, hibernation is one specific type of dormancy, but its popular association with bears is somewhat...misleading. But before I get into that, I'd like to introduce the two basic categories of dormancy.

OK. So basically, you can think of dormancy as a period of rest for the animal's body, oftentimes extreme rest, which you'll see later in the case of hibernation. Animals enter these dormant periods in order to avoid something in their environment. Usually, we're talking about temperature extremes. It could also be Q4(C) **a lack of water or food.** These are conditions that...um, if an animal had to face them, it might not survive. So what that animal does is become dormant. It ceases all physical activity, its heart rate and metabolism slow...its body temperature drops. In this dormant state, the animal is conserving its resources. It can survive for long periods sheltered from the outside world...without taking in food or water. Got it?

Student B (male) That makes sense, Professor. But you were saying there're two categories of dormancy...?

Professor Right. So...there are two ways an animal can enter dormancy, and the, the first is called predictive. That means it anticipates its environment is about to turn inhospitable...and

Q1讲义文的主要内容是？
(A) 有助于动物应对恶劣环境的休眠形式
(B) 哺乳动物应对冬季的适应形态
(C) 不同哺乳动物的冬眠类型
(D) 预测休眠与相应休眠的区别

Q2教授为什么提起北美花栗鼠？
(A) 为了说明花栗鼠与熊之间的联系比大多数人认为的更加紧密
(B) 为了说明为什么只有小型哺乳动物才能进入休眠状态
(C) 为了介绍陆生哺乳动物新陈代谢方面的背景知识
(D) 为了举例说明冬眠对特定动物会产生何种影响

MP3·321
adaptation 适应，顺应
evolve 使进化，使发展
dormancy （动物或植物的）休眠状态
（←**dormant** 休眠状态的）
hibernate 冬眠
（←**hibernation** 冬眠）
association 联系，关联
misleading 误导的，使人误解的
oftentimes 经常，有时
temperature extremes 极端温度状态（平均气温范围内的最高温度和最低温度）
cease 使停止，停止
heart rate 心律
metabolism 新陈代谢
conserve 保存，维持
shelter 避难，躲藏
predictive 预测的
anticipate 预期，预料

it becomes dormant before this happens. Q4(D) **For example, as the animal observes a steady drop in temperature and a, a decrease in day length, it knows winter is approaching and can enter dormancy early to make sure it avoids those conditions.** Q6 MP3·311 **Um, now the opposite is called consequential dormancy, and... well, what do you think that means?**

Student B Uh, I'd guess that's when the animal becomes dormant after the conditions occur...as a response or something.

Professor Yes, that's exactly it. Consequential dormancy occurs as a result—a consequence—of extreme conditions the animal is already experiencing.

Student A Professor...I'm sorry. I'm still curious about the hibernation of bears being misleading. Can you talk about what you mean by that?

Professor Sure, let's move on to that now. So...hibernation is one, um, one manifestation—one kind of dormancy. And, as you probably all know, it happens during the winter. Um, hibernation can be either predictive or consequential, depending on the species. In other words, some animals sense winter coming and they go into hibernation. Q4(C) **Others...um, they may wait until it really gets cold and food becomes scarce...then they'll start to hibernate.**

Q2 **And, um, what happens to animals when they hibernate? Their bodies go through some major changes. Heart rate, metabolism, temperature...all these go way down. Let's take the chipmunk as an example. Ordinarily, chipmunks breathe around 100 times a minute and their body stays at about 100 degrees Fahrenheit. But in hibernation, they breathe less than once a minute, and their body temperature falls to 39 degrees. We're talking major changes here, right? They've completely shifted their life processes so they can get by on as few resources as possible, and they're very, very hard to, to rouse from this state.** OK...and in mammals, it's usually only the smallest species

Q3关于熊，教授介绍了什么？
(A) 它们会经历一种相应休眠状态。
(B) 休眠是熊与其他大型哺乳动物的不同之处。
(C) 因为怕热，在气温非常高的夏季有可能会进行夏眠。
(D) 冬季会进入休眠状态，但并不是真正的冬眠。

Q4下列选项哪些是讲义文中介绍的诱发休眠的原因？请判断并点击相应的空格。
(A) 温度高于平均气温的时候 **(YES)**
(B) 相应地区出现新的天敌 **(NO)**
(C) 降水量不足与食物短缺 **(YES)**
(D) 季节性光照，时间减少 **(YES)**
(E) 非季节性的气温变化 **(NO)**

MP3·321
inhospitable （与环境或状态等）不适宜的，不友好的
approaching （季节或特定时期）即将来临的
consequential 结果的，结果性的
manifestation 表现，明显的症状
depending on 根据…
scarce 稀少的，稀有的
chipmunk 北美花栗鼠
shift 换，变换
get by on 靠…勉强维持
rouse from （从睡梦中）醒来

that experience true hibernation.

Student A Q3 **So you're saying bears don't hibernate?**

Professor **Well, technically they don't. You don't see nearly as much change in body functions in bears. They...um, it's more like they're in a very sound sleep. Their heart rate...temperature...these don't drop much, they don't stay asleep all winter like chipmunks. No, they'll get up and look for food on warm days...and, um, females of some species actually give birth during the winter. So, while you can say bears become dormant in winter, it's not correct to say they hibernate.** Understand?

Student A Yeah. That's certainly a big misconception, because I think most people call bears hibernators.

Professor Yes, you're right. Now, before we run out of time today, I want to mention another kind of dormancy...one that scientists know a lot less about. It's called estivation and, as opposed to hibernation...um, estivation occurs in the summer. Any ideas why?

Student B Well, in hot climates like deserts, the summer months bring extreme temperatures...less rainfall. Some animals probably can't survive in that.

Professor Uh-huh. Temperature and lack of water are the main conditions causing species to estivate. Um...like I said, we don't know too much about estivation, but it's probably a consequential form of dormancy. Q4(A) **So whenever there's a period of higher-than-normal temperature,** Q4(C) **or less-than-average rainfall...this triggers estivation in many reptiles especially, since they're very vulnerable to heat.** Insects, uh, the lungfish...a couple of squirrel and lemur species...they estivate too. Just as in other types of dormancy, their body functions slow, allowing their temperatures to fall and helping them survive on less food and water.

Q5教授为什么这么说？
[thinking about how to phrase her response] **Well, um...uh, kind of.**
(A) 为了鼓励学生详细说明自己举出的例子
(B) 为了表明对此问题尚有争论
(C) 为了表明学生的话并不十分准确
(D) 为了给学生改正错误的机会

Q6教授这样说的意思是？
well, what do you think that means?
(A) 她认为学生不熟悉“相应休眠”这一术语
(B) 她不想花费太多时间解释相应休眠
(C) 她想提醒学生上节课学过的内容
(D) 她认为学生们能猜测出相应休眠的意思

MP3-321
sound （睡眠）充足的，深的
misconception 错误的常识，误解
run out of time 时间到了
estivation 度夏，夏眠
as opposed to 与…形成对比，对照
rainfall 降水量，降雨量
trigger 诱发，触发
reptile 爬行类
be vulnerable to 易受…伤害的
lungfish 肺鱼
lemur 狐猴

passage 2

 MP3・312 **[1~6] Listen to part of a lecture in a zoology class.**

Professor (female)

Q2 **Well, class...are you ready to continue our discussion of North American carnivores? Good. Um, so far we've covered a lot of the larger animals—bears, canines like the wolf and the coyote, and the, the big cats...mountain lion and lynx. And, um, chances are you already knew a lot about these species. They get a lot of, uh... well, a lot of publicity, because they're seen as majestic somehow. But today we're gonna shift gears a bit and focus on a smaller, less-appreciated carnivore—the American badger.**

You all know what a badger generally is, don't you? It's in the same family of mammals as the ferret and the weasel...and the wolverine too. They're stocky little animals, standing low to the ground on short, sturdy legs. They grow to be between 23 and 30 inches long, with the females weighing around, um 15 pounds...and the males averaging 20 pounds. Badgers are very talented diggers. Q4(D) **Um, their paws are equipped with long, curved claws that they use to remove dirt, either for making a burrow for shelter or for catching prey.** Uh...badgers can't run very fast, so they catch most of their food by going after it under the ground. Squirrels, worms, frogs, insects, snakes...um, these are some of the badger's most common food options. They catch most of them at night—they're nocturnal.

Dictation 开始 OK, so that's a [1] *basic description of the American badger* for you. Q1 **But what I'm going to focus on today is more about their physical appearance...specifically, their coloration.** Because badgers..., um, this isn't just true for American badgers, other species in Europe and Asia share [2] *many of the same physical traits*—badgers have a very interesting color pattern in their fur.

Let's see. So, most of the badger's body is a single, solid color: grayish-silver usually. But, um, when it comes to their heads...things get more interesting. See, badgers have a very interesting pattern of black and white stripes on their faces. Q5 MP3・313 **Their cheeks are [3] *white with a brownish or black patch*...um, this patch is also called a badge and may have something to do with how the animal got its name.** Each cheek has a darkish patch. Then, the center of the face [4] *is primarily dark but has a bright white stripe* that starts at the

Q1 讲义文的主要内容是？
(A) 不同类型的獾及其特征
(B) 獾可以熟练挖地的适应性特征
(C) 獾与大型食肉动物之间的相似点
(D) 獾皮毛的颜色类型

Q2 教授是怎样开始讲解獾的？
(A) 通过提及大家熟悉的几种北美食肉动物
(B) 通过罗列獾特殊的身体特征
(C) 通过反驳大家对獾最常见的误解
(D) 通过提问学生对这种哺乳动物已知的信息

Q3 针对獾面部的面具形图案，教授介绍了什么？
(A) 这是对臭鼬颜色的模仿进化而来的。
(B) 不同种类的獾具有不同特点。
(C) 这是为了警告天敌不要接近它们。
(D) 这是为了显示獾对部分猎食者来说有致命性。

snout and runs straight up between the eyes and onto the top of the head. Um...in some species, this stripe [5]*extends all the way down the animal's back.*

This pattern of colored fur makes for a very distinctive face...also called a mask. And the big question is: why do badgers have these strange masks? What [6]*evolutionary principle was at work* here? Q6 MP3·314 **Well, to answer that question, I have to explain the idea of aposematism.** **Um...you might have heard of this [7]*biological concept by another name*—warning coloration.** Q3 **Basically, some species develop distinctive color patterns that serve as visual warnings to other animals—particularly predators—to stay away.** You know...for example, certain moths display color patterns that [8]*let predators know they taste bad*...that they aren't worth catching and eating. Or, um, poisonous snakes and frogs may be brightly colored to warn animals that any encounter with them will mean trouble. That's aposematism.

Oh, and another good example of this is the skunk, which is actually similar in many ways to the badger. Um, the skunk has its own color patterns of black and white stripes...and this warns other animals that it's capable of defending itself. [9]*By spraying a potent and unpleasant scent.* Now, the badger does have glands that produce a similar scent, but it can't actually spray it like the skunk. Q3 **Instead, the badger's mask is warning predators that it's a fierce fighter and will defend itself and [10]*its young to the death.*** Dictation 结束 Q4(A) **Their large, sharp fangs and powerful jaws are perfectly designed for battle. Badgers have been known to successfully fight off much larger animals...even bears.** So when a would-be predator sees that black and white badger mask, it knows it better look elsewhere for a meal.

Q4讲义文中提到了獾的哪两个特征？请选择两项正确答案。
(A) 在驱逐天敌方面使用的锋利的牙齿和有力的下巴。
(B) 适应快速奔跑的结实的腿和巨大的脚。
(C) 覆盖身体大部分的红褐色皮毛。
(D) 为了适应挖地及取食而进化的有力的爪子。

Q5教授暗示了什么？
(A) 獾不是唯一带有此类斑点的动物。
(B) 对于“badger”一词的由来有些不确定。
(C) “badger”一词最初可能是对这一类动物的统称。
(D) 通常，獾皮毛的特点是三种颜色排列。

Q6教授这样说的理由是？
Um...you might have heard of this biological concept by another name—warning coloration.
(A) 为了提醒学生记下要点。
(B) 为了向学生介绍他们更为熟悉的术语。
(C) 为了提醒学生在另一节课上已经学过关于警戒色的内容。
(D) 为了鼓励学生了解生物学的一个概念。

MP3·322

carnivore 食肉动物；食虫动物
canine （狗，狼等）犬科动物
lynx 山猫，猞猁
get [receive] publicity 广为人知
majestic 雄伟的
shift gears 改变方向
badger 獾
ferret 雪貂，白鼬
weasel 黄鼠狼
stocky 矮胖的，健壮结实的
sturdy 健壮的，结实的
burrow （兔、狐等挖的）洞穴
nocturnal 夜行性的
solid 无花纹的
patch 斑点；补片
snout （动物的）鼻子，嘴
aposematism
（生物的生存方式之一）警戒
warning coloration
（生物的）警戒色
moth 蛾，飞蛾
poisonous 致命的，有毒性的
potent 有力的，有效力的
gland 分泌腺，腺
fang 尖牙，尖齿

passage 3

 MP3·315 **[1~6] Listen to part of a lecture in a biology class.**

Professor (male)

Class, um, could everyone take their seats? I'm ready to get started. Today we're going to be discussing a special phenomenon in the world of biology: bioluminescence. It's the production of, um, of light through a chemical reaction. Q2 **Oh—this might be new to you—*luminescence* refers to light that's produced at low temperatures. Um, it's distinct from *incandescence*, which is light emission that results from high temperatures. Obviously, luminescence is more efficient than incandescence because it doesn't use or produce much heat.**

So...what kinds of animals luminesce? Anyone? You may be accustomed to thinking of bioluminescence as a—an aquatic phenomenon, which is reasonable since around 90 percent of deep-sea marine life produces bioluminescence. But the reality is that bioluminescence can be found all over the planet...among all sorts of organisms. On land, the trait's less common than in the oceans, but there're still plenty of—of different examples of bioluminescence. Fireflies and glow worms are probably the best known...but there're lots of insects and arachnids that can glow.

Dictation 开始 Q1 **If you're wondering [1]*why organisms luminesce*—why they glow, you're not the only one. Scientists have long been studying the purpose of, um, of bioluminescence.** There's been a lot of progress, but we're still uncertain about some things. Q3(A) **For example, there're a couple of species of earthworms that, that [2]*secrete this luminescent material*—and we just don't know why. I mean, there isn't any apparent reason to it.** Q3(B) **Oh, and in the ocean there's the mystery of dinoflagellates—single-celled plankton—that glow when disturbed, often lighting up huge areas in the ocean. Think the size of the state of Connecticut.** Q6 MP3·316 **Anyway, we're not, um, [3]*really sure why these tiny organisms glow.* But—that's enough about what we don't know. Why don't we move on to our, um, theories about the function of bioluminescence?**

All right. Q1 **One main purpose of bioluminescence is camouflage...um, particularly among marine organisms.** The ability to glow helps these organisms [4]*blend in with their environment.* It sounds counterintuitive, doesn't it? That glowing could actually help an animal blend in...but that's how it works. Just imagine you're swimming underwater in the ocean. What do you see when you look below you? Everything is dark and murky, right? What

Q1 教授主要从哪个方面介绍了生物发光？
(A) 具有生物发光现象动物的特点
(B) 生物发光作为伪装在动物身上的使用
(C) 不同种类生物发光的作用
(D) 解释生物发光的进化论起源

Q2 教授是如何解释“发光”这一术语的？
(A) 通过解释比起在陆地上，发光在水中更常见的原因
(B) 通过解释引起发光的化学反应
(C) 通过提供一个更简单、更常见的词汇
(D) 通过比较发光与另一种形式的光制造

Q3 科学家们尚未能解释的生物发光例子是什么？请选择两项正确答案。
(A) 某种蚯蚓
(B) 海洋中微小的浮游生物
(C) 某种萤火虫
(D) 昆虫与蛛形纲动物

MP3·323

bioluminescence 生物发光（生物体自动发光的现象）
luminescence 发光，冷光（←**luminesce**白炽光，高温发光）
incandescence 炽热
be accustomed to 对…熟悉
firefly 萤火虫
glow worm 萤火虫，萤科昆虫
arachnid （蜘蛛，蜱等）蛛形纲动物
secrete 分泌，排出
dinoflagellate 腰鞭毛虫类（一种单细胞植物性浮游生物）
camouflage 伪装，掩饰

if you look upward, toward the surface? It's very bright...isn't it? **Q4(C)** **When viewed from below, organisms in the ocean really** [5]***stand out as dark silhouettes against the bright background.*** **However...if they emit light on the underside of their bodies, they're better able to** [6]***fool predators looking up at them from below.***
OK. **Q1** **Another very important use of bioluminescence is for communication.** If you've ever seen fireflies flashing outside at night, you've witnessed this. Male and female fireflies exchange flashes [7]*in order to find a mate.* They use their flashes to locate one another. **Q5** **The interesting thing about firefly flashes is that they're species-specific. I mean, different species have different flash patterns—that way no one, um,** [8]***accidentally attracts a mate of a different species.***
Q1 **Actually, I guess the behavior of fireflies that I just mentioned is very similar to another function of bioluminescence: attraction.** Fireflies use their bioluminescent capabilities to attract mates, while **Q4(D)** **other types of organisms—especially marine ones—they luminesce in order to attract prey.** The anglerfish...maybe you've seen pictures of anglerfish before—they've got a very odd, very distinctive appearance, so I'm sure you'd remember it. See...they have this, this [9]*lure that protrudes from their head.* It's a filament that has a little bioluminescent growth at the end of it. The anglerfish can [10]*wiggle the glowing lure around* in order to attract prey.Dictation 结束
Q1 **I think we're about out of time for today, but before we finish up I'd like to add one more function of bioluminescence. It's essentially the, um, the opposite of attraction: repulsion.** **Q4(A)** **Some squid possess luminescent chemicals they can release to scare off or confuse an attacker. Similarly, on land, firefly larvae glow because it helps discourage or repel predators who might be interested in eating them.**
Class, please do the reading I assigned in your syllabus—next time we'll be talking about another unusual biological phenomenon: chromatophoral color changes.

Q4在讲义文中，教授介绍了动物利用生物发光的一些具体用途，请判断下列项目是否属于这些用途并点击相应的空格。
(A) 驱逐攻击者 **(YES)**
(B) 散播食物源的信息 **(NO)**
(C) 使得游动在上方的天敌鱼不容易被发现 **(YES)**
(D) 引诱潜在的食物接近 **(YES)**
(E) 帮助一种生物在黑暗的水域中凸显 **(NO)**

Q5根据教授的介绍，为什么不同种类的萤火虫发出的光不同？
(A) 为了与刚出生的幼虫交流
(B) 为了在交配季节弄清特定种类萤火虫的领地
(C) 为了防止天敌吃掉它们的幼虫
(D) 为了确保同类萤火虫相互交配

Q6教授为什么这样说？
But—that's enough about what we don't know.
(A) 为了表示对某些与生物发光有关的科学数据的质疑
(B) 为了表明学生已学习过相关主题
(C) 为了告诉学生对这一问题的介绍已经结束了
(D) 为自己在生物发光方面知识的不足道歉

MP3·223
blend in with （不区别地）与…混合
counterintuitive 非直观的
murky 黑暗的，阴郁的
species-specific 某个种类特有的
anglerfish 琵琶鱼
lure 诱惑物，诱饵，引诱
protrude from 从…突出
wiggle 摆动，扭动身体
repulsion 击退，反驳
scare off 吓跑
larva 幼虫，幼体（***pl.*** **larvae**）
repel 击退，驱除
syllabus 教学大纲
chromatophoral 色素细胞的，色素体的

Answer case example > 1 (D) 2 YES → (A), (C) / NO → (B) 3 (B) 4 (A) 5 (A) 6 (C)
passage 1 > 1 (C) 2 (D) 3 (B) 4 (D) 5 (B)
passage 2 > 1 (C) 2 (C) 3 (D) 4 (A) 5 (D) 6 (B)
passage 3 > 1 (B) 2 (B) 3 (C) 4 (D) 5 (B) 6 (D)

case example

 MP3·324 **[1-6] Listen to part of a talk in a geography class.**

Professor (female)

All right, class. Q1 **Today we're going to be talking about the formation of valleys.** This topic was used as the essay question on the final exam last year, so it's definitely a good idea to pay close attention. It's a, uh, really important and interesting topic. Q1 **So, uh, anyway, there are basically two ways that valleys are formed. There's fluvial formation—that's formation by a river—and there's glacial formation.**

We'll start by looking at fluvial formation, because it's a little more complex. The first thing I want you to note is the shape of river valleys. Q2(A) **If you took a cross section of one, you'd notice it would come to a narrow point at the bottom, right? So, uh, this is why river valleys are known as V-shaped valleys.** Q6 MP3·325 **They get their shape because of downcutting. You all know what I mean by downcutting, don't you? *[surprised]* No?** ***[annoyed]*** **It was one of the main topics in this week's reading...** ***[pause]*** **Downcutting is the vertical erosion that is caused by rivers.** You see, rivers flow down a gradient, from their highest point to their base level—that is, the lowest level at which they can still flow, either sea level or else the elevation of the lake which it flows to. Anyway, as the river flows, it picks up rocks and sand from the bottom and takes them downstream, where they're deposited in a wide floodplain. The channel of the stream gets deeper and deeper as more material is eroded from the riverbed, and over time, this creates a valley.

Q2(C) **Of course, the steeper the gradient of the river, the faster this process occurs, and the steeper the valley is, too.** So, uh, take the Black Canyon of the Gunnison National Park, as an example. It's one of the steepest and most impressive valleys in North America—it's uh, really breathtaking. If you ever get a chance to visit that part of the country, I recommend you pay it a visit. *[pausing before getting*

Q1讲义文的主要内容是？
(A) 高山地带冰川的形成
(B) 河流侵蚀作用的影响
(C) 美国与欧洲的地理差异
(D) 河谷的形成方式

Q2根据讲义文中提供的信息，请判断下列哪些叙述符合河流侵蚀型河谷的形成特点并点击相应空格。
(A) 它们呈清晰的V字形。**(YES)**
(B) 大小主要取决于河流的深度。**(NO)**
(C) 河流的倾斜度影响河谷的形成速度。**(YES)**

Q3根据教授的介绍，大峡谷是哪种典型的河谷？
(A) 一条倾斜度大的河流塑造的河谷。
(B) 在向上隆起和向下侵蚀的共同作用下形成的河谷。
(C) 最深处在海平面以下的河谷。
(D) 冰川经过后留下的河谷。

MP3·337
formation 形成，构成
fluvial （依据河流向下流动的作用）河流侵蚀型的
glacial 冰川的
cross section 断面，截面
downcutting 向下侵蚀

back on track] Anyway, the Black Canyon formed that way because the, uh, Gunnison River—the river that created the valley—has an incredibly steep gradient. It drops about 43 feet per mile. That's about five times faster than the descent the Colorado River makes. Q3 **But, uh, speaking of the Colorado...it helped create the Grand Canyon, which is a good example of another type of valley. You see, other dramatic river valleys can occur when there is also geological uplift in the region. We say this, uh, "rejuvenates" the river. So, the Colorado River had reached its base level thousands of years ago, but then there was uplift created by the Rocky Plateau. This increased the Colorado's gradient, and then it started downcutting again. At the same time, the land kept being pushed up by the collision of two tectonic plates, and, uh, with a combination of these forces, we ended up with the Grand Canyon.**

Q4 **Oh, and just before we move on to talk about glacial valley formation, there's one further point I'd like to cover: how the type of material on the riverbed can have an impact on the shape of a river valley. It's pretty obvious, really. Some types of rock are more resistant to erosion than others. So, uh, a riverbed comprised mainly of soft rocks like limestone for instance, tends to erode very quickly. On the other hand, harder stone erodes pretty slowly. So, uh, some of the tributaries that run into the Finger Lakes of New York, for instance, have created fairly wide and flat-bottomed valleys, even though their gradients are fairly steep.**

OK, so that's all clear? Good. Let's take a look at glacial formation now then. Rather than a V-shape, glaciers tend to form U-shaped valleys. This is because glacial ice exerts an enormous amount of pressure and force as it slowly moves down slope. Q5 **In fact, I want you to think about glaciers as being like giant bulldozers. I use this image because a glacier has so much weight and power behind it. You see, using this massive force, it acts like a bulldozer on the earth around it. Like a bulldozer, it flattens everything in its path, gouging out a huge divot where it has been. Then, when the glacier recedes, the wide, flat bottomed U-shaped divot remains—and we have a valley.** Uh, one of the most famous U-shaped valleys is the Yosemite Valley in California, which has been filled by large glaciers on and off for 30 million years.

And, uh, one last point of difference—you'll want to write this down—the size and shape of a glacial valley is determined by the size of the glacier. For instance, if the ice in the glacier was deep, then the valley is high. Or if it was wide, the valley it left behind is wide, too. So, while the Yosemite is very big, there are, for example, a number of smaller U-shaped valleys in Scotland, known locally as

Q4根据教授的介绍，通常河底的石头种类对什么有影响？
(A) 河谷的形态
(B) 漫滩的面积
(C) 河流的倾斜度
(D) 运河的长度

Q5教授如何解释冰川中冰的作用？
(A) 通过将其比喻为现代的一种机器
(B) 通过介绍U字形河谷的规模
(C) 通过与其他自然现象对比
(D) 通过比较不同大小的冰川

Q6教授的意思是什么？
***[annoyed]* It was one of the main topics in this week's reading...**
(A) 她认为这周的阅读资料不难。
(B) 她希望学生下周阅读资料。
(C) 她认为学生应该已经知道了这个信息。
(D) 她不想复习以前的资料。

MP3-337
erosion 侵蚀（作用），侵蚀（←**erode**侵蚀）
gradient 倾斜，斜坡
elevation 高度，海拔
downstream 向下流的
deposit 使沉积，堆积
floodplain 漫滩
channel 水路，海峡
riverbed 河底
breathtaking 壮观的，非常惊人的
pay a visit 访问，拜访

"glens." They were created by smaller glaciers during previous ice ages. It, uh, it has nothing to do with the steepness of the glacier's gradient.

MP3·337

descent 下降，降下
uplift [地质]隆起（高高立起的部分）
rejuvenate 返回原状态，回复
collision 冲突，对立
tectonic plate [地质]地壳板块（形成大陆并移动的地壳表面）
be resistant to 抵抗…
limestone 石灰岩
tributary 支流（河流的分流）
exert 施加（力量），行使（压力）
flatten 使平坦
gouge out 挖去…
divot 挖（草皮等）留下的痕迹
recede 后退，远去
glen 溪谷，峡谷
have nothing to do with 与…没有任何关系

passage 1

MP3·326 **[1-5] Listen to a conversation between a student and a professor.**

Student (female) Professor Chang? Hi, I'm Gillian Willis from your advanced chemistry class.

Professor (male) Oh, yes. Hi, Gillian. What can I do for you?

Student Well, I was hoping to steal a minute of your time. Q1 **It's just...I've been thinking about the report we have to write before mid-semester break, and, well, I need a bit of help.**

Professor No problem, Gillian. You've caught me at a good time. I was supposed to go to a departmental meeting, but it's been postponed.

Student That's lucky. Q5 MP3·327 **Uh...look, I know you said we could write about anything from the course...**

Professor **Yeah, I don't want to impose any limits on you guys. Once students get to the advanced level, I think it's good for them to explore the topic for themselves.**

Student Q1 **I get that, but, uh, I'm having a hard time picking just one thing to focus on. I was hoping**

Q1学生为什么来找教授？
(A) 为了了解清楚课程论文的要求
(B) 为了理解教授对她期中报告的反馈
(C) 为了寻求课题主题选择方面的帮助
(D) 为了请求延长项目的截止时间

MP3·338

mid-semester break 学期中（短暂的）假期
impose A on B 把A强加于B，让B负担A

you'd have some advice.

Professor OK, what have you narrowed it down to?

Student Well, I'm interested in inorganic reactions, and I, ah, I also enjoyed the class on thermochromism. I've been reading ahead in the textbook, and, ah, spectroscopy looks like a fascinating topic, too.

Professor Q2 **Well, I'm pleased you're going ahead and doing some extra reading, but, uh, I wouldn't recommend getting into the stuff about spectroscopy just now. We're going to cover that in much more detail after the mid-semester break.** And, ah, as for inorganic reactions...well, there's nothing wrong with the topic itself, it's just that about half the students in the class do their reports on that. You know, it's hard to be original. But thermochromism...that sounds like a topic with a lot of potential.

Student OK...but would it be better to just talk about thermochromism generally? You know, I could just give a definition and then focus on some of the most important details like, uh, comparing the use of liquid crystals and leuco dyes, or something like that.

Professor *[sounding worried]* Well, it's important to know the broad differences between the two—that leuco dyes produce more vibrant colors, but are more sensitive and difficult to work with. But, uh...

Student *[interrupting]* Oh, don't worry professor. I'll cover it in a lot more detail than that.

Professor Q3 ***[still unimpressed with the proposal]*** **Yeah, but...well, in my experience, the best reports are normally the ones that focus on a specific application. They're often a lot more fun to write about, and I certainly enjoy reading them more, too.**

Student You think so?

Professor For sure. Especially with a topic like thermochromism, because there are a ton of things to choose from. For example, you could talk about mood rings, which change color depending on the temperature of the wearer. Or, uh, the color

Q2教授为什么建议她不要选光谱学？
(A) 它在教材中没有涉及。
(B) 他不是此方面的专家。
(C) 作为课题的主题缺乏原创性。
(D) 还没有在课上学习过光谱学。

Q3关于一般性的报告，教授暗示了什么？
(A) 写它们很具有挑战性。
(B) 通常它们读起来很无聊。
(C) 它们不够具体。
(D) 它们太过宽泛，不能很好地概括事件。

Q4学生决定集中于哪些方面？
(A) 无色染料与液晶的区别
(B) 显示电量的颜色指示器
(C) 关于热变色性质的一般性介绍
(D) 随着温度变色的瓶标签

MP3-338

narrow down 缩小范围
inorganic reactions 无机反应
thermochromism 热变色性（物质的颜色随温度变化的性质）
spectroscopy 光谱学（分析光谱，研究物质性质的光学领域）
liquid crystal 液晶
dye 染料，颜料
vibrant 鲜明的，有活力的
a ton of 相当多的
mood ring 情绪戒指（随着人的感情或体温，颜色会发生变化的戒指）
color indicator 颜色指示器
run out （电力或燃料等）用尽
trust A to *do* 以为A会…，很明显会…

	indicators on batteries that let you know when the battery is running out.
Student	**Q4 Or what about that thing you talked about in last week's lecture? You know, those new labels on beer bottles—the ones that change color so you can tell if your beer's still cold or not.**
Professor	*[laughing]* Trust you to remember that example. But yeah, beer bottle labels could make for a really interesting report.
Student	**Q4 Great. I'll start working on it.**
Professor	Excellent. And, ah, if you have any problems or questions, you know where my office is.
Student	Thanks, professor.

Q5教授为什么这样说？
Once students get to the advanced level, I think it's good for them to explore the topic for themselves.
(A)为了告诉学生高级课程非常固定
(B) 为了说明自己不向学生提供具体指导的决定
(C) 为了暗示学生自己不是给予建议的合适人选
(D) 为了强调主题的范围有多广

passage 2

 MP3•328 **[1-6] Listen to part of a lecture in a geology class.**

Professor (male)

So...class. OK, everyone please take out your books. Let's get started. **Q1 Um, the topic this afternoon is—um, it's about Mars... but, well, a specific part of Mars: a volcano.** Q5 MP3•329 **<u>Now, I wouldn't be surprised if some of you have heard of this volcano before</u>—it's the largest volcano in the whole solar system. So that makes it pretty important, huh? Q1 The name of this volcano is Olympus Mons.**

So just how big is Olympus Mons? It's twenty-seven kilometers high...and...let's compare it to the tallest peak on Earth, Mt. Qomolangma. Olympus Mons is three times taller than Qomolangma, but the most noteworthy aspect of the volcano's size is its width. It's got a huge girth. In fact, Olympus Mons is as wide as the whole state of Missouri. So we covered height and width...and there's one more thing I want you to keep in mind when we're talking about the size of this Martian volcano. You see, it's extremely large for the, uh, the size of the planet. Um, Mars is actually three times smaller than Earth...so you can imagine that this volcano is just huge relative to the size of the planet.

OK. So, Olympus Mons is categorized as a shield volcano. Now, on Earth, shield volcanoes are some of the biggest volcanoes we have. **Q2 Typically, uh, these volcanoes are very wide, with a relatively gentle slope—more like a, a hill rather than a sharp peak. They're**

Q1讲义文的主要内容是？
(A) 地壳板块在火山形成中的作用
(B) 地球和火星上热点的存在
(C) 奥林帕斯火山与地球上盾状火山的区别
(D) 夏威夷岛上的盾状火山

Q2根据教授的说法，为什么比起山峰，盾状火山更像小丘？
(A) 因为它们经历了数百万年的侵蚀。
(B) 因为它们不经常产生爆炸性喷发。
(C) 因为它们喷出的熔岩流动性很强。
(D) 因为比起陆地，它们更常在海里形成。

Q3教授为什么讨论板块构造论？
(A) 为了强调地球上的火山比火星上的更多。
(B) 为了描写盾形火山喷发前会发生的现象。
(C) 为了说明作用于奥林帕斯

not real steep, and, um, that's because the lava that typically comes out of shield volcanoes is very fluid. It flows right downhill, so there isn't much buildup of material at the top of the volcano. The lava cools and expands the, um, the width of the volcano rather than the, the height. Dictation 开始 Another thing about these shield volcanoes is that they don't really...uh...explode, when erupting. So the lava coming out of shield volcanoes isn't, isn't [1]*explosively bursting up into the air.* Do you understand? The, the Hawaiian Islands are examples of shield volcanoes on Earth.

Q1 Q3 **But, you might ask, why is Olympus Mons so much larger than volcanoes on Earth? Well, we think it's probably related to plate tectonics.** As you know, Earth's surface is composed of these huge tectonic plates that are constantly moving. And, as far as anyone can tell right now, Earth is [2]*the only planet in the solar system* that experiences this. We aren't really sure, but it's possible that some planets might have once had, um, this kind of plate-tectonic activity in the past...but probably, probably with some differences from what we see on Earth. OK, uh...but that's not really the topic for today, Q1 **so let me get back to comparing Olympus Mons with Earth volcanoes.**

You see, many shield volcanoes are formed over "hotspots," which are [3]*fixed places on the globe* where, where conditions deep within the planet cause volcanic activity at the surface. For example, the Hawaiian Islands are over one of Earth's hotspots. Now, the reason I mentioned plate tectonics is that, on Earth, tectonic plates keep the [4]*surface crust in constant motion* over a hotspot. So no single area of crust is ever...uh...permanently over a hotspot. Q6 MP3·330 **And this means that, over time, um, volcanoes that were [5]*created by the hotspot become dormant.* Right? Because the tectonic plate they're on moves away from the heat source—the hotspot.**

Actually, the Hawaiian Islands illustrate this fact beautifully. See, this island chain has been formed as its tectonic plate—the Pacific plate—has slowly moved over a hotspot. Now, the speed of the plate is, of course, uh, pretty slow...about 52 kilometers per every million years. But as a result of this, um, movement, we can [6]*see a trail of islands* that are actually the remains of volcanoes that formed as the tectonic plate traveled over the hotspot. Q4 **Hawaii, the big island, is the youngest...so it's still right over the hotspot, and it, it hasn't [7]*had very much time to erode.* Older islands at the end of the chain are smaller because they've become dormant and had a longer time to erode.**

Q3 **So that's why there's a limit to the size of these volcanoes on Earth. They remain over hotspots for...for a period of time, and**

火山形成的力量。
(D) 为了解释地球上的火山为什么比奥林帕斯火山小。

Q4对于夏威夷岛群岛末端的岛屿，教授暗示了什么？
(A) 很久之前，它们处于热点之上。
(B) 它们未来有可能再次变为活火山。
(C) 它们尚未通过热点。
(D) 它们过去比现在的夏威夷岛大。

Q5教授这样说的意思是？
Now, I wouldn't be surprised if some of you had heard of this volcano before—
(A) 他希望听听学生对这件事的看法。
(B) 他希望提供一些令学生吃惊的新信息。
(C) 他认为今天的话题会引起学生的兴趣。
(D) 他认为学生有可能对话题很熟悉。

MP3·339

Olympus Mons 奥林帕斯火山（位于火星上的太阳系最大火山）
noteworthy 值得关注的，显著的
girth 周长；尺寸
Martian 火星的；火星人
relative to 与…比较
be categorized as 分类为…
shield volcano 盾状（盾牌形）火山
lava 熔岩
fluid 流动的，液体性的
buildup 累积的东西，沉积物

then they [8]*move away and start to erode.*[Dictation 结束] But scientists think that the, um, the situation on Mars is different. Well, you see, they don't think Mars has tectonic plates...which would mean that Olympus Mons has remained over a hotspot for its entire existence. So, of course, it had the opportunity to get a lot bigger than, for example, the Hawaiian Islands could.

Q6教授这样说的意思是？
Actually, the Hawaiian Islands illustrate this fact beautifully.
(A) 他希望学生了解夏威夷群岛已经有一段时间停止活动了。
(B) 他认为夏威夷群岛是一个很好的例子，能够体现地壳板块对火山造成的影响。
(C) 他想讨论一个与板块构造论没有直接关联的要点。
(D) 他认为夏威夷群岛有访问的教育价值。

MP3·339
erupt 喷发，爆发
explosively 爆炸性地
burst up into 突然喷发到
plate tectonics 板块构造
tectonic plate （地质学）地壳构造板块
hotspot 热点
surface crust （地壳的）表层
in constant motion 处于不断运动中
permanently 永久性地，永恒地
dormant 休眠的，蛰伏的
trail of islands 岛屿轨迹
remains 剩余物，残余

passage 3

 MP3·331 **[1-6] Listen to part of a discussion in an astronomy class.**

Professor (male) Now, when astronomers first set out to map the, uh, way galaxies are distributed in the sky, they found something that was...pretty strange. Of course, they were expecting to see a relatively random scattering of galaxies, but they observed something...uh...pretty different. Any guesses about what these astronomers might have, um...noticed?

Student A (female) Well, from what you've said, I've gathered that the distribution of galaxies wasn't totally even... which makes me think that there was an area where there were far more or far fewer galaxies than anywhere else...

Professor Good. You're on the right track.

Student A **Q5** MP3·332 **Are you talking about those huge clouds where stars form? Nebulae?**

Professor **No...actually, I think we may be having some slight...confusion. Nebulae are components of galaxies.** I'm not talking about the distribution of stuff within a single galaxy...I'm talking about the distribution of galaxies themselves, a much

Q1讲义文的主要内容是？
(A) 贯穿宇宙的银河分布。
(B) 天空看起来好像没有银河的部分。
(C) 利用紫外线和X射线对银河的观测。
(D) 银河回避带的形成。

Q2根据教授的介绍，银河回避带的形成原因是什么？
(A) 地球大气圈内的气体
(B) 银河内的物质
(C) 巨大的黑洞
(D) 宇宙中星体形成的巨大云团

	bigger scale.
Student A	Oh, right. I see what you're saying. OK.
Professor	Dictation开始 Q6 MP3·333 **Any other guesses, then?**
Student B (male)	[1]***I'll venture another...*****how about a region where there just weren't any galaxies?**
Professor	That's it. Q1 **The astronomers discovered this ...this band in the sky where there were hardly any galaxies. Pretty strange, they thought. They** [2]***ended up giving it a name,*** **uh, the "zone of avoidance" because it's...it's almost as though, um, as though galaxies just avoid the region. What do you think the cause of this...this zone of avoidance might be?**
Student B	Well, could it be like...like a huge black hole or something?
Professor	Uh...no. Let me give you a hint. The zone of avoidance isn't [3]*caused by the absence of galaxies...*
Student B	Maybe there's something covering up the galaxies...so that we can't see them, even though they're there.
Professor	Yes. That's correct. So...what is it that's covering up [4]*this band of sky from astronomers' telescopes?*
Student B	Is there something in the Earth's atmosphere that's...that's [5]*obscuring our view of space?*
Professor	No...it's not in the Earth's atmosphere. Any last guesses?
Student A	Oh, I think I know. Is it our galaxy that's causing the problem? I mean, is it part of the Milky Way that's preventing us from seeing clearly outside our own galaxy?
Professor	That's exactly what the problem is. See, the Milky Way is very large. I mean, it's between 80,000 and 100,000 light years wide. And about, um, about 1,000 light years thick. Q2 [6]***It's a big spiraled disk with*** **a lot of gas and dust floating around in the plane of the disk, so there's an awful lot of stuff in the way if you're trying to look out across the, uh, the plane of the Milky Way** [7]***to see what's beyond.*** **That's what the zone of avoidance is...it's the dust and gas clouds in the band of the Milky Way. It**

Q3根据讲义文的介绍，高能量的X光线可以做什么？
(A) 它们可以探知遥远银河中的黑洞。
(B) 它们可以重新接收红外线信号并且储存信息。
(C) 它们可以穿透银河系中的灰尘和气体。
(D) 它们可以发射电磁波。

Q4教授为什么提起2MASS和钱德拉X光线的观测？
(A) 为了提供发现银河回避带的背景知识
(B) 为了说明科学家不能进行贯穿银河的观测的原因
(C) 为了举例说明银河回避带妨碍天文发现的方法
(D) 为了表明科学家对银河回避带另一边存在的物质有一定了解

MP3·340
astronomer 天文学家
set out to *do* 开始…
map 绘制…的地图
galaxy 银河系
be distributed in 在…分布
random 随机的
scatter 散布，分散
be on the right track 在做正确的考虑
nebula 星云（像云模样分布开的天体）(**pl. nebulae**)
venture 大胆提出，大胆说出（意见或想法）
band 带，绳
end up *doing* （没有计划地）最终…
zone of avoidance 银河回避带（在银河系中因为星体间尘埃的消光作用而无法看到的外部银河部分）
cover up 覆盖…，遮挡…
obscure 使变暗，使模糊

blocks about 20 percent of the sky beyond our galaxy.

Student B Wow. So we don't have any information about 20 percent of the sky outside the Milky Way?

Professor Well, not exactly. See, even though we can't see through it, uh—[8] *infrared radiation can detect* a lot more of what's behind all the dust and gas. **Q4 Between, um, 1997 and 2001, the Two Micron All-Sky Survey, also known as "2MASS,"** [9] ***mapped out the whole sky* and discovered new galaxies that had been, well, hidden behind the zone of avoidance.** Dictation 结束

Q3 X-rays...high-energy x-rays can also pass through a lot of the gas and dust. Q4 In 2001, astronomers used the Chandra x-ray observatory to see through all of those layers of clouds and dust. The...the Chandra observation took place in the year 2000 and lasted for...for 28 hours. It was aimed at the zone of avoidance and collected light from the stars behind the blank spot.

Student B So, what did the Chandra observation tell us about, uh, about what lies beyond the zone of avoidance?

Professor **Q4 The Chandra x-ray observatory recorded thirty-six new galaxies beyond the Milky Way.** I'd like to talk more about this next time, but for now we're out of time. For homework, I'd like everyone to research the results of the Chandra observation.

Q5教授为什么这样说？
No...actually, I think we may be having some slight... confusion.
(A) 为了表明没有理解学生的意思
(B) 为了表明学生的回答错了
(C) 为了表明对于这一问题还存在科学上的疑虑
(D) 为了引导学生进一步说明

Q6学生这样说的意思是什么？
I'll venture another...
(A) 他希望进入下一个要点
(B) 他确信自己的猜测正确
(C) 他希望教授重复一下问题
(D) 他在给出一个建议

MP3·340

Milky Way 银河，银河系(=**our galaxy**)
light year [天文]光年
spiral 成螺旋形
disk （扁平的）圆盘，圆盘模样的物体
float around 在周围飘浮，在周围流传
plane 平面，水平面
infrared radiation 红外线
observatory 观测所
blank 空的，没有内容的
out of time 时间用尽了

Answer passage 1 > 1 (C) 2 (B) 3 (D) 4 (C) 5 (A)

passage 2 > 1 (C) 2 (B) 3 (B) 4 (C) 5 (D) 6 (B)

passage 3 > 1 (C) 2 (B) 3 (A) 4 (D) 5 (A) 6 (C)

MP3·341 **passage 1. [1-5] Listen to part of a conversation between a student and a professor.**

Professor (female) Q1 **Are you here to pick up last week's take-home exam? The one you were absent for?**

Student (male) **That's right. I heard from someone in the class that we could drop by your office between 2:00 and 4:00 to pick it up.**

Professor You heard correctly. The exams are in a pile on the table by the door. Go ahead and grab one.

Student Q4 MP3·342 **OK. *[pause]* So I...*[looking for more information]* I just go home and take the test and...**

Professor **This must be your first take-home exam?**

Student **Yeah. I've never done one of these before. Just in-class exams. I'm not really sure what I've got to do.**

Professor OK. Why don't you take a seat right here and I'll go over the rules for take-home exams.

Student I appreciate it. Thanks.

Professor Well, what you're gonna be doing with this exam is describing an environmental contaminant in two different environments.

Student Right. I remember you saying that would be the topic of the exam.

Professor Now, I want you to compare and contrast the two environments in as many ways as you can come up with.

Student Any way? Can you give me some examples?

Professor There are some examples on the exam, actually. You can check them out when you start researching your topic.

Student Great.

Professor This is your opportunity to impress me with the amount of information you've retained from our class. So try to be creative about fitting in topics, procedures, principles, and things that we've gone over in class. And you'll want to put as much quantitative data into the paper as you can. If you include a calculation, I want to see the numerical data. Graphics are OK to use, too.

Student All right. Is there a word length...or a page length?

Professor *[remembering suddenly]* Oh, yes. Q2 **There certainly is a page length...a maximum page length. It should be less than ten pages long. And there's no minimum length.** I want you to be concise. Cover all the important points, but don't include any irrelevant commentary.

Student I see.

Professor **Q3 Don't forget to cite all of the sources you consult.**

Student **Q5** MP3·343 **Of course. Are there a certain number of sources I have to use? Are Internet sources acceptable?**

Professor **As for sources—use your judgment.** **How many sources do you think are necessary to support your paper?** And Internet sources are OK to use, but make sure that you don't rely on Internet sources exclusively.

Student No problem.

Professor You should use footnotes in the paper, too.

Student All right. I can do that.

Professor OK. There's just one final thing I want to add. Obviously you're going to be using outside sources to write your paper. So that's fine. But I would prefer that you don't talk to other people in the class to find out how they did the exam. Just do what you think is best. I mean, use sources of your choosing, use a topic that you're interested in...I don't want you getting your ideas from someone else, got it?

Student Yes. So I have to have it back to you in twenty-four hours, right?

Professor Yes. That's right. You can email it to me if you'd like, or you can bring a printed copy here to my office.

MP3·350

take-home exam 把试卷带回家里进行的考试
drop by 顺便来访
contaminant 污染物质
compare and contrast 对比与对照
come up with 想出，找出（方法或主意等）

retain 保持，保留
procedure 程序，步骤
principle 原则，原理
quantitative 数量（上）的
calculation 计算
numerical 数字的，用数字表示的
concise 简洁的
irrelevant 无关的

commentary 说明，注释
cite 引用
source 材料，资料
consult 咨询，商议
rely on 依靠…，依赖…
exclusively 独占地
footnote 脚注
a printed copy 复印件，复印本

◎ 解析

1. 学生为什么拜访教授？
   (A) 为了了解“家中考试”的主题。**(not correct)**
   (B) 为将要写的随笔寻找思路。**(not correct)**
   (C) 为了拿“家中考试”的试卷。
   (D) 为了说明下周将要缺席考试的原因。**(not mentioned)**

Main Idea

教授问：“Are you here to pick up last week's takehome exam?（你是来领上周的“家中考试”试卷的吗？）”学生回答了”that's right（是的）”，由此可见正确答案选(C)。讲义文中也提到了有关“家中考试”主题以及考试随笔的论述构思的内容，但这些都不是学生去找教授的主要原因，因此(A)和(B)选项错误。

2. 对于报告的长度，教授说了什么？

(A) 没有对长度的正式要求。**(not correct)**

(B) 报告长度不应超过10页。

(C) 有最低的页数要求，但是没有最高的页数限制。**(not correct)**

(D) 最少写5页。**(not correct)**

Detail

请看标记Q2处的内容。对于报告的长度，教授说："It should be less than ten pages long. And there's no minimum length.（长度应该在十页以内。但是没有最低页数限制。）"由此可见，最多只能写9页。因此正确答案是(B)。因为没有最低页数要求，而有最高页数要求，所以(C)选项内容与原文内容正好相反。与提交随笔、报告相关的写作分量等是重要的细节信息，因此听的时候要格外注意。

---

3. 对于参考材料，教授说了什么？

(A) 可以和课上的其他学生商量。**(not correct)**

(B) 不允许使用网络资料。**(not correct)**

(C) 引用外部材料不合适。**(not correct)**

(D) 对于所有的引用材料，都要表明出处。

Detail

请看标记Q3处的内容，教授明确说道："Don't forget to cite all of the sources you consult.（别忘了标明所有参考材料的出处。）"因此正确答案选(D)。cite一词的意思是"从其他参考材料中引用"，因此在与写作报告等相关内容中经常出现。教授说不要询问别人考试相关事项，引用外部材料也没关系，因此(A)与(C)选项不正确。教授只说不能完全依赖网上的资料，而不是说完全不可以使用网络资料，因此(B)也不正确。

---

4. 学生这样说的意思是什么？

So I...[looking for more information] I just go home and take the test and...

(A) 他希望教授知道自己的考试计划。

(B) 他希望教授知道他要在哪考试。

(C) 他希望教授提供更加详细的指导。

(D) 他认为教授应该再宽限几天写作报告的时间。

Attitude

听了学生这句话，教授问他是不是第一次进行"家中考试"。学生做了肯定的回答并表示不清楚要做什么。另外，通过学生的语气也可以听出学生比较犹豫，没有自信。由此可以推测出他应该是需要更多关于新考试形式的信息，因此正确答案选(C)。

---

5. 教授为什么这样说？

How many sources do you think are necessary to support your paper?

(A) 为了告诉学生他需要自己决定参考资料的数量。

(B) 为了了解学生想使用参考资源的数量。

(C) 为了在决定资料数量之前询问学生的意见。

(D) 为了暗示学生他应该已经知道至少要使用的参考资料的数量。

Function

回放部分提到"As for sources-use your judgment.（你们自己判断参考材料的问题吧）"。通过这一表现可以看出，教授并不是想听学生对自己问题的回答，而是想让学生们自己决定需要的参考资料的数量。因此，正确答案选(A)。在此类询问话者意图的话题中，经常考查的是话语的隐含意，而非话语的字面意思。

 MP3·344 **passage 2. [1-6] Listen to part of a discussion in an astronomy class.**

Professor (male) If you've been following along the course outline, Q1 **you'll know that today we're going to be talking about Trojan asteroids. Right.** Can anyone offer up a guess to why these asteroids have such a name?

Student A (female) Ah, I guess maybe it has something to do with the Trojan War.

Professor Right, the Trojan War. You all know about that, right? The war between the Greeks and the Trojans from Greek mythology. I'm sure some of you've covered it in uh, classics or literature classes. Q5 MP3·345 **But how do you think the asteroids might relate to the Trojan War?**

Student B (male) **Is it because they have unique core compositions...like something is hidden inside? Kind of like the famous Trojan Horse.**

Professor **Great try, but I'm afraid the answer is more mundane than that... It's just due to the names of the asteroids. Pretty obvious, huh?** Q2 **You see the guy who discovered the first of these asteroids was a German astronomer named Max Wolf. He had a really simple, but effective technique to find asteroids. Basically he would take photographs of the night sky, then compare two photos taken on different nights to see if any stars had moved. Can you imagine that? Such a basic observation and yet, yet he was able to discover many asteroids.** Anyway, Max Wolf named the first one he found Achilles, after the great Greek hero from the Trojan War stories. And, uh, well, the trend continued from there. All subsequent discoveries were named after a famous character from either the Greek or Trojan camps. And here's the thing, just like the Trojan War characters are divided into two camps—the Greeks and the Trojans—the Trojan asteroids are also divided into clusters.

Student B I guess that means all the asteroids with Trojan names are in one cluster, and all the ones with Greek names are in another.

Professor Bingo! OK, Q1 **now we've covered the origin of the name, we really need to get onto the more detailed astronomical stuff. So, uh, the interesting thing about these asteroids is that they follow the same circular orbit as Jupiter...**

Student A A circular orbit? That's not what normally happens with asteroids, is it? I thought they tended to follow an elliptical orbit.

Professor Right, but not the Trojans. What happens is, the combined gravitational pull of the sun and Jupiter act on these asteroids. So, uh, you've got the sun pulling them in from the center, but you've also got the gravity of Jupiter pulling at them from the side, too. The overall effect keeps their position fixed on Jupiter's circular orbit.

Student A Is that why the asteroids are in two camps? Like, each cluster has been pulled onto either side of Jupiter?

Professor Exactly. The two clusters are positioned at what we call in astronomical jargon Lagrangian Points. Uh, Lagrangian Points are places where the combined gravitational pull of two relatively larger masses provides the exact amount of centripetal force required for the small object to rotate on their orbital axes. The Trojan camp, they're at L4—Lagrarian Point 4 on Jupiter's orbit. And the Greeks, they're at L5.

Student B *[sheepishly]* So, well, I hope this isn't a stupid question... Q4 **But if the asteroids are clustered at set points on the orbit, then why don't they, like, collide with Jupiter? You know, when it crosses them in its orbit.**

Professor ***[realizing he might be going too fast for some students]*** **Ah, sorry. I should've made it clear that the asteroid clusters also circle the sun. L4 and L5 aren't fixed points on the orbit.** ***[with emphasis]*** **They're fixed points relative to Jupiter on the orbit.** Do you see what I'm saying?

Student B *[still unclear]* Um, well, I think so...

Professor Q3 OK...***[thinking about how to explain it]*** **Here's a good way to look at it. Just imagine that Jupiter's orbit is the face of a clock. Then the Trojan camp is always 2 hours ahead of Jupiter on this clock, and the Greek camp, it's always 2 hours behind. So when Jupiter is at 10 o'clock on the orbit, the Trojan camp is at 12, and the Greek camp is back at 8.**

Student B Q4 **Ah, now I get it! So the clusters orbit the sun at exactly the same speed as Jupiter.** *[with emphasis]* Relative to Jupiter, the asteroids don't look like they're moving.

Professor Yeah. I mean, actually it's a little more complicated than that. The asteroids sort of arc within a small area on the orbit. Like, if you see a picture of the Trojan or Greek camps, you'll notice there's a slightly elongated distribution of asteroids along the orbit. Q6 MP3•346 **This is caused by perturbations from other large bodies, usually other planets in the solar system.** ***[stopping himself from getting too sidetracked]*** **But, uh, these arcs are very minor in the scheme of things, and I'm worried it might all be a bit overwhelming. Um...all you need to know at the moment is that the asteroids are pretty much stationary relative to Jupiter.**

MP3•351

Trojan asteroids 特洛伊小行星群
mythology 神话
classics 古典
core [地质]中心核
composition 组成物质
mundane 平凡的
subsequent 随后的，后来的
name after 以…的名字起名
cluster 群，团，群聚
astronomical 天文学上的
circular orbit 圆形轨道

elliptical 椭圆形的
gravitational 重力的（←**gravity**重力）
jargon （专门）用语
Lagrangian point [天文]拉格朗日点（两天体之间引力和离心力达到平衡的点）
mass 大量的
centripetal force 向心力
rotate on 以…为中心旋转
axis 轴(**pl. axes**)
collide with 与…冲突
face （钟表等的）正面，前面

relative to 关于…的，和…比较起来
arc 画弧线，弧
elongated （很长地）延长的，加长的
distribution 散布，分布
perturbation [天文]摄动（由于近距离经过的天体的引力或与之的碰撞而产生的天体运动偏差）
scheme 体制，体系
overwhelming 巨大的，压倒性的
stationary 不懂的，静止的

◎ 解析

1. 讲义文的主要内容是什么？
   (A) 最近发现的特洛伊小行星群 **(minor)**
   (B) 特洛伊战争与天文学之间的相似点 **(not mentioned)**
   (C) 特洛伊小行星群的位置与分布状态
   (D) 远古以后天文学的发展过程 **(not mentioned)**

Main Idea

教授在讲义文开头说："today we're going to be talking about Trojan asteroids（今天我们要学习关于特洛伊小行星群的内容。）"他通过这句话，直接揭示了讲义文的主题是关于特洛伊小行星群的。然后，教授又在接下来的讲义文中介绍了特洛伊小行星群名称的起源，它处于木星轨道上的原因以及它在轨道上的分布。因此正确答案选(C)。

2. 马科斯·沃尔夫探测小行星的技术的有趣之处是什么？
   (A) 需要特殊的摄影设备。 **(not correct)**
   (B) 它是十分基础的技术。
   (C) 直到今天，还有天文学家使用这一方法。 **(not correct)**
   (D) 它被保守了几年的秘密。**(not mentioned)**

Detail

请看标记Q2处的内容。教授评价马科斯．沃尔夫探测小行星的方法是"really simple, but effective technique（非常简单但是有效的方法）"，之后又定义它是"basic observation（基础性的观测方法）"。而选项(B)中的rudimentary是设备或技术等毫不复杂，非常简单的意思。这是对马科斯·沃尔夫探测小行星的技术最合适的形容，因此正确答案选(B)。

3. 教授是如何说明特洛伊小行星群的轨道的？
   (A) 通过与其它小行星群的轨道进行比较。
   (B) 通过以日常家居用品为例。
   (C) 通过向学生提供统计数据。
   (D) 通过与木星轨道对照。

Organization

请看标记Q3的内容。教授说："Just imagine that Jupiter's orbit is the face of a clock.（想象木星的轨道是时钟的表面。）"为了让学生更容易理解木星与小行星轨道之间的关系，教授借用时钟指针的转动原理进行了一番说明。因此正确答案选(B)。选项中使用"household object"对原文中的时钟进行了表述。这是用大家熟知的事物对学术上较难的概念进行说明。

4. 为什么特洛伊小行星群不会碰撞木星？
   (A) 因为比起木星，小行星群被太阳拉得更近。**(not correct)**
   (B) 因为小行星群不是环绕圆形轨道，而是绕着椭圆形轨道旋转。**(not correct)**
   (C) 因为小行星群以与木星相同的速度围绕太阳旋转。
   (D) 因为小行星群在移动时会受到其他天体运动的影响。**(not correct)**

Detail

请看标记Q4处的内容。教授说："the asteroid clusters also circle the sun."他介绍了小行星群也像木星围绕太阳公转一样围绕太阳旋转，因此两者之间不会发生碰撞。听了教授的说明之后，学生再次确定地说："So the clusters orbit the sun at exactly the same speed as Jupiter.（所以小行星群以与木星相同的速度围绕太阳旋转。）"因此正确答案选(C)。小行星群的Trojan camp与Greek camp将木星夹在中间，以与木星相同的速度移动，因此从木星的角度来看，它的轨道是确定的。但是从整个太阳系来看，它的轨道就不是确定的。

5. 教授为什么这样说？
but I'm afraid the answer is more mundane than that...
(A) 为了提前告知叙述主题较难。
(B) 为了进一步讨论特洛伊木马。
(C) 为了显示出对学生的回答感到失望。
(D) 为了告诉学生这一术语的来源极其简单。

Function
请看标记Q5处的内容。这一小行星群之所以被命名为Trojan asteroids，是因为其中的小行星都是以特洛伊战争中的出场人物命名的。这一解释与之前学生猜测的原因相比更加简单，因此教授就是为了指出这一点。因此正确答案选(D).

6. 教授这么说时，可以推测出他？
***[stopping himself from getting too sidetracked]* But, uh, these arcs are very minor in the scheme of things, and I'm worried it might all be a bit overwhelming.**
(A) 他觉得在做进一步评论之前，有必要确认事实根据。
(B) 他不想让学生因为细节感到迷惑。
(C) 他认为学生已经知道这一信息了。
(D) 他想下节课再谈这点。

Attitude
请看标记Q6部分的内容。在回放部分的最后，教授说："all you need to know at the is that the asteroids are pretty much stationary relative to Jupiter（你们目前只要了解一点就好。就是相对木星来说，小行星可以说是静止的。）"从这句话可以看出，教授怕如果讲得太细，枝节的内容会混淆讲义文的重点。因此正确答案选(B).

MP3·347 **passage 3. [1-6] Listen to part of a lecture in a biology class.**

Professor (female)

Alright class, let's get started. Q1 **Today you're going to learn about the very unique characteristics of, um, mangroves.** Q2 **As you should know from your geography class, the word "mangroves" is often used to define a saltwater forest that grows on coastal mud flats—basically waterlogged swamps—and this fragile area is flooded with water usually, uh, once or twice a day, depending on the local tide periods. Anyway, I'm not really going to be talking about the mangrove ecosystem, but rather...yeah, rather we're going to look at the mangrove trees themselves.** This is the species that is indigenous to this habitat. Q1 **These mangrove trees live in areas where everything is constantly in flux—like water levels and salinity—they've evolved over time and developed many special features to help them adapt.**

The most important feature is their upward growing roots, known as aerial roots. Not only do they provide support for the trees in such unstable soils, enabling them to withstand strong currents and storms, but they also help in breathing. Q3 **On the surface of these aerial roots, uh, they have special tiny pores called lenticels. Water and soil can't penetrate these lenticels, uh, only air can. Also, the lenticels contain large pockets of air that provide a reservoir of air during periods of**

high tide, when all the aerial roots are, um, underwater. So, the function of the aerial roots is to, to absorb air and provide structural support.

Q5 MP3·348 **The biggest problem mangroves face is their nutrient uptake. Barely any free oxygen is available in the damp, muddy soil and definitely not in the water. So, uh, in addition to having roots that breathe air, they also have root modifications that block salt and draw in water, carbon dioxide, oxygen, and other nutrients essential to photosynthesis. The gases the aerial roots absorb and store get sent down to the roots that grow in oxygen-deficient parts of the soil.**

Hopefully you haven't forgotten your middle school science...photosynthesis requires fresh water, right? So um, obviously in the kind of environment mangroves inhabit, this can be a bit of a problem. However, the mangrove has developed a few solutions. It can block salt from the root system, create high tissue salt concentrations, and secrete excess salt. Actually, most mangroves, they um, they block out most of the salt right at the root system. The mangroves just then dispose of the remaining salt by depositing it in bark or leaves that have grown out of maturity. Some of the plants even secrete salt directly out of the leaves. On their underside there are these specialized pores that use hairs to guide the concentrated salt solution away from the plant while keeping in the freshwater for the leaves. It's really an amazing adaptation.

Q6 MP3·349 **OK, let's focus now on one of the mangroves' most distinct aspects —as if their roots weren't special enough, right?** Well, mangroves actually reproduce viviparously. Can anyone guess what viviparous reproduction is? No? Well, this means a mangrove tree produces seeds that germinate on the plant, unlike most botanical species. They do this via the production of a propagule. This, um, propagule requires water and carbon dioxide from its parent, so it grows directly on it. However, the propagule can actually photosynthesize on its own. Eventually it falls off the parent tree and drops into the water, where it can travel great distances. The wonderful thing for these propagules is that they can survive desiccation—uh, that's when they sort of dry out—they can survive and remain in this kind of dormant state for more than a year until they arrive in a suitable environment. And uh, once a propagule has found this environment and is ready to root, it will change its floating position from horizontal to vertical so that in this elongated shape, it can lodge into the mud and root more easily. Q4 **It actually can change its density to determine if it will float horizontally or vertically! So uh, yeah, if the propagule doesn't root, it can revert again to a horizontal position to float off again in search of better rooting conditions.**

MP3·352

mangrove 红树属树木，海榄雌（生存于热带湿地中的森林植物）
mud flat 泥滩
waterlogged 水浸的
swamp 湿地，沼泽
fragile 易碎的，脆的
indigenous 土生土长的
habitat 栖息地，住处
flux 变动，变化
salinity 盐分，盐度
aerial root [植物]气根（不在土壤里，暴露在空气中行使机能的根）
unstable 不稳定的
withstand 经受，承受
pore 毛孔，气孔
lenticel 皮孔
penetrate 穿过，渗入
reservoir 贮藏处，贮水池
uptake 吸水，上吸
barely 几乎不，仅仅
damp 潮湿的
modification 更改，修改
photosynthesis 光合作用（←**photosynthesize** 进行光合作用）
deficient 不足的
tissue 组织
concentration 浓度，含量（←**concentrated** 浓缩的）
secrete 排出，分泌

MP3 • 352

dispose of 将…处理掉，除掉
salt solution 盐溶液
viviparous [植物]胎生的，在母株上萌发的
reproduction 繁殖
germinate 萌发，（使）发芽

botanical 植物学的
propagule 能发育成植物体的芽，繁殖体
desiccation 干燥，脱水
dormant 休眠的
horizontal 水平的

vertical 竖直的
lodge into 存放，暂住，位于
density 密度
revert 回复到（原来状态）

◎ 解析

1. 讲义文的主要内容是什么？
   (A) 红树根的不同功能 **(minor)**
   (B) 威胁红树林生存的因素 **(not mentioned)**
   (C) 红树为了生存而进行的适应性进化
   (D) 繁殖体繁殖的优点 **(minor)**

Main Idea

在讲义文的开头部分，教授说："Today you're going to learn about the very unique characteristics of, um, mangroves.（今天，我们将对红树林十分不同寻常的特点进行学习。）"用这句话揭示了主题之后，又说道："they've evolved over time and developed many special features to help them adapt.（红树随着时间的流逝不断进化，并且为了适应进化出许多特别的属性。）"这句话将议论的主题引至红树为适应环境而进化的生物学功能。因此正确答案是(C)。(A)与(D)虽然在讲义文中提及，但只是红树许多适应方法中的一部分，不能看做是整篇文章的主题。

2. 教授为什么以介绍盐水森林和浸水湿地的方式开始讲课？
   (A) 为了复习以前课上学过的关于红树林生存地的内容
   (B) 为了明确他将要讨论红树林的哪些方面
   (C) 为了回答上节课有人提出的问题
   (D) 为了比较红树以及其他的盐水植物

Organization

请看标记Q2部分的内容，教授明确说了今天的课中将了解学习"the mangrove trees themselves（红树本身）"。教授默认学生们在地理课上已经学过有关红树的内容，提出今天的课上将不讨论如saltwater forests或waterlogged swamps一类的"the mangrove ecosystem"地理性问题，而是要讨论红树的生物学层面的内容。为了明确这一点，教授就说了这句话，因此正确答案选(B)。

3. 根据教授的介绍，皮孔为什么很重要？

(A) 因为它使得植物可以吸收并贮存空气

(B) 因为它可以将从盐水中寻找、收集到的养分转化 **(not mentioned)**

(C) 因为它可以固定植物周围的土壤 **(not correct)**

(D) 因为它有助于增加地上大气中的氧气含量 **(not mentioned)**

Detail

请看标志Q3部分的内容。教授说："the lenticels contain large pockets of air that provide a reservoir of air（皮孔起着空气贮存处的作用，具有很大的空气囊。）"由此可见，植物皮孔的作用是提供空气。因此正确选项为(A)。此外，皮孔的作用并不是固定周围的土壤，而是吸收空气，支撑植物成长，因此(C)选项不正确。

---

4. 根据教授的介绍，繁殖体（珠芽）有何特别之处？

(A) 通过母株植物进行光合作用。 **(not correct)**

(B) 在几乎所有种类的土壤中都可以生根。 **(not correct)**

(C) 通过叶上的特殊气孔排出多余的养分。 **(not correct)**

(D) 它们可以改变自身密度漂浮或生根。

Detail

这题要求选择教授提到的繁殖体所具有的特征。请看标记Q4部分的内容，教授说："It can actually can change its density to determine if it will float horizontally or vertically!(事实上，繁殖体甚至可以改变自身的密度来决定是水平飘浮，还是竖直浮动。)"因此正确答案是（D）。此外，繁殖体可以不依靠母株独立进行光合作用，在找到合适的植根环境之前会一直漂浮，因此(A)和(B)都不正确。而(C)不是对红树的繁殖体，而是对普通红树的说明，因此不正确。

---

5. 教授为什么这么说？

Hopefully you havent't forgotten your middle school science.

(A) 为了表明她希望学生知道这一基本信息

(B) 为了暗示课程材料对学生来说太简单了

(C) 为了让学生对之前学过的某种理论提出质疑

(D) 为了激发学生对她讲课的反响

Function

请看标记Q5处的内容，教授在说了这句话之后，又提到了光合作用需要淡水的事实。教授希望通过这点考查学生是否掌握有关光合作用的基础知识，因此正确答案为(A)。

---

6. 教授这么说的意思是？

—as if their roots weren't special enough, right?

(A) 具体讨论根系太过复杂的问题。

(B) 红树的繁殖是一个更加有趣的话题。

(C) 红树具有很多独特之处

(D) 繁殖系统与根的结构紧密相关。

Detail

请看标记Q6处的内容，这是教授在之前对红树根的特征进行过说明之后，为了将话题转向其他特征而说的一番话。通过这一部分，可以推测出红树不仅在根部具有很多特征，在其他部位也能发现很多独特属性。实际上，教授在说了这些话之后，立刻介绍了红树独特的在母株上萌发的繁殖方式。因此正确答案为(C)。

Answer case example > 1 (B) 2 (C) 3 (C) 4 (A) 5 (B)
passage 1 > 1 (D) 2 (C) 3 (C) 4 (A) 5 (B)
passage 2 > 1 (D) 2 (A) 3 (B), (C) 4 (C) 5 (B)
passage 3 > 1 (A) 2 (D) 3 (B), (C) 4 (C) 5 (D)

case example

MP3·353 **[1-5] Listen to part of a conversation between a student and a librarian.**

Librarian (female) Q4 MP3·354 **Can I help you find something in the library's film and music collections?**

Student (male) **Um, I'm not sure. I've actually never been to this part of the library before.** **<u>This is Media Collections, right?</u>**

Librarian Yep. We occupy the entire ground floor of the Norton-Oliver Library. We have videos, DVDs, CDs, LPs...Are you, um, just browsing around or are you looking for something specific? I can answer whatever questions you have about the film and music resources here.

Student Thanks. Q5 MP3·355 **Um, what's the circulation policy for, um, for items in Media Collections?**

Librarian **Well, that depends. Are you a student here?**

Student **<u>Uh, no. I just live in the community. *[concerned]* Am I ineligible to borrow from the library?</u>**

Librarian Well...I'm afraid you won't be able to take any films or music outside the library if you don't have valid university identification.

Student *[disappointed]* Oh, I see.

Librarian However, you're welcome to use the viewing rooms here in the library to watch or listen to anything you like.

Student Really?

Librarian Yes. It's just—we can't loan you any media items for use outside the library...unless you're a student at the college.

Student Well, that could work. See, Q1 **I'm taking a**

Q1这位男子需要从图书馆获得什么？
(A) 通过在线目录，查询电影收藏。
(B) 和同学一起观看西班牙语电影。
(C) 更换一张学院图书馆的借阅卡。
(D) 有关图书馆借阅规定的信息。

Q2关于在线目录这位女士暗示了什么？
(A) 这个男子应该在去图书馆之前查好。
(B) 其中没有包含多媒体收藏的列表。
(C) 它比本人亲自查询要方便。
(D) 学生可以用它来借图书和电影。

MP3·368
collection 收藏，收集，（一批）收藏品
occupy 占领，占(空间、时间等)
browse around 浏览（书籍），随便逛逛
resources 资源，财力，办法，策略
circulation （货币、消息等的）流通，发行量
That depends. 要视情况而定
be ineligible to *do* 没有资格做…
valid 有根据的，有法律效力的
loan 贷款，借出

	Spanish class at the community college—
Librarian	*[interrupting]* At CCN?
Student	That's right.
Librarian	Well, CCN is one of our affiliate institutions. If you can present a CCN ID, you can check out materials from Media Collections.
Student	That's great. I happen to have my CCN ID on me right now. So I can check out anything I want?
Librarian	As long as it's not reserved for a class or something like that.
Student	OK. Q1 **Well, I'm looking for three Spanish films my teacher said I could find here.** Do you have, like a, a foreign-language section?
Librarian	Yes, we do, but, um...I'm afraid affiliate borrowers are only permitted to check out two items at once.
Student	That's OK. I'll just pick up the third one when I return the first two.
Librarian	OK, sounds good. As for the films you're looking for...just give me the titles, and I'll look them up and make sure we have them and they're available for checkout.
Student	OK. The first one's called *Como agua para chocolate.*
Librarian	Let me just type that in here. *[while typing]* Q2 **Are you familiar with the online catalogue? You can view all of our books and DVDs and videos online by going to the library website and clicking on the link to the catalogue. That way you can check the status of a book or film or whatever before you come over to the library. You know...to make sure it's not already checked out.**
Student	OK, great. I'll do that next time.
Librarian	Ah ha. Directed by Alfonso Arau?
Student	Um, yeah.
Librarian	Yes, we do have *Como agua para chocolate,* and it's currently available. The call number is DVD 726.
Student	Great. The other one I'd like to check out if possible is *Días contados.*
Librarian	All right. Let me look. *[typing] Días contados.* Yes...we have a listing for it. Directed by Imanol

Q3为什么这个男子现在只借一部电影了？

(A) 他发现其他的都被一个班预定了。

(B) 他打算在图书馆的放映室看另外一部。

(C) 他不能在规定时间内看两部电影。

(D) 他一次只能借一部。

Q4为什么这个男子要这样说：**This is Media Collections, right?**

(A) 以确认他处在正确的区域。

(B) 以询问那个女士一些事情。

(C) 以解释他来到图书馆的原因。

(D) 以便让那个女士知道他迷路了。

MP3-368

affiliate 使紧密发生联系，使附属

institution 机构，制度

check out （在图书馆）借书，（在酒店、餐馆）结账

happen to 发生在…身上

status 状态；身份

retrieve 取回，挽回，补偿

hang on one second. 稍等一会儿

	Uribe, right?	
Student	Yes. Is it currently available?	
Librarian	Yeah. So you'll take them both?	
Student	Right. Where do I find them?	
Librarian	Our DVDs are stored out back—I'll retrieve them for you. Just hang on one second.	
Student	Thanks. Oh, wait a minute. Q3 **How long can I check them out for?**	
Librarian	**Um, you get them for one night. They have to be back by noon tomorrow.**	
Student	**Oh, really? I don't think I'm going to have enough time to watch two films tonight. I'd better just check out one of them.**	
Librarian	Which one would you prefer to check out first?	
Student	Uh, how about *Como agua para chocolate*?	
Librarian	OK. I'll be right back with the DVD.	
Student	Thank you so much.	

Q5当男子这样说的时候可以推测出什么？
Uh, no. I just live in the community. *[concerned]* Am I ineligible to borrow from the library?
(A) 他希望那个女士为他破例。
(B) 他担心自己不能使用图书馆。
(C) 他听到女士给他的信息很高兴。
(D) 他不准备从图书馆借书。

passage 1

MP3·356 **[1-5] Listen to part of a conversation between a student and a Residence Life clerk.**

Clerk (male)	Hi. Can I help you with something today?
Student (female)	*[frustrated]* Um...maybe. I'm having an issue with the campus maintenance department. But I thought maybe you guys at Residence Life could help.
Clerk	Are you a resident of Claremont Hall?
Student	Yeah, um, I live here in the undergraduate wing.
Clerk	Then I may be able to help you out. What's the problem?
Student	Dictation 开始 Q1 **Um, the paint in the common room of my suite is peeling off all over the place.** [1]***Paint chips are getting everywhere.*** **My roommates and I have been trying to get maintenance up to our suite to repaint the wall, but it's been more than two weeks and nothing's happened.**
Clerk	I see. Q4 MP3·357 **When** [2]***did you submit your request?***
Student	**Actually, we submitted two requests. One right after it happened...um, on the 21st. And then we submitted a second request on the 28th.**

Q1这位女士为什么要去见住宿生活中心的工作人员？
(A) 去和宿舍的油漆匠保持联络。
(B) 去要求换到另一个学生公寓。
(C) 去叫工作人员打开她的房间让油漆匠进去。
(D) 去咨询一个维修项目延迟的相关情况。

Q2为什么那两个油漆匠不能在墙上工作？
(A) 没有向正确的办公室申请表格。
(B) 他们拿到了错误的地址。
(C) 没有人让他们进去。
(D) 他们比预定的时间到得晚。

It's already November 4th and we still haven't seen anyone from the maintenance department.

Clerk OK. Let me just look for [3]*the maintenance request documents you submitted,* and I'll see if I can figure out what the problem is here. What's your name?

Student It's Sam Russo, but I didn't submit the documents. It was my roommate, Denise Lombardi.

Clerk *[looking through some papers]* OK. Denise Lombardi... *[pause]* Are you in suite 301?

Student Yeah, that's our suite.

Clerk OK. Yeah, I have the documents here. One submitted on the 21st and the other submitted on the 28th. *[scanning the documents]* Q5 MP3·358 **Um...it looks like** [4]***everything's in order with these forms.* And according to what it says here, two painters were sent to suite 301 after all.**

Student ***[surprised]* What? Then why hasn't** [5]***our wall been repainted yet?***

Clerk Well, I'm not sure. Let me give the maintenance department a call and find out what happened. This will just take a minute... I'll be right back. *[pause]* Q2 **I spoke with the maintenance department on the phone, and they said the first painter went to the suite on Thursday the 23rd at 10:30 in the morning, and the second painter went up there on Wednesday the 29th at two in the afternoon.**

Student **Oh. Well no one was home then.** [6]***We're all in class during the middle of the day.* Couldn't someone from Residence Life here let the painters into our suite?**

Clerk **Well, yes, we can do that. If we have the permission of someone in the suite. But when your roommate...um, when Denise filled out the form she didn't check the permission box to let us** [7]***unlock your suite for maintenance personnel.***

Student Oh...so that's the problem.

Clerk Q3 **Yeah. Just an oversight. Would you like to fill out another request form? Hopefully** [8]***this time things will work out.*** Dictation 结束

Student **Yes. I suppose I'd better fill out another form.**

Q3为什么这位女士填了另外一张维修申请表？
(A) 为了抱怨维修的员工。
(B) 为了在她上漆的套间里加一堵墙。
(C) 为了纠正前一张表的疏漏。
(D) 为了把她的名字加到同屋那里。

Q4从这个女士那里可以推测出什么？
(A) 她为不得不反复地提交申请感到沮丧。
(B) 她满怀希望地认为那个男子会帮她提交申请。
(C) 她认为那个男子应该知道申请提交的时间。
(D) 她记不清楚提交申请的时间了。

MP3·369
maintenance department 维修部门
undergraduate 本科生，本科的；未毕业的
wing 区域
common room （学校里教师和学生的）公共休息室
suite （酒店的）套房；（有两至三间房的）套间
peel off 剥离；脱下
chip 碎片，薄片
submit a request 提交申请
figure out 弄明白，想清楚
in order 按顺序，整齐
fill out a form 填表
personnel 员工
oversight 疏忽
work out 解决

Clerk	**OK, sure. Here you go.**
Student	**So I just check this box right here?**
Clerk	**Yeah, that's the one. This time, when a maintenance employee shows up we'll be able to let him or her right into your suite, even if no one's home.**
Student	Thanks a lot. I'm so relieved that we'll finally get the walls repainted.
Clerk	Yeah, I'm sorry it's taken so long.
Student	Well, I know it's not your fault. Thanks for helping me figure out the issue.
Clerk	No problem. Is there anything else I can help you with today?
Student	No—I think that's it. Thanks.

Q5为什么这个女士要这样说：
***[surprised]* What?**
(A) 为说了误解那个男子的话道歉。
(B) 为了表现对男子所分享信息的惊讶。
(C) 为了表示她没有听到男子的话。
(D) 为了询问该男子以便再次核对信息。

MP3·369
relieved 如释重负的

passage 2

MP3·359 **[1-5] Listen to part of a conversation between a student and a bookstore employee.**

Student (female)	Um...hi. This is the section for English courses, isn't it?
Employee (male)	Yes, that's right.
Student	Oh, that's what I was afraid of. Q1 **Um...do you think you could help me find something?**
Employee	Well, I can certainly try. Q4 MP3·360 **What are you looking for?**
Student	**It's right over here. Or... <u>I mean, it should be.</u> It's a book for Professor Lawson's class on literary theory. I think the course number is... yeah, E-N, 4-1-9.**
Employee	Hmm...yeah, I see where it should be. There's the tag with the course information. The class is called Contemporary Literary Analysis?
Student	Right.
Employee	Well, I don't think there are any more left.
Student	Don't you have any other copies out back in storage or something?
Employee	No, I'm sorry. The semester's two weeks old now, so most students already have all the books they need. We haven't had a chance to reorder anything yet. Q2 **Why did you wait so long to come look for this?**

Q1为什么要与书店店员接触？
(A) 以便决定她的英语课需要哪本书。
(B) 为了确认能否从出版商处定书。
(C) 为了搞清楚去哪儿买二手书。
(D) 以便寻求帮助挑选她课上用的书。

Q2为什么这个学生买书买晚了？
(A) 她在学期开始之后才参加了这个课程。
(B) 她的教授本应该为她定一本复印件。
(C) 她没有意识到这门课程需要一本教材。
(D) 劳森教授最近才布置了这本书。

Student **Oh...I just transferred into the class yesterday. Yeah, I didn't realize when I arranged my schedule last semester, but it turns out I need this class to graduate.** So...um, I really need this book. It's the main text for the whole class. What am I supposed to do?

Employee Q5 MP3·361 **Well, it shouldn't be any problem to order another one for you. Let me just take down the ISBN number from the tag here, and I can...wait a minute... *[inspecting something]*** **Oh, that's unfortunate.**

Student Why...what is it?

Employee This book was specially ordered by your professor. I mean, he ordered it from the publisher directly. And, uh, we had nothing to do with it here at the bookstore.

Student OK, but what does that mean?

Employee Well, it's up to your professor to order more copies. We can't do it. Q3(C) **So...I'm afraid you'll have to go talk to him about getting a copy for you.** And, um, usually...it usually takes longer to get in orders made by professors than the stuff we order. You know, because we have a special system set up with the publisher, and your professor doesn't.

Student *[dismayed]* Oh, no. How long will it take?

Employee About one to two weeks, I think.

Student That's so long. I won't be able to do any of the reading assignments until I get the book. This is really going to affect my grade... I can't believe it...

Employee Well...hold on. You have some other options here.

Student *[curious]* I do? What do you mean? What else can I do?

Employee Um, there's always the used bookstores downtown. A lot of times, students will sell their books at those stores once they finish the semester. So there might be some used copies there from students who took the class last term.

Student A used copy? I don't know. I don't like using books that someone else has already written

Q3店员对这个女士的问题给出了哪两种可能的解决方案的建议？
(A) 从图书馆借书。
(B) 去看学生信息板。
(C) 让教师为他定一本复印件。
(D) 从学校书店预定。

Q4当这个学生这样说的时候她暗示：
I mean, it should be.
(A) 书籍没有按顺序上架。
(B) 店员应该知道书在哪儿。
(C) 她在找的书不在常规位置。
(D) 她已经知道那本书放在哪儿了。

MP3·370
tag （商定里的）标签；标记
contemporary 当代的；同代人
copy 复印，复印本
transfer 转让
turn out 结果是…
what am I supposed to do? 我应该做什么？
take down 记下
publisher 出版商，出版人
have nothing to do with 没有什么事情可做
be up to A 由A来决定
hold on （打电话或者谈话时）等一下，别着急
used bookstore 二手书店

	in. I take a lot of notes in mine, so I need all the blank space I can get.
Employee	Well, that still might be your best bet if you're looking to get the book quickly.
Student	I suppose so... It's just that, um...not only that, but all the stores in town are kind of inconvenient to get to. I'd have to take the bus... then walk a ways. It's such a hassle.
Employee	Uh...you know, you might not have to go all the way there to get a used copy. There's always a chance that a student here on campus might be looking to sell one. That happens sometimes... like maybe someone just transferred out of the class. If so, they're probably looking to get rid of the book, since they don't need it anymore. Q3(B) **Why don't you check the student message boards around campus and see if anyone's advertising it?**
Student	Hey, that's not a bad idea.
Employee	I mean...you have a better chance finding one downtown, but it couldn't hurt to check on campus first.
Student	Yeah, definitely. I'll go do that right now.
Employee	Good. I hope you find what you're looking for.
Student	Thanks. So do I.

Q5为什么店员会这样说：
Oh, that's unfortunate.
(A) 以便让这个学生知道她还有其他的选择。
(B) 为了表示预定图书时可能出现了错误。
(C) 为了表达对这个学生处境的同情。
(D) 为没有事先定书而道歉。

MP3·370
best bet 最好的办法
hassle 激烈的争论

passage 3

MP3•362 **[1-5] Listen to part of a conversation between a student and a basketball coach.**

Coach (male)	Kim, can I talk to you for a minute?
Student (female)	Sure, Coach. What is it?
Coach	Well, first of all, how was your visit with your family over the weekend?
Student	Oh...it was great, thanks. Unfortunately, my flight was delayed, so I didn't arrive at my parent's place until Saturday. But once I actually got there, it was a lot of fun.
Coach	Hmm...that's too bad about the flight, but I'm glad you had a good time.
Student	Dictation 开始 Thanks. Q1 **I hope I didn't miss too much at practice while I was away.**

Q1为什么教练想跟这位女士交谈？
(A) 为了让她知道她不在时的决定。
(B) 为了知道她回家是否愉快。
(C) 为了了解她关于更换球队队服的意见。
(D) 为了谈论为何她错过了最近一次训练。

Coach	**Actually, that's why I need to talk with you. You see, there was a team meeting after practice on Saturday afternoon, and...well, the rest of the girls [1]*expressed their interest in changing* our team uniforms.**
Student	Ah, you talked about that already? Q2 **Yeah, we were all thinking that it'd be better to have uniforms that feature the school colors more... instead of the plain purple ones we have now.** But I didn't realize the team was going to [2]*bring it up so soon.*
Coach	Yeah, they felt it'd be best to get started on it as soon as possible.
Student	So...what did you think of the idea?
Coach	I think it's fantastic. In fact, I've already spoken with the university athletic director, Mr. Sato. [3]*He's approved our proposal*...um, the new design and everything. The new uniforms should be here in time for our first game.
Student	*[excited]* Oh, that's great! Well, then, I'm glad the girls brought it up with you...even if I had to miss the discussion.
Coach	Q4 MP3·363 **Good. Now...there was one other thing that was decided during the team meeting. And...um, it has [4]*a great deal to do with you.***
Student	***[surprised and nervous]* M—me?**
Coach	You were [5]*elected to be team captain* this year!
Student	*[shocked]* Ah! Really? I can't believe it! That's so wonderful!
Coach	I thought you'd be excited.
Student	You bet I am. Oh, that's such a wonderful honor. I mean...I know I've been on the team for three years and a lot of the girls look up to me, but... I just can't believe it.
Coach	Well, you should. You [6]*certainly deserve to be captain,* and I can't think of anyone else I'd rather have in the position.
Student	Thanks so much, Coach. That means a lot.
Coach	Now, it's not simply a title, you know. Q3 **There're a lot of [7]*duties and responsibilities that come with* being team captain.** Dictation 结束
Student	OK, I'm ready. What exactly do I need to do?

Q2为什么球队想要更换队服?
(A) 以便让设计简化。
(B) 以便得到更多舒服的队服。
(C) 以便突出大学的吉祥物。
(D) 以便让学院的颜色更加突出。

Q3教练提到队长的两项职责是什么？选择两个选项
(A) 在球队训练时组织训练活动。
(B) 协调教练和球队的沟通。
(C) 在面对困难时帮助球员保持乐观的态度。
(D) 选择新球员加入。

MP3·371
feature 特征
plain 平的，什么也没有的
bring up 提出（计划，方案等）
approve 同意
in time 及时
have a great deal to do with 与…有很大关系
you bet 你说对了
look up to 尊重
deserve to *do* 理应（做…）

Coach Q3(B) **Well, most importantly, you have to be the link between me and the team. If there are ever any problems or concerns among the girls, I'll expect you to tell me about them immediately.**

Student I understand.

Coach Q3(C) **You're also going to have to get used to acting as a leader; help out the younger players during practices and games, boost morale, give them guidance for developing their skills... that kind of thing.** Q5 MP3·364 **As captain, they're all going to be looking at you to take control and direct the dynamic of the group, understand?**

Student **I think so. I just hope I have what it takes to be there for them.**

Coach **Well, I know you do.** So...for your first task as team captain, I'd like you to give everybody the happy announcement about the uniforms. Let them know that Mr. Sato gave the plan a green light. OK? They should all be in the locker room getting dressed for practice by now.

Student OK, Coach. Thanks so much for all your support. I'm really excited about my new position...and the new uniforms!

Coach Good, Kim. I know we're going to have a great year.

Q4为什么这个学生要说这些：***[surprised and nervous]*** **M—me?**

(A) 为了确定教练在这里和她说话。

(B) 为了表达对这个决定的不同意。

(C) 为了促使教练解释他的意见。

(D) 为了向教练表明她明白他的意思。

Q5从教练身上可以推断出什么？

(A) 他害怕这个学生没有时间领导全队。

(B) 他希望这个学生考虑他所说的话。

(C) 他理解这个学生对担任队长的疑惑。

(D) 他对这个学生可以领导全队有信心。

MP3·371

link 联系

concern 担心

get used to doing 习惯做…

boost morale 提高士气

dynamic 动力

have what it takes to be 做到应有的那样

give a green light 为…开绿灯，特许做…

Answer

case example > 1 (C) 2 (A) 3 YES → (B), (C), (E) / NO → (A), (D) 4 (B), (C) 5 (B) 6 (D)

passage 1 > 1 (D) 2 YES → (A), (D) / NO → (B), (C) 3 (A) 4 (B), (E) 5 (B) 6 (B)

passage 2 > 1 (B) 2 (B) 3 YES → (A), (D) / NO → (B), (C), (E) 4 (C) 5 (D) 6 (B)

passage 3 > 1 (D) 2 YES → (A), (B), (C) / NO → (D), (E) 3 (B) 4 (B), (C) 5 (A) 6 (D)

case example

MP3·372 **[1-6] Listen to part of a talk in a paleontology class.**

Professor (male) I have a question for you, class. Q1 **Dinosaurs—were they warm-blooded or cold-blooded?**

Student A (female) Q5 MP3·373 **Um—they were cold-blooded, of course.**

Professor **Are you sure?**

Student A **[uncertainly] Well, that's what I'd always assumed. But, uh, I guess you wouldn't have asked us if it were that simple.**

Professor Well, up until about the 1970s, it was sort of generally assumed that dinosaurs were, um, were huge lumbering creatures that were... well, slow and dumb. But in the past couple of decades, most of the evidence we've been finding suggests that the opposite might actually have been true. Dinosaurs might've been fast and active, with high metabolisms.

Student A Um...but what does that have to do with them being warm- or cold-blooded?

Professor Err, if an animal has a high metabolism, there's a good bet that it's warm-blooded because its body is generating its own heat.

Student A Q2 **OK. So what caused scientists to reconsider their belief about dinosaurs being cold-blooded?**

Professor **Well, a young paleontologist named Robert Bakker had a lot to do with it. He published an article in 1968 called "The Superiority of Dinosaurs," which suggested that dinosaurs were much more active than generally believed...and warm-blooded. Bakker's assertions generated a lot of interest, and soon**

Q1教授主要讨论了恐龙的哪些方面?
(A) 有些种类与其他的种类不同的原因。
(B) 它们如何在上百万年中进化出了特殊的特征。
(C) 它们是哪两种生物学物种。
(D) 它们如何能够产生自身的温度。

Q2教授是如何纠正恐龙一定是冷血动物的误解的?
(A) 通过讨论过去几十年古生物学家的工作。
(B) 通过解释动物新陈代谢的过程。
(C) 通过提出与这种观念相矛盾的证据。
(D) 通过列举一种类似的现代动物。

MP3·387
warm-blooded 温血的
(↔**cold-blooded** 冷血的)
assume 假定，承担
(↔**assumption** 假设，承担)
metabolism 新陈代谢
good bet 较大的几率
generate 产生，生成
superiority 优越性
assertion 断言

others began looking into the possibility that dinosaurs may have been, um, warm-blooded creatures.

Um, before I go on, I'd like to just introduce some more specific terminology to talk about the physiology of dinosaurs. The words "warm-blooded" and "cold-blooded" aren't really accurate enough for our purposes. First, there's endothermic, which refers to animals that, like birds and mammals, generate internal heat to control their body temperature. Then there's ectothermic, which means an animal uses its external environment or its behavior to regulate its body temperature. Um, most reptiles are ectothermic. So that's some better terminology for you to use in our conversation today.

Student B (male) Professor, could you go over some of the specific pieces of evidence that support, um, the hypothesis that dinosaurs are, um... endothermic?

Professor Absolutely. Q3(E) **First, when we look at the range of modern animals around the globe, there's a certain trend: metabolic rate is proportional to speed. From what we know about dinosaurs, it seems that they were designed to move at fast speeds.** Q6 MP3·374 **So there's a natural assumption, then, that dinosaurs might've also had high metabolic rates, as that would fit the trend we see among modern animals.**

Student B **Well, that doesn't really seem like, um, hard evidence.**

Professor True. It's not. Honestly, we just don't know enough about dinosaurs to make definite conclusions about them. So keep that in mind as I go on. There're problems with every one of the, um, lines of evidence that I'm presenting here. Q3(B) **So, another piece of the puzzle that would seem to support the hypothesis of endothermy is their posture. It's erect—you know, more up and down than side to side. There's sort of a general correlation between upright posture and endothermy. If you look at modern animals, it's pretty much only, um, endotherms like**

Q3在课上，教授列出了支持恐龙是温血动物的理论依据。指出下列各项是否是证明这个理论的证据。勾选每个选项所对应的正确方框。
(A) 周围的环境控制着它们的体温。**(NO)**
(B) 它们的四肢让它们直立。**(YES)**
(C) 大多数的种类很大并且寿命相对较短。**(YES)**
(D) 它们的新陈代谢率在本质上是会变化的。**(NO)**
(E) 现今行动迅速的物种大多数都是温血的。**(YES)**

Q4教授给出的恐龙会是冷血的两个理由是什么？点击选择两个答案。
(A) 它们生长得很快。
(B) 那时的气候很热。
(C) 它们的皮肤跟现代的冷血动物相类似。
(D) 现代的爬行动物表现出了相似的行为特征。

MP3·387

terminology 术语
accurate 精确的，准确的
endothermic 温血的
（↔**ectothermic** 冷血的）
regulate 管理，控制
hypothesis 假说，假设
range of …的范围
metabolic rate 新陈代谢率（动物在新陈代谢时的速率）
be proportional to 与…成比例
hard evidence 铁证
definite 明确的
posture 姿势
correlation 相关关系
upright 垂直的，竖直的
（=**erect**）

birds and mammals that have erect limbs. **Q3(C) Oh, and another factor that supports the endothermic theory is their growth rate. As you know, some of them grew to be extremely large, so they probably had to grow quite quickly. What we know about modern animals tells us that endothermic animals grow faster than ectothermic animals.** From what we can tell, dinosaurs seem to have had faster growth rates than similarly sized modern reptiles, and similar growth rates to modern endothermic animals. Does everyone follow?

Student A But do we know how long dinosaurs usually lived? Could they have been ectothermic animals that grew slowly but had long lives, so they reached very large sizes?

Professor Yeah, that's certainly a possibility. We don't know for sure how long dinosaurs lived. **Q3(C) However, the oldest Tyrannosaurus we've come across so far was 28 years old. And the oldest sauropod was 38...so it seems that they had rather short lifespans.**

Student B So does everyone pretty much agree that dinosaurs are, um, endotherms? Or is there still some controversy?

Professor Oh, well sure. Nothing's been decided yet. **Q4(B) Some people look at the climate of the Mesozoic era—which was probably a lot warmer than today's climate—and they take that as a sign that dinosaurs probably didn't need to be endothermic because the climate was so mild. They would've been warm enough. Q4(C) Furthermore, from what we can tell about dinosaurs' skin, they had scales...which is just like today's modern ectotherms.**

In light of the evidence that's available, paleontologists have taken a number of different positions on the issue of endothermy and ectothermy in dinosaurs. Yes, some believe that dinosaurs were endotherms...others think that maybe they were something in between modern endotherms and ectotherms. And still others believe that dinosaurs must've been

Q5当这个女士这样说的时候可以推测出什么？
***[uncertainly]* Well, that's what I'd always assumed. But, uh, I guess you wouldn't have asked us if it were that simple.**
(A) 她确信她最初的答案是正确的。
(B) 她正在重新考虑她对这个问题的看法。
(C) 她误解了教授的问题。
(D) 她不同意教授的评价。

Q6为什么那个男子这么说：
Well, that doesn't really seem like, um, hard evidence.
(A) 为了确保他理解了教授说的是什么。
(B) 为了表达他对教授观点的认同。
(C) 为了表示他对这个讨论有所补充。
(D) 为了对教授的争论提问。

MP3-387
limb 肢
reptile 爬行动物
lifespan 寿命
controversy 争议
Mesozoic era 中生代
scale 范围
in (the) light of 由于，鉴于

ectotherms. We just don't know...and we may never know.

passage 1

MP3•375 **[1-6] Listen to part of a lecture in a marine biology class.**

Professor (male)

OK, everyone. Q1 **I'm looking forward to today's lecture, which is about one of my favorite underwater creatures—the octopus.** Q5 MP3•376 **Now, there're about 300 individual species, but I'm just gonna discuss those in the suborder of Incirrina.** **Do I need to write that on the board? *[writing]* Here it is.** Um, the Incirrina suborder includes most octopus species...and they're the ones you're probably most familiar with. The body is made up of two basic parts—the mantle and the arms. The mantle is the large... um, bulbous part where the eyes are located, and the mouth. It also houses the octopus's vital organs. Then you have the arms shooting off from the mantle. How many are there? Yes...eight, of course. Each arm is equipped with a double row of suction cups... I'll talk more about those later.

One of the most interesting things about the octopus, though, is what it lacks—solid structures. Pretty much the entire body is soft... no shells, no bones...um, the only solid structure is the beak. You know, like a bird's beak...that's what the octopus uses to smash the shells of its prey—mostly crabs and scallops. Q2(A) **Anyway, with no rigid body parts, the octopus can do some amazing things... like squeeze its body through tiny cracks in rocks or coral to escape predators.** Q1 **And, um...this is what I want to focus on—characteristics of the animal that help it survive.**

Dictation 开始 Let's continue with the idea of escaping predators for a minute. Um, what does an octopus do if there aren't any rocks or coral around to hide in? How can it get away? Q2(D) **Well, it turns out the animal is [1] *a very gifted impersonator*...it can make itself appear to be something else. For example, say an octopus is crawling along the seafloor...which, by the way, is how they usually travel. Um, so it's crawling along, and suddenly a predator shows up. The octopus can arrange its body in such a way that [2] *it looks like a clump of seaweed*...or some other uninteresting piece of debris.** Moving slowly, in sync with the waves, it'll gradually just drift away, and the predator will be none the wiser.

Pretty neat. Q6 MP3•377 **But what if the predator isn't fooled?** In that case, [3] ***the octopus might shift into high gear.*** It

Q1这个讲义文主要讲了什么？
(A) 章鱼的智商和记忆力
(B) 无鳍亚目中常见的伪装方式
(C) 章鱼捕获猎物的方式
(D) 章鱼设法逃避捕食者的方法

Q2指出下列各项是否在讲义文中作为章鱼的求生技能出现过。勾选各个选项所对应的正确方框。
(A) 从岩石或珊瑚的小口中滑走。**(YES)**
(B) 释放出一股黑色液体来混淆猎物的注意。**(NO)**
(C) 从一只触角中分泌出一种毒液。**(NO)**
(D) 呈现出一种无生命的废墟的样子。**(YES)**

Q3为什么教授提到了章鱼的视力？
(A) 为了强调章鱼感官与众不同的特性。
(B) 为了把章鱼的受体和其他相似的感官进行比较。
(C) 为了描绘水生动物为适应环境所做的特殊努力。
(D) 为了解释章鱼需要这么多防御诀窍的原因。

has another method of locomotion, which, um...it's called jet propulsion. It'll draw in water through its gills, and then [4]*blast it out at high pressure through* its mouth. This'll send the creature shooting forward at up to 25 miles per hour. That's pretty fast, but the drawback is the octopus can only use its jet propulsion for a short time before tiring out.

Luckily, it has [5]*a few more defensive tricks.* One of these...the octopus can release a cloud of dark ink into the water. Um, not only does this obscure the vision of the predator, it also obscures smell...important since a lot of [6]*marine predators rely on scent* during hunting. So the ink cloud basically throws the predator off the octopus's trail. OK, then...one more. In, um, [7]*in extreme circumstances,* the octopus will actually detach one or more of its arms. That's right...just let them go. They'll wiggle around in the water, [8]*hopefully distracting the predator long enough* for the octopus to escape. Oh...and conveniently, the arms grow back.

Q3 **Now...how about avoiding predators all together? This is where the octopus's [9]*somewhat unique senses come into play.* First of all, it has fairly good eyesight...which is a bit unusual for undersea creatures.** Um...its eyes aren't positioned like ours. They're [10]*located on opposite sides of its mantle*, greatly increasing its field of vision. Dictation 结束 And then...remember those suction cups I mentioned? Each one has a chemoreceptor—an organ that senses and analyzes chemical particles...kind of similar to our senses of smell and taste. Um, mostly the octopuses use this when touching objects to identify prey, but recent studies show it can also sense chemicals in the water...from a distant source.

All right...there's one more characteristic I should mention...and it's certainly related to the octopus's survival abilities. Q4 **Unlike other invertebrates...and, well, most other marine animals...um, the octopus is very intelligent. Some people place it on the same level as a house cat.** Q4(E) **It has a good memory,** Q4(B) **and it's highly advanced at solving problems.** Just ask someone who's kept one as a pet, um...they may've had a hard time keeping it in the tank.

Q4根据教授的说法，章鱼是怎样与其它无脊椎动物区分开来的？勾选两个答案。

(A) 它可以察觉到水中化学物质的出现。

(B) 它有很好的解决问题的能力。

(C) 它有嗅觉和味觉。

(D) 它有很多特别的求生技能。

(E) 它有记忆信息的能力。

Q5教授说这些话时表达的是什么意思？

Do I need to write that on the board?

(A) 他想要学生为即将进行的测验学习这个单词。

(B) 他认为这个术语学生们可能不太熟悉。

(C) 他不想学生把时间花在写术语上。

(D) 他认为学生已经学习过这个术语了。

Q6为什么教授要这样说：

But what if the predator isn't fooled?

(A) 为了暗示存在着与他刚才所讨论过的东西不同的观点。

(B) 为了介绍另一种章鱼从捕食者处逃生的方法。

(C) 为了把章鱼的智力和它的捕食者进行比较。

(D) 为了让学生猜测章鱼的行为。

MP3-388

octopus 章鱼
suborder 亚目
Incirrina 无鳍亚目
mantle 罩住，覆盖
bulbous 球茎的
house 房屋，躲藏
shoot off from 从…击落
a row of 一排
suction cup 吸杯
beak 鸟嘴，喙
smash 粉碎
scallop 扇贝
squeeze 挤，榨，握（手）

coral 珊瑚
impersonator 演员，模拟艺人的人
crawl along 一直爬行
a clump of 一块，一丛
debris 残骸，废墟
in sync with 与…一致
drift away （人）渐渐离开，（烟）慢慢散去
none the wiser 毫不明白的
shift into high gear 转换到更高的一档
locomotion 运动，移动
jet propulsion 喷射推进
gill 鳃
blast out 炸开
tire out 使…疲劳
obscure 模糊的
scent 气味
in extreme circumstances 在极端的环境下
detach 使分离
wiggle 扭动
distract 转移注意力，使分心
come into play 开始活动
chemoreceptor 化学受体
invertebrate 无脊椎的（动物）

passage 2

MP3·378 **[1-6] Listen to part of a lecture in an environmental studies class.**

Professor (female)

Well, class, we've been going over the global fishing industry...and the environmental problems that it causes. Today, let's get more specific. I'm going to give you some information about a particular species of fish...one that's quite popular with consumers: salmon. If you eat fish, you've probably sampled this one. Q1 **But did you know the world's wild salmon populations are in big trouble? They've been on the decline since the beginning of the twentieth century, but, um, recently this trend has picked up alarming speed.** There're two major wild salmon populations...based on geography. One is the Atlantic, living along the eastern coasts of the U.S. and Canada. The other is the Pacific. These guys are found from California up to Alaska...and then over on the other side, off the coast of Russia and down by Japan. Q2 **The Atlantic population is certainly worse off...in fact, it's pretty much disappeared.** Take the U.S. Every river north of Connecticut used to be full of salmon. Now...it's estimated only 50 to 100 individuals inhabit this region. Quite a change. Q2 **Pacific wild salmon...the situation's not as dire for them, but they're struggling**—particularly in the southern reaches...California, Japan, and Q1 **to explain why this fish is vanishing...there're quite a few factors, most of them human related.**

OK. Q3(A) **Issue number one is dams.** Here's how the salmon lifecycle works: They're born far upstream in a river and swim down into the sea. They stay there until it's time to mate...then, in one of nature's amazing feats, they battle the current and swim back

Q1这个讲义文主要关于什么？
(A) 近年来野生大马哈鱼是如何回归自然的。
(B) 野生大马哈鱼数量的减少是人类的活动造成的。
(C) 大马哈鱼农场和环境的关系
(D) 野生和人工饲养的大马哈鱼的数量有何不同。

Q2关于大西洋的野生大马哈鱼教授说了什么？
(A) 它们没有太平洋的同类耐寒。
(B) 它们的处境比太平洋的野生大马哈鱼更悲惨。
(C) 它们现在只在受保护的河流和湖泊中能被发现。
(D) 它们的数量在二十世纪初急剧地减少了。

upstream to where they were born. Once there, they mate...and die. And what does this have to do with dams? Q3(A) **Well, when you dam the rivers, the salmon can no longer make it back to their birthplaces to reproduce. No reproduction, no more salmon population. So that's a huge problem.**

What else? Q3(D) **Um...habitat loss. With an increase in human activities, you tend to see a decrease in salmon habitat. Logging, farming, urban development...all of these are changing the environment. Um, agricultural pesticides and other waste products filter into the rivers, killing off salmon or, um, or otherwise disrupting their migrations.** And where habitat remains, you have the problem of overfishing...people taking out more salmon than can be replaced by natural processes.

And...OK, the last cause of wild salmon decline I want to mention is an interesting one. Q5 MP3•379 **All this time, I've made sure to specify that we're talking about wild salmon,** because...um, **as any of you who've bought salmon at the grocery store probably know, there's wild salmon and there's farmed salmon. Those are salmon raised in specially designed facilities—farms...with the sole purpose of producing consumable fish.** But the interesting thing is, these farmed salmon may be contributing to the decline of wild populations. Studies show wild populations living near salmon farms are shrinking faster than populations that don't have a salmon farm in the area. Why? Q4 **Well, we think that when farmed salmon escape the farms...which they, um, almost certainly do...when this happens, they mix with nearby wild populations and introduce all kinds of strange parasites and diseases. Diseases that were born in the close confines of the farm and which the wild salmon have no immunity to.** That poor salmon that manages to escape the farm...he's actually responsible for killing off a lot of his wild relatives.

Good. So you understand the problem. Q6 MP3•380 **But you still might be asking, why should we care about wild salmon populations? Well, apart from the human interest here—the economy revolving around salmon is huge...** **I mean billions-of-dollars huge.** Um, apart from that, there're some significant issues hinging on the disappearance of wild salmon. Salmon are really one of the biological foundations of their ecosystems. All of those fish migrating upstream to the headwaters of these rivers... they're bringing vital nutrients to habitats that otherwise...uh, wouldn't have many. They provide food to all kinds of animals—birds, bears...many of which are vanishing themselves. And when the salmon die...you know, after reproducing...um, their carcasses

Q3指出下列各项在讲义文中是否被作为造成野生大马哈鱼数量减少的因素出现。勾选每个选项正确的题框。

(A) 河流筑坝，阻碍了大马哈鱼的繁殖。**(YES)**

(B) 把野生大马哈鱼引入到大马哈鱼场的捕获行为。**(NO)**

(C) 由于熊和鸟的消失造成的水分中营养成分的缺乏。**(NO)**

(D) 由于人类发展所导致的栖息地的丧失和恶化。**(YES)**

(E) 由近几十年来旱灾的时间延长引起的水流失。**(NO)**

Q4根据教授所说的，人工饲养的大马哈鱼是如何影响野生大马哈鱼的？

(A) 与其抢夺食物和其他资源。

(B) 补充正在日益减少的大马哈鱼的数量。

(C) 引入了它们没有免疫能力的疾病。

(D) 给基因库加入了更多灵活的基因。

Q5当教授这样说的时候她暗示了：

All this time, I've made sure to specify that we're talking about wild salmon,

(A) 大马哈鱼的处境并不像一开始所设想的那么糟糕。

(B) 她的讨论将会只集中在野生大马哈鱼上。

(C) 其他的鱼类野生物种也正在减少。

(D) 野生的和人工饲养的大马哈鱼要应付不同的环境状况。

provide nutrients to all the plants and animals living in the rivers. Without salmon, entire river ecosystems could very likely collapse, and no one would argue that's a good thing.

Q6为什么教授要这样说：
I mean billions-of-dollars huge.
(A) 为了量化人工饲养的大马哈鱼所引起的环境破坏。
(B) 为了强调大马哈鱼产业的经济价值。
(C) 为了鼓励学生更加严肃认真地对待这个问题。
(D) 为了更正她之前对野生大马哈鱼的评论。

MP3·389

sample 样本
inhabit 栖息
dire 悲惨的
reach 达到
feat 功绩，成就
habitat 栖息地
logging （木材）采运作业
agricultural pesticide 农药
filter into 滤入
disrupt 使中断
facilities （使事情便利的）设备，工具
parasite 寄生虫
confine 限制，使禁闭
apart from 除了
carcass 尸体

passage 3

 MP3·381 **[1-6] Listen to part of a lecture in a biology class.**

Professor (female)

Good morning, everyone. I'd like to get started right away because we've got a lot to cover. I thought we'd go over neurons today and, um...then we'll get into neurology a little bit. Q1 **Um, I think it'd be helpful to start with something in the way of a reminder about what neurons are...their structure and their function in our bodies.** Q5 MP3·382 **I know you've probably learned about them already in your, um, your introductory biology courses,** **<u>but how about a refresher?</u>**

Dictation 开始 So...a general explanation of neurons is that they're cells that make up the nervous system. The nervous system—this [1]*includes the central nervous system,* basically the spine and the brain...and then there's the peripheral nervous system, which includes nerves that run throughout the body. Q1 **Anyway, um, neurons...they [2]*have the job of transmitting information* within the nervous system.**

But let's get a little more specific, OK? Starting with the structure of neurons. You can break them down into three parts: the cell body, the axon, and the dendrites. Is any of this sounding familiar to you? The cell body has the [3]*typical cell components,* like DNA, ribosomes, and mitochondria. Q2(C) **The axon is sort of like a long strand... and it's the axon that's [4]*responsible for sending signals* to other neurons.** Then there are the dendrites—little branch-like threads that, um, stick out of the neuron. Q2(A) **Most neurons have thousands of dendrite branches, and, um, their job is to receive messages from**

Q1这个讲座主要讲了什么？
(A) 神经元有如此的结构的原因
(B) 神经病学历史上的重大突破
(C) 新近发现的治疗严重的神经性疾病的方法
(D) 神经元在人类神经系统中传递信息的途径

Q2在讲座中，教授描述了突触传输的过程。指出下列各项是否在这个过程中发生了。为每个选项勾选正确的方框。
(A) 一个神经元的树状突接收一个信号 **(YES)**
(B) 通过神经元之间的缝隙传递的信号被称为突触 **(YES)**
(C) 一个神经元的轴突把一条信息传递给另一个神经元 **(YES)**
(D) 一个神经元的细胞体直接与突触通信 **(NO)**
(E) 大脑接收单个神经元发出的信号 **(NO)**

other neurons. Axons send, dendrites receive. Got it?

Q1 OK, that [5]***brings us to synaptic transmission***...which is the **process by which neurons transmit information.** So...what's a synapse? Q2(B) **Well, you see...neurons aren't actually in physical contact with each other. They're separated by a small gap, and it's this gap that's called a synapse.** Um, synapses essentially [6]*connect neurons into a network* that, um, that makes the components of our nervous system function, for example, our brain. Q2(B) **What happens is** [7]***electrical and chemical messages cross this gap*** **in order to travel from one neuron to the next.** There're 100 billion neurons in the brain, all making connections with other neurons... and that's, um, basically how our brains work—how we think. Fascinating, isn't it? I mean, your entire nervous system is actually [8]*a system of separate cells*—separate neurons that aren't, um, physically connected. And yet they can [9]*communicate with each other via* synaptic transmission.

Actually, you know...at one point, we used to think the brain was more of a connected, um, meshwork. Q3 **It wasn't until the late nineteenth century that the breakthrough discovery of neurons was made. It was a Spanish physician named Santiago Ramón y Cajal who first realized that—that neurons were separated by gaps—synapses.** His theory about neurons became [10]*known as the neuron doctrine*...and now it's pretty much universally accepted, though it did [11]*take a little while to catch on.* Dictation 结束

Great. Q6 MP3 • 383 **So how is all this knowledge about neurons being applied today? Well, a big subject of study in medical fields right now deals with neurologic diseases...with, um, with a prominent example being Alzheimer's.** And diseases such as Alzheimer's have a lot to do with our neurons...or, actually the damage that's caused to them. Um, there's a lot we still don't know about Alzheimer's...but what we have found is that it, it damages brain cells. Q4(C) **Um, it results in the loss of neurons and synapses in the brain...in the cerebral cortex, which is the part of the brain that handles memory, attention, thought, and language. This causes the brain to lose some of its ability to perform synaptic transmission...so not as much information is being shared between neurons...**or, um, perhaps incorrect information is being shared. Over time, a person suffering from Alzheimer's may develop symptoms like, um, like disorientation, difficulty with abstract thinking, problems finding the right word...let's see, personality changes too, Q4(B) **and problems doing familiar tasks.** Because the necessary information just isn't making it where it needs to go.

Um, that's a quick overview of Alzheimer's. Unfortunately, I don't

Q3为什么教授要提到圣地亚哥·拉蒙·卡哈尔?
(A) 为了确认神经病学的奠基人。
(B) 为了给神经元和突触的发现提供一个时间范围。
(C) 为了描述科学家研究神经元的过程。
(D) 为了暗示神经元的研究仍然存在争议。

Q4讨论中提到的老年痴呆症的特征是什么?勾选两个答案。
(A) 它有可能引发帕金森综合症。
(B) 它使人们在做熟悉的事情时都会有困难。
(C) 它阻断了大脑中突触的传播。
(D) 它的主要症状是逐渐丧失对运动功能的控制。

Q5为什么教授要说这些:
but how about a refresher?
(A) 为了显示她会复习一下某些学生已经学过的知识。
(B) 为了确保学生是否已经完成了生物学引介部分的课程。
(C) 为了询问学生对她所讲述的一些知识的观点。
(D) 为了暗示学生理解讲座的话题可能会有困难。

have time to tell you more about it...or other neurological diseases such as Parkinson's. But maybe we can revisit the topic again next class, OK?

MP3·390

neuron 神经元
neurology 神经病学
reminder 提醒物(=**refresher**)
introductory 介绍性的
central nervous system 中枢神经系统
spine 脊椎
peripheral 周围的
run throughout 匆匆离去
transmit 传输
break down into 分解成
cell body 细胞体
axon 轴突
dendrite 树突
ribosome 核糖体
mitochondrion 线粒体
(**pl. mitochondria**)
strand （线等的）一股，一缕
stick out of 穿过
synaptic transmission 突触传递
synapse 突触
meshwork 网状组织
breakthrough （科学等的）重大突破
doctrine 教条，学说
catch on 流行起来，理解
prominent 卓越的，杰出的
Alzheimer's 阿尔茨海默症(即老年痴呆症）
cerebral cortex 大脑皮层
symptom 症状
disorientation 混乱，错乱
abstract 抽象的，深奥的
Parkinson's 帕金森综合症(发生于中年以上成人黑质和黑质纹状体通路变性疾病）

Q6从教授那里可以推断出什么？
(A) 她想批评有关神经元的知识是如何被应用的。
(B) 她认为学生熟悉现有的医学研究。
(C) 她认为学生应该把阅读神经性疾病的相关知识作为作业。
(D) 她想开始关于神经病学另一个方面的讨论。

P.274

Answer
case example > 1 (B) 2 (C) 3 (D) 4 Corporation → (A), (C) / Partnership → (D) / Neither → (B) 5 (A) 6 (B)
passage 1 > 1 (A) 2 (C) 3 (A), (C) 4 YES → (B), (C), (E) / NO → (A), (D) 5 (A) 6 (A)
passage 2 > 1 (B) 2 (B) 3 (B) 4 YES → (A), (B) / NO → (C), (D), (E) 5 (D) 6 (C)
passage 3 > 1 (B) 2 (C) 3 (B), (D) 4 Ancient Sumer → (B), (E) / Qin Dynasty → (A), (C) 5 (A) 6 (C)

case example

MP3·391 **[1-6] Listen to part of a lecture in a business studies class.**

Professor (female)

I'd like to...to take a step back from our ongoing discussion of the global economy to give you a little background on something that's so, um, fundamental to us that it's...it's hard not to take it for granted. Q1 **I'm talking about the company. Where did companies come from...and why?**

The concept is actually a pretty old one. I mean, businesspeople figured out early on that there were some basic advantages to forming a company. First of all, it gave their business a life of its own. Even if the founders of the business died, the, uh, the company would live on. Also, it set out a fair and structured method for entrepreneurs to pool their resources in order to conduct their business more effectively.

Q5 MP3·392 **So, um...it's no wonder then that we see companies appearing well over 2,000 years ago—in India, ancient Rome of course...perhaps even before that.** We don't know a whole lot about these early companies, but it's clear they were formed for the purpose of conducting business. Moreover, they were subject to certain laws that were drawn up with the specific intent of...of governing such organizations.

Q1 讲义文的主要内容是？
(A) 公司最初得以发展的原因
(B) 公司的历史和类型
(C) 股份公司和公司的区别
(D) 三种最流行的公司类型

Q2 教授为什么提起英国东印度公司？
(A) 为了强调公司的全球影响力。
(B) 为了指明公司对英国殖民成功的贡献。
(C) 为了举出一个著名的殖民公司的例子。
(D) 为了暗示公司是古老的存在实体。

MP3·404
take a step back 采取让步措施，退一步想
ongoing 前进的，进行的
fundamental 基础的，根本的
take it for granted 认为…理所当然
founder 创立者，建立者
set out 制定，阐述
entrepreneur 企业家，承包商
pool resources 集资，公用财产
a whole lot 很多
be subject to 服从于
intent 意图，目的
govern 管理，治理

Moving forward...it wasn't really until the colonial period that we started seeing companies with a lot of the features we might recognize today. Shareholders, limited liability...I'll talk more about these ideas in a minute. Um, these companies were chartered; founded—with permission from their home government, and their purpose was basically to go into other parts of the world and make money by extracting resources and monopolizing trade there. Q2 **Think of the British East India Company...probably the most famous example of this type of business organization—and the most powerful. For about 250 years, it ruled over England's colonies in Asia and made tremendous profits.**

OK, then...um, the rise of the modern company really took off after the Industrial Revolution, which, um...it made so many new technologies possible, and companies stepped in to deliver these countless new products to the public. Q3 **In recent history, we've seen a trend toward consolidation. That is, a powerful company will buy up other smaller companies and form a super-company**...and I'm sure you can come up with many examples of these, but we don't have time for that right now.

Q1 **What I do want to talk about quickly are the...the three most common types of companies in today's world...at least, in the U.S.** Um...often when we call an organization a "company," we're really talking about a "corporation." Q4(A) **The key feature of corporations is they exist independently of their founders, their employees, and their shareholders. They're legally defined as separate entities.** What does that mean? Well, everyone involved with the corporation enjoys something called limited liability. In other words, if the corporation goes bankrupt, no single person is fully responsible for it. The shareholders—the people who invest in the corporation by buying shares—um, they'll lose the money they invested, and the corporation's employees...they'll lose their jobs. Q4(C) **But beyond that, no one is financially responsible for the corporation's failure.** Understand?

Q3教授关于当今世界的公司是怎么说的？
(A) 税务问题正促使大部分公司的管理模式发生改变。
(B) 消费品激增致使更多小公司诞生。
(C) 开始于工业革命时期的趋势很大程度上已经结束。
(D) 最大的公司经常收购一些小公司。

Q4教授阐述了股份公司与合资公司的区别。标示出以下的各项在讲义文中提到哪些作为股份公司或者合资公司的特征。在各短语对应正确的一栏中做出标记。
(A) 独立于它的所有者并作为一个合法的实体。**(Corporation)**
(B) 倘若破产，保护股东免于失去他们的投资。**(Neither)**
(C) 任何人都不会在经济上为公司的失败负责任。**(Corporation)**
(D) 允许公司所有者在纳税问题上省钱。**(Parthership)**

MP3-404

colonial 殖民的
shareholder 股东
limited liability 有限责任
charter（写明某组织或机构的主要职责与原则的）章程，宪章
extract 摘录；榨取
monopolize 垄断
East India Company 东印度公司
rule over 统治，管理
take off 取消，起飞
the Industrial Revolution 工业革命
step in to 介入，干预
consolidation 统一，合并
come up with（针对问题等）提出，想出
corporation 股份公司，法人

Now, contrast that with a partnership. In a partnership, the owner or owners are fully responsible for the company. If it goes into debt, the partners are legally required to pay all the money owed by the company. So...um, they could potentially lose not only the money they invested in the company, but also any other, uh, personal savings or assets they have. Obviously, being a partner is much less secure than being a shareholder, right? Because legally the company is a part of you; it's not a separate entity like a corporation. Q4(D) **But, um, then partnerships also have some benefits that corporations lack...mainly dealing with the taxes they have to pay. In short, corporate profits are often taxed twice—once as income for the corporate entity, and again as income for the shareholders. General partnerships...their income's only taxed once.**

Q6 MP3•393 **OK, very quickly...there're also limited liability companies, and these basically combine the good points of both corporations and partnerships. Um, owners have limited liability, but they also get the tax benefits enjoyed by partnerships. That's a very simplified explanation, but I'm afraid it's all we have time for today.**

Q5教授暗示了什么？

(A) **她提到的那些原因促使古代生意人组成公司。**

(B) 现代学者并不十分确定最初的公司以那样的方式发展的原因。

(C) 古印度和古罗马在最初公司的发展中是相对晚的。

(D) 公司这一概念在印度和罗马是同步发展的。

Q6当教授说这些时，她的意思是？

That's a very simplified explanation, but I'm afraid it's all we have time for today.

(A) 她认为这一概念容易理解。

(B) **她想要之后扩展这个解释。**

(C) 她想要学生在这个问题上自己有更多探索。

(D) 她认为这个问题不重要。

MP3·404

entity 存在，实体
go bankrupt 破产
share 股票
contrast A with B 把A和B作对比
partnership 合资公司
go into debt 欠债(=**owe**)
savings 存款
assets 财产

passage 1

 MP3·394 **[1-6] Listen to part of a talk in a psychology class.**

Professor (male) Q1 Class, I'd like to begin by asking you for a definition of a—a keyword in today's lecture: Inhibition. Would someone be willing to provide a definition for the word "inhibition?"

Student A (female) Um, I can. Inhibition is...um, the control of our basic, our basic intuitive impulses or reactions; self-control.

Professor Yes. Q2 Self-control—that's a good way to describe it. I'm sure all of you have experienced a situation like this: um, you're at the post office, waiting in a long line, when someone cuts in front of you. Your initial reaction might be very angry, but instead of swearing or yelling or making a scene, you politely direct the person to the back of the line. Uh, in this situation, your social inhibition—your self-control—has caused you to, um, to tone down your initial reaction and to respond in a way that's more socially acceptable. Do you see what I'm saying?

Student B (male) Q4(C) You mean social inhibition is what helps us, um, behave in socially acceptable ways?

Professor Yes, that's right.

Student B Q6 MP3·395 So if self-control is closely related to, um, to social behavior and expectations... wouldn't that mean that it's really affected by, um, culture? Since different cultures have different social rules and norms?

Professor Yes, certainly. Self-control is measured differently in different cultures...and even in different time periods within the same culture. I mean, the social expectations that guided your grandparents are different than the ones you're familiar with.

OK. Um...I think I should give you a brief overview of the history of the research in this field of social psychology—the study of social inhibition. One of the most famous researchers is Walter Mischel, a psychologist

Q1讲义文的主要内容是？
(A) 一种控制人类行为的心理现象
(B) 心理学家研究的不同的冲动控制紊乱
(C) 一个有争议的理论的标志性实验
(D) 文化影响人类自制力的方式

Q2教授是怎样引出他自己关于自制力的解释的？
(A) 通过介绍这类研究历史的细节。
(B) 通过暗示自制力已经在很多动物中得到观察。
(C) 通过详述一个普遍的实验作为例子。
(D) 使学生联想起在教室里发生的情景。

MP3·405
inhibition 禁止，抑制（←**inhibit**禁止）
intuitive 直觉的，本能的
impulse 冲动，一时的念头（←**impulsiveness** 冲动）
reaction 反应，反抗
self-control 自制，自我克制
cut in 切入，插嘴
initial 开始的，最初的
swear 发誓，诅咒
make a scene 大吵大闹
direct 直接的，坦率的
tone down 缓和，柔和
acceptable 可接受的
norm 准则，规范
brief overview 简洁概述

associated with Columbia University. Well, um, in the 1960s, he carried out his famous "marshmallow experiment," which tested the self-control of young children. Here's how it worked. Children were given a marshmallow and told that they could eat it whenever they wanted...but if they waited for a certain period of time to eat it, like 15 or 20 minutes, they'd get another marshmallow. Q3(C) **The marshmallow experiment showed that different people have different levels of self-control.** Some children were able to wait long enough to receive a second marshmallow, while others weren't able to wait. They didn't control their desire to eat the first marshmallow.

Student A OK. I get the experiment, but I don't really understand the significance. So some people have more self-control than others. Does it really matter all that much?

Professor Well, that's a valid question. The truth is, most of the research approaches the issue with the belief that self-control is better than, um, impulsiveness. Self-control is, um, viewed as a desirable personality trait. Actually, there's good reason for this belief. So in the marshmallow experiment, for example, children who demonstrated more self-control grew up to be better adjusted and more dependable. Q3(A) **They even averaged higher scores on the SAT.**

Student A That's interesting. Q4(B) **So self-control, in our society at least...it, uh, seems to influence how successful you are.**

Student B I'm curious about something. Are humans the only animals who have this ability or do other animals exhibit—control as well?

Professor Good question. It's tempting to assume that self-control is exclusively a, um, a human skill... but that's not the case. In fact—remember that marshmallow experiment I told you about? Well, researchers replicated that same kind of experiment with pigeons—and they came up with similar results to Mischel's experiment. Evidently, self-control in pigeons is quite similar

Q3讲义文中提到的沃尔特·米契尔进行的的棉花糖实验有哪两个重要发现？标出两个答案。
(A) 自制力与智力测试的表现有关系。
(B) 鸽子的自制力不如人类。
(C) 人类的能力在控制行为时有变化。
(D) 社会把自制力的价值看得比冲动更高。

Q4在讲义文中，教授阐述了人类的社会自制力的一些作用。标示出下列各项是不是社会自制力的一种作用。在各短语对应正确的一栏中做出标记。
(A) 提高自然生存本能。**(NO)**
(B) 增加在生活中体验成功的机会。**(YES)**
(C) 允许用积极的方式与别人互相合作。**(YES)**
(D) 帮助区分正确和错误。**(NO)**
(E) 帮助制定计划、理顺思路。**(YES)**

MP3-405

carry out 实行，执行
valid 有根据的；合法的
personality trait 个性品质，人格特质
well adjusted 完全适应环境的，乐观的
dependable 可靠的，可信赖的
exhibit 展览，展示
tempting 引诱人的，吸引人的
replicate 复制，摹写

to self-control in humans. Pretty interesting, huh? Um, does anyone else have any questions?

Student A Um, getting back to human self-control...what happens when a person has a problem with self-control?

Professor Well, there's no simple answer... Q5 **but self-control appears to be linked to psychological disorders like, um, obsessive gambling, or attention-deficit/hyperactivity disorder.** With attention-deficit/hyperactivity disorder, researchers and experts are starting to recognize that Q4(E) **self-control, which helps people plan, organize, and think...** Q5 **self-control may be behind some of the symptoms of the condition**—like the inability to pay attention in certain situations.

Um, I'm afraid we've got to stop here for today. Please read chapter 11 in your textbooks—it picks up where we're leaving off and discusses other impulse-control disorders in more depth.

Q5关于着迷于赌博和多动症，教授暗示了什么？
(A) **它们很可能是自制力缺乏的结果。**
(B) 它们通过心理治疗可以治愈。
(C) 它们是由痛苦的儿童事件引起的。
(D) 它们是由其他冲动控制失调症导致的。

Q6教授为什么这么说？
I mean, the social expectations that guided your grandparents are different than the ones you're familiar with.
(A) **为了支持她提出的论点。**
(B) 为了暗示人们已经熟悉这个话题。
(C) 为了质疑那个人的结论。
(D) 为了纠正那个人的错误。

MP3·405
be linked to 与…有关
psychological disorder 心理混乱
obsessive gambling 着迷于赌博
attention-deficit/ hyperactivity disorder 注意障碍/多动症

passage 2

 MP3·396 **[1-6] Listen to part of a talk in a history class.**

Professor (female) Q1 **OK, class, as we've been learning over the past few weeks, the world's ancient civilizations invented many of the everyday objects that're so important in our lives today: paper, pottery, the wheel... Well, today, I'd like to add one more item to the list—glass.**

Q1讲义文的主要内容是？
(A) 两种古老文明的发明
(B) **制作玻璃的发展历史**
(C) 古代社会手工艺的使用
(D) 在玻璃制造业中的两项突破

Student A (male) You mean ordinary glass, like we use in windows ...and to make things like bottles?

Professor Um...yes, but the earliest glass didn't, uh, didn't look much like the consistent, clear varieties we're used to. Furthermore it was nowhere near as common as it is today. In fact, it was quite rare and therefore very valuable.

Student B (male) Q6 MP3·397 **So where did glass first appear? Was it in China, India...the Middle East?**

Professor **Well, that's the question everyone would like to have answered.** Unfortunately, we might never learn the truth, because there just isn't enough evidence to prove when and where glass manufacturing first occurred. However, we do have a rough idea.

Student A Professor...doesn't glass occur naturally, like in volcanic eruptions and other, um, natural events?

Professor Yes, you're right about that. We also know that ancient humans sculpted natural glass into things like knife blades...and maybe jewelry. Q2 **But what I want to focus on right now is the actual manufacture of glass by humans.** OK, where was I? Right. Dictation 开始 Q2 [1]***The earliest evidence of manmade glass* we have comes in the form of pottery glaze...the stuff added to the outside of ceramic pottery that** [2]***gives it that bright sheen.*** We're talking as early as 5000 BC here.

Student B Are glazes considered to be glass? The two things sound pretty different to me.

Professor Yes, well, that's very true. But what the glazes represent is the ability to create glass, because the ingredients are pretty much the same. There's the silica first of all—sand, in other words. Then to that you add [3]*certain substances that lower the melting point* and add strength and color. Q3 **So, as I was about to say, the first true human-made glass appeared around 2500 BC** [4]***in the form of decorative beads.*** Q4(B) **The problem for historians, though, is they're found in both Egypt and Mesopotamia...and no one knows for sure where they appeared first.**

Q2 教授为什么提到陶器上的釉?
(A) 为了举出在玻璃制作之前出现的一种工艺。
(B) 为了指出人造玻璃的第一个证据。
(C) 为了解释只有很少的早期玻璃可以研究的原因。
(D) 为了介绍玻璃的构成成分。

Q3关于公元前2500年的玻璃珠子,教授是怎么说的?
(A) 它们是由火山形成的玻璃雕刻出的。
(B) 它们是第一个真正的合成玻璃的例子。
(C) 它们早于欧洲的陶器。
(D) 它们在埃及和美索不达米亚还未被发现。

MP3·406
consistent 一贯的,始终如一的
rough 粗糙的,粗略的
volcanic eruption 火山爆发
sculpt 雕刻
blade 刀刃
glaze 釉
sheen 光泽,光辉
ingredient 成分,原料
silica 硅石,矽土
melting point 熔点
decorative 装饰性的
bead 珠子,滴,
crafter 工匠
hollow 空的,虚伪的
core 核心,
mold 模子,模型
dip A into B 把A滴进B中

For the next 1,500 years, development in glassmaking in both of these places seems to [5]*have followed a similar course.* In 1500 BC, glass crafters figured out how to make hollow containers out of glass. They did this [6]*by creating a core mold from hardened clay,* then either dipping this core into melted glass...uh, or spreading the liquid glass over the core with a special tool. Once the glass cooled, the clay core would be removed. Now...this often worked better in theory than reality. A lot of times, it was impossible to remove the core completely, [7]*leaving patches of residue that made the glass pretty impure.* So, as I was saying earlier, the first glass looked a lot different from the stuff we're used to.

But back to the big debate. We're just not sure [8]*whether these innovations in glassmaking* happened in Egypt or Mesopotamia.

Student B Why is it so hard to tell?

Professor Q4(A) **Well, these civilizations were very close to one another, and they traded with each other all the time.** So, for example, if Mesopotamian glassmakers figured out [9]*how to make hollow glass vases,* this knowledge would've been very quickly transported to Egypt, [10]*and vice versa.*Dictation 结束

Some historians claim that Egyptians never actually produced their own glass, they just purchased it from Mesopotamia and worked with it to create different objects. But when the ruins of the Egyptian city Amarna were uncovered in the late 1800s, archaeologists found the remains of what many believe was a glassmaking facility. So certainly there's evidence for Egyptian glass manufacturing.

Student A Professor, you mentioned earlier that glass during this time was pretty rare. When did it become more commonplace?

Professor Good question. Q5 **There were a couple of key events that led to an explosion in glass manufacturing, and the first was the discovery of glassblowing in the first century BC.** This

Q4指出下列哪些是讲义文中提到的造成制作玻璃的起源地很难确定的因素。在各短语对应正确的一栏中做出标记。
(A) 美索不达米亚和埃及的贸易联系紧密。**(YES)**
(B) 历史学家在两个不同地方都找到了早期的玻璃。**(YES)**
(C) 在埃及发现了玻璃制造设备，而美索不达米亚则没有。**(NO)**
(D) 火山玻璃早在人们学会制作玻璃之前就存在了。**(NO)**

Q5关于使得玻璃成为一种普通产品的革命，教授暗示了什么？
(A) 它是走向更大的工业革命的重要一步。
(B) 它得到欧洲和中东文化交流的帮助
(C) 它因在欧洲社会宗教影响力的提高而得到促进。
(D) 它是促使更高效玻璃制造新技术产生的结果。

Q6教授这样说的理由是？
Well, that's the question everyone would like to have answered.
(A) 为了找出其他学生是否也在思考同一件事。
(B) 为了暗示玻璃的历史还未被完全研究清楚。
(C) 为了表明没人能确定这个事实。
(D) 为了鼓励学生自己去探索这个问题。

occurred somewhere along the Mediterranean's east coast. Basically, by creating intricate molds and blowing molten glass into them with thin metal tubes, the process of producing glass items was revolutionized.

Then, as the Roman Empire expanded across much of the known world, it took the knowledge of glassblowing with it, and many cultures adopted the craft. Throughout the next millennium, new innovations took place slowly in Europe and other parts of the world. Sheet glass first started to appear in northern Europe in the 11th century, leading to the first use of glass in windows. Stained glass production became a major industry...which, um, is still evident in old European churches. Later, the Industrial Revolution made possible the mass production of glass, turning it into the everyday object we're familiar with.

MP3·406

patch 补丁，小片
residue 残渣，剩余
impure 不纯的，肮脏的
vice versa 反之亦然
ruins 遗址，遗迹
uncover 揭开，揭露
remains 遗址，废墟
commonplace 平常的，一般的
explosion 爆炸，激增
glassblowing 吹制玻璃
intricate
blow A into B 把A吹进B里
molten 熔化的
revolutionize 变革
sheet glass 玻璃片
mass production 大量生产

passage 3

MP3·398 **[1-6] Listen to part of a lecture in a politics class.**

Professor (male)

Q2 Are any of you members of the armed forces? Even if you're not, you still probably know a little bit about the military and can picture what the organizational structure is like, right? The military is known for its rules and its hierarchy. It's also a good example of a sociological concept that Q1 I want to discuss today: bureaucracy. Q5 MP3·399 Do all of you understand what I'm talking about when I say "bureaucracy?" The word carries with it a negative connotation, doesn't it? In the United States at least, our popular culture represents bureaucracies as inefficient and—and negative. So let me clarify: Dictation 开始 **Q2 Bureaucracy is simply the formal control structure found in large organizations...like the military, as I mentioned,** and also in organizations like governments, corporations, schools...that kind of thing. In a bureaucracy, there's 1) *a set of standardized regulations* that control how just about all the procedures within the organization are carried out. Bureaucracy also 2) *divides the organization into a hierarchy and allocates different powers* to different, um, offices or groups within the organization. The, um, the point of bureaucracy is to, to have everything organized

Q1 讲义文的主要内容是？
(A) 与官僚有关的问题和危险
(B) 官僚的历史和特征
(C) 现在对官僚的普遍误解
(D) 世界上最早的官僚机构的发展

MP3·407

armed forces 武装力量
hierarchy 等级制度，层级
bureaucracy 官僚机构
negative connotation 消极含义
popular culture 通俗文化
inefficient 效率低的
clarify 澄清，阐明
standardized regulations 标准条例
procedure 程序，手续
office 处，所
allocate A to B 把A分配给B

in the most efficient way possible.

Q3 **One of the most famous scholars of bureaucracy, Max Weber ...he identified certain characteristics that, um, that define a bureaucracy. Here they are:** Q3(D) **First, it has written rules that help [3]*ensure operations in the organization run smoothly.***

Q6 MP3·400 **Second, there's a clear hierarchy—** **you know what I mean by "hierarchy," right? Good.** Third, power in the organization is associated with certain positions and offices, not the individuals themselves. Fourth, new employees are hired [4]*based on their expertise or their performance* on an entrance examination. Fifth, record keeping and communication within the organization must be [5]*formal and impartial.* Q3(B) **And finally...um, staff within the organization must be paid for their work.**

Q1 **OK, so now you have a basic idea of what bureaucracy is, and some of its features. Let's move on and talk a little bit about [6]*how this concept originated.*** Well...the term itself came from the word "bureau," which, um, during the 18th century, was used in Western Europe to mean an office. The second half of the term, the "cracy" part, comes from the Greek "kratos," um, which means something like "power" or "rule."

Now, although the concept of bureaucracy has changed over time, the basic idea has been around for quite a while. Q4(B) **In fact, its development seems to be [7]*closely linked to the origin of writing.*** Q4(E) **One of the earliest examples of, um, of bureaucracy can be found back in ancient Sumer, where a bureaucracy made up of priests developed to deal with, well, property-related issues and to collect taxes.** That sort of thing. Q4(B) **Of course, none of this would've been possible without written records...and the Sumerians are [8]*considered to have one of the oldest written languages.*** They used picture-like characters known as cuneiforms, which they inscribed on, uh, on clay tablets to produce the official written records for their early bureaucracy.[Dictation 结束]

A more, um, modern style of bureaucracy arose under the Qin Dynasty in China...um, which lasted from 221 BC to 206 BC. Q4(C) **The Qin created a, um, a central bureaucracy and established an intricate code of law that listed punishments for all sorts of crimes.** The bureaucracy that formed during this period of time was adopted by later successful dynasties. Q4(A) **Later on, imperial entrance examinations became an important part of bureaucratic life in China, and scholar-bureaucrats had to, um, to pass these difficult exams before they could become officials.**

After the Industrial Revolution, bureaucracies became larger and more complex...and, naturally, some problems developed. In

Q2教授为什么提到军队？
(A) 为了确认"bureaucracy"这个词的起源。
(B) 为了将军队的目的与其他官僚机构的目的相比较。
(C) 为了解释官僚组织这一概念。
(D) 为了解释官僚机构被普遍批评的原因。

Q3根据学者马克斯·韦伯，官僚机构的两个特征是什么？请选择两项正确答案。
(A) 它们的成员是根据书面推荐来选择。
(B) 它们由挣工资的雇员管理。
(C) 权利集中于特定的个别成员。
(D) 它们的管理按照成文的规定进行。

Q4在讲义文中，教授介绍了在古代苏美尔和中国秦朝历史上的官僚机构的功能。将每种功能对应正确的文明。其中一个选项将不会用到。点击相应正确的空格。
(A) 建立一种官员选拔考试制度。**(Qin Dynasty)**
(B) 促进书面语的发展。**(Ancient Sumer)**
(C) 设立一种犯罪惩罚制度。**(Qin Dynasty)**
(D) 控制政府部门的腐败。
(E) 帮助税务征收。**(Ancient Sumer)**

MP3·407
identify 确认，识别
expertise 专门知识（或技能等），专长
performance on 在…上的表现
record keeping 记录保持
impartial 公平的，公正的
priest 教士，神父
property 财产，所有物
collect tax 收税

government bureaucracies, this meant that there was more and more money involved, and so corruption became a bigger and bigger issue. Actually, around the end of the 19th century, it became necessary to actually, um, impose some reforms to deal with the problems of corruption in government bureaucracies. In the United States, the Pendleton Civil Service Reform Act was created in 1883 to help make sure that government employees were being hired because of their qualifications and service records...not just because they voted for the people in power. Nonetheless, the word "bureaucracy" still conjures a negative image...as I was saying earlier.

Q5教授为什么这样说？
The word carries with it a negative connotation, doesn't it?
(A) 为了证明对一个词的普遍偏见。
(B) 为了将美国和其它国家进行比较。
(C) 为了提出自己对官僚机构的看法。
(D) 为了对一种流行观点提出怀疑。

Q6当教授这样说时，她的意思是？
You know what I mean by "hierarchy," right? Good.
(A) 他认为这个概念对讲义文主题不重要。
(B) 他想要学生密切注意下一个观点。
(C) 他认为自己不必解释这个词。
(D) 他认为这个时候不适合解释这个词。

MP3-407

cuneiform 楔形文字
inscribe 题写，铭刻于
clay tablet 粘土桌子
arise 产生，出现
Qin Dynasty 秦朝
imperial 帝国的，帝王的
bureaucrat 官僚主义者
corruption 腐败
impose 强加于，征(税等)
reform 改革，变革
the Pendleton Civil Service Reform Act 彭德尔顿法文官制度改革法
conjure （令人）想起

Answer case example > 1 (D) 2 YES → (A), (B), (E) / NO → (C), (D) 3 (B) 4 (D) 5 (B) 6 (A)
passage 1 > 1 (D) 2 (B), (C) 3 (D) 4 (B) 5 (A)
passage 2 > 1 (A) 2 (D) 3 (B) 4 YES → (B), (C) / NO → (A), (D), (E) 5 (C), (D) 6 (A)
passage 3 > 1 (C) 2 (D) 3 YES → (B), (D) / NO → (A), (C), (E) 4 (C) 5 (C) 6 (C)

case example

MP3·408 **[1-6] Listen to part of a talk in an American history class.**

Professor (female) Well, class. I think we did a pretty good job last time summing up the political achievements of Thomas Jefferson. Who wants to list some of those, just to refresh our memories?

Student A (male) Um...well, he was the third U.S. president...

Professor And...?

Student A And he concluded the Louisiana Purchase with France that pretty much doubled the size of the country at the time.

Student B (male) Also, he was the main author of the Declaration of Independence. So he played a major role in, in helping the country achieve independence from England.

Professor Very good. And don't forget his influential views on the philosophy known as republicanism. Q1 **But today I want to shift our focus slightly. Because...it's obvious Jefferson had a profound impact on America as a politician. You see, he was also a philosopher—a thinker...and one of the subjects he contributed greatly to was architecture.** Q5 MP3·409 **In fact, one of his designs has been recognized by the American Institute of Architects as being the country's most significant architectural achievement.** **But I'll get to that in a second.**

What's interesting to think about is that Jefferson was a, a self-taught architect. Yes, he attended college, but at that time there were no programs in the U.S. concentrating on architecture. So he ...most of his knowledge on the subject came

Q1讲义文的主要内容是？
(A) 杰弗逊对美国学术界的影响
(B) 杰弗逊在美国建立过程中所起的作用
(C) 杰弗逊做驻法大使的经历
(D) 杰弗逊作为美国建筑师的成就

Q2判断下列哪些是讲义文中提到的新古典主义的特征。在各短语相应正确的一栏中做出标记。
(A) 在法国建筑中能够见到。**(YES)**
(B) 从古罗马主题中受到启发。**(YES)**
(C) 结合了欧洲和亚洲传统的特征。**(NO)**
(D) 诞生于新兴美国这一理想。**(NO)**
(E) 为了与现代相联系。**(YES)**

MP3·422
sum up 总结，概括
refresh A's memory 恢复某人的记忆
conclude 缔结，结束
the Declaration of Independence 独立宣言
republicanism 共和主义
shift focus 转移焦点
profound 深远的，渊博的
contribute to 对…做出贡献

from books, especially those written by the Italian Renaissance architect Andrea Palladio. Then of course, Jefferson also go to—well, hold on. Q6 MP3·410 **He was also able to study classical architecture firsthand, and you all should be able to tell me when that was. Anybody?**

Student B Um...he...went to France, right? As the U.S. ambassador? That was in the 1780s, I think. Maybe he got to study some of the architecture over in Europe.

Professor Right...that's exactly what I meant. As we discussed, Jefferson was the American ambassador to France from 1785 to '89. Q2(A) **So some of the architectural styles he read about—um, much of which belonged to the school of neo-classicism—a lot of that type of architecture was on display in Paris and other parts of France.** Do you all know what neo-classicism refers to?

Student A Q2(B) **It's based on, um, Roman ideals, isn't it? Styles and, and ideals that were popular in ancient Rome?**

Professor **Yeah, pretty much. "Ideals" is a good word. Neo-classicism emphasizes the ideals of the classical world...ancient Greece and Rome, but** it doesn't just seek to copy those ideals. Q2(E) **Proponents of neo-classicism wanted to take them and reinterpret them for modern times.** That's something Jefferson was very interested in. After all...he was closely involved with the founding...the "design," we could say, of a brand-new nation, right?

Student B So...what are some examples of Jefferson's architectural work? Are any of his buildings still around?

Professor Yes, they sure are. I mentioned just a minute ago that one of his works has been called the most significant architectural achievement in America, remember? And that would be the central campus of the University of Virginia, a school which Jefferson actually founded.

Student A You're saying he founded it and designed the

Q3关于弗吉尼亚大学的建筑教授说了什么？
(A) 它们用来表现希腊和罗马庄严的历史。
(B) 它们用来激发讨论和思考。
(C) 它们的设计主要是法国风格。
(D) 它们是模仿华盛顿重要建筑建造的。

Q4教授为什么提起美国联邦办公大楼？
(A) 为了阐明她之前提到的新古典主义思想的意义。
(B) 为了暗示杰弗逊的政策影响他的建筑风格。
(C) 为了列举杰弗逊的一些不大知名的建筑作品。
(D) 为了说明弗吉尼亚大学在美国建筑业中的重要性。

MP3·422

concentrate on 集中于，专心于
Italian Renaissance 意大利文艺复兴
firsthand 直接地，第一手
school （中、小）学校，学院，大学
neo-classicism 新古典主义
ideal 理想，典范
proponent 支持者，拥护者
reinterpret 重新解释
found 创立，创办
brand-new 全新的，崭新的

buildings?

Professor Correct. Let me describe the layout of this campus. There's a rectangular open area called the Lawn. On either side of the Lawn, there's a row of buildings...intended to be places where both students and professors would live, teach, and learn. And these buildings show a variety of influences, from Greek to French to Italian... even some Chinese themes are thrown in there. But everything is synthesized into a very neo-classical arrangement. Then, at the north end of the Lawn stands the main structure, the Rotunda...pretty much a miniature replica of the Pantheon in Rome. This houses the library. Jefferson referred to this campus as his "academical village," where residents could devote themselves to the pursuit of knowledge. Q3 **All the diverse styles he included in the buildings...they were meant to inspire debate and encourage academic investigation.**

Student B OK, I think I understand what Jefferson was going for... Q4 **but why is this campus considered to be the most important work in American architecture?**

Professor **Because it really determined the direction of American design. That's why most government buildings in the U.S., from town halls to courthouses to the federal buildings in Washington...as well as college campuses everywhere—they all feature this strikingly neo-classical style. The Greek pillars...the symmetrical shapes.** Jefferson is largely responsible for the adoption of this style throughout the country.

There's also the Virginia State Capitol building, which Jefferson modeled after the Maison Carree, an ancient Roman temple he saw in France. And of course his home, Monticello, which features many of the same neo-classical elements. These are just the most famous examples of Thomas Jefferson's architecture. I mean, he created many other designs for buildings that he never got around to

Q5教授为什么这样说？
But I'll get to that in a second.
(A) 为了对杰弗逊的一个具体设计展开讨论。
(B) 为了表明她还没准备好讨论这个重要观点。
(C) 为了暗示之前的评论与讲义文无关。
(D) 为了让学生了解下面课程的目的。

Q6当教授这样说时她的意思是？
Anybody?
(A) 她想让学生推断杰弗逊是学习建筑的过程。
(B) 她认为学生对该主题的了解应该比他们看似了解的多。
(C) 她想让学生们对古典建筑给出一个定义。
(D) 她认为某些学生已经学过古典建筑。

MP3-422
layout 安排，设计
rectangular 长方形的，矩形的
a row of 一排，一行
synthesize 综合，合成
arrangement 安排，布置
replica 复制品
house 议院，房子
devote oneself to 献身于…
courthouse 法院
federal 联邦政府的
strikingly 引人注目地，显著地，突出地
pillar 柱子
symmetrical 对称的，均匀的
adoption 采用，收养
model after 仿照
get around to *doing* 着手干…

constructing. But, as I've explained, the work he did complete had a huge impact.

passage 1

MP3·411 **[1-5] Listen to part of a conversation between a student and a librarian.**

Student (male) Hello, I was wondering if you could help me with something.

Librarian (female) Oh, of course. What is it you need help with today?

Student Q1 **Um...I'm just getting started on my senior thesis.**

Librarian **OK, so you're looking for resources to help you map out your project?**

Student **Right. Um, my professor said that I should come to the library and look through some journals in order to get an idea of, um, of what I might want to spend the rest of the year writing about.**

Librarian That's good advice. So, have you narrowed down your, um, your subject at all?

Student Well...the thing is, I couldn't really find many journals here in the library. I mean, I saw a handful of options...but I guess I was expecting that there'd be a lot more to look through.

Librarian Well, we've got tens of thousands of e-journals available... *[pause]* You browsed around the library's online database?

Student *[confused]* Online database? No...I was just looking through the journals up on the third floor, in the Sheldon Wing.

Librarian *[understanding]* Oh, well that's the problem, yeah, we really don't have many journals up there...just a couple current issues of some of the most popular ones. For specialized research—like the kind you'll be doing for your thesis—it's not very helpful. You'll be doing most of your research through the online database.

Student Oh.

Librarian See, these days the library just can't afford to

Q1这个人需要从图书馆得到什么？
(A) 图书馆保存的一系列学术杂志。
(B) 进入图书馆期刊数据库的许可。
(C) 怎样检查期刊的建议。
(D) 为一个重要任务查阅资料。

Q2根据这个女人所说的，数字期刊代替印刷杂志有哪两个好处？选出两个答案。
(A) 数字期刊包含最新的文章。
(B) 在数字期刊中更容易看到整个文章。
(C) 数字期刊节省图书馆的空间。
(D) 保存数字期刊不需要花费图书馆任何费用。

MP3·423
senior thesis 学士论文
map out 详细制定，筹划
journal 杂志，期刊
narrow down （论文等）缩小范围
a handful of 一把，一小撮
look through （从头至尾）浏览，详尽核查
browse (around) 逛逛，随便看看
wing 翼，翅膀
specialized 专业的，专业化的
can't afford to *do* 负担不起

house all of the journals we'd like to offer our students. Q2(C) **There're so many academic journals out there—we just don't have space here for comprehensive archives.**

But lucky for us, many journal titles have been digitized—it's much more efficient to subscribe to online sources like JSTOR and LexisNexis. See, these kinds of archives have the same benefit as physically storing journals in the library: having them available for long-term use. Q2(B) **But with online archives there's an additional benefit—it's a lot easier to search the full text of articles.**

Student Yeah, I see how that makes sense for the library... Q4 MP3•412 **but, well, I've actually visited the JSTOR site online before...but you have to pay to access the articles.**

Librarian **Oh no, no. As long as you're a student here, you have free access.** The university pays for a subscription, so we can offer our students free access to all of the journals in the database. It's easy to log in with the computers in the lab on the third floor. Um, there's an icon on the desktop for the e-journal page of the library website. Q5 MP3•413 **From there, you can browse online journals that are available for students through different sources...and if you'd like to look at the full text of an article, all you have to do is enter your university ID and password. Got it?**

Student **Uh...OK. *[sounding uncertain]* So, uh, I go to the library website, and, uh, then I click on...uh...**

Librarian **Here, let me show you on my computer.** Just click on the button that says "e-research." It's that easy. Let's go even further and find a journal that might be useful for your thesis. What's your field of study?

Student Oh, I'm an American history major. As far as my thesis goes...um, I read this really interesting article over spring break about, um, Karr v. Schmidt—you know, that, um, that case in the '70s about that student who wasn't allowed to enroll in school because his hair was too

Q3这个人的毕业论文主题是?
(A) 美国教育系统的最新进展
(B) 数字期刊中科研刊物的特征
(C) 美国法院在19世纪60、70年代的决策
(D) 美国少数群体的言论自由

Q4她为什么这么说?
Oh no, no.
(A) 为了暗示他不需要访问JSTOR网站。
(B) 为了表明他不需要付费。
(C) 为了拒绝他使用在线网络的请求。
(D) 为了解释他没资格进入网站。

MP3•423

house 房屋，议院
comprehensive 综合的
archive 档案
digitize 使数字化
subscribe to 订阅
(←**subscription**预订，预约)
physically 按照自然规律，物理上
long-term 长期的
access 入口，通道
field 领域
spring break 春假
enroll in 成为…的一员，报名参加

long... Q3 **Well, that got me thinking about the history of freedom of expression...in the '60s and '70s, um, especially as it pertains to, to social groups that have faced persecution in American culture, like the gay community...and black students. I'd really love to write about that for my thesis,** but I just wasn't sure if there'd be enough, um, enough source material to work with.

Librarian Well, I just did a quick search and came up with a couple of possibilities. Here's an article called *Personhood: The Right to be Let Alone*, and here's another one: *Flaunting the Freak Flag: Karr v. Schmidt and the Great Hair Debate in American High Schools, 1965–1975*. Seems like that one might be pretty useful for you.

Student Thanks, that's a great place to start.

Librarian If you need to do a little more brainstorming on your topic and need some inspiration, you might want to check out *Reviews in American History*, *The Journal of American History*, and *The American Historical Review*. They're all great journals.

Student I really appreciate your help. I think I'll go up to the third floor computer lab and see what kind of sources I can find.

Q5关于这个男人，能够推断出？

(A) 他对这个女人介绍的程序感到迷惑。

(B) 他对自己的电脑技术没信心。

(C) 他怀疑这个女人的介绍不正确。

(D) 他不太确定怎样进入图书馆网站。

MP3-423

pertain to 从属，隶属
persecution 迫害
come up with 提出，想出
personhood 人格
flaunt 夸耀，（厚颜无耻地）炫耀
freak 怪物
brainstorming 头脑风暴
inspiration 灵感

passage 2

 MP3·414 **[1-6] Listen to part of a lecture in an American art class.**

Professor (female)

Class, we've been talking about the Inca all this month, but today I'd like to focus on another culture, one that occupied that same region...uh, roughly modern-day Peru. Only, they were there long before the Inca. I'd like to spend today's period discussing the Nazca.

Q2 **Maybe some of you are familiar with the Nazca culture because you've seen a documentary about—or even visited, maybe—the Nazca lines in Peru.** Um, in case you haven't heard of the Nazca lines before, they're these huge geoglyphs—drawings on the ground in the high desert of Peru. They're really impressive—drawings of monkeys, hummingbirds, fish...and other animals too. The images were made by, uh, by removing the dark-colored pebbles that cover the desert surface...which exposed a contrasting lighter-colored surface beneath. But enough about that—um, it's just one part of the Nazca culture...and it's not the main focus of my lecture today.

OK. Well. It's important to point out that the Nazca culture fits into a period in the history of the Andes region known as the Early Intermediate Period, when societies like the Nazca and its contemporaries were developing advanced artistic heritages. In fact, we sometimes refer to them as "Master craftsman" cultures, since the quality of their art is so impressive. Q1 **And it's one of their art forms that I want to talk about today, in fact, their pottery.**

Nazca ceramics are referred to as polychrome, which literally means "many colored." When we're talking about pottery, polychrome refers to work that's, uh, that's got three or more colors on it. So keep that in mind as we go on. Dictation 开始 Um, Nazca pottery is known for its use of color. Q3 **It's also important to note that the Nazca had no system of writing. Instead, they used iconography—or symbolic signs and images—to communicate.** In studying Nazca pottery...um, it gives us a chance to study [1] *all kinds of examples of their iconography.* Some of the iconography seen on Nazca ceramics is based in nature, with motifs like, uh, like plants, animals, birds—that sort of thing. Then [2] *there're supernatural themes,* which sort of anthropomorphize or give human-like features to the different spirits the Nazca believed in.

Q6 MP3·415 **From what we can tell, Nazca ceramics were used for [3] *a pretty wide variety of purposes.* Oh, some of it was ceremonial...some of it was used in burial contexts...and some of it**

Q1 教授主要讨论的是纳斯卡人的哪个方面？

(A) 他们制作的陶艺的特征

(B) 他们与印加人和安迪斯山脉地区人们的关系

(C) 他们的肖像研究对陶器设计的影响

(D) 在他们的艺术中找到的一些中心主题

Q2 教授为什么提到纳斯卡线条？

(A) 为了介绍所有纳斯卡艺术中体现的某种概念。

(B) 为了给出纳斯卡环境的背景知识。

(C) 为了解释纳斯卡文明消失的原因。

(D) 为了说明学生可能听说过纳斯卡文明的原因。

Q3 关于纳斯卡陶器上装饰的图案，教授说了什么？

(A) 它们是用单色制作的。

(B) 它们用在书面语的地方。

(C) 它们在经历几个世纪变迁后没有很大的变化。

(D) 它们与纳斯卡线条上图案的不同。

MP3·424

geoglyph 地理学

hummingbird 蜂鸟

pebble 卵石

contrasting 形成鲜明对比的，截然不同的

fit into 适应，符合

contemporary 当代的

heritage 遗产

master craftsman 巨匠

polychrome 多色的，彩饰的

iconography 图解，图解书

shows scratches and wear from use—so [4]*obviously not all of it was devoted to*, um, burial practices and such.
OK, moving on... Oh, we haven't talked much about the shapes of Nazca pottery, so let's do that. Well, there're the kind of [5]*utilitarian forms most of us are familiar with*, like bowls and jars and plates and things like that, but there're also interesting effigy vessels, which resemble human or animal figures. The most esteemed shape of all was the, uh, the double spout bottle—sort of like a round jug with two spouts on top. These jugs generally had the [6]*most detailed drawings of supernatural features* of all the Nazca pottery forms. Q4(C) **And there was also an assortment of other types of ceramic shapes, like panpipes, drums, and whistles.**
As you might imagine, Nazca pottery changed over time. Q4(B) **The culture began around 100 BC, and early Nazca pottery was** [7]***mostly plain and undecorated***, usually, um—**thin-walled vessels... most commonly bottles in the shape of a human effigy.** Sometimes it would be adorned with, uh, thick and uneven slip—uh, that's a [8]*decorative paint made out of watery clay*. Q5(D) **Um, and remember how I said Nazca pottery is polychrome? Well, at first only three colors were used—red, white, and black. But later on, as many as 12 colors were used.** Q5(C) **For quite some time, um, naturalism and realism prevailed in Nazca ceramic designs. Eventually, though,** [9]***supernatural motifs became more prominent.*** Later pottery designs suggest that the culture experienced some changes in social organization as well...and they perhaps [10]*witnessed a transfer of power from the coastal region to the highlands.* Dictation 结束
Um, we're out of time for now. Next time, we're going to pick up where we're leaving off today and talk about some specific Nazca motifs, like, uh, the Mythical Killer Whale...and the Harvester.

Q4在讲义文中，教授描述了纳斯卡陶器的特点。判断哪些是纳斯卡陶器的特点。在相应的一栏中标记出来。
(A) 大部分类似植物、动物和其它的自然形态。**(NO)**
(B) 早期瓶子做成了人类身体的形状。**(YES)**
(C) 一些陶器用来发出声音。**(YES)**
(D) 葬礼仪式上使用的是双嘴的罐子。**(NO)**
(E) 它们大都用于实际生产 **(NO)**

Q5一直以来纳斯卡陶器的风格以哪两种方式改变？选出两项正确答案。
(A) 从强调神话虎鲸到注重收割者。
(B) 从只展示港口主题到包含不同高地景象。
(C) 从专注于现实设计到更多的超自然主题。
(D) 从运用三个标准色到更多颜色。

Q6教授这样说的理由是？
Oh, we haven't talked much about the shapes of Nazca pottery,
(A) 为了暗示她接下来会讨论。
(B) 为忽略一些信息而道歉。
(C) 为了确认一个普遍的误解。
(D) 为了确保学生已经完全理解了。

MP3·424

motif 主题，主旨
supernatural 超自然的
anthropomorphize 人格化，赋与人性
burial 葬礼
context 上下文，环境
be devoted to 忠诚于
utilitarian 功利的
effigy vessel 雕像容器
esteemed 受尊敬的
spout 喷出，滔滔不绝地说
jug 水壶，监牢
assortment 分类
panpipe 牧羊神的笛子，排笛
whistle 哨子
adorn 装饰
uneven 不平坦的，不均匀的
slip 滑倒，溜走
prevail 盛行，获胜
highland 高地
leave off 停止，中断
mythical 神话的
killer whale 虎鲸
harvester 收割者

passage 3

MP3•416 **[1-6] Listen to part of a talk in an American history class.**

Professor (male) Class, I'm pretty excited today, because we're going to be exposing one of the biggest misconceptions about American history. Are you ready? Q5 MP3•417 **So...someone please tell me when democracy was introduced to America.**

Student A (female) **Well, that would be 1776, wouldn't it? With the Declaration of Independence and the...uh, the formation of the new American government.**

Professor **That's exactly what I wanted you to say ...but I'm afraid your answer isn't correct.** You see, as I'm about to explain, democracy existed in America long before the colonists decided to, uh—break from England.

Student B (male) Professor, are you referring to Native American societies? I've read that they were run in a pretty democratic way.

Professor No, that's not the topic for today, but I'm glad you brought it up. You're right—most Native American tribes made decisions very democratically. You'll learn all about that in our next unit. Q1 **But, no...today's lecture is dedicated to the forms of government established by British American colonists—in the original thirteen colonies.**

Student A Q6 MP3•418 **Oh...so you're saying the colonies were democracies, even though they were part of England?**

Professor **That's right. But, um...let me just make sure we're clear on something.** **The term "democracy" is pretty broad.** I mean, there're several different types. Take ancient Greece, for example...which is where this form of government first appeared. The Greek city-states were examples of direct democracies. In other words, each person had one vote on all issues. Obviously, that's different than the democracies we know today, yes?

Student B Yeah, I think modern democracies are mostly

Q1讲义文的主要内容是？
(A) 民主的美洲印地安人社会
(B) 1776年美国政府的建立
(C) 殖民地时期的美国政府体系
(D) 英国议会的结构

Q2教授为什么提到英国议会？
(A) 为了指出美国与英国民主的不同。
(B) 为了暗示英国继承了希腊的民主。
(C) 为了强调共和与君主制的联系。
(D) 为了让学生注意英国议会的一个民主要素。

MP3·425

misconception 误解
democracy 民主
(←**democratic**民主的)
the Declaration of Independence 独立宣言
colonist 殖民地居民，殖民者
Native American 美洲印地安人
tribe 部落，种族
be dedicated to 致力于…
city-state (古代)城邦
direct democracy 直接民主制

representative democracies, right?

Professor Dictation 开始 Exactly. And what's a representative democracy?

Student B Um, [1] *the general public elects certain people* to represent them...and their interests. Like the U.S. Congress.

Professor Uh-huh. And these representatives, while they're [2] *charged with representing the interests of the people,* they don't just carry out [3] *the exact will of the people.* No. They have the power to take actions that they feel will benefit the people they represent. And that's what we mean by representative democracy.

Student A Q3(B) **So I guess the governments of the American colonies were representative democracies...not direct ones.**

Professor **Yes, that's right.** Any idea why that would be? Where that influence came from? No? Well, England of course. I mean, the people founding these colonies were English after all. So when it came time to [4] *choose a method of governance*...they simply went with what they knew. Q2 **And England—it was a monarchy, yes, but partially democratic as well. There was the English Parliament, [5] *a body of elected ministers responsible for,* um, for passing laws and such. We saw something similar in the colonies.**

Student B So all of the colonies shared the same type of government?

Professor Well...they were all similar in that they were representative democracies. But beyond that there were actually a lot of differences. Because... um, each colony was founded by a different group...and for a different purpose. Take, uh, the Jamestown colony in Virginia. That was set up in 1607 by a commercial organization... [6] *in the pursuit of profit from agriculture.* Shortly after that, in New England, several colonies were established with a focus on religion. But then...in both of these cases, the colonists chose to form representative democracies based on the English model.

Q3判断哪些是讲义文中提到的美国殖民政府的特征。在相应正确的一栏中做出标记。
(A) 允许每个公民在政治问题上投票。**(NO)**
(B) 功能相当于间接民主制。**(YES)**
(C) 建立是为了从国内农业中获得利润。**(NO)**
(D) 在本地的小问题上作出裁决。**(YES)**
(E) 在17世纪卷入与英国君主制的冲突中。**(NO)**

Q4根据教授的介绍，为什么英国一开始允许美国殖民地自治？
(A) 殖民地答应仿照英国政府。
(B) 英国不可能在海外强制实施自己的法律。
(C) 英国暂时担忧国内混乱。
(D) 自治比远距离统治更加有效率。

MP3·425

representative democracy 代表制民主
representative代表性的，代议制的，典型的
be charged with 被指控
carry out 实行，实施
take action 采取行动，提起诉讼
governance 统治，支配
monarchy 君主制，君主政体
partially 部分地，局部地
parliament 议会，国会
minister 大臣，部长
pass a law 通过法案
commercial 商业的
the pursuit of profit 追逐利润

Student B **Q4 Why did England let the colonies have their own governments in the first place? It seems like they'd want to have more control over them...you know, [7]*by governing them directly*.**

Professor **Yeah, that's a good point. In fact, the colonies were given a lot more liberties than you'd expect, partly because England was [8]*somewhat preoccupied at the time.*** Dictation 结束 **See, not long after most of these colonies were founded, English society got caught up in civil conflict.** Interestingly enough, the issue at the center of the conflict had to do with democracy. It was basically the king versus the parliament, with parliament wanting more limits on the king's power and the king...well, he obviously wanted to keep his power. This struggle turned into an all-out civil war in 1642. So on the one hand, England was too busy at home to exercise total control in America.

Then on the other hand...um, the fact is that ultimate control of the colonies was still in England's hands. **Q3(D) Um, yes, the colonies had their own representative governments, but these were involved only with local issues.** All major decisions were made by the colonial governors—who were appointed by England... or by the English Parliament. And, as you probably already know, the colonies didn't get to elect representatives to the parliament in England.

Student A That's what led to the Revolutionary War, I think.

Professor Yes, that was a big part of it. The English Parliament started passing these tax laws to get more money from the colonists. And the colonists thought that was pretty unfair since their interests weren't being represented in parliament. And, um, the rest is history.

Q5教授这样说的是因为？
That's exactly what I wanted you to say...but I'm afraid your answer isn't correct.
(A) 学生本应该密切关注这个问题。
(B) 学生没有为上课做好准备。
(C) 学生提出了他想揭露的误解。
(D) 学生的答案几乎正确。

Q6教授为什么这样说？
The term "democracy" is pretty broad.
(A) 为了表明民主制是一种经过广泛实践的政府形式。
(B) 为了界定一个学生可能不太了解的词语。
(C) 为了提醒学生他们对民主的理解可能不太全面。
(D) 为了让学生解释民主政府这一概念。

MP3·425
preoccupied 心事重重的
get [be] caught up in 陷入，卷入
civil conflict 文明冲突
versus 与
struggle 斗争，奋斗
all-out war 全面战争
exercise control 实行控制
ultimate 最终的
governor 统治者，管理者
appoint 派遣
the Revolutionary War 独立战争

DAY21 Review Test IV

P.310

Answer passage 1 > 1 (B) 2 (D) 3 (B) 4 (C) 5 (C)

passage 2 > 1 (D) 2 YES → (A), (C), (D) / NO → (B), (E) 3 (B) 4 (A) 5 (D) 6 (C)

passage 3 > 1 (C) 2 (A), (B) 3 YES → (A), (C) / NO → (B), (D) 4 (A) 5 (D) 6 (D)

MP3·426 **passage 1. [1-5] Listen to part of a conversation between a student and an administrator.**

Student (male) Q4 MP3·427 **Hi. This is the Information Technology Services Center, isn't it?**

Administrator (female) **Yes, it is. But if you're here to use a computer, you have to go to the lab down the hall. This is just the office. For like technical questions and networking issues.**

Student OK. Actually, that's what I'm here for.

Administrator Well then, come on in. How can I help you?

Student Q1 **I'm thinking about setting up a webpage, and heard that every student at the university has space on the servers here. So I was wondering how I take advantage of it.**

Administrator Well, you're right. A lot of the students don't take advantage of the server space allocated to them unless they're in a technology class, but it's true that everyone has some space.

Student *[excited]* That's great. So, what do I have to do?

Administrator First of all, you have to make sure you know your username and password.

Student Where do I find that information?

Administrator Well, you may already know them. Do you use your campus e-mail address?

Student Yeah, I do.

Administrator Well, you should just use the same login name and password. They give you access to your university web space.

Student OK. So once I have those...what's next?

Administrator *[thinking]* Next...um, you use them to access the ITSC Login Service—oh, but first you have to make sure you have access to the ITSC Login Service. Uh, do you live on campus?

Student Yeah, I live over in Purham Hall.

Administrator Ah, great. Then you'll have no problem with that. All the campus dorms have access to the ITSC Login Service. So, what you'll do is log in to the server and then...um, wait, maybe I can find you some instructions for doing that. It's a little bit complicated the first time. You might want to have some written instructions to refer to.

Student That would be great, thanks.

Administrator Q5 MP3·428 ***[looking through papers, trying to find the appropriate instructions]*** **If you don't mind my asking, what are you creating a webpage for?** **I'm guessing it's not for a class—you'd probably already have all this information.**

Student	No, it's not for a class, just an independent project. Q2 **I'm thinking about starting up a knitting company with a couple of people who live in my dorm. Just something really small. We've been selling stuff locally, and it's going pretty well so far. So we thought we'd use our free university web space to try selling our stuff online.**
Administrator	*[interested]* Huh, that's really an interesting idea. Good luck with that. Here...I found the instructions I was telling you about. This sheet of paper has everything you need to know about using the ITSC Login Service.
Student	Great! Thanks.
Administrator	Those're pretty much the basics. Next, you just have to design the actual webpage. Have you, um, ever designed a webpage before? Q3 **If you've never done it before, you might find it a little bit overwhelming...** but it's nothing you can't handle. There are tons of resources online...lots of tutorials. And once you're done with that, you'll use the ITSC Login Service to upload your webpages...and that's it.
Student	I really appreciate your help. Thanks so much!
Administrator	Oh, sure. When you get your webpage up and running, I'd love to check it out.
Student	All right, I'll drop by sometime and let you know how it turns out.

MP3 • 435

set up 建立，创立
take advantage of 运用[利用]…，获得利益
allocate A to B 把A分配给B
have access to 进入（电脑系统等）(=**access**)
on campus 校内的

instructions 〈复数形式〉说明书，指示
complicated 复杂的
refer to 参考…
knitting （织毛线等）针织，织物
locally （特定）区域内
overwhelming 压倒性的，费力的

tons of 大量的
nothing you can't handle 不是无法处理的程度
tutorial （有使用方法等的）说明书
up and running （机器等）开始启动
turn out 出现结果，结果是…

◎ 解析

1. 学生为什么去信息科技服务中心？
   (A) 去询问他是否可以使用实验室里的计算机。**(not correct)**
   (B) 为了了解怎样使用分配给自己的大学服务器空间。
   (C) 为了询问学校邮件地址及密码。**(not correct)**
   (D) 为了制作个人主页需要的说明书。**(not correct)**

Main Idea

学生拜访教授或大学职员的原因通常在对话的开头出现。请看标记Q1处的内容。学生在提到分配给自己的服务器之后，又说“So I was wondering how I take advantage of it.（所以我想知道该怎么用那东西。）”由此可见，正确答案为(B)。(A)是职员对学生来访原因的推测。而(C)和(D)是学生在制作网络主页时需要的东西，并不是学生来访的目的，因此为错误选项。

2. 学生为什么想开设个人主页？

(A) 因为他希望多了解一些网页设计。**(not correct)**

(B) 因为这是一项需要完成的作业课题。**(not correct)**

(C) 为了建立宿舍的网上社区。**(not correct)**

(D) **为了通过它在网上卖东西。**

Detail

请看标记Q2处。学生说：" So we thought we'd use our free university web space to try selling our stuff online（所以我们觉得可以利用学校的免费网络空间在线出售东西。）" 因为想与同学一起建立knitting company（针织品公司）在线出售商品，需要制作网页，因此他们会使用学校免费提供的服务器空间。所以正确答案选择(D)。

3. 关于制作网页，女职员说了什么？

(A) 大学主页上有很多相关资源。 **(not correct)**

(B) **没有经验做起来可能会感觉困难。**

(C) 没有正式的指导培训不可能完成。**(not mentioned)**

(D) 她可以向学生提供书面说明。**(not correct)**

Detail

请看标记Q3处的内容。学校的行政人员说：" If you've never done it before, you might find it a little bit overwhelming...（如果你之前没做过，你可能会觉得有点难…）" 可见，正确答案选(B)。不是大学的主页，而是网上有很多说明书，因此(A)选项不正确。此外，职员并没有提到这是只有在修完正式课程后才可以进行的工作。并且职员找给学生的说明书是指导登陆网络科技中心使用服务的，而不是关于网页制作的，因此(C)和(D)选项均不正确。

4. 可以推测出职员？

(A) 她猜测学生可能有一个技术性问题。

(B) 她希望学生去找计算机实验室的人谈谈。

(C) **她认为学生是为用计算机实验而来的。**

(D) 她不想帮助学生解决问题。

Attiude

职员告诉了学生计算机实验室的位置，说明了服务中心的业务。由此可见，她认为学生是要去计算机实验室的，找错了地方来到了这里。因此正确答案选(C)。

5. 职员这样说是为了暗示什么？

I'm guessing it's not for a class—you'd probablyalready have all this information.

(A) 学生要想得到这些信息需要上一门课。

(B) 她不清楚学生目前有哪些课。

(C) **教授在课上会进行解释说明。**

(D) 学生自己寻找这些信息也很容易。

Inference

职员说："好像不是上课要求的…如果是因为课程要求，肯定已经知道这些东西了。" 从这句话可以看出，如果学生是因为课业要求而开设网页的话，教授在上课时应该已经告诉了他们相关的注意事项。因此，正确答案选（C）。

 MP3・429 **passage 2. [1-6] Listen to part of a talk in an American history class.**

Professor (male) In the United States, the bald eagle is considered to be an important symbol. Uh, some people feel like it represents the nation. Q1 **Actually, the bald eagle has even earned itself the, um, the title of "National Emblem," which means, um, you know...it's the official symbol of the nation.** Uh, back in 1782, the bald eagle became the national emblem because it was believed to be long-lived, strong, um, good-looking...and, um, people incorrectly assumed that it only lived in North America. This isn't true...but, um, Q5 MP3・430 **I think of the 100,000 bald eagles that currently exist, um, about half that population lives in Alaska. So North America does have a... sizable population of bald eagles.** ***[uncertainly]*** **I think that's right... <u>does anyone have their book open?</u>**

Student A (female) Uh, I have a different question...I don't really understand why the United States adopted a national emblem in the first place. What purpose does it serve?

Professor Uh...the national emblem...well, it actually came into being when the U.S. designed the Great Seal of the United States. Do you know what I mean by seal? It's a kind of meaningful picture that, uh, represents a person or group of people. And it's often made into a stamp. So the Great Seal is like an official seal that's used to, um...for one thing, to stamp government documents...to show that they're authentic...that sort of thing.

I guess many of you already know what the American national seal looks like. Before I give you a more detailed description of it, let me show you a slide of it first. *[pause while he looks for it]* Here it is. So, as you can see, the Great Seal is circular in shape, and in the middle there's a design that features the bald eagle. Q2(A) **The, um, the wings and feet of the bald eagle are, um, fully extended.** Q2(C) **In one claw, the, um, the eagle has a bunch of arrows. There are thirteen arrows, which—does anyone know what the thirteen arrows stand for?**

Student B (male) **Probably the thirteen original American colonies.**

Professor **Right.** Now, in the other claw, the bald eagle has an olive branch...and that, um, that of course symbolizes peace. Q2(D) **On the breast of the bald eagle there's a shield. It, um, it kind of looks like the U.S. flag.** Uh, with a blue part on top and then some red and white stripes. Again, there are thirteen stripes...for the thirteen original colonies. Um, in its beak, the bald eagle has a yellow ribbon...or banner, or something, and it's got the Latin words *E pluribus unum* on it...which means "out of many, one." OK, finally, above the eagle there's a circular design with white stars on a blue background. So, that's the Great Seal of the United States...and that's the, um, the first instance of the eagle being used as a national symbol. The national emblem, as I mentioned earlier.

Student A Uh, so I'm just wondering...that little symbol on the one-dollar bill, that's the Great Seal, right?

Professor Right, exactly. Q3 **The Great Seal isn't just used by government officials, it's something that's pretty visible to us all. It's also on passports. And, uh, you can see the bald eagle—I mean, not as part of the Great Seal—you can see it on coins like the dollar and the half-dollar.**

Student B Professor, there's something I heard once, um...the bald eagle may look impressive and everything, but, um, isn't it just a scavenger bird? I don't really understand why a nation would want to adopt that kind of animal as its, um, what did you call it? National seal?

Professor National emblem. Well, you're not the only person to express dissatisfaction with the, um, the decision to make the bald eagle the national emblem. Q4 **One notable objector was Benjamin Franklin. Um, there's this famous letter he wrote, um, to his daughter, I think...anyway, he explains all about how he thinks the bald eagle is an inappropriate choice. I have a few quotes from his letter...there're actually some pretty harsh, uh, criticisms of the bird.** Let me read a little to you.

OK, he starts off by saying that the bald eagle is "a bird of bad moral character." Then he describes how the bald eagle makes a living dishonestly, um, and gives an example of how the bald eagle watches the hawk do its fishing, and then, uh, when the hawk gets a fish, the bald eagle goes after the hawk and steals the fish away. Q6 MP3•431 **Franklin says a little more about how the bird is lousy and then adds, "Besides he is a rank coward."** ***[amazed]*** **I'm not kidding—that's actually in the letter.** Next, Franklin suggests that maybe the turkey would make a better, um, a better national bird than the bald eagle. Interesting, huh? How do you think the U.S. would be different today if, uh, if the turkey were its national emblem?

MP3•436

bald eagle 秃鹰
represent 代表，表现
national emblem 国徽
assume 推测，假定
currently 现在，目前
sizable 相当多的，相当大的
in the first place 首先
serve 达成，满足（目的、目标）
come into being 形成
the Great Seal 国玺
authentic 真实的，可靠的
detailed 详细的
circular 圆形的，循环的
extended 延伸的，扩张的
claw（野兽的）锋利的爪子
a bunch of 一束，一群
stand for 代表…，象征…
colony 殖民地
shield 盾牌，防护物
beak（鸟类的）嘴，喙
scavenger 食腐动物，食腐鸟类
notable 值得注意的，著名的
objector 反对者
inappropriate 不适当的，不适合的
quote 引用，引用文
harsh 粗糙的，辛辣的，刺耳的
dishonestly 不当地，不正直地，不诚实地
hawk 鹰
lousy 卑劣的，非常糟的
rank 臭气难闻的，严重的
coward 懦夫，胆小鬼

◎ 解析

1. 讲义文的主要内容是什么？
   (A) 美利坚合众国国玺的由来 **(minor)**
   (B) 北美地区白头秃鹰的历史 **(not mentioned)**
   (C) 国玺设计的象征意义 **(minor)**
   (D) 作为美国国家象征来使用的白头秃鹰

Main Idea

请看讲义文开头标记Q1处的内容。通过这段内容，可以推测讲义文将要针对美国的国家象征物白头秃鹰展开叙述。在正文中，教授介绍了选择白头秃鹰作为国家象征的原因以及国玺设计中蕴含的象征意义，这是在补充开始提出的主题。因此正确答案选(D).

2. 下列各项是否是讲义文中提及的国玺中蕴含的形象？请判断并点击正确空格。

(A) 舒展翅膀和脚的鹰	√	
(B) 有鹰栖息的橄榄树 **(not correct)**		√
(C) 象征殖民地的箭	√	
(D) 刻有与国旗设计相似图案的盾牌	√	
(E) 象征和平的带有线条图案的旗帜 **(not correct)**		√

Connecting Contents

请看标记Q2(A)处的内容，教授说国玺上镌刻的白头秃鹰的翅膀和腿呈fully extended（完全展开的）状态。而在标记Q2(C)处，他又介绍了白头秃鹰爪子所抓的箭象征着组成美利坚合众国的13块殖民地。在标记Q2(D)处，他介绍说白头秃鹰的胸部画有kind of looks like the U.S. flag（像美国国旗似的）shield（盾牌）。因此，(A)、(C)和(D)选项为YES。白头秃鹰没有栖息在橄榄树上，而是爪子里攥着olive branch（橄榄枝），因此(B)选项为NO。此外，不是线条图案的旗帜，而是“a yellow ribbon...or banner（仿佛黄丝带旗帜）”，并且象征和平的是橄榄枝，因此(E)选项也是NO。

3. 教授提到了哪些关于国徽的内容？
   (A) 它一开始是为作为国旗设计策划的。**(not correct)**
   (B) 它既可以作为国玺的一部分使用，也可以独立使用。
   (C) 它被选来象征和平与道德。**(not mentioned)**
   (D) 政府花了很长时间挑选国徽。**(not mentioned)**

Detail

请看标记Q3的内容，国徽不仅使用在政府文书中，也在护照或硬币等处使用。因此正确答案为(B)。国徽不是设计国旗时，而是设计国玺时第一次使用的。而讲义文中没有提到它象征道德或挑选时耗费了很长时间，因此(A)，(C)和(D)选项均不正确。

4. 教授为什么介绍本杰明·富兰克林写的一封信？
   (A) 为了说明有些人不赞成使用白头秃鹰作为国徽。
   (B) 为了提供关于国徽选择与制作国玺过程的细节。
   (C) 为了表明秃鹰从建国开始就一直被用作国徽。

Organization

当讲义文中出现特定的人名或地名等固有名词并且接下来有与之相关的说明时，很可能会有题目考查那些关键词。本杰明·富兰克林是反对使用白头秃鹰作为国徽象征的一位“notable objectors（知名反对者）”，他在信中强调了白头秃鹰不适合作为国家象征使用的原因。因此正确答案选(A)。学生问了

(D) 为了回答学生的问题，解释选择鸟作为国徽的原因。

为什么一定要选择白头秃鹰，但是教授并没有做出明确回答，因此选项(D)不正确。

5. 教授为什么这样说？
does anyone have their book open?
(A) 为了不让学生参考书本。
(B) 为了了解学生是否都读了。
(C) 为了解释教材中的一部分内容。
(D) 为了确定一个特定的统计数值。

Function
教授说" I think that's right..." 这句话时语气不太确定。由此可以推测，他询问是否有人打开了教材的原因是想确认自己刚刚提到的信息是否与书中的内容相符。因此正确答案选(D)。

6. 当教授这么说的时候，可以推测出他？
[amazed] I'm not kidding-that's actually in the letter.
(A) 他认为那封信是个玩笑。
(B) 他希望学生严肃一些。
(C) 他认为信的内容出人意料地尖锐。
(D) 他认为信中有一处错误。

attitude
富兰克林批评作为国家象征使用的动物为" a rank coward（气味难闻的胆小鬼）"，这里应该选择对此评价最恰当的反应。教授介绍这点时语气十分惊讶，再加上强调这一评价确实在信中出现，可见教授认为这一评价十分尖锐。所以正确答案选(C)。

 MP3·432 **passage 3. [1-6] Listen to part of a lecture in an environmental studies class.**

Professor (female)

Q1 **OK, um, tonight I wanted to start off with a discussion of charcoal.** I'm sure you're all familiar with the substance? You're all familiar with it. You've most likely seen charcoal being used at—at a barbecue. And if so, you're acquainted with charcoal as a form of fuel. You see, its use as a fuel is one of the major functions of charcoal. Charcoal has been used as a—as a fuel source for a really long time. Some people claim that, um, that it was used in Europe more than 5,000 years ago. That's quite a long time ago.

Q1 **It, um—when it burns, charcoal is cleaner than wood, and it burns at a higher temperature, too. Um...I'll tell you more about that in a second, but first I'll give you some information about, uh, about how charcoal is made.** What's it made from? Wood. The key to making charcoal is burning wood but, um, depriving it of oxygen at the same time. The most basic way to accomplish that is by covering a pile of—of wood with dirt before burning it. Of course, there're also special ovens that are, um, designed for this purpose. You see, the main thing is, you don't want the carbon in the wood to—to burn. But now, um, what this "baking" process does do is burn away a lot of, um, of things you don't want in a fuel source. Q2(A) **See...water in the wood gets burned away—and that's good because the, um, the presence of water lowers the temperature at which your fuel burns.** Q2(B) **Other bad stuff that you get rid of in the charcoal-making process—are, um, methane, hydrogen, and, tars...** When the process is finished, what's left is about 20 to 25 percent of the original size—of the wood. And it's mainly carbon. As I said before, this product burns cleaner and hotter than wood...so that's why people go through the effort of making charcoal—even though they could just use wood as a fuel source.

Q1 I'd like to spend a minute, um, going over the advantages of burning charcoal, um, instead of wood. Q5 MP3·433 OK...let's look at a place that currently burns a lot of wood for fuel... um, such as sub-Saharan Africa. Their reliance on wood creates some big problems...You know, it's estimated that by 2030, almost, um, almost 10 million people in the region will die from, um, from exposure to wood smoke. *[concerned]* That's a shocking statistic. And there's another issue—pollution. Scientists expect that cooking fires fueled by wood will release 6.7 billion tons of carbon into the atmosphere. And you know what that means—we've talked before about the, um, the effects of greenhouse gases in the atmosphere. So, in light of the negative effects of using wood as a fuel source, it makes sense to convert wood into cleaner-burning charcoal, doesn't it? **Q3 I do have to point out a couple of problems associated with charcoal, though. Q3(A) You see, back when charcoal was extremely popular in Great Britain, um, the demand for charcoal led to a lot of—of trees being cut down, because the raw wood was needed to make charcoal. So charcoal use is linked to, um, to deforestation. Q3(C) The other drawback of using charcoal is that you still have a lot of pollution that's created when you bake the wood to make charcoal. Remember how I told you about all the—the bad stuff that gets burned off? Well that bad stuff, of course, pollutes the air.**

So then, what's the point? **Q6 MP3·434 What's the point of making charcoal if you still have some pretty bad drawbacks to deal with? Well, it comes down to deciding which fuel source is the cleanest...the lesser of two evils. And that's charcoal. Q1 Despite the negative consequences, um, with a little planning, charcoal can still be an overall better option.** If you implement responsible forestry practices, the impact of—of deforestation can be reduced. And the other thing—it's possible to minimize the pollution from processing charcoal. Uh, there's technology out there that can control the emissions. So, if we use better forestry management and more sophisticated kilns, um, charcoal is a much better fuel than wood. **Q4 Getting back to the example of sub-Saharan Africa... scientists think that switching from wood to charcoal would, um, would prevent around 3 million premature deaths...and it would, um, lower the region's greenhouse-gas emissions by 65 percent.**

MP3·437

charcoal 炭，木炭
substance 物质，材料
be acquainted with 对…很熟悉
deprive A of B 从A中夺去B，从A除去B
a pile of 一堆…
fuel source 燃料源
methane 甲烷，沼气
tar 焦油，沥青（蒸馏煤炭、木材等可得的黑色油状液体）
sub-Saharan Africa 位于撒哈拉沙漠以南的非洲
reliance 依存度，依赖
estimate 预想，预测
wood smoke 木材烟雾，木材烟尘（燃烧木柴等木头时产生的烟气）
release 释放
greenhouse gas 温室气体（二氧化碳或甲烷等导致温室效应的气体）
in light of 从…的方面来看
convert A into B 把A转化为B
be linked to 与…连系
deforestation 森林破坏
drawback 缺点，短处
come down to 归结为…
evil 邪恶，恶
consequence 结果，后果
overall 全部的，整体的
implement 履行，执行
forestry 森林，林业
practice （事业等的）惯例，例行
minimize 最小化
process （技术性的）处理，加工
emission 排放，排出
sophisticated 尖端的，精密的
kiln 窑炉，窑
switch from A to B 把A转换为B，转移A至B
premature death 过早死亡

◎ 解析

1. 讲义文的主要内容是什么？

(A) 木头用作燃料使用的负面作用 **(minor)**

(B) 撒哈拉沙漠以南的非洲地区燃料使用的来源 **(minor)**

(C) 木炭的生产及其优点

(D) 木炭在欧洲及非洲的使用史 **(not mentioned)**

Main Idea

开始，教授说道： “tonight I wanted to start off with a discussion of charcoal.（今晚的课上，首先讨论有关木炭的话题。）”由此可见，讲义文的主题是charcoal木炭。但是，只知道这点仍然无法选出正确答案。关键是通过讲义文的整体内容，掌握教授具体介绍了木炭的哪些方面。在讲义文中，教授首先介绍了木炭的制造过程，之后又说明了木炭的亲环境特点，因此正确答案选(C)。讲义文中提到了木炭用作燃料使用的缺陷以及撒哈拉沙漠以南的非洲地区把木头当做燃料使用的内容，但是它们并不是整体性的内容，因此(A)与(B)选项也不正确。

2. 为了制造木炭而烤制木头的过程中会产生哪两种有益的事情？请选择两项正确答案。

(A) 水分含量减少。

(B) 除去了甲烷，氢元素及焦油成分。

(C) 碳含量降低。 **(not correcr)**

(D) 燃点降低。 **(not correcr)**

Detail

标记Q2(A)处写道“water in the wood gets burned away（木头中的水分都被蒸发）”，标记Q2(B)处写道“Other bad stuff that you get rid of in the charcoal-making process（在制造木炭的过程中除去其它的有害物质）”并举出了methane, hydrogen与tars等例子。因此正确答案为(A)和(B)。请留意，教授提到为了制造木炭，保持碳元素含量十分重要，木炭几乎完全是由碳构成的。除此之外，木炭比木头的燃点更高，是一种清洁燃料，因此(C)与(D)选项都不正确。

3. 下列哪些项目是在讲义文中提到的将木炭作为燃料来源使用时产生的损失？请点击正确的空格。

(A) 木炭的原料是木头，因此可能导致森林破坏。	√	
(B) 燃烧木炭时排出的有毒气体 **(not correcr)**		√
(C) 木炭燃烧时排出的各种污染物质	√	
(D) 为了建造加工设施而产生的高费用。**(not mentioned)**		√

Connecting Contents

在标记Q3(A)处，教授提到英国因为过度使用木炭而导致了森林破坏——“So charcoal use is linked to, um, to deforestation（木炭的使用与森林破坏有直接关系）”。而在标记Q3(C)处，教授又提到为了制造木炭而燃烧木头时，会产生有害气体“that bad stuff, of course, pollutes air（那些有害物质都会污染大气）。”因此(A)与(C)选YES。在讲义文中，没有提到燃烧木头会产生有毒气体与建造加工设施时会产生费用的内容，因此(B)与(D)选NO。

4. 教授为什么提起撒哈拉沙漠以南非洲地区人们的过早死亡？

(A) **为了强调以木炭取代木头使用的重要性。**

(B) 为了比较那一地区与其它地区的死亡率。

(C) 为了支持撒哈拉沙漠以南非洲地区丰富的燃料使用。

(D) 为了强调依赖木炭作为燃料的严重缺陷。

Organization

请看标记Q4的部分。教授认为那一地区如果使用木炭代替木头做燃料，就可以预防近300万件的早期死亡案例。教授的意思是木炭可以拯救很多人的生命，可见他正在强调使用木炭代替木头作为燃料的重要性。因此，正确答案选(A)。

---

5. 教授这么说的时候，可以推测出她？

[concerned] That's a shocking statistic.

(A) 她确信情况并没有看起来的严重。

(B) 她希望有解决问题的办法。

(C) 她怀疑结果的准确性。

(D) **她对那一地区的情况感到担忧。**

Attitude

在撒哈拉沙漠以南的非洲地区，人们暴露于wood smoke（木材烟尘）之中，这可能导致在不久的将来，约一千万人死亡。这个例子是为了说明木材作为燃料使用的危险性。根据教授的语气，以及统计数据的严重性可以看出教授十分担忧。因此，正确答案选(C)。

---

6. 从教授的话中可以推测出什么？

(A) 木炭和木头都不是可持续使用的燃料来源。

(B) 木炭作为燃料来源使用时，有几点无法克服的缺陷。

(C) 现在，大部分人都使用可替代燃料代替木炭的使用。

(D) **把木头转化成木炭是值得的。**

Inference

教授说"the cleanest...the lesser of two evils（最清洁的，危害更小的东西）"就是木炭。即，木炭作为燃料使用虽然也有缺陷，但是比起木头，它更清洁，负面影响更小，因此是一个更好的选择。由此可见，教授认为费力将木材转换为木炭这一过程虽然麻烦，但也是值得的。因此正确答案选(D)。

type A

Answer

01 **debris** 碎片，残骸
02 **implant** 移植
03 **intertwined** 纠缠的
04 **redeeming** 补偿的
05 **trigger** 触发，引起
06 **potent** 有力的
07 **protrude** 使突出
08 **erosion** 腐蚀
09 **exert** 施加（压力等）
10 **gradient** 倾斜度，梯度
11 **exclusively** 排他的，专门的
12 **elongated** 细长的，拉长了的
13 **indigenous** 本土的，土生土长的
14 **circulation** 循环
15 **retrieve** 挽回，恢复
16 **morale** 士气，斗志
17 **proportional** 成比例的
18 **correlation** 相互关联
19 **locomotion** 移动
20 **extract** 提取
21 **monopolize** 垄断
22 **intuitive** 直觉的
23 **consolidation** 巩固，加强
24 **trait** 特征，特点
25 **conjure** 施魔法
26 **browse** 浏览
27 **persecution** 虐待，迫害
28 **assortment** 分类
29 **preoccupied** 全神贯注的，被抢先占有的
30 **deforestation** 滥伐森林

type B

Answer

01 (A) **02** (C) **03** (A) **04** (C) **05** (C) **06** (B) **07** (A) **08** (B) **09** (D) **10** (B) **11** (C) **12** (B)
13 (A) **14** (C) **15** (A) **16** (C) **17** (A) **18** (B) **19** (B) **20** (D) **21** (A) **22** (C) **23** (D) **24** (D)
25 (B) **26** (C) **27** (A) **28** (B) **29** (A) **30** (C)

type B [SCRIPT]

01 a regular allowance granted to students

(A) stipend(薪金) (B) feat(功绩) (C) fund(基金) (D) practice(练习)

02 be more advanced and delicate

(A) patterned(被组成图案的) (B) virtual(实质上) **(C) sophisticated(精密的)** (D) supposed(假定的)

03 looking up to someone or worshipping them

(A) reverence(尊敬) (B) deity(神性) (C) temptation(诱惑) (D) increment(增加)

04 being able to use various skills

(A) established(既定的) (B) numerous(数目多的)
(C) versatile(多才多艺的) (D) encouraging(鼓励的)

05 the rearrangement of the parts of something

(A) fracture(使…破碎) (B) dependence(依赖) **(C) reconfiguration(重新配置)** (D) realization(实现)

06 being colored brightly in order to be easily noticed

(A) diverse(不同的) **(B) flamboyant(艳丽的)** (C) sufficient(充足的) (D) cheerful(快活的)

07 acting differently from what you say or claim to believe

(A) hypocritical(伪善的) (B) irrelevant(不相关的) (C) redeemable(可换成现款的) (D) elective(选举的)

08 a course that must be taken to gain entry to an advanced course

(A) admission(录取) **(B) prerequisite(先决条件)** (C) manual(手册) (D) provision(供应)

09 to go under water

(A) descend(下降) (B) surge(使汹涌奔腾) (C) waver(减弱) **(D) submerge(潜入水中)**

10 a substance produced by part of a plant or animal

(A) core(果核) **(B) secretion(分泌物)** (C) production(生产) (D) creature(生物，动物)

11 payments made after a war by a defeated country

(A) remains(剩余物) (B) details(细节) **(C) reparations(赔偿)** (D) premises(地基)

12 the processing of food by the body to generate energy

(A) physiology(生理学) **(B) metabolism(新陈代谢)** (C) capability(能力) (D) immunity(免疫)

13 eating both plants and meat

(A) omnivorous(杂食的) (B) ambivalent(矛盾的) (C) bilingual(双语的) (D) egalitarian(平等主义的)

14 the state of being completely filled with something so that no more can be added

(A) replenishment(补充) (B) congestion(拥挤) **(C) saturation(饱和)** (D) opposition(反对)

15 to surround something with a material that prevents electricity or heat from entering or escaping

(A) insulate(使…绝缘) (B) offend(冒犯) (C) protect(保护) (D) circulate(循环)

16 to destroy or dispose of something completely

(A) buttress(扶壁) (B) repeal(废止) **(C) eradicate(根除)** (D) invade(入侵)

17 not offering pleasant conditions, making it difficult to stay

(A) inhospitable(冷淡的) (B) reliant(依赖的) (C) covert(隐蔽的) (D) local(当地的)

18 active at night

(A) impressive(印象深刻的) **(B) nocturnal(夜行的)** (C) inferior(劣等的) (D) deluxe(豪华的)

19 a glowing light

(A) bloom(开花) **(B) luminescence(发光)** (C) enlightenment(启蒙) (D) infection(感染)

20 the way an animal's coloration or shape makes it difficult for others to see it

(A) reproduction(繁殖) (B) inference(推断) (C) disease(疾病) **(D) camouflage(伪装)**

21 deserving attention as something which is interesting or important

(A) noteworthy(值得注意的) (B) responsive(易感应的) (C) calculating(计算) (D) relentless(冷酷的)

22 not currently active, but may possibly become active again later

(A) geographical(地理的) (B) sterile(无菌的) **(C) dormant(睡眠状态的，静止的)** (D) logical(有逻辑性的)

23 brief, containing no unnecessary words

(A) exceptional(例外的) (B) opposing(对面的) (C) fragile(脆弱的) **(D) concise(简明的)**

24 to start to grow or develop

(A) consider(考虑) (B) peruse(精读) (C) occur(发生) **(D) germinate(发芽)**

25 the part of a substance that is left after most of it has gone

(A) silence(沉默) **(B) residue(残渣)** (C) dispersion(散布) (D) property(资产)

26 going in separate directions

(A) urgent(紧急的) (B) distinct(显著的) **(C) divergent(有分歧的)** (D) impeccable(完美的)

27 the shape of the outline of something

(A) contour(轮廓) (B) measurement(衡量) (C) impact(影响) (D) physique(体格)

28 having a common center

(A) repellant(击退的) **(B) concentric(同中心的)** (C) reflective(反映的) (D) defective(有缺陷的)

29 bold and bright

(A) vibrant(活跃的) (B) convex(凸面的) (C) located(位于) (D) intentional(有意的)

30 a short story about a real personal experience

(A) fable(寓言) (B) bibliography(传记) **(C) anecdote(轶事)** (D) conjecture(推测)

郑重声明